lonely planet

D0339247

Devon & Cornwall

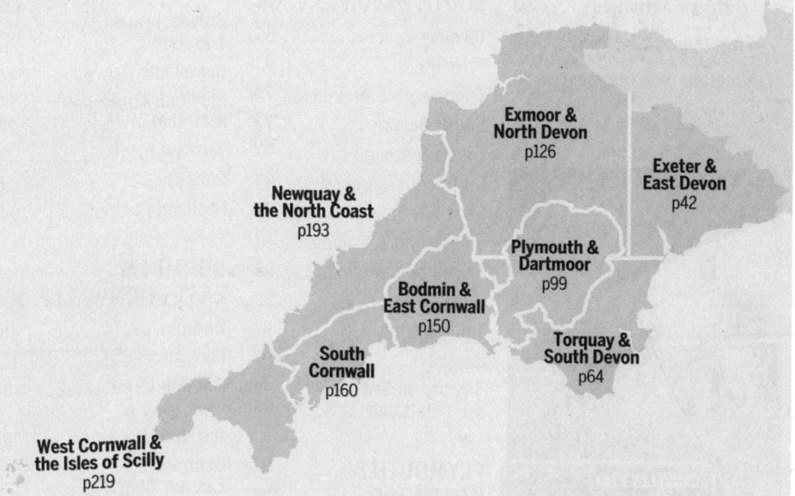

Exmoor &
North Devon
p126

Exeter &
East Devon
p42

Newquay &
the North Coast
p193

Plymouth &
Dartmoor
p99

Bodmin &
East Cornwall
p150

South
Cornwall
p160

Torquay &
South Devon
p64

West Cornwall &
the Isles of Scilly
p219

THIS EDITION WRITTEN AND RESEARCHED BY

Oliver Berry,
Belinda Dixon

Contents

PLAN YOUR TRIP

Welcome to
Devon & Cornwall 4

Devon & Cornwall Map . . . 6

Devon & Cornwall's
Top 16 8

Need to Know 16

If You Like.... 18

Month by Month 21

Itineraries 24

Outdoor Activities 30

Travel with Children. . . . 36

Regions at a Glance. . . . 38

CLOVELLY P147

TREEN & LOGAN ROCK
P234

ADAM BURTON / GETTY IMAGES ©

GUY EDWARDES / GETTY IMAGES ©

ON THE ROAD

EXETER & EAST DEVON 42

Exeter 43
East Devon 54
Topsham 55
Exmouth 57
Sidmouth 59
Beer & Around 61

TORQUAY & SOUTH DEVON 64

Torquay 65
Brixham 73
Teignmouth & Around 75
South Devon 77
Totnes & Around 77
Dartmouth & Around 83
Start Bay 89
Kingsbridge & Around 91
Salcombe & Around 93
Hope Cove 96
Thurlestone 97
Bantham 97
Bigbury-on-Sea
& Burgh Island 98

PLYMOUTH & DARTMOOR 99

Plymouth 100
Dartmoor
National Park 110
Tavistock & Around 113
Princetown 117
Postbridge & Around 118
Widecombe-
in-the-Moor 119
Ashburton 120
Moretonhampstead 120
Chagford 121
Lydford 123
Okehampton 125

EXMOOR & NORTH DEVON 126

Exmoor
National Park 128
Dulverton 130
Exford & Around 132
Dunster & Around 132
Porlock & Around 134
Lynton & Lynmouth 137
North Devon 138
Ilfracombe 139
Croyde, Braunton
& Around 141
Barnstaple & Around 144
Bideford, Appledore
& Around 145
Westward Ho! 147
Clovelly 147
Hartland Peninsula 148

BODMIN & EAST CORNWALL . . 150

Bodmin 151
Lanhydrock 153
Bodmin Moor 153
Camelford &
the Northern Moor 153
Central &
Eastern Moor 156
Liskeard &
the Southern Moor 158

SOUTH CORNWALL . . 160

Falmouth, Truro & the
Roseland 161
Falmouth 161
Trebah, Glendurgan &
the Helford River 167
Penryn 168
Flushing & Mylor 169
Restronguet Creek
& Devoran 169
Trelissick Gardens 169

Contents

Truro 170
The Roseland 174
Southeast Cornwall . . . 180
Charlestown 180
Mevagissey &
Gorran Haven 181
Lost Gardens
of Heligan 182
Eden Project 182
Lostwithiel 183
Fowey 183
Golant 187
Polperro 187
Looe 188
The Rame Peninsula 190
Tamar Valley 191

**NEWQUAY &
THE NORTH COAST . . 193**
**Bude & the Atlantic
Highway 195**
Bude 195
Crackington Haven 196
Boscastle 196
St Juliot 197
Tintagel 198
Port Isaac 198
Padstow & Around 200
Rock & Polzeath 200
Padstow 201
Wadebridge 206
Newquay & Around 206
**Perranporth to
Portreath 213**
Perranporth 213
St Agnes &
Chapel Porth 213
Porthtowan 216
Portreath 216
Tehidy Woods 216
Camborne, Redruth &
the Mining World
Heritage Site 216

**WEST CORNWALL &
THE ISLES OF
SCILLY 219**
West Cornwall 220
St Ives 220
Gwithian &
Godrevy Towans 226
Hayle 226
The Penwith
Peninsula 227
Penzance 235
Newlyn 240
Mousehole 241
Marazion 241
Perranuthnoe to
Praa Sands 244
The Lizard 245
Helston 245
Trelowarren 246
Porthleven &
the Loe 246
Gunwalloe 246
Mullion 247
Lizard Point & Around . . . 247
St Keverne & Around 248
The Helford 249
Isles of Scilly 250
St Mary's 251
Tresco 253

UNDERSTAND

Devon & Cornwall
Today 258
History 260
Food & Drink 268
The Arts 273
Environment 277

**SURVIVAL
GUIDE**

Directory A–Z 282
Transport 288
Index 296
Map Legend 303

SPECIAL FEATURES

Off the Beaten Track . . . 28
Outdoor Activities 30
Travel with Children . . . 36
Food & Drink 268
The Arts 273
Environment 277

Welcome to Devon & Cornwall

When it comes to white sand, wild surf and wide-open skies, nowhere in Britain can compare to Devon and Cornwall.

Coast & Countryside

Flung out on Britain's westerly edge, these side-by-side counties are celebrated for their natural charms: craggy cliffs cloaked in gorse, rocky tors on empty moors, golden beaches washed by surf. Every year millions of visitors flock here to feel the sand between their toes and paddle in the briny blue, and with miles of coastline, countryside and clifftops to explore, it's no wonder. And while the West Country's popularity inevitably means crowds, with the help of a decent map and an adventurous spirit, you'll always be able to find a patch of sand to call your own.

History & Culture

While the scenery is undoubtedly the star attraction, there's more to Devon and Cornwall than shining sands and wrap-around views. Thousands of years of history have left an indelible mark on the landscape, from neolithic monuments and Bronze Age villages to lonely minestacks and medieval castles. History buffs can explore the region's many houses and gardens, while culture vultures can immerse themselves in a packed calendar of festivals, celebrations, street parties and artistic events.

Cooking Up A Storm

More recently, the West Country has made a name for itself as one of Britain's gastronomic hot spots. Thanks to the fabulous produce on its doorstep, Devon and Cornwall can now claim some of the nation's most innovative restaurants and talented chefs. Whether it's cracking open a fresh crab, barbecuing some just-caught fish on the beach or tucking into a genuine Cornish pasty, there's a wealth of foodie experiences waiting out west.

Outdoor Adventures

If you want to experience the region's stunning landscapes at their best, you'll need to ditch the car and get active. Hiking trails and cycling paths criss-cross the countryside, and the South West Coast Path winds its way through a kaleidoscope of secret beaches, windblown dunes and majestic clifftops. But there are plenty more outdoor activities on offer, from coasteering over rocky crags, kayaking down a wooded creek or stargazing under Exmoor's night skies. It's a landscape just waiting to be explored.

Why I Love Devon & Cornwall
by Oliver Berry

Cornwall is my home county, so it's the place I know better than anywhere else. I've travelled all over the globe, but there's something special about Cornwall, and I always find myself drawn back sooner or later. I reckon I've discovered pretty much every beach there is over the years, but there's always something new to see: the light, the weather and the changing seasons all bring out a different side to the Cornish landscape. For me, the Lizard and the Penwith coastline are every bit as spectacular as the more exotic places I've visited.

For more about our authors, see p304.

Above: Bedruthan Steps (p206), Cornwall

Devon & Cornwall

ROAD DISTANCES (miles)

Note: Distances are approximate

	Exeter	Newquay	Penzance	Plymouth	St Ives	Torquay
Newquay	80					
Penzance	108	31				
Plymouth	43	49	77			
St Ives	108	31	9	74		
Torquay	21	80	108	31	105	
Truro	86	12	27	55	24	86

ATLANTIC

OCEAN

Lundy Island

North Coast
Find your own secret patch
of sand (p193)

Widemouth Bay

Eden Project
Experience the world's
biodiversity here (p182)

Bossiney Boscastle
Haven
Tintagel

Camelford
Port Isaac

Polzeath

Newquay
Catch a wave in Cornwall's
surf central (p206)

Padstow Rock

Wadebridge

Bedruthan Steps

Bodmin Moor

Eden Project

Newquay

Perranporth

St Ives
Delve into Cornwall's artistic
heritage (p220)

St Agnes

St Austell Fowey

Charlestown St Austell Bay

Lost Gardens of Heligan

Mevagissey

Portreath

St Ives Bay

Truro

Redruth

Trelissick Garden

Isles of Scilly
Relax on this remote
archipelago (p250)

St Ives

Gwithian & Godrevy Towans

Hayle

Camborne

Penryn

Roseland Peninsula

Penwith Peninsula

Penzance Marazion

Newlyn

Falmouth

Falmouth Bay

Mousehole

Porthleven

Helston

Constantine

Isles of Scilly

Land's End

Gunwalloe

The Lizard

St Keverne

Mullion

Lost Gardens of Heligan
Discover one of Cornwall's
great garden estates (p182)

Lizard Point

St Michael's Mount
Cross the causeway to an
island abbey (p244)

The Lizard
Get lost among glorious cliffs,
coves and villages (p245)

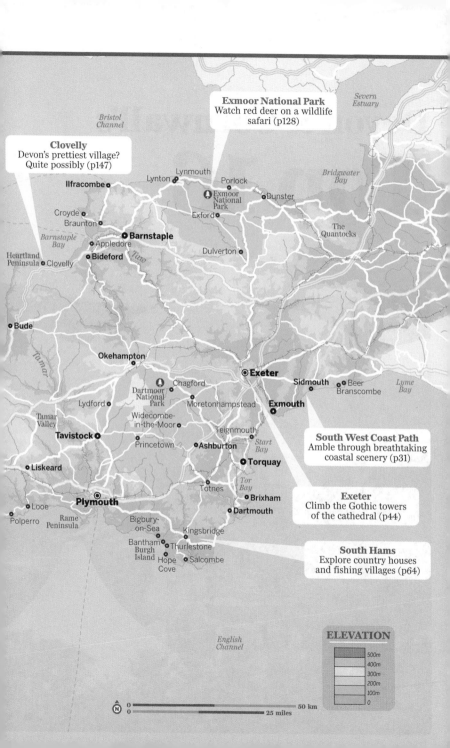

Exmoor National Park
Watch red deer on a wildlife
safari (p128)

Clovelly
Devon's prettiest village?
Quite possibly (p147)

South West Coast Path
Amble through breathtaking
coastal scenery (p31)

Exeter
Climb the Gothic towers
of the cathedral (p44)

South Hams
Explore country houses
and fishing villages (p64)

Bristol
Channel

Severn
Estuary

Bridgwater
Bay

Lynmouth
Lynton
Ilfracombe
Porlock
Exmoor
National
Park
Dunster

Croyde
Braunton
Exford

Barnstaple
Bay
Barnstaple
Appledore
The
Quantocks

Heartland
Peninsula
Clovelly
Bideford
Taw
Dulverton

Bude

Tamar

Okehampton

Dartmoor
National
Park
Chagford
⊙ **Exeter**
Sidmouth
Beer
Branscombe
Lyme
Bay

Lydford
Moretonhampstead
Exmouth

Tamar
Valley
Widecombe-
in-the-Moor

Tavistock
Princetown
Teignmouth
Start
Bay

Ashburton
Torquay

Liskeard
Totnes
Tor
Bay
Brixham

Looe
Plymouth
Dartmouth

Polperro
Rame
Peninsula
Bigbury-
on-Sea
Kingsbridge

Bantham
Burgh
Island
Thurlestone
Hope
Cove
Salcombe

English
Channel

ELEVATION

	500m
	400m
	300m
	200m
	100m
	0

N
0   50 km
0   25 miles

Devon & Cornwall's
Top 16

Eden Project

1 Rising from a Cornish claypit just outside St Austell, these futuristic biomes have become an iconic symbol of Cornwall's creative renaissance. Housing an outlandish array of plants, trees and botanical curiosities from across the globe, the greenhouses are the largest anywhere on earth. It's now more than a decade since they first graced the Cornish skyline, but there's a reason to visit Eden (p182) in every season, whether it's a spring flower show, a summer gig, an autumn food fest or a wintertime ice-skate. Whatever you do – don't miss it.

Isles of Scilly

2 Scattered across the Atlantic, 28 miles from Land's End, this remote island archipelago (p250) is Cornwall's answer to the Caribbean. Of the 140-odd islands, only five are permanently inhabited, leaving the rest to seabirds, seals and the occasional basking shark. Blessed with a laid-back lifestyle, electric-blue water and some of the best beaches anywhere in Britain, the islands are hard to leave – especially once your internal clock has switched over to Scilly time.

GLENN BEANLAND / GETTY IMAGES ©

ROBERT HARDING PRODUCTIONS / GETTY IMAGES ©

Dartmoor National Park

3 Bleakly bewitching, the heather-clad heaths and granite tors of Dartmoor (p110) have an edge of wildness about them that feels quite different from the rest of Devon. It's a place where nature still holds sway, and the only sign of human habitation is a few scattered farmhouses and drystone walls. Hiking and biking are the main draws here, and it's one of the few areas in Britain where wild camping is still legal, where you can pitch a tent just about anywhere and sleep out under wild skies.

Exeter Cathedral

4 A dose of Gothic grandeur in the centre of Devon's oldest city, this mighty cathedral (p44) is the region's foremost house of worship. Largely built during the 13th century, its most notable features are the decorative facade and a fabulous vaulted ceiling – but it's the chance to climb up the towers that excites most visitors. Unsurprisingly, there's a wrap-around view from the top, stretching right across Exeter; on a clear day, you might even spy Dartmoor and the Devon coast.

St Ives

5 When it comes to seaside settings, St Ives (p220) really does take some topping. Tucked in beside a grand curve of coastline, with a jumble of slate roofs, narrow lanes and golden beaches, it's quite simply one of Cornwall's most beautiful sights. The town is famous for its artistic connections, too: Barbara Hepworth established an artists' colony here in the 1930s, and the town is still home to a wealth of studios, galleries and workshops – not to mention the historic Leach Pottery studio and the renowned Tate St Ives.

South West Coast Path

6 No matter where you go in Devon and Cornwall, you'll never be too far from the South West Coast Path (p31). Winding through a string of cliffs, coves, villages, peninsulas and headlands, this fabulous footpath is one of the region's must-experience attractions. Hardcore hikers tackle the whole route, a truly epic ramble of more than 450 miles that also takes in the coastlines of Dorset and Somerset. Others focus just on the Devon or Cornwall sections, but really, an hour's stroll is every bit as stunning. Top right: Hartland Point lighthouse (p149), Devon

Cream Teas

7 There are few better things on a sunny southwest afternoon than a pot of tea accompanied by hot scones, homemade jam and lashings of clotted cream. The main problem you'll face is the thorny issue of how to spread your scone – Devon says it's unquestionably cream then jam, while Cornwall maintains it's definitely jam followed by cream. Look out for another Cornish twist on the theme known as 'thunder and lightning', in which the jam is replaced by treacle.

JAMES OSMOND / GETTY IMAGES ©

Clovelly

8 Tumbling down a formidably steep hillside on the north Devon coast, Clovelly (p147) feels like a step back into a more pastoral time. Bisected by a cobbled street lined by cob houses and fishermen's cottages, it's a vision of village life that could have been lifted straight out of a film set. It's a place that is awash with lots of photo opportunities, especially in the late evening when the winding lanes are at their quietest and quaintest.

Surfing at Newquay

9 If you're looking to catch a wave, then you're in luck – the coastlines of Devon and Cornwall have some of the most reliable surf anywhere in Europe. The surfing epicentre is Newquay (p206), with Croyde in Devon coming a close second, but you'll find lots of quieter surf spots scattered around the region's shores. You can learn the basics in a day, but mastering the art takes years of practice. The only drawback is the water temperature, which is rather bone-chilling – but with a decent wetsuit you won't feel the chill.

Cornish Pasties

10 It's been a long time coming, but Cornwall's most celebrated culinary invention has finally achieved Protected Geographical Indication status (in other words, only pasties made in Cornwall can now be called 'Cornish pasties'). It's about time too, as nothing tastes quite like a true Cornish pasty. Stuffed with beef, swede, potatoes and onions, wrapped in pastry and crimped on the side, pasties are Cornwall's original takeaway snack; they were developed as a portable lunchbox for men working in the local fields and tin mines.

Lost Gardens of Heligan

11 From colourful magnolias to rare rhododendrons, the West Country's gardens bloom with horticultural interest. Its temperate climate and subtropical valleys provide the perfect growing conditions for exotic trees, plants and flowers, including many species that can't survive anywhere else in Britain. Each has its own special attraction: the Lost Gardens of Heligan (p182) are particularly impressive, with a landscape of kitchen gardens and wild jungle valleys that have been carefully restored by a team of dedicated gardeners.

St Michael's Mount

12 Cornwall's answer to Mont St-Michel occupies a rocky island opposite the old harbour of Penzance. The abbey (p244) was originally built by Benedictine monks, but has served many roles over the years (including a coastal fort, stately home and even an ammunition dump). It's now the family home of the St Aubyn family, although it's officially owned by the National Trust. Don't miss the chance to walk across to the island along its famous cobbled causeway, which only reveals itself at low tide.

The Lizard

13 This peculiarly named peninsula (p245) juts out from Cornwall's southern coastline like a rocky finger, and was notorious as one of Cornwall's most treacherous headlands – countless ships met their end on its hidden reefs and inky cliffs down through the centuries. These days it's a place to wander the cliffs, explore the coves and watch wildlife – if you're really lucky, you might spot Cornwall's symbolic bird, the red-beaked chough, which is thriving again here after years of decline. Top: Kynance Cove (p248)

South Hams

14 Sandwiched between Plymouth Sound and Torbay, this swathe of countryside encapsulates everything that's green and good about Devon. Hatched by fields, spotted with villages and riverside towns, it's tailor-made for touring. Along the way you'll encounter Agatha Christie's holiday home at Greenway (p83), the stately homes of Coleton Fishacre (p88) and High Cross House (p77), and the smart marinas of Salcombe (p93) and Dartmouth (p83). Bottom: River Dart, Dartmouth

Exmoor National Park

15 Britain's smallest national park (p128) straddles the Devon/Dorset border. While it might not quite have the epic quality of Dartmoor, Exmoor has charms all of its own, from a unique water-powered railway at Lynton to the panoramic viewpoint of Dunkery Beacon. But, as always, it's the landscape that's Exmoor's selling point: it's a photogenic patchwork of medieval fields, ancient oak woods and plunging coombes (valleys), and is one of the best places in Britain to spot herds of wild red deer.

North Coast Beaches

16 If there's one experience everyone is after when they visit this corner of Britain, it's the chance to lounge on the sand and paddle in the briny blue. Devon and Cornwall's beaches are rightly one of the region's major attractions, and range from world-famous sands to little-known gems you'll need local knowledge and an OS map to find. The beaches of Cornwall's north coast are perhaps the most beautiful of all, particularly the string of spectacular coves dotted between Bude (p195) and Padstow (p201). Bottom: Polzeath (p200)

Need to Know

For more information, see Survival Guide (p281).

Currency
Pound – also called 'pound sterling' (£)

Language
English and Kernewek (Cornish)

Visas
Not required by most citizens of Europe, Australia, NZ, USA and Canada.

Money
ATMs widely available in main towns, but scarce in small villages.

Mobile Phones
Signals can be very patchy outside main towns.

Time
GMT

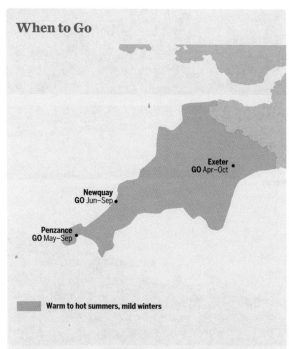

When to Go

Exeter
GO Apr–Oct

Newquay
GO Jun–Sep

Penzance
GO May–Sep

Warm to hot summers, mild winters

High Season
(Jun–Aug)

➡ Prices are high, and hotels, B&Bs and campsites are usually full.

➡ Beaches and attractions can be uncomfortably crowded

➡ Expect heavy traffic, especially around bank holidays

Shoulder
(Mar–May & Sep–Oct)

➡ Peak prices drop and seasonal deals are available

➡ Weather can be more settled than in summer

➡ Quietest during school term-times; half-terms are always busy

Low Season
(Nov–Feb)

➡ Rates for B&Bs and hotels at their lowest

➡ Some sights and attractions close or operate shorter hours

➡ Accommodation and trains are booked out for Christmas and New Year

Useful Websites

Visit Cornwall (www.visitcornwall.co.uk) The official tourist site: accommodation, activities and more.

Visit Devon (www.visitdevon.co.uk) Similar info but for Devon.

Simply Scilly (www.simply-scilly.co.uk) The lowdown on the Isles of Scilly.

Traveline SW (www.travelinesw.org.uk) Public transport info for the southwest.

Important Numbers

England (and UK) country code	☑44
International access code	☑00
Emergency (police, fire, ambulance, mountain rescue or coastguard)	☑999

Exchange Rates

Australia	A$1	£0.65
Canada	C$1	£0.65
Europe	€1	£0.85
Japan	¥100	£0.77
New Zealand	NZ$1	£0.54
USA	US$1	£0.66

For current exchange rates see www.xe.com

Daily Costs
Budget
Less than £80

➡ Hostel bed £15-20

➡ Campsite pitch £10-20

➡ Public transport £5-10

➡ Pasty and a pint £6-7

Midrange
£80-150

➡ Double room in a B&B £80-120

➡ Lunch and dinner in local restaurants £20-30

➡ Admissions and activities £10-20

➡ Petrol per day £10-20

Top End
More than £150

➡ Room in a luxury hotel £150+

➡ Meals in top-end restaurants £50-70

Opening Hours

Opening hours vary throughout the year. We've provided high-season opening hours; hours will generally decrease in the shoulder and low seasons.

Banks 9.30am-5pm Monday to Friday, 9.30am-1pm Saturday.

Museums Smaller museums may close Monday and/or Tuesday, and close on weekdays in the low season.

Post offices 9am-5pm Monday to Friday, 9am-12.30pm Saturday (main branches to 5pm).

Pubs 11am-11pm Sunday to Thursday, later on Friday and Saturday. Some rural pubs close from 3-6pm.

Restaurants Lunch noon to 3pm, dinner 6-11pm.

Cafes & teashops 9am-5pm.

Shops 9am-5.30pm Monday to Saturday, 10am to 4pm Sunday. Rural shops open shorter hours.

Arriving in Devon & Cornwall

Exeter Airport (p289) Budget flights covering the UK and some Continental destinations. Bus 56 runs from Exeter's bus station and St David's train station to the airport.

Newquay Airport (p289) Regular flights to London, Belfast, Birmingham, Cardiff, Edinburgh and the Isles of Scilly. Bus 556 runs to the airport from Newquay bus station.

Getting Around

Getting around by public transport is perfectly possible in Devon and Cornwall; there's a decent bus network between main towns, plus several wonderfully scenic train lines.

Bus Convenient for reaching smaller towns and villages, but can be infrequent outside summer. Many buses don't run on Sundays.

Train Main towns, including Exeter, Plymouth, St Austell, Truro and Penzance, are on the main line from London Paddington. Branch lines serve several smaller towns.

Bike Rural lanes and dedicated bike trails make for great cycling, but be prepared for hills. Most large towns have bike hire outlets.

Car Having your own wheels is the best way to explore, but you'll need to factor in traffic, parking, petrol and narrow lanes.

Boat Ferries cross most of the region's big rivers, including the Fal, Fowey, Helford, Dart and Tamar; some carry bikes and cars, others are pedestrian-only.

For much more on **getting around**, see p288

If You Like...

Views

It doesn't take too long travelling around the southwest to realise that for every knockout view, there's another waiting just around the corner – so whatever you do, don't forget to pack the wide-angle lens.

Land's End As far west as you can get on mainland Britain: next stop, the Scilly Isles. (p233)

Carn Brea Panoramic views from a craggy hilltop in the heart of Cornwall's mining country. (p215)

Brown Willy The highest hill in Cornwall, in the middle of Bodmin Moor. (p153)

Exeter Cathedral Climb the spire for a bird's eye perspective on Exeter. (p44)

Dunkery Beacon Hike to the highest point on Exmoor for a 360-degree outlook. (p132)

The Jurassic Coast Rust-red, fossil-rich cliffs, best-viewed between Beer and Branscombe. (p58)

Lizard Point The most southerly headland in Britain, craggy and spectacular. (p247)

Beaches

When it comes to beaches, few corners of Britain can match Devon and Cornwall. There are hundreds to explore, whether you're planning to paddle in the surf, delve into the rock-pools or don a wetsuit and brave the waves.

Fistral Britain's best-known surfing beach, and a great place to learn – as long as you don't mind crowds. (p207)

Perranporth Over a mile of family-friendly sands on Cornwall's north coast. (p213)

Porthminster The biggest of three sandy beaches just a stone's throw from St Ives. (p221)

Kynance Cove The Lizard's postcard cove, framed by cliffs and islands. (p248)

Porthcurno A perfect pocket of sand beneath the Minack Theatre. (p234)

Croyde Surf-central in Devon, and just as exciting as Fistral. (p141)

Bantham South Devon's finest overlooks Burgh Island. (p97)

Salcombe Strings of sandy coves connected by ferries. (p93)

Outdoor Adventures

With miles and miles of unspoilt countryside and coast, getting out and about in the great outdoors is guaranteed to be a highlight of your trip.

Cycling Cornwall's **Camel Trail** is the best-known bike path, but the West Country has many more trails to pedal. (p203)

Surfing Newquay (p208) and Croyde (p141) are the surfing hotspots, but there are quieter places to find some waves.

Hiking The wild grandeur of Dartmoor (p111) makes for epic

IF YOU LIKE... STARGAZING

If you like nothing better than lying back and gazing up at a star-spangled sky, then you're in luck: since 2011, Exmoor has been Europe's only designated Dark Sky Reserve, a recognition of the quality of the moor's nighttime skies and the lack of light pollution. Stargazing safaris and organised nighttime walks are offered by the National Park Authority (NPA), or you can just bring a pair of binoculars and do your own star-spotting.

hikes, and the South West Coast Path (p31) is never far away.

Swimming Take a dip in the outdoor pools of **Plymouth** (p104) and **Penzance** (p237).

Kayaking The region's tidal estuaries such as the River Fowey are ideal for exploring by kayak. (p185)

Coasteering A cross between rock-climbing, wild swimming and rockpooling; Newquay (p208) is a good place to try it.

Eating Like A Local

Eating your way around the southwest is one of the best ways to experience life through local eyes. From fresh pasties to just-caught fish, there's a smorgasbord of flavours to savour.

Philps Bakery Said to be Cornwall's best pasty-maker – although the competition's fierce. (p227)

Riverford Field Kitchen Sustainable home-grown farm grub just outside Totnes. (p82)

Trevaskis Farm One of the best of Cornwall's many farm shops, near Gwithian. (p227)

Jelbert's Ices Only one flavour at this Newlyn ice-cream maker – old-school vanilla made with clotted cream. (p240)

Newlyn fishmongers Get your crab, lobster and fish literally straight off the boats. (p240)

Beer Buy some fish and do like the locals do: barbecue it on the beach. (p63)

Salcombe Smokies Tuck into locally wood-smoked mackerel. (p95)

PLAN YOUR TRIP IF YOU LIKE...

(Top) Ladram Bay (p58), Jurassic Coast
(Bottom) St Michael's Mount (p244), Cornwall

Rummaging around in the undergrowth for some edible grub is becoming a real trend in the southwest, and there are lots of places where you can do it. Two of the best are Fat Hen near Penzance, which offers foraging courses followed by an alfresco feast; and 7th Rise near St Mawes, where you can hone your rabbit-hunting, spear-fishing, fire-lighting and foraging skills. (p235) (p180)

Historic Houses

Great estates and gardens litter the countryside, a reminder of the days when Devon and Cornwall were the playground of the landed gentry. These days, many are owned by the National Trust.

St Michael's Mount Cornwall's island abbey, star of a million postcards. (p244)

Lanhydrock Quintessential English Victoriana, from smoking rooms to cavernous kitchens. (p153)

Port Eliot This arty estate in southeast Cornwall is only open for a few weeks a year. (p191)

Arlington Court A Regency house known for its fabulous collection of horse-drawn carriages. (p144)

Coleton Fishacre Glorious art deco house in south Devon, with gardens to match. (p88)

Artistic Locations

Countless poets, painters and philosophers have been inspired by the region's landscapes down the centuries.

Greenway Play Hercule Poirot in Agatha Christie's summer retreat. (p83)

St Ives Barbara Hepworth was one of many artists who made this coastal town their home. (p220)

Exmoor Get moody on the windswept hills where RD Blackmorne set *Lorna Doone*. (p128)

Newlyn Stanhope Forbes and the other artists of the Newlyn School turned this fishing port into an artists' haven. (p240)

Trebetherick John Betjeman loved Cornwall with a poet's passion, especially the area around Daymer Bay. (p200)

Getting Away From It All

Devon and Cornwall are popular destinations, especially in peak season in July and August, but there are always places to escape the throngs.

Penwith Moors Few people explore these wild western moors, with their hill forts and ancient monuments. (p227)

Fal River Cruising down this lovely river makes a peaceful retreat from Cornwall's crowded beaches. (p170)

Uninhabited Isles of Scilly Isolated islands that are 100% people-free. (p254)

Lundy Island Two hours from North Devon, this wildlife-filled island feels like another world. (p140)

Dartmoor Strap on your boots and a backpack – Dartmoor's empty horizons are a hike away. (p111)

Braunton Burrows Well off the beaten track, this is Devon's largest dune system. (p141)

Camping

Nothing beats a night under the stars, and you'll find superb campsites scattered all over Devon and Cornwall – from tap-and-toilet sites to glamping spectaculars.

Treloan Spacious camping on the rural Roseland. (p174)

Lovelane Caravans Retro caravans that'd make your granny green with envy. (p249)

Henry's Wacky, wonderful, and just a walk from Lizard village. (p248)

Cornish Tipi Holidays The original tipi site in Cornwall, in a delightful wooded setting. (p201)

Blackdown Yurts Posh camping, complete with wood burners and compost loos. (p53)

Wood Life Woodland camping in a luxury handmade tent. (p53)

Vintage Vardos Three restored gypsy wagons on a private Devon farm. (p144)

Dartmoor wild camping Pick your spot, pitch your tent, and you'll have Dartmoor to yourself. (p112)

Month by Month

TOP EVENTS

'Obby 'Oss Festival, Padstow

Flora Day, Helston

British Fireworks Championships, Plymouth

Port Eliot Festival, near St Germans

Eden Sessions, near St Austell

February

February is a quiet time: spring is months away and old man winter still holds the west in his icy grip.

☆ Animated Exeter

Cartoons and animations aplenty come to Exeter for this three-day festival in late February – and there are workshops if you secretly fancy yourself as the next Walt Disney.

March

Daffodils and snowdrops in the hedgerows provide the first hint that winter might be on its way out, while Shrove Tuesday marks the beginning of the Easter festivities.

🏃 St Columb Hurling

An ancient Cornish free-for-all in which the townsfolk of St Columb chase around town in pursuit of a silver ball. It kicks off on Shrove Tuesday and, yes, it's as dangerous as it looks.

✨ St Piran's Day

Various events take place on 5 March in honour of Cornwall's patron saint, St Piran. One of the largest is a mass march across the sands of Perranporth to the tumbledown chapel known as St Piran's Oratory, buried among the dunes.

April

The weather's usually warming up by April, so this is often a good month to soak up some early rays of sunshine.

🍴 Southwest Food & Drink Festival

The southwest's largest foodie celebration is held in late April in Exeter, and stages everything from chefs' demos to produce markets.

May

Traditionally seen as the beginning of spring, May is welcomed in with several festivals that can trace their roots back to pagan times.

✨ 'Obby 'Oss

One of the southwest's most colourful (and chaotic), Padstow's May Day festivals is on 1 May, and involves two colourful 'osses' (blue and red) twirling around the town's streets, followed by a procession of singers, musicians and inebriated revellers. It's riotous, raucous, and royally good fun.

✨ Flora Day

Cornwall's other famous spring festival takes place in early May. Townsfolk take to Helston's streets in formal dress, and enact the age-old Furry Dance – a waltz-like dance accompanied by its own special tune.

🏃 World Pilot Gig Championships

This huge Scilly regatta in early May revolves around racing pilot gigs, the long multi-man rowboats that were once a common sight around the southwest's shores. Teams from across the world come to compete.

⚜ Devon County Show

In early May Devon's farmers and food producers congregate for this annual agricultural show, which has been one of the main events on the county calendar since 1872.

⚜ Fowey Festival

This litfest began life as the Daphne du Maurier Festival, but it's now rebranded itself to encompass other literary luminaries, as well as the odd bit of theatre, dance and music.

June

Usually a good month to travel, with reliable weather, some interesting events and relatively few grockles and emmets (local terms for tourists in Devon and Cornwall).

⚜ Royal Cornwall Show

Cornwall's biggest agricultural show happens in early June on a purpose-built showground just outside Wadebridge. Expect food stalls, cooking displays and cultural events alongside parades of prize-winning livestock.

⚜ Golowan Festival

Penzance's premier summer party and arts festival runs over several days in mid-June to celebrate the Festival of St John. Music, parades, plays, parties – and an almighty knees-up on Mazey Day.

✕ Rock Oyster Festival

Staged in the grounds of Dinham House between Rock and Wadebridge, this outdoor festival has mushroomed into one of Cornwall's big summer events. The focus is on food, but there's live music and activities for kids, too.

☆ Maker Festival

A small-scale music festival staged on the lovely Rame Peninsula, with views of the sea along with the bands. Mid-June.

☆ Falmouth Sea Shanty Festival

Hooray, and up she rises... The sound of sea shanties fills the air in Falmouth in this mid-June singing celebration, but you'll have to bring your own bottles of rum and pieces of eight.

July

The crowds are still relatively thin in early July, but things hot up as soon as the school holidays begin in mid-July. Weatherwise, the month can be unpredictable: sunny one year, rainy the next.

⚜ Ways With Words

Book readings, author talks and literary discussions in the appropriately scholarly setting of Dartington Hall. Held in the first week of July.

☆ Eden Sessions

Big-name bands play a series of outdoor gigs in the shadow of Eden's biomes.

The concerts are normally held over successive weeks in July and August.

⚜ Port Eliot Festival

Blending literature, arts, dance, poetry and live music, this magical festival takes place in the sweeping grounds of a Cornish country house in St Germans, Cornwall.

August

Peak season: on sunny days, it can seem like half of Britain has decided to make a break for the southwest's shores. Expect heavy traffic, human and automotive – but don't be surprised if you're caught in a summer shower.

☆ Sidmouth Folk Week

Held in the first week of August since 1955, this week-long festival continues to attract top names from the folk world.

☆ Dartington International Summer School

A month-long classical music festival staged in the stately surrounds of Dartington Hall near Totnes. There are concerts and recitals galore, plus music lessons if you fancy having a go.

🏃 Rip Curl Boardmasters

The largest surf, skate and music festival in Europe. Surfing and extreme sports take place on Newquay's Fistral Beach, while bands play on the bluffs above Mawgan Porth.

✕ Newlyn Fish Festival

Newlyn's fish market and harbour overflows with food stalls during this seafood extravaganza, and there's plenty of opportunities to sample the wares.

☆ British Fireworks Championships

Plymouth's skies are filled with bursts of colour for this two-night fireworks contest in mid-August. It's spectacular, loud and best of all, completely free.

🏃 Beer Regatta

A week-long party in the pretty Devon village of Beer, celebrating local connections with the sea. The festival highlight is the Beer Lugger races, in which local lugger boats battle it out in the bay.

🏃 Dartmouth Regatta

Boats and ships of all shapes and sizes descend on riverside Dartmouth for this annual sailing celebration, which always begins on the last Friday of August.

September

The summer hordes have mostly left for home by September, which makes this a good month to explore if you're allergic to crowds.

☆ St Ives September Festival

A lively mixed-arts festival encompassing literature, music, theatre and more,

held in various venues around the picturesque Cornish town of St Ives in early September.

✕ Cornwall Food & Drink Festival

Culinary-themed events in a marquee on Truro's Lemon Quay. Stock up on chutneys, chocs and charcuterie, watch chefs work their gastronomic magic, and meet some of Cornwall's top food producers.

🏃 Torbay Week

Yachts and dinghies race across the waters of the English Riviera during this September sailing festival.

October

October paints the West Country in autumnal colours, making this a great month to visit the region's landscaped gardens and country estates.

✕ Falmouth Oyster Festival

Mass oyster eating on Falmouth's quayside, plus cookery demos, boat races and concerts. Held in late October.

November

There's always a nip in the air by November, so wrap up warm and bring a brolly.

🎆 Blazing Tar Barrels

The unhinged locals of Ottery St Mary carry flaming

tar barrels through packed-out streets on 5 November each year, while paramedics and health-and-safety officials look on in abject horror.

☆ Cornwall Film Festival

Cornwall's annual cinematic shindig stages workshops, directors' talks and discussions, as well as plenty of film screenings.

December

Cold nights, late-night shopping and street processions mark the festive month of December: chestnuts and mulled wine are essential.

🎆 City of Lights

Huge wicker lanterns are paraded through the streets of Truro to celebrate the start of the festive season in early December.

🎆 Time of Gifts

The Eden Project builds a giant ice-rink beside the biomes in December, and hosts a range of festive events, from food-tasting to wreath-making.

🎆 Montol Festival

This pagan-themed festival in Penzance celebrates the winter solstice, with a masked parade overseen by the spooky Lord of Misrule.

◉ Christmas Lights

The tiny Cornish fishing village of Mousehole lights up the festive season in truly stunning style.

Itineraries

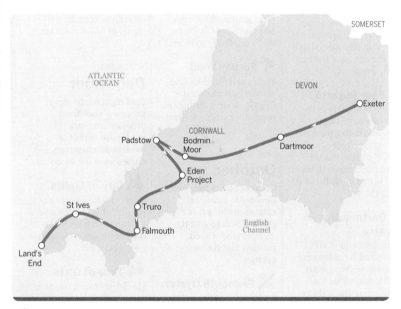

West Country Classics

This end-to-end road-trip factors in the must-see sights of Devon and Cornwall. Begin in the city of **Exeter**, where you can get a grandstand view from the top of the cathedral's towers. Then head west into the wilds of **Dartmoor**, a strange landscape of open heaths, twisted tors, and pretty villages such as Chagford and Widecombe-in-the-Moor. More wide-open scenery unfolds as you travel over windswept **Bodmin Moor** en route to **Padstow**, the little port that has reinvented itself as Cornwall's culinary hotspot.

South of Padstow, in a disused claypit, loom the giant greenhouses of the **Eden Project**, which house trees and plants from across the globe. Heading southwest brings you via the Cornish capital of **Truro** to the historic harbour of **Falmouth**, a lively university town where you can explore the county's sea-going heritage at the National Maritime Museum. Next comes arty **St Ives**, awash with art galleries and crafts shops, as well as the renowned Tate St Ives. Finish up with a stroll along the headland at **Land's End**, last stop on mainland Britain.

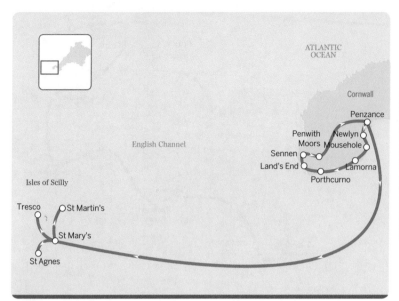

 2 WEEKS West to the Isles

This journey begins in the far, far west and just keeps on going. **Penzance** is the start point, a historic harbour town which still has many Georgian buildings and a distinctly alternative, arty vibe. Nearby **Newlyn** is still home to Cornwall's biggest fishing fleet, so it's a great place to pick up fresh crabs and lobsters straight off the boats, and you can investigate its artistic connections at the century-old Newlyn Art Gallery. Just along the coast, **Mousehole** is an essential detour; it's arguably the prettiest village in west Cornwall, with its slate-roofed cottages, winding alleyways and horseshoe-shaped harbour.

Next comes more coastal exploring via the coves of **Lamorna** and **Porthcurno**, where you can watch an unforgettable clifftop play at the famous Minack Theatre, carved directly into the granite cliffs. From here it's a short hop to **Land's End** and the gorgeous cove at **Sennen**, from where you can strike out along the coast path and seek out some seriously out-of-the-way beaches. If time allows, the nearby **Penwith Moors** are littered with ancient hillforts, strange stone circles and abandoned minestacks: perfect hiking country.

Then it's over the sea to the **Isles of Scilly**. You can either catch the ferry from Penzance, or take a plane from the tiny Land's End Airport. Either way, you'll arrive at the main island of **St Mary's**, the largest and liveliest of the 140-odd islands that make up the archipelago. From here, it's a simple matter of catching one of the regular inter-island boats to the other islands, including **Tresco**, a privately-owned island that's known for its subtropical gardens, established by medieval monks and bursting with exotic blooms. The islands of **St Martin's**, **Bryher** and **St Agnes** are even quieter than Tresco, and home to only a handful of residents: these are the ones to visit if you like your beaches empty and your coastline quiet. But if you're still not quite far enough from civilisation, you could charter a boat to visit one of the hundred or so **Uninhabited Isles**, where gannets and gulls will be your only company.

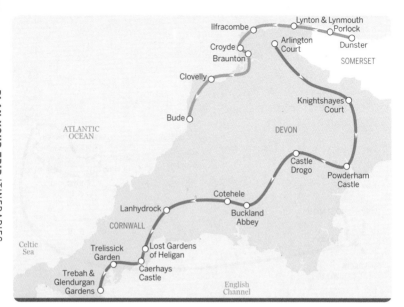

North Coast Explorer

Wild views and sea-smacked shores characterise this coastal road-trip, which starts on Exmoor and winds west onto Cornwall's stunning north coast. Kick things off in **Dunster** with a visit to the ruby-red castle, then head west through the village of **Porlock** to take the spectacular hairpin road over Porlock Hill. Follow the road along the moor's north coast to the twin seaside towns of **Lynton** and **Lynmouth**, and factor in time for a walk along the beautiful Valley of the Rocks.

Continue west to take in some old-fashioned seaside atmosphere in **Ilfracombe**, a classic candy-floss resort known for its Victorian villas and busy beaches, as well as an unexpectedly arty side thanks to Damian Hirst, who owns a restaurant in town. Further west brings you to beachy **Braunton** and **Croyde**, where you can learn the surfing basics or just stroll through the dunes. Next comes **Clovelly**, a lost-in-time village lined with cob cottages and cobbled streets, before you cross the Cornish border to **Bude**, another seaside town that's surrounded by sandy beaches, including family-friendly Summerleaze and cliff-backed Crackington Haven.

Great Estates

This tailored trip links some of the southwest's most impressive country houses and gardens. It begins with vintage carriages at **Arlington Court**, then heads southeast to visit the Victoriana-filled halls of **Knightshayes Court** and the battlements of **Powderham Castle**, both easy day-trips from Exeter. To the west lies **Castle Drogo**, an architectural fantasy built during the early 20th century, while **Buckland Abbey** boasts an older heritage: it was Francis Drake's former home.

Over the Cornish border, **Cotehele** is a mostly Tudor manor with a wonderful old quay. On the edge of Bodmin Moor, Grade I-listed **Lanhydrock** mixes 17th and 19th century styles: look out for the Great Hall and the magnificent Victorian kitchens. To the south are the **Lost Gardens of Heligan**, forgotten for the best part of a century until they were rediscovered by Tim Smit, creator of the Eden Project. Nearby **Caerhays Castle** is famous for its rhododendrons, but is only open for a few months in spring; for year-round displays, head for the trio of extravagant gardens around Falmouth: **Trelissick**, **Trebah** and **Glendurgan**.

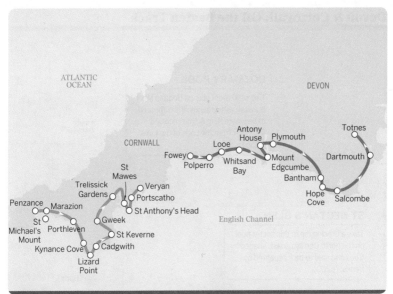

ATLANTIC
OCEAN

DEVON

CORNWALL

Antony
House

Totnes

Plymouth

Looe

Fowey

Dartmouth

Polperro

Whitsand
Bay

Mount
Edgcumbe

St
Mawes

Bantham

Trelissick
Gardens

Veryan

Hope
Cove

Salcombe

Penzance

Portscatho

Marazion

St Anthony's Head

English Channel

St
Michael's
Mount

Porthleven

Gweek

Kynance Cove

St Keverne

Cadgwith

Lizard
Point

 Two Peninsulas

This itinerary takes in two of Cornwall's
most picturesque peninsulas, the Lizard
and the Roseland. Start in **Penzance** and
head round Mount's Bay to **Marazion**,
where you catch a boat or walk along
the causeway to the island abbey of **St
Michael's Mount**. Alternatively, continue
on to the harbour of **Porthleven**, where
you'll find several excellent restaurants.

Then it's onto the Lizard, a wild,
empty peninsula known for its wildlife
and treacherous coastline. Stop to see
the iconic view of **Kynance Cove** before
exploring the headland at **Lizard Point**
and the thatched village of **Cadgwith**. Try
homemade ice cream at Roskilly's Farm
near **St Keverne**, then head along the
Helford River to **Gweek** and its seal-rescue
sanctuary.

From here, it's on to the rolling grounds
of **Trelissick**, and a trip aboard the King
Harry Ferry to the **Roseland Peninsula**. Essential stops here include chic **St
Mawes** and its Tudor castle, the nearby
lighthouse at **St Anthony's Head** and the
photogenic villages of **Portscatho** and
Veryan.

 Over the Tamar

This itinerary spans the Tamar Estuary,
the age-old boundary between Devon and
Cornwall. **Fowey** makes a fine start, with
its pastel-coloured houses, riverside pubs,
and Daphne du Maurier connections.
Head east via the olde-worlde harbour of
Polperro to **Looe**, a breezy seaside town
divided by the River Looe. Beaches abound
nearby, including the massive sweep of
Whitsand Bay.

Then it's on to the **Rame Peninsula** and the country estates of **Mount
Edgcumbe** and **Antony House** before
catching the Torpoint Ferry across the
Tamar to **Plymouth**. Devon's biggest city
might not be pretty, but it's packed with
history – especially around the historic
Barbican. The city also has a growing
foodie scene, with several celebrity chefs
setting up shop around town.

From Plymouth, it's a leisurely spin
into the South Hams for a paddle at **Bantham** and **Hope Cove**, a saunter around
Salcombe and a day of dining in **Dartmouth**. Finish with vintages at Sharpham
Vineyard and lunch at the Riverford Field
Kitchen before reaching journey's end in
quirky **Totnes**.

Devon & Cornwall: Off the Beaten Track

DOZMARY POOL
This windswept lake on Bodmin Moor is awash with legends: it's rumoured to be where King Arthur received Excalibur from the Lady of the Lake. (p156)

ST NECTAN'S GLEN
Take a bracing dip in this secret pool on the north Cornish coast, shaded by trees and said to be frequented by fairies. (p200)

ATLANTIC OCEAN

GOLITHA FALLS
Trek to a gorgeous wooded waterfall near St Neot on the southern edge of Bodmin Moor: perfect picnic territory. (p159)

ROCHE ROCK
Discover a forgotten medieval chapel in the wilds of mid-Cornwall, supposedly once inhabited by a local hermit. (p182)

MÊN-AN-TOL
This weird hollow stone is said to have magical properties, but you need to crawl all the way through it to benefit. (p230)

LANTIC & LANSALLOS
Leave the crowds far behind on these hard-to-reach beaches on the south Cornish coast, or just explore the spectacular stretch of coast path. (p189)

Lundy Island

Bude
Widemouth Bay

ST NECTAN'S GLEN
Launceston
DOZMARY POOL
Wadebridge
GOLITHA FALLS
Bodmin
Newquay
ROCHE ROCK
Liskeard
Perranporth
St Austell
LANTIC & LANSALLOS
St Ives
Redruth
Truro
MÊN-AN-TOL
Land's End
Hayle
Penzance
St Just-in-Penwith
Mousehole
Helston
Falmouth
The Lizard

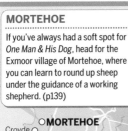

MORTEHOE

If you've always had a soft spot for *One Man & His Dog*, head for the Exmoor village of Mortehoe, where you can learn to round up sheep under the guidance of a working shepherd. (p139)

EXMOOR NATIONAL PARK

Exmoor's newfound status as a 'Dark Sky Reserve' makes this one of the southwest's best places for star-spotting. (p128)

EXETER LIVESTOCK MARKET

Soak up the sights (and smells) of an authentic livestock market, held twice-weekly just outside Exeter. (p49)

DITTISHAM

This pretty south Devon cove is well worth a detour, with a great seaside cafe and ferries to Agatha Christie's nearby house at Greenway. (p86)

Plan Your Trip

Outdoor Activities

Devon and Cornwall were made for adventure. Their national parks and stunning shores see you hiking iconic coast paths, surfing England's best waves, cycling desolate moors. Trot on a horse, escape on a yacht, clamber over rocky tors. Your break could spark a new passion or the rediscovery of an old.

Best Outdoors

Best Long-Distance Hikes

The epic 360-mile South West Coast Path; Devon's Two Moors Way; Cornwall's Saints Way; Exmoor's Coleridge Way.

Best Places for Short Walks

Dartmoor and Exmoor National Parks; Bodmin Moor; countless coast path hikes.

Best Surfing Beaches

Surf-central Newquay draws the crowds. For less-frenetic wave-riding try Polzeath, Bude and Sennen Cove in Cornwall, plus Croyde and Bantham in Devon.

Best Cycle Trails

The West Country Way links Exmoor to North Cornwall. There's Devon and Cornwall's Coast to Coast routes, Devon's Granite Way and Tarka Trail, and Cornwall's Camel Trail.

Best Horse-Riding Spots

Dartmoor and Exmoor National Park offer wilderness trotting; Exmoor has equine-friendly Coleridge Way.

Key Information Sources

Active Exmoor (www.activeexmoor.com)

Active Dartmoor (www.dartmoor.co.uk/active-dartmoor)

Adventure Activities Cornwall (www.adventure-cornwall.co.uk)

Bodmin Moor (www.bodminmoor.co.uk)

Cornwall Area of Outstanding Natural Beauty (AONB; www.cornwall-aonb.gov.uk)

Dartmoor National Park Authority (DNPA; www.dartmoor.gov.uk)

Exmoor National Park Authority (ENPA; www.exmoor-nationalpark.gov.uk)

National Trust (NT; ☑0844 800 1895; www.nationaltrust.org.uk)

South Devon Area of Outstanding Natural Beauty (AONB; www.southdevonaonb.org.uk)

Southwest Tourism (www.visitsouthwest.co.uk)

Torbay Coast and Countryside Trust (www.countryside-trust.org.uk)

Walking

The sheer diversity of landscapes in Devon and Cornwall gives walkers itchy feet. Britain's longest national trail, the South West Coast Path, dazzles and challenges as it careers around the shores. Dartmoor, Exmoor and Bodmin Moor deliver hundreds of miles of wilderness walks rich in archaeology and laced with myth. Meanwhile, an irresistible network of less-trodden footpaths meanders across the counties' rural heartlands, opening up green lanes, woodlands and drovers' trails.

The South West Coast Path

It's billed as a 630-mile adventure – and it is. The South West Coast Path (SWCP) takes in the entire shore of Devon and Cornwall on its journey from Poole in Dorset to Minehead in Somerset. En route are cliffs crowned by tin mines, sparkling bays, pretty fishing villages and swathes of rural idyll. It's so gorgeous you'll forgive it the painful combined gradient of three Everests. In metric it's even more impressive: 1014km.

A whopping 65% of the trail is within AONBs (Areas of Outstanding Natural Beauty); over half is Heritage Coast and 5% is National Park. Bird life is particularly impressive; expect to see peregrine falcon, gannet, fulmar, kittiwake and guillemot. Seals, dolphins and sharks are often seen close to shore. The region's wildflowers are outstanding in spring and summer: a palette of pink thrift, creamy bladder campion, purple heather and yellow gorse.

Day Walks

Superb, shorter clifftop hikes abound. Here are some local favourites:

➡ **Lynmouth–Combe Martin** (13 miles) The realm of the red deer, where vertiginous cliffs meet open moor.

➡ **Pendeen Watch–Sennen Cove** (9 miles) Cracking views and the working Levant Mine.

➡ **Sennen Cove–Porthcurno** (6 miles) From surfing beaches to a cliffside theatre, via Land's End.

➡ **Salcombe–Hope Cove** (8 miles) Happy wanderings from a chic sailing port to an enchanting Devon fishing village.

➡ **Portreath-Trevaunance Cove** (9 miles) Mining heritage, a surfers' beach, sandy cove and 192m-high headland.

➡ **Branscombe to Beer** (2 miles) From fishing village, via remarkable geology, to shipwreck beach. Bring a swimsuit.

Planning

Few people tackle the whole trail in one go; leave around eight weeks (56 consecutive walking days) if you do. Many return to cover different sections year-on-year, with some stretches providing testing, exhilarating days or weeks. The trail's official website (www.southwestcoastpath.com) has an excellent overview, and a distance calculator. It also profiles day walks. The South West Coast Path Association (www.swcpa.co.uk) produces the *South West Coast Path Guide* (£10), which details the route, transport and on-trail accommodation.

Safety

Some sections of the path pose dangers ranging from live firing by the military to cliff falls. The trail website details any affected sections; on the ground, observe warning signs. Check locally before attempting to wade across rivers; it can be fatal. You'll also need to carry water, a hat and weather-proof clothing.

Practicalities

The path can be walked all year but it's at its best from April to September, although in July and August beds and tranquillity are at a premium. In winter, conditions are often very wet and muddy with severe gales. Way marking is in the form of acorn symbols. Sometimes they're missing and crossing cities, towns and large villages can be complicated. Carrying OS maps is a good idea.

Accommodation ranges from five star to seaside-chic and old-fashioned B&B; many hikers opt for youth hostels to keep costs down. The walking itself, in all its inspirational, exhausting glory, is absolutely free.

Dartmoor National Park

The 368 sq miles of Dartmoor are the emptiest, highest and wildest in southern England. Rounded hills, or tors, pepper a rolling, primitive landscape. Hiking here takes in stone circles and rows, burial mounds and massive Bronze Age settlements; you'll also encounter free-roaming Dartmoor ponies, sheep and cows.

The DNPA can advise on day hikes and runs a program of guided walks themed around history, legends and geology. They cost £4 for adults (free for children); details are online (www.dartmoor-npa.gov. uk) and in the free *Enjoy Dartmoor* visitor guide.

Longer, self-guided hikes that encompass Dartmoor include the 117-mile Two Moors Way (p32) and the 18-mile (two to three day) Templar Way.

Good bases for hikers are Princetown, with its key visitor centre, Okehampton and Widecombe-in-the-Moor.

Exmoor National Park

While Dartmoor is bigger, 267-sq-mile Exmoor National Park has a different asset – the sea. A compelling 34 miles of jaw-dropping, leg-testing coastline. Add ancient woods, time-warp villages, red deer and Exmoor ponies and you have a winner for walkers.

The ENPA runs a superbly varied program of guided walks (adults £3 to £5; children free). These include deer watching at dawn, stargazing, nighttime navigation and fungi foraging. The ENPA also produces a series of walking cards outlining day hikes; staff can also advise.

Long-distance, self-guided hikes linked to Exmoor include the 117-mile Two Moors Way (p32), and the 36-mile Coleridge Way (p32).

Two of Exmoor's best bases for hikers are the twin, coastal villages of Lynton and Lynmouth, both starting points for splendid gorge-side hikes. Sleepy Dulverton on the moor's southern edge opens up a cracking 12-mile circular walk via Tarr Steps. Picturesque Exford is a good centre-of-the-moor walking base.

Bodmin Moor

Not to be outdone, Cornwall has its own moor, Bodmin. Ruined tin mines dot an atmospheric, mystical landscape of bogs, Stone Age sites and high tors (hills), making for a moody hiking environment. Highlights include walks from the ancient mining village of Minions, with its own stone circle, and the high tors of Rough Tor and Brown Willy.

A logical base is Bodmin, which has the distinct feel of a moorland settlement.

Other Walking Routes

Two Moors Way (www.devon.gov.uk/walking/two_moors_way) A coast-to-coast epic (117 miles, eight days) from Lynmouth on Exmoor, across Devon and Dartmoor to Wembury, on the south coast.

Coleridge Way (www.coleridgeway.co.uk) This 36-mile (three- to four-day) jaunt runs from Exmoor to the Quantocks, in the footsteps of the poet, Samuel Taylor Coleridge.

Saints' Way A 30-mile (three- to four-day), cross-Cornwall, former pilgrims' route, from Padstow in the north to Fowey in the south.

Templar Way Leisurely stroll (18 miles, two days) from Haytor to seaside Teignmouth.

Walking Festivals

These guided walks and events enable in-depth explorations of the areas' geography, history and wildlife. They're also held at quieter (cheaper) times of year.

Walk Scilly (www.simplyscilly.co.uk) Late March to early April.

Ivybridge Walking Festival (www.iwcdevon. org.uk) Late April to early May.

North Devon and Exmoor Walking Festival (www.exmoorwalkingfestival.co.uk) Late April to early May, and early October.

Fal River Walking Festival (www.falriver. co.uk/whats-on/walking-festival) Late October to early November.

Safety & the Environment

Some of Devon and Cornwall's walking environments, especially the moors, have their dangers. Note the military uses part of Dartmoor for firing practice using live ammunition. On some of the southwest's trails (especially Dartmoor) there's little signposting; carrying a map and compass, and knowing how to use them is recommended. Region-wide the elements could catch you out: warm waterproof clothing, water, hats and sunscreen are essential.

You have a legal right to walk on footpaths, bridleways and byways. In national parks you can often walk on other areas deemed 'open country'; check with NPAs and local authorities if in any doubt. Along with usual guidelines, hikers are asked to leave historic sites undisturbed, not to feed ponies or other animals, and to consider leaving the car behind.

Water Sports

Few regions are so rich in idyllic places to get on, and in, the water. Here find hundreds of miles of beautiful beaches, scores of historic sailing ports and an array of sheltered estuaries. In Cornwall, add the most consistent quality surf in England and you have endless opportunities to surf, bodyboard, sail, kayak and dive.

These experiences also offer an insider's insight into life along the shore: secret coves, seal's-eye views of soaring cliffs and wildlife-watching galore.

Surfing

The southwest's surf culture has helped power its reinvention as a cool holiday hotspot. Surprisingly, the roots reach back more than a century – sepia archive images show people surfing in the region in 1904. The sport really took off in the 1950s, and now racks of wetsuits and boards tempt thousands into the waves.

The self-styled surfing (and party) capital is Newquay. More relaxed surf hubs include Polzeath, Perranporth, Bude and Sennen Cove in Cornwall, and Croyde, Woolacombe and Bantham in Devon.

Braunton, near Croyde, also has a UK first – the ultra-cool Museum of British Surfing (p141) is the county's only permanent, wave-riding-related heritage display.

Learning to Surf

Beginners are likely to spend a lot of time simply trying to stand up and lessons are highly recommended. **Surfing GB** (www.surfinggb.com), formerly the British Surfing Association, accredits schools countrywide. Lesson costs start from around £30 for 2½ hours; at least two sessions are normally needed to get the best results.

Hire outlets are sited at all of Devon and Cornwall's popular surfing beaches. It costs around £10 to rent a wetsuit for a half-day; the same for surfboards. Another option is a much easier-to-manage bodyboard; hire stands are easy to find, and costs are similar to those of surfboards.

Be aware, each year people get into difficulties in the water and sadly some drown; head for an RNLI-patrolled beach (the main ones are) and follow the lifeguards' advice.

Thicker wetsuits mean you can surf year-round; perversely the biggest swells usually come amid autumn and winter low-pressures. Good surf in the summer sunshine is not uncommon but can't be guaranteed.

Cornwall and Devon's north shores tend to enjoy better conditions, but wind and swell directions mean different beaches on either coast can be better on the day. Check the latest surf conditions with Magic Seaweed (www.magicseaweed.com).

Kitesurfing & Windsurfing

Kitesurfing's growing popularity sees fleets of brightly coloured canopies sweeping the southwest's skies on windy days. The **British Kite Surfing Association** (☑01305-813555; www.britishkitesurfingassociation.co.uk) lists approved schools; prices start from around £90 for a half-day. Exmouth, in Devon, is a particularly good place to learn.

Windsurfing also remains popular; the Royal Yachting Association (p34) details courses. Taster sessions start from around £45. Places with approved centres include Bude and Falmouth in Cornwall, and Plymouth and Exeter in Devon.

White Water

Dartmoor's deep, steep gorges ensure heavy winter rains turn stretches of the

---

BEST UNSPOILT BEACHES

Saunton Sands Three miles of undeveloped North Devon shore backed by the UK's biggest dune system.

Porthcurno One of west Cornwall's most atmospheric beaches: a sand-filled cove framed by dramatic cliffs.

Slapton Sands South Devon's immense, spray-dashed pebble beach edging a watery nature reserve.

Gwithian & Godrevy Escape the crowds in Cornwall's largest stretches of sand.

Bantham Rural, dune-backed south Devon beach with a vast expanse of golden grains at low tide.

Perranporth A 3-mile sweep of sands, backed by grassy dunes.

River Dart into foaming, fast-flowing water – riding them is a truly thrilling experience. The rapids are only open between October and March. Winter kayaking also takes place on the Rivers Barle and East Lyn on Exmoor. The DNPA and ENPA can advise.

The **British Canoe Union** (BCU; ☑0845 370 9500; www.bcu.org.uk) approves training centres; many require you to be BCU two-star standard before you can head onto 'moving water'. Prices start at £40 for a half-day.

Kayaking

The southwest's sheltered estuaries and rugged coasts make paddling tempting, as do regular sightings of seals, dolphins and basking sharks. At many popular beaches you can hire out sit-on-top kayaks; prices start at around £15 per hour (per day from £40).

If you prefer closed-cockpit boats, the British Canoe Union details approved schools. There are training centres in Falmouth, St Mawes, Plymouth, Exeter, Okehampton and Bude. You can also head out on a Canadian canoe on the Fal River.

For longer-distance paddling, Sea Kayak and SUP (p94) in Salcombe runs a two-day beginners course for £180. Falmouth-based **Sea Kayaking Cornwall** (www.seakayakingcornwall.com) stages one-day introductory sessions (£95) and two-to-five day expeditions (from £234). North Devon–based **Sea Kayaking South West** (☑01271-813271; www.seakayakingsouthwest.co.uk) does a two-day beginners course for £160 and also organises mini-expeditions (per three days from £250).

Sailing

The southwest's past is inextricably bound up with sail-power: Iron Age tin traders; 17th-century fishermen working the Newfoundland cod banks; an expansionist Royal Navy; fast clippers racing to the Azores to trade in fresh fruit; and fleets of boats fishing closer to home.

Learning to Sail

The **Royal Yachting Association** (RYA; ☑023-8060 4100; www.rya.org.uk) lists approved schools. Many are in the region's traditional maritime centres, including Falmouth, Mylor, St Mawes, Fowey, Rock and the Isles of Scilly in Cornwall; and Salcombe, Dartmouth, Torquay and Plymouth in Devon.

Half-day sessions in smaller craft (eg a topper) cost about £40. A weekend, live-aboard course for a RYA qualification costs from around £200 per person.

Diving

The number of wrecks off the southwest coast makes sailors nervous. But couple them with reefs and crystal-clear waters and you have a great area to dive. Wrasse, conger eels and dogfish float past face masks in a watery world that drifts from shallow reefs to deeper waters.

The big dive attraction is the **Scylla** (www.divescylla.com). This gutted former Royal Navy warship was sunk near Plymouth by the National Marine Aquarium in 2004 in order to study how reefs form. Devon and Cornwall's coasts have more than 4600 wrecks; the Isles of Scilly alone has a remarkable 150 recognised dive sites.

The **British Sub Aqua Club** (☑0151-3506200; www.bsac.com) approves training centres. Popular dive bases include Exmouth, Plymouth and the Isles of Scilly. A half-day taster is around £50; four-day training courses start at £375.

WATER-SPORTS SPOTS

Newquay Learn to surf at buzzing Fistral Beach or nearby Watergate Bay.

Croyde North Devon's chilled-out surfing hub, fringed by quaint thatched cottages.

Widemouth Bay Another beautiful Cornish surfing hot-spot, 3 miles south of Bude.

Bantham & Bigbury Learn to surf, try stand-up paddleboarding or hire a sit-on-top kayak.

Perranporth Fancy harnessing wind *and* waves? Try kiteboarding here.

Salcombe South Devon yachting haven; learn to sail or head out on a sea-kayak expedition.

Cycling

Traffic-free routes and varied landscapes make the southwest one of the best cycling regions in the country. Many of the paths are on former rail or tram lines and snake amid extinct mines or quarries.

Dartmoor has good routes; the DNPA sells a map (£13). Exmoor's mountain-bike trails are graded, ski-run style, in *Exmoor for Off-Road Cyclists* (£10).

Top Cycle Routes

West Country Way Part of this trail stretches from Exmoor, via Bodmin, to Padstow in north Cornwall.

Devon Coast To Coast (p128) Ilfracombe to Plymouth, 102 glorious miles; 70 of them traffic-free.

Camel Trail (p203) A 17-mile, car-free trip from Bodmin Moor to the north Cornwall coast.

Granite Way (p124) Eleven spectacular miles on a former Dartmoor railway line.

Cornwall Coast to Coast (p169) An 11-mile jaunt along the route of an old mineral tramway.

Tarka Trail (p146) A delightful, 30-mile loop through north Devon's lowlands.

Multi Activity Centres

These providers offer a range of adrenaline sports, ranging from abseiling and mountain biking, to coasteering.

Adventure Okehampton (www.adventure okehampton.com) Based in Dartmoor National Park

BF Adventure (www.bfadventure.org) Based in Falmouth National Park

Exmoor Adventures (www.exmooradventures. co.uk)

Mountains+Moor (www.mountainsandmorr. co.uk) Based in Exmoor National Park

Outdoor Adventure (www.outdooradventure. co.uk) Based in Bude

Rock Climbing

Strings of challenging crags stretch across Devon and Cornwall. Dartmoor alone has scores of accessible climbs with multi- and

PLACES TO WATCH WILDLIFE

Exmoor Head out on a dawn stag-watching walk.

Penwith Cornwall's westerly tip is prime shark-spotting territory.

Dartmoor Herds of sturdy Dartmoor ponies roam this windswept wilderness.

Isles of Scilly Head out on a 'snorkelling with seals' safari.

Topsham One of the best places to watch birds in Devon and Cornwall.

single-pitch routes; the DNPA produces a free leaflet. Torbay and Bodmin are other good focus points.

The **British Mountaineering Council** (☎0161-4456111; www.thebmc.co.uk) has a database of indoor and outdoor climbs. For tuition try the Rock Centre (p110) and Adventure Okehampton (p110) in Devon. Expect to pay around £20 per half-day.

Horse Riding

Devon and Cornwall help riders achieve that dream of cantering across open countryside. Diverse environments include dappled bridleways, spectacular moorland or the ride-through-the-surf beloved of films.

Although you can't ride horses on public footpaths, you can trot on the vast network of bridleways – Exmoor (p128) alone has 400 miles of them. Much of the common land on Dartmoor (p112) is open to horse riders, as are some of the region's other trails, such as the Coleridge Way (p32). Wherever you plan to head out, always check whether riding is permitted.

Many stables on Dartmoor and Exmoor are either on, or within very easy reach of, the open moors. They cater to novices and experienced riders alike – expect to pay around £40 for a two-hour hack. The **British Horse Society** (☎02476-840500; www. bhs.org.uk) lists approved stables.

Many riding centres offer accommodation. This can range from luxurious farmhouses to basic camping; some will even put your horse up for the night, too.

Travel with Children

It's good to know in our digital, virtual world that channelling incoming tides around sandcastles still provides great joy. And wraparound beaches aren't Devon and Cornwall's only child-friendly assets. Rafts of activities and bucketloads of attractions ensure they're an absolute delight for kids, and adults re-connecting with child-like joys.

Best Regions For Kids

Newquay & the North Coast
Water-sports magnet with beaches galore, an aquarium, farm attraction and puffing steam trains. Investigate Bude, Perranporth and St Agnes, too.

Torquay & South Devon
Torquay offers oodles of beaches plus an eco zoo, giant al fresco aviary, prehistoric caves and a model village. South Devon serves up surfing beaches and river trips.

South Cornwall
Head here for the Eden Project, a shipwreck museum, child-friendly maritime museum, and incredibly cute seal and monkey sanctuaries.

Exmoor & North Devon
North Devon dishes up superb surfing, huge dune-backed beaches, and the mega-attraction the Big Sheep. Exmoor offers deer-watching and wildlife discovery days.

Devon & Cornwall for Kids

A plethora of child-focused attractions and activities ensure the southwest delivers fantastic family holidays. Attractions are well attuned to the needs of parents and children: displays are targeted at young minds, cafes feature kid-friendly meals, and baby-changing rooms are common. Many hotels, pubs and restaurants cater well for kids, but it pays to check. As elsewhere some people will frown on breastfeeding, while others will barely notice.

Safety

The beaches of Cornwall and Devon are glorious, but do present safety issues; sadly fatalities are not unknown. Most of the key tourist beaches have lifeguards; head for one that does, then follow the lifeguards' advice. Be especially wary of rip currents and fast-rising tides. Lifeguard cover is seasonal (often Easter to September) and tends to finish at 5pm or 6pm. The RNLI website (www.rnli.org) lists which beaches it covers and when.

Some sections of the Devon and Cornwall coast are prone to cliff-falls; keep an eye out for warning signs.

Children's Highlights

Family-Friendly Attractions

➡ **Paignton Zoo**, Torquay (p66)

➡ **Flambards**, Helston (p246)

➡ **The Big Sheep**, north **Devon** (www.thebigsheep.co.uk)

➡ **Crealy Adventure Parks** (www.crealy.co.uk) One in Devon, one in **Cornwall**

➡ **Land's End Theme Park**, Land's End (p233)

Rainy-Day Attractions

➡ **Eden Project, South East Cornwall** A heated eco-attraction with a playful feel. (p182)

➡ **National Marine Aquarium, Plymouth** Underwater walkways reveal sharks, turtles and huge rays. (p103)

➡ **Kents Cavern, Torquay** Cavemen, a devil's toe nail and Stone Age handprints. (p66)

➡ **National Maritime Museum, Cornwall** Crammed with hands-on activities. (p163)

➡ **Underground Passages, Exeter** Prowl ancient tunnels and hear stories of ghosts and cholera. (p45)

Kid-Friendly Heritage Sites

➡ **Arlington Court, north Devon** Estate with horse carriages, peacocks and bats. (p144)

➡ **Pendennis Castle, Falmouth** Battlements, a Tudor Gun Room, and hands-on exhibits. (p163)

➡ **RAMM, Exeter** Fun, child-friendly displays at the 2012 museum of the year. (p46)

➡ **Geevor Tin Mine, Pendeen** Go on an underground tour, then pan for minerals at this iconic Cornish mine. (p229)

➡ **Castle Drogo, Dartmoor** Crenellations and playhouses at the last castle to be built in England. (p121)

➡ **Porthcurno Telegraph Museum** Secret wartime tunnels and a whirring telegraphy kit. (p234)

Planning

When To Go

School holidays see accommodation demand, and prices, spike. But summer, Easter and half-term also see attractions extend their opening hours, often putting on special family-friendly events. And if the summer holiday storm clouds *do* gather, there are plenty of rainy-day attractions where you can get dry.

Accommodation

Families fare well for sleep spots in Devon and Cornwall; we outline B&Bs and hotels offering family rooms throughout the guide. Some accommodation providers can provide put-me-up beds.

Self-catering and camping offer great flexibility. Watch out for the new breed of 'comfy camping' options, where Romany caravans and safari-style tents come with their own fire pits.

Child-Savvy Organisations

All over Cornwall and Devon, organisations run superb child-focused events. Pirate parades, rockpool rambles, nighttime hikes and archery days: these family experiences can define your trip.

Cornwall Wildlife Trust (www.cornwallwildlifetrust.org.uk)

Dartmoor National Park Authority (DNPA; www.dartmoor.gov.uk)

National Trust (NT; www.nationaltrust.org.uk)

English Heritage (EH; www.english-heritage.org.uk)

Exmoor National Park Authority (ENPA; www.exmoor-nationalpark.gov.uk)

South Devon Area of Outstanding Natural Beauty (AONB; www.southdevonaonb.org.uk)

Torbay Coast & Countryside (www.countrysidetrust.org.uk)

Useful Websites

Cornwall Beach Guide (www.cornwallbeachguide.co.uk)

Day out with the Kids (www.dayoutwiththekids.co.uk) Activity directory, searchable by region.

Visit Cornwall (www.visitcornwall.com) Draws together child-friendly info.

Visit Devon (www.visitdevon.co.uk) Has subsections on attractions and free days out.

Visit South West (www.visitsouthwest.co.uk) Has an extensive family holidays section.

Regions at a Glance

Coast and countryside, cities and villages, bluffs and bays – the sheer variety of Devon and Cornwall's landscapes is one of the region's major draws. Every corner has its own unique selling point, from surfing on the north Cornish coast to savouring fine wines in South Devon. The main problem you'll have is deciding which area to explore first.

The region's compact dimensions mean that it's easy to explore, too, regardless of whether you choose to do it by road or rail, biking or hiking. Make sure you leave time for the journey, though – getting from A to B is all part of the experience, and you're guaranteed to discover some unexpected gems along the way.

Exeter & East Devon

History
Coastline
Countryside

Exeter Cathedral

Centring on its huge Gothic cathedral, the elegant city of Exeter has a history stretching back to Roman times. Don't miss the beautiful cathedral close and the city's spooky underground passages.

Jurassic Coast

The rust-red cliffs of east Devon form part of the Jurassic Coast, an ancient landscape known for its fragile cliffs and fossil-hunting possibilities.

East Devon Countryside

The landscape of east Devon is wonderfully varied, ranging from the marshy banks of the Exe Estuary to the salty old harbours of Sidmouth and Branscombe.

p42

Torquay & South Devon

Beaches
History
Countryside

Torbay's Seaside

Billing itself as the English Riviera, the Torbay area is one of the region's holiday hotspots, and it's tailor-made for an old-fashioned bucket-and-spade break by the sea.

Stately Homes

Some of Devon's loveliest country houses are hidden away in the south Devon countryside: the Modernist-era High Cross House, the Regency pomp of Coleton Fishacre and Agatha Christie's Dartmouth hideaway, Greenway.

South Hams

The South Hams is the quintessential Devon landscape, encompassing fields, woods, rivers, harbours and sleepy hamlets. Dartmouth and Salcombe are both riverside beauties, while Totnes has an alternative edge.

p64

Plymouth & Dartmoor

Activities
Food & Drink
History

Outdoor Adventures

Whether it's hiking the tors of Dartmoor, cycling the Tarka Trail or windsurfing on Plymouth Sound, this is a great corner of Devon to get out and active.

Foodie Plymouth

It's not quite on the foodie radar yet, but Plymouth has a growing number of top-notch bistros, with leading lights such as Hugh Fearnley-Whittingstall, Garry Rhodes and the Tanner Brothers all catering to the city's diners.

Maritime Past

Plymouth has a long history as a maritime hub: Francis Drake spotted the Spanish Armada from here, and the Pilgrim Fathers set out for the New World from the Barbican's quayside.

p99

Exmoor & North Devon

Villages
Activities
Scenery

Towns & Villages

From farming hamlets to seaside harbours, North Devon has scores of villages crammed with history. Lynton, Ilfracombe, Porlock and Clovelly are classic seaside destinations, while Dulverton, Challacombe and Exford have a more rural vibe.

Exploring the Moors

There are endless ways to explore Exmoor's landscapes: saddle up for a horse-ride, strap on your hiking boots, hire a mountain bike or book a wildlife safari.

Sea & Country

Exmoor has a split personality: it's half coast, half countryside. Spend the morning swimming, go hiking in the afternoon, then head out for late-night stargazing.

p126

Bodmin & East Cornwall

Views
Nature
Ancient Sites

Cornwall's Rooftop

A pocket of proper wilderness between Cornwall's north and south coasts, Bodmin Moor has a stark beauty all its own. Hikers head for the high points of Brown Willy and Rough Tor.

Moorland Wildlife

The moor is a haven for rare wildlife, from adders and lizards to stonechats and skylarks. It's also supposedly stalked by the Beast of Bodmin Moor, a large catlike creature that's allegedly been spotted many times.

Stone Circles

During neolithic times, the moor was woodland, and many prehistoric people made their home here. Their legacy remains in the shape of several stone circles.

p150

South Cornwall

Beaches
Countryside
Villages

South Coast

Cornwall's south coast beaches are gentler than the ones on the north coast: here the golden crescents are more likely to be backed by green fields than craggy cliffs.

Peninsular Splendour

Two of Cornwall's prettiest peninsulas jut out from its southern coastline: the rural Roseland, spotted with pretty hamlets and farms; and the remote Rame Peninsula with a collection of great estates.

Seaside Towns

Picture-perfect villages are strung all along Cornwall's south coast. Most were established to serve the county's once-great fishing industry. While only a handful of boats remain, they're still full of maritime atmosphere.

p160

Newquay & North Coast

Beaches
Watersports
Food & Drink

Classic Coastline

The north coast is home to Cornwall's classic beaches: golden sweeps of sand, backed by dunes and rocky cliffs. Fistral, Perranporth and Gwithian are busy in summer, but there are secret ones to discover, too.

Newquay Surfing

Unsurprisingly, the Atlantic coastline is blessed with Cornwall's biggest waves, so this is ground central if you want to learn to surf. Newquay's the premier spot, but Bude, Perranporth and Polzeath are equally good.

Classy Cuisine

Celeb chefs are ten-a-penny (Jamie Oliver, Rick Stein, etc), but don't overlook the lesser-known restaurants, as there are some real gems to dig up.

p193

West Cornwall & the Isles of Scilly

History
Coastline
Islands

Prehistoric Sites

The Penwith moors have more prehistoric sites than almost anywhere else in the West Country. You'll find numerous stone circles here, as well as many quoits, dolmens, menhirs and hillforts.

Last Stop

The wild west is also where the land finally runs out of steam. Land's End is mainland Britain's most westerly point, and the sea-smacked coast here has an extra-special grandeur.

Island Escapes

Scilly and its low-lying island archipelago are 28 miles west of Land's End. With fine beaches, unique flora and only a handful of residents, it's an idyllic escape from the outside world.

p219

On the Road

Exmoor &
North Devon
p126

Exeter &
East Devon
p42

Newquay &
the North Coast
p193

Plymouth &
Dartmoor
p99

Bodmin &
East Cornwall
p150

Torquay &
South Devon
p64

South
Cornwall
p160

West Cornwall &
the Isles of Scilly
p219

Exeter & East Devon

Includes ➡

Exeter 43
Around Exeter 52
East Devon.................. 54
Topsham..................... 55
Exmouth 57
Sidmouth.................... 59
Beer & Around.............61

Best Places to Eat

➡ River Cottage HQ (p61)

➡ Salutation (p57)

➡ Rusty Bike (p50)

➡ River Exe Cafe (p59)

➡ Pebblebed Wine Cellar (p57)

Best Places to Stay

➡ Magdalen Chapter (p49)

➡ Wood Life (p53)

➡ Reka Dom (p57)

➡ Salty Monk (p60)

➡ Bay View (p63)

Why Go?

Heritage city, rural idyll, spectacular shores – Devon's eastern corner delivers them all. On the Jurassic Coast, wave-carved cliffs range from russet-red to creamy-white. In between sit long pebble beaches, genteel resorts and quaint fishing villages; perfect for hiking, kitesurfing, fishing or strolling along the prom. In history-rich Exeter discover Roman walls, a fine cathedral and lively arts scene. The snaking River Exe estuary is ripe for exploration by boat, bike or on foot. Behind, rolling red-soil hills shelter tucked-away villages and stately homes. Fine food and drink abounds, from vineyards and celebrity-chef-run eateries to the beach barbecue of mackerel you've just caught yourself. Sleep in Mongolian yurts, luxury safari tents or chic city retreats. It's also a place to really experience other ways of life as they're lived, whether at a livestock market, village beach party or rural pub.

When to Go

➡ **Jul–Aug** In theory, warmer, dryer weather. School holidays swell visitor numbers, accommodation costs rise, roads and resorts become congested. Beer holds its fiesta-like village regatta.

➡ **Jun & Sep** Prime visiting time: fewer crowds and less traffic, but all attractions are open. September brings the warmest seas, and the weather is often quite good, too.

➡ **Apr–May** The holiday season gets underway from Easter; sights, campsites and boat trips swing into action. In late April foodies flock to Exeter's South West Food and Drink Festival.

➡ **Oct–Nov** Many attractions close, but accommodation prices plummet. A great time for coastal storm-watching, too.

EXETER

POP 119,600

Exeter is steeped in evidence of its centuries-old role as the spiritual and administrative heart of Devon. Relics include its ancient cathedral and chunks of winding Roman wall. But the city also has a youthful vibe, visible in bursts of ultramodern construction and a thriving arts scene. Down by the River Exe, the atmospheric quayside is a launch pad for explorations by bike or kayak. Add a movie museum, the chance to go on subterranean tours and stylish places to stay and eat, and you have a relaxed but lively touring base.

History

Exeter's past can be read clearly in its buildings. In around AD 55, invading Romans built a fortress ringed by a 2-mile defensive wall. Saxon and Norman times saw growth: a castle went up in 1068, the cathedral 40 years later. The Tudor woollen boom brought Exeter riches and half timbered houses; all those sheep in surrounding fields meant wool was brought to the city, dyed, and the cloth exported via Exeter Quay to Europe.

By the late Georgian era, Exeter was a genteel urban centre, its merchants busy building elegant town houses, many of which now house hotels and B&Bs. The Blitz of WWII brought devastation. In just one night in 1942, 156 people died and 12 hectares of the city were flattened. The postwar years saw an ambitious rebuild in red brick and cream stone; see its clean lines above the main street shopfronts. Fast forward to the 21st century and the attention-grabbing £220-million Princesshay Shopping Centre.

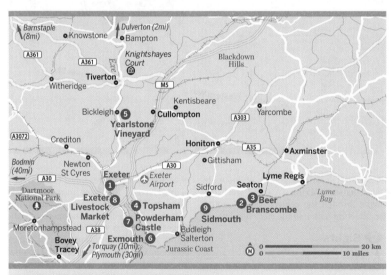

Exeter & East Devon Highlights

❶ Walking along the rooftop of the glorious Gothic **Exeter Cathedral** (p48)

❷ Hiking the extraordinary, millennia-old **Jurassic Coast** (p62) around Branscombe

❸ Catching your own supper, then cooking it on the beach at **Beer** (p61)

❹ Exploring the marsh-fringed Exe estuary, then enjoying a superb meal in pretty **Topsham** (p55)

❺ Sipping fine vintages, then tucking into fine food at picturesque **Yearlstone Vineyard** (p52), near Bickleigh

❻ Getting a real natural high **kitesurfing** (p58) off Exmouth

❼ Glimpsing life below stairs at stately **Powderham Castle** (p52)

❽ Experiencing the bustle – and the bidding – at the twice-weekly **Exeter Livestock Market** (p49)

❾ Joining an impromptu jam session during **Folk Week** (p60) at Sidmouth

Exeter

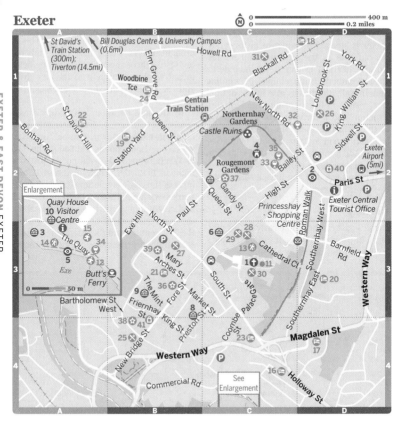

Part blue cubes, part echoes of 1950s designs, its shimmering glass and steel lines snake through the centre, adding another architectural notch in the city's timeline.

⊙ Sights

★ **Exeter Cathedral**   CHURCH
(☏01392-285983;   www.exeter-cathedral.org.uk;
The Close; adult/child £6/free; ⊙9am-4.45pm Mon-Sat) Magnificent in warm, honey-coloured stone, Exeter's Cathedral Church of St Peter is framed by lawns and wonky half-timbered buildings. It's a quintessentially English scene peopled by picnickers snacking to the sound of the bells. The site has been a religious one since at least the 5th century but the Normans started the current building in 1114; the towers of today's cathedral date from that period. In 1270 a 90-year remodelling process began, introducing a mix of Early English and Decorated Gothic styles. Outside, above the Great West Front, scores of weather-worn figures line a once brightly painted screen that now forms England's largest collection of 14th-century sculpture.

Inside, the ceiling is mesmerising; the longest unbroken Gothic vaulting in the world, it sweeps up to meet ornate ceiling bosses in gilt and vibrant colours. Look out for the 15th-century Exeter Clock in the north transept: in keeping with medieval astronomy it shows the earth at the centre of the universe with the sun, a fleur-de-lys, travelling round. Still ticking and whirring, it chimes on the hour.

The huge oak canopy over the Bishop's Throne was carved in 1312, while the 1350 minstrels' gallery is decorated with 12 angels playing musical instruments. Cathedral staff will point out the famous sculpture of the lady with two left feet and the tiny St James Chapel, built to repair one destroyed in the Blitz – its unusual carvings include a cat, a mouse and, oddly, a rugby player.

Exeter

◉ **Top Sights**
1 Exeter Cathedral........................C3
2 Underground Passages D2

◉ **Sights**
3 Customs House.............................A3
4 Exeter Castle................................C2
5 Exeter Quay.................................A3
6 Guildhall.......................................C3
7 RAMM...C2
8 Spacex..B3
9 St Nicholas Priory........................B3
10 Wharfinger's House.....................A2

◉ **Activities, Courses & Tours**
11 Exeter Cathedral Roof Tours...............C3
12 Exeter Cruises.............................A3
13 Redcoat Tours Cathedral
    Departures.................................C3
14 Redcoat Tours Quay Departures.........A3
15 Saddles & Paddles......................A3

◉ **Sleeping**
ABode, Royal Clarence ....(see 29)
16 Globe Backpackers......................C4
17 Magdalen Chapter.......................D4
18 Raffles..D1
19 Silversprings...............................B2
20 Southernhay House.....................D3

21 St Olaves.....................................B3
22 Townhouse..................................A1
23 White Hart....................................C4
24 Woodbine.....................................B1

◉ **Eating**
25 @Angela's....................................B4
26 Harry's..D1
27 Herbies...B3
28 MC Cafe, Bar & Grill C3
29 Michael Caines............................C3
30 Refectory.....................................C3
31 Rusty Bike....................................C1

◉ **Drinking & Nightlife**
32 Old Firehouse...............................D2
33 Old Timers....................................C2
34 On the Waterfront.........................A3
35 Timepiece....................................C2

◉ **Entertainment**
36 Bike Shed Theatre........................B3
37 Exeter Phoenix.............................C2
38 Exeter Picturehouse.....................B4
39 Mama Stone's...............................B3

◉ **Shopping**
40 Real Food Store............................D2
41 The Real McCoy............................B4

As well as the superb Roof Tours (p48), the cathedral also runs free 45-minute guided **tours** (☉11am & 12.30pm Mon-Sat, plus 2.30pm Mon-Fri). Evocative Choral Evensong services are held at 5.30pm Monday to Friday, and 4pm on Saturday and Sunday.

★**Underground Passages**   UNDERGROUND
(📞01392-665887; www.exeter.gov.uk/passages; Paris St; adult/child £5/3.50; ☉9.30am-5.30pm Mon-Sat Jun-Sep, 11.30am-4pm Tue-Sun Oct-May) Prepare to crouch down, don a hard hat and even get spooked in what is the only publicly accessible system of its kind in the country. These medieval, vaulted tunnels were built to house pipes bringing fresh drinking water from local springs into the city. The pipes often sprang leaks and, unlike modern utility companies, the authorities opted to have permanent access for repairs, rather than dig up the streets each time – genius.

Entertaining guides lead you through part of this vast, dank network of passages, telling tales of ghosts, the Civil War, escape routes, the Blitz and cholera outbreaks. The hard hat comes in handy when navigating the rock arches and narrow bends. One section involves a real bent-knees scramble; those who are too big (or too unwilling) can take an easier detour.

The last tour is an hour before closing. The passages get very busy; it's best to turn up, book a tour, then come back at the appointed time.

Bill Douglas Centre   MUSEUM
(📞01392-724321; www.exeter.ac.uk/bdc; Old Library, Prince of Wales Rd; ☉10am-5pm Mon-Fri; P) **FREE** A delightful homage to film and fun, this movie museum is a lively celebration of all things celluloid. Collections include 18th-century magic lanterns, zograscopes, shadow theatres and a hand-held panorama reel of George IV's coronation. You even get to glue an eye to a saucy 'what the butler saw' machine.

Movie memorabilia includes programs, posters, sheet music, games and toys – highlights include Charlie Chaplin bottle stoppers, Ginger Rogers playing cards and *Star Wars* merchandise. Alongside, thought-provoking displays cover a wealth of subjects ranging from Disneymania to Cinema as Institution and the Cult of Celebrity.

The Bill Douglas Centre is a 15-minute walk northwest from the city centre, on the University of Exeter campus.

RAMM
MUSEUM

(Royal Albert Memorial Museum & Art Gallery; ☑ 01392-265858; www.rammuseum.org.uk; Queen St; ⊙ 10am-5pm Tue-Sun) **FREE** The imposing red-brick exterior looks every inch the Victorian museum, but a £24-million pound revamp has brought the exhibits bang up to date. Interactive displays focus on Exeter's heritage from prehistory to the present, and on global exploration and the concept of collecting. You get to see Exeter's Roman-era artefacts and Tudor carvings, plus striking ethnographic displays; highlights include African masks, samurai armour and the mummy of Shep en-Mut. The **Museum Cafe** (Queen St; ⊙ 10am-4.30pm Tue-Sun) overflows with Devon-made pies, cakes and bread.

St Nicholas Priory
HISTORIC BUILDING

(☑ 01392-265858; www.exeter.gov.uk/priory; Mint Lane; adult/child £3.50/1.50; ⊙ 10am-5pm Sat, plus Mon-Fri school holidays) For a vivid insight into life inside a late-Elizabethan town house head to this former Benedictine monastery. Built out of russet stone 900 years ago, its striking interiors now sparkle with the kind of trappings that would have surrounded the wealthy Hurst family when they lived here in 1602. Expect brightly coloured furnishings, elaborate plaster ceilings and intricate oak panelling.

Guildhall
HISTORIC BUILDING

(☑ 01392-265524; www.exeter.gov.uk/guildhall; High St) **FREE** The earliest parts of Exeter's Guildhall date from 1330, making it the oldest municipal building still in use in the country. An ornate barrel roof arches above wooden benches and crests of dignitaries. The mayor still sits in the huge throne-like chair at the end. It's often open on weekdays, depending on civic functions; call or check the website.

Exeter Quay
WATERFRONT

(The Quay; ℗) On fine sunny days the people of Exeter head to the quay. Here cobbled paths lead between former warehouses that have been converted into antique shops, quirky stores, craft workshops, restaurants and pubs (popular spots for al fresco drinks and people watching).

The quay features evidence of the city's woollen processing and export business which, by the 18th century, had made Exeter the country's third most important trade centre. Look out for the stately 17th-century, red-brick **Customs House** (complete with cannons) and the gabled 18th-century **Wharfinger's House**, home to the man who collected the wharfing fees.

The nearby **Quay House** was built in 1680 as a wool store and today houses the Quay House Visitor Centre. Wool-trade-related exhibits include 'tillet blocks' – carved wooden tiles used by merchants to stamp their crests onto fabric. One shows a weaver sitting at a loom. The centre also stocks leaflets detailing other stops on Exeter's Woollen Trail.

The quay is also the springboard for walks, and bike and canoe voyages. Boat trips and summer-time free guided tours leave from here too. To cross the river head for bathtub-like **Butt's Ferry** (The Quay; adult/child 30/20p; ⊙ 11.30am-4.30pm daily Jun-Aug, Sat & Sun Easter-May & Sep), which is propelled by a ferryman pulling on a wire.

Spacex
GALLERY

(☑ 01392-431786; www.spacex.org.uk; 45 Preston St; ⊙ 10am-5pm Tue-Sat) **FREE** A leader among Exeter's buoyant visual arts scene, cutting-edge but friendly Spacex has a reputation for consistently strong, accessible contemporary art exhibitions. It also offers engaging workshops for adults and children, and regular free artists' talks.

Activities

The foot and cycle paths that head southeast from Exeter Quay join the **Exe Valley Way**, shadowing both the Exeter Canal and an ever-broadening River Exe towards the sea, around 10 miles away. They make for good biking, hiking and kayaking trips; the first 3 miles are a blend of heritage city, countryside and light industrial landscape; the later sections are more rural.

The Quay House Visitor Centre stocks Exe Valley Way leaflets. The trail itself leads south from Exeter Quay. About 1½ miles downstream, the route reaches the laid-back **Double Locks pub** (www.doublelocks.com; Canal Banks), which features real ale and a waterside terrace.

The Royal Society for the Protection of Birds' (RSPB) **Exminster Marshes Nature Reserve** starts about 2 miles further on. Around 2 miles inside the reserve, the waterside Turf pub (p57) clings to a slither of land, and is an idyllic setting to enjoy

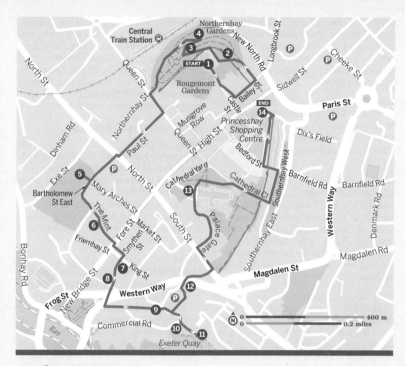

🏃 City Walk
Exeter City Walls

START EXETER CASTLE
END ROMAN WALK
LENGTH 2 MILES; 2.5 HOURS

Start at the gatehouse to **1 Exeter Castle**, built by the Normans after an 18-day siege. A plaque commemorates three Devon women, hanged after being tried here for witchcraft in 1685. In Northernhay Gardens, take the path along the wall which is crowned by **2 Civil War–era parapets**; in an era of shifting loyalties Exeter had to defended itself against both Royalists and Parliamentarians.

Duck through the arch of 12th-century **3 Athelstan's Tower**. Here the Roman wall survives to its original height; clues are the uniform texture and pebbly mortar. Head right down the slope; then cut right again, to go through a **4 gate** back into Northernhay Gardens. Queen St and Paul St lead to **5 Bartholomew Cemetery**, a swathe of green. Stepping through the gate here sees you standing on top of 19th-century catacombs.

At Bartholomew St's right-hand bend, wind into The Mint, stopping by **6 St Nicholas Priory** (p46), with its recreation of late-Elizabethan life. Turn right down Fore St, before cutting left down a lane which leads to the delightful slope of cobbled **7 Stepcote Hill**, where half-timbered houses lead to a russet-red **8 St Mary's Steps Church**, complete with ornate figure-flanked clock.

Cross busy Western Way. Then pass some of **9 city wall** on the left, making for atmospheric **10 Exeter Quay** (p46); here **11 On the Waterfront** (p50) is a good refreshment stop. Next, climb the hill, cutting left up steps to the car park; the footpath on its eastern edge runs on top of the historic wall. Climb steps to the footbridge, looking down to see **12 Roman facework** and volcanic blocks.

From South St, branch off into the Palace Gate to admire the architecture of **13 Cathedral Close**. On the walkways of the Princesshay Shopping Centre, finish your walk alongside a well-preserved Roman section of wall, on aptly named **14 Roman Walk**.

good grub and summer barbecues. From there a rougher trail connects with a path to appealing Powderham Castle (p52). You can also navigate much of the above route by kayak, making an enjoyable, non-tidal paddle past pubs.

Saddles & Paddles BICYCLE RENTAL, KAYAKING
(☑ 01392-424241; www.sadpad.com; 4 King's Whaf, Exeter Quay; ☺ 9.30am-5.30pm) Rents out bikes (adult per hour/day £6/15), kayaks (£10/35) and three-person Canadian canoes (£15/50).

Exeter Cruises CRUISES
(☑ 07984 368442; Exeter Quay; adult/child/family return £6/3.50/14; ☺ hourly 11.30am-4.30pm, daily Jun-Aug, Sat & Sun only Easter-May & Sep) The *Southern Comfort* makes the 45-minute trip down the Exeter Ship Canal from Exeter Quay to the Double Locks pub. Boats leave the quay on the half hour, and the pub on the hour.

Quay Climbing Centre ADVENTURE SPORT
(☑ 01392-426850; www.quayclimbingcentre.co.uk; Haven Rd; per hr £13; ☺ 10am-10pm Mon-Fri, noon-8pm Sat & Sun) The wealth of climbing options at this huge indoor centre range from kid-friendly inflatable towers to a 15m-high, expert-level wall. The Leap of Faith involves lunging for an almost-out-of-reach handle, a real test of nerve, despite the harness. The centre's just south of Exeter Quay.

☞ Tours

Redcoat Tours WALKING TOURS
(☑ 01392-265203; www.exeter.gov.uk/guidedtours; ☺ 2-5pm daily) **FREE** Exeter's rich history emerges in fine style on these 1½ hour guid-

---

EXETER CATHEDRAL ROOF TOURS
....
For a sensational view of Exeter Cathedral book one of these high-rise, 75-minute, guided walks (☑ 01392-285983; www.exeter-cathedral.org.uk; adult/child £10/5; ☺ 2pm Tue-Thu, 11am Sat Apr-Sep). Climb 251 steps up a spiral staircase, head out onto the sweeping roof to stroll it's length, then gaze down on the city from the top of the North Tower. They're popular so book at least two weeks ahead. The price of the tour includes cathedral admission (under 11s aren't allowed).

---

ed tours. Themes range from the Romans, religion and riots, to plague and trade, and crime and punishment. Tours leave from either outside the Royal Clarence Hotel on Cathedral Yard, or Exeter Quay. The evening Ghosts and Legends tour (leaving Cathedral Yard at 7pm on Tuesdays, year-round) is a particularly spooky treat.

🎉 Festivals & Events

Animated Exeter FILM
(www.animatedexeter.co.uk) The country's leading festival of its type, this week-long celebration of all things animated takes place over February half term. Some 140 films are shown, workshops range from stop motion to games jams, and past speakers have included the people behind Wallace and Gromit, Aardman Animations.

South West Food & Drink FOOD
(www.exeterfoodanddrinkfestival.co.uk) The marquees of this three-day, late-April foodie fiesta fill Exeter's Northernhay Gardens with an irresistible array of prime West Country produce. You'll also encounter presentations by leading chefs, pop-up branches of some of the region's best restaurants, and music nights curated by cool Exeter venue, Mama Stone's.

🛏 Sleeping

Raffles B&B £
(☑ 01392-270200; www.raffles-exeter.co.uk; 11 Blackall Rd; s/d/f £48/78/96; P ☎) Creaking with antiques and awash with Victoriana, this B&B is a lovely blend of old woods and tasteful modern fabrics. Plant stands, dado rails and Pear's Soap adverts add to the turn-of-the-century feel. Largely organic breakfasts, a walled garden and much coveted parking seal the deal.

White Hart INN £
(☑ 01392-279897; www.whitehartpubexeter.co.uk; 66 South St; s/d £50/70; P ☎) They've been putting people up here since the Plantagenets were on the throne in the 1300s. The courtyard is a wisteria-fringed mass of cobbles and the bar is book-lined and beamed. Rooms are tasteful modern affairs with suede chairs, honey and gold hues and glinting bathrooms. The deals on Sunday night doubles (from £50) can be a steal.

Townhouse B&B £
(☑ 01392-494994; www.townhouseexeter.co.uk; 54 St David's Hill; s/d/f £40/80/100; P ☎) Expect

simple but delightful rooms with stripped wooden floors and clean, pared-down lines, spiced up by dashes of intense colour. The Victorian exterior drips with ivy and all the rooms are named after literary characters – will you opt for Moneypenny, Lorna Doone or Darcy?

Woodbine B&B £
(☑ 01392-203302; www.woodbineguesthouse. co.uk; 1 Woodbine Tce; s/d £38/66; P 🛜) A surprise sits behind the door of this archetypal flower-framed terrace: fresh, modish rooms with low beds and burgundy flashes – there's even underfloor heating in the bathrooms.

Globe Backpackers HOSTEL £
(☑ 01392-215521; www.exeterbackpackers.co.uk; 71 Holloway St; dm/d £17.50/43; 🛜) Rightly a firm favourite among budget travellers, this spotlessly clean, relaxed, rambling house boasts three doubles, roomy dorms and wet room showers that are positively luxurious.

Silversprings APARTMENT ££
(☑ 01392-494040; www.silversprings.co.uk; 12 Richmond Rd; 1/2 bedroom apt per night £85/95; P 🛜) There are so many reasons to make these serviced apartments your Exeter pied-á-terre. Tucked away off a square a short walk from the city centre, each one comes with bedroom(s), lounge and mini-kitchen, plus home comforts like DVD players and satellite TV. Furnishing are fabulous: Isca is modern and sleek; Richmond sports rococo frills; while St Just is all Edwardian elegance, with wood-panelled walls and a bell for the butler (manservant not included).

St Olaves HOTEL ££
(☑ 01392-217736; www.olaves.co.uk; Mary Arches St; d £85-130, ste £100-160, f £170; P) The swirling spiral staircase at St Olaves is so gorgeous it's tempting to sleep beside it. But you better opt for the 18th-century-with-contemporary-twists bedrooms: expect ornate mirrors, brass bedsteads and plush furnishings.

★Magdalen Chapter BOUTIQUE HOTEL £££
(☑ 01392-281000; www.themagdalenchapter. com; Magdalen St; d £150-250; @ 🛜 ⊠) Undoubtedly Exeter's coolest hotel (staff wear converse trainers and low-slung slacks), the Magdalen is replete with funky flourishes. Lush purple corridors lead into dove-grey bedrooms, each with iPad, coffee machine and mood-lighting ranging from bright

---

OFF THE BEATEN TRACK

EXETER LIVESTOCK MARKET

The red hills around Exeter are prime agricultural territory; often generations of the same family have farmed the same patch of land. Although the scenery is beautiful, it can be hard to get a sense of what life is really like at the end of the farm lane. Find out at the twice-weekly auctions at Exeter Livestock Market (☑ 01392-251261; www.kivells.com; Matford Park Rd, Exeter; ⊙ sales usually 9.30am Mon & Fri, check for details) FREE. You get to join the farmers leaning on the showing rings' circular rails, while the auctioneer's sing-song chant raises the price. Then have lunch with the buyers and sellers in the on-site eatery. Full of specialised language (prime stock and store stock, suckler cows and breeding bulls) and ripe smells of the farm, it's an authentic insight into rural Devon life.

Welcome, to dimmed-down Relax. But the best bit is a tiny heated pool that flows from the outside into an indoor enclave made toasty by its very own log burner.

Southernhay House BOUTIQUE HOTEL £££
(☑ 01392-439000; www.southernhayhouse.com; 36 Southernhay East; r £150-240; 🛜) In the 1800s, this was a prestigious gentleman's residence; now it's an impeccably run, luxury sleep spot. Antiques and velvet furnishings cosy up to slate walls and exotic artefacts, and curving wooden banisters wind towards immense flat-screen TVs. Perhaps the pick of the rooms is Sugar, where the art deco theme echos styling at Burgh Island (p98), the Southernhay's jazz age, south Devon sister hotel.

ABode, Royal Clarence HOTEL £££
(☑ 01392-319955; www.abodehotels.co.uk/exeter; Cathedral Yard; r £150-330; @ 🛜) At ABode, Georgian grandeur meets minimalist chic. Wonky floors and stained glass combine with recessed lighting, pared-down furniture and neutral tones. The rooms range from 'comfortable' and 'enviable' to 'fabulous'. The last is aptly named: bigger than most people's flats, its slanted ceilings frame a grandstand view of the cathedral. Prices depend on availability; book ahead to bag the bargains.

✗ Eating

Herbies VEGETARIAN £
(15 North St; mains £6-10; ⊘ 11am-2.30pm Mon-Sat, 6-9.30pm Tue-Sat; ✍) Cosy and gently groovy, Herbies has been cheerfully feeding Exeter's vegetarians for more than 20 years. Tuck into delicious butterbean and vegetable pie, Moroccan tagine, cashew nut loaf or broad bean, thyme and squash risotto. The grilled vegetable salads are a work of art and they take good culinary care of vegans, too.

Refectory CAFE £
(Cathedral Green; mains £7; ⊘ 10am-5pm Mon-Sat; ✍) In Exeter Cathedral's refectory you can tuck into cakes, quiches and soups at trestle tables surrounded by vaulted ceilings, stained glass and busts of the great, the good and the dead.

★ Rusty Bike MODERN BRITISH ££
(☑ 01392-214440; www.rustybike-exeter.co.uk; 67 Howell Rd; mains £14; ⊘ 6-10pm daily, plus noon-3pm Sat & Sun) The retro fussball table and bashed-about chairs create the air of a beatnik hang-out but the cooking is pure stylish-rustic cuisine. Menus change daily depending on what an array of quality local suppliers bring in. Expect rarities like pressed venison and mallard; beef chuck and carrots; and beetroot, horseradish and pheasant – delivered, of course, by the local gamekeeper.

MC Cafe, Bar & Grill BISTRO ££
(www.michaelcaines.com; Cathedral Yard; mains £10-20, 2-/3-course lunch £11/16; ⊘ 9am-10pm) The MC in the title stands for acclaimed chef Michael Caines, so prepare for bistro classics with creative twists: mushroom and Devon Blue cheese risotto, and fish encased in batter made with local Otter Ale. Leave room for the classically creamy crème brûlée.

Harry's BISTRO ££
(☑ 01392-202234; www.harrys-exeter.co.uk; 86 Longbrook St; mains £10; ⊘ noon-2pm & 6-11pm daily) Harry's is the kind of welcoming neighbourhood eatery you wish was on your own doorstep but rarely is. The decor is all wooden chairs, blackboard menus and gilt mirrors; the food includes Spanish ham with marinated figs, crispy pizzas and a hearty three-bean chilli.

Michael Caines FINE DINING £££
(☑ 01392-223638; www.michaelcaines.com; Cathedral Yard; mains £25; ⊘ noon-2.30pm & 6-9.30pm Mon-Sat) This restaurant's eponymous chef has two Michelin stars at his other Devon eatery, Gidleigh Park (p123), and that style filters through here: expect a complex fusion of West Country ingredients and full-bodied French flavours. Try the celeriac and truffle oil soup, or the salad of Devon quail with smoked bacon, quail egg and caramelised hazelnuts. The seven-course meals (£65; £96 with wines) really are ones to linger over; the early evening menus (two/three courses £17/23) are some of the best deals in town.

@Angela's MODERN BRITISH £££
(☑ 01392-499038; www.angelasrestaurant.co.uk; 38 New Bridge St; dinner mains £21; ⊘ 6-9.30pm Mon-Sat, bookings-only lunch Fri & Sat) Dedication to sourcing local ingredients sometimes sees the chef here rising before dawn to bag the best fish at Brixham Market; his steamed John Dory with scallops is worth the trip alone. The lamb and beef were raised in Devon fields, while a memorable dish is local duck with a rich caramelised orange sauce.

🍷 Drinking & Nightlife

Mama Stone's LIVE MUSIC
(www.mamastones.com; 1 Mary Arches St; ⊘ 6pm-midnight, 9pm-3am when bands play) An uber-cool venue showcasing everything from acoustic sets to pop, folk and jam nights; many of the acts have been schooled at the artist development program that operates alongside. Mama Stone's daughter, Joss (yes, *the* Joss Stone), plays sometimes too.

Old Firehouse PUB
(www.oldfirehouseexeter.co.uk; 50 New North Rd; ⊘ noon-1.30am Sun-Thu, to 2.30am Fri & Sat) Step into the snug, candle-lit interior of this Exeter institution and feel instantly at home. Dried hops hang from rafters, the floors are flagstone while the walls are exposed stone. The range of draft ciders and cask ales is truly impressive, and the pizzas, which are served after 9pm, have helped keep countless students fed.

On the Waterfront BAR
(www.waterfrontexeter.co.uk; The Quay) In 1835 this was a warehouse; now its red-brick, barrel-vaulted ceilings stretch back from a thoroughly modern bar. The tables outside are a popular spot for a riverside pint.

Old Timers WINE BAR
(www.oldtimersexeter.co.uk; Little Castle St) Scuffed floorboards, crowded-in tables and

walls smothered in an eyebrow-raising array of collectables set the scene at this atmospheric drinking den.

Timepiece CLUB
(www.timepiecenightclub.co.uk; Little Castle St) DJ sets range from Salsa (Tuesdays) and World Music (Sunday), to indie, anthems and electro (Friday), and pop, dubstep, house, R&B and hip-hop on Saturday nights.

☆ Entertainment

Exeter Picturehouse CINEMA
(☎0871 902 5730; www.picturehouses.co.uk; 51 Bartholomew St West; ☏) An intimate, independent cinema, screening mainstream and art-house movies; the licensed cafe is a hang-out of choice for on-trend movie goers.

Exeter Phoenix ARTS CENTRE
(☎01392-667080; www.exeterphoenix.org.uk; Bradninch Pl, Gandy St; ⊙10am-11pm Mon-Sat, snacks to 9pm; ☏) Exeter's art and soul, the Phoenix is a buzzing blend of indie cinema, performance space, galleries and a cool cafe-bar.

Bike Shed Theatre THEATRE, BAR
(www.bikeshedtheatre.co.uk; 162 Fore St) The Bike Shed is the new kid on Exeter's cultural block, profiling emerging writers in a rough 'n' ready subterranean, brick-lined performance space. Its vintage cocktail bar makes a cool setting for Friday-night live music, and DJ sets on Saturdays.

🛍 Shopping

The Real McCoy VINTAGE
(www.therealmccoy.co.uk; 21a McCoy's Arcade, Fore St) This Aladdin's cave of retro threads has long been a magnet for Exeter's fashionistas. It proudly proclaims stock spanning a hundred years (1880s to 1980s): downstairs has everything from cricket blazers and cravats to beaded evening gowns, while upstairs is the domain of 1950s leather jackets, '70s jeans and checked shirts galore.

Real Food Store FOOD
(www.realfoodexeter.co.uk; 11 Paris St; ⊙9am-6pm Mon-Fri, to 5pm Sat) Boxes and bags full of field-fresh veg, racks of fragrant bread, ranks of local cheeses and piles of cured meat and fish – some 70% of the goods in this community-run cafe-cum-store are from Devon, and the other 30% is from the wider southwest. That kind of commitment to local produce earned it a finalist's place in Radio 4's Food & Farming awards.

ℹ Information

Exeter Central Tourist Office (☎01392-665700; www.heartofdevon.com; Dix's Field; ⊙9.30am-4pm Mon-Sat)

Quay House Visitor Centre (☎01392-271611; www.heartofdevon.com; The Quay; ⊙10am-5pm daily Easter-Oct, 11am-4pm Sat & Sun only Nov-Easter)

ℹ Getting There & Away

TO & FROM THE AIRPORT

Exeter International Airport (p289) is 5 miles east of the city. Regular UK and European flights include those from Amsterdam, Belfast, Dublin, Glasgow, Manchester, Paris, Newcastle and the Isles of Scilly. A key operator is FlyBe (p288).

Bus 56 runs from the bus station and Exeter St David's train station to Exeter airport (20 to 30 minutes, hourly until 6pm, 5pm on Saturday).

BUS

Bude (£6.50, 2 hours, five Monday to Saturday) Bus X9; runs via Okehampton.

Exmouth (30 minutes; two to four per hour) Bus 57; runs via Topsham (15 minutes).

Moretonhampstead (1 hour, five daily Monday to Saturday) Bus 359.

Plymouth (£6.50, 1¼ hours, every two hours Monday to Saturday, every three hours on Sunday) Bus X38.

Sidmouth (1 hour, one to three per hour) Bus 52A/B, via Sidford.

Totnes (1 hour, nine daily Monday to Saturday, two on Sunday) Bus X64.

Jurassic Coastlinx (Bus X53) Runs five to seven services daily to Beer and onto Lyme Regis and Weymouth.

Transmoor Link (Bus 82) On summer Saturdays and Sundays only (mid-May to mid-September), this service makes one trip from Exeter to Tavistock via Moretonhampstead, Postbridge, Princetown and Yelverton.

TRAIN

Main-line and branch-line trains run from Exeter St David's and Exeter Central stations:

Barnstaple (£10, 1¼ hours, one to two hourly)

Bristol (£16, 1¼ hours, half-hourly)

Exmouth (£5, hourly, 40 minutes)

London Paddington (£40, 2½ hours, half-hourly)

Paignton (£7, 50 minutes, half-hourly)

Penzance (£18, 3 hours, hourly)

Plymouth (£8, 1 hour, half-hourly)

Topsham (£4, hourly, 15 minutes)

Torquay (£6, 45 minutes, half-hourly)

Totnes (£6, 35 minutes, half-hourly)

EXETER & EAST DEVON EXETER

❶ Getting Around

CAR

Exeter is at the southern end of the M5 motorway; junctions 29 and 30 provide useful, if congested, routes into the city. Most major car-hire firms have branches in the city or at the airport. The very centre of Exeter is off-limits to cars, but not buses.

PARKING

The Cathedral and Quay car park often has places when others are full. Park-and-ride buses run from Sowton (near M5, junction 30), Matford (near M5 junction 31) and Honiton Rd (near M5, junction 29) every 10 minutes, Monday to Saturday from around 7am to 6pm. The parking itself is free; you just pay the bus fare (adult/child return £2.25/1.50).

TAXI

Ranks are at St David's train station and on the main street. Other options include **Capital Taxis** (☑ 01392-434343; ☺ 24hr), **Club Cars** (☑ 01392-213030; ☺ 24hr) and **Gemini** (☑ 01392-666666; ☺ 24hr).

Around Exeter

North of Exeter, Devon's rural heartland takes over. In this hilly, pastoral landscape, vivid green and yellow fields are interspersed with flashes of bright red soil. It's one of the least touristy parts of the county and delivers an insight into everyday farming life. The superb stately homes at Powderham Castle and Knightshayes Court are also within easy reach, as are a microbrewery, a vineyard, and horse-drawn canal trips.

❂ Sights & Activities

★**Powderham Castle**   HISTORIC BUILDING
(☑ 01626-890243; www.powderham.co.uk; adult/child/family £11/8.50/33; ☺ 11am-4.30pm Sun-Fri Apr-Oct, plus Sat in Aug; Ⓟ) Somehow this crenellated manor house manages to be both stately and homely. The historic seat of the Earl of Devon, it was built in 1391, damaged in the Civil War and remodelled in the Victorian era. Today it has some of the best-preserved Stuart and Regency furniture around. Highlights include the fine wood-panelled great hall, glimpses of life 'below stairs' in the Victorian kitchen, and parkland with 650 deer. The Earl and Countess of Devon are still resident and, despite all that grandeur, for delightful fleeting moments it feels like you're actually wandering through someone's sitting room.

Powderham is on the River Exe near Kenton, 8 miles south of Exeter. Bus 2 runs from Exeter (30 minutes, every 30 minutes Monday to Saturday), or you can walk or cycle along the canal and river paths.

★**Yearlstone Vineyard**   WINERY
(☑ 01884-855700; www.yearlstone.co.uk; Bickleigh; admission £3; ☺ 11am-4pm Wed-Sun Easter-Nov; Ⓟ) The owners proudly point out this vineyard is on the same latitude as the Moselle Valley. It's certainly as picturesque, set amid an amphitheatre of deeply wooded, sharply sloping hills above a rushing River Exe. Its range of award-winning white, red, rosé and sparkling wines includes the pale gold Vintage Brut, the light and fruity red Yearlstone No 4 and the tangy, dry white Yearlstone No 1. Tours range from guide-yourself affairs (£3.50) to detailed explorations of the wine-making process, complete with lunch and a complementary bottle of wine (£50). All involve a tutored tasting. The deli-style food in the cafe (p54) is definitely worth a detour. Yearlstone is on the outskirts of the village of Bickleigh, 10 miles north of Exeter on the A396.

Knightshayes Court   HISTORIC BUILDING
(NT; ☑ 01884-254665; www.nationaltrust.org.uk; Bolham; adult/child £7.20/3.15; ☺ 11am-5pm daily early-Feb–Oct; Ⓟ) For a full-blooded dose of Victorian excess, head to Knightshayes Court. It was designed by the eccentric architect William Burges for the Tiverton MP John Heathcoat Mallory in 1869. Burges' obsession with the Middle Ages resulted in a plethora of stone curlicues, ornate mantles and carved figurines, plus lavish Victorian decoration (the smoking and billiard rooms feel just like a gentlemens' club).

The gardens feature a waterlily pool, imposing topiary, terraces with extensive views and an inspirational kitchen garden. Knightshayes is 1 mile east of Tiverton at Bolham; bus 398 runs to Bolham from Tiverton (10 minutes, seven daily Monday to Saturday).

Grand Western Canal   CANAL
(☑ 01884-254072; www.devon.gov.uk/grandwestern-canal; Canal Hill, Tiverton; ☺ open access; Ⓟ) Built in 1814, the canal that meanders around the hills above Tiverton provides an intriguing insight into life on man-made inland waterways. Tub boats carrying limestone from local quarries worked this

waterway for 130 years before the network declined. This 11-mile stretch is all that's left. In November 2012 severe flooding and storms caused a massive breach of the canal at Halberton; water thundered into the surrounding fields and 20 families were evacuated from their homes. Engineers dammed the canal either side of the fractured embankment, and the local council pledged £3 million to rebuild it before the canal's 200th anniversary in 2014.

The breach hasn't affected activities at the canal basin near Tiverton. Here waterside displays chart its history; there's also the sweet Ducks Ditty (⊙noon-4pm Tue-Sun Apr-Oct) canal-boat cafe-bar and a boat hire office (☑01884-253345; www.tivertoncanal. co.uk; ⊙noon-3.30pm Tue-Sun May-Sep, from 10.30am Sun-Fri July & Aug), which rents out motor boats (one/four hours £40/90), row boats (one/four hours £10/25) and Canadian canoes (one/four hours £15/30). Or journey on a brightly painted horse-drawn barge (☑01884-253345; www.tivertoncanal.co.uk; adult/child from £9.50/7; ⊙1-2 trips daily May-Sep). On these all you'll hear is gurgling water and clip-clopping horses' hooves as you look out for moorhens, kingfishers, little grebes and roe deer.

The Grand Western Canal and Country Park is on the outskirts of Tiverton. Tiverton is 15 miles north of Exeter on the A396.

🛏 Sleeping

★Wood Life CAMPSITE £
(☑01392-832509; www.thewoodlife.org; The Linhay, near Kenn; 5 nights for 6 people £500-620, 7 nights £620-1150; ⊙Apr-Oct; P) 🍃 The trappings that come with this luxurious, six-person safari-style tent don't just include brass bedsteads draped with Egyptian cotton and thick rugs on the decked floors. There's also a fire pit (complete with campfire kettle), tub of fresh herbs, and vintage games chest. Add firewood-warmed showers, a set of hurricane lamps and your very own 3.5 hectare wood, and you have a slice of comfy camping heaven. It's tucked away on the outskirts of Kenn village, 7 miles south of Exeter.

Blackdown Yurts CAMPSITE £
(☑01884-266699; www.blackdownyurts.co.uk; near Kentisbeare; 4-person yurt per week £400-480; ⊙Apr-Sep; P) 🍃 These authentic Mongolian yurts are utterly irresistible. Brightly painted wood is framed by vivid fabrics, and a central wood burner adds a warm glow.

Each one comes complete with compost loo, field kitchen and fire pit. A communal, covered cooking-cum-dining area and hot showers add to the appeal, while your welcome basket includes tea, coffee and a complimentary bottle of wine. It's all hidden away on a sleepy smallholding around 15 miles southeast of Tiverton.

Fisherman's Cot INN £
(☑01884-855237; www.fishermanscot-bickleigh. com; Bickleigh; d/f £73/92; P 🗢) For a picture-postcard setting it's hard to beat the Cot, a cavernous thatch overlooking the rushing River Exe. There's white linen and chocolate brown throws in the bedrooms; for maximum character ask for a water-view room above the pub. The menu is packed with bar food standards (mains £11, meals served noon to 9pm), while the waterside beer garden (open 11am to 11pm) is a prime spot to watch the water tumble beneath Bickleigh's famous five-arched 17th-century bridge.

Bickleigh Castle B&B ££
(☑01884-855363; www.bickleighcastle.com; Bickleigh; s/d/f £60/120/140; P 🗢) How often do you get to kip in the grounds of a castle? Snug bedrooms set in thatched cottages frame a flower-filled central courtyard; the 11th-century fortifications rise behind. Expect beams, country-cottage furnishings and total tranquility. The village of Bickleigh is less than a mile away. At these prices, this is a steal.

Halsbeer Farm SELF-CATERING ££
(☑018842-66699; www.halsbeerfarm.co.uk; 4-person cottage per week £340-900; P 🗢🏊) 🍃 Stay here for a week or two and you might find it hard to leave. Fluffy bathrobes and drapes sit alongside weathered beams; phenomenally well-equipped kitchens allow you to cook up a storm. Then there's the long, comfy conservatory (complete with wood burner), the games room (with pool and table-tennis tables) and the small, covered, heated swimming pool. Situated near Kentisbeare.

Combe House HISTORIC HOTEL £££
(☑01404-540400; www.combehousedevon.com; Gittisham, near Honiton; d £215-450; P) The sumptuous Combe House is more like a National Trust property than a hotel. The great hall of this Elizabethan country manor has floor-to-ceiling wood panels, ancient oak furniture and original Tudor paintings

everywhere. Indulge your taste for crisp cottons, monogrammed towels, rain showers and deluxe throws – one room even has a vast copper washtub for a bath. The acclaimed restaurant (three-course lunch/dinner £33/52, open noon to 2.30pm and 7pm to 9.30pm daily) rustles up exquisite creations that draw heavily on local suppliers. It all sits on a 1400-hectare estate with Arabian horses roaming the grounds. You'll find it 14 miles east of Exeter.

Eating & Drinking

Deli Shack Cafe   BISTRO £
(📞 01884-855700; www.delishackcafe.co.uk; Yearlstone Vineyard, Bickleigh; mains £9; ⊘ 11am-4pm Wed-Sun, Easter-Nov; 🖘) At Yearlstone Vineyard's eatery, the sweeping views down the lush Exe Valley are gorgeous, the wines are from the vines in front of you and the food is full of flavour. Try lemon sole with soused veg, pasta with hot smoked salmon, and roasted vine tomato and basil tart. Pick this perfect lunch spot on a warm day to join diners sipping vintages on the sun-filled terrace.

Beer Engine   BREWERY, PUB
(📞 01392-851282;   www.thebeerengine.co.uk; Newton St Cyres; mains £11; ⊘ bar 11am-11pm; meals noon-2.15pm daily, 6.30-9.15pm Tue-Sat, to 8.15pm Sun & Mon) A dream-come-true for ale aficionados: a pub that brews its own beer. The decor is varnished floorboards, leather settles and exposed red brick, but the best bit is downstairs: the gleaming stainless-steel tubs and tubes of the fermenting process. The building's past as a railway hotel inspires the brews' names: the fruity Rail Ale, sharp and sweet Piston Bitter and the well-rounded Sleeper Heavy. Flavoursome food includes slow-cooked shoulder of West Country lamb, a range of ploughman's lunches made with local Quickes cheddar, and steak and Sleeper Ale pie.

Newton St Cyres is on the A377, 5 miles north of Exeter. Or go car free: train services from Exeter often chug into the village in time for supper; the one that tends to return just after 11pm (10.30pm on Sunday) is very handy indeed.

ℹ Information

Tiverton Tourist Office (📞 01884-255827; www.discovertiverton.co.uk; Phoenix Lane; ⊘ 9.15am-3pm Mon-Sat)

ℹ Getting There & Away

Bus 55/55A/55B runs from Exeter to Tiverton (one hour, half-hourly Monday to Saturday, eight on Sundays), via Bickleigh.

Tiverton Parkway station is on the mainline London Paddington–Penzance train route, and has hourly connections to Exeter (15 minutes). The station is 10 miles from Tiverton; hourly buses (20 minutes) connect the two.

EAST DEVON

East of Exeter, Devon's red-soil fields and red-rock cliffs undulate towards Dorset. A few miles south of the city lies Topsham, a charming, ancient port overflowing with fine places to eat and stay. Next comes the faded resort of Exmouth, launch pad for Jurassic Coast cruises and adrenalin sports. Regency Sidmouth delivers old-world seaside charm, stargazing and an irresistible equine sanctuary. Captivating Beer offers the chance to land your own lunch and an ancient network of caves. Meanwhile, the River Cottage eateries of TV chef Hugh Fearnley-Whittingstall lie inland, rustling up truly memorable meals.

ℹ Information

Exmouth Tourist Office (📞 01395-222299; www.exmouth-guide.co.uk; 3 Rolle St; ⊘ 9am-5pm Mon-Fri, to 4pm Sat)
Sidmouth Tourist Office (📞 01395-516441; www.visitsidmouth.co.uk; Ham Lane; ⊘ 10am-5pm Mon-Sat, to 4pm Sun May-Oct, 10am-1.30pm Mon-Sat Nov-Apr)

ℹ Getting There & Away

BUS

X53 Jurassic Coastlinx Runs between Exeter and Weymouth (five to seven daily), stopping at Beer and Lyme Regis.

Bus 57 (two to four per hour) Runs between Exeter, Topsham (15 minutes) and Exmouth (30 minutes).

Bus 157 Links Exmouth with Sidmouth (one hour, hourly Monday to Saturday, four on summer Sundays).

Bus 52A/B Connects Exeter with Sidmouth (one hour, one to three hourly) and Sidford.

TRAIN

Hourly branch-line services run from Exeter to Topsham (15 minutes) and Exmouth (25 minutes); Axminster is on the well-served Exeter–Waterloo intercity route.

Topsham

POP 5520

Topsham stretches languidly down the banks of the River Exe, its atmospheric Fore St flanked by heritage buildings, and its long waterfront providing picturesque views of an estuary widening towards the sea. Despite being just 4 miles south of Exeter, this appealing settlement has retained a market-town feel. Add an exceptional selection of places to dine and sleep, an irresistible vineyard and some compelling boat trips, and you have a very attractive edge-of-Exeter base.

◎ Sights

Historic Topsham   HISTORIC BUILDINGS

Topsham has been an important port since the medieval era, and its wealth is evident in the Dutch gable merchants' houses that march through the middle of town. Explore by heading down the dog-legging Fore St into the Strand, before heading back beside the water. You'll encounter independent shops, eateries, the town museum and ferry trips along the way.

Pebblebed Vineyard   WINERY

(☑ 07814 788348; www.pebblebed.co.uk; Clyst St George, near Topsham; per person £15) You get more than a whiff of southern Europe on these winery tours – south-facing slopes, neatly staked vines and the heady aroma of fermenting grapes. The hour-long strolls end with a tutored tasting of four wines: a fruity red, fresh rosé, dry white and Devon sparkling. Tours only run in the summer and a few times a week – book ahead. If you do miss out, head for their Topsham wine cellar and sample the vintages there.

Topsham Museum   MUSEUM

(25 Strand; ◎ 2-5pm Sat-Mon & Wed Apr-Oct) FREE Artefacts from Topsham's salty past fill this 17th-century, waterfront building, including model sailing ships, shipwrights' tools and tub-like historic boats. And there is also a surprise: a Vivien Leigh Room (she was the sister-in-law of the museum's founder), where the memorabilia includes the nightdress the film star wore in *Gone With The Wind*.

⚹ Activities

Sea Dream   CRUISE

(www.topshamtoturfferry.co.uk; The Quay; adult/child return £5/3; ◎ 4-6 sailings daily Apr-Sep) For a true taste of Topsham's maritime links, on

AGRICULTURAL SHOWS

Devon's annual agricultural shows are when country folk come together to compete, gossip and showcase their wares. Along with barns full of cattle, sheep, goats and pigs, expect marquees and food stalls overflowing with prime produce, huge beer tents, show jumping rings, terrier races and pony club games. All in all, they're entertaining, in-depth insights into rural life. The biggest is the three-day **Devon County Show** (www.devoncountyshow. co.uk), held near Exeter each May.

These one-day shows are well worth a visit, too:

Mid Devon (www.middevonshow.co.uk) Late July, near Tiverton.

Totnes (www.totnesshow.com) Late July.

North Devon (www.northdevonshow. com) Early August, near Barnstaple.

Okehampton (www.okehamptonshow. co.uk) Early August.

Kingsbridge (www.kingsbridgeshow. co.uk) Early September.

board the Sea Dream and glide past mudflats and marsh land, passing a panorama of the town. The 15-minute trip leads to a tiny slither of land jutting out from the River Exe's south bank, and the lovely Turf pub. From there you can stroll a mile further downstream to visit stately Powderham Castle. Or walk upstream, beside the canal and mudflats, to the Topsham Ferry, which shuttles back to Topsham.

Topsham Ferry   BOAT TRIP

(adult/child £1/50p; ◎ 9.30am-5.30pm Wed-Mon Easter-Sep, 10am-5pm Sat & Sun Oct-Easter) A blink-and-you'll miss it trip from Topsham to the south bank of the Exe, crossing the river at its narrowest point. Tranquil waterside paths lead 2 miles downriver to the Turf pub, where the Sea Dream ferry sails back to Topsham.

Bowling Green Marsh   BIRDWATCHING

(RSPB; www.rspb.org.uk; Bowling Green Rd; ◎ open access) FREE As the main high-tide roost on the River Exe, this is one of the best places to spot birds in Devon and Cornwall. Follow signs to the hide and in summer look out for greenshank, ringed plover and little egret; winter brings masses of wigeon, pintail and

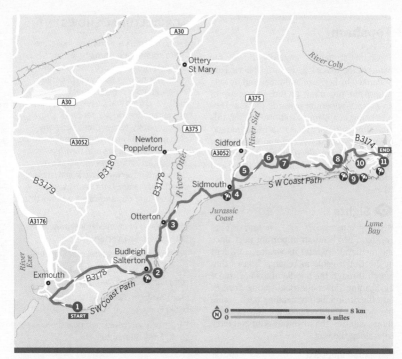

Driving Tour
The East Devon Coast

START ORCOMBE POINT, EXMOUTH
END BEER
LENGTH 20 MILES; ONE DAY

Many bypass them in favour of speedier A roads, but east Devon's steep, hedge-backed lanes lead to hidden villages and views of the sea. Park at the end of the seafront and stroll to ❶ **Orcombe Point**, the Jurassic Coast's western tip, where a Geoneedle contains rocks spanning 185 million years. The B3178 meanders to ❷ **Budleigh Salterton**, where the main street features an array of architectural styles and the beach boasts cliffs and 250-million-year-old Triassic-era pebbles. As the B3178 to Sidmouth heads north out of Budleigh, divert right; a rural route snakes to ❸ **Otterton**, where well-kept thatches and tearooms line more road-side leats. From here back roads wind to Regency ❹ **Sidmouth** (p59), where strolling along the Esplanade reveals ornate architecture, red cliffs and eateries galore. Next, avoid the main route to Sidford; instead hug the shore up steep Sal-

combe Hill Rd, past the ❺ **Norman Lockyer Observatory** (p60). After the sharp descent to sleepy ❻ **Salcombe Regis**, the lane dog-legs through the village, past ancient cottages and a picturesque church. Soon, the irresistible ❼ **Donkey Sanctuary** (p60) demands a detour. At the mini-roundabout, pick up signs to Branscombe, a flatter, straighter route. Then the hills return in an idyllic drive along steep, single-track lanes lined with high hedges, interspersed with passing places and first gear bends. At ❽ **Branscombe**, a string of thatches winds to a central triangle; pause at the Mason's Arms for lunch. Then fork right (signed Beach) to picturesque ❾ **Branscombe Mouth**, the perfect spot for a dip or paddle in the sea. As the signs suggest, the climb east out of Branscombe is narrow and steep. The rise crested, next comes the descent to ❿ **Beer Quarry Caves** (p61), a compelling stop. The eateries and B&Bs in ⓫ **Beer** (p63) village itself are superb. For a coastal hike, try our circular walk between Beer and Branscombe.

teal, as well as black-and-white avocet. For best views, time a visit to the approach of high tide. The reserve is at the end of the Goat Walk path, at the end of the Strand.

Sleeping

★ Reka Dom B&B ££

(☎01392-873385; www.rekadom.net; 43 The Strand; d £80-100; P) The views from the 4th-floor lounge of this rambling B&B's tower suite are extraordinary – 360-degree viwes of river, hillside and heritage town. Water vistas fill the windows of the cabin-like bedroom and gorgeous bathroom. The two-bedroom Powderham suite boasts a mini-lounge with views of the river and the eponymous castle. Breakfasts are convivial affairs, served round a central table stocked with fresh fruits, home-baked bread and home-made jam.

Globe INN ££

(☎01392-873471; www.theglobetopsham.co.uk; Fore St; d £100; P 📶) The deeply worn doorsteps at this fine coaching inn give a clue to its grand old age (16th century). The bar features sloping floors, wood panelling and wrought iron candelabras, while the bedrooms are much more modern: white-painted beams, smartly tiled bathrooms and soft golden throws.

Eating & Drinking

★ Salutation FINE DINING ££

(☎01392-873060; www.salutationtopsham.co.uk; 68 Fore St; tasting menus 5/9 courses £38/92, with wines £66/150; ⏰6.30-9pm Mon-Sat; P) You can almost taste the ambition at this exquisite restaurant-with-rooms: chef Tom Williams-Hawkes has worked with the Rothschilds, Gordon Ramsay and at double-Michelin-starred Gidleigh Park. The fine dining restaurant delivers highly technical tasting menus, while the bistro (mains £8 to £13, open 7.30am to 5pm Monday to Saturday) rustles up River Exe moules and slow-braised stews. Or just head in for coffee and cake; the Paris-quality patisserie comes at Devon prices (£3). The bedrooms (doubles £126 to £165) are as delicious as the food: contemporary-chic in grey and black candy-stripes and crisply designed lines.

★ Pebblebed Wine Cellar WINE BAR

(www.pebblebed.co.uk; Ferry Rd; ⏰5-10pm Fri & Sat, plus 11am-2pm Sat) Add this to your must-visit list. Trestle tables, whitewashed walls and ranks of balanced bottles lend this vaulted wine cellar an air of rustic charm. Food comes in the form of pizzas, and local cheese and meat platters (£7), but the stars of the show are the vintages from Pebblebed's own local vineyard – get sipping at a tutored tasting (6pm on Friday and Saturday, noon on Saturday).

Petite Maison FINE DINING ££

(☎01392-873660; www.lapetitemaison.co.uk; 35 Fore St; 2/3 courses £32/38; ⏰7-9.30pm Tue-Sat) The focus here is on intensifying the flavours of already flavour-filled ingredients. Duck comes confit, local meats are slow-roasted or smoked, vegetables are glazed, and fish comes with rich shellfish-based sauces. Then there are the puddings – indulgence doesn't come more tempting than the warm-baked chocolate mousse cake.

Turf PUB ££

(☎01392-833128; www.turfpub.net; mains £9; ⏰meals noon-2.30pm Mon-Fri, to 3pm Sat & Sun Easter-Oct, winter hrs vary) The location of this former lock-keeper's house is simply superb: book-ending a slender finger of land that snakes between River Exe mudflats and the Exeter Canal. The views from the tables on the lawns are stunning, the interior is cosy, the bar food is better than average, and there's camping (£5 per person) and a rustic-chic B&B. Access is either by the Sea Dream ferry, or a mile-long footpath from the RSPB's Exminster Marshes Nature Reserve. It's well worth the journey, either way.

Avocet CAFE £

(86 Fore St; mains £7; ⏰9am-5pm Mon-Fri, to 1pm Sat) It's not just the huge homemade cakes that are top notch in this snug cafe; the light bites are a treat for the taste buds, too. Expect rareties such as cured trout with onion relish, plus hearty sarnies (try the local crab) and soups.

Exmouth

POP 47,950

Exmouth is a curious combination of well-worn Georgian resort and adrenalin frenzy. The town's exposed position at the mouth of the River Exe draws fleets of wind and kite-surfers who whip across the water on gusty days. The area also has a unique pint-sized National Trust property and is the beginning, or the end, of the Jurassic Coast.

In the 1800s Exmouth was a fashionable, elegant watering hole with a whiff of scandal. Mary Ann Clarke, the Duke of York's mistress, lived here; in later life Lady Nelson resided here (after Horatio ran off with Lady Emma Hamilton); while Lady Byron (whose husband was quite the Don Juan himself) lived a few doors down.

◎ Sights & Activities

À la Ronde   HISTORIC BUILDING

(NT; ☑ 01395-265514; www.nationaltrust.org.uk; Summer Lane; adult/child £7.50/3.80; ⊙1-5pm Tue-Thu Apr-Oct, plus Sun Jun-Aug; Ⓟ) This delightfully quirky 16-sided cottage is a DIY job with a difference. It was built in 1796 for two spinster cousins to house a mass of curiosities acquired on a 10-year European grand tour. Its glass alcoves, low lintels and tiny doorways mean it's like clambering through a doll's house. Hunt out the intricate paper cuts (the cousins' own work), a delicate feather frieze in the drawing room and the gallery plastered with a thousand seashells on the top floor. The house is dressed as if the inhabitants just might come back at any moment, so you can play on the grand piano, stroll into a dining room where the table is laid out for a meal, and see a nightshirt hanging off a wardrobe, ready for bed. The house is 2 miles north of Exmouth on the A376; bus 57 (two to four per hour) runs close by.

Edge Kitesurfing   WATER SPORTS

(☑ 01395-222551;   www.edgewatersports.com; 3 Royal Ave) At Exmouth, the wind whips across the mouth of the River Exe's wide estuary, creating prime kite and windsurfing conditions. A series of sandbanks also ensures plenty of shallow, flat-water areas that are ideal places to learn. Lessons run by Edge include kite surfing, for both beginners (per 3 hours £95) and intermediates (per hour £50); and wakeboarding for beginners (per hour £40). Experienced wakeboarders can hire a boat and driver for £65 per hour.

Stuart Line   CRUISE

(☑ 01395-222144;   www.stuartlinecruises.co.uk; adult/child 2-3hr cruise £8/6; ⊙1-3 per week Apr-Oct) Stuart Line runs a string of trips from Exmouth Marina. The voyage up the River Exe is a pleasant cruise, especially when the weather's too rough to head out to sea. But the pick of the trips are the sailings along Devon's Jurassic Coast past the rust-red cliffs, and the impressive sea stacks that emerge at Ladram Bay. The chance of dolphin sightings adds to the appeal.

JURASSIC COAST

The kind of massive, hands-on geology lesson you wish you'd had at school, the Jurassic Coast is England's first natural World Heritage site, putting it on a par with the Great Barrier Reef and the Grand Canyon. This striking shoreline stretches from Exmouth in East Devon to Swanage in Dorset, encompassing 185 million years of the earth's history in just 95 miles. It means you can walk, in just a few hours, many millions of years in geological time.

It began when layers of rocks formed, their varying compositions determined by different climates. Desert conditions gave way to higher then lower sea levels before massive earth movements tilted all the rock layers to the east. Next, erosion exposed the different strata, leaving most of the oldest formations in the west and the youngest in the east.

The differences are very tangible. Edging east out of Exmouth the rusty-red Triassic rocks are 200 to 250 million years old, and are at their most striking at Orcombe Point, Ladram Bay and Sidmouth. In between, Budleigh Salterton's famously pebbly beach is made up of some of the coast's oldest rocks: nuggets of quartzite that are slowly being released from the cliffs and smoothed by the sea. Then comes the geological quirk at Beer, where a creamy-white segment of cliff interrupts the rose-red line. This is chalk from the Cretaceous period – a mere 65 million years old. It survived at Beer because the earth's forces folded this layer down, so it wasn't worn away, as it has been elsewhere. That legacy can be seen at the fascinating Beer Quarry Caves (p61) and a stunning hike between Branscombe and Beer (p62).

The website www.jurassiccoast.org is an excellent information source; also look out locally for the highly readable *Official Guide to the Jurassic Coast* (£4.95), or buy it at www.jurassiccoasttrust.org.

ExePlorer Water Taxi
BOAT TRIP

(☑07970 918418; www.exeplorer.co.uk; Exmouth Marina; adult/child return £4/2.50; ☺8am-5pm daily Apr-Sep) To really get a feel for the sheer width of the River Exe at its mouth, take this tub-like, red-and-blue water taxi for the 15-minute cross-estuary trip to the Dawlish Warren Nature Reserve (p75), a wind-whipped slither of sand that juts out into the river. The taxi will also shuttle you to the excellent, floating River Exe Cafe. The taxi is normally at Exmouth Marina on the hour and half past.

🛏 Sleeping

New Moorings
B&B £

(☑01395-223073; www.newmoorings.co.uk; 1 More-ton Rd; s £30, d £60-70; ℗🛜) The unfussy but charming rooms here are decked out in neu-tral gingham and sanded wood. The bath-rooms are small but spotless, the breakfast menu is extensive, and the hosts are past masters at warm welcomes – the sign on the front door says, simply, 'Smile!'

Dolphin
HOTEL £

(☑01395-263832; www.dolphinhotelexmouth.co.uk; 2 Morton Rd; s/d £40/80; ℗🛜) The bedrooms here may be supremely simple but they're also quite sweet; choose from warm red and pine, or blue and cream. There's an im-pressive number of single and family rooms, too.

Royal Beacon
HOTEL ££

(☑01395-264886; www.royalbeacon.co.uk; The Beacon; s £65, d £105-145; ℗🛜) Exmouth's classiest sleep spot sits proudly on Ex-mouth's classiest street – a villa-backed rise overlooking the sea. It exudes that warming feel of a well-run, long-established hotel. Plush furnishings, soft lighting and discreet service keep comfort levels high, and the cracking sea views could occupy your eyes for hours.

🍴 Eating & Drinking

⭐River Exe Cafe
MODERN BRITISH ££

(☑07761 116103; www.riverexecafe.com; near Exmouth; mains £10-15; ☺Apr-Oct) It's idyl-lic: a chilled-out, chalet-style restaurant on a barge floating in the wide waters of the River Exe. Luckily the super-fresh food lives up to the setting: roasted scal-lops, clams steamed in lime and chilli, Channel squid with tzatziki, and locally for-aged samphire and ceps wild mushrooms.

Unless you have your own boat, book the water taxi from Exmouth along with your table; handily it runs until 11pm.

Les Saveurs
FUSION ££

(☑01395-269459; www.lessaveurs.co.uk; 9 Tower St; mains £17; ☺7-10pm Tue-Sat) Succulent sea-food leads the way at this intimate, shabby-chic Exmouth eatery; look out for brill, sole and scallops from neighbouring Lyme Bay. The style is French-influenced and gutsy. Expect black-pudding and kidney alongside prime cuts of local lamb, pork and beef, while rich sauces might feature Madeira, marsala or champagne.

Sidmouth
POP 13,135

The select resort of Sidmouth is the English seaside at its most stately, serene and salu-brious. Here it's not so much kiss-me-quick as have a nap before a stroll. Hundreds of listed buildings line up elegantly behind its Esplanade, freshly painted pillars support bright-white balconies, and well-tended flowers tumble from window boxes. But this slice of old England also offers a frenetic folk festival, an incredibly cute animal sanctuary and the chance to gaze at the stars.

The village of Sidford, with its eateries and B&Bs, sits on the busy A3052, 2 miles to the north.

◉ Sights

Historic Sidmouth
HISTORIC BUILDING

The town's tourist office (p54) sells *Historic Sidmouth* (£2), a guide to the resort's 30 blue plaques. Follow it, or just investigate ones that catch your eye; the Esplanade is a good hunting ground. At the far west end, Clifton Place is a strip of pretty, largely Geor-gian cottages set right beside the sea; look out for the Swiss-chalet style Beacon Cot-tage (1840) with its pointed black-framed windows, long verandas and crowning of thatch.

Heading east, a crenellated red-stone gateway signals the Belmont Hotel; further down the all-cream Riviera Hotel (1820) has a grand bowed entrance, while the vast lemon-yellow Kingswood Hotel (c 1890s) was formerly the location of the hot and cold brine baths. The white and black Beach House was built in 1790 and revamped in Gothic style in 1826; it was a fashionable meeting spot for the gentry.

Towards the Esplanade's east end is the Royal York & Faulkner (1810), Sidmouth's first purpose-built hotel, with its blue and white pillars and long veranda. Notable guests have included Edward VII when he was Prince of Wales.

Donkey Sanctuary WILDLIFE CENTRE
(☑ 01395-578222; www.thedonkeysanctuary. org.uk; Sidmouth; ☺9am-dusk; 🅿) FREE An attraction with a strong feel-good factor, the sanctuary is home to around 400 donkeys, some rescued from mistreatment or neglect, others retired from working the beaches. Walkways pass fields full of the creatures happily grazing, trotting round and rolling in the grass. In the main yard you can mingle freely with animals specially chosen for their fondness of people. Signs alongside explain donkey body language (head down is resting; ears up is interested; a swishing tail means don't come any closer), while collars bearing names and ages allow you to know who you've just met. Because donkeys bond with each other, if they come into the sanctuary together they're kept together for life. When one goes into the veterinary hospital, their friends go in to keep them company.

Norman Lockyer Observatory OBSERVATORY
(☑ 01395-579941; www.normanlockyer.com; Salcombe Hill Rd; adult/child £6/3; ☺2-6 times a month, hrs vary; 🅿) Because of relatively low light pollution, high cliffs and an expanse of sea, east Devon is prime stargazing territory. Many remote coastal spots reveal good displays, but for truly mesmerising views spend an evening at the Norman Lockyer Observatory, where high-powered telescopes reveal astonishing clusters of constellations. Evening openings are timed to coincide with celestial events, perhaps Saturn at opposition, Mercury and Venus or the Perseid meteor shower. Book your place and hope for clear skies. The observatory is a few minutes' drive east from the centre of Sidmouth.

Sidmouth Museum MUSEUM
(☑ 01395-516139; Church St; ☺10am-4pm Tue-Sat Apr-Oct) FREE East Devon's history emerges in engaging style here, from the interactive Jurassic Coast exhibit and Iron Age mirror, to displays on Sidmouth's architecture and the extensive collection of local, hand-made lace (known as Honiton lace); there's even an intricate collar worn by Queen Victoria.

☆ Festivals

Sidmouth Folk Week MUSIC
(www.sidmouthfolkweek.co.uk) Early each August Sidmouth is transformed by this vibrant festival of world and traditional music. Around 700 sessions are staged in scores of venues around town – including pubs and beer gardens – with impromptu performances often spilling over into the streets.

⌨ Sleeping & Eating

★**Salty Monk** B&B ££
(☑ 01395-513174; www.saltymonk.co.uk; Church St, Sidford; s £85, d £130-180; 🅿🛜) There's an irresistible air of indulgence at the sublime Salty Monk. Super-stylish baths are beautifully lit, and sumptuous fabrics and antiques surround ancient beams. De-stress in the hot tub, sauna and massage room, then opt for fine dining (think roast pigeon tartlets with game jus; three courses £43) or brasserie fare (duck with garlic mushrooms; mains £13 to £22); it's assured cooking with quality local ingredients whichever you choose. Food is available from noon to 1.30pm Thursday to Sunday, and 6.30pm to 9pm daily.

Lavenders Blue B&B ££
(☑ 01395-576656; www.lavendersbluesidmouth. com; 33 High St, Sidford; d £90; 🅿) The fresh, light-filled rooms here are fragrant with the scent of flowers, and colour schemes range from lemon-yellow to zingy purple and aquamarine. One even has a sea view. Breakfasts are a feast of good-for-you treats: the tropical salad comes with melon, pineapple and grapes drizzled with fresh lime.

Longhouse B&B ££
(☑ 01395-577973; www.holidaysinsidmouth.co.uk; Salcombe Hill Rd, Sidmouth; d £85-95; 🅿) For truly remarkable views, head to this flint-fronted B&B set high on the hills above Sidmouth. Book the Garden Room for your own terrace plus picture window; restful decor adds to the effect. It's right next door to the Norman Lockyer Observatory, so you could get some stargazing in too.

Royal York & Faulkner HOTEL ££
(☑ 01395-513043; www.royalyorkhotel.co.uk; The Esplanade, Sidmouth; d £125-180; 🅿🛜) From the phenomenally creaky revolving door to the *Daily Telegraph* in the reception rooms, this Regency sea-front hotel provides a glimpse of Sidmouth's golden age. Furnishings are resolutely old fashioned and some

RIVER COTTAGE EATERIES

East Devon's rolling farmland and glittering bays overflow with fine produce – no surprise then that campaigning TV chef Hugh Fearnley-Whittingstall has set up two eateries here focusing on local, sustainably-sourced ingredients, as well as a cookery school that teaches everything from butchery to foraging.

The **River Cottage HQ** (☏ 01297-630300; www.rivercottage.net; near Axminster; 4-course lunch/dinner £50/80; ☺ noon-4pm Fri-Sun, 7.30-11pm Fri & Sat, booking required; ☏) delivers a true taste of HFW's 21st-century take on *The Good Life*. Hop on the tractor trailer, bounce down the farm track, then tuck into complex dishes packed with the flavours of Devon's hills and shores. It's a friendly affair, replicating the communal scene you've seen on the small screen: the warm fuzzy glow people get when they come together to enjoy fantastic food.

The **River Cottage Canteen** (☏ 01297-631715; www.rivercottage.net; Trinity Sq, Axminster; mains £6-10; ☺ 9am-5pm daily, 6.30-9pm Wed-Sat; ☏) is set in the middle of market town Axminster. Here a rustic-chic former pub is the setting for hearty dishes including cured wild boar, venison scotch eggs, and sharing platters of local meats, fish and cheese. Drinks include Stinger Beer, brewed from (carefully) handpicked Dorset nettles – it's spicy with just a hint of tingle. In Plymouth there's another River Cottage Canteen (p106).

fittings a little tired, but opt for a sea-front room with balcony, and the views of those crumbling, rosy cliffs are simply superb.

Drinking

Anchor PUB
(Old Ford St) During Folk Week, music overflows from the Anchor, with fiddlers, singers and accordion players creating a festival atmosphere inside and out. The rest of the year it's still a great spot, a convivial place for a pint with the locals.

Beer & Around

POP 1500

Set in a deep fissure in creamy-white cliffs, Beer manages to be thoroughly picturesque and a proper, working fishing village (not an imitation of one) at the same time. Multicoloured, snub-nosed boats line its steeply sloping beach beside the winches and wires used to haul them ashore; deck chairs and crab pots lie scattered around. Water-filled leats and chalk- and flint-faced buildings frame the main street (Fore St). With its unusual cave network, superb coast path and appealing places to stay and eat, the village is a charismatic base for east Devon explorations.

The picture-postcard-pretty village of **Branscombe** is just 3 miles west, a ribbon of thatches, tearooms and pubs that meanders behind a cliff-backed beach called Branscombe Mouth.

Sights & Activities

Beer Quarry Caves CAVES, TOUR
(☏ 01297-680282; www.beerquarrycaves.co.uk; Quarry Lane, Beer; adult/child/family £7/5/22; ☺ 10am-4.30pm Easter-Sep, to 2.30pm Oct) The geological pressure that ensured Beer's chalky cliffs stand out from the surrounding red, also created an accessible seam of high-quality masonry material called Beer Stone. It's been used in countless famous buildings, including 24 cathedrals, the Tower of London and Windsor Castle. The Romans began the network, which was then developed continually from the Middle Ages to the early 20th century.

Before setting off on the evocative underground tour of this maze of quarry tunnels you don a hard hat. Look out for 2000-year-old tool marks on the walls and tales of smuggling, including 18th-century excise-dodger Jack Rattenbury, who snuck barrels of French brandy ashore and secreted them in the caves. Beer's caves also evoke harsh working conditions: the incessant ringing of hammer and chisel gave rise to the phrase 'stone deaf'.

Fishing Trips FISHING
For the ultimate find-your-own-food experience, sign up for a mackerel fishing trip (per hour adult/child £8/5) from Beer beach. A wheeled jetty is rolled partway into the sea, allowing you to hop aboard. Your fisherman-cum-guide then putters about hunting out the best spots, perhaps just around the

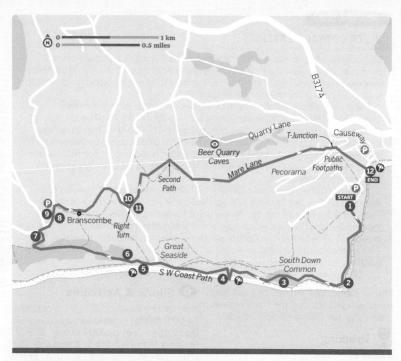

Coast Walk
Beer to Branscombe

START CLIFF TOP CAR PARK, BEER
END BEER
LENGTH 6 MILES; FOUR HOURS

For this breathtaking hike, climbing cliff paths and crossing beaches, wear good boots and take your swimsuit. From Beer's southerly **1 Cliff Top car park**, the flint-studded coast path leads up to **2 Beer Head** and extraordinary views. Behind you are Beer's trademark creamy-white cliffs, ahead the Jurassic Coast's russet-red shoreline undulates to Exmouth. Next comes the **3 Hooken Landslip**, a sunken swathe of coast where 150 million tonnes of cliff slid down one night in 1790. Take the path forking left here, down the cliff edge (signed Branscombe Mouth). This insanely steep, improbable-looking track of steps and switchbacks descends into the landslip itself – a tree-shaded landscape where birdsong replaces the sounds of the sea. Soon, a path cuts left to the pebble **4 beach**, a tempting spot for a dip. The huge anchor beside the beach at **5 Branscombe Mouth** belonged

to the MSC *Napoli*; a 62,000 tonne cargo ship that beached offshore in January 2007. Nearly 60 containers, carrying everything from BMW motorbikes to cat food, washed ashore in Branscombe Bay; the ensuing mad scramble to raid their contents became international news. It took 18 months to clean up the wreckage. A path heads up grassy **6 West Cliff Hill**, heading diagonally inland, before cutting right towards Branscombe village, emerging at **7 St Winifred's Church**, a beautiful, barrel-vaulted Norman church. Turn right, down past the **8 National Trust Bakery** and the working **9 Blacksmith's Forge**. The lane winds past the **10 Mason's Arms**, which is a good spot to refuel. Take the next right turn, signed Beach, then a switchback left, then a right, steeply up **11 Stockham's Hill**. When two paths appear, take the second path, leading to a lane sweeping downhill, revealing gorgeous Lyme Bay views. Where Mare Lane reaches a T-junction, turn left, then immediately after, on the bend, turn right onto two, easy-to-miss public footpaths, leading down between houses, back to **12 Beer village**.

chalky-white cliffs at Branscombe. If the fish bite, ask the skipper to gut your catch, then settle down for a barbecue on the beach. Fishermen who'll take you out include Paul (07779 040491), Cyril (07815 669796) and Kim (07989 631321).

Festivals & Events

Beer's big bash is the mid-August regatta (www.beer-regatta.co.uk), a week-long party crammed full of lugger races, fishing competitions, sea shanties, scavenger hunts, raft building contests, fancy dress, and lots and lots of beach barbecues.

Sleeping

Durham House
B&B £
(01297-20449; www.durhamhouse.org; Fore St; s/d £45/80; P ?) The rooms in laid-back, airy Durham House are a chilled combo of cream, light beams, wicker chairs and reclaimed pine. It's all topped off with dashes of period charm: an arched doorway, bright tiles and stained glass. For breakfast choose from croissants and cinnamon toast, or a full-blown cooked feast.

Colebrooke
B&B £
(01297-20308; www.colebrookehouse.com; Fore St, Beer; s/d/f £45/75/85; P) Expect bright, pine-and-cream rooms, sweet ornaments and some original fireplaces in this tall Victorian town house. The family bedrooms are particularly spacious.

★ Bay View
B&B ££
(01297-20489; www.bayviewbeer.com; Fore St; s/d £43/98; P) The causeway to the beach is just 10 yards away from this cosy B&B's front door, while four of the rooms have smashing sea views. Inside it's all brass bedsteads, cream-painted woods and chi chi bathrooms. Breakfast treats include smoked haddock, and waffles with maple syrup.

Sea Shanty
CHALET ££
(01297-625710; www.seashantyholidays.co.uk; per week £775-875; P ?) For a peaceful, cliffside holiday hideaway, Sea Shanty is hard to beat. Set on the Beer to Branscombe coast path, the two-bedroom chalets Osprey and Avocet are tucked into an uncrowded site. Both have verandas and sweeping views of the sea. It's just a 5-minute walk to the beach at Branscombe Mouth.

Mason's Arms
INN ££
(01297-680300; www.masonsarms.co.uk; Branscombe; d £80-180; meals noon-2.15pm & 6.30-9pm; P ?) With their patches of exposed stone, oak beams and neutral tones these are deeply tasteful rooms. Gleaming bathrooms sport posh toiletries, while the horsebrass and tankard framed bar (mains £14) dishes up locally sourced delights such as potted Branscombe crab, and Creedy Carver duck. Branscombe beach is just a 20-minute walk away.

Eating & Drinking

On a sunny summer's day Beer is made for al fresco, DIY dining. Buy a disposable barbecue from the Village Stores (Fore St; 8am-6pm Mon-Sat 9am-1pm Sun), grab some just-landed fish at the beachside Fishmonger's Shack (Fore St; 8.30am-4.30pm Mon-Sat, from 10am Sun), pick up bread rolls from the bakery (Fore St; 10am-5pm), and oil and lemon from Woozies Deli (01297-20707; Fore St; 10am-4pm, closed Tue). Then dine on the beach with a cracking view.

Seafood Platter
MODERN BRITISH ££
(01297-20099; www.theseafoodplatter.co.uk; Fore St; mains £13; noon-2pm & 6-9pm) A clue is in the name: net-fresh fish is the speciality at this appealing gastropub. The eponymous seafood platter for two (£60) comes crammed with local lobster and crab, while other dishes include cider-braised belly pork and hake rarebit; tangy West Country cheeses come with pumpkin chutney and homemade bread.

Steamers
MODERN BRITISH ££
(01297-22922; www.steamersrestaurant.co.uk; New Cut, Beer; mains £12-20, two/three courses £15/18; noon-2pm & 7-9pm Tue-Sat) At Steamers, produce from local hills and bays makes its way onto the innovative menu – classy creations include Seaton Bay crab with mango, chargrilled Devon pork with orange and brandy, and some seriously sticky puddings. Canny local foodies book in for the great-value set lunches and dinners.

Anchor Inn
PUB
(Fore St) Surely one of the best sea-view beer gardens in Devon. The Anchor's grassy terrace stretches to the very cliff edge, providing views of the wide bay and fishing boats on the pebbly beach below.

Torquay & South Devon

Includes ➡

Torquay 65
Brixham 73
Teignmouth & Around .. 75
South Devon 77
Totnes & Around 77
Dartmouth & Around .. 83
Start Bay 89
Kingsbridge & Around .. 91
Salcombe & Around 93
Bantham 97

Best Places to Eat

➡ Riverford Field Kitchen (p82)

➡ Room in the Elephant (p72)

➡ Seahorse (p88)

➡ Millbrook Inn (p93)

➡ Britannia @ the Beach (p91)

Best Places to Stay

➡ Burgh Island (p98)

➡ Pippin (p79)

➡ Cary Arms (p72)

➡ Alf Resco (p86)

➡ Seabreeze (p89)

Why Go?

This chunk of Devon is holiday heaven. The breezy, family-friendly resort of Torquay can claim bundles of beaches, unique attractions, stylish sleep spots and top-notch eateries. Boat trips and zoos, saucy postcards and fishing ports, palm trees and proms – you'll find them all here.

Outside the resort, the character changes. Paved esplanades give way to soaring cliffs, and amusement-backed beaches become untamed stretches of sand. In the scenic South Hams, you'll discover chic yachting havens, prime surf breaks, hip eco-hang-outs, Miss Marple-esque villages and historic homes. Plus some absolutely superb places to eat and stay. Kayak up a tranquil creek, catch crabs on a harbour wall, go barefoot beachcombing on a huge sweep of sand. Whether you go resort or rural, you'll get a cracking bit of coast either way.

When to Go

➡ **Apr & May** Attractions open and boat trips start. Hotels and B&Bs aren't yet charging top rate.

➡ **Jul & Aug** High season equals high accommodation prices, but the weather should be better. Torquay and Dartmouth regattas set sail; major literature and music festivals start in Totnes.

➡ **Sep** Summer crowds melt away; accommodation bills edge down. Attractions remain open and the seas are at their warmest.

➡ **Oct** Dartmouth's food festival brings top-name chefs to town.

➡ **Feb & Mar** The surf tends to be better. Accommodation prices plummet in many top-end hotels.

TORQUAY

It may face the English Channel, rather than the Med, but the coast around Torquay has long been dubbed the English Riviera, famous for palm trees, piers and russet-red cliffs. At first glance, Torquay itself is the quintessential faded English seaside resort, beloved by both the coach-tour crowd and stag- and hen-party animals. But a mild microclimate and an azure circle of bay have also drawn a smarter set and Torquay now

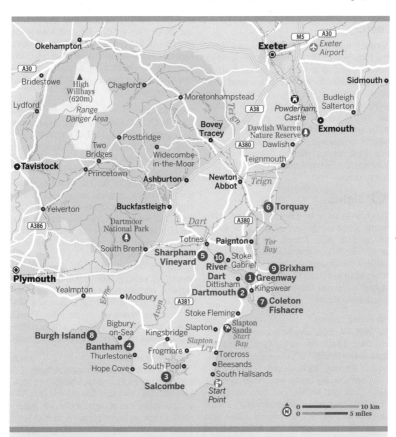

Torquay & South Devon Highlights

❶ Cracking the clues at Agatha Christie's bewitching holiday home, **Greenway** (p83)

❷ Gazing at gorgeous architecture and feasting on fine foods at picture-postcard-pretty **Dartmouth** (p83)

❸ Hopping on a ferry to a sublime sandy cove at chic yachting haven, **Salcombe** (p95)

❹ Standing up, and falling in, as you learn to surf at chilled-out **Bantham** (p97)

❺ Drinking in the views and sampling fine wines at picturesque **Sharpham Vineyard** (p77)

❻ Having family fun in **Torquay** (p65), with its eco-zoo, prehistoric caves and model village

❼ Experiencing jazz-age glamour at the house

and gardens at **Coleton Fishacre** (p88)

❽ Riding the world's only sea tractor en route to wave-dashed **Burgh Island** (p98)

❾ Seeing how your supper was landed in a behind-the-scenes tour at **Brixham Fish Market** (p73)

❿ Losing the crowds and discovering tranquil secret spots as you kayak the **River Dart** (p78)

competes with foodie-hub Dartmouth for fine eateries. The area also boasts unique attractions that range from an immense aviary to prehistoric caves. Add an Agatha Christie connection, fishing ports and steam trains, and it all adds up to some grand days out beside the sea.

History

Torquay has been a holiday hotspot since the French wars of the 18th century fired its development as a watering place; touring Europe was suddenly not such a good idea. In the Victorian era, rows of seaview villas popped up (look out for them still stacked up like dominoes on the steeply sloping hills) and the Prince of Wales bagged a few sailing victories in the regattas. Their modern incarnation, during August's Torbay Week, still sees hundreds of vessels competing in races.

◉ Sights

Torquay leads into Paignton a few miles south along the shores of Tor Bay (not to be confused with Torbay, the local council area). The fishing port of Brixham is 5 miles further south again. The resort of Teignmouth is 8 miles north of Torquay, while the nature reserve at Dawlish Warren is 5 miles north from there.

★ Living Coasts   ZOO
(⊅ 0844 474 3366; www.livingcoasts.org.uk; Beacon Quay; adult/child/family £10/8/32; ⊙ 10am-5pm, to 4pm Nov-Mar; ℗) Clinging to the cliffs beside Torquay Harbour, the open-plan Living Coasts aviary brings you closer to exotic birds than ever before. The immense enclosure features a series of underwater viewing tunnels and mocked-up microhabitats that include Penguin Beach, Auk Cliff and Fur Seal Cove. The result is an up-close view of free-roaming penguins, punk-rocker-style tufted puffins and disarmingly cute bank cormorants. The Local Coasts feature reveals the starfish, bizarre-looking cuttlefish and appealing seahorses that inhabit the water just offshore. For optimum squawking and waddling, time your visit to coincide with penguin breakfast (10.30am) or lunch (2.30pm).

Beaches   BEACH
Torquay boasts 20 beaches and a surprising 22 miles of coast. Holidaymakers flock to the central Torre Abbey Sands, which is covered by water at very high tides; the locals opt for the sand-and-shingle beaches beside the 73m red-clay cliffs at Babbacombe. These can be accessed by a glorious 1920s funicular railway (⊅ 01803-328750; www.babbacombecliffrailway.co.uk; Babbacombe Downs Rd; adult/child return £2/1.30; ⊙ 9.30am-4.45pm Feb-Oct, to 6pm Jun-Sep), a memorable trip in a tiny wooden carriage that shuttles up and down rails set into the cliff. Meadfoot Beach is a long strip of pebbles and sand; Livermead Sands is compact and relatively quiet; while further west, Paignton seafront has a wide russet-tinged stretch called Paignton Sands.

Paignton Zoo   ZOO
(⊅ 0844 474 2222; www.paigntonzoo.org.uk; Totnes Rd, Paignton; adult/child/family £13/10/41; ⊙ 10am-5pm, to 4pm Nov-Mar; ℗) A conservation charity runs this innovative zoo, set on an 32-hectare site dotted with spacious enclosures recreating habitats as varied as savannah, wetlands, tropical forest and desert. Highlights are the orang-utan island, the vast glass-walled lion enclosure, and a lemur wood, where you walk over a plank suspension bridge as the primates leap around in the surrounding trees.

But the real must-see is the crocodile swamp: a steamy enclave overflowing with tropical vegetation, where raised pathways wind over and beside Nile, Cuban and saltwater crocs, some up to 6m long. There's also a glass-free zone where a 10m reticulated python sits, hopefully, just out of reach.

Torquay Museum   MUSEUM
(⊅ 01803-293975; www.torquaymuseum.org; 529 Babbacombe Rd, Torquay; adult/child £5/3; ⊙ 10am-5pm Mon-Sat, 11am-4pm Sun Jul–mid-Sep) The unique collection of Agatha Christie memorabilia here includes photos and handwritten notes, plus display cases devoted to her famous detectives. It also does a superb job of evoking the genteel turn-of-the-20th-century watering hole Torquay was when Christie was a child.

Kents Cavern   UNDERGROUND
(⊅ 01803-215136; www.kents-cavern.co.uk; 89 Ilsham Rd, Torquay; adult/child £9/8; ⊙ 9am-5pm Apr-Oct, 10am-4.30pm Nov-Mar; ℗) Expect stalactites to drip water on your head and temperatures to dip to 14°C amid these atmospheric caves. Hour-long guided tours lead through a maze of rusty-red, uneven tunnels linking rock galleries, arcades and chambers, some of which soar to impressive heights.

Bones found here revealed evidence of Torbay's prehistoric animals – cave lions, giant mammoths and sabre-tooth cats. There are also hyenas' lairs and cave bears' dens; look out for the skull of a cave bear (*ursus deningeri*), embedded in the rock in the Water Gallery.

Kents Cavern is also the oldest recognisable human dwelling in Britain. Flint hand axes unearthed here have been dated to 450,000 years old, while the discovery of a 35,000-year old jawbone makes it the oldest directly dated human bone in Britain.

Babbacombe Model Village MINIATURE VILLAGE
(☑ 01803-315315; www.model-village.co.uk; Hampton Ave, Torquay; adult/child/family £10/8/33; ☉ 10am-dusk; P) Thousands of tiny buildings and even tinier people pack an absorbing attraction chock-full of English eccentricity. The imagination and attention to detail is remarkable with Lilliputian tableaux that are in turns witty, bizarre and unnerving.

Settings include a small-scale Stonehenge, football stadium, beach (complete with nude sunbathers), animated circus, castle (under attack from a fire-breathing dragon) and thatched village where firefighters are tackling a blaze. Visit in the evening for illuminations; think Piccadilly Circus, complete with flashing banner ads.

Cockington Country Park PARK
(☑ 01803-520022; www.countryside-trust.org.uk; Cockington, Torquay; ☉ open access; P) FREE
At 182 hectares, Cockington provides a welcome oasis of calm, green space, just a mile from Torquay's seafront bustle. Walking trails wind through fields, woods and parkland surrounding a 17th-century manor house, walled garden and craft studios.

A heavily thatched village comes complete with forge, mill, gamekeeper's cottage, 14th-century church as well as a real architectural rarity: a thatched pub that was designed by Sir Edwin Lutyens, the 1936 **Drum Inn** (☑ 01803-690264; www.vintage inn.co.uk/thedruminncockington; mains £7-12; ☉ meals 11am-10pm, to 9.30pm Sun). Check to see if there's a match taking place on Cockington's cricket pitch (summer weekends offer the best chance).

TORQUAY & SOUTH DEVON TORQUAY

TORQUAY'S AGATHA CHRISTIE CONNECTION

Torquay is the birthplace of a one-woman publishing phenomenon: **Dame Agatha Mary Clarissa Christie** (1890–1976), a detective writer who is beaten only by the Bible and William Shakespeare in terms of sales. Her characters are world famous: Hercule Poirot, the moustachioed, immodest Belgian detective; and Miss Marple, the surprisingly perceptive busybody spinster.

Born Agatha Miller in Torquay's Barton Rd, the young writer had her first piece published by the age of 11. By WWI she'd married Lieutenant Archie Christie and was working at the Red Cross Hospital in Torquay Town Hall, acquiring the knowledge of poisons that laces countless plot lines, including that of her first novel *The Mysterious Affair at Styles* (1920). Christie made her name with the cunning plot device she used in *The Murder of Roger Ackroyd* six years later. Then came 1926 – in one year her mother died, Archie asked for a divorce and the writer mysteriously disappeared for 10 days, her abandoned car prompting a massive search. She was eventually discovered in a hotel in Harrogate, where she'd checked in under the name of the woman her husband wanted to marry. Christie always maintained she'd suffered amnesia; some critics saw it as a publicity stunt.

Christie later married again, this time to the archaeologist Sir Max Mallowan, and their trips to the Middle East provided masses of material for her work. By the time she died in 1976, Christie had written 75 novels and 33 plays.

Christie connections crop up all over south Devon, in Torquay and near Dartmouth, where you can visit her holiday home, Greenway (p83). A combined **vintage boat and bus service** (☑ 01803-844010; www.greenwayferry.co.uk; adult/child return £15/11; ☉ one daily Apr-Oct) also runs there from Torquay. Dartmouth's Royal Castle Hotel (p87) is the Royal George in *Ordeal by Innocence*, while Burgh Island Hotel (p98) features in fictional form in *And Then There Were None* and *Evil Under the Sun*. For further investigations, there's the comprehensive *Exploring Agatha Christie Country* (£4), by David Gerrard.

Torquay

BABBACOMBE

Redgate Beach

Anstey's Cove

Babbacombe Rd

Oddicombe Beach

Babbacombe Beach

Lincombe Rd

Ilsham Rd

Cedars Rd

Sutherland

Old Torwood Rd

Quinta Rd

Babbacombe Downs Rd

Babbacombe Rd

Reddenhill Rd

Kenwyn Rd

Hatfield Rd

Hampton Ave

St Marychurch Rd

Warbro Rd

Dunmere Rd

Manor Rd

Orestone Hotel (1.8mi);
Teignmouth (6mi);
A379

Westhill Rd

St Marychurch Rd

Hatfield Rd

ST MARYCHURCH

Warren Rd

Hele Rd

Teignmouth Rd

Lymington Rd

Abbey Rd

Sheddenhill

Croft Rd

Union St

Tor Hill Rd

Belgrave Rd

Hele Rd

Hele Rd

Torwood St

Meadfoot Rd

Park Hill Rd

Rock End Ave

Mill La

Falkland Rd

Avenue Rd

Sherwell La

Huxtable Hill Rd

Nut Bush La

Riviera Way

Exeter (20mi);
A380

Hele Rd

The Strand

Torquay
Tourist
Office

Fleet St

Victoria Pde

Park Hill Rd

Beacon Cove

Living Coasts

Warren Rd
Rock Walk

Greenway

Ferry Torbay Rd

Princess Pier

Harbour

Haldon Pier

Enlargement

1 km
0.5 miles

400 m
0.2 miles

Torquay

◎ Top Sights
1 Living Coasts B3

◉ Sights
2 Babbacombe Model Village.................E1
3 Cockington Country Park A4
4 Funicular Railway................................F1
5 Kents Cavern G4
6 Torquay Museum.................................C2
7 Torre Abbey Gardens.........................C5

⊕ Activities, Courses & Tours
8 English Riviera Centre........................C4
9 Torquay–Brixham Ferry A2

⊜ Sleeping
10 Cary Arms..F2
11 Haven House C4
12 Headland View F2
13 Hillcroft..D4
14 Lanscombe House.............................A5
15 Osborne...F5
   Seabreeze...................................(see 12)

⊗ Eating
   Elephant Brasserie ....(see 20)
16 Gemelli D4
17 Number 7..B3
18 Old Vienna...F5
19 Orange Tree.......................................B2
20 Room in the Elephant.........................B3

⊕ Drinking & Nightlife
21 Hennessy...C2
22 Hole in the Wall.................................B2

⊕ Entertainment
23 Bohemia..C2

Paignton Pier   AMUSEMENTS
(☑ 01803-522139; www.paigntonpier.co.uk; Paignton Sands, Paignton) Here's the chance to indulge in pure holiday nostalgia: on this grand old Victorian pier you can parade along the long wooden deck, jump in a dodgem, bounce around on a trampoline and have a game of crazy golf.

Torre Abbey Gardens   GARDENS
(www.torre-abbey.org.uk; King's Dr; admission £2.50; ⊙ 10am-5pm Easter-Sep) The gardens here feature the Potent Plant plot, a collection of species which can be used to make the poisons that feature in Agatha Christie novels. Particularly deadly are the prunus family (its fruit stones can be used to make one of Christie's favourites: cyanide), foxglove and monkshood.

🏃 Activities

Dartmouth Steam Railway
and River Boat Co   RAILWAY
(☎01803-555872; www.dartmouthrailriver.co.uk; Torbay Rd, Paignton; adult/child/family return £13.50/7.50/36; ⊙4-9 trains daily Mar-Nov) Chugging from seaside Paignton to the beautiful banks of the River Dart, this train trip effortlessly rolls back the years to the age of steam. The 7-mile, 30-minute journey starts with a long coastal stretch beside Goodrington Sands (look out for dolphins), then cuts inland. The final section sees trains steaming beside the River Dart, stopping at Greenway Halt (near Agatha Christie's former home), then the village of Kingswear, where regular ferries shuttle across to picturesque Dartmouth.

The engines powering the smartly-liveried, vintage coaches date from the 1920s and 1950s; some are former heavy coal trains from the Welsh valleys, while others pushed Great Western Railway passenger services.

Other trips are available; one involves cruising to Dartmouth by boat, then taking the steam train back to Paignton (adult/child/family £17.50/10.50/47).

Torquay–Brixham Ferry   FERRY
(Greenway Ferry; ☎01803-882811; www.greenwayferry.co.uk; Princess Pier; adult/child return £3.50/2.50; ⊙12 sailings daily Apr-Oct) Tor Bay encompasses 16 sq miles of open sea. The sheer scale becomes apparent from the pleasure boats that make the half-hour Torquay–Brixham trip. The voyage chugs from Torquay's old harbour, past marinas, packed beaches and Paignton Pier, beside crumbling cliffs and grand Victorian hotels to the bustling fishing port of Brixham. Several other operators work the route – competition can cause prices to dip wildly; check out the stands lining Torquay's harbour.

English Riviera Centre   SWIMMING
(☎01803-206345; www.rivieracentre.co.uk; Chestnut Ave; each session per person £9; ⊙7am-9.30pm Mon-Sat, 9am-6pm Sat & Sun) When the weather turns foul, the wave machine and giant flumes of the pool at the English Riviera Centre draw the crowds. There's a sauna and steam room too. A seven-day pass costs £15.

✦✦ Festivals & Events

Torbay Week   SAILING
(www.torbayweek.co.uk) Now one of the most popular sailing regattas on the south coast, Torbay Week attracts hundreds of competitors each August to take part. Racing ranges from yachts and keel boats to dinghies. The horseshoe-shaped bay delivers plenty of vantage points, while funfairs ensure amusements ashore, too.

🛏 Sleeping

Headland View   B&B £
(☎01803-312612; www.headlandview.com; 37 Babbacombe Downs Rd; s/d £57/72; P🖥) Set high on the cliffs at Babbacombe, this delightful terrace is peppered with subtle nautical flourishes, from jaunty model lighthouses to boat motifs on the curtains. The wicker chairs on the tiny balconies have grandstand views of a beautiful stretch of sea.

Seabreeze   B&B £
(☎01803-322429; www.seabreezebabbacombe.co.uk; 39 Babbacombe Downs Rd; s £55-75, d £65-85; P🖥) The smart rooms here are done out in cheery colours, choose from sea-themed aquamarine or bright 'n' breezy red, white and blue. Swish bathrooms and mini bay-view balconies seal the deal.

Haven House   B&B £
(☎01803-293390; www.havenhotel.biz; 11 Scarborough Rd; s £35, d £55-65; P🖥) There's not a doily in sight in simple rooms done out in subtle colours and tinted throws. The large, mounted soft-toy moose head above the front door (a nod to *Fawlty Towers*) adds a dash of comedy.

Orestone   HOTEL ££
(☎01803-328098; www.orestonemanor.com; Rock House Lane; d £95-200; ⊙meals noon-2pm & 7-9pm; P🖥) The Georgian-era Orestone is chock-full of country house charm – winter brings blazing log fires, and summer sees breakfast on a sea-backed terrace. At dinner, a pianist tinkles the ivories as you tuck into classy cuisine (mains £17, 7pm to 9pm). Lunch is also available. In the bedrooms, period elegance meets modern comforts: muted blues and greens surround snazzy bathrooms and fluffy bathrobes, and all have views of the bay. The Orestone is tucked into a wooded valley 3 miles north of Torquay.

Lanscombe House   B&B ££
(☎01803-606938; www.lanscombehouse.co.uk; Cockington Lane; d £95-115; P) Laura Ashley herself would love the design: a 19th-century house filled with lashings of tasteful fabrics, four-poster beds and free-standing slipper baths. Set on the edge of Cockington Village, it has a lovely English cottage garden where you can hear owls hoot at night.

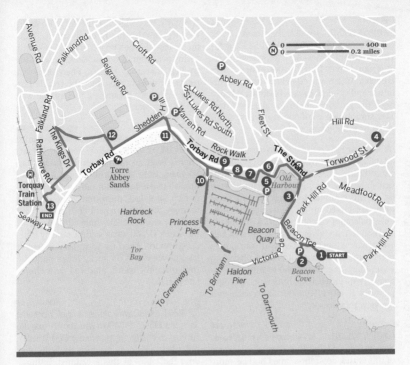

Town Walk
Agatha Christie's Torquay

START IMPERIAL HOTEL
END GRAND HOTEL
LENGTH 2 MILES; THREE HOURS

Begin deductions with a drink on the terrace of the **1 Imperial Hotel** (Miss Marple would choose tea; Poirot a tisane), a fine establishment that appears in three Christie novels: as the Majestic in *Peril at End House* and *The Body in the Library*, and as itself in *Sleeping Murder*. Next take a peep at the waters of **2 Beacon Cove**, where Agatha had to be rescued from drowning as a girl. Stroll beside the **3 Old Harbour**, past souvenir shops and boards promoting boat trips, before heading up Torwood St to **4 Torquay Museum** (p66). Here you can take in the evocative displays in the Agatha Christie Gallery. Look out for the story of how she worked in the resort first as a nurse during WWI, then as a pharmacy dispenser – which is where she acquired that famous knowledge of poisons. Back at the harbour, cut in beside the **5 Tourist Office** (p73) – there's more

Christie merchandise inside – and past the **6 Christie bust**, which was put up to commemorate her centenary year. Next comes the **7 Pavilion**, a shadow of its former glory. It was here that Archie Christie proposed to Agatha at a classical music concert in 1913. Neighbouring **8 Princess Gardens** crop up in *The ABC Murders*. As **9 Rock Walk** rears steeply on the right, divert left onto the late-Victorian **10 Princess Pier**, one of Agatha's favourite roller-skating spots when she was a girl. At **11 Torre Abbey Sands**, turn inland, strolling past tennis courts and pitch 'n' put greens to **12 Torre Abbey Gardens** (p69), where you can discover plants that can be used to produce the poisons that feature in Christie's plots. Next cut down beside more playing fields, past the train station to the suitably named **13 Grand Hotel**. This is where Agatha honeymooned with first husband Archie after they married secretly on Christmas Eve in 1914. A pilot in the Royal Flying Corps, he was back at the front by Boxing Day. Time, perhaps, for another cup of tea.

Hillcroft B&B ££

(☑ 01803-297247; www.thehillcroft.co.uk; 9 St Lukes Rd; s £75-80, d £75-90, ste £115-130; @ 🛜) The bedroom styles here represent a bit of a world tour. Chic themes either reflect French antiques and crisp lines or Asian furniture and exotic fabrics – bathrooms range from the grotto-esque to the sleekly styled. The sumptuous top-floor suite has broad views over the town.

⭐ **Cary Arms** BOUTIQUE HOTEL £££

(☑ 01803-327110; www.caryarms.co.uk; Babbacombe Beach; d £225-275, ste £375) The great British seaside has just gone seriously stylish. At this boutique bolt-hole New England tones are jazzed up by candy-striped cushions; balconies directly overlook the beach and children are given a fishing net and bait on arrival. A stick of rock with the hotel's name running through it is even placed on your pillow. There's a cluster of gorgeous cottages (two/three/six/eight-person cottages per week £1550/1950/2500/3000), each with sea-view terrace, too.

Osborne HOTEL £££

(☑ 01803-213311; www.osborne-torquay.co.uk; Hesketh Cres; d £140-230; P 🛜 ⛱) The terrace of this grand, crescent-shaped hotel is more St Tropez than Torquay: think palm trees, white parasols and utterly bewitching sea views. Rooms feature brown leather and neutral tones, beds range from four poster to brass-framed and sleigh. Work out in the gym, swim in the cliff-side heated pool, then settle back in a bay-view room, which comes with binoculars to watch the boats go by.

🍴 **Eating**

Number 7 SEAFOOD ££

(☑ 01803-295055; www.no7-fish.com; 7 Beacon Tce; mains £15; ⊙ noon-1.45pm Wed-Sat year round, 7-9pm daily Jul-Sep, Tue-Sat Oct-Jun) Fabulous smells fill the air in this buzzing harbourside fish bistro. The menu is packed with super-fresh fruits of the sea, with specialities including local crab, lobster, skate and monkfish, often with an unexpected twist. Try the king scallops with vermouth, or fish and prawn tempura.

Elephant Brasserie MODERN BRITISH ££

(☑ 01803-200044; www.elephantrestaurant.co.uk; 3 Beacon Tce; mains £17, 2-/3-course lunch £17/20; ⊙ noon-2pm & 6.30-9pm Tue-Sat) The setting may be less formal, but the bistro below

Torquay's Michelin-starred eatery (Room in the Elephant) is still supremely smart. Treatments include open ravioli of ham hock with spring pea foam, and poached haddock with truffled macaroni cheese. There are real treats for dessert fans, too: the treacle tart with vanilla ice cream is a memorable way to end the meal.

Orange Tree MODERN BRITISH ££

(☑ 01803-213936; www.orangetreerestaurant.co.uk; 14 Park Hill Rd; mains £15-25; ⊙ from 7pm Tue-Sat) There's been an eatery here for more than 30 years, time enough to perfect a style of English-meets-European cuisine. Dishes focus on local fish, meat and game; prepare to enjoy the rich Brixham crab bisque with scallops, sea bass with smoked pancetta or the south Devon steak with a punchy blue-cheese sauce. Then try to resist the dessert trio: clever twists on sticky toffee pudding, rhubarb and custard, and iced dark chocolate parfait.

Old Vienna EUROPEAN ££

(☑ 01803-380180; www.oldvienna.co.uk; 7 Lisburne Sq; mains £15-22; ⊙ 7-10pm Wed-Sun) It may be run by an engaging Austrian called Werner, but plenty of local produce finds its way onto the tables at this acclaimed, intimate eatery. The result is an unusual menu where smoked mackerel, ruby red Devon beef, and pheasant sits alongside sauerkraut, goulash soup and Linzer torte.

Gemelli ITALIAN ££

(☑ 01803-294183; www.gemellirestaurant.co.uk; 172 Union St; pizzas £8, mains £13; ⊙ noon-2pm & 6.30-9pm Wed-Mon; 🍴) There's a welcome feeling of eating in someone's home at this snug, family-run restaurant. Goodies range from authentic pizzas and golden pasta, to dishes that mix local produce with a dash of the Med – look out for Devon fillet steak with prawn and mushroom sauce, and baked sea bass with pesto. The extensive meat-free menu will make vegetarians smile.

⭐ **Room in the Elephant** FINE DINING £££

(☑ 01803-200044; www.elephantrestaurant.co.uk; 3 Beacon Tce; 2/3/7 courses £45/56/70; ⊙ 7-9pm Tue-Sat Apr-Sep) A restaurant to remember. Torbay's Michelin-starred eatery is defined by imaginative flavour fusions: halibut with smoked eel and lovage; Brixham crab with mango and sweet-pea panna cotta; chilled bitter chocolate fondant with salted-butter caramel ice cream. The sumptuous cheese-board is weighted with the very best West Country offerings, while the window frames bright marina views.

Drinking & Nightlife

Torquay has one of the busiest nightlife scenes in Devon – the area around the harbour gets particularly hectic, especially at weekends.

Hole in the Wall   PUB
(6 Park Lane) Dating from around 1540, this heavily beamed, Tardis-like boozer claims to be the oldest pub in Torquay – the part-cobbled floor is actually listed. At the front there's a tiny alley-cum-terrace on which to enjoy an al fresco pint.

Hennessy   COCKTAIL BAR
(www.hennessyrestaurant.com; 41 Torwood St; ⊘6pm-midnight Tue-Sun) Gilt chairs, leather banquettes and mock flock wallpaper set the scene at this busy cocktail bar.

Bohemia   CLUB
(www.bohemianightclub.com; ⊘41 Torwood St) The three rooms here pulse to diverse sounds; expect R&B, hip-hop, chart, indie and dance anthems.

Information

Torquay Tourist Office (☑01803-211211; www.theenglishriviera.co.uk; Vaughan Pde; ⊘9.30am-5pm Mon-Sat, plus Sun Jun-Sep) Now covers Torquay, Paignton and Brixham.

Getting There & Around

BUS
Brixham (35 minutes, every 20 minutes) Bus 12 runs via Paignton.
Dartmouth (1¼ hours, every 2 hours Monday to Saturday) Bus X81.
Totnes (1 hour, hourly to four daily) Bus X80/81.
Teignmouth (40 minutes, eight daily Monday to Saturday) Bus 11.

CAR
Torquay and Paignton are circled by the A380 ring road; it heads onto Brixham as the more minor A3022. A slower seafront road also winds between all three.

FERRY
Regular ferries (p70) shuttle between Torquay and Brixham.

PARKING
A seven-day permit costs £33, allowing parking in all council car parks (but not on-street parking) in Torquay, Paignton and Brixham. It's available from the tourist office (and the website).

TRAIN
A branch line runs from Exeter (on the London Paddington–Penzance main line) via Torquay (£8, 50 minutes, hourly) to Paignton (£7, 52 minutes). Many services stop at Teignmouth, Dawlish and Dawlish Warren.

Another branch line runs at least hourly from Newton Abbot (also on the London–Penzance mainline) to Torquay (20 minutes) and on to Paignton (10 minutes).

The Dartmouth Steam Railway and River Boat Co also puffs to Kingswear, on the opposite side of the river to Dartmouth; ferries link the two locations.

Brixham

An appealing, pastel-painted tumbling of fishermen's cottages leads down to Brixham's horseshoe harbour, signalling a very different place from the resort towns to the north. Here gently tacky arcades co-exist with winding streets, brightly coloured boats and one of Britain's busiest fishing ports. Although picturesque, Brixham is far from a neatly packaged destination and its brand of gritty charm offers a more authentic glimpse of life along Devon's coast. The port also recently made it onto TV screens worldwide as the location for Sky Atlantic's fly-on-the wall documentary, *Fish Town*.

⊙ Sights & Activities

Fish Market   TOUR, MARKET
(☑0741 0617931; www.brixhamtourismpartnership.co.uk; The Quay; tour £8; ⊘twice monthly late-Jun–Sep) With more than 100 boats landing catches totalling £25 million, Brixham is one of the UK's busiest fishing ports. These early-morning, behind-the-scenes tours provide a unique insight into a world that's normally off-limits to visitors. Fishermen guide you past buyers and sellers in white coats, and ice-lined plastic trays full of fish, before the bustling auction itself begins. Then comes breakfast at the Fishermen's Mission with those who work in the trade. Tours are only open to people over 13; they're hugely popular so book well in advance. If you miss the tours, head down to the fish market around 5am to 6am and make for the **viewing platform** to watch the fleet's manoeuvrings.

Fishing Trips
FISHING

(✆ 01803-882811; www.greenwayferry.co.uk; The Quay; adult/child £12/7; ☉ 4 daily Easter-Oct) In a town so steeped in the fishing industry, even visitors not normally interested in trying to land a catch can be tempted to have a go. On these two-hour mackerel fishing trips you'll learn how to bait the hook, zip it into the water and wait for a bite. Boats are likely to head south to Berry Head or into the middle of Tor Bay; look out for special evening angling trips, too.

Golden Hind
SAILING SHIP

(✆ 01803-856223; www.goldenhind.co.uk; The Quay; adult/child £4/3; ☉ 10am-4pm Mar-Sep) Tied up alongside Brixham Harbour is something straight out of *Pirates of the Caribbean*: a full-sized replica of the vessel commanded by Devon explorer Sir Francis Drake during his 16th-century circumnavigation of the globe. Though remarkably small, the original ship had a crew of 60. Today, you get to walk across a gangplank, peer inside the tiny captain's cabin, prowl around the poop deck and listen to tales of life in the officer's quarters delivered in suitably 'arrr, me-hearties' tones. Youngsters can enjoy the Pirate Days, most Thursdays in the school holidays.

Brixham Heritage Museum
MUSEUM

(✆ 01803-856267; www.brixhamheritage.org.uk; New Rd; adult/child £2/free; ☉ 10am-4pm Tue-Sat Apr-Oct, to 1pm Nov-Mar) The town's salty history is explored here, with an eclectic collection of exhibits on sail boats, smuggling, ship-building and sea rescues.

🛌 Sleeping

Sampford House
B&B £

(✆ 01803-857761; www.sampfordhouse.com; 57 King St; d £60-74, cottage per night £75-90; P 🛜) Book a harbour-view room at this 18th-century cottage and you'll probably see seals bobbing around in the waters below. Winding staircases lead to compact but cute bedrooms with cherry wood furniture and brass bedsteads. There's also a neighbouring two-up-two-down cottage, complete with galley kitchen, bathroom, bedroom and lounge with cracking water views.

Harbour View
B&B £

(✆ 01803-853052;www.harbourviewbrixhambandb .co.uk; 65 King St; s/d £50/80; P 🛜) A sensitive conversion has turned the downstairs of this 18th-century cottage into a spacious two-storey guest lounge. The narrow staircases feature exposed stone and rope handrails, while bedrooms are all modern, with movement sensitive lighting and sleek fitted cabinets. Still, it's the absorbing harbour views that steal the show.

Trefoil
B&B £

(✆ 01803-855266; www.trefoilguesthouse.co.uk; 134 New Rd; s £25-42, d £60-70; P 🛜) It's worth staying here for the breakfasts alone. Former chef Pam's speciality is cheese and black pepper muffins with bacon and poached eggs, and the sideboard groans with fresh strawberries, melon, pineapples and prunes. The rooms are smashing as well: stylish in slate grey, duck-egg blue or gentle gold. Each has posh biscuits and fluffy bathrobes, too.

🍴 Eating & Drinking

David Walker & Son
SEAFOOD £

(www.davidwalkerandson.com; Unit B, Fish Market; ☉ 9am-3pm Mon-Fri, 8am-4pm Sat) A chance to connect with Brixham's fishing industry *and* stock up for your barbecue: the ice-filled counters here are piled high with what's just been landed. Picnic goodies include huge, cooked shell-on prawns (£9 per 500g) and dressed crab (from £6 each).

Beamers
SEAFOOD ££

(✆ 01803-854777; www.beamersrestaurant.co.uk; 19 The Quay; mains £16-23; ☉ 6pm-late Wed-Mon; 🍴) Each morning head chef Simone strolls over to Brixham Fish Market to select the best of the day's catch. The result? Supremely fresh, superbly cooked fish. Perhaps the top pick is the platter of the day boat fish for two (£35). Saffron, Pernod and pear spring some menu surprises, while bagging a window table secures a captivating harbour view.

Poop Deck
SEAFOOD ££

(✆ 01803-858681; www.poopdeckrestaurant.com; 14 The Quay; mains £17; ☉ noon-2.30pm Thu-Sun, 6.30-9.30pm Tue-Sat) Decisions, decisions – here the catch of the day is landed just yards away, so it's tempting to have it simply grilled with garlic butter or olive oil. Or opt for the sea bass with brandy sauce, but that would mean missing the hot shellfish platter, a steaming pile of lobster, crevettes, scallops and crab...

Maritime
PUB

(79 King St, Brixham) Quirky doesn't even begin to describe this pub full of full-blooded English eccentricity. Thousands of key rings, stone jugs and chamber pots smother this ancient pub's walls, while a vast whiskey

selection stacks up behind the counter. The best feature though is Mr Tibbs, a parrot who wanders around the bar saying 'hello' to customers (literally).

ℹ Getting There & Away

BUS

Torquay (35 minutes, every 20 minutes) Bus 12 runs via Paignton.

Kingswear (20 minutes, every 30 minutes to hourly) Bus 22. Ferries then connect to Dartmouth.

FERRY

Regular ferries (p70) shuttle between Brixham and Torquay.

Teignmouth & Around

POP 14,750

Hugging the shore where the River Teign meets the sea, Teignmouth has all the trappings of a well-worn resort. Georgian terraces back a seafront lined with rough, red-gold sand, and a classic Victorian pier juts proudly out to sea. But the town is also home to a small port that plies a coaster trade, and the tiny network of nearby lanes, with their candy-coloured fishermen's sheds and seafarer's pubs, lend the place a bustling, nautical air. A ferry chugs resolutely across the river, while the Dawlish Warren nature reserve – an elemental mass of wind-blasted dunes – is just a short coastal hike away.

◉ Sights & Activities

Teign Ferry   FERRY
(☏ 07896-711822; www.teignmouthshaldonferry. co.uk; Back Beach; adult/child return £3/1.40; ◷ 8am-dusk mid-Jul–Aug, to 6pm Apr–mid-Jul, to 4.30pm Nov-Mar) The open-topped Teign Ferry shuttles from Teignmouth to the appealing village of Shaldon on the south bank. The ferry service began life around the 10th century, while the distinctive black-and-white colour scheme of the current boat is Elizabethan. It's an evocative crossing – you embark by walking up a gangplank. The voyage itself brings a crumbling, red headland ever closer. Once in Shaldon hunt out Ness Beach, accessed via a smugglers' tunnel that's been hacked out of the rock.

The ferry sails from Teignmouth's River (or Back) Beach, just behind the Point (seafront) car park. The schedule can be affected by the weather; times are posted on beachside boards.

Teignmouth & Shaldon Museum   MUSEUM
(Teign Heritage Centre; www.teignheritage.org. uk; 29 French St; adult/child £2.50/free; ◷ 10am-4.30pm Tue-Sat Feb-Oct, plus 2-5pm Sun Jul & Aug) It's as far from a fusty old museum as you can get, with engaging exhibits filling a stylish new building. Step into a Victorian bathing machine, feel the weight of a cannonball, and have a go at being a Punch 'n' Judy puppeteer. Look out for cannons from a 16th-century Venetian shipwreck (found by a local lad); and displays on Admiral Pellew, the inspiration for CS Forester's *Hornblower* series.

Dawlish Warren   WILDLIFE RESERVE
(www.dawlishwarren.co.uk; The Warren; ◷ open access; Ⓟ) **FREE** Clinging to the coast on the southern shore of the mouth of the River Exe, the curling sand spit here reaches far out into the water, offering exhilarating views up the river and out to sea. The variety of habitats is remarkable, ranging from dunes and grasslands, to salt marshes and mudflats, and the reserve is a key roost for wildfowl and wading birds. It has more than 30 nationally rare species of flora including the Sand Crocus. Also look out for Black Spleenwort, Adder's-tongue and Hart's-tongue Fern.

Dawlish Warren is 5 miles north of Teignmouth by road, and trains shuttle between the two roughly hourly (12 minutes). A water taxi (p59) runs to the reserve from Exmouth, or hike the spray-spattered coast path from Teignmouth (6 miles).

A DAY AT THE RACES

In a glorious collision of smartly dressed county set and hard-bitten gambling fraternity, the 19-fixture jumps season at Newton Abbot Racecourse (☏ 01626-353235; www. newtonabbotracing.com; Newton Rd, Newton Abbot; ◷ 3 meetings a month Apr-Sep) lasts all summer long. It's a flat, oval, left-hand circuit, with seven fences in just over a mile. Opt for the pricier Paddock Enclosure ticket (£18) for close-up views of the Parade Ring and winning post, or head for the Course Enclosure (£12) for more-distant views of the whole track. Either way there'll be posh frocks, tweeds, silks, thundering horses and, of course, champagne.

Walks WALKING

The 6-mile stretch of coast between Teignmouth and the nature reserve at **Dawlish Warren** is edged by red sandstone cliffs that have been eroded into a series of bizarre stacks, coves and undulating headlands. Here the coast path is sandwiched between the sea and a train line that is itself squeezed in alongside rocks. It makes for an atmospheric hike – taking the coast path north out of Teignmouth actually involves walking on the breakwater. About a mile along, the trail cuts sharply inland, skirting the striking **Parson and Clerk** rock formation, before descending steeply to the seafront at the resort of **Dawlish**, a mile further on. Look out for the weirdly shaped **Horse**, **Old Maid** and **Cowhole rocks** on the way. From Dawlish, a 2-mile stroll leads past deeply eroded russet cliffs, a wide beach and a cluster of fairground rides to the Dawlish Warren Nature Reserve itself.

If the walk back seems too far, you could ride the route instead: there are train stations at Dawlish Warren, Dawlish and Teignmouth (times vary so it's best to check).

Sleeping

Old Salty House B&B £

(☎01626-879574; www.oldsaltyhouse.co.uk; 21 Northumberland Place; s/d £40/60) With its oh-so-suitable name, Old Salty is hidden away in the warren of lanes bordering Teignmouth's atmospheric Back Beach; ancient warehouses and fishermen's pubs lie all around. Inside it's a cosy, comfy affair, all sanded wood, wicker and painted floorboards; buttered crumpets and warm potato cakes are among the breakfast treats.

Bay HOTEL £

(☎01626-774123; www.bayhotelteignmouth.co.uk; 15 Powderham Tce; s £40-46, d £70-80, f £105, penthouse £160; P 📶) Reproduction Georgian furniture and soothing colours fill the bedrooms at this rangy seafront hotel. The best come with views of Teignmouth's russet sands, while the four-person penthouse is charming: slanting ceilings, an oval bathtub and a vast deck-cum-balcony, with top-notch views of the waves.

Thomas Luny House B&B ££

(☎01626-772976; www.thomas-luny-house.co.uk; Teign St; s £60-75, d £80-102; P) The essence of refined, restrained luxury, this 200-year-old town house is graced by heavy fabrics, antiques, wooden trunks and old sailing prints. The patio garden is an oasis of quiet calm.

Eating & Drinking

Blue Hut KIOSK, SEAFOOD £

(Back Beach; snacks from £3; ⏲11am-5pm Easter-Sep) Sandwiched between brightly painted fishermen's sheds beside the Point car park, the Blue Hut sells cockles, winkles, mussels and rolls crammed with freshly picked crab, best enjoyed with a cuppa and great estuary views.

Crab Shack SEAFOOD ££

(☎01626-777956; www.crabshackonthebeach.co.uk; Back Beach; mains £11-20; ⏲noon-2pm Wed-Sun, 7-9pm Wed-Sat) The location couldn't be better for super-fresh fish: overlooking the sheltered Teign estuary, and the fleet that brought your supper ashore. The restaurant even owns a couple of fishing boats. Grab a table on the lobster-pot-framed terrace, then feast on moules, a whole grilled lobster or a bucket of garlic-roasted crab claws.

The Owl and The Pussycat MODERN BRITISH ££

(☎01626-775321; www.theowlandpussycat.co.uk; 3 Teign St; mains £17; ⏲10am-2.30pm Mon-Sat, 6-9.30pm Mon-Sun) A stylish, crisp restaurant that's brimming with West Country produce. South Devon beef is combined with truffle oil, the Creedy Carver duck is infused with ginger and port, and the tasty bouillabaisse overflows with locally landed fish.

Ship Inn PUB

(www.shipteignmouth.co.uk; 2 Queen St, Teignmouth) Rustic tables, beams and wooden floors help make the mellow Ship one of the most atmospheric pubs in town – its beers (including two local Otter Ales) are well kept, too. On a summer's evening its waterside terrace is perfect for enjoying tasty pub grub (mains from £8; meals noon to 2.30pm and 6pm to 9pm), a tangy pint and memorable sunset views.

Information

Teignmouth Tourist Office (☎01626-215666; www.visitsouthdevon.co.uk; The Den; ⏲10am-5pm Mon-Sat, plus 10am-4pm Sun Jul-Aug)

Getting There & Away

BUS

Exeter (1 hour, every 20 minutes Monday to Saturday) Bus 2.

Torquay (40 minutes, eight daily Monday to Saturday) Bus 11.

TRAIN

Exeter (30 minutes, half hourly)

Torquay (20 minutes, half hourly)

SOUTH DEVON

South of Torquay, Devon is transformed. Candyfloss, promenades and arcades give way to green fields and soaring cliffs. Here historic Totnes is home to Tudor architecture, a superb vineyard and a counterculture vibe. Charismatic Dartmouth delivers Agatha Christie's house and nautical history, while to the south, Salcombe offers boat trips, beaches and sailing. Here you'll also find the soothing villages of Hope Cove and Bantham, the tranquil market town of Kingsbridge, and at Burgh Island, a sumptuous art deco hotel. Acclaimed eateries are scattered throughout. It's a winning combination: sophistication and simplicity; peace and space; undeveloped beaches and sparkling bays.

ℹ Information

Visit South Devon (www.visitsouthdevon.co.uk) A good information source.

South Devon AONB (☑ 01803-861384; www.southdevonaonb.org.uk) Runs inspiring events.

Totnes & Around

POP 7450

After Torbay's kiss-me-quick delights, Totnes is decidedly different. It's got such a reputation for being alternative that locals scrawled 'twinned with Narnia' under the town sign. But as well as shops stacked with tie-dye and incense, this New Age haven is packed with history and architecture ranging from the Normans to the 1920s. Add a vineyard, a jazz-age architectural gem, some great places to sleep, and an award-winning eco-restaurant, and you have a vibrant south Devon base.

History

The Normans built a castle here in the 11th century, realising access to the River Dart lent Totnes strategic importance. Tudor times brought wealth through the tin trade; one legacy is the 60 merchants' houses lining the main streets. Totnes' transition to alternative hub began in 1925 when Dorothy and Leonard Elmhirst bought the nearby Dartington Estate, setting up an experiment in rural regeneration and a progressive school. Dartington College of Arts opened in 1961, reinforcing the town's New Age image. The college decamped to Falmouth in 2010, but the pioneering environmental movement, Transition Town Totnes, continues the sustainability theme.

◉ Sights

★**Sharpham Wine & Cheese** WINERY
(☑ 01803-732203; www.sharpham.com; ⊘ 10am-5pm daily May-Sep, closed Sun Jan-Apr; **P**) The ranks of vines on the steeply sloping banks of the curving River Dart are more reminiscent of Chablis than south Devon. The winery's most expensive tour (£65) involves an expert-led walk, an explanation of vinification techniques, a tutored tasting, light lunch and a bottle of Dart Valley Reserve. A full guided tour and tutored tasting costs £20, while a self-guided walk and instructed tasting costs £8. Sharpham also makes cheese, so you can nibble that while sampling vintages. Be sure to book a table for lunch in its award-winning cafe, too. Sharpham Vineyard is 3 miles south of Totnes, and signposted off the A381, but walking the Dart Valley Trail from Totnes is a more enjoyable way to arrive.

High Cross House HISTORIC BUILDING
(NT; ☑ 01803-842382; www.nationaltrust.org.uk; Dartington Estate; adult/child £7.20/3.70; ⊘ 10.30am-5pm Wed-Sun; **P**) This elegant blue and white creation is one of the most important Modernist-era houses in England. Designed by William Lescaze in 1932, its rectilinear and curved lines are deeply evocative of the period, as is the interior of pared-down furniture and smooth wood. It was created as a 'machine for living' and

---

TRANSITION TOWN TOTNES

In 2005 in Totnes, the seeds of an almighty eco-project were sown. The first experiment of its kind in the UK, Transition Town Totnes (www.transitiontowntotnes.org) looked ahead to a world with less oil and then examined the impact on every aspect of our lives, from food and car use to health care and schools. Since then more than 400 Transition initatives have sprung up across the UK.

In Totnes, look out for low-impact community housing (Transition Homes), food foraging walks, and – at Totnes' Saturday Market – Dr Bike (he'll fix non-major faults for free, time swap or donations). Plus there's the Totnes Pound (www.totnespound.org), a local currency you can 'buy' in Totnes, then spend in local shops.

mirroring that today you're encouraged to experience the space: play the piano, sit on the chairs and browse the art books. But be warned: having settled into one of the streamlined 1930s sofas, it is rather hard to leave.

Totnes Castle
CASTLE

(EH; ☑01803-864406; www.english-heritage.org. uk; Castle St; adult/child £3.60/2.20; ☉10am-6pm Apr-Sep, to 5pm Oct) The outer keep of Totnes' Norman motte-and-bailey fortress crowns a hill at the top of town, providing engrossing views over higgledy-piggledy rooftops and the river valley. Hunt out the medieval loo, too.

Historic Buildings
ARCHITECTURE

Totnes has one of the best collections of Tudor architecture in Devon, with impressive buildings lining its steep, central High and Fore Sts. Towards the top, where Castle St meets the High St, look out for Poultry Walk. This wonky row of Tudor jettied buildings, propped up by an array of columns, was where the town's poultry market was held. Downhill, on the left, the 16th-century Butterwalk used to shelter

---

DARTINGTON ESTATE

It was quite some wedding gift: Henry VIII gave this 800-acre estate to two of his wives (Catherines Howard and Parr). Now it's home to B&B accommodation, the 1930s High Cross House, the Barn art house cinema, the affable White Hart pub and a medieval great hall that hosts events ranging from classical music to literature festivals.

Dartington's 14th-century manor house frames a grassy space reminiscent of an Oxbridge quadrangle. In the landscaped gardens impressive terraced banks line a tiltyard, while flower-filled borders lead down to glades, meadows and thatched cottages. Amid the tiny paths and secret benches, hunt out the carved stone *Memorial Figure* by Henry Moore, the swirling bobbles of *Jacob's Pillow* by Peter Randall Page and the bronze donkey by Willi Soukop. The Japanese Garden, complete with raked gravel and cedar wood shelter, is beside the ruined church.

The estate is 1½ miles northwest of Totnes.

---

dairy markets. Many of the houses have elaborate Tudor plasterwork ceilings; two of the best preserved are at Bogan House, in the Totnes Fashion and Textile Museum. Church Close cuts sharply left off the High St, leading beside the red Devon sandstone of the 15th-century St Mary's Church. Hidden in behind is the ancient Guildhall. Ramparts Walk curves around the church, tracing the line of the original Saxon town boundary. At the bottom of Fore St, Bank Lane features an ornate, lemon-yellow 18th-century house built in a style known as Strawberry Hill Gothic.

Guildhall
HISTORIC BUILDING

(☑01803-862147; Ramparts Walk; adult/child £1.25/30p; ☉10.30am-4pm Mon-Fri Apr-Oct) Parts of this atmospheric structure were the kitchens of the town's Norman priory; inside look out for cells, ceremonial robes and an elaborate council chamber.

Elizabethan Garden
GARDEN

(Fore St; ☉9am-5pm) FREE Signs in this tiny walled garden cast a light on 16th-century medical thinking, outlining which herb cured which ailment – soapwort for syphilis, woad to staunch bleeding, bay for bee stings. It's accessed via an easy-to-miss gate and cobbled alley at the side of the Totnes Elizabethan Museum.

Totnes Fashion & Textile Museum
MUSEUM

(43 High St; adult/child £2/80p; ☉11am-5pm Tue-Fri May-Sep) Beautifully displayed 18th- to 20th-century garments, set in one of Totnes' finest Tudor Merchant's houses.

🏃 Activities

★Totnes Kayaks
KAYAKING

(☑07799 403788; www.totneskayaks.co.uk; The Quay, Stoke Gabriel; per 1/3/6hr £10/24/35; ☉10am-5pm Apr-Oct) The best way to explore the gentle River Dart is to head to sleepy Stoke Gabriel (5 miles southeast of Totnes), then paddle out between unspoilt hills. A top tip is to go with the tide (owner Tom will advise), which may take you upriver to Sharpham Vineyard and Totnes, or downriver to charming Dittisham. It's gorgeous either way.

Canoe Adventures
CANOEING

(☑01803-865301; www.canoeadventures.co.uk; adult/child £22/17) 🛶 Voyages in 12-seater Canadian canoes – the monthly moonlit paddles are a treat.

South Devon Steam Railway
RAILWAY

(☑01364-644370; www.southdevonrailway.org; adult/child return £12/7; ☺4-9 trains daily Apr-Oct) The privately run South Devon Railway chuffs from Totnes to Buckfastleigh, on the edge of Dartmoor.

⭐ Festivals & Events

Ways With Words
LITERATURE

(☑01803-867373; www.wayswithwords.co.uk; Dartington Estate) Key authors attend this classy lit fest each July, where venues include the Tudor Great Hall and the restored Barn. The central, grassy courtyard is dotted with book-signings, food stalls and people reading and chatting in deckchairs.

Dartington International Summer School
CLASSICAL MUSIC

(☑01803-847070; www.dartington.org/summer-school; Dartington Estate) Courses at this month-long festival (starting in late July) include everything from composition and conducting an orchestra, to vocal techniques and perfect piano skills. Around three public concerts a day are also held; expect early music and full-blown opera, as well as tango, junk music and tea dances.

🛏 Sleeping

⭐Pippin
CAMPSITE ££

(☑01275-395447; www.canopyandstars.co.uk; Cleave Farm, near Totnes; 3/7 nights £265/605; Ⓟ) ✿ It really doesn't get much more idyllic than this: a brightly painted Romany caravan in the heart of an orchard where birdsong is the only sound. Snuggle down beside the wood burner or cook up a storm on the fire-pit, then soak in the al fresco hot tub, gazing up at the stars. The welcome basket includes organic cider made from the apples around you, and breakfast eggs come direct from the hen house. Ducks and peacocks roam the grounds. It's a popular spot so make sure you book.

Dartington Hall
B&B ££

(☑01803-847000; www.dartington.org; Dartington Estate; s £39-104, d £99-209; Ⓟ) ✿ The wings of this exquisite, ancient manor house have been carefully converted into bedrooms that range from heritage-themed to deluxe-modern. Ask for one overlooking the grassy, cobble-fringed courtyard and settle back for a truly tranquil night's sleep.

Sea Trout
INN ££

(☑01803-762274; www.theseatroutinn.co.uk; Staverton, near Totnes; d £102-109, ste £140; Ⓟ📶)

Most of the rooms here are the epitome of carefully judged, comfortable, contemporary good taste. All that changes dramatically in the feature room; a deliberately over-the-top rococo delight, where ornate black-wood furniture sits alongside mock-chandeliers and a slipper bath. An annex houses a mini-suite, while the great-value restaurant (open noon to 2pm and 6pm to 9pm daily; mains £15) regularly notches up awards.

Royal Seven Stars
HOTEL ££

(☑01803-862125; www.royalsevenstars.co.uk; The Plains; s £85-95, d £119-150; Ⓟ📶) They've been putting up travellers here since Charles II's day, and this grand old coaching inn in the heart of Totnes is all 17th-century charm. Bay windows, bowed ceilings and slanting floors give it atmosphere, while rich throws, solid wood furniture and fancy bathrooms ensure modern comforts. (Book online; it's more than £10 a night cheaper)

Steam Packet
INN ££

(☑01803-863880; www.steampacketinn.co.uk; St Peters Quay; s/d/f £75/95/110; Ⓟ) It's almost as if this wharfside warehouse's minimalist rooms have been plucked from the pages of a design magazine, so stylish are the painted wood panels, nautically themed trimmings, and orange-and-red throws. Ask for a river-view room, then sit back and watch the world float by.

Maltsters Arms
B&B ££

(☑01803-732350; www.tuckenhay.com; Tuckenhay, near Totnes; d £80-125, f £95-140; Ⓟ) Stretched out along the bank of tranquil Bow Creek, the Maltsters is hard to resist. Subtle oatmeal and bursts of burgundy define the bedrooms; opt for a nicer by far river-view one and get a sofa bed, beams and, in some, struts made from an ancient ship's mast. The delightfully snug restaurant (noon to 2.30pm and 6.30pm to 9pm) specialises in local fish and meats, while the waterside beer terrace is a perfect spot for a pint. It's 4 miles south of Totnes.

Old Forge
B&B ££

(☑01803-862174; www.oldforgetotnes.com; Seymour Pl; s £63, d £80-90, f £100; Ⓟ📶) In this 600-year-old former jail, comfort has replaced incarceration: deep reds and sky-blue furnishings cosy up to bright throws and spa baths. The delightful family room even has its own decked sun terrace. It's a 10-minute walk to town.

Beaches

Hidden coves, wooded inlets, sandy harbours, epic bays: the southwest has a beach to suit all moods. Around its 630-mile coastline, you'll find everything from family-friendly resorts to secret sands known only to a chosen few. Take your pick – and don't forget to pack the flip-flops.

2

STEPHEN SHEPHERD / GETTY IMAGES ©

4

JON ARNOLD / GETTY IMAGES ©

1. Treen & Logan Rock (p234)
Strange geological formations watch over crystal-clear waters.

2. Saunton Sands (p141)
This 3-mile beach is backed by the UK's biggest sand dunes.

3. Kynance Cove (p248)
A gem on the Lizard Peninsula, this National Trust–owned cove offers caves and islands to explore.

4. Perranporth (p213)
Perran's sundial overlooks the magnificent stretch of beach.

3

IAN LEWIS / GETTY IMAGES ©

✗ Eating & Drinking

Willow
VEGETARIAN £

(☑ 01803-862605; 87 High St; mains £8; ☉ 10am-5pm Mon-Sat, 6.30-9pm Wed, Fri & Sat; ☑) ✎ This rustic vegetarian cafe sums up the spirit of New Age Totnes. Wobbly tables dot its bright dining room, and the menu is an array of couscous, quiches, hotpots, homemade cakes and fair-trade drinks. It's strong on vegan dishes, too.

★ Riverford Field Kitchen
MODERN BRITISH ££

(☑ 01803-762074; www.riverford.co.uk; Wash Barn; 3-course lunch/dinner adult £23/27, child £11/13; ☉ noon-3pm daily, from 7.30pm Mon-Sat; ☑) ✎ As one of Britain's leading veg-box suppliers, Riverford is synonymous with organic, sustainable food. Fittingly, its eco-bistro is set in the middle of a farm, meaning minimal food miles. Vegetables are picked to order from the fields outside, and meats are organic and locally sourced. Big trestle tables fill a futuristic hangar-like canteen, with diners passing around platters laden with richly flavoured food. Imaginative treatments might include marinated, grilled Moroccan lamb and British veg transformed by cumin or saffron. You have to book and take a self-led or guided tour of the fields. The Field Kitchen is 3 miles west of Totnes.

Sharpham Vineyard Café
BISTRO ££

(☑ 01803-732178; www.vineyardcafe.co.uk; Sharpham Estate; mains £10-15, snacks £4-7; ☉ noon-2pm May-Oct; ☑) Rustic, organic fare fills the tables of this decked cafe, anchored just yards from Sharpham's vines. Treats include smoked fish or charcuterie boards, local crab salads and hearty fare such as belly pork and bean cassoulet. And, of course, the vineyard's own, simply superb cheese and wine. It's 3 miles south of Totnes.

White Hart
PUB ££

(☑ 01803-847111; www.dartingtonhall.com; Dartington Estate; tapas £5, mains £12-17; ☉ tapas noon-9pm, dinner 6-9pm; ☑) To its already-acclaimed gastropub dishes, the White Hart has added a British tapas menu, so you can graze on mini-bundles of flavour washed down with a carafe of wine. Menus change daily, but ham hock, lamb cutlets, scallops or wild mushroom risotto might pop up. Winter brings a blazing fire; on fine evenings the lawnside tables are the place to be.

Rumour
PUB ££

(☑ 01803-864682; www.rumourtotnes.com; 30 High St; mains £7-18; ☉ noon-3pm Mon-Sat, 6-9pm daily; ☑) ✎ Rumour is a local institution – a narrow, cosy pub-restaurant with low lighting, funky local art and free newspapers. Famous for its crispy pizzas (£7), it also rustles up stylish cuisine, such as pollock roasted with avocado butter, and irresistible 28-day matured 8oz steaks.

☆ Entertainment

Barn
CINEMA

(www.dartington.org/barn-cinema; Dartington Estate) An atmospheric independent cinema with a good program.

🔒 Shopping

Totnes Market
MARKET

(Civic Sq; ☉ 9am-4pm) Each Friday and Saturday scores of stalls, selling everything from vintage goods to fudge, fill the Civic Sq. On the third Sunday of the month one of Devon's biggest food markets is set up here.

Shops at Dartington
SHOPPING CENTRE

(www.dartington.org/shops; Dartington Estate; ☉ 10am-5pm) Jewellery, kitchenware, books, glassware, clothes, toys, fine foods and a Cranks cafe fill the attractive outbuildings of this former cider press.

Riverford Farm Shop
FOOD

(www.riverfordfarmshop.co.uk; 38 High St; ☉ 9am-5.30pm Mon-Sat, 10am-4pm Sun) Plot your picnic here, among piles of organic local veg, pies, pasties, bread and cheese.

ℹ Information

Tourist Office (☑ 01803-863168; www.totnes-information.co.uk; Coronation Rd; ☉ 9.30am-5pm Mon-Fri & 10am-4pm Sat Apr-Oct, 10am-4pm Mon-Fri & to 1pm Sat Nov-Mar)

ℹ Getting There & Away

BOAT
Boats (p85) shuttle downriver to Dartmouth.

BUS
Torquay (1 hour, hourly to four daily) Bus X80/81.

Dartmouth (45 minutes, hourly, Monday to Saturday) Bus X81.

TRAIN
Trains go at least hourly to Exeter (£6, 35 minutes) and Plymouth (£6, 30 minutes). The South Devon Steam Railway puffs up to Buckfastleigh.

BERRY POMEROY CASTLE

Even the most level-headed are set to get spooked at the immense 17th-century ruin of Berry Pomeroy (EH; ☑ 01803-866618; www.english-heritage.org.uk; adult/child £5/3; ◷ 10am-6pm Apr-Sep, to 5pm Oct), 2 miles east of Totnes. The crumbling walls of its roof-less shell soar up to three floors high. Individual rooms are still clearly outlined, making it feel both partly normal and as if something has gone horribly wrong at the same time. The sense of menace increases at St Margaret's Tower, a circular well-like structure where Lady Margaret Pomeroy is said to have been imprisoned and starved to death by her jealous sister. Her ghost (apparently) roams the battlements today.

Dartmouth & Around

POP 7500

A bewitching blend of primary-coloured boats and delicately shaded houses, Dartmouth is irresistible. Buildings cascade down steep, wooded slopes towards the River Dart, and 17th-century shops with splendidly carved and gilded fronts line narrow lanes. Its charms have drawn a yachting crowd and a string of top-notch eateries, but fleets of fishing vessels, ferries and pleasure boats ensure it's still a busy working port with an authentic tang of the sea. Hiking trails lead up the river or onto the cliffs, while a unique art deco house and Agatha Christie's Greenway estate wait in the wings. The pastel-painted village of Kingswear sits on the opposite bank.

History

Dartmouth's history is salty and compelling: ships headed off on the Crusades from here in the 12th century, and the Pilgrim Fathers sailed for America from here in 1620 – only putting in to Plymouth, to later depart from the much more famous Mayflower Steps, because one of the boats sprang a leak. Then in WWII thousands of American servicemen set off from Dartmouth for the carnage of the Normandy landings. Echoes of that martial past are still present; the hills above town are home to the Britannia Royal Naval College, the imposing 100-year-old mansion where the Royal Navy still trains all its officers.

◉ Sights

★ Greenway   HISTORIC BUILDING
(NT; ☑ 01803-842382; www.nationaltrust.org.uk; Greenway Rd, Galmpton; adult/child £9/5; ◷ 10.30am-5pm Wed-Sun mid-Feb–Oct, plus Tue late-Jul–mid-Sep) High on Devon's must-see list, the captivating summer home of crime writer Agatha Christie sits beside the placid River Dart. Christie owned the property between 1938 and 1959 and a visit is a unique experience: part-guided tours allow you to wander between rooms where the furnishings and knick-knacks are much as she left them. So you can check out the piles of hats in the lobby, the books in her library, the clothes in her wardrobe, and even listen to her speak (via a replica radio) in the drawing room.

The gardens are also a delight. Woods speckled with splashes of magnolias, daffodils and hydrangeas frame the water, while the planting creates intimate, secret spaces – the boathouse and views over the river are sublime. In Christie's book *Dead Man's Folly*, Greenway doubles as Nasse House, with the boathouse making an appearance as a murder scene.

The property is hugely popular. Entrance to the house is by timed ticket, and there's only very limited parking, which has to be booked well in advance. The best way to arrive is by boat, train or on foot. The Greenway Ferry (☑ 01803-882811; www.greenwayferry.co.uk) runs regularly from Dartmouth (adult/child return £7/5, eight daily), Totnes (adult/child return £12/9, one daily) and Torquay (adult/child return £15/11, one daily); the latter involves a ride on a heritage ship and a vintage bus. Services only operate when the house is open and it's best to book.

Alternatively, take the Dartmouth Steam Railway from Kingswear to Greenway Halt (adult/child return £8.50/5.50, four to nine daily March to November), then walk a mile through the woods. Or hike along the leafy Dart Valley Trail from Kingswear (4 miles), or walk the west bank of the River Dart from Dartmouth to Dittisham, then cross by the Dittisham to Greenway ferry (☑ 0845 489418; www.greenwayferry.co.uk; adult/child return £4/3; ◷ 9.30am-4.30pm).

Dartmouth

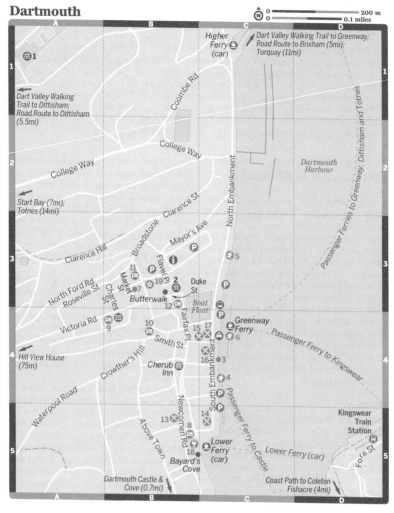

**Britannia Royal
Naval College**   HISTORIC BUILDING

(☑ 01803-834224; College Way; adult/child £12/5; ⊙ tours Mon & Wed Apr-Oct) The imposing building crowning the hills above Dartmouth is where the Royal Navy trains all its officers. Built in 1905, it replaced two training hulks that were anchored in the Dart. Guides lead you around the stately rooms and grounds, recounting the building's history and tales of its students (alumni include Princes Charles and Andrew); it's also where the Queen first met the Duke of Edinburgh in 1939. Visits are by pre-booked guided tour only (the pick-up point is in central Dartmouth); contact the tourist office.

Dartmouth Castle   CASTLE

(EH; ☑ 01803-833588; www.english-heritage.org. uk; Castle Rd; adult/child £5/3; ⊙ 10am-6pm Apr-Sep, to 5pm Oct, 10am-4pm Sat & Sun Nov-Mar; ℗) The atmospheric boat trip to this fortification at the mouth of the River Dart is part of its huge appeal. The tiny, open-top **Castle Ferry** (www.dartmouthcastleferry.co.uk; adult/child return £4/2; ⊙ 10am-4.45pm Apr-Oct) putters the mile downriver from Dart-

Dartmouth

⊙ Sights
1 Britannia Royal Naval College............ A1
2 Dartmouth Museum............................ B3

🔴 Activities, Courses & Tours
3 African Queen..................................... C4
4 Castle Ferry C4
5 Dartmouth Boat Hire..........................C3
6 Dartmouth to Dittisham Ferry C4
7 Monty Halls Great Escapes B3

🛏 Sleeping
  Alf Resco .... (see 13)
8 Bayard's Cove B5
9 Brown's Hotel......................................B4
10 Charity House.......................................B4
11 Just B..B3
12 Royal Castle...B3

🍴 Eating
13 Alf Resco B5
14 Annabelles Kitchen.............................C5
15 Crab Shell...B4
16 Rockfish C4
17 Seahorse..C4

🍷 Drinking & Nightlife
18 Dartmouth Arms..................................B5

🎭 Entertainment
19 Flavel..B3

mouth's South Embankment, providing unbeatable views of the houses and woods lining the steep banks. The picturesque castle itself started life in the 14th century to protect the harbour from seaborne raids. It was commissioned by Dartmouth's privateering mayor, John Hawley – said to be the inspiration for the 'Shipman' in Chaucer's *Canterbury Tales*. The fortification saw additions in the 15th century, the Victorian era and WWII. Today its maze of passages, guardrooms and battlements provides an evocative insight into life inside; there's also an audiovisual recreation of a Victorian gun drill.

Historic Dartmouth   ARCHITECTURE
Dartmouth has an impressive array of half-timbered houses lining the South Embankment, Fairfax Place, Duke St and the streets framing the boat float. Many date from the 17th century and have brightly painted crests and gilded motifs. Look out for the 14th-century Cherub Inn, up steps off Fairfax Place, and the towering building opposite the entrance to Church Close,

whose carvings include vivid bunches of grapes, a popular design for Dartmouth wine traders.

Beside the boat float, the Butterwalk is a row of incredibly slanting 17th-century shops. It's home to the Dartmouth Museum (📱01803-832923; www.dartmouthmuseum.org; Duke St; adult/child £2/50p; ⊙10am-4pm Tue-Sat Apr-Oct, noon-3pm daily Nov-Mar), which beautifully evokes the town's nautical past via model ships, boats in bottles and sepia photos.

The quaintly cobbled Bayard's Cove, just south of the lower ferry, is where the Pilgrim Fathers stopped off en route from Southampton to America in 1620.

🏃 Activities

Boating
Beautiful from the banks, Dartmouth is even more beguiling from the water. The Greenway Ferry company's boat trips include ones to Agatha Christie's summer house, Greenway, and the village of Dittisham. A series of car and passenger ferries also regularly shuttle between Dartmouth and Kingswear, on the opposite bank, and to Dartmouth Castle.

⭐Dartmouth Steam Railway
& River Boat Co   BOAT TRIPS, RAILWAY
(📱01803-555872; www.dartmouthrailriver.co.uk) Running memorable River Dart cruises between Dartmouth and Totnes (adult/child £12/7.50, two to four daily February to November), the same firm also operates the Kingswear Castle, the UK's last working coal-fired paddle steamer. It shuttles to Totnes one to four times a week between mid-June and mid-September (adult/child £15/10). The company also runs a wide range of steam train-boat trip combinations.

Monty Halls Great Escapes   BOAT TOURS
(📱01803-431858; www.montyhalls.co.uk/greatescapes; 4 Market St; per person £30; ⊙10am-4pm Thu-Sun) Trips run by the TV marine biologist (not always led by him personally) include a 90-minute wildlife-spotting voyage (one to four weekly) aboard a rigid inflatable boat (RIB), heading upriver or along the coast.

African Queen   FISHING
(📱07885 246061; www.theafricanqueen.co.uk; South Embankment; per adult £17; ⊙2 per day Apr-Sep) Four-hour mackerel fishing trips that head towards Start Point Lighthouse.

OFF THE BEATEN TRACK

DITTISHAM

Dittisham is one of those enchanting, water-side villages that makes you wonder if, really, living anywhere else is such a good idea after all. A cluster of rough-stone cottages gathers along a riverbank dotted with yachts, a pontoon lined with dinghies stretches out from a cracking pub and the Anchorstone Cafe (p87). Agatha Christie's holiday home, Greenway, sits on the opposite bank, connected by the Dittisham to Greenway Ferry (p83). If it's not in sight when you arrive, summon it by ringing the ship's bell beside the pontoon. You can drive to Dittisham (pronounce it '*Dit-shm*' and feel like a local); it's 5 miles north of Dartmouth, but a much more memorable arrival is on the **Dartmouth to Dittisham Ferry** (🖸01803-882811; www.greenwayferry.co.uk; adult/child return £7.50/5; ☺7 daily Wed-Sun Feb-Oct).

Dartmouth Boat Hire
BOATING
(🖸01803-834600; www.dartmouth-boat-hire.co.uk; North Embankment; per hr/day £45/140; ☺Apr-Oct) Chug about the Dart on a hired motorboat.

Beaches

Castle Cove
SWIMMING
For a close-to-Dartmouth-swim, clamber down the steps and join the bathers at the tiny Castle Cove, just round from Dartmouth Castle.

Blackpool Sands
BEACH
Sun-loving locals head 3 miles south of Dartmouth to this long curl of coarse sand, lured by beautiful views, kayaking (per hour/day £15/40) and an organic, licensed cafe. Take bus 93 from Dartmouth (25 minutes, hourly Monday to Saturday, every 2 hours Sunday).

Walks

For a short circular walk, catch the Higher Ferry from Dartmouth to the east bank, stroll a mile downriver to Kingswear, then catch the Lower Ferry back. Or hike the Dart Valley Trail to Dittisham (5 miles) and cross the river to Greenway on the Dittisham to Greenway Ferry, then walk down to Kingswear before crossing back to Dartmouth by ferry.

✷✷ Festivals & Events

Dart Music
MUSIC
(www.dartmusicfestival.co.uk) Held in mid-May, the three days of music-making encompasses folk, classical and jazz.

Royal Regatta
SAILING
(www.dartmouthregatta.co.uk) Dartmouth's big annual party falls on August Bank Holiday weekend. Expect plenty of partying and contests ranging from sailing and rowing, to swimming and tennis. It packs out the town; book ahead for accommodation.

Dartmouth Food Festival
FOOD
(www.dartmouthfoodfestival.com) One of Devon's biggest; held in late October.

🛏 Sleeping

Just B
ROOMS £
(🖸01803-834311; www.justbdartmouth.com; reception 17 Foss St; r £68-92) The 11 chichi options here range from bedrooms with bathrooms to mini-apartments, all featuring snazzy furnishings, crisp cottons and comfy beds. They're scattered over three central properties, and the 'just B' policy (no '&B' means no breakfast) keeps the price down.

Hill View House
B&B £
(🖸01803-839372; www.hillviewdartmouth.co.uk; 76 Victoria Rd; s/d £47/70; P🖕🛜) 🖉 At this price, you'll be asking, 'what's the catch?' There isn't one. Lloyd loom-style furniture and angle-poise lamps sit in relaxed, beautifully styled rooms above a retro guest lounge. It's a 10-minute walk into Dartmouth.

Charity House
B&B ££
(🖸01803-832176; Collaford Lane; s/d £62/82) Quirky collectibles pepper this 17th-century guesthouse in an artful array of driftwood, Panama hats and gleaming bits of boats. Classy bedrooms team stylish fabrics and modern bathrooms with views of a historic church – it's right in the heart of town, too.

★ Alf Resco
B&B ££
(🖸01803-835880; www.cafealfresco.co.uk; Lower St; d £65-85, flat £95) Where better to sleep in Dartmouth than above the town's best beatnik cafe? There's a cosily quirky double and a cute (but pint-sized) bunk-bed room. But the best by far is the spacious, log-cabin-like, top-floor self-contained flat, where upmarket furniture and vintage knick-knacks come with a balcony with grandstand estuary views. Breakfast is included; it'll be a feast.

Bayard's Cove
B&B ££

(☑ 01803-839278; www.bayardscoveinn.co.uk; 27 Lower St; d £115-150, ste £135-150, f from £155; ☎) Crammed with character and bursting with beams, a night at the Bayard's Cove sees you sleeping amid whitewashed, rough stone walls and huge church candles. As well as grand double beds, the gorgeous suites feature mini-cabins, complete with bunk beds and tiny TVs (the kids will love them), and rooms even have estuary glimpses.

Greenway
APARTMENT £££

(☑ 0844 800 2070; www.nationaltrustcottages. co.uk; Greenway Rd, Galmpton; P ➹) How's this for a truly memorable place to stay: Agatha Christie's Greenway estate. The house's stately top-floor apartment (three/seven nights £2000/3000) sleeps 10 and comes with its own pool; pretty, three-person Greenway Lodge (two/seven nights £670/1115) links straight into the magical gardens; while South Lodge (two/seven nights £980/1633), which sleeps six, has remarkable views onto the River Dart.

Brown's Hotel
BOUTIQUE HOTEL £££

(☑ 01803-832572; www.brownshoteldartmouth. co.uk; 29 Victoria Rd; d £145-185, ste 250; P) Somehow this smoothly sumptuous hotel manages to combine leather curtains, pheasant-feather lampshades and animal-print chairs, and make it all look classy. Breakfasts are laid-back affairs, with organic bread, freshly squeezed orange juice and homemade marmalade. Prices are up to £65 cheaper if you avoid weekends.

Royal Castle
HOTEL £££

(☑ 01803-833033; www.royalcastle.co.uk; The Quay; s £120, d £153-207, f from £163; ☎) The Castle has stood plum on Dartmouth's waterfront for 500 years. The library is full of battered, leather-bound books, timbers from a Spanish man-o-war prop up the bar, and antique chaises longues, massive carved chairs and velvet curtains dot the rooms. Pack a copy of Agatha Christie's *Ordeal by Innocence;* the crime writer used the hotel as inspiration for the Royal George in the novel.

✖ Eating

Alf Resco
CAFE £

(☑ 01803-835880; www.cafealfresco.co.uk; Lower St; mains from £6; ⊙ 7am-2pm) Tucked under a huge canvas awning, this cool cafe brings a dash of chilled-out cosmopolitan charm to town. Rickety wooden chairs and old street signs are scattered around a front terrace, making it a great place for brunch alongside the riverboat crews.

Crab Shell
SANDWICHES £

(1 Raleigh St; sandwiches £4; ⊙ 10.30am-2.30pm Apr-Dec) The shellfish in the sarnies made here has been landed on the quay a few steps away, and much of the fish has been smoked locally. Opt to fill your bread with mackerel and horseradish mayo, kiln roast salmon with dill, or classic, delicious Dartmouth crab.

Anchorstone Café
BISTRO £

(☑ 01803-722365; www.anchorstonecafe.co.uk; Manor St, Dittisham; mains from £7; ⊙ noon-4pm Wed-Sun May-Oct) It's hard to know what's best: the view or the food. Tucked away in the village of Dittisham, the dining terrace here is right beside the creek. Watch the ferry shuttling across to Greenway, tuck into succulent Dartmouth crab and lobster, sip some local Sharpham wine. You can cruise to this waterside idyll by boat (p86) too. It's open daily and evenings (7pm to 9pm Wednesday to Sunday) during the school summer holidays.

Rockfish
SEAFOOD ££

(☑ 01803-832800; www.rockfishdevon.co.uk; 8 South Embankment; mains £6-17; ⊙ noon-9.30pm) Weathered boarding and a chilled soundtrack lend this award-winning fish and chip shop the air of a boho boathouse. The menu is a cut above your average chippy; along with cod and haddock there's also monkfish, local calamari, oysters and good wine. Eat in (enjoy the atmosphere) or take away (fight the seagulls).

Annabelles Kitchen
MODERN BRITISH ££

(☑ 01803-833540; www.annabelleskitchen.co.uk; 24 South Embankment; mains £14-24; ⊙ 12.30-2pm Thu-Sat, 6.30-9pm Tue-Sat) Top-class local produce combines with creative treatments at this smart restaurant. The scallops come with black pudding, the catch of the day comes with brown shrimp, and a table at the picture window comes with views of a river lined with pastel-painted houses.

Blackpool Sands
CAFE ££

(☑ 01803-770209; www.lovingthebeach.co.uk; Blackpool Sands; mains £10-20; ⊙ 8am-5pm daily, to 9pm Thu-Sat May-Sep) In the summer the huge doors open directly onto the beach; in the winter there's a warming log fire. All

WORTH A TRIP

COLETON FISHACRE

There's more than a touch of showbiz magic about the charming Arts and Crafts–style Coleton Fishacre (NT; ☎ 01803-842382; www.nationaltrust.org.uk; Brownstone Rd, near Kingswear; adult/child £9/5; ☺ 10.30am-5pm Sat-Thu mid-Feb–Oct; ℙ). It was built in 1926 for the D'Oyly Cartes, a family of theatre impresarios and owners of London's Claridge's and Savoy Hotel. Art deco embellishments are everywhere: Lalique tulip uplighters, comic bathroom tiles and a saloon that's reminiscent of a stage set, complete with tinkling piano (if you can play they'll probably let you tap out a tune). It's easy to imagine living here: sitting on the monochrome furnishings in Lady Dorothy's bedroom, working at the desk in the well-stocked library or tucking into an al fresco lunch in the sea-view verandah.

The grounds are like a three-act play, from the grassy croquet terrace where games were played to the scratch of a gramophone, to the sharply slanting subtropical gardens and the suddenly revealed vistas of the sea. Expect to come across bamboo, New Zealand tree ferns and succulents from the Canary Islands. Spring brings azaleas, magnolias and camellias; summer swaths of blue hydrangeas.

Coleton Fishacre is 3 miles from Dartmouth on the Torquay side of the estuary. You can hike to the property along a dramatic stretch of cliff path from Kingswear (4 miles) or drive.

year organic Devon goodies stack the menu: try the garlic crab bisque, tender Start Bay lobster or succulent Riverford beef steaks, washed down with locally produced Ashridge vintage cider.

 Seahorse SEAFOOD £££
(☎ 01803-835147; www.seahorserestaurant.co.uk; 5 South Embankment; mains £17-28; ☺ noon-2.30pm Wed-Sun, 6-10pm Tue-Sat) The seafood served at Mitch Tonks' eatery is so fresh, the menu changes twice a day. So, depending on what's been landed at Brixham (7 miles away) or Dartmouth (a few yards), you might get cuttlefish in Chianti, sea bream with roasted garlic, or fried local squid with garlic mayonnaise. A Seahorse speciality is sublime charcoal-roasted fish, and the two-course lunches (£20, Wednesday to Sunday) are a bargain.

🍷 Drinking & Entertainment

Dartmouth Arms PUB
(www.dartmoutharmsinn.co.uk; 26 Lower St) As an antidote to Dartmouth's sailing chic, join the locals for an unpretentious pint in an ancient bar smothered in polished wood; navigational lights and cross-sections of ships dot the walls. Summer-time drinking spills over onto Bayard's Cove outside.

Flavel ARTS CENTRE
(www.theflavel.org.uk; flavel Pl) Hosts small-scale theatre and dance, plus live music and films.

ⓘ Information

Tourist Office (☎ 01803-834224; www.discoverdartmouth.com; Mayor's Ave; ☺ 10am-5pm Mon-Sat, to 4pm Sun Apr-Oct, 10am-4pm Mon, Tue & Thu-Sat Nov-Mar)

ⓘ Getting There & Away

BOAT

Fleets of pleasure boats set sail from Dartmouth; as well as being picturesque boat trips (p85), these can also be handy ways to travel from A to B.

Dartmouth–Kingswear Ferries (www.dartmouthhigherferry.com; single foot passengers 50p-£1.10, single car incl passengers £4-4.70; ☺ 8am-10.45pm) Dartmouth's **Higher** and **Lower Ferries** both take cars and foot passengers, shuttling across the river to Kingswear every 6 minutes. The slightly bigger Higher Ferry crosses the river 300m north (upstream) of the town centre, but both services connect to the main road into Kingswear, on the east bank.

BUS

Kingsbridge (1 hour, hourly Monday to Saturday, every 2 hours Sunday) Bus 93.

Torquay (1¼ hours, every 2 hours Monday to Saturday) Bus X81.

TRAIN

The Dartmouth Steam Railway and Riverboat Company runs a steam train from Paignton to Kingswear (adult/child return £11/6.50).

Start Bay

Start Bay curves out in an elongated crescent just south of Dartmouth. This is one of Devon's most spectacular sections of coast; the road climbs steeply in a series of hairpin bends, fields roll up to precipitous cliffs and villages cluster beside the sea.

It's a landscape most people bypass, but it offers unforgettable places to stay and unusual sights to explore, from a ruined village and a lighthouse to a massive freshwater lake.

◎ Sights & Activities

Start Point Lighthouse   LIGHTHOUSE
(☑ 01803-771802; www.trinityhouse.co.uk; Start Point; adult/child £4/2.50; ☉ 11am-5pm Sun-Thu Jul & Aug, noon-5pm Wed & Sun Apr & May, noon-5pm Wed, Thu & Sun Jun & Sep; ℙ) Sitting on one of England's most exposed peninsulas on the English coast, the 200,000 candela beam of this bright-white lighthouse can be seen for 25 nautical miles. It was built in 1836, went electric in 1959 and was manned right up until 1993; it's now controlled automatically from Trinity House's HQ in Essex.

Tours last 45 minutes and wind up hundreds of steps, through tiny circular rooms. The highlight is the final climb, by ladder, to the top platform where you stand alongside the massive optics and look out over 360-degree views, down onto a boiling sea.

South Hallsands   HISTORIC SITE
(South Halsand; ☉ open access; ℙ) **FREE** The shells of the handful of houses that cling to the cliff here are all that remain of a thriving fishing village. In 1917 one severe storm literally swept this community out to sea. More than 20 cottages, a pub and a post office were lost overnight; remarkably, none of the 128 residents were killed. You can't wander amid the ruins themselves, but you can see them clearly from a cliff-side viewing platform where signs feature evocative sepia images of the village and its indomitable inhabitants.

Slapton Sands   BEACH
(ℙ) The name is misleading. Slapton Sands is actually a spectacular pebble ridge, and at 3 miles long you can find solitude here on even the busiest days. It's backed by the southwest's largest freshwater lake, Slapton Ley, with only just enough room for a narrow strip of road between the ley and the sea. At the southern Torcross end, you'll quite often come across fishing folk casting their lines from the shore.

Slapton Ley   NATURE RESERVE
(Slapton Sands) Slapton Ley's broad sweep of water is ringed by a nature reserve and fringed by reedbeds and woods. To explore, park at the Memorial Car Park halfway along Slapton Sands and walk across the road (signed Slapton village). The reserve entrance is on the left, immediately after the bridge. A 1¾-mile trail skirts the ley, crossing reed beds via a series of boardwalks. While walking, look out for yellow iris, tufted ducks, great crested grebes and – if you're lucky – otters. Soon the path heads up to Slapton itself, a quintessential Devon village where houses huddle around mazelike lanes. It has a time-warp village shop, robust church and 14th-century ruined tower; the Tower Inn is just next door. From the village, a path beside the road takes you back to the coast and your car.

Sherman Tank   MEMORIAL
(Torcross; ℙ) Wave-dashed as they are today, Slapton Sands have an even more dramatic past. During WWII, thousands of American servicemen trained here for D-Day using live ammunition. On one rehearsal in 1944, Exercise Tiger, a German torpedo boat sank several landing craft; more than 700 American servicemen died.

One of the tanks that sank during the exercise has been winched from 65ft of water just offshore. Painted black, it now sits beside the car park at Torcross as a memorial. Signs alongside outline the remarkable role this area played in WWII; from 1943 the residents of seven local villages, including Slapton, were evacuated from their homes for a year while the D-Day rehearsals took place.

🛏 Sleeping

★**Seabreeze**   B&B ££
(☑ 01548-580697; www.seabreezebreaks.com; Torcross; d £100-140; ℙ) Fall asleep to a real-life soundtrack of the waves at this funky former fisherman's cottage, just metres from the sea wall. Bedrooms have white-painted beams, real pebbles tiling the bathroom floor and window seats facing straight onto Start Bay. The cool cafe downstairs rejoices under the slogan: 'best buns on the beach'.

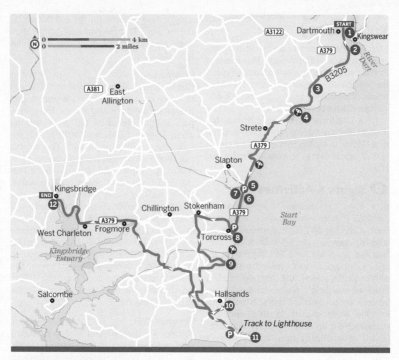

🏃 Driving Tour
Dartmouth to Kingsbridge

START DARTMOUTH SOUTH EMBANKMENT
END KINGSBRIDGE QUAY
LENGTH 21 MILES; ONE DAY

From Dartmouth's pretty **1** **South Embankment** turn right for Dartmouth Castle, a steep route revealing the gorgeous River Dart. At **2** **Warfleet Pottery** fork right, making for the A379 towards Torcross. Dog-leg through quaint **3** **Stoke Fleming**, emerging for buzzard's-eye views of Start Bay's scalloped coves. At **4** **Blackpool Sands** perhaps pause for a swim, before driving up 16% gradient, switchback, view-framed bends. After Strete's pastel-painted cottages, the 3-mile pebble ridge of Slapton Sands suddenly fills the windscreen; watery Slapton Ley is just behind. U-bends and a brake-burning descent lead to a glorious, flat, straight strip of land between sea and ley called the Slapton Line; persistent erosion could see it washed away within decades. Pull into the **5** **Memorial Car Park**, then clatter down the pebbles to drink in long views at **6** **Slapton Sands Beach**. Next, stroll inland around reed-filled **7** **Slapton Ley** (p89). Back in the car, pause at the poignant WWII **8** **Sherman Tank Memorial** (p89). Curl around the head of the ley, passing cottages and fields, before turning off towards **9** **Beesands**. This ever-narrowing route through steep, twisting lanes spills you out at this ancient fishing village, strung out on a pot-lined shore. For lunch, Britannia @ the Beach offers net-fresh seafood, while the Cricket Inn has more restaurary surroundings. Next, it's back in the car and out of Beesands for **10** **South Hallsands**. Stroll to the viewing platform to see more startling evidence of this deeply eroded shore. Then drive south to **11** **Start Point**'s wind-swept lighthouse, clambering to the very top for extraordinary views. Afterwards, narrow lanes lead through a string of villages, past chequerboard fields and stretches of creek to **12** **Kingsbridge**. If it's fine the river-side terrace of the Crab Shell is a tempting option, while the Old Bakery delivers foodie delights galore.

Cricket
INN **££**

(📋 01548-580215; www.thecricketinn.com; Beesands; s £80-110, d £90-120, f from £145; 🐾) Smart and sleek, with cream-painted tongue-and-groove panels and crisp cotton sheets, most of the rooms here overlook Start Bay; ask for the one with the bay window, and settle down to watch the waves

Start Point Lighthouse
COTTAGE **£££**

(📋 01386-701177; www.ruralretreats.co.uk; Start Point; 7 nights £1345-1840; 🅿) Worth booking the babysitter for: two cosy former lighthousekeeper's cottages full of old sea chests and comfy sofas. One (Beacon) even has its very own deck, directly overlooking the sea. They sit beside a working lighthouse, so bring ear plugs (the signal sounds once a minute in fog) and hope for a clear night. The apartments sleep five to six people; because of the lighthouse setting, no children under 11 are allowed.

✖️ Eating

★ Britannia @ the Beach
BISTRO **££**

(📋 01548-581168; www.britanniaatthebeach. co.uk; Seafront, Beesands; mains £13-25; ⊘ 9am-8.45pm) They've tacked a smashing, pocket-sized eating terrace onto this old beach-side fishmonger's shack, so now you can tuck into perfectly cooked shellfish, bass, bream and monkfish just yards from where it was hauled ashore. The bring-your-own wine system (free corkage) keeps the price down. On fine summer evenings diners spill out onto tables lining the sea wall (they'll even loan you a blanket to keep your legs warm).

Cricket
PUB **££**

(📋 01548-580215; www.thecricketinn.com; Seafront, Beesands; mains £11-18; ⊘ noon-8.30pm) Fishermen started supping here in 1867 and, despite the smart re-vamp, still do – one of the regulars in the corner probably caught your lunch. The beautifully cooked lobsters, crab and scallops come straight out of Start Bay, a pebble's throw away. It's classic cooking, but expect some surprises: you might get seaweed and ginger butter on your lemon sole.

Laughing Monk
BISTRO **££**

(📋 01803-770639; www.thelaughingmonkdevon. co.uk; Totnes Rd, Strete; mains £17-22; ⊘ 5-9.30pm Mon-Sat Apr-Oct, 6.30-9pm Tue-Sat Nov-Mar) Although the produce is overwhelmingly local, the flavours are from much further afield; delight in Chanel squid with punchy chilli dressing, Dartmouth crab with zingy guacamole or free-range chicken in a gutsy Madeira casserole. The cheeseboard features four classic West Country varieties, best sampled with some port (from £4 a glass).

Tower Inn
PUB **££**

(📋 01548-580216; www.thetowerinn.com; Church Rd, Slapton; lunch £5-11, dinner £16; ⊘ noon-2pm daily, 7-9pm Mon-Sat) It's a bit of a winner: rich flavours (think pigeon, woodland mushrooms and black pudding) combine with innovative treatments (sea bass in vodka batter) at an atmospheric inn, where the beer garden overlooks a 14th-century tower.

ℹ️ Getting There & Away

Bus 93 runs from Dartmouth to Strete (20 minutes, hourly, four on Sunday) and on to Torcross (30 minutes) and Kingsbridge (1 hour).

Kingsbridge & Around

POP 4400

Despite being on the same estuary as chi chi Salcombe to the south, Kingsbridge has preserved the feel of a sleepy, waterside market town. It offers a genuine glimpse of rural Devon life and browsing its independent shops or lingering by its quay is a pleasant way to spend a few hours.

👁️ Sights & Activities

Singing Paddles
CANOEING, KAYAKING

(📋 07754 426633; www.singingpaddles.co.uk; per 2hr/day £25/75) 🛶 These memorable, chilled-out kayak and canoe tours range from family safaris to expedition training days, and often involve wildlife-watching, beachside brews, hot sausages and cakes. They run from Bowcombe Creek (near Kingsbridge), Slapton Ley (in Start Bay) and Aveton Gifford (near Bantham).

Cookworthy Museum of Rural Life
MUSEUM

(📋 01548-853235; www.kingsbridgemuseum.org. uk; 108 Fore St; adult/child £2.50/1; ⊘ 10.30am-4pm Mon-Sat May-Oct) An engaging collection of school desks, cooking ranges, wagons and ploughs; plus a particularly fine photographic archive.

🛏 Sleeping

Seaflowers
B&B **££**

(☎ 01548-531107; www.seaflowers.co.uk; Frogmore; d £100-130; P 🛜) The long terrace of this contemporary B&B stretches out beside a photogenic sweep of Frogmore Creek. Light streams from skylights onto smart white rooms finished with bursts of burgundy and lime. Ask for the water-facing bedroom, where patio doors open beside your own section of water. It's in the small village of Frogmore, 3 miles east of Kingsbridge.

Buckland Tout-Saints
LUXURY HOTEL **£££**

(☎ 01548-853055; www.tout-saints.co.uk; Goveton; d £185-215, ste £310; P 🛜) It may take an age to find among south Devon's high hedge-backed lanes, but it's worth it when you do. History oozes from this manor house's wood-panelled walls and plasterwork ceilings. Rooms range from sombre four-poster suites to contemporary designs – they're deeply luxurious either way. It's 2 miles north of Kingsbridge.

🍴 Eating

Mangetout
CAFE, DELI **£**

(☎ 01548-856620; www.mangetoutdeli.com; 84 Fore St; mains from £5; ⊙ 8am-5pm Mon-Sat; 🍴) Hike to the top of town for a diet-defying deli-cum-cafe with a smorgasbord of goodies. Choose from Devon hams, chorizo, zesty salads, olives, fresh breads, cakes and croissants. The cheeses are a who's who of local producers: Devon Oke, Ticklemore, Sharpham brie, Quickes Cheddar and the pungent Devon, Beenleigh and Exmoor blues.

Old Bakery
CAFE, BISTRO **££**

(☎ 01548-855777; www.theoldbakerykingsbridge. co.uk; The Quay; tapas £3-8, mains £12-17; ⊙ 9am-9pm Mon-Sat; 🍴) Huge pieces of modern art combine with battered leather sofas; huge bowls of olives sit alongside piles of home-baked bread. Tapas-style grazing dishes include smokey baba ganoush, mounds of charcuterie and garlic-laced seafood. The lunch-time Spuntino five-dish platters (£10 with glass of wine) are a treat.

Crabshell
PUB **££**

(www.thecrabshellinn.com; The Quay; mains £10-18; ⊙ food noon-3pm & 6-9pm) On a sunny day, in-the-know locals make a beeline for the waterside beer terrace of the Crabshell, to watch boats and stand-up paddleboarders glide by. Lunch might be fig and Cornish blue cheese salad, local mussels steamed in white wine or a hamburger of tender south Devon beef, washed down with some carefully chosen wines.

☆ Entertainment

Reel
CINEMA

(☎ 01548-856636; www.thereelcinema.co.uk; Fore St) A sweet, independent three-screen movie house, towards the top of Fore St.

🛍 Shopping

A healthy range of independent shops line Kingsbridge's Fore St as it winds up from the Quay.

Harbour Bookshop
BOOKS

(www.harbourbookshop.co.uk; 2 Mill St; ⊙ 9am-5pm Mon-Sat) Well-stocked, independent bookseller, with a good range of literary fiction, crime and childrens's titles.

@11's
FOOD

(11 Fore St; ⊙ 9am-5pm Mon-Sat) Bakery specialising in award-winning pastries; their freshly-made bread, pasties and sarnies are pretty irresistible too.

Choc Amour
FOOD

(20 Fore St; ⊙ 9am-5pm Mon-Sat) At this tradi-tional confectioners ranks of sweet jars line the counter and your purchase is still measured out in scales.

Catch of the Day
FOOD

(54 Fore St; ⊙ 9am-4pm Mon-Wed & Fri, 9am-1pm Thu & Sat) Staff smoke the famous Salcombe Smokies (mackerel) at this fishmongers; try the flavoursome smoked salmon and prawns, too.

ℹ Information

Kingsbridge Tourist Office (☎ 01548-853195; www.welcomesouthdevon.co.uk; The Quay; ⊙ 9am-5pm Mon-Sat) Volunteer run, so times occasionally vary.

ℹ Getting There & Away

Dartmouth (1 hour, hourly Monday to Saturday, every two hours Sunday) Bus 93, via Start Bay (30 minutes).

Hope Cove (40 minutes, two daily Monday to Saturday) Bus 162, via Thurleston (15 minutes).

Plymouth (1¼ hours, hourly Monday to Saturday, every 2 hours Sunday) Bus 93.

Salcombe (20 minutes, hourly Monday to Saturday) Bus 606.

WORTH A TRIP

MILLBROOK INN

Mix together one French chef, an ancient British inn and piles of choice Devon produce and what do you get? Gutsy, classically influenced food served up in the quaint old **Millbrook Inn** (☑01548-531581; www.millbrookinnsouthpool.co.uk; South Pool, near Kingsbridge; mains £12-18, snacks from £5; ⊘noon-1.45pm & 7-8.45pm; ☑). There's a nose-to-tail ethos here; flavour-packed dishes include home-cured ox tongue and salted belly pork, plus potted south Devon crab and gooey, grilled goat's cheese dotted with walnut and pear. Rich puddings round things off nicely (don't miss the dark chocolate fondant), and to wash it all down, you'll be treated to largely French wines and very local ale. Look out for that other excellent French invention: the (bargain) *menu du jour* (two/three courses £10/12).

Salcombe & Around

POP 7100

Oh-so-chic Salcombe sits charmingly at the mouth of the Kingsbridge estuary, its network of ancient, winding streets bordered by sparkling waters and sandy coves. Its beauty has edged it into the UK's Top Ten millionaire towns, with almost one-third of properties commanding seven-figure price tags. Around 40% of houses here are second homes, and out of season Salcombe can have a ghost-town feel. Nevertheless, the port's undoubted appeal remains, offering tempting opportunities to catch a ferry to a beach, head out kayaking and soak up some nautical history.

◎ Sights

Beaches BEACH
A string of beautiful beaches frame Salcombe's shores, many linked to the town by ferries. The best are the sands on the opposite, East Portlemouth, side, where a long strip of sand emerges as the tide falls. At high tide, head south on the lane backing the shore to sand-filled Mill Bay.

On the Salcombe side a waterside walk south along Cliff Rd leads to compact North Sands (even smaller at high water), then broader, but still-tidal South Sands, with its mini-watersports centre, cool cafe and chic hotel.

Overbeck's HISTORIC BUILDING
(NT; ☑01548-842893; www.nationaltrust.org.uk; Sharpitor; adult/child £7.50/3.80; ⊘11am-5pm mid-Feb–Oct; ☑) An Aladdin's cave of curios, Edwardian country house Overbeck's crowns the cliffs at Salcombe's estuary mouth. It's set in 3 hectares of lush, subtropical gardens, with exotic plants framing wide views. It's named after former owner

Otto Overbeck, an inventor who pioneered a machine called the Rejuvenator, which claimed to cure disease using electric currents – one of these Heath Robinson-esque devices is on display.

Rooms are packed with Otto's quirky collections of stuffed animals, snuff boxes and nautical bits and pieces. Look out for displays about the *Herzogin Cecilie*, a beautiful four-masted barque that sank in 1936 at Starehole Bay, just a mile to the south; a dramatic coast path leads to the spot.

You can drive to Overbeck's or walk the steep 2¼ miles from Salcombe; keep heading south on Cliff Rd until you see the sign.

Maritime Museum MUSEUM
(www.salcombemuseum.org.uk; Market St; adult/child £1.50/50p; ⊘10am-12.30pm & 2.30-4.30pm Apr-Oct) Here be treasure: the highlight haul of the local shipwrecks is the 500 glittering Moroccan gold dinars from the Salcombe Canon site, dating from the 13th to the 17th centuries. There are also evocative tools of the shipbuilders' trade: stretching hooks, caulking irons and drawing knives. Models of the boats they helped build sit alongside.

Historic Salcombe ARCHITECTURE
Today Salcombe is a smart holiday hotspot, but in the 17th century the town had a very different trade. Salcombe's fishermen worked the Newfoundland Banks. By the 1800s scores of shipyards built fast fruit schooners bound for the Azores. In those days the area immediately around the central Whitestrand Quay contained four boat yards and streets full of sail lofts, landing quays and warehouses. All competed for a precious section of shore, resulting in the long, thin buildings, set side-on to the harbour. Many of these remain, framed by

Salcombe

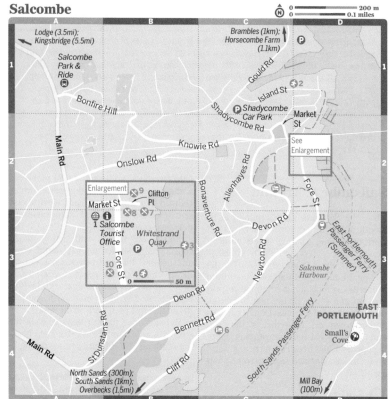

Salcombe

◎ Sights
1 Maritime Museum A3

✈ Activities, Courses & Tours
2 ICC D1
3 South Sands Ferry B3
4 Whitestrand......................................B3

🛏 Sleeping
5 Ria View..C2
6 Sunny Cliff C4

🍴 Eating
7 Casse-Croute....................................B3
8 Salcombe Fishmongers.....................B3
9 Salcombe Yawl.................................B2
10 Victoria B3

🍷 Drinking & Nightlife
11 Ferry Inn...D3

incredibly narrow lanes; it's worth heading down a few to see where they lead. The Maritime Museum sells an 1842 map of the town; or just hunt them out between Fore St and the water, especially near Clifton Place and the Ferry Inn.

🏃 Activities

Boating

Sea Kayak & SUP Salcombe KAYAKING, SAILING
(☎01548-843451; www.southsandssailing.co.uk; South Sands) Rents out sit-on-top kayaks (per hour/day £17/80), sea kayaks (per three hours/day £35/80), stand-up paddleboards (SUP; per hour/day £17/80) and topper sailing dingies (per hour/day £27/100).

Whitestrand BOATING
(☎01548-843818; www.whitestrandboathire.co.uk; Whitestrand Quay) Rents out motorboats (per hour/day from £25/85).

ICC
SAILING

(☎ 01548-844300; www.icc-salcombe.co.uk; Island St) Long-established school running RYA sailing courses ranging from beginners (per three days £207) to advanced (per five days £345) and powerboating (per day £160).

Ferry Trips

East Portlemouth Ferry
BOAT TRIP

(☎ 01548-842061; return adult/child £3/1.80; ⊙ 8am-5.30pm) The half-hourly East Portlemouth Ferry (passenger only) chugs to the sandy shores opposite Salcombe. Between Easter and October it goes from Ferry Pier (off Fore St), and from November to Easter from Whitestrand Quay.

South Sands Ferry
BOAT TRIP

(☎ 01548-561035; www.southsandsferry.co.uk; Whitestrand; s adult/child £3.30/2.30; ⊙ 9.45am-5.15pm Apr-Oct) This yellow-and-blue passenger boat shuttles from Whitestrand Quay to South Sands, where an ingenious motor-powered landing platform trundles into the water to help you ashore. The ferry runs every half-hour, the trip takes 20 minutes.

Walks

For an exhilarating and incredibly steep coastal hike, head south from South Sands along the coast path to Bolt Head (2 miles). En route you'll pass towering rock formations and sheer-sided cliffs. Then you can either head back the same way, or strike out on footpaths inland to complete a circular walk. The tourist office can advise.

🛏 Sleeping

Ria View
B&B £

(☎ 01548-842965; www.salcombebandb.co.uk; Devon Rd; d £70-90; ℙ 🛜) The panorama on offer at this B&B is so scenic the rooms almost come as an extra. Effortlessly stylish decor blends cream, peach and hints of dull gold; wicker sofas are scattered around. The front rooms and the flower-filled deck have captivating views down onto floating boats and a rising and falling tide.

Brambles
B&B £

(☎ 01548-843167; bramblesbandb@hotmail.com; Higher Batson; d £80; ℙ) When your host says, 'really, we just like spoiling people', you tend to be onto a winner. Expect a tea tray full of treats, quality furniture, cotton bedlinen and your very own mini-terrace overlooking an unspoilt field. It's charming, totally tranquil and a 20-minute walk into Salcombe (they even provide torches to light your way home).

Lodge
B&B £

(☎ 07850 513336; www.lodge-churchills.co.uk; Malborough; d £70, f £85-110; ℙ 🛜) They leave you to your own devices here, from the let-yourself-in check-in to the well-stocked, make-yourself-a-meal kitchen (breakfast is extra: per adult/child £6/3.50). Sweet, white bedrooms feature the odd exposed stone wall and powder-blue painted beam. It's in the hill-top village of Malborough, 4 miles northwest of Salcombe.

Horsecombe Farm
B&B ££

(☎ 01548-842233; horsecombefarm@gmail.com; Higher Batson; d £130; ℙ 🏊) The flower-framed heated pool here alone could clinch a stay, but then there's the hill-view decking, fire pit on the terrace, Aga-cooked, locally sourced breakfasts, and posies of lavender in the beautifully furnished rooms. The pick has its own mini-balcony, with creek glimpses. Salcombe is a 25-minute walk away through the lanes.

Sunny Cliff
APARTMENT ££

(☎ 01548-842207; www.sunnycliff.co.uk; Cliff Rd; d £130-145, ste £255, 4/6 bedroom apt per week £2000/2200; ℙ 🛜 🏊) The thing that overwhelms everything else here is the view; your cliff-side apartment looks straight onto a sparkling river, sandy coves, tree-clad hills, ferries and sailboats. Which is a shame, because the fresh New England-style rooms deserve more than a second glance, as does the waterside terrace, complete with pool.

South Sands
BOUTIQUE HOTEL £££

(www.southsands.com; South Sands; d £205-375, ste £435; ℙ 🛜) It's hard to imagine a better beach-side retreat; set right on the edge of a golden cove, sandy shoes pile up beside the front door. Plush rooms are pure driftwood-chic, with subtle, coral-themed fabrics and 'I'd rather be at South Sands' mugs. The best is number 10, with a roomy bay-view balcony; twin, window-side, claw-footed baths; and the biggest bed you've seen in your life. Prices fall by £55 to £115 a night in low season.

🍴 Eating & Drinking

Salcombe is strong on gourmet picnic supply outlets. Salcombe Fishmongers (www.salcombeboathire.co.uk; 11 Clifton Pl; ⊙ 9am-5.30pm Mon-Sat), at the foot of Market St, offers tempting seafood platters and classy crab sandwiches. Next door, the Chelsea-style deli Casse-Croute (☎ 01548-843003; 10 Clifton Pl; ⊙ 8.30am-5.30pm, 8.30am-4.30pm winter) is packed with charcuterie and organic artisanal breads; the sarnie options include chicken with sweet lime chilli. Opposite, the Salcombe Yawl (www.salcombeyawl.co.uk; 10a Clifton Pl; ⊙9am-5pm) is stacked with homity pies (open veggie pies), Scotch eggs and huge Cornish pasties.

Victoria PUB £
(☑01548-842604; www.victoriainn-salcombe. co.uk; Fore St; mains from £8; ⊙noon-9pm; ☎) It may not be as fancy as some Salcombe eateries, but this is a proper local pub, serving proper local pub food – the beef for the Sunday lunch comes from within 5 miles, and the fish in the batter has been landed by Salcombe or Brixham boats. Drinks range from well-kept real ales to champagne, and there's a sunny, terraced beer garden.

Bo's Beach Cafe CAFE
(www.southsandssailing.co.uk; South Sands; ⊙9am-5pm Apr-Oct) Caffeine-laden, espresso-based coffees, tempting cakes, a chilled vibe, water views and sandy feet. Perfect.

Beachside MODERN BRITISH ££
(☑01548-845900; www.southsands.com; South Sands; mains £15-28; ⊙noon-3pm & 6-9pm) Acclaimed restaurateur and fishmonger Mitch Tonks, of Dartmouth's Seahorse (p88), devised the menus at this cove-side eatery set in the South Sands hotel. Inevitably seafood features strongly; char-grilled monk fish, Salcombe crab and West Country lobster sit alongside ranks of pork and beef steaks. The cooking is assured; it has to be to compete with the mesmerising bay views.

Winking Prawn BISTRO ££
(☑01548-842326; www.winkingprawn.co.uk; North Sands; mains £15-24; ⊙9-11am Fri-Mon, plus 11.30am-4pm & 6-9.30pm daily, reduced hrs Nov-Mar) Overflowing with distressed driftwood-chic, this brasserie features huge rowing oars, red ensigns and a seaview deck. It's a perfect spot to sample sautéed scallops with bacon, sea bream with sweet pepper, and goat's cheese–themed veggie options. That or work through a pitcher of Pimm's. Summer sees them busy barbecuing mackerel, steaks, haloumi and prawns (from 4pm to 8.30pm).

Ferry Inn PUB
(Fore St) If the sun is shining it's an unbeatable location: the beer terrace clings to the waterfront providing cracking harbour views.

ℹ Information

Salcombe Tourist Office (☑01548-843927; www.salcombeinformation.co.uk; Market St; ⊙10am-5pm Apr-Oct, 10am-3pm Mon-Sat Nov-Mar)

ℹ Getting There & Away

CAR
A **Park & Ride service** (⊙10am-6pm Easter, Bank Holidays & Jun-Aug) runs in peak times.

BUS
Kingsbridge (20 minutes, hourly Monday to Saturday) Bus 606.

Hope Cove

West of Salcombe the south Devon coast features undeveloped cliffs, golden beaches and the tucked-away village of Hope Cove. A couple of pint-sized sandy bays, a tiny harbour and a gathering of thatches – there's not much to Hope Cove, but what there is is delightful. And what more do you need than beaches, a pub and a couple of places to stay?

🛏 Sleeping & Eating

Sun Bay HOTEL ££
(☑01548-561371; www.sunbayhotel-hopecove. co.uk; Hope Cove; d £95-105, f from £125; [P]☎) The airy rooms may be simple (think crisp furnishings and brass bedsteads) but the location is a winner. It's just a short stroll from Hope Cove's sands, and you can see them from most bedroom windows and the long bar on the terrace.

Cottage HOTEL £££
(☑01548-561555; www.hopecove.com; Hope Cove; d £156-196; [P]☎) Set high on a hill, this venerable hotel has a pleasantly old-fashioned feel, with family curios scattered around. Rear-facing bedrooms are fairly basic, but the floral-themed front-facing ones boast wide sea views (some also have balconies). The long, thin terrace is a perfect spot to combine wave-watching with afternoon tea. Prices include a five-course dinner.

Hope and Anchor PUB ££
(☑01548-561294; www.hopeandanchor.co.uk; Hope Cove; mains £13; ⊙meals noon-2pm & 6-8.30pm) The street-side beer terrace here is *the* place where everyone gathers for a pint. The kitchens dish up good-quality bar food.

ℹ Getting There & Away

Kingsbridge (40 minutes, two daily Monday to Saturday) Bus 162, via Thurlestone (30 minutes).

Thurlestone

A few miles west of Hope Cove, a compact rock arch rises from the centre of Thurlestone Bay. South Milton Sands edges the water, a long, coarse-grain beach backed by dunes that shelter a prime shore-side eatery. Inland lies sleepy Thurlestone village, with its atmospheric old pub and a swish modern hotel.

🛏 Sleeping & Eating

Thurlestone   LUXURY HOTEL **£££**
(☑ 01548-560382; www.thurlestone.co.uk; Thurlestone; d £310-450; P 🔊 🌉) Smart blue parasols dot the grounds, glass screens shelter the almost-infinity pool and supreme luxury reigns in rooms, with super-fluffy bathrobes, crisp linens and balconies with sweeping sea views. Prices drop by around £80 a night in spring and autumn.

Beachhouse   BISTRO **££**
(☑ 01548-561144; www.beachhousedevon.com; South Milton Sands; mains £6-15; ☺ 9am-5pm Apr-Oct, to 9pm Jul & Aug; 10am-4pm, plus to 9pm Fri & Sat Sep-Mar) Great seafood and great sea views. One of Devon's best beach-shack eateries is a funky, chilled-out place. Watch the waves while feasting on cracked crab, steaming moules and juicy local beef burgers, followed by scoops of Salcombe Dairy Ice Cream.

Village Inn   PUB **££**
(☑ 01548-860382; www.thurlestone.co.uk; Thurlestone; mains £6-17; ☺ meals noon-2pm & 6-9pm Mon-Fri, noon-9pm Sat & Sun) A snug study in stone and wood, with benches and settles inside and picnic tables outside. The food is firmly local, with fish brought in daily from Brixham for platters that also feature smoked seafood. Or plump for a sarnie or the West Country Aberdeen Angus steaks.

ℹ Getting There & Away

Kingsbridge (20 minutes, two daily, Monday to Saturday) Bus 162, also runs to Hope Cove (30 minutes).

Bantham

This pocket-sized village has the best surf spots in south Devon – and hardly anything else. Tucked in at the east side of the River Avon, its scattering of buildings, including an inn and a shop, stretches back from rolling dunes.

◉ Sights & Activities

Bantham Beach   BEACH
(www.banthamdevon.co.uk; Bantham; parking per day May-Sep £5, Feb-May & Oct £3.50, Nov-Jan free; P) Bantham is, arguably, south Devon's finest beach. Set at the mouth of the River Avon, this undeveloped, dune-backed sweep of sand has views onto picturesque Burgh Island on the estuary's other side. At high tide a ring of sand frames the sea; at low tide it becomes a golden expanse, dotted with pockets of ankle-deep water. But do be aware: the rip currents here can be dangerous. Note the warning signs and the lifeguards' advice (lifeguard cover runs from 8am to 6pm from May to October).

Bantham Surfing Academy   SURFING
(☑ 01548-853803; www.banthamsurfingacademy.co.uk; Bantham Beach) Two-hour sessions (per one/four lessons £35/120) cater to all skill levels, and also include special child-friendly Kiddie Classes (per hour £25). They also hire out wetsuits (per 2 hours/day £5/15), bodyboards (per 2 hours/day £5/10) and longboards (2 hours/day £10/15).

🛏 Sleeping & Eating

Sloop Inn   B&B **£**
(☑ 01548-560489; www.thesloop.co.uk; Bantham; d/f £80/100; P 🔊) Just a sandy stroll from the beach, this 14th-century inn makes a chilled-out base. The simple rooms are decked out in neutral tones and wood-grained furniture; choose from views over rolling fields or dunes stretching to the sea. The bar offers a log fire, good pub grub (noon to 2pm and 6.30pm to 9pm Monday to Saturday) and a legendary Sunday lunch (2pm to 4pm Sunday).

Gastrobus   FAST FOOD **£**
(www.thegastrobus.co.uk; Bantham Beach car park; snacks from £4; ☺ 10am-7pm May-Oct; ☑) Street food comes to south Devon, with this funky, fabulous pop-up al fresco cafe. Tuck into powerful espressos, melting chocolate

TORQUAY & SOUTH DEVON THURLESTONE

brownies, gourmet blue cheese burgers, and goat's cheese and grilled veg salads but leave some room for the early-evening charcoal barbecues.

ⓘ Getting There & Away

Buses don't run to Bantham. A (very) part-time passenger ferry shuttles between Bantham village slipway and Bigbury-on-Sea.

Bigbury-on-Sea & Burgh Island

From towering cliffs lined with impressive houses, Bigbury-on-Sea rolls down suddenly to a sandy beach. The village is more developed than Bantham on the other side of the Avon Estuary, but it has an ace in the pack: the intriguing Burgh Island, complete with jazz-age hotel, which sits just offshore.

◉ Sights & Activities

Burgh Island   ISLAND

(www.burghisland.com; Bigbury-on-Sea; ⊙ open access) FREE A slanting chunk of grass-topped rock, 10-hectare, tidal Burgh Island is connected to Bigbury-on-Sea by a stretch of sand at low tide. At high water the journey is made by a sea-tractor (single £2), an eccentric device where the passenger platform is perched on stilts 6ft above the tractor's wheels and the waves.

It takes around 30 minutes to walk around the island. Bear right once ashore, taking the cliff path that edges rocky coves as it heads uphill. At the summit you'll find the remains of a huer's hut, where lookouts used to spot lucrative pilchard shoals then raise the alarm (hence: 'hue and cry'). The gorgeous, art deco Burgh Island Hotel sits on the side nearest the shore, with the Pilchard Inn just alongside.

Discovery Surf School   SURFING

(☑ 07813-639622; www.discoverysurf.com; Bigbury-on-Sea lower car park) Offers two-hour sessions of surfing tuition (per one/four lessons £35/120).

Venus   KAYAKING

(☑ 01803-712648; www.lovingthebeach.co.uk; Bigbury-on-Sea lower car park) Rents out sit-on-top kayaks (per hour/day £15/40) and does two-hour stand-up paddleboard (SUP) sessions (hire plus 45 minutes tuition £45), and SUP hire (per hour/day £15/40).

🛏 Sleeping

Henley   B&B ££

(☑ 01548-810240; www.thehenleyhotel.co.uk; Folly Hill, Bigbury-on-Sea; s £85, d £120-145; P 🛜) This charming Edwardian holiday cottage clings to the cliffs just inside the Avon estuary. Lloyd Loom furniture, leafy house plants and exotic rugs dot the interior, and the views down onto Bantham are extraordinary. Steps (150 of them) lead to the beach below.

★ **Burgh Island**   LUXURY HOTEL £££

(☑ 01548-810514; www.burghisland.com; Burgh Island; s £310, d £400-640; P 🛜) Pack your dinner jacket or your flapper frock – at glamorous art deco Burgh Island, guests definitely dress for dinner. The gleaming-white palace sits gracefully on its own tidal island, and the guest list has included Agatha Christie (who penned *And Then There Were None* here), Noel Coward, 'Fruity' Metcalfe and Josephine Baker. Rooms have sublime views and are frankly fabulous: 1920s-style sofas and fabrics meet geometric rugs, slipper baths and retro radios. It's perfect for cocktails and croquet, and feeling delightfully marooned.

🍴 Eating & Drinking

Pilchard   PUB £

(Burgh Island; snacks £6; ⊙ meals 11am-5pm) What a spot to sip a pint and watch the waters rise. The atmospheric 14th-century Pilchard Inn (think beams and open fire) sits on the shores of Burgh Island, so it's cut off from the mainland at high tide. Which somehow makes the real ale and baguettes all the more flavoursome.

Oyster Shack   SEAFOOD ££

(☑ 01548-810876; www.oystershack.co.uk; Milburn Orchard Farm, Stakes Hill; mains £18; ⊙ noon-9pm Apr-Oct, winter times vary) The laid-back terrace of this idyllic bistro is *the* place to indulge in local oysters, mussels, monkfish and crab; treatments range from grilled and traditional to spicy and Spanish. Local seafood packs the barbecue and picnic chests, while the weekday, three-course set menus are a bargain (£12). The shack lies just off the tidal road between Bigbury-on-Sea and Aveton Gifford.

ⓘ Getting There & Away

Plymouth (1¼ hours, one per week) Bus 875.
River Avon Passenger Ferry (☑ 01548-561196; ⊙ 10-11am & 3-4pm Mon-Sat May–mid-Sep) Runs between Bigbury-on-Sea and the Bantham village slipway.

Plymouth & Dartmoor

Includes ➡

Plymouth.................. 100

Dartmoor
National Park............. 110

Tavistock & Around.... 113

Princetown 117

Widecombe-
in-the-Moor 119

Moretonhampstead .. 120

Chagford..................... 121

Lydford 123

Okehampton 125

Best Places to Eat

➡ Gidleigh Park (p123)

➡ River Cottage Canteen & Deli (p106)

➡ Browns (p116)

➡ Royal William Bakery (p105)

➡ White Horse (p121)

Best Places to Stay

➡ Agaric @ Tudor House (p120)

➡ Horn of Plenty (p114)

➡ Tor Royal Farm (p118)

➡ St Elizabeth's House (p105)

➡ 22 Mill Street (p121)

Why Go?

There may only be 10 miles between them, but Plymouth and Dartmoor feel like different worlds. In the vibrant, waterfront city of Plymouth, must-see attractions meet tempting boat trips. Add ranks of restaurants (two headed by celebrity chefs), the region's top theatre and a lively nightlife and you have a compelling city break.

Then, within a 20-minute drive, there is Dartmoor National Park – a wilderness escape, where gorges cut between hills and ponies roam beside the road. Eat at one of the country's best restaurants or an ancient inn warmed by a fire. Hike, cycle or ride a horse, then doze off in a country house pile – or go wild camping beneath a sky full of stars.

Plymouth and Dartmoor couldn't be more different. We've combined them because geography makes each a springboard for the other; their contrasting natures only add to their appeal.

When to Go

➡ **Easter–May** Attractions open across Dartmoor and Plymouth, the city's best boat trips re-start.

➡ **Jun** Butterflies surround Dartmoor's tors (exposed rocky peaks).

➡ **Jul–Aug** Lidos (outdoor swimming pools) in Plymouth and across Dartmoor warm up. Colour explodes in Plymouth's skies as firework firms battle to be named Britain's best. Foodies flock to the city for Flavour Fest.

➡ **Sep** Tradition-packed Widecombe Fair profiles Dartmoor life. The tors turn purple and yellow as heather and gorse bloom. Plymouth's Marine City Festival celebrates seafood, swimming and cinema.

➡ **Feb–Mar** Dartmoor's white-water rivers offer rafting and kayaking thrills.

➡ **5th Nov** Plymouth's entire population (it seems) heads to the Hoe for fireworks and an immense Bonfire Night pyre.

PLYMOUTH

POP 258,700

For decades, some have dismissed Plymouth as sprawling and ugly, pointing to architectural eyesores and sometimes palpable poverty. But the arrival of two celebrity chefs (Hugh Fearnley-Whittingstall and Gary Rhodes) and on-going waterfront regeneration begs a rethink. Yes, the city (an important Royal Naval port) suffered WWII

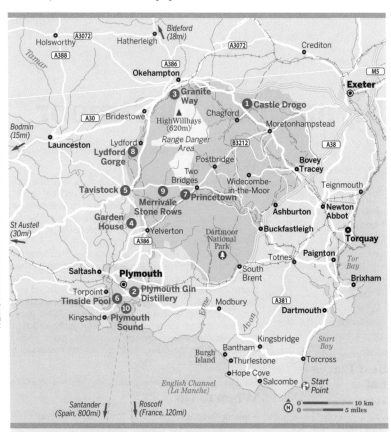

Plymouth & Dartmoor Highlights

① Wandering the rooms and imagining you live at exquisite, jazz-age **Castle Drogo** (p121)

② Strolling past stills and tasting a tipple at the **Plymouth Gin Distillery** (p101)

③ Swooping over a 165m-wide viaduct as you cycle the **Granite Way** (p124)

④ Savouring the scents and the blooms at the beguiling **Garden House** (p114)

⑤ Rummaging for shabby-chic antiques in the Victorian **Pannier Market** (p116) in Tavistock

⑥ Plunging into a 1930s lido for a retro dip in **Tinside Pool** (p104) in Plymouth

⑦ Feeling chilled by crimes at **Dartmoor Prison Heritage Centre** (p117) in Princetown

⑧ Scrambling over rocks to a 30m-high waterfall at exhilarating **Lydford Gorge** (p123)

⑨ Playing history detective amid the **Merrivale Stone Rows** (p117)

⑩ Catching a **Plymouth Boat Trip** (p104) and heading out for a hike around the shores of Plymouth Sound

ART ON THE BARBICAN

Plymouth's Barbican, with its scattering of galleries, is a place to track down works by two very different Plymouth painters. The representational artist Robert Lenkiewicz (1941–2002; www.lenkiewiczfoundation.org), likened by some to a modern-day Rembrandt, was the son of European Jewish refugees. This brooding, eccentric philosopher was a fixture of the Barbican for decades and developed a special bond with alcoholics, drug addicts and homeless people, often offering them a meal and a bed for the night. The painter also, notoriously, embalmed the body of a local tramp. Lenkiewicz's murals still dot the Barbican. The Elizabethan Mural, the biggest and also the most peeling, sits in the Parade, alongside his former studio. Another huge painting, the *Last Judgement*, is outside the Barbican Pannier Market (5 Southside St). In Prete's Café (15 Southside St) you can sip a coffee while looking up at his *Last Supper*.

In an utterly different artistic vein, Plymouth-based Beryl Cook (1926–2008; www.berylcook.org) was renowned for her cheerful depictions of brash, large ladies sporting unfeasibly small clothes. Her exuberant, almost comic-book artwork features a dizzying variety of Barbican scenes and a popular local game is to try and spot (in the flesh) the type of characters that people her paintings. To get an insight into this breezy, slightly saucy world head for the gloriously unreconstructed Dolphin (p106) for a pint. Cook immortalised this Barbican institution in several paintings, famously often sitting on one of the well-worn settees as she gathered material for her work; some of her paintings still hang on the walls.

bomb damage, and today it's still sometimes more gritty than pretty, but Plymouth is also packed with possibilities. You can swim in an art deco lido, tour a gin distillery, learn to kayak, roam an aquarium, take a boat trip across the bay, then see a top-class theatre show and party till dawn. And the ace in the pack? Plymouth Hoe – a cafe-dotted, wide grassy headland offering captivating views of a boat-studded bay.

History

Plymouth has long been the port of choice for explorers and adventurers. It farewelled Sir Francis Drake on his circumnavigation of the globe, Sir Walter Raleigh on his colony-building trip to Virginia, the fleet that defeated the Spanish Armada, the pilgrims who founded America, and countless boats carrying emigrants to Australia and New Zealand.

During the 1940s Plymouth, a Royal Dockyard, suffered horrendously at the hands of the Luftwaffe. More than 1000 civilians died in the Blitz and the city centre was reduced to rubble. The crisp lines of the post-bombing rebuild can be seen above the shopfronts lining pedestrianised streets. In the 21st-century the defence sector remains crucial; Devonport Dockyard employs 2500 people, while scores of Royal Navy vessels and hundreds of troops are still Plymouth-based.

◉ Sights

★ **Plymouth Gin Distillery** DISTILLERY
(☑ 01752-665292; www.plymouthdistillery.com; 60 Southside St; tours from £7; ⊗ tours hourly 10.30am-4.30pm) They've been concocting gin at this heavily-beamed distillery since 1793, making it the oldest producer of the spirit in the world. The Royal Navy was responsible for taking it around the world in countless officers' messes, while in the 1930s Plymouth Gin featured in the first recorded recipe for a dry martini. Tours thread past stills and huge copper vats, and you'll sniff the sometimes surprising raw ingredients (called botanicals) and indulge in a tutored tasting, before retiring to the medieval bar for a complementary G&T. The Connoisseur's Tour (£20) involves comparing other styles of gin, while the Master Distiller's Private Tour (£40) will have you creating and distilling your very own recipe; you can take a bottle of it home as a souvenir. Bookings required.

★ **Plymouth Hoe** NEIGHBOURHOOD
To get under Plymouth's skin, head for the Hoe. Crowned by the former lighthouse, Smeaton's Tower, this grassy headland provides 180-degree views of rolling hills and a glittering Plymouth Sound – the huge natural harbour. It's where Plymothians come to stroll, fly kites, kick a football, roller skate or watch the boats in the bay. It's always been the

PLYMOUTH & DARTMOOR PLYMOUTH

Plymouth

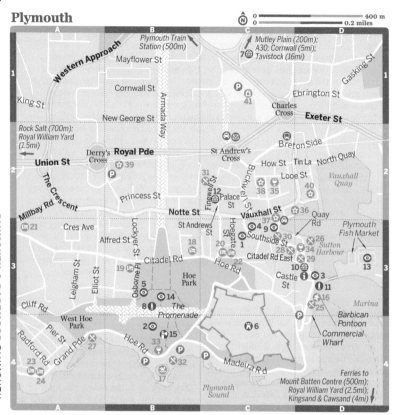

N 0 ———————— 400 m
0 ———————— 0.2 miles

Plymouth Train
Station (500m)

Mutley Plain (200m);
A30; Cornwall (5mi);
Tavistock (16mi)

Mayflower St

Western Approach

Cornwall St

Gasking St

King St

New George St

Armada Way

Ebrington St

Charles
Cross

Exeter St

Rock Salt (700m);
Royal William Yard
(1.5mi)

Derry's Cross **Royal Pde**

Union St

St Andrew's
Cross

Breton Side

How St Tin La North Quay

Princess St

The Crescent

Millbay Rd

Notte St

St Andrews
St

Looe St

Vauxhall
Quay

Vauxhall St

Quay
Rd

Plymouth
Fish Market

Cres Ave

Alfred St

Citadel Rd

Southside St

Citadel Rd East

Sutton
Harbour

Leigham St

Elliot St

Osborne Pl

Lockyer St

Hoe Rd

Castle
St

Hoe
Park

Cliff Rd

West Hoe
Park

The
Promenade

Marina

Pier St

Radford Rd

Grand Pde

Hoe Rd

Barbican
Pontoon
Commercial
Wharf

Madeira Rd

Ferries to
Mount Batten Centre (500m);
Royal William Yard (2.5mi);
Kingsand & Cawsand (4mi)

Plymouth
Sound

PLYMOUTH & DARTMOOR PLYMOUTH

focus of the city's community spirit – locals staged morale-boosting open-air dances here during WWII and thousands still fill it at New Year and on Bonfire Night.

The Hoe is also, supposedly, where Sir Francis Drake insisted on finishing his game of bowls before setting off to defeat the advancing Spanish Armada. The fabled green on which he lingered was probably the spot where his statue now stands. A few steps away, today's enthusiasts play on a modern bowling green.

The biggest of the Hoe's many war memorials, the immense Plymouth Naval Memorial, commemorates Commonwealth WWI and WWII sailors who have no grave but the sea. It lists a total of 23,186 men. Bunches of flowers are still often propped up beside individual names. The Royal Citadel, the imposing 17th-century fort at the Hoe's east end, is still home to local troops. Also look out for some of the scores of Plymouth-

based warships (see www.qhm.mod.uk/plymouth/movements), which can often be seen in Plymouth Sound.

Barbican NEIGHBOURHOOD
(www.plymouthbarbican.com) In Plymouth's historic Barbican district, part-cobbled streets are lined with Tudor and Jacobean buildings, galleries, restaurants and funky bars. The Mayflower Steps commemorate the final UK departure of the Pilgrim Fathers, a band of Puritans who sailed to the New World in 1620 in search of greater religious freedom. Having left Southampton, they were forced into Dartmouth by an unseaworthy ship and eventually left Plymouth (England) on board the *Mayflower*, going on to found New England's first permanent colony at Plymouth (Massachusetts). The Pilgrims' approximate departure point is marked by a heavily weathered honey-coloured Doric arch and flapping American and British flags.

Plymouth

◉ Top Sights
1 Plymouth Gin Distillery C3
2 Plymouth Hoe B4

◉ Sights
3 Barbican D3
4 Barbican Pannier Market C3
5 Bowling Green B3
6 Citadel C4
7 City Museum and Art Gallery C1
8 Drake Statue B3
9 Elizabethan Mural C3
10 Island House D3
11 Mayflower Steps D3
12 Merchant's House C2
13 National Marine Aquarium D3
14 Plymouth Naval Memorial B3
15 Smeaton's Tower B4

◉ Activities, Courses & Tours
16 Mount Batten Ferry D3
   Plymouth Boat Trips .... (see 16)
17 Tinside Pool B4

◉ Sleeping
18 Acorns & Lawns B3
19 Bowling Green B3
20 Casa Mia C3
21 Duke of Cornwall A3
22 Four Seasons C3

23 Rusty Anchor A4
24 Sea Breezes A4

◉ Eating
   Barbican Kitchen .... (see 1)
25 Boathouse Cafe D3
26 Cap'n Jaspers D3
27 Coffee Shack A4
28 Harbourside Fish & Chips C3
29 Platters D3
30 Prete's Café C3
   Rhodes @ the Dome .... (see 33)
31 Tanners Restaurant C2
32 Terrace B4

◉ Drinking & Nightlife
33 Bar Rhodes B4
34 Dolphin D3
35 Minerva C2

◉ Entertainment
36 Annabel's D2
37 H2O C2
38 Plymouth Arts Centre C2
39 Theatre Royal B2
40 Vauxhall Quay D2

◉ Shopping
41 Drake Circus Shopping
   Centre C1

Plaques alongside mark the departures of the first emigrant ships to New Zealand, Captain Cook's voyages of discovery, the arrival of the first-ever transatlantic flight in 1916 and, five decades later, the first solo circumnavigation of the globe by boat.

Nearby, the **passenger list** of the *Mayflower* is displayed on the side of **Island House**. Look out for the descriptions of passengers as either 'Saints' (Puritan pilgrims) or 'Strangers' (those hired to support the expedition).

Smeaton's Tower LIGHTHOUSE
(📞 01752-304774; The Hoe; adult/child £2.60/1.30; ⊙10am-noon & 1-4pm Tue-Sat Apr-Sep) The red-and-white stripes of Smeaton's Tower rise from the middle of Plymouth Hoe. The whole 70ft structure used to stand on the Eddystone Reef, 14 miles offshore, and was transferred here, brick by brick, in the 1880s. For an illuminating insight into the lives of past lighthouse keepers, head up the winding stone stairs and through a series of circular rooms. Some 93 steps later you'll emerge onto an open-air platform with stunning views of the city, Dartmoor and the sea.

National Marine Aquarium AQUARIUM
(📞0844 893 7938; www.national-aquarium.co.uk; Rope Walk; adult/child/family £12.75/8.75/37; ⊙10am-5pm, to 6pm Apr-Sep) The futuristic glass lines of this innovative aquarium are wittily sited next to the city's pungent Fish Market – an interesting dead-fish/live-fish juxtaposition. Here sharks swim in coral waters teeming with moray eels and vividly coloured fish – there's even a loggerhead turtle called Snorkel who was rescued from a Cornish beach. Walk-through glass arches ensure huge rays glide over your head, while the immense Atlantic Reef tank reveals just what's lurking a few miles offshore. The aquarium focuses on conservation; look out for tanks containing home-reared cardinal fish, corals and incredibly cute seahorses.

City Museum and Art Gallery MUSEUM
(📞01752-304774; www.plymouthmuseum.gov.uk; Drake Circus; ⊙10am-5pm Tue-Sat) [FREE] The imaginative displays conjure up Plymouth's rich history. Look out for Napoleonic-era bone model ships and the skis of doomed Antarctic explorer Captain Robert Falcon Scott – a Plymouth man.

SIR FRANCIS DRAKE

Sir Francis Drake (1540–96) was a man with a dashing image that belies a complex reality. To Tudor England he was a hero, explorer and adventurer. To his Spanish counterparts he was 'Drake the master thief'. He was also involved, albeit briefly, in slavery when he sailed with his relative, John Hawkins; the first English captain to ply the triangular 'slave trade'. In 1580 Drake sailed into Plymouth aboard the *Golden Hind*, having become the first man to circumnavigate the globe. His vessel was full of treasure looted from Spanish colonies, securing the favour of Queen Elizabeth I and the money to buy Buckland Abbey (p114) on the outskirts of Plymouth. Eleven years later, Drake (legend has it) calmly insisted on finishing his game of bowls on Plymouth Hoe, despite the advancing Spanish Armada. The first engagement happened just off Plymouth, the second at Portland Bill – eventually the Spanish fleet was chased to Calais and attacked with fire ships. Many escaped but were wrecked off the Scottish coast. Drake died of fever in 1596 while fighting in Spanish territories in the Caribbean and was buried at sea off modern Panama. His statue, which looks more dignified than piratical, stands on Plymouth Hoe.

Merchant's House HISTORIC BUILDING
(☏ 01752-304774; 33 St Andrews St; adult/child £2.60/1.30; ⊙ 10am-noon & 1-5pm Tue-Sat Apr-Sep) Curiosities pack this 17th-century building – from manacles, truncheons and a ducking stool, to a replica 19th-century school room and a Victorian pharmacy where you can try old-fashioned pill rolling.

🏃 Activities

Swimming

⭐ **Tinside Pool** SWIMMING
(☏ 01752-261915; www.plymouth.gov.uk/tinside lido; Hoe Rd; adult/child £3.90/2.80; ⊙ noon-6pm Mon-Fri, from 10am Sat & Sun late-May–early-Sep, from 10am daily in school holidays) Taking a dip at this jazz age, open-air swim-spot is an unforgettable experience. Its 1935, art deco design sees cream curves and light-and dark-blue tiles sweep gracefully out from the foot of the Hoe. Plunge into the chilly salt water to join the regulars doing laps and the youngsters larking around beside the fountains, then recline on a sun lounger on the circular rim, looking straight out over Plymouth Sound.

Boating

Along with the following Barbican-based firms, the Cremyll Ferry (p105) also provides another great boat connection to Cornwall.

Plymouth Boat Trips BOAT TRIP
(Barbican Pontoon) The pick of this firm's trips is the 30-minute blast-across-the-bay to the quaint, pub-packed Cornish fishing villages of Kingsand and Cawsand (adult/child return £8/4, four daily mid-April to October). They also offer one-hour harbour cruises (adult/child £7.50/4, four daily mid-April to October) to the warships at Plymouth's naval base, and fishing trips (per three-hour cruise £25); have your catch turned into a meal at their funky, sustainable fish-focused Boathouse Cafe (www.theboathousecafe.co.uk; 2 Commercial Wharf; mains £6-18; ⊙ 5am-5pm Sun-Thu, 8am-9pm Fri & Sat) for £15 extra.

Mount Batten Ferry BOAT TRIP
(☏ 01752-408590; www.mountbattenferry.com; Barbican Pontoon; adult/child return £3/2) A little yellow ferry shuttling from the Barbican Pontoon across to the Mount Batten Peninsula (10 minutes, half-hourly).

Mount Batten Centre SAILING, KAYAKING
(☏ 01752-404567; www.mount-batten-centre.com; 70 Lawrence Rd, Mount Batten Peninsula) Two-hour taster sessions include those in sailing dinghies (£20) and sit-on-top kayaks (£18). Two-day courses include kayaking (£90), sailing (£165), windsurfing (£140) and powerboating (£225).

🛏 Sleeping

Sea Breezes B&B £
(☏ 01752-667205; www.plymouth-bedandbreakfast.co.uk; 28 Grand Pde; s/d/f £40/70/95) At this deeply comfortable guesthouse, fresh decor ranges from subtle gingham to groovy swirls. The bathrooms gleam, the towels are fluffy and the breakfasts feature melon, strawberries and hand-cut toast. Bag a front-facing bedroom (go for the one with the window seat) for smashing sea views.

Acorns & Lawns
B&B **£**

(📞 01752-229474; www.acornsandlawnsguesthouse.com; 171 Citadel Rd; d £60-75; 🐾) Simplicity and serenity seem to seep from the walls here. The guest lounge and breakfast room are all light colours and varnished floors; a bright-white stairwell leads to light-coloured, light-filled rooms. Ask for a front-facing bedroom to look out over the lower slopes of grassy Plymouth Hoe.

Bowling Green
HOTEL **£**

(📞 01752-209090; www.thebowlinggreenplymouth.com; 10 Osborne Pl; s/d £50/75; 🅿️🐾) Some of the smart cream-and-white rooms in this cosy, family-run hotel look out onto the modern incarnation of Drake's famous bowling green. If you tire of watching people throw woods after jacks, you can play chess in the conservatory.

Four Seasons
B&B **£**

(📞 01752-223591; www.fourseasonsguesthouse.co.uk; 207 Citadel Rd East; s £38-48, d £65; 🐾) Treats are everywhere here, from the big bowls of free sweets to the mounds of Devon bacon for breakfast. They've got the basics right, too: tasteful rooms decorated in gold and cream.

Rusty Anchor
B&B **£**

(📞 01752-663924; www.therustyanchor-plymouth.co.uk; 30 Grand Pde; s/d/f £35/70/80; 🐾) Decorative driftwood and shells lend this relaxed B&B a flavour of the sea; four rooms have views of Plymouth Sound's wide waters. Owner Jan will try to meet your breakfast requests, be they kippers, pancakes or homemade rolls.

Casa Mia
B&B **£**

(📞 01752-265742; www.casamiaguesthouse.co.uk; 201 Citadel Rd East; s/d/f £40/75/85) A riot of colourful flowers outside and a highly polished brass step hint at what to expect: a cheerful, traditional and spotlessly clean B&B. It's in a great location, tucked away from main roads and only a few minutes' walk to the Barbican and to town.

⭐ St Elizabeth's House
BOUTIQUE HOTEL **££**

(📞 01752-344840; www.stelizabeths.co.uk; Longbrook St, Plympton St Maurice; d £140-160, ste £180-250; 🅿️🐾) In the 17th-century St Elizabeth's was a manor house, now it's a luxury enclave overflowing with boutique chic. Free-standing slipper baths, oak furniture and Egyptian cotton grace the rooms; the suites feature palatial bathrooms and private terraces. It's set in the suburb-cum-village of Plympton St Maurice, 5 miles east of Plymouth.

Duke of Cornwall
HOTEL **£££**

(📞 01752-275850; www.thedukeofcornwallhotel.com; Millbay Rd; s £104, d £140-250, f from £150; 🅿️🐾) Turret-topped, dotted with balconies and lined with Gothic gables – the Duke of Cornwall is certainly arresting. The rooms are massive, if a touch old-fashioned. The four-poster suite comes with complimentary champagne, but for a unique sleep, plump for the panoramic tower room. With its wrap-around views of the city and the shore, it even has a telescope to help you take it all in.

Eating

Royal William Bakery
CAFE, BAKERY **£**

(www.royalwilliambakery.com; Royal William Yard; mains £5; ⊙ 8.30am-8pm; 🚗) Piles of huge, just-cooked loaves, tureens full of soup, crumbly pastries and irresistible cakes: this is a bakery like few others. After 5pm, they'll even rustle you up a bespoke, huge slab of

PLYMOUTH & DARTMOOR PLYMOUTH

ROYAL WILLIAM YARD

In the 1840s, this cluster of waterfront warehouses supplied stores for countless Royal Navy vessels. Today it's home to sleek apartments, a relaxed pub, a chic wine lounge (p106) and a burgeoning cluster of eateries; the best being River Cottage Canteen (p106) and the Royal William Bakery (p105). A simple exhibition (⊙ 9am-4pm Mon-Thurs, to noon Fri) FREE outlines the yard's history; roaming past the former slaughterhouse, bakery, brewery and cooperage underlines just how big the supplies operation was. The yard is 2 miles west of the city centre, hop on bus 34 (8 minutes, one-to-two hourly) or, better still, catch the hourly ferry (📞 07771 544394; www.royalwilliamyardharbour.co.uk; adult/child single £3/1.50; ⊙ 10.30am-4pm Apr-Sep) that runs from the Barbican Pontoon. A 10-minute walk north of the yard, the Cremyll Ferry (📞 0774 6199508; www.cremyll-ferry.co.uk; Admirals Hard; adult/child return £2.60/1.30; ⊙ half-hourly) chugs across the Tamar to Cornwall, and the historic house and fine walks of the Mount Edgcumbe (p190) estate.

pizza. The serve-yourself style is so laid-back you don't get a bill, just tell them what you've eaten and they'll tot it up at the end.

Cap'n Jaspers CAFE **£**
(www.capn-jaspers.co.uk; Whitehouse Pier, Quay Rd; snacks £2-5; ⊗8am-midnight) Unique, quirky and slightly insane, this Barbican institution has been delighting tourists and locals alike for decades. Motorised gadgets whirr around and the teaspoons are attached to the counter by chains. The menu is of the burger and bacon butty school – trying to eat the 'half a yard of hot dog' is a Plymouth rite of passage. Or scoff a fresh crab roll, the filling could have been caught by the bloke sitting next to you; his boat's probably tied up alongside.

Harbourside Fish & Chips FAST FOOD **£**
(www.barbicanfishandchips.co.uk; 35 Southside St; mains £7; ⊗11am-10pm, to 11pm Fri & Sat) That customers are often queuing out the door signals this is a top-quality 'chippy'. Either eat in (in a pocket-sized dining space), take away (watch out for diving seagulls), or ferry your meal to the neighbouring Dolphin pub, to tuck in as you down a drink.

★ **River Cottage**
Canteen & Deli MODERN BRITISH **££**
(✆01752-252702; www.rivercottage.net; Royal William Yard; mains £8-15; ⊗noon-3pm daily, 6.30-9.30pm Tue-Sat; ✐) Television-chef Hugh Fearnley-Whittingstall has long campaigned for flavourful, local, sustainable, seasonal, organic produce – and that's exactly what you get here. Expect meats roasted in front of an open fire, fish simply grilled and familiar veg given a revelatory makeover.

Rhodes @ the Dome MODERN BRITISH **££**
(✆01752-266600; www.rhodesatthedome.co.uk; Hoe Rd; mains £12-20; ⊗noon-2.30pm & 5.30-9.30pm) TV chef Gary Rhodes' new eatery boasts a prime site in the middle of the Hoe overlooking Plymouth's vast bay. Dishes are complex, classy and often unusual: smoked mackerel linguine; roast chicken with crystalised walnuts; and braised lamb squab (which, surprisingly, comes with clotted cream).

Rock Salt MODERN BRITISH **££**
(✆01752-225522; www.rocksaltcafe.co.uk; 31 Stonehouse St; mains £12-20, snacks from £4; ⊗10am-9.30pm Tue-Sat, to 4pm Sun; ✆✐) They bill it as good honest food, and it is: great ingredients and creative flavour-combos

delivered with flair in a chilled-out brasserie. Its piled-high all day breakfasts and in-between-meal snacks have won legions of local fans too. It's set slightly south of Plymouth's edgy nightclub strip, Union St.

Barbican Kitchen MODERN BRITISH **££**
(✆01752-604448; www.barbicankitchen.com; 60 Southside St; mains £11-20; ✐) The decor at this cool eatery teams wood and stone with bursts of shocking pink and lime. The food is attention grabbing too. Try the curried West Country crab, or the sticky, maple-roast belly pork with pears. The express menu, served at lunch and early-evening, is a great deal (two/three courses £11/15).

Platters SEAFOOD **££**
(✆01752-227262; www.platters-restaurant.co.uk; 12 The Barbican; mains £15; ⊗noon-10pm) A long-established eatery with fish so fresh it's just stopped flapping. Treats include the scallops sautéed in garlic butter and the succulent grilled skate.

Tanners Restaurant FINE DINING **£££**
(✆01752-252001; www.tannersrestaurant.com; Finewell St; mains £20; ⊗noon-2.30pm & 6.30-9pm Tue-Sat) The surroundings are gorgeous, and so is the cuisine. A beautifully-lit medieval building sets the scene for reinvented British and French classics; Bodmin moor venison carpaccio, risotto with wild garlic and Vulscombe goat's cheese. Considering the quality, the set lunch (Tuesday to Saturday only) is a bargain (two/three courses £14/17).

🍷 Drinking

A proper Navy city, Plymouth has a very lively nightlife. Union St is clubland, Mutley Plain and North Hill have a studenty vibe, while on the Barbican there are more restaurants amid the packed-out bars. All three areas get very rowdy, especially on the weekends.

Dolphin PUB
(14 The Barbican) This wonderfully unreconstructed Barbican boozer is all scuffed tables, padded bench seats and an authentic, no-nonsense atmosphere. Feeling peckish? Get a fish and chip takeaway from nearby Harbourside, then settle down with your pint.

Vignoble WINE BAR
(www.levignoble.co.uk; New Cooperage, Royal William Yard; ⊗noon-11pm Sun-Thu, to midnight Fri & Sat)

PLYMOUTH'S CAFE CULTURE

On a sunny summer's day the people of Plymouth head for a waterside cafe to watch the world drift by. The **Terrace** (www.theterracecafebar.co.uk; Hoe Rd; snacks £3-6; ⊙10am-6pm), is a firm local favourite. Tucked away beside Tinside Pool, it boasts panoramic views across Plymouth Sound and a chilled soundtrack. To the west, the tables and chairs of the **Coffee Shack** (Hoe Rd; ⊙7am-5pm) are scattered alongside the waterside promenade; classical music floats from the speakers.

From both, watch out for strings of yachts, dinghy races, lone canoeists, dive boats, cross-channel ferries, warships, submarines, gig boats and fishing trawlers. On a fine day it helps explain why Plymothians, although the first to admit their city is far from perfect, do tend to think of it with a sneaking sense of pride.

Perhaps the perfect way to explore the world of wine. At this chilled-out hang-out you buy a £10 card and a high-tech gizmo delivers seven-to-eight taster-sized glasses of your chosen vintages. There are zingy Juiceology soft drinks, and cheese and charcuterie platters too (£7 to £13). Their expert-led tasting evenings (£15 a head) are worth booking a taxi for.

Minerva　　　　　　　　　　PUB
(www.minervainn.co.uk; 31 Looe St) Stone walls, wooden benches, chunks of sailing ships, real ales, live music and Thursday night jam sessions make this 16th-century drinking den a local favourite.

Bar Rhodes　　　　　COCKTAIL BAR
(www.rhodesatthedome.co.uk; Hoe Rd) Expect grandstand water views and a tempting range of Plymouth Gin cocktails (from gimlets and martinis to Singapore Slings) at Gary Rhodes' sleek bar, which is at the same address as his Rhodes @ the Dome eatery.

☆ Entertainment

Annabel's　　　　　CABARET, CLUB
(www.annabelscabaret.co.uk; 88 Vauxhall St; ⊙8.30pm-2am Thu-Sat) The stage spots in this fabulously quirky venue are filled by an eclectic collection of acts (expect anything from comedy or tango to burlesque). Crowd-pleasing tunes fill the dance floor while classy cocktails fill your glass.

Vauxhall Quay　　　　CLUB, BAR
(www.thevauxhallquay.com; Little Vauxhall Quay) Just round from the heart of the Barbican, the terrace of this cool club-cum-bar-cum-pizzeria is ideal for a waterside drink. Tuesdays, Thursdays and Fridays see live music, often with an acoustic theme, while on Saturdays DJs blend chart, pop, indie and '80s.

H2O　　　　　　　　　　　CLUB
(https://en-gb.facebook.com/H2OBarClubPlymouth; 11a The Parade) A hit with Plymouth's night owls, playing everything from rock, ska and reggae, to the latest club anthems and drum and bass.

Theatre Royal　　　　　THEATRE
(☑01752-267222; www.theatreroyal.com; Royal Pde) One of the nation's highest grossing theatres, the Theatre Royal stages acclaimed home-grown productions as well as large-scale touring shows that include West End musicals, ballet and opera. Its award-winning studio **Drum Theatre** is renowned for experimental shows and developing new writing.

Plymouth Arts Centre　　　CINEMA
(☑01752-206114; www.plymouthartscentre.org; 38 Looe St; ⊙10am-8.30pm Tue-Sat, 4-8.30pm Sun) An atmospheric, independent cinema with great scheduling and irresistibly comfy seats; plus a groovy bar and bistro, and innovative gallery spaces too.

ℹ Information

Tourist Office (☑01752-306330; www.visitplymouth.co.uk; 3-5 The Barbican; ⊙9am-5pm Mon-Sat & 10am-4pm Sun Apr-Oct, 9am-5pm Mon-Fri & 10am-4pm Sat Nov-Mar)

ℹ Getting There & Around

BUS

Birmingham (£38, five hours, four daily) National Express

Bristol (£15, three hours, four daily) National Express

Exeter (£7, eight daily Monday to Saturday, three on Sunday) Bus X38, runs via Ashburton

London (£32, five to six hours, four daily) National Express

Outdoor Activities

Devon and Cornwall feature Britain's best natural adventure playgrounds, where you can surf amazing waves, hike along spectacular coastal paths, canter across moors or sail between beautiful bays. Whether you're after exhilaration or relaxation, you'll find it here.

ANDY STOTHERT / GETTY IMAGES ©

STEVE ALLEN / GETTY IMAGES ©

1. Pony Trekking & Horse Riding, Exmoor National Park (p128)

Exmoor provides superb riding opportunities through lush landscapes and vast moors.

2. Cycling, Grand Western Canal (p52)

This 1814 canal has cycling paths, horse-drawn barges and boat hire.

3. Walking

The Cornish coast between Newquay and Padstow offers great walking paths with stellar views.

4. Surfing, Newquay (p208)

One of Britain's best spots for surfing and kiteboarding.

DAVID EPPERSON / GETTY IMAGES ©

Paignton (1¼ hours, hourly Monday to Saturday, two-hourly on Sunday) Bus X80, runs via Totnes

Penzance (£9, 3½ hours, four daily) National Express

Tavistock (one hour, hourly) Bus 83/84/86, runs via Yelverton

CAR

Plymouth sits just south of the A38 dual carriageway, which leads west to Cornwall, and east to Exeter and the motorway network, 43 miles away.

PARKING

Multistorey car parks include **Drake Circus shopping centre** (per two/four hours £2.80/4.80) and the **Theatre Royal** (per two/four hours £2.40/4.80). There's also metered parking on the Hoe, and on city streets (per two/four hours £2.40/4.80).

TRAIN

Plymouth is on the London Paddington–Penzance main line.

Bristol (£25, hours, two or three per hour)
Exeter (£8, one hour, two or three per hour)
London (£45, 3¼ hours, half-hourly)
Penzance (£8, two hours, half-hourly)
Totnes (£5, 30 minutes, half-hourly)
Truro (£10, 1¼ hours, hourly)

DARTMOOR NATIONAL PARK

Dartmoor is an ancient, compelling landscape, so different from the rest of Devon that a visit feels like falling straight into Tolkien's *Lord of the Rings* trilogy. Exposed granite hills (called tors) crest on the horizon, linked by swathes of honey-tinged moors. Streams tumble over moss-smothered boulders in woods of twisted trees. The centre of this 368-sq-mile national park is the higher moor; a vast, treeless expanse.

On sunny, summer days Dartmoor is idyllic. With ponies wandering at will and sheep grazing beside the road, it's a cinematic landscape that prompted Steven Spielberg to film the WWI epic *War Horse* here. But Dartmoor is also a mercurial place where the urban illusion of control over our surroundings is stripped away and the elements are in charge. So it's also the setting for Sir Arthur Conan Doyle's *The Hound of the Baskervilles*, and in sleeting rain and swirling mists you suddenly see why: the moor morphs into a bleak wilderness where tales of a phantom hound can seem very real indeed.

Dartmoor's settlements range from brooding Princetown, picturesque Widecombe-in-the-Moor, and tiny Postbridge, to genteel Chagford and Ashburton. In between lies a natural breakout zone offering superb hiking, cycling, riding, climbing and white-water kayaking, rustic pubs and fancy restaurants, wild camping nooks and cosy country-house hotels – perfect boltholes when the fog rolls in.

ℹ️ Information

Dartmoor National Park Authority (DNPA; ☑ 01822-890414; www.dartmoor.gov.uk) runs a string of tourist offices (known locally as DNPA Visitor Centres). The main one is at Princetown (p117), and others include Postbridge (p119) and **Haytor** (☑ 01364-661520; Haytor Vale; ☺ 10am-5pm Apr-Sep to 4pm Oct & Mar, 10.30am-3.30pm Thur-Sun Nov-Feb). There are also council-run tourist offices at Okehampton (p125) and Tavistock (p116). The official tourism website is www.dartmoor.co.uk.

🏃 Activities

Dartmoor is packed full of adventurous possibilities (p31). The DNPA is a good source of supplementary information.

Climbing

All those looming granite tors are irresistible to climbers. Experienced crag scramblers will have to book at some popular sites; the DNP can provide a free leaflet and further advice.

Adventure Okehampton   OUTDOORS
(☑ 01837-53916; www.adventureokehampton.com; Klondyke Rd, Okehampton; per half day from £18) Runs both indoor and outdoor climbing sessions, plus bike hire and activities including archery, abseiling and bushcraft, from its base at Okehampton YHA.

Rock Centre   ROCK CLIMBING
(☑ 01626-852717; www.rockcentre.co.uk; Rock House, Chudleigh; per hr £40) Stages climbs on the moor itself (per three-hour session for four people £80) and individual sessions indoors (per 1½ hours £15).

Cycling

Tackle tough terrain or freewheel down a hill – on Dartmoor there are routes for everyone. You can cycle on roads and public bridleways, but not on footpaths or across open countryside. The DNPA sells an off-road map and can advise about other routes. Tourist offices sell the Dartmoor Cycling Map (£13). Here are some of the key cycle routes:

Plym Valley Trail A traffic-free, 7-mile route leading from the moor to Plymouth.

Granite Way An 11-mile, off-road trail between Okehampton and Lydford tracing the route of a former railway line (p124).

Princetown & Burrator Mountain Bike Route This challenging, 13-mile moorland circuit sweeps along tracks and bridleways, taking in Princetown, Sheepstor village and Burrator Reservoir.

Dartmoor Way (www.dartmoorway.org. uk) A 90-mile, round-Dartmoor walking and cycling route with an option to detour across the middle of the moor.

Bike Hire

Adventure Okehampton (p110) rents out bikes (per half/full day adult £6.50/8.50, per half/full day child £5.50/7.50) from the Youth Hostel at the start of the Granite Way.

Devon Cycle Hire   BICYCLE RENTAL (☑ 01837-861141; www.devoncyclehire.co.uk; Sourton Down, near Okehampton; per half/full day adult £12/14, per half/full day child £8/10; ☺ 9am-5pm Thu-Tue Easter-Sep) On the Granite Way.

Princetown Cycle Hire   BICYCLE RENTAL (Fox Tor Cafe; ☑ 01822-890238; www.princetown-cyclehire.co.uk; Two Bridges Rd, Princetown; half/full day adult £10/18, half/full day child £5/8; ☺ 9am-5pm) Handy for the Princetown & Burrator Mountain Bike Route.

Walking

Some 730 miles of public footpaths criss-cross Dartmoor's heaths and rocky tors. Crimson's *Dartmoor Walks* (£12) has 28 hikes of up to nine miles, while their *Dartmoor Short Walks* (£8) focuses on 2-to 6-mile family-friendly treks. Tourist offices can advise on self-guided trails or DNPA-run guided walks (www.dartmoor.gov.uk/visiting; £4). Themes for these include: archaeology, military history, quarrying, and bird and animal life. Regular child-friendly events include butterfly strolls and den building.

A wealth of day trails is on offer, along with some testing long-distance routes:

Templer Way An 18 mile, two- to three-day leg stretch from Haytor to Teignmouth.

West Devon Way This 36-mile trek runs between Okehampton and Plymouth.

> ### WARNING
>
> The military has three training ranges on Dartmoor where live ammunition is used. DNPA staff can explain their precise locations; they're also marked on Ordnance Survey maps. When walking you're advised to check if the route you're planning falls within a range; if it does, check if firing is taking place via the Firing Information Service (☑ 0800 458 4868; www.mod.uk/access). In the day, red flags fly at the edges of in-use ranges; red flares burn at night. Even when there's no firing, beware of unidentified metal objects lying in the grass – do not touch anything that you find; just note its position and report it to the police or the Commandant (☑ 01837 657210).

Dartmoor Way Circles from Buckfastleigh in the south, through Moretonhampstead, northwest to Okehampton and south through Lydford to Tavistock. Ninety miles in total.

Two Moors Way An epic going 102 miles from Ivybridge, across Dartmoor and Exmoor to Lynmouth on north Devon's coast.

Most trails aren't waymarked, so carry a map and compass. Be aware too, the military uses some sections of moor for live firing. The Ordnance Survey (OS) Explorer 1:25,000 map No 28, Dartmoor (£7.99), is the most comprehensive and shows park boundaries and MOD firing-range areas.

Dartmoor's weather is notoriously fickle, so be prepared for an upland environment: warm, waterproof clothing, water, hats and sunscreen are essential.

White-water Rafting

The raging River Dart makes Dartmoor a top spot for thrill seekers. You can ride in a raft without any experience but to shoot a rapid in a kayak you need more skill (BCU 2 star) and, if you're organising it yourself, a permit.

Environmental safeguards mean rivers are only open between October and March.

CRS Adventures   WATER SPORTS (☑ 01364-653444; www.crsadventures.co.uk; River Dart Country Park, near Ashburton) Runs thrilling, three-hour sessions on inflatable rafts (per two people £100).

Dartmoor National Park

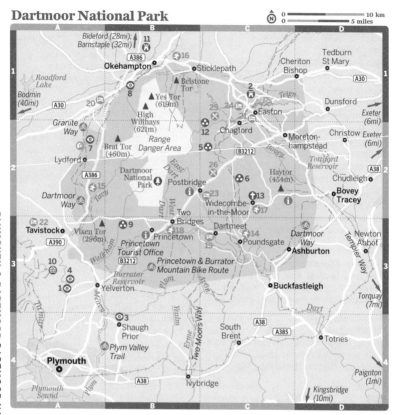

Pony Trekking & Horse Riding

There's a frontier feel to parts of the moor which makes it perfect for saddling up and trotting out. Riding costs around £20/36 per hour/half-day.

Babeny Farm   HORSE RIDING
(☎ 01364-631296; www.babenystables.co.uk; Pounds-gate, near Ashburton) All experience levels.

Cholwell   HORSE RIDING
(☎ 01822-810526; www.cholwellridingstables.co.uk; Mary Tavy, near Tavistock) Caters for novices and experts.

Eastlake   HORSE RIDING
(☎ 01837-52515; www.eastlakeridingstables.co.uk; Eastlake, near Okehampton) Rides available by the hour, or day.

Shilstone Rocks   HORSE RIDING
(☎ 01364-621281; www.dartmoorstables.com; Wide-combe-in-the-Moor) Beginners welcome.

Tor Royal   HORSE RIDING
(☎ 01822-890189; www.dartmoorhorseriding. co.uk; Princetown) Caters to all experience levels.

🛏 Sleeping

From spoil-yourself-silly luxury to lovely thatched cottages to snoozing under the stars, Dartmoor has a wide range of sleeping options.

The **YHA** (www.yha.org.uk) has a hostel at Postbridge, two at Okehampton, plus three bare-bones camping barns, including one near Postbridge. Independent hostels and bunkhouses include those at Moretonhampstead and Princetown.

Dartmoor is also perfect for 'wild camping'; pitching a tent on some sections of open moor is allowed provided simple but strict rules are followed, DNPA tourist offices can advise.

Dartmoor National Park

⊙ Sights
1	Buckland Abbey	A3
2	Castle Drogo	C1
3	Dewerstone	B4
4	Garden House	A3
5	Grey Wethers & Fernworthy Circles	C2
6	Grimspound	C2
7	Lydford Gorge	A2
8	Meldon Viaduct	B1
9	Merrivale Stone Rows	B3
10	Morewellham Quay	A3
11	Okehampton Castle	B1
12	Scorhill Stone Circle	C2
13	St Pancras Church	C2

⊙ Activities, Courses & Tours
14	Babeny Farm Riding Stables	C3
15	Cholwell Riding Stables	A2
16	Eastlake Riding Stables	B1
17	Shilstone Rocks Riding Stables	C2
18	Toy Royal Riding Stables	B3

⊙ Sleeping
19	Brimpts Farm	C3
20	Collaven Manor	A1
21	Easton Court	C1
22	Horn Of Plenty	A3
23	Runnage YHA	C2
24	Sandy Park	C1

⊙ Eating
25	Gidleigh Park	C1
26	Warren House Inn	C2

✕ Eating

Dartmoor caters for all tastes and budgets. Its restaurants include one with two Michelin stars, and there's also a wealth of fine dining in country-house hotels. Chagford and Tavistock make great bases for gourmet breaks. The ancient settlements of Widecombe, Ashburton and Moretonhampstead house eateries dishing up stylish modern food, while scattered all around are timewarp pubs serving up hearty grub, and tearooms that have perfected the art of cream teas.

❶ Getting There & Around

BUS
Onto the Moor
Bus X38 (eight daily Monday to Saturday, three on Sunday) To Ashburton from Plymouth or Exeter.

Bus 83/84/86 (hourly) To Tavistock from Plymouth, via Yelverton.

Bus 118 (two to five daily) To Tavistock from Barnstaple (2¼ hours), via Lydford and Okehampton.

Bus 359 (two hourly Monday to Saturday) To Moretonhampstead (one hour) from Exeter.

Around the Moor
There are several key routes around the Moor, be warned: some are seasonal.

Bus 98 (three daily, Monday to Saturday) A year-round service, which runs from Tavistock to Merrivale and Princetown; one bus a day goes onto Two Bridges and Postbridge.

Transmoor Link/Bus 82 Runs on summer Saturdays and Sundays only (mid-May to mid-September) between Tavistock and Exeter, stopping at Yelverton, Princetown, Two Bridges, Postbridge, Warren House Inn and Moretonhampstead. One bus each way covers the whole route; with two services each way running between Postbridge and Tavistock (stopping at Princetown and Two Bridges). The service is particularly prone to annual changes, so check for updates.

Haytor Hoppa Runs on summer Saturdays only (adult/child/family £5/2/10; Easter to October), providing four buses between Newton Abbot train station, Haytor, Widecombe-in-the-Moor and Bovey Tracey.

Passes
Dartmoor Sunday Rover (adult/child/family £7.50/5/16; ⊙ Jun-Sep) Gives unlimited Sunday travel on most moorland bus routes; buy from drivers or at Plymouth train station.

CAR
The A38 and A30 dual carriageways frame Dartmoor, while the single-lane B3212 carves a path across the centre, linking Moretonhampstead, Postbridge and Princetown.

Countless single-track lanes lead away from these central routes, some becoming very steep and narrow; signs only sometimes indicate when that is the case. Much of the moor is unfenced grazing and has a 40mph speed limit. Be warned: you're likely to come across sheep, ponies and even cows on the road.

PARKING
Many moorland towns and villages have pay-and-display car parks. On the moor itself, there are numerous, free car parks; sometimes they're little more than lay-bys for half a dozen cars. The surface is rough to very rough.

Tavistock & Around

POP 12,300

Peaceful and prosperous, Tavistock is graced by crenellated, turreted constructions built in the late 1800s out of warm, grey stone.

The rugged landscape around the town is home to three worth-a-detour sights: the former mine at Morewellham Quay; Sir Francis Drake's former manor house, Buckland Abbey; and the intimate horticultural delight that is the Garden House.

◉ Sights

Garden House GARDENS
(☑01822-854769; www.thegardenhouse.org.uk; Buckland Monachorum, near Yelverton; adult/child £7/2.70; ⊙10.30am-5pm Mar-Nov; Ⓟ) The enchanting blend of landscapes here make this garden one of the best in Devon. Its 8 acres encompass wildflower meadows and South African planting, Acer glades and a walled cottage garden. Terraces cluster around the picturesque ruins of a medieval vicarage, while clambering up its 16th-century tower reveals views of sweeps of blue flax, poppies and buttercups. Everywhere tucked-away benches hide in flower-filled nooks – soothing spots to drink in the fragrance and watch the bees buzz by. The cafe serves rustic treats: goat's cheese sandwiches with onion relish, and salads scattered with pomegranate seeds. The Garden House is 5 miles south of Tavistock.

Buckland Abbey HISTORIC BUILDING
(NT; ☑01822-853607; www.nationaltrust.org.uk; near Yelverton; adult/child £9/4; ⊙noon-4pm daily mid-Feb to Oct, Fri-Sun only Nov & Dec; Ⓟ♿) There's a tangible sense of history at this honey-coloured, manor house. It started life in the 13th-century as a Cistercian monastery and abbey church. After the Dissolution, it was turned into a family residence by Sir Richard Grenville before being bought by his cousin and nautical rival Sir Francis Drake in 1581. A sumptuous interior includes Tudor plasterwork ceilings in the Great Hall and Drake's Chamber, where Drake's Drum is said to beat by itself when Britain is in danger of being invaded. There's also a monastic barn, a fine Elizabethan garden, extensive woodland walks and a great program of events – look out for the Tudor archery days or the charcoal-making weekends. Buckland Abbey is located 7 miles south of Tavistock.

Morwellham Quay HISTORIC SITE
(☑01822-832766; www.morwellham-quay.co.uk; Morwellham, near Tavistock; adult/child/family £9/7/26; ⊙10am-5pm Easter-Oct, to 4pm Nov-Easter; Ⓟ) Morwellham Quay is part of the southwest's Mining World Heritage Site and offers an intriguing insight into the copper boom that gripped west Devon in the 1860s. Then, this port beside the River Tamar saw tonnes of ore loaded onto masted vessels. Recently, the BBC filmed its series *Edwardian Farm* here. You can explore the cottages, smithy and cooperage of this lost community as well as pan for copper, try on a bonnet or waistcoat and watch potters and farriers in action. Costumed guides show you around but the highlight is the atmospheric trip into a copper mine on a little underground train (adult/child £3.50/2.50). The last entry is two hours before closing. Morwellham Quay is 5 miles southwest of Tavistock.

Tavistock Museum MUSEUM
(☑01822-612546; www.tavistockmuseum.co.uk; Court Gate; ⊙11am-3pm Easter-Oct) FREE Remnants from Tavistock's now vanished abbey sit in this traditional but excellent museum alongside artefacts of the town's copper mining heydays. Look out for clogs, shovels and photos revealing the harsh conditions masked by the mines' lyrical names: Virtuous Lady, Queen of the Tamar and Lady Bertha. You'll also see why there's a local place called Chipshop. A clue: its nothing to do with fried fish.

🛏 Sleeping

April Cottage B&B £
(☑01822-613280; www.aprilcottagetavistock.co.uk; 12 Mount Tavy Rd, Tavistock; d £70; Ⓟ📶) The sweet, knick-knack-packed rooms of this compact cottage are festooned with floral prints. But the best bit is the rushing River Tavy, which tumbles along beside a tiny deck and summer house. Ask for the river-view double, crank open the window, and the sounds of water will soothe you to sleep.

★ Horn of Plenty LUXURY HOTEL ££
(☑01822-832528; www.thehornofplenty.co.uk; Gulworthy, near Tavistock; s £115-215, d £125-225; Ⓟ) The swish rooms at this sumptuous country-house hotel boast claw-foot baths, canopied beds, warm wooden floors and scattered antiques. Most have balconies or terraces from which to gaze out at rolling countryside. A book-lined library and tranquil terrace complete the classy, rural retreat effect; it all makes it very hard to leave.

Browns BOUTIQUE HOTEL ££
(☑01822-618 68; www.brownsdevon.com; 80 West St, Tavistock; s £88, d £107-263; Ⓟ📶) Browns

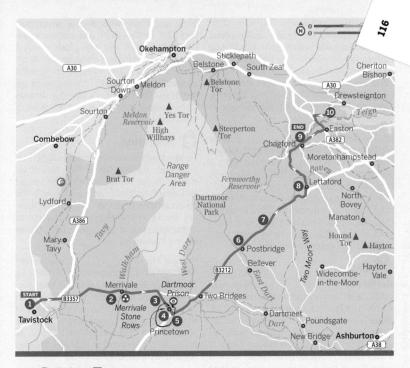

🏃 Driving Tour
A Dartmoor Road Trip

START TAVISTOCK
END CHAGFORD
LENGTH 20 MILES; ONE DAY

Driving on Dartmoor is like being inside a feature film: compelling 360-degree views are screened all around. This scenic, west-to-east transmoor traverse sweeps up and through this wilderness, taking in genteel towns, a bleak prison, prehistoric remains, a rustic pub and a quirky castle. Start by strolling among **1 Tavistock's** fine 19th-century architecture, perhaps dropping by its Pannier Market to rummage for antiques. Next take the B3357 towards Princetown. It climbs steeply, crosses a cattle grid (a sign you're on the moor 'proper') and crests a hill to reveal swathes of honey-coloured tors. Soon you're at **2 Merrivale**. Park up on the right, just after the Dartmoor Inn, and stroll over the rise (due south) to discover a snaking stone row; a tiny stone circle and a standing stone are just 100m further on. Back in the car, after a short climb, turn right towards Princetown,

glimpsing the brooding bulk of Dartmoor Prison (you can't stop here; there's a better vantage point later). Call in at the **3 Dartmoor Prison Heritage Centre** (p117) to explore the jail's grim story. Cut through rugged **4 Princetown**, perhaps taking tea at the Fox Tor Cafe, before picking up the B3212 towards Two Bridges; the **5 lay-by** immediately after you leave Princetown provides prime Dartmoor Prison views. As you follow signs for Moretonhampstead, an expansive landscape unfurls. At **6 Postbridge**, park and stroll over the 700-year-old bridge, then dangle hot feet in the cold River Dart. A few miles further on, the **7 Warren House Inn** (p119) makes an atmospheric spot for lunch. Around **8 Lettaford** take one of the signed, plunging lanes to **9 Chagford** to visit its quaint, thatch-dotted square. Scour some of its wonderfully old-fashioned shops, then head to **10 Castle Drogo** (p121) to explore a unique 1920s stately home. Finish the day back at Chagford at 22 Mill Street, a truly classy spot to eat and sleep.

bursts with boutique-chic. At this 17th-century coaching inn beams and exposed stone sit alongside stained glass and Middle Eastern flourishes. The best bedrooms have mustard-coloured armchairs and antique-effect writing tables; the cheaper rooms can be small, but are still luxurious; Egyptian cotton and Molton Brown toiletries come as standard.

Rockmount
B&B ££

(☑0744 5009880; www.rockmount-tavistock.com; Drake Rd, Tavistock; s £49-55, d £70-110; P 🐾) A real surprise sits behind this hillside B&B's conventional exterior – supremely stylish, streamlined rooms, done out in dark wood, crisp white and flashes of lime. Breakfast (full English or Continental) comes delivered to your door; the views down onto Tavistock will entertain your eye.

✖ Eating

Gortons
BRASSERIE ££

(☑01822-617581; www.gortons-tavistock.co.uk; 19 Plymouth Rd, Tavistock; lunch 2/3 courses £20/25, dinner 2/3 courses £35/42; ⊙noon-2pm Wed-Sat, 7-9pm Tue-Sat) The same chef runs both this smart bistro and the sumptuous Horn of Plenty country-house hotel. This in-town outpost also makes imaginative use of local foodstuffs; the roasted wood pigeon comes with mushroom risotto; the pork tenderloin with a rich port sauce. Take a tip from the locals and book in for a Tuesday pot-luck supper (2/3 courses £25/30); knocking £10 to £12 off the price of each meal.

Browns
BISTRO, FINE DINING ££

(☑01822-618686; www.brownsdevon.com; 80 West St, Tavistock; ⊙bistro 11.30am-9pm, restaurant noon-2.30pm & 7-9pm) With its flagstone floors and squishy sofas, the bistro (mains £6 to £17) at Browns is a top spot to peruse the paper before sampling some gutsy moorland ingredients; perhaps Dartmoor rabbit terrine, or pheasant hot pot with spiced red cabbage. The restaurant (mains £20, six courses £70) cranks the culinary skill up to another level: try the confit chicken with truffled egg yolk, or a real rarity: fallow deer tartare.

Horn of Plenty
FINE DINING £££

(☑01822-832528; www.thehornofplenty.co.uk; Gulworthy, near Tavistock; 3-course lunch/dinner £25/50; ⊙noon-2pm & 7-9pm) Local foodies love the classic, locally sourced, seasonal cuisine at this fine hotel. Flavours are rich: poached duck eggs come with truffled asparagus; beef fillet with ox cheek and marrow crust. Faultless service and the plush, hushed surroundings reinforce a country-house atmosphere that starts when you're greeted by name on the doorstep, having swept up the drive. Their Pot Luck Monday dinners (three courses £29) are a steal. It's 3 miles from Tavistock.

🛍 Shopping

Tavistock offers an appealing insight into moorland market town life. Non-chain stores line the streets, while on the second and fourth Saturday of each month the produce-laden stalls of Tavistock Farmers Market (www.tavistockfarmersmarket.com; ⊙9am-1pm), one of the region's best, fill the central Bedford Sq.

Pannier Market
MARKET

(www.tavistockpanniermarket.co.uk; Bedford Sq, Tavistock; ⊙9am-4.30pm Tue-Sat) A vast, Victorian covered hall that's home to hundreds of stalls stacked with an eclectic range of shabby-chic goodies; there's everything from silver cutlery and second-hand books, to moleskin trousers and tweed caps. Tuesday is particularly good for antiques.

Country Cheeses
FOOD

(www.countrycheeses.co.uk; Market Rd, Tavistock; ⊙9.30-5pm Mon-Sat) Ripe, cheesy aromas wash over you as you step into this award-winning shop. The counters are stacked with oozing, crumbling golden delights. Many are made locally; look out for Slow Tavy (washed in Plymouth Gin), Trehill (with garlic) and Little Stinky (says it all).

ℹ Information

Tavistock Tourist Office (☑01822-612938; The Archway, Bedford Sq; ⊙10am-4pm Mon, Tue, Fri & Sat year round, plus 10am-5pm Mon-Sat Aug & Sep)

ℹ Getting There & Away

Plymouth Bus 83/84/86 (one hour; hourly) Via Yelverton.

Barnstaple 118 (two to five daily) Via Lydfordand Okehampton.

Princetown Bus 98 (25 minutes, six daily, Monday to Saturday)

Postbridge Bus 98 (one daily, Monday to Saturday) Via Two Bridges.

Bus 82/Transmoor Link (p113) Summer weekends only, runs across the moor to Exeter.

Princetown

POP 1767

Set in the heart of the remote, higher moor, Princetown is dominated by the grey, foreboding bulk of Dartmoor Prison. The jail has dictated the town's fortunes for hundreds of years. Princetown began falling into decline when the jail stopped housing prisoners of war in the early 1800s, and parts of the town still have a bleak, neglected feel. But the settlement also offers an intriguing insight into the hard realities of moorland life and makes an atmospheric base for some excellent walks.

◉ Sights & Activities

Dartmoor Prison Heritage Centre MUSEUM
(⌨01822-322130; www.dartmoor-prison.co.uk; Princetown; adult/child £3/2; ◷9.30am-12.30pm & 1.30-4pm; P) Dartmoor jail was built in 1809 to hold first French, then American, prisoners of war. It became a convict prison in 1850, and today is a category C jail, with capacity for 653 inmates. Just up from its looming gates, the Dartmoor Prison Heritage Centre provides a chilling insight into life inside. Look out for the disturbing makeshift knives made by modern prisoners, as well as mock-up cells, straight jackets and manacles. Escapes feature too in the form of sheets tied into ropes and chair legs hammered into grappling hooks. Then there's the tale of Frankie 'the mad axeman' Mitchell, who was supposedly sprung by the '60s gangster twins, the Krays. The centre also sells the bizarrely cheerful garden ornaments made by the prisoners; don't miss the (presumably ironic) neighbourhood-watch figurines.

Princetown Tourist Office HERITAGE CENTRE
(DNPA; ⌨01822-890414; ◷10am-5pm Apr-Sep, to 4pm Oct & Mar, 10.30am-3.30pm Thu-Sun Nov-Feb) Princetown's Tourist Office and Visitor Centre is the main one for the whole moor. Along with leaflets, moorland books and outdoor clothing, it also has worth-visiting heritage displays, including one outlining the links between Princetown and the Sherlock Holmes story, *The Hound of the Baskervilles*. The book's author, Sir Arthur Conan Doyle once stayed at Princetown's Duchy Hotel (now the tourist office itself). Local lore recounts Dartmoor man Henry Baskerville took Conan Doyle on a carriage tour, and the brooding landscape he encountered, coupled with legends of a huge phantom dog, inspired the thriller.

Walks

As the inspiration for *The Hound of the Baskervilles*, the moor around Princetown still evokes the book's locations. From the village centre, the lonely track heading southeast from beside the Plume of Feathers pub leads to Foxtor Mires (the book's Grimpen Mire) 2½ miles away. Many see the nearby Nun's Cross Farm as Merripit House (where the Stapletons lived); and the hut circles half a mile southwest of Princetown (beside the B3212) as the ruins Holmes camped in. To explore, kit yourself out with a compass and an OS map; staff at the Princetown Tourist Office can also advise.

🛏 Sleeping & Eating

Prince of Wales HOSTEL, PUB £
(⌨01822-890219; www.theprinceofwalesprincetown.co.uk; Tavistock Rd; dm £12, breakfast £5; ◷meals noon-2.30pm & 5.30-8pm) The pick of

---

ARCHAEOLOGICAL SITES

With an estimated 11,000 monuments Dartmoor is ripe for archaeological explorations. It has the largest concentration of Bronze Age (c 2300-700 BC) remains in the country, 75 stone rows (half the national total), 18 stone circles and 5000 huts.

The **Merrivale Stone Rows**, near Princetown, are a handy one-stop-shop for many monument types, boasting a parallel stone row, a stone circle, a menhir, burial chambers and dozens of hut circles. To the north east, near Chagford, the **Grey Wethers** stone circles stand side by side on a stretch of open moor; another stone circle is 400m away near Fernworthy. At nearby Gidleigh, **Scorhill Stone Circle** is sometimes called the Stonehenge of Dartmoor, although only half of the original stones remain. The biggest site is the huge Bronze Age village of **Grimspound**, just off the B3212, where you can wander inside the ruins of several round houses, and the circular stone wall that surrounded the entire settlement.

The DNPA runs a series of archaeology-themed walks (£3 to £8) all over the moor, and sells mini-guides to some sites (£4).

Dartmoor's bunkhouses, this former brewery boasts central heating and double glazing (on the moor, this matters), great showers, a sloping-ceilinged crash room and – joy of joys – a drying room. The rustic pub (mains £5 to £16) next door is famous for its three open fires, mixed grill platters the size of tea trays and pints of own-brewed, full-bodied, Jail Ale.

★**Tor Royal Farm**   B&B **££**
(☑ 01822-890189; www.torroyal.co.uk; Tor Royal La, near Princetown; s £55, d £80-100; ℗) Just what a middle-of-the-moor retreat should be: an easy-going, farmhouse packed with lived-in charm. It was built in 1785 for a Secretary to the Prince of Wales and heritage features are everywhere, from the royal, fleur-de-lys plumes on the cornices, to the smart, country-cottage styled bedrooms. The farm's own pork appears on the breakfast table, and you can book horse-riding lessons at their stables just next door.

Two Bridges   LUXURY HOTEL **££**
(☑ 01822-892300; www.twobridges.co.uk; Two Bridges; s £95-120, d £140-190; ℗ 🛜) Walking into this classic moorland hotel feels like slipping on a favourite pair of shoes – everything fits, perfectly. Tuck into a cream tea (£8 to £13) in front of a huge inglenook fireplace, or chill out in classically furnished bedrooms with views out over the tors. Former guests Wallace Simpson, Winston Churchill and Vivien Leigh probably liked it too. Two Bridges is 1.5 miles northeast of Princetown.

Fox Tor Cafe   CAFE **£**
(www.foxtorcafe.com; Two Bridges Rd; mains £5-10; ⊙ 9am-5pm, from 7.30am Sat & Sun; 🚲) Everybody gravitates to Princetown's FTC: hikers, horse riders and cyclists, and local families out for a meal. They're drawn by an open fire, superb coffee, homemade cakes and a surprisingly wide-ranging menu that features hearty chilli and home-cooked ham, egg and chips, as well as mushroom stroganof and a tasty lentil wedge.

❶ Getting There & Away

Bus 98 (three daily, Monday to Saturday) links Princetown with Tavistock, one service a day goes on to Two Bridges and Postbridge.

For summer Sunday services east across the moor, see the Transmoor Link (Bus 82; p113).

Postbridge & Around

The hamlet of Postbridge owes its popularity, and its name, to its medieval stone slab or clapper bridge. This 13th-century structure has four, 3m-long slabs propped up on sturdy columns of stacked stones. Walking across takes you over the rushing East Dart river; paths alongside provide picturesque spots to sit, whip off your boots and plunge your feet into what may feel like the coldest water in the world.

🛏 Sleeping & Eating

Brimpts Farm   CAMPSITE, B&B **£**
(☑ 0845 0345968; www.brimptsfarm.co.uk; site per person £2.50, s/d/f £33/55/82; ℗) The brightly painted, rustic bedrooms above this farmhouse have views over *War Horse* location, Combestone Tor. Converted barns provide another batch of rooms (some self-catering) and there's back-to-nature camping too. Brimpts is also one of the best moorland cream tea venues, offering freshly baked scones, homemade jams and utterly gooey clotted cream (£4.50). The cafe is open 11.30am to 5.30pm weekends and school holidays. The farm is signed off the B3357, Two Bridges–Dartmeet road.

Bellever YHA   HOSTEL **£**
(☑ 0845 371 9622; www.yha.org.uk; d/dm £35/18; ℗ 🛜) A characterful former farm on the edge of a conifer plantation, with a huge kitchen, lots of rustic stone walls, snug doubles and comfy dorms. It's a mile south of Postbridge down an unmarked lane, and is signed off the B3212.

Runnage YHA   HOSTEL **£**
(☑ 0800 0191 700; www.yha.org.uk; dm £9.50; ℗) At this converted hayloft set on a working farm, you'll be rolling out your sleeping bag to a soundtrack of bleating sheep. It's 1.5 miles east of Postbridge: take the 'Widecombe' turning off the Moretonhampstead road.

Lydgate House   B&B **££**
(☑ 01822-880209; www.lydgatehouse.co.uk; Postbridge; s £45-55, d £85-120; ℗ 🛜) Just arriving at this beautifully furnished Victorian house is an atmospheric experience – it's hidden away at the end of a moss-lined track. There are rich tapestries, linens and antique furniture inside; birdsong, a rushing river and total tranquility outside. It's a 10-minute walk from Postbridge.

Warren House Inn PUB £
(www.warrenhouseinn.co.uk; mains £8-12; ⊙bar 11am-11pm, meals noon-8.30pm) This former tin miner's haunt exudes the kind of hospitality you only get in a pub in the middle of no-where. A Dartmoor legend, its stone floors, trestle tables and hearty food are given an extra glow by a fire that's been crackling non-stop since 1845. Try its warrener's (rab-bit) pie; named after the men who used to farm the creatures on the moor. It's on the B3212, two miles north of Postbridge.

ℹ️ Information

Postbridge Tourist Office (☎01822-880272; Postbridge; ⊙10am-5pm Apr-Sep, to 4pm Oct)

ℹ️ Getting There & Away

Bus 98 (one daily, Monday to Saturday) runs to Princetown. Postbridge is also served by the Transmoor Link (p113).

Widecombe-in-the-Moor

POP 566

Widecombe is archetypal Dartmoor, right down to the ponies grazing on a village green framed by honey-grey buildings and a 14th-century church. Widecombe (the 'in-the-Moor' is dropped locally) is commemo-rated in the traditional English folksong, *Widecombe Fair*; the event of the same name takes place on the second Tuesday of September.

◉ Sights

St Pancras Church CHURCH
St Pancras' immense 37m tower has seen it dubbed the Cathedral of the Moor. Inside, search out the brightly painted ceiling boss-es; one near the altar has the three rabbits emblem adopted by Dartmoor's tin miners. Look out too for the antique wooden boards telling the fire-and-brimstone tale of the vio-lent storm of 1638 – it knocked a pinnacle from the roof, killing several parishioners. As ever on Dartmoor the devil was blamed and said to be in search of souls.

🛏️ Sleeping & Eating

Higher Venton Farm B&B £
(☎01364-621235; www.ventonfarm.com; near Widecombe-in-the-Moor; s/d £40/70; ℗) Higher Venton could be used to define the archi-tectural style 'picture-postcard thatch'. A 16th-century farmhouse with low lintels

and a tightly winding staircase, there's not a straight line in the place. Some rooms share bathrooms. It's on a road heading south out of Widecombe; follow Rugglestone Inn signs, and it's half a mile beyond.

Manor Cottage B&B £
(☎01364-621218; www.manorcottagedartmoor. co.uk; Widecombe-in-the-Moor; d £50-60; ℗ 🌐) Roses climb round the doorway of an an-cient Dartmoor cottage that's just a sheep's bleat from Widecombe's picturesque village green. The best billet is a bedroom-bathroom suite at the top of its own spiral staircase (two other doubles share a bathroom). Breakfasts feature berry compote, local sausages, and eggs freshly laid by the hens clucking around outside.

Rugglestone Inn PUB ££
(www.rugglestoneinn.co.uk; Widecombe-in-the-Moor; mains £10; ⊙meals noon-4pm & 6.30-8pm) For a taste of traditional Dartmoor, head to the Rugglestone Inn. Two of the three tiny rooms are warmed by real fires; unvarnished wood-en tables and ancient chairs are scattered around. The flavoursome food is homemade; expect hearty ploughman's, and beef and ale or steak and Stilton pies. Many of the ingredi-ents are provided by local farmers, you'll often find them eating here too.

MYTHICAL DARTMOOR

Dartmoor is laced with myth, and tales of evil forces form a central part of its heritage. Often inspired by the moor's shifting mists and stark, other-worldly nature, many revolve around the Dewer (the Devil). According to legend, he leads his pack of phantom Wisht Hounds across the moor at night, rounding up sinners before driving them off a 100m granite outcrop called the **Dewerstone**. You can stroll to the Dewerstone from **Shaugh Prior**; an idyllic, but also at times chilling, half-mile riverside walk through woods of moss-smothered trees. Shaugh Prior is 12 miles southeast of Tavistock.

Many think tales of the Wisht Hounds inspired *The Hound of the Baskervilles* by Sir Arthur Conan Doyle. More devilish tales crop up at Lydford Gorge (p123), and the St Pancras Church (p119) at Widecombe-in-the-Moor.

ⓘ Getting There & Away

Bus 672 (one weekly, Wednesday) Calls at Buckfastleigh (40 minutes), Ashburton (50 minutes) and Newton Abbot (1 hour).

Bus 193 (twice weekly, Wednesday and Friday) Runs to Newton Abbot and Ashburton.

On summer Saturdays, Widecombe is served by the Haytor Hoppa (p113).

Ashburton

POP 4051

Ashburton is an appealing blend of traditional, edge-of-the-moor town and rustic-chic retreat. Elegant terraces line its winding roads and granite buildings sit beside slate-hung shops where you can buy everything from rucksacks and camping stove fuel, to stylish homewares and upcycled antiques. With some top eat and sleep spots, the town makes a comfortable base for exploring the southern moor.

⬛ Sleeping & Eating

Gages Mill   B&B **£**
(☏ 01364-652391; www.gagesmill.co.uk; Buckfastleigh Rd; s/d/f £60/80/100; Ⓟ) Walk into this easy-going, 14th-century farmhouse and feel instantly at home. The guest lounge is framed by arches of exposed stone, while cheery bedrooms sport gingham checks and the occasional beam. There's a garden to picnic in by day, and a well-stocked honesty bar by night.

⭐ **Agaric @ Tudor House**   B&B **££**
(☏ 01364-654478; www.agaricrestaurant.co.uk; 30 North St; s £58, d £124-140) They may be on the fringe of Dartmoor, but Agaric's impeccable rooms wouldn't be out of place in Soho. Decor ranges from gentleman's club (hard woods and writing desks) to boudoir-esque glam (reclaimed furniture, and glinting lights set in the bathroom floor). A local-food breakfast is cooked as late as you like, and you can help yourself from the tins of homemade cookies on the kitchen shelves.

Agaric Restaurant   BISTRO **££**
(☏ 01364-654478; www.agaricrestaurant.co.uk; 30 North St; 2-course lunch £16, dinner mains £16-23; ⊙noon-2pm Wed-Fri, 7-9pm Wed-Sat) Some of the food you tuck into here has been forraged by the owners, some is dropped off by locals when they have a surplus crop. That sums up Agaric's approach: first-class, local, seasonal produce transformed into fabu-

lous tasting, unfussy food. And whether you tuck into cured meat, terrines, ice cream or cheese, it'll all be homemade.

ⓘ Getting There & Away

Bus X38 (eight daily Monday to Saturday, three on Sunday) goes to Plymouth and Exeter.

Bus 193/672 Runs on Wednesday and Friday (one or two a day) to Widecombe and Newton Abbot.

Moretonhampstead

POP 1786

Moretonhampstead has made a living from through-traffic for centuries but these days a mini-bypass leads many passing cars and tractors away from its central square. The village centre is a pleasant jumble of Georgian houses, shops, pubs and restaurants, and its bustle can be welcome after the remoteness of the higher moor.

⬛ Sleeping

Walled Garden   B&B **£**
(☏ 01647-441353; www.moretonwalledgarden.co.uk; Mount Pleasant; s/d £45/65; Ⓟ🛜) In-vogue bathrooms, snazzy furnishings (think burgundy, blue, or chocolate and gold) and a large, tranquil garden with an outdoor chess set, make this an agreeable, central sleep spot.

Old Post House   B&B **£**
(☏ 01647-440900; www.theoldposthouse.com; 18 Court St; s/d/f £45/60/70) Expect bright prints, colours ranging from pink to cream and simple bedrooms in this village-centre terrace. The huge family room has sweeping, fringe-of-moor views.

White Hart   HOTEL **££**
(☏ 01647-440500; www.whitehartdartmoor.co.uk; The Square; s £65-75, d £110-130; ⊙meals 12.30-2.30pm & 6.30-9pm; Ⓟ🛜) The mail coaches used to change horses here in Georgian days; today it's a comfortable hotel with beams and bow ceilings and tartan carpets. The restaurant does classy bar food (mains £11 to £20).

✕ Eating

Michael Howard   DELI **£**
(www.michael-howard-butchers.co.uk; 7 Court St; ⊙9am-5pm Mon-Sat) The perfect moorland refueling stop: olives and local cheeses sit alongside pasties, pies and tempting cakes. They do takeaway hot drinks too.

★**White Horse** GASTROPUB **££**
(📞01647-440242; www.whitehorsedevon.co.uk; 7 George St; mains £5-19; ⊙12.30-2.30pm Tue-Sat, 6.30-9pm daily) With a style somewhere between boho-chic and casual country house, this funky gastropub makes for a chilled-out hang-out. Mediterranean-themed goodies crowd a menu that ranges from pizzas and Dartmoor beef bresaola, to (worth-forking-out-for) à la carte.

ℹ Getting There & Away

Exeter Bus 359 (50 minutes, five daily, Monday to Saturday).
Chagford Bus 173/178 (15 minutes, three daily, Monday to Saturday)
Transmoor Link (p113) Summer weekends only.

Chagford

POP 1479
With its wonky thatches and cream-and white-fronted buildings, Chagford gathers round a busy square, apparently every inch a timeless moorland town. But the purveyors of waxed jackets and hip flasks have also been joined by health-food shops, contemporary pottery galleries, and some supremely stylish places to eat and sleep.

◉ Sights

Castle Drogo HISTORIC BUILDING
(NT; 📞01647-433306; www.nationaltrust.org.uk; near Drewsteignton; adult/child £8.70/4.30; ⊙11am-5pm mid-Feb to Oct; 🅿) This gorgeous, stately home is the last castle to be built in England. The imposing grey edifice was designed by Sir Edwin Lutyens for self-made food-millionaire Julius Drewe, and was constructed between 1911 and 1931. The brief was to combine the medieval grandeur of a castle and the comforts of a 20th-century country house. The result is a delightful blend of crenellated battlements, cosy carpeted interiors and (how practical) a good central-heating system. The gardens are influenced by Gertrude Jekyll and the woodland trails have alpine-esque views over Dartmoor and the plunging Teign Gorge. Castle Drogo is 3 miles northeast of Chagford.

🛏 Sleeping

Easton Court B&B **£**
(📞01647-433469; www.easton.co.uk; Easton; s/d £65/80; 🅿🛜) It's worth staying here just for the breakfasts: choices include fresh fish or soufflé omelette. The rooms are lovely too, with their cast-iron beds, soft sofas and views of wooded hills. It's 1½ miles from Chagford.

Sandy Park INN **£**
(📞01647-433267; www.sandyparkinn.co.uk; Sandy Park, near Chagford; d £60-70; ⊙meals noon-2.30pm & 6-9pm Mon-Fri, noon-9pm Sat & Sun; 🅿🛜) Part pub, part chic place to stay, at this 17th-century thatch you can sip a pint of real ale in an atmospheric, exposed-beam bar, sample cracking Dartmoor fare in the restaurant (mains £12), then totter upstairs to sleep amid plump pillows and bright furnishings.

★**22 Mill Street** B&B **££**
(📞01647-432244; www.22millst.com; 22 Mill St; d £130-170; 🅿🛜) The super-sleek rooms of this boutique beauty feature exposed stone walls, wooden floorboards and slatted blinds, offset by satin cushions and bursts of modern art. Molton Brown toiletries dot the bathrooms and Chagford's quaint village centre is just outside the front door.

Gidleigh Park LUXURY HOTEL **£££**
(📞01647-432367; www.gidleigh.com; Gidleigh, near Chagford; d £345-550, ste £575-1195; 🅿🛜) A prestigious oasis of ultimate luxury, Gidleigh teams crests, crenellations and roaring fires with shimmering sanctuaries of blue marble, waterproof TVs and private saunas. Impeccable but unstuffy service and countless thoughtful touches (your own decanter of port; an always-raidable guest pantry) help you feel at home. The restaurant is double-Michelin-starred, and the tennis courts, bowling greens and croquet lawns help keep you trim. It's 2 miles from Chagford.

DARTMOOR'S OUTDOOR POOLS

Considering its 368-sq-miles of land-locked hills, Dartmoor might not seem like an ideal spot for an al fresco dip. But it is. Moretonhampstead, Chagford, Bovey Tracey, Buckfastleigh and Ashburton each have small and elegant outdoor pools, which swarm with local families once the temperatures soar. They're often solar heated, admission is normally a few pounds, and they tend to be open from June to August. Times vary; local tourist offices can advise.

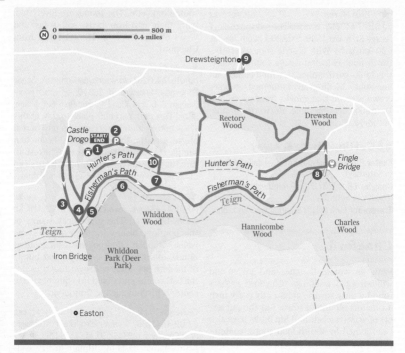

Walking Tour
Dartmoor's Teign Gorge

START CASTLE DROGO
END CASTLE DROGO
LENGTH 4 MILES; FIVE HOURS

Tree-clad and sheer-sided, the spectacular Teign Valley also boasts a unique stately home, an unspoilt village and a classic inn.

After exploring intriguing **1 Castle Drogo** (p121), pick up Teign Valley Walk signs from the **2 car park**, onto the (signed) Hunters Path, down rough-earth steps towards Iron Bridge (later signed Dogmarsh Bridge). This skirts the slopes in front of the castle, revealing cracking views of Dartmoor and the plunging gorge. Head towards Fisherman's Path, past thatched **3 Gib House**, ponds and bluebell woods. It's a steep descent around **4 Hunter's Tor** to the Fisherman's Path (don't cross the bridge); next scramble over tree roots beside the River Teign and head towards Fingle Bridge, looking out for dipper, kingfisher, salmon and trout. Soon **5 Drogo Weir** appears. Designed by Castle Drogo's architect, Sir Edwin Lutyens, it powered the castle's own hydroelectric power station; the weir's **6 Turbine House** is further on, hidden in the trees on the opposite bank. Scramble up steep steps around **7 Sharp Tor**. At three-arched **8 Fingle Bridge**, refuel at the namesake inn which offers warm fires, riverside terraces and food all day. Head away from the bridge, then switchback left up Hunter's Path to climb sharply up the gorge. Crest a rise and see the steep tree-covered valley, the River Teign far below (listen for its tumblings) and the Dartmoor's hills.

Now head sharp right, following signs for Drewsteignton, and onto the Drewston/Rectory Woods walk. It leads through conifers to **9 Drewsteignton** village; a cluster of thatches, traditional stores and a 15th-century church. If the Drewe Arms has re-opened perhaps pause for a drink. Next head towards Hunter's Path, turning right once you reach it (signed Road Near Drogo). Drink in more spectacular views, before skirting the top of Sharp Tor then cutting up through **10 Piddledown Common**, and back to your car.

Eating

22 Mill Street
RESTAURANT ££

(☑ 01647-432244; www.22millst.com; 22 Mill St, Chagford; lunch mains £15, dinner 2/3/5 courses £20/25/70; ☺ noon-2.30pm & 7-9pm Wed-Sat) The imaginative dishes rustled up by this intimate little restaurant are packed with produce from the moors and the shores. Look out for smoked potato soup, spiced Cornish venison, and Brixham John Dory with cockles. Round it all off with the textured chocolate and dark-ale ice cream.

★ Gidleigh Park
FINE DINING £££

(☑ 01647-432367; www.gidleigh.com; Gidleigh, near Chagford; 2-/3-course lunch £42/55, 3-/8-course dinner £110/135; ☺ noon-2.30pm & 7-9.30pm) Welcome to Devon's top eatery: a double-Michelin-starred restaurant set in a luxury Arts and Crafts–era hotel. Classic French techniques transform local ingredients; Devon quail, Brixham scallops and Dartmoor lamb are all accompanied with purée, velouté or jus – the effect is stunning and the meals truly memorable. The wine cellar has some 1100 prestige bins; you can even book a personal tour.

❶ Getting There & Away

Moretonhampstead Bus 173 (15 minutes, twice a day, Monday to Saturday)

Exeter Bus 173 (1 hour, five daily Monday to Saturday)

Okehampton Bus 178 (40 minutes, one daily, Monday to Saturday)

Lydford

POP 376

A winding string of ancient granite cottages, plus a ruined castle and a gorgeous gorge; Lydford makes for a perfectly peaceful night's stop. This tranquil backwater was once the administrative centre of the whole moor, and in the Saxon times of Aethelred II, royal coins were also minted here.

◉ Sights & Activities

Lydford Gorge
WATERFALL

(NT; ☑ 01822-820320; www.nationaltrust.org.uk; Lydford; adult/child £6/3; ☺ 10am-5pm mid-Mar to Sep, to 4pm Oct; ℗) Three miles of trails zigzag down what is the deepest river gorge in the southwest. Oak woods close in on all sides and the temperature drops. The riverside route leads to the 30m-high **White Lady Waterfall**, an impressive cascade that thunders down from sheer rocks. Rugged trails also weave past a series of bubbling whirlpools; you can actually walk out over the fearsome **Devil's Cauldron**, which seems to have been scooped out of the surrounding mossy rocks.

Lydford Castle
CASTLE

(☺ open access) **FREE** Lydford's diminutive 13th-century castle sits in the heart of the village. Now a compact, roofless cube, it used to double as a jail and helped make 'Lydford Law' notorious as a 'hang 'em first, ask questions later' system.

🛏 Sleeping & Eating

Dartmoor Inn
INN ££

(☑ 01822-820221; www.dartmoorinn.com; Moorside, Lydford; d £100; ☺ meals noon-2.30pm & 6.45-9pm, plus noon-2.30pm Sun; ℗) They've pulled off the ancient-meets-modern trick superbly here. Flagstone floors, roaring open fires and horse brasses hung from beams surround crowds of diners tucking into elegant gastropub cooking (mains £13 to £22), while distressed furniture, lavish fabrics and Roberts radios fill chic bedrooms. Irresistible.

Castle
INN ££

(☑ 01822-820241; www.castleinndartmoor.co.uk; Lydford; d £60-100; ☺ meals noon-9pm; ℗ 🛜) The bedrooms in this Elizabethan inn range from small and simple to spacious and luxurious – bag room 1 for a double shower, private deck and Lydford Castle views. The bar is the ultimate snug: lamp-light bathes bow ceilings and high-backed benches, while the food is hearty Dartmoor pub fare (mains £8 to £22).

Lydford Country House
B&B, SELF CATERING ££

(☑ 01822-820347; www.lydfordcountryhouse.co.uk; Lydford; s £75, d £115-150, f £145-155; ℗ 🛜) Sleek rooms dotted with gleaming, mango-wood furniture overlook tor tops while antiques and deep sofas fill the vast guest lounge. A four-person self-catering apartment takes up the entire top floor (per week £700), the Granite Way cycle path snakes past the door, and you can stable your horse here too.

❶ Getting There & Away

Bus 118 (two to five daily) runs north to Okehampton (15 minutes) and onto Barnstaple, and south to Tavistock (30 minutes).

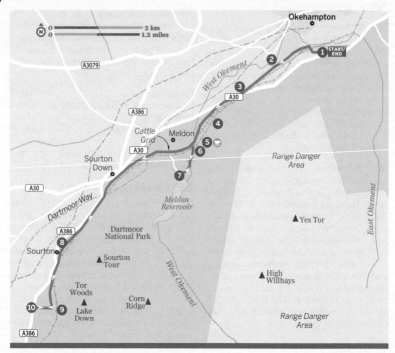

🚴 Cycling Tour
Granite Way

START OKEHAMPTON YHA
END OKEHAMPTON YHA
LENGTH 12 MILES (RETURN); FOUR HOURS

Dartmoor's now tranquil wilderness used to bustle with quarrying and mining; this traffic-free, relatively level ride teams striking scenery with insights into that past.

The Granite Way traces the route of a railway line, built to shuttle industrial cargoes off the moor. Hire a bike from ❶ **Adventure Okehampton** (p110) and head downhill, under the railway bridge, turning left onto the Granite Way (National Cycle Route 27). Shadow the railway line, forking left under a stone bridge; soon ❷ **Okehampton Castle's** (p124) ruins emerge on your right. A bit further on, head left through the ❸ **gate**, under the busy A30. After ❹ **Meldon Quarry's** *Dr Who*-esque landscape of rocks and waste piles, a ridge of tors emerges, including Dartmoor's highest point: High Wilhays (621m). ❺ **Meldon Buffet**, a cafe/visitor centre in former railway carriages makes an unusual

tea stop, just before the ❻ **Meldon Viaduct**; an 1874 steel structure spanning 165m with views of the deep tor-fringed valley ahead. Next detour left (signed Meldon Reservoir) to 45m high ❼ **Meldon Dam**, a reservoir with waterside walking trails. Back on the main Granite Way, cycle south, dog-legging beside a cattle grid, where the landscape suddenly widens, exposing open moorland sweeping up to Sourton Tors. Explore the 14th-century ❽ **St Thomas a Becket church** at Sourton, which pops up beside the track. Eventually multi-arched, granite ❾ **Lake Viaduct** appears; a stunning structure offering more gorse moorland views. Soon, a sign points left towards the Bearslake Inn; a steep path onto a rough track which leads under the viaduct itself, over wooden bridges and beside a stream, before emerging at the thatched ❿ **Bearslake Inn**, which serves classy bar food (12.30pm to 2pm and 6pm to 9pm). Then, retrace your steps back to the Granite Way, and Okehampton. You're nearly home when the precarious ruins of Okehampton Castle peel into view.

Okehampton

POP 5922

Okehampton has a staging post feel. The town huddles on the edge of an uninhabited tract of bracken-covered slopes and granite tors – a mind-expanding landscape known as the higher moor. With traditional shops and pubs, it's a good place to stock up before a foray into the wilderness.

Sights & Activities

Okehampton Castle   CASTLE

(EH; ☑ 01837-52844; www.english-heritage.org.uk; Castle Lodge, Okehampton; adult/child £4/2.30; ☺ 10am-5pm Apr-Oct, to 6pm Jul & Aug) For a picturesque slice of history, it's hard to beat these towering, crumbling walls teetering on the top of a wooded spur just above the cascading River Okement. Although started as a motte-and-bailey affair by the Normans, it also has 14th-century additions and at one time was the largest castle in Devon. Paths and flights of steps trace between its reputedly haunted walls, revealing views of bracken-covered moors in the distance.

Finch Foundry   HISTORIC SITE

(NT; ☑ 01837-840046; www.nationaltrust.org.uk; Sticklepath; adult/child £5/2; ☺ 11am-5pm mid-Mar to Oct; ℗) The last working water-powered forge in England dates from the 19th-century and still rings to the sound of metal being hammered. It sits at the end of a 5-mile hike through a boulder strewn river-valley along the Tarka Trail from Okehampton.

Sleeping & Eating

White Hart   INN £

(☑ 01837-52730; www.thewhitehart-hotel.com; Fore St; s/d £72/87; ☺ pizzas 6-9.30pm Wed-Sat; ℗) Coaching inns don't come much more established than this 17th-century town-centre hostelry. Some bathrooms may need a little TLC, but bedrooms are comfy, with wrought-iron candelabras, warming pans and beams scattered all round. Its freshly made pizzas (£9) help satisfy carb cravings after a day out on the moors.

Bracken Tor YHA   HOSTEL £

(☑ 0844 293 0555; www.yha.org.uk; Saxongate; d/dm £25/20; ℗ @) A perfect base for hikes – this 100-year-old country house sits in 1.6 hectares of grounds on the fringe of the higher moor. It's a mile south of Okehampton. Note, there's another hostel in Okehampton itself, which is also home to Adventure Okehampton (p110), which runs adventure activities.

Collaven Manor   B&B ££

(☑ 01837-861522; www.collavenmanor.co.uk; Sourton, near Okehampton; d £98-140; ℗) At this delightful, clematis-clad mini-manor house a wooden chandelier crowns a 16th-century hall, while restful bedrooms are lined with tapestries and window seats – soothing places to enjoy tor-top views. Collaven Manor is 5 miles west of Okehampton.

Eat Toast   CAFE £

(www.eattoast.co.uk; Market St; mains from £6; ☺ 9.30am-5pm Mon-Sat) It's a winning combination: a quirky kitchenware shop that shares a cavernous, brick-lined space with a laid-back cafe. The aroma of freshly ground coffee fills the air, brightly coloured utensils fill the shelves, while the big leather sofas are the perfect spot for a latte and cake or a charcuterie plate.

Information

Tourist Office (☑ 01837-53020; www.okehamptondevon.co.uk; Museum Courtyard, 3 West St, Okehampton; ☺ 10am-4.30pm Mon-Sat Easter-Oct, 10am-4.30pm Mon, Tue, Fri & Sat Nov-Easter)

Getting There & Away

Bus X9 (six daily Monday to Saturday) Runs to Exeter (55 minutes) and Bude (one hour).

Bus 178 (one daily, Monday to Saturday) Goes to Chagford (30 minutes) and Moretonhampstead (one hour).

Bus 118 (two to five daily) Runs to Lydford, Tavistock and Barnstaple.

PLYMOUTH & DARTMOOR OKEHAMPTON

Exmoor & North Devon

Includes ➡

Exmoor
National Park............128

Dulverton................... 130

Dunster & Around 132

Porlock & Around 134

Lynton & Lynmouth....137

North Devon 138

Ilfracombe 139

Croyde, Braunton &
Around........................ 141

Bideford, Appledore
& Around 145

Hartland Peninsula 148

Best Places to Eat

➡ Mason's Arms (p144)

➡ Woods (p130)

➡ Terra Madre (p145)

➡ Rising Sun (p138)

➡ Reeve's (p134)

Best Places to Stay

➡ Vintage Vardos (p144)

➡ Millers at the Tors (p137)

➡ Berridon Farm (p148)

➡ Broomhill Art Hotel (p144)

➡ Tarr Farm (p130)

Why Go?

Thousands of holidaymakers peel past this region on their way to the (undeniably lovely) holiday spots further west. So they miss Exmoor, an enchanting national park, where heather-clad hills are roamed by wild ponies and red deer. Villages huddle cosily beside precipitous cliffs; dramatic headlands plunge towards mossy gorges; sturdy towns deliver an authentic slice of rural life.

North Devon's charms are also worth the detour: classic surf breaks; a wild, jagged coast with vast expanses of sand; plus pretty villages, striking modern art, fine gardens and stately homes. Everywhere, restaurants serve just-caught seafood and produce fresh from furrow and farm, while sleep options range from comfy camping and vintage caravans, to art-packed boutique hotels. That's why your Exmoor and North Devon detour just might end up being your destination.

Much of Exmoor is in Somerset, but some is in Devon, so for complete coverage we've included the whole national park in this guide.

When to Go?

➡ **Apr & May** Vivid bluebells carpet woods; bright yellow gorse dots Exmoor. At Easter, attractions open.

➡ **Jun–Aug** By late-July, blooming heather turns Exmoor into a sea of purple. Expect (possibly) warmer days, but also more demands on accommodation.

➡ **Sep & Oct** Holiday crowds disperse, leaving (hopefully) reasonable weather and warmer seas, and definitely cheaper sleeping bills. Freshly gathered mushrooms enliven restaurant menus. Early October brings the spectacle of stags battling it out, as Exmoor's deer rut begins.

➡ **Dec** Short winter days reveal north Devon and Exmoor's exceptionally dark skies. Enjoy the magical, mischievous Dunster by Candlelight celebrations.

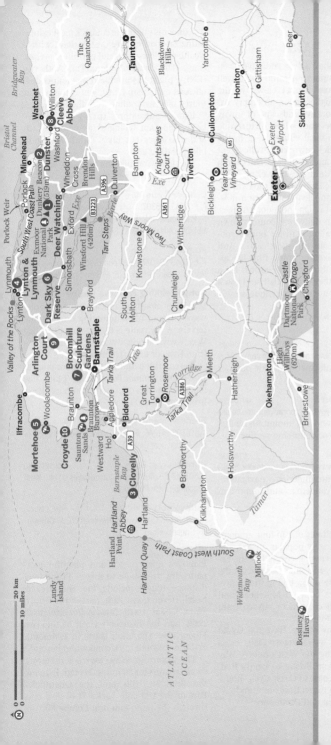

Exmoor & North Devon Highlights

1 Seeing stags lock antlers in **Exmoor National Park** (p129)

2 Exploring the heritage at the **castle** (p133) in Dunster

3 Strolling the steep, cobbled streets of the supremely pretty fishing village of **Clovelly** (p147)

4 Rattling up sheer cliffs in a water-powered **railway** (p137) at Lynton and Lynmouth

5 Seeing a shepherd and sheepdog herd their flock around **Mortehoe** cliffs (p139)

6 Marvelling at star displays in Europe's first **International Dark Sky Reserve** (p133)

7 Finding 300 contemporary art works in the **Broomhill Sculpture Gardens** (p144)

8 Roaming the Cistercian site of **Cleeve Abbey** (p133)

9 Discovering a horse-drawn carriage collection at **Arlington Court** (p144)

10 Riding the waves at Devon's surf-central **Croyde** (p141)

EXMOOR NATIONAL PARK

Exmoor is more than a little addictive. Even when you get home, your mind could well return to its broad, russet views. In the middle sits the higher moor, an empty, expansive, other-worldly landscape of tawny grasses and huge skies. Here picturesque Exford makes an ideal village base. In the north, sheer, rock-strewn river valleys cut into the plateau and coal-black cliffs lurch toward the sea. Amid these towering headlands, charismatic Porlock, and the twin villages of Lynton and Lynmouth are atmospheric places to stay. On the moor's fringes, relaxed Dulverton delivers a country town vibe, while appealing Dunster boasts cobbled streets and an arresting castle. And everywhere on Exmoor you'll find life attuned to the rhythm of the seasons; it's a glimpse into another world. Visit, and you'll be preparing to return before you leave.

Activities

Adventure

Active Exmoor OUTDOORS
(☑01398-324599; www.activeexmoor.com) Has comprehensive information about outdoor activities.

Exmoor Adventures OUTDOORS
(☑01643-863536; www.exmooradventures.co.uk) Runs kayaking, canoeing, mountain biking, coasteering and rock climbing sessions.

Mountains+Moor OUTDOORS
(☑07773 215 657; www.mountainsandmoor.co.uk) Lessons in mountaineering, navigation, rock climbing, canoeing, and mountain biking.

Cycling

Despite the sometimes one-in-four gradient hills, cycling is hugely popular on Exmoor. The pick of the scenery is covered by the Exmoor Cycle Route, a 56-mile loop tracing the 2007 Tour of Britain leg, taking in the precipitous gradients between Minehead and Lynmouth, and a cross-moor stretch from Lynton and Wheddon Cross.

Several sections of the National Cycle Network (NCN; www.sustrans.org.uk) cross the park, including the West Country Way (NCN route 3) from Bristol to Land's End, and the Devon Coast-to-Coast Cycle Route (NCN route 27) between Ilfracombe and Plymouth, via Exmoor and Dartmoor.

Exmoor is one of the county's most exhilarating off-road cycling destinations, with a wealth of bridle-paths and permitted cycling tracks. The Exmoor National Park Authority (ENPA; p129) has produced a colour-coded, off-road cycle map (£10); you can buy it at tourist offices or online from the ENPA.

Exmoor Adventures (p128) runs a five-hour mountain biking skills course (£50) and also hires out bikes (adult mountain bike per day £25).

The following bike hire outlets are also recommended:

Exmoor Cycle Hire BIKE RENTAL
(☑01643-705307; www.exmoorcyclehire.co.uk; 6 Parkhouse Rd, Minehead; adult per day/week £14/50, child day/week £8/28)

Pompys BIKE RENTAL
(☑01643-704077; www.pompyscycles.co.uk; Mart Rd, Minehead; per day £15; ⊙9am-5pm Mon-Sat)

Pony Trekking & Horse Riding

With open moorland and 300 miles of bridleways, Exmoor offers tempting horse-riding terrain. A key route is the 36-mile Coleridge Way (www.coleridgeway.co.uk), which winds from Exmoor to the Quantocks.

You can ride a diminutive Exmoor pony at Dulverton's Exmoor Pony Centre (p130). The following stables offer pony and horse treks from around £40 for a 2-hour ride:

Brendan Manor Stables HORSE RIDING
(☑01598-741246; www.ridingonexmoor.co.uk; Brendon Manor, near Lynton)

Burrowhayes Farm HORSE RIDING
(☑01643-862463; www.burrowhayes.co.uk; West Luccombe, near Porlock)

Outovercott Stables HORSE RIDING
(☑01598-753341; www.outovercott.co.uk; Outovercott, near Lynton)

Walking

Exmoor's open moors and plentiful footpaths are irresistible to hikers. Prime long distance routes include the Somerset & North Devon Coast Path, part of the South West Coast Path (www.southwestcoastpath.com), and the Exmoor section of the Two Moors Way. The latter starts in Lynmouth and travels south to Dartmoor and beyond.

The Coleridge Way (www.coleridgeway.co.uk) weaves for 36 miles through Exmoor, the Brendon Hills and the Quantocks. Part of the 180-mile Tarka Trail also cuts through the park; join it at Combe Martin,

WILDLIFE WATCHING

Exmoor supports one of England's largest wild red-deer populations, best experienced in autumn when the annual 'rutting' season means stags can be seen bellowing, charging and clashing horns in an attempt to impress their prospective mates. Despite their numbers, these skittish creatures are notoriously difficult to spot without some local knowledge. Two to four times a month, the ENPA runs memorable early morning and evening Deer Search Walks (£3 to £5), which involve scrabbling around the moors and combes, talking in whispers, trying to spot the animals.

You can also head out on an organised jeep safari to combine scenic sightseeing with a couple of hours of off-road wildlife-spotting. Experienced companies include the following:

Barle Valley Safaris (☑ 07977 571 494; www.exmoorwildlifesafaris.co.uk; Fore St, Dulverton; safari £30)

Discovery Safaris (☑ 01643-863444; www.discoverysafaris.com; Porlock; safari £25)

Exmoor Safari (☑ 01643-831229; www.exmoorsafari.co.uk; Exford; safari £33)

Red Stag Safari (☑ 01643-841831; www.redstagsafari.co.uk; location varies; safari £25-38)

---

hike along the cliffs to Lynton and Lynmouth, then head across the moor towards Barnstaple.

The Exmoor National Park Authority (p129) organises walks throughout the year. Its autumn dawn safaris to view rutting stags are superb, as are its summertime evening deer-watching hikes. Pick up the *Exmoor Visitor* magazine for full details.

🛏 Sleeping

The only YHA hostel inside the national park boundaries is at Exford, although there is one at Minehead. For more basic accommodation, there are also camping barns at Northcombe Farm and at Mullacott Farm; you'll need all the usual camping supplies.

ℹ Information

TOURIST OFFICES

There are three Exmoor National Park Authority (ENPA) tourist offices around the park – the main one is in Dulverton. All are open from 10am to 5pm daily in Exmoor's main tourist season (late-March to October), with more limited hours in winter.

Dulverton Tourist Office (ENPA; ☑ 01398-323841; www.exmoor-nationalpark.gov.uk; 7-9 Fore St)

Dunster Tourist Office (ENPA; ☑ 01643-821835; www.exmoor-nationalpark.gov.uk; Dunster Steep)

Lynmouth Tourist Office (ENPA; ☑ 01598-752509; www.exmoor-nationalpark.gov.uk; The Esplanade) Recently moved to a new home, near the Cliff Railway.

WEBSITES

Exmoor National Park Authority (ENPA; www.exmoor-nationalpark.gov.uk) The official ENPA site.

Visit Exmoor (www.visit-exmoor.info) Useful advice on activities, events, accommodation and eating out, on this official tourist website.

What's On Exmoor (www.whatsonexmoor.com) General information.

ℹ Getting Around

BUS

Various buses serve Exmoor's main towns and villages, all of which are listed at the useful **ExploreMoor** (www.exploremoor.co.uk) website. Be aware, some services are seasonal.

Some key routes:

Bus 398 (six daily Monday to Saturday) Year round, cuts through the moor from Minehead to Tiverton via Dunster, Wheddon Cross and Dulverton. One bus a day stops at Exford.

Bus 300 (three daily May to October, no Sunday service November to April) Heads along the coast from Minehead to Lynmouth, via Porlock.

Bus 309/310 (nine daily, Monday to Saturday) Year round, runs from Barnstaple, via Parracombe to Lynmouth.

MoorRover (☑ 01643-709701) On-demand minibus that can take you anywhere on Exmoor. Prices range from £10 to £30, depending on distances involved. It'll also carry bikes and provide a luggage transfer service. Book at least a day ahead.

TRAIN

The West Somerset Railway (p133) runs between Taunton and Minehead via Dunster (April to October, four to seven trains daily).

Dulverton

POP 2500

The southern gateway to Exmoor National Park, Dulverton is tucked into the base of the Barle Valley near the confluence of two key rivers: the Exe and Barle. A traditional country town, its home to a collection of gun-sellers, fishing-tackle stores and gift shops, and makes an attractive edge-of-moor base.

Sights

Tarr Steps LANDMARK

Exmoor's most famous landmark is an ancient, 17-span stone bridge, whose huge slabs rest on stone columns sunk into the River Barle. It's the longest clapper bridge in England and local folklore declares it was built by the devil for sunbathing. Early versions probably date from Tudor times; in 2012 it had to be re-built after flood damage.

The steps are 7 miles northwest of Dulverton, and are signed off the B3223 Dulverton-Simonsbath road.

Exmoor Pony Centre WILDLIFE RESERVE

(☑01398-323093; www.exmoorponycentre.org.uk; Ashwick, near Dulverton; ☺10am-4pm Sun-Fri Easter-Oct; ᴘ) FREE You'll see them cantering across the open hills, but this is the best way to get up close to Exmoor's stubby ponies. Originally bred as beasts of burden, despite their diminutive size they're famously hardy. Simply visit the stables, or book for a half-day pony experience (£45), where you groom and tack up, then go on a two-hour moorland hack (for competent riders under 82.5kg only).

Sleeping

Tarr Farm HOTEL ££

(☑01643-851507; www.tarrfarm.co.uk; Tarr Steps; s/d £90/150; ᴘ🛜) This is the place to really lose yourself: a charming farmhouse nested among the woods near Tarr Steps, 7 miles from Dulverton. The nine rooms are spacious and luxurious, with spoil-yourself extras such as organic bath goodies and homemade biscuits.

Streamcombe Farm B&B, CAMPSITE ££

(☑01398-323775; www.streamcombefarm.co.uk; www.exmoorgreenandwild.co.uk; Streamcombe La, near Dulverton; camping per person £10, d £85-110; ᴘ) You can't get much more rural than this enchanting 18th-century farmhouse. Rustic, gingham-themed bedrooms feature chimney breasts and reclaimed joists. The only sounds are the sheep, dear and pheasants outside. There's also back-to-nature woodland camping, a two-person, shabby-chic shepherd's hut (£65), and a cookery school in the barn.

Town Mills B&B ££

(☑01398-323124; www.townmillsdulverton.co.uk; High St; s/d £65/95; ᴘ🛜) The top choice if you want to stay in central Dulverton. The bedrooms in this converted, riverside mill are thoroughly contemporary, with creamy carpets, magnolia walls and bits of floral artwork. A covetable collection of Tintin artwork lines the stairs.

Three Acres B&B ££

(☑01398-323730; www.threeacrescountryhouse.co.uk; Brushford, near Dulverton; d £90-120; ᴘ🛜) Home to a retired army officer in the 1930s, evidence of that era is everywhere: from the pith helmet on the hat rack to the overstuffed armchairs in the lounge. The colour schemes reflect Exmoor's landscape: soft heather-purple, dusky green and russet browns. There's also wortleberry jam for breakfast, a peaceful sun-terrace, and homeade sloe gin in the bar.

Eating

Exclusive Cake Co BAKERY £

(www.exclusivecakecompany.co.uk; 19 High St; from £3; ☺9am-4pm Mon-Fri, 8am-2pm Sat) Gourmet goodies stack the shelves, with classy versions of regular loaves and cakes, plus real rarities: leek, feta and cheddar bread; ginger chocolate tiffin; venison and port pie (note the typically-Exmoor warning: 'Game pies may contain lead shot').

Mortimers CAFE £

(☑01398-323850; 13 High St; mains from £6; ☺9am-5pm Thu-Tue) Top-class and exotic teas, plus crumbly cakes and Dulverton rarebits. It opens late for pizzas in summer (till 9pm Thursday to Saturday).

Woods BISTRO ££

(☑01398-324007; www.woodsdulverton.co.uk; 4 Bank Sq; mains £11-17; ☺noon-2pm & 6-9.30pm) Woods has got rustic chic down to a fine art, both in its decor and its dishes. Deer antlers hang on rough stone walls, trestle tables sit beside wood-panelled booths. Exmoor beef, lamb, pigeon and cheeses fill the menu, often with intriguing accompaniments – look out for mozzarella, pickled wild mushrooms and samphire.

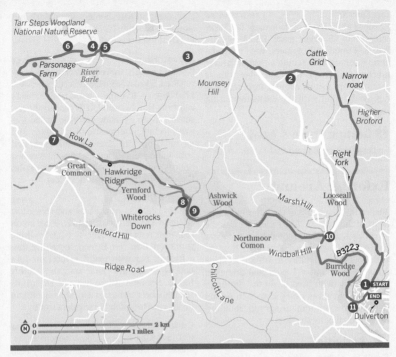

Tarr Steps Woodland National Nature Reserve

Parsonage Farm

River Barle

Mounsey Hill

Cattle Grid

Narrow road

Higher Broford

Right fork

Row La

Great Common

Hawkridge Ridge

Yernford Wood

Ashwick Wood

Marsh Hill

Looseall Wood

Whiterocks Down

Venford Hill

Northmoor Comon

Windball Hill

B3223

Ridge Road

Chilcott Lane

Burridge Wood

START

END

Dulverton

2 km
1 miles

🚶 Walking Tour
Exmoor's Tarr Steps

START DULVERTON CHURCH, FORE ST
END FORE ST, DULVERTON
LENGTH 12 MILES; EIGHT HOURS

High heathland, wild ponies, wooded glens, an ancient inn and Exmoor's most famous beauty spot – see it all on this classic walk.

Skirt the south side of **1 Dulverton church**, joining the up-hill track. Ignore the path leading left to Marsh Bridge, instead cross the field, take the right fork, then climb to turn left onto a narrow road. Cut left onto a blue-labelled footpath, past **2 Higher-combe Farm** and onto the moor. Head right at the road, then straight on at the cattle grid. Soon there's another road and cattle grid; cut left here, onto the open moorland and **3 Winsford Hill**'s lower slopes. The valley views are fabulous; look out for the free-roaming Exmoor ponies with anchor brands on their backs.

Eventually high moorland gives way to a wooded river valley, where a right fork leads to the mighty stone slabs of **4 Tarr Steps**

(p130). After an icy paddle (if the river isn't flooded), the **5 Tarr Farm Inn** (p132) is an idyllic spot for lunch.

Cross the Barle via those massive stone steps, then peel right following the blue waymarked route up **6 Parsonage Farm drive**. At the road, go straight on through the fields (by now following yellow waymarks) into the village of **7 Hawkridge**. Head past the church to fork right down Row Lane, joining the Exe Valley Way to Dulverton. This plunges back into the tranquil woodland framing the river: a mossy, Tolkien-esque landscape of ancient trees, that's home to dormice, frogs and otters. As you cross the stone footbridge at **8 Castle Bridge**, the wood-fringed embankments of the Iron Age hillfort **9 Mounsey Castle** rise from the opposite bank. The footpath then hugs a river that snakes to **10 Marsh Bridge**; stay on the south side of the waterway here. Follow it back to Dulverton, walking over the **11 River Barle bridge**, up Bridge St, then High St and back to Fore St.

Tarr Farm Inn RESTAURANT ££
(☎ 01643-851507; www.tarrfarm.co.uk; Tarr Steps; snacks from £5, dinner mains £11-23; ◷ noon-2pm & 6-9pm) All comers are welcome here: walkers and families devour hearty lunches and cream teas, after-dark diners sample more formal country fare, which is deservedly a hit with the Barbour-wearing regulars.

❶ Getting There & Away

For buses to/from Dulverton, see p129.

Exford & Around

POP 500

Tucked into the banks of the River Exe at the heart of the moor, Exford's pleasing muddle of cottages and slate-roofed houses cluster around a village green. Although hunting with hounds was banned in 2005, the village remains the base of Devon and Somerset Staghounds (who used to do the hunting); they ride out three times a week in season (late-summer/autumn to spring), monitoring and managing the deer.

🏃 Activities

Exmoor's highest point is 4 miles north-east of Exford, at Dunkery Beacon (519m). An 8-mile trail to the summit climbs from Wheddon Cross, 5 miles east of Exford, revealing stunning views. Look out for Exmoor ponies and red deer on the way.

Or hike from Wheddon Cross to the local beauty spot of Snowdrop Valley (www.wheddoncross.org.uk/snowdropvalley.htm), which is carpeted by snow-white blossoms in spring.

🛏 Sleeping & Eating

Exford YHA HOSTEL £
(☎ 0845-371 9634; www.yha.org.uk; Exe Mead; dm/d £14/40; ℗) One of Exmoor's best budget bases, this brick Victorian house is just a few paces from Exford's pubs. The dorms are small and a smidgen institutional, but the hordes of hikers and cyclists aren't too bothered.

Exmoor House B&B ££
(☎ 01643-841432; www.exmoorhouse.com; Wheddon Cross; d £82; ℗) Edwardian dark wood panels line the hallway, sedate rooms sit above a cosy, book-stacked lounge, while the restaurant (three-course dinner £26; booking required) rustles up classy country specials: trout paté, home-smoked duck and slow-cooked lamb. It's 5 miles east of Exford, in Wheddon Cross.

Edgcott House B&B, SELF CATERING ££
(☎ 01643-831162; www.edgcotthouse.co.uk; Edgcott Road, Exford; s £65, d £75-115, cottage per week £750; ℗ 🖥) A 10-minute stroll from Exford's centre is this beautiful 17th-century house, set in private riverside gardens. Period features include a terracotta-tiled hallway and an amazing 15m 'Long Room' decorated with hand-painted murals. A whitewashed holiday cottage, the picturesque, six-person Cascade House, sits just next door.

Exmoor White Horse INN ££
(☎ 01643-831229; www.exmoor-whitehorse.co.uk; Exford; d £85-105, mains £14-22; ◷ bar meals noon-9pm, restaurant 7-9pm; ℗ 🖥) Everything you want from an Exmoor coaching inn: a friendly bar with real fire, local produce packed restaurant and smoothly comfy rooms. Set right in the heart of Exford, its riverside beer terrace is a local hang-out; an idyllic spot to watch horse riders trot by.

Crown Hotel INN ££
(☎ 01643-831554; www.crownhotelexmoor.co.uk; Chapel St; s/d £80/140; mains £8-14; ◷ meals noon-2.30pm & 6-9.30pm; ℗) For a taste of true Exmoor try the Crown, where hunting prints and stags' heads preside over leather armchairs, while traditional bedrooms feature racing-green and cream. Despite the back-country vibe, the food is surprisingly adventurous: try sea bream on ratatouille or the light, twice-baked cheese soufflé.

❶ Getting There & Away

For bus travel to Exford, see p129. Plus on school days the 412 bus runs once each way between Exford and Dulverton.

Dunster & Around

POP 1220

Dunster, one of Exmoor's oldest villages, gathers around a scarlet-walled castle and a medieval yarn market, an attractive tumbling of bubbling brooks, packhorse bridges and cobbled streets. Tucked away on the edge of the northern moor, its varied sleeping and eating options make it an attractive base. Three unusual attractions nearby are also worth a detour.

The family-friendly resort of Minehead is 3 miles north east of Dunster.

◉ Sights

Dunster Castle CASTLE
(NT; ☎ 01643-821314; www.nationaltrust.org.uk; Castle Hill, Dunster; castle adult/child £9/4.40, garden & park £5.20/2.50; ⏰ 11am-5pm Mar-Oct; **P**) Rosy-hued Dunster Castle sits atop a densely wooded hill. Built by the Luttrell family, who once owned much of northern Exmoor, the oldest sections are 13th century, although the turrets and exterior walls are 19th-century additions. Inside, look out for Tudor furnishings, 17th-century plasterwork and a ridiculously grand staircase; outside, the terraced gardens have views across Exmoor's shores. Stay alert for spooks; the castle is one of England's most haunted.

Cleeve Abbey HISTORIC SITE
(EH; ☎ 01984-640377; www.english-heritage.org.uk; Abbey Rd, Washford; adult/child £4.40/2.60; ⏰ 10am-5pm Apr-Oct, to 6pm Jul & Aug; **P**) Most visitors zip straight past tiny, tumbledown Cleeve Abbey but it's well worth visiting for the insight it offers into the lives of monks who lived here 800 years ago. Despite being largely torn down during Henry VIII's dissolution, the impressive cloister buildings, original gatehouse, refectory and monks' dormitory are among the best preserved in England. It's five miles east of Dunster.

West Somerset Railway RAILWAY
(☎ 01643-704996; www.west-somerset-railway.co.uk; 24hr rover ticket adult/child £17/8.50) The chugging steam trains of this vintage railway are one of the best ways to see the Somerset countryside. The 20-mile route runs from Minehead to Bishops Lydeard, with stops including Dunster, Watchet and Williton. There are four to seven trains daily from March to October, with a much more limited service for the rest of the year. Bikes can be carried on board for £2.

Bakelite Museum MUSEUM
(☎ 01984-632133; www.bakelitemuseum.co.uk; Orchard Mill, Williton; adult/child £5/2.50; ⏰ 10.30am-6pm Thu-Sun Easter-Oct, daily in Jul & Aug) The endearingly weird Bakelite Museum, 7 miles east of Dunster, houses the nation's largest collection of Bakelite (otherwise known as polyoxybenzylmethylenglycolanhydride), one of the earliest plastics. This wonder material was used to make everything from telephones to radios, letter openers, egg cups, vacuum cleaners, toasters and even false teeth, and the museum has a treasure

OFF THE BEATEN TRACK

STAR GAZING ON EXMOOR

All over Exmoor people are, rightly, clearly chuffed to bits that it's been named Europe's first International Dark Sky Reserve, in recognition of the night-time inky blackness overhead. But what does that mean in practice? Namely, a whole host of local organisations striving to limit light pollution; plus, for visitors, some simply spectacular star displays. The ENPA runs unforgettable, free, night-time navigation and stargazing walks – eerie hill-top hikes illuminated only by mesmerising constellations. The authority has also produced Dark Sky Discovery leaflets, complete with star charts and maps pinpointing the best light-free spots. For optimum star gazing, central, higher Exmoor is best – try Brandon Two Gates (on the B3223), or Webber's Post (just north of Dunkery Beacon).

trove of pieces showcasing the material's myriad applications. The pièce de résistance has to be the full-size Bakelite coffin – pity the pall-bearers who had to lug that one around...

St George's Church CHURCH
(www.stgeorgesdunster.co.uk; Church St, Dunster) Dunster's beautiful church dates mostly from the 15th century and boasts an intricately carved fan-vaulted rood screen. Just behind the church is a 16th-century dovecote, used for breeding edible squabs (young pigeons) for the dinner table at Dunster Castle.

Dunster Watermill HISTORIC BUILDING
(☎ 01643-821759; www.dunsterwatermill.co.uk; Mill Lane, Dunster; adult/child £3.50/2.50; ⏰ 11am-4.45pm Apr-Oct) This working 18th-century mill still has most of its original cogs, wheels and grinding stones. You can buy stone ground wholemeal flour from its shop, and there's also a sweet riverside tearoom.

🛏 Sleeping

Mill Stream Cottage B&B £
(☎ 01643-821966; www.millstreamcottagedunster.co.uk; 2 Mill Lane, Dunster; s £55, d £74-84) In the 1600s this was Dunster's workhouse, now it's a sweet-as-pie guesthouse with country-cottage style rooms. You get homemade cakes on arrival and home-baked biscuits on

the tea tray, plus a sofa-filled guest lounge, where you can doze off in front of the wood-burner.

Dunster Castle Hotel HOTEL **££**
(☑ 01643-823030; www.thedunstercastlehotel.co.uk; 5 High St, Dunster; d £90-150; ⊘ meals noon-2.30 & 6-9pm; ⓢ) Everything feels rich in this former coaching inn, from the dark purple furnishings and gleaming wooden furniture, to the plush, heraldic-style throws. The bar is suitably comfy, while the buzzy *restaurant* (mains £13-20) specialises in intense flavours. Expect beef with chorizo, butternut squash with Parmesan, and scallops with air-dried ham.

Spears Cross B&B **££**
(☑ 01643-821439; www.spearscross.co.uk; 1 West St, Dunster; d £93-103; ⓢ) One for the connoisseur – of cuisine and beams. Gorgeous antique elm supports and panels are everywhere, framed by floral furnishings and the occasional raspberry-red wall. But it's also worth staying for breakfast alone: Bucks Fizz (with freshly squeezed orange juice and champagne), their own cured bacon, locally smoked trout and spelt-and-honey artisanal bread.

Luttrell Arms INN **££**
(☑ 01643-821555; www.luttrellarms.co.uk; High St, Dunster; s £100-130, d £130-160; ⊘ meals noon-3pm & 7-9pm; ⓟ) Sleeping here is more like kipping in a baronial pile: something to do with the monumental stone fireplaces and arching beams, the paneled doors and sheepskin throws. Huge flagstones, heavy armchairs and faded tapestries dot the bar – a perfect fit for the hearty food (mains £13).

 Eating

Cobblestones CAFE **£**
(www.cobblestonesofdunster.co.uk; High St, Dunster; mains £6-14; ⊘ noon-3pm daily, 6.30-8.30pm Fri-Sun) Plump for the daily roast or farmhouse pâté and crusty bread, or better still just drop in for a superior cream tea.

Reeve's MODERN BRITISH **££**
(☑ 1643-821414; www.reevesrestaurantdunster.co.uk; 22 High St, Dunster; mains £18; ⊘ noon-1.30pm Sat & Sun, 7-9pm Tue-Sat) This seriously stylish restaurant dishes up Dunster's best food in an attractive dining room full of fairy lights and stripped-wood floors. Its dishes are complex and satisfying: think piled-up grilled venison, fragrant stacks of monk fish, and a gooey dark chocolate pudding with a dollop of clotted cream.

ⓘ Getting There & Away

For bus 398 to Dulverton, see p129. Bus 28 (one to two per hour) shuttles to Minehead, where you can pick up buses west along the Exmoor coast.

The West Somerset Railway (p133) stops at Dunster during the summer.

Porlock & Around
POP 2350

The small village of Porlock is one of the prettiest on Exmoor's coast. The thatched cottages lining its main street is framed on one side by the sea, on the other by houses clinging to the steep slope behind. Winding lanes lead to the picturesque quay at Porlock Weir, a collection of pubs, shops and hotels, 2 miles to the west.

Coleridge's famous poem *Kubla Khan* was written during a brief sojourn in Porlock (helped along by a healthy slug of laudanum and a vicious head cold), and the villages are popular with tourists, as well as walkers hiking the South West Coast Path and Coleridge Way.

◉ Sights & Activities

Porlock Weir HARBOUR
Porlock Weir's granite quay curves around a pebble beach backed by pubs, fishermen's storehouses and seasonal stores. A lock gate leads to Turkey Island, where a row of thatched cottages sit encamped on the shore – here back gardens merge into the beach. The weir has been around for almost 1000 years (it's named in the Domesday Book as 'Portloc') and boasts stirring views across the Vale of Porlock. It's a popular lunch spot, and also the springboard for some excellent walks. An especially scenic section of coast path leads west towards Gore Point and the pint-sized church at Culbone, reputed to be the smallest in England at just 7.6m long. The shingle beach at the weir's west end forms part of the Porlock Ridge and Saltmarsh Site of Special Interest (SSSI), a popular spot for local birdwatchers.

Exmoor Owl & Hawk Centre WILDLIFE RESERVE
(☑ 01643-862816; www.exmoorfalconry.co.uk; Allerford, near Porlock; adult/child £9/6.50; ⊘ 10.30am-4.30pm Tue-Sun Feb-Oct, plus Mon in school holidays; ⓟ) Even with the best guide, you can't always bank on catching sight of Exmoor's more elusive residents, unless you head for the Exmoor Owl & Hawk Centre. From April to September it holds daily displays – catch the owl show in the medieval barn (between 11.30am and 1pm) or the flying displays in the open

fields (2.30pm to 3.45pm). You can even book your own private flying session (from £60), or the kids could hitch a ride on the farm's Shetland ponies, donkeys and alpacas.

Holnicote Estate HISTORIC BUILDINGS
(NT; ☑ 01823-451587; www.nationaltrust.org.uk; near Porlock; ⊘ open access; **P**) **FREE** The 5060-hectare Holnicote Estate is the largest NT-owned area of land on Exmoor and sweeps south east out of Porlock, taking in a string of impossibly pretty, thatched villages. First comes **Bossington**, where **Kitnors** (mains from £4; ⊘ 11am-4.30pm Apr-Oct) is *the* quintessential tea room (thatched, of course). Charming **Allerford** boasts a photogenic ford and 15th-century packhorse bridge. **Selworthy** offers striking Exmoor views and picturesque cob-and-thatch cottages that cluster around the village green. The estate has some cracking walks, including the steep, 3-mile circular hike from Webber's Post up the lower slopes of Dunkery Beacon (Exmoor's highest point), and back along the East Water valley.

🛏 Sleeping

Sea View B&B £
(☑ 01643-863456; seaview.porlock@btconnect. com; High Bank, Porlock; d £60-65; 🛜) The furniture- and picture-packed bedrooms of this charming B&B are full of thoughtful touches: muscle-soak bath salts and blister bangages for walkers tackling Porlock's precipitous hills. Bespoke breakfasts feature dry-cured bacon and vegan scones, while the front-facing windows frame the sea by day, and the lights of South Wales by night.

★ Millers at the Anchor BOUTIQUE HOTEL ££
(☑ 01643-862753; www.millersuk.com/anchor; Porlock Weir; s £65-95, d £90-140; 🛜) Stuffed with random antiques, overflowing with piled-up books, and scattered with exotic rugs, Millers delivers an enjoyably overwhelming dose of English eccentricity. Gilt-framed mirrors jostle with marble busts in rooms boasting vast beds and captivating views of Porlock Weir, but the tomes in the library, chess set in the lounge and quirky home cinema may tempt you out of your room. It's all run by the man behind the eponymous antiques guides and gin label – it's a winning combo here.

🍴 Eating & Drinking

Ship Inn INN £
(Top Ship; www.shipinnporlock.co.uk; High St, Porlock; d/f £70/80, mains £8-15; ⊘ meals noon-2.30pm & 6-9pm; **P**) Coleridge and pal Robert Southey both downed pints in this fabulous, thatched Porlock pub – you can even sit beside the regulars in 'Southey's Corner'. Substantial pub food, mainly steaks, roasts and stews, are served in the bar, and there are 10 light rooms in pine and cream.

Ship Inn PUB £
(Bottom Ship; www.shipinnporlockweir.co.uk; Porlock Weir; mains from £8; ⊘ meals noon-3pm & 6-8.30pm) Confusingly, both Porlock and Porlock Weir have a pub called the Ship. This one, at the foot of the hill at Porlock Weir, is nick-named the Bottom Ship. At lunchtime its beer garden fills up with locals and hikers.

Culbone RESTAURANT, INN ££
(☑ 01643-862259; www.theculbone.com; near Porlock; d £75-100, mains £9-22; ⊘ meals noon-10pm Mon-Sat, to 9pm Sun; **P** 🛜) The menu at this smart restaurant-with-rooms is stuffed with local produce; from the 28-day aged Devon Red steaks (choose from three different cuts or a huge *chateaubriand* for two) and Exmoor lamb, to the Somerset goat's cheese risotto. The setting is pure contemporary-chic, with slate floors and black leather chairs – a vibe which runs into the upstairs rooms. Its on the A39, situated 4 miles west of Porlock.

Cafe Porlock Weir RESTAURANT, HOTEL ££
(☑ 01643-863300; www.thecafeporlockweir.co.uk; Porlock Weir; lunch mains £5-11; dinner mains £10-25; ⊘ noon-8pm Wed-Sun) The dining room views of sea-blown Porlock Weir are pretty special, and the food is full of Exmoor character too. Lunch might be goujons of beer-battered fish and chips. Dinner could see you tucking into terrines of Withycombe pork with toasted brioche, while the seafood platter (£30 per person) is piled high with lobster, crab, oyster, scallops and crevettes. The upstairs rooms (doubles £88 to £138) are surprisingly plain.

ℹ Information

Porlock Tourist Office (☑ 01643-863150; www.porlock.co.uk; West End, High St, Porlock; ⊘ 10am-12.30pm & 2-5pm Mon-Sat, 10am-1pm Sun Easter-Oct) In the winter it's open in the morning only.

ℹ Getting There & Away

For bus travel to Porlock see p129. Bus 39 (seven daily, Monday to Saturday) shuttles between Porlock, Porlock Weir and Minehead.

EXMOOR & NORTH DEVON PORLOCK & AROUND

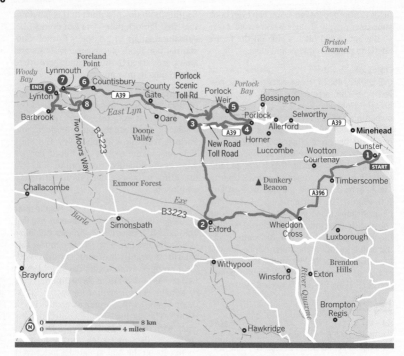

Driving Tour
Dunster to Lynton

START DUNSTER
END LYNTON
LENGTH 32 MILES; ONE DAY

From ❶ **Dunster** motor south, with Exmoor's hills rising to the west. After turning at Wheddon Cross, ❷ **Exford**'s village green provides an excuse for a stroll. Drive uphill, past Exford post office, following Porlock signs. After a cattle grid, the road climbs, gorse takes over, and buzzards soar. Next comes a long, glorious drive across open moorland; depending on the season it's heather-purple or honey-brown. Crest a hill, and the sea and beach far below emerge. At the A39, choose from two routes to Porlock. The first involves a £2.50 toll: turn left, and just under a mile later make a right onto the ❸ **New Road Toll Road**, a scenic route that sweeps through pine forests and round u-bends, revealing stretches of shore. (To avoid the toll, turn right onto the A39 for a second gear descent down the infamous, 1:4 Porlock Hill; expect hairpin bends, escape lanes and

'try your brakes' signs). Park and wander ❹ **Porlock**'s shopping street, before driving down to ❺ **Porlock Weir** for a beach-side stroll and lunch at the Bottom Ship. Next, drive up the lane between the pub and the cafe on the Weir – it cuts sharply right, signed Worthy and Ashley Combe. At the white gate below the thatched stone arch, pay your £2. A bouncing road now climbs beside a wooded stream, sea glimpses emerge below. At the A39, motor towards Lynmouth through a moorland plateau framed by the sea, wind-bent trees and tufted grass. ❻ **Countisbury Hill** plunges down; a cliff-clinging, brake-burner descent. Signs speak volumes: 'Rockfalls', '12% gradient', 'Cyclists Advised to Walk'. Stroll beside ❼ **Lynmouth's harbour**, discovering the town's tragic, flood-related past at the Memorial Hall. Next take the A39 towards Lynton, via Watersmeet – another first- and second-gear ascent, which hugs the steep-sided and mossy gorge. At ❽ **Watersmeet** stop for the half-mile stroll to the waterfalls. Next drive up to ❾ **Lynton**; the Vanilla Pod is an ideal spot for supper.

Lynton & Lynmouth

POP 4900

With precipitous cliffs and steep, tree-lined slopes, the landscape surrounding pretty, harbour town Lynmouth is striking. It was also in part to blame for a flash flood in the 1950s which claimed scores of lives – memory of the disaster remains strong in the village.

From Lynmouth's souvenir stores, a rocky headland winds up to the Victorian resort of Lynton. You can get there via a remarkable water-operated railway, or a stiff cliff path climb.

◎ Sights

★ Cliff Railway   RAILWAY
(☑ 01598-753486; www.cliffrailwaylynton.co.uk; single/return adult £2.30/3.20, child £1.40/2; ☺ 10am-6pm Easter-Oct) This extraordinary piece of Victorian engineering was designed by George Marks, believed to be a pupil of Brunel. Two cars linked by a steel cable descend or ascend the sloping cliff face according to the amount of water in the cars' tanks. All burnished wood and polished brass, it's been running like clockwork since 1890 (a history display at the Lynmouth station details its ingenious creators), making for an unmissable ride.

Flood Memorial Hall   INTERPRETATION CENTRE
(The Esplanade, Lynmouth; ☺ 9am-5pm Easter-Oct) FREE At breakfast time on the 16th of August, 1952, a huge wave of water swept through Lynmouth after a day of torrential rain. The devastation was immense – 34 people lost their lives, and four bridges and countless houses were swept away. The memorial hall's exhibition features a scale model of the village before the flood, photos of the buildings that were destroyed, and the personal testimonies of those involved.

Lyn & Exmoor Museum   MUSEUM
(Market St, Lynton; adult/child £1/50p; ☺ 10.30am-1.30pm & 2-5pm Mon-Fri, 2-5pm Sun Apr-Oct) Interesting archaeological finds and a collection of tools, paintings and archive photos.

☆ Activities

Popular hiking trails amongst Lynton and Lynmouth's spectacular scenery include ones to the lighthouse at Foreland Point, to Watersmeet (2 miles east of Lynmouth, reached via the gorgeous East Lyn river glade) and along the scenic Glen Lyn Gorge.

Valley of the Rocks   WALKING
The dramatic geology in this valley was described by poet Robert Southey as 'rock reeling upon rock, stone piled upon stone, a huge terrifying reeling mass'. Many of the formations have evocative names such as Devil's Cheesewring and Ragged Jack, and you might even spy a feral goat or two wandering along the banks. It's a mile's walk west of Lynton along a cracking coast path.

🛏 Sleeping

Castle Hill   B&B £
(☑ 01598-752291; www.castlehill.biz; Castle Hill,, Lynton; d £65-95, f £130; ☎) Most of the rooms in this hill-top guesthouse are smoothly modern. Expect oatmeal, solid wood furniture and the odd cherry-red settee. The mini-suites have bijou balconies with views of the town and the hills. The location, amid Lynton's shops, is good too.

St Vincent House   B&B £
(☑ 01598-752244; www.st-vincent-hotel.co.uk; Castle Hill, Lynton; d £75-85; ℗ ☎) Built by a compatriot of Nelson, at this former sea-captain's house all the rooms are named after famous battleships. Gleaming satins elevate them above navy-style functionality, while the pocket-sized front garden is a delight.

★ Rock House   B&B ££
(☑ 01598-753508; www.rock-house.co.uk; Manor Green, Lynmouth; s £45, d £100-120) The setting is simply superb: sitting right on Lynmouth's pocket-sized harbour, russet hills slope up on three sides. Contemporary rooms sport leather headboards, lilac scatter-cushions and mini-armchairs. All have extraordinary views; but the best is from number four, where the window is right next to the beach.

Millers at the Tors   BOUTIQUE HOTEL ££
(☑ 01598-753236; www.millerslynmouth.co.uk; Tors Park, Countisbury Hill, Lynmouth; d £130-260; ℗) With its plethora of exotic artefacts, eccentric doesn't even begin to describe this swish, objet d'art-packed enclave. It's run by Martin Miller, of the *Miller's Antiques* books, which explains the delightfully over-the-top furnishings. It's set part of the way up precipitous Countisbury Hill, which accounts for the wrap-around views.

Seawood   B&B ££
(☑ 01598-752272; www.seawoodhotel.co.uk; North Walk, Lynton; s £70, d £110-135, ste £165; ℗ ☎) You can't get any closer to the cliff edge than at this boutique beauty where the views are

extraordinary, the sea stretches to south Wales, and Exmoor's russet hills are to one side. Bedrooms blend Victorian coving, dark polished woods and snazzy fabrics. As you breakfast on the sun-trap terrace, look out for pods of dolphins far below.

North Walk House
B&B **££**

(☑01598-753372; www.northwalkhouse.co.uk; North Walk, Lynton; s £41, d £98-160; P 🛜) Stripped wooden floors, stripy bedspreads and colourful rugs help give North Walk House a gently funky feel. The views over the Bristol Chanel and the Foreland Point's rugged cliffs are fantastic, while the organic breakfasts feature Exmoor bacon and sausages, and Aga-baked eggs.

Old Rectory
BOUTIQUE HOTEL **£££**

(☑01598-763368; www.oldrectoryhotel.co.uk; Martinhoe; d £160-170, ste £185, 3-course dinner £36) You suspect the vicar (hence the name) wouldn't quite know what to make of it: a supremely plush, boutique-style hotel. Despite lashings of luxury (think elegant baths and silky fabrics), the place retains a laid-back, country house air. That even extends to the unstuffy table d'hôte restaurant, which simply features fabulous food and wine.

✗ Eating

Charlie Friday's
CAFE **£**

(www.charliefridays.co.uk; Church Hill, Lynton; from £2; ⊙10am-5pm Feb-Nov) A funky, friendly hang-out serving melting pastries and fairtrade, two-shot espressos that really pack a punch.

Captain's House
CAFE **£**

(www.thecaptainshouseinlynmouth.co.uk; 1 Tors Rd, Lynmouth; from £4; ⊙9am-4pm May-Oct) Tucked away from Lynmouth's main parade of gift shops, this tiny, riverside tea garden serves pasties, ploughman's, cakes and barley water.

★ Rising Sun
GASTROPUB **££**

(☑01598-753223; www.risingsunlynmouth.co.uk; mains £12-18; ⊙6-9pm daily) It's only a quick walk uphill from the touristy Lynmouth seafront, but this thatched pub is a world away from pasties-from-a-bag. The dishes here delight in combining West Country produce with European flavours: expect soft, seared scallops with crisp pancetta, and crab with coriander and lime. The building itself has plenty of character too, with higgledypiggledy floors and hefty beams.

Vanilla Pod
BISTRO **££**

(☑01598-753706; 10 Queen St; mains £10-18; ⊙10am-3pm & 6-9.30pm; 🛜🍴) You could eat every meal of the day here. Breakfast might be golden eggs benedict with Devon ham, while lunch could be a black Waxed Curworthy (hard cheese) ploughmans, then a Devonshire cream tea. The evening menu springs some surprises: local crab ravioli, game terrine, and warm flatbreads with yoghurt and Harissa dip.

☆ Entertainment

Lynton Cinema
CINEMA

(☑01598-753397; www.lyntoncinema.co.uk; Lee Rd; ⊙1-2 performances a day) A small (capacity: 68) but beautifully old-fashioned movie house – an usherette with a torch shows you to your seat.

ℹ Information

Lynmouth has an ENPA tourist office (p129). **Lynton Tourist Office** (☑0845 4583775; www.lynton-lynmouth-tourism.co.uk; Lynton Town Hall, Lee Rd; ⊙10am-5pm Mon-Sat, to 4pm Sun)

ℹ Getting There & Away

For buses to/from Lynton and Lynmouth, see p129.

NORTH DEVON

Intensely rugged and in places utterly remote, north Devon has a coast to inspire. Drastically concertinaed cliffs frame atmospheric fishing villages while long sandy beaches stretch out alongside. It offers a smorgasbord of delights, from surfing lessons at cool Croyde to Damien Hirst's artistry in Ilfracombe. Here, swimming experiences range from snorkelling safaris to Victorianstyle bathing while sleep spots encompass safari-style tents and vintage Romany caravans. Then there's Braunton's immense sand dunes, impossibly pretty Clovelly, Hartland's phenomenal rock formations, and (sitting on the horizon 10 miles out to sea) Lundy Island – a truly get-away-from-it-all escape.

The twin villages of Lynton and Lynmouth fall within Devon, but are also in Exmoor National Park; for clarity we cover them in that section.

ℹ Information

Visit North Devon (www.northdevon.com)

Ilfracombe

POP 19,150

Ilfracombe's geology is startling. Precipitous headlands plunge down to pint-sized beaches; waterfront walkways cling to the sides of sheer cliffs. It seems at first a classic, well-worn Victorian watering hole. Steep streets slope to a historic harbour lined by touristy shops; formal gardens and ropes of twinkling lights line the prom. But the resort also has a snazzier side, as evidenced by a string of smart eateries and places to sleep, a surprising Damien Hirst connection and an utterly unusual heritage swim spot.

◎ Sights & Activities

Verity   LANDMARK
(The Pier) Pregnant, naked and holding aloft a huge spear, Verity, Damien Hirst's 20m statue, towers above Ilfracombe's harbour mouth. On the seaward side her skin is peeled back, revealing sinew, fat and foetus. Critics say she detracts from the scenery, the artist says she depicts truth and justice. Either way, she's drawing the crowds.

Tunnelsbeaches   SWIMMING
(☎ 01271-879882; www.tunnelsbeaches.co.uk; Bath Place; adult/child/family £2.50/1.95/8.50; ☺ 10am-5pm or 6pm Easter-Oct, to 7pm Jul & Aug) A unique attraction: Victorian tidal swimming pools which beautifully evoke Ilfracombe's heyday. Passageways hacked out of solid rock lead to part-natural, part-man-made lidos and a strip of beach where you can still plunge into the sea. Sepia photos depict the pools in the 19th century, conveying a world of woollen bathing suits, segregated swimming and boating etiquette ('Gentlemen who cannot swim, should never take ladies upon the water').

Nick Thorn Surf School   SURFING
(☎ 01271-871337; www.nickthorn.com; Woolacombe Beach; per half-/full day £30/55; ☺ 9am-5pm Apr-Sep) Stationed at the best local surf beach, Woolacombe, which is 5 miles west of Ilfracombe.

Ilfracombe Princess   BOAT TOUR
(☎ 01271-879727; www.ilfracombeprincess.co.uk; The Pier; adult/child £12/6; ☺ one to four trips daily Easter-Oct) Hop aboard this cute little yellow tub-boat for 1½ hour seal cruises along a dramatic shore.

Ilfracombe Aquarium   AQUARIUM
(☎ 01271-864533; www.ilfracombeaquarium.co.uk; The Pier; adult/child £4.25/3.25; ☺ 10am-4.30pm, to 5.45pm late-Jul & Aug) This small but beautifully executed aquarium recreates aquatic environments stretching from Exmoor to the Atlantic, via estuary, rock pool and harbour – hunt out the fearsome lobster and graceful stingrays.

🛏 Sleeping

Olive Branch   B&B £
(☎ 01271-879005; www.olivebranchguesthouse.co.uk; 56 Fore St; s £45, d £75-99; ☎) Georgian trimmings (bay windows and ceiling roses), meet modern furnishings (oval armchairs and beautifully carved wood) to make this a swish, in town retreat. All rooms but one have grandstand views over the bay and the steeply-sloping Capstone Hill.

Norbury House   B&B ££
(☎ 01271-863888; www.norburyhouse.co.uk; Torrs Park; d £80-110, f £125-145; P ☎) Each of the delightful rooms in this gorgeous guesthouse is done up in a different style: choose from pop art, art deco or contemporary chic. Fabulous soft furnishings, a light-filled sitting room (complete with baby grand piano), and cracking sea-and-town views add to the appeal. Bovril, the black labrador, will even walk you along the cliff-path to the Grampus pub.

Westwood   B&B ££
(☎ 01271-867443; www.west-wood.co.uk; Torrs Park; d £80-125; P ☎) Modern, minimal and marvellous, this B&B is a study of neutral tones

EXMOOR & NORTH DEVON ILFRACOMBE

OFF THE BEATEN TRACK

SHEPHERDING EXPERIENCE

For an authentic insight into the lives of those who live and work amid north Devon's extraordinarily craggy scenery, sign up for one of these memorable two-hour walks (☎ 01271-870056; www.boroughfarm.co.uk; Borough Farm, near Mortehoe; adult/child £10/5; ☺ 6pm Thurs Apr-Sep). Shepherd David Kennard and adorable collie Fly steer you around the precipitous cliffs at Mortehoe, demonstrating the intricacies of safely herding their sturdy sheep. The man-dog team-working is touching, the skill levels remarkable, and the scenery breathtaking. Book.

and dashes of vivid colour. It's also graced by pony-skin chaise longues and stand-alone baths; some rooms have sea glimpses.

Lundy House B&B ££
(☎01271-870372; www.lundyhousehotel.webvilla.net; Chapel Hill, Mortehoe; d £75-105, 4-6 person apt per week £1000; P) The location is simply stunning: clinging to a cliff between Morthoe and Woolacombe. The restrained rooms boast glittering black and white bathrooms, but the best bits are the view (a plunging shoreline, dancing waves and the smudge of Lundy Island), and the decked garden.

Eating & Drinking

Grampus PUB £
(☎01271-862906;www.thegrampus-inn.co.uk;mains £8; ⏲food: noon-3pm daily, 7-9pm Mon-Sat) A proper, old fashioned Devonshire pub with a warm welcome, hearty food, an open fire, pub games and quality beers – try Ilfracombe's own Lundy Gold. It's in the village of Lee, 3 miles west of Ilfracombe. Hiking the coast path is the best way to arrive.

George & Dragon PUB
(www.georgeanddragonilfracombe.co.uk; Fore St; mains £9; ⏲meals noon-3pm & 6.30-9pm) Ilfracombe's oldest pub (c 1366) has flagstone floors, a beam-crossed ceiling, home-cooked crab on the menu and fine Exmoor Ales in your glass.

Espresso BISTRO ££
(☎01271-855485; www.seafoodrestaurantilfracombe.co.uk; 1 St James Pl; mains £9-35; ⏲noon-3pm & 6-9.30pm Mon-Sat, noon-8pm Sun) What a delight: an easy-going eatery serving succulent, net-fresh fish, charcuterie platters and rib-eye steaks. Or just opt for some grilled and garlicky north Devon lobster and champagne by the glass.

11 The Quay EUROPEAN ££
(☎01271-868090; www.11thequay.com; 11 The Quay; mains £6-25; ⏲noon-2.30pm & 6-9pm) Full of Chelsea-chic, this distinctive eatery is owned by the artist Damien Hirst, a man famous for exhibiting dead cows and sharks. The menu's less controversial – sample pan-roasted Exmoor chicken breast or sea bass with ginger, while admiring Hirst's artwork. It includes his *Pharmacy* installation and, with delicious irony, fish in formaldehyde.

Information

Ilfracombe Tourist Office (☎01271-863001; www.visitilfracombe.co.uk; Landmark Theatre, the Seafront; ⏲10am-4.30pm daily, closed Sun Oct-Mar)

Getting There & Away

Barnstaple (30 minutes, two per hour) Bus 21/21A, runs via Braunton
Lynton (45 minutes, one to two daily May to October, weekends November to April) Bus 300

LUNDY ISLAND

For a castaway, get-away-from-it-all bolthole, try Lundy Island. This slab of granite three miles long and half-a-mile wide is anchored on the horizon, a two-hour ferry ride from north Devon's coast. In May and June puffins nest on the 122m-high7 cliffs, Lundy ponies, sika deer and Soay sheep roam the cliffs and basking sharks float by offshore. Pack a swim suit as the wardens here lead snorkelling safaris. There are standing stones, a 13th-century castle and a couple of lighthouses to explore. Car-free, it's an extraordinarily peaceful place and its rich star displays lend it a magical quality at night.

Lundy has a shop and a welcoming pub, the **Marisco Tavern** (☎01237-431831; mains from £6; ⏲meals noon-2pm & 6-8.30pm). You can camp near the tavern (per two person tent site £20) or try one of 23 self-catering apartments which include cottages at the castle, apartments in a former lighthouse and the single-bed Radio Room. In peak season prices are around £200 for two nights in a two-person cottage, or £970 for a 4-person let for a week. Book though the **Landmark Trust** (www.landmarktrust.org.uk), which runs the island. The **Lundy Shore Office** (☎01271-863636; www.lundyisland.co.uk; ⏲9am-5pm Mon-Fri, plus 9am-1pm Sat April-Oct) doubles as the tourist office.

Between April and October the *MS Oldenburg* sails to the island from Ilfracombe or Bideford (day return adult/child £35/16, 2 hours, three to four sailing a week). If you stay overnight, the return fare rises to £62 for an adult and £30 for a child. Between November and March, a helicopter flies from Hartland Point (adult/child return £105/55). It only runs on Mondays and Fridays and can't be done as a day-trip. Book transport though the Lundy Shore Office.

Croyde, Braunton & Around

POP 8360

Croyde has the kind of cheerful, chilled vibe you'd expect from its role as north Devon's surf central. Here old world meets the new surfing wave washing these shores – thatched roofs peep out over racks of wet suits and crowds of hip dudes in board shorts sip beer outside 17th-century inns. Powerful waves line up to roll in towards acres of sand.

This mini-Maui is reached through traffic-choked Braunton 2 miles inland, which boasts Britain's first surf museum. From Croyde, a jaw-dropping coast road (and coast path) winds down to Saunton Sands, a 3-mile stretch of golden beach.

◉ Sights & Activities

Museum of British Surfing   MUSEUM
(☑ 01271-815155; www.museumofbritishsurfing.org.uk; Caen St, Braunton; adult/child £4/2.50; ☺ 10am-5pm Tue-Sun) Few museums are quite this cool. Vibrant surfboards and vintage wetsuits line the walls, sepia images catch your eye. The stories are compelling: 18th-century British sailors riding Hawaiian waves; England's home-grown surf pioneers of the 1920s; and the wetsuit innovators of the 1960s – here heritage meets hanging ten.

Braunton Burrows   WILDLIFE RESERVE
(www.brauntonburrows.org; ☺ open access) FREE
The vast network of dunes here is the UK's largest. Paths wind past sandy hummocks, salt marshes, purple thyme, yellow hawkweed and pyramidal orchids. The burrows were also the main training area for American troops before D-Day. Mock landing craft are still hidden in the tufted dunes near the car park at its southern tip.

Surfing   SURFING
The water's hard to resist. **Ralph's** (☑ 01271-890147; Hobbs Hill, Croyde; surfboard & wetsuit per 4/24hrs £12/18, bodyboard & wetsuit per 4/24hr £10/15; ☺ mid-Mar–Dec 9am-dusk) is among those hiring equipment. Lessons are provided by **Surf South West** (☑ 01271-890400; www.surfsouthwest.com; Croyde Beach; per half-/full day £30/58; ☺ Apr to mid-Nov) and **Surfing Croyde Bay** (☑ 01271-891200; www.surfingcroydebay.co.uk; 8 Hobbs Hill, Croyde; per half-/full day £40/80).

🛏 Sleeping & Eating

Croyde gets very busy in the summer. Book ahead, even for campsites.

Mitchum's   CAMPSITE £
(☑ 07891-892897; www.croydebay.co.uk; site per two adults £33-63; ☺ Jun-Aug; Ⓟ) Mitchum's has superb facilities at two sites, one next to Croyde village, the other overlooking the sandy beach. There's a two-night minimum booking in July and August.

Bay View Farm   CAMPSITE £
(☑ 01271-890501; www.bayviewfarm.co.uk; Croyde; site per two adults £24; Ⓟ) One of the area's best campsites, with laundry, showers and surf-view pitches. Requires a week's minimum booking in summer.

Thatch   B&B, PUB ££
(☑ 01271-890349; www.thethatchcroyde.com; 14 Hobbs Hill, Croyde; d £60-110, f £130; Ⓟ) This cavernous, thatched pub is a legendary surfers' hang-out. Trendy bedrooms feature delicate creams, browns and subtle checks; the owners also run similar rooms above another wave-riders' pub and in the cottage opposite. The pick though are their bedrooms at the nearby (quieter) Priory, where elegant wooden beams frame exposed stone.

Chapel Farm   B&B ££
(☑ 01271-890429; www.chapelfarmcroyde.co.uk; Hobbs Hill, Croyde; s/d/tr £40/80/110; 2/6 person apt per week £550/650; Ⓟ🛜) Walls and ceilings shoot off at atmospherically random angles in this cosy, thatched cobb farmhouse, formerly a home to monks. Some of the light, pretty rooms share bathrooms. Neighbouring, similarly styled self-catering cottages are available too.

Saunton Sands   HOTEL £££
(☑ 01271-890212; www.sauntonsands.co.uk; Saunton Sands; d £260-350; Ⓟ🛜⛱) Wedding-cake-white and all clean lines and curves, the art deco Saunton Sands Hotel dominates the cliffs just south of Croyde. The 1930s style doesn't extend to the slightly uniform bedrooms, but the pool and the mind-expanding beach views are superb.

Hobb's   BISTRO ££
(☑ 01271-890256; www.hobbsincroyde.co.uk; 10 Hobb's Hill, Croyde; mains £14-23; ☺ 6-9.30pm Tue-Sun) Heavily beamed eatery rustling up specialties including carpetbagger steaks (with mussels and brandy sauce), local seafood paella, and a grenadine rhubarb crumble.

Seaside Villages

Devon and Cornwall remind you that magical coastal communities are not just figments of your imagination. Cobbled lanes snake down steep hills, cottages cluster beside the shore, floating boats nudge harbour walls, and your fish supper is hauled ashore. Experience it at Clovelly, Mousehole, Fowey, St Mawes, Mevagissey, Port Isaac and Beer.

1. Clovelly (p147)

Cobbled streets and fishermen's cottages cling to the steep hills of this historic seaside village.

2. Mousehole (p241)

This pretty harbour town is the home of the stargazy pie.

3. Bantham Beach (p97)

The best beach in South Devon is situated at the mouth of the River Avon and offers excellent surfing opportunities.

4. Beer (p61)

An active fishing village that has an amazing network of caves.

ℹ️ Information

Braunton Tourist Office (📞01271-816688; www.visitbraunton.co.uk; Caen St; ⊙10am-3pm Mon-Fri, plus 10am-1pm Sat Jun-Dec) Inside the town's (free) museum.

ℹ️ Getting There & Away

Barnstaple (40 minutes, hourly Monday to Saturday, five on Sunday) Bus 308, goes from Croyde via Saunton Sands and Braunton

Ilfracombe (30 minutes, two per hour) Bus 21, runs from Braunton

Barnstaple & Around

POP 30,920

The commercial and administrative centre of north Devon, Barnstaple is also its transport hub. The ripe-smelling farmland around it house attractions both stately and arty, and places to eat and sleep that range from a Michelin-starred restaurant, to a campsite of Romany caravans.

◉ Sights

★**Broomhill Sculpture Gardens**   GARDENS
(📞01271-850262; www.broomhillart.co.uk; Muddiford Rd; adult/child £4.50/1.50; ⊙11am-4pm; 🅿️) It's a magical effect: 300 often quirky sculptures hidden away in a 10-acre wooded valley. Slivers of burnished steel, painted columns and a series of mystical figures pop out from behind trees; sculptural silhouettes emerge from flood planes and 25 polished stone Zimbabwean Shona statues sit on a plateau. There's a fairy tale, often comic feel to much of it – Greta Berlin's 23ft-tall, red-leather stiletto tends to raise a smile. Broomhill also has a slow-food restaurant, and an art hotel. It's all 3 miles north of Barnstaple at Muddiford, on the B3230.

★**Arlington Court**   HISTORIC BUILDING
(NT; 📞01271-850296; www.nationaltrust.org.uk; Arlington; adult/child £9/4.50; ⊙11am-5pm daily mid-Feb–Oct; 🅿️) When you arrive at the door of this honey-grey Regency manor house you're invited to ring the bell, so you can be welcomed as a guest. Arlington exudes charm, from the model ships and shells collected by the owners, to the produce-packed walled kitchen garden. Its stables house the **National Trust Carriage Collection**, and the burnished leather and plush fabrics of its 40 vehicles summon up an era of stately transport, as do the daily harnessing demonstrations and trips in jangling, rattling carriages. Search out the tiny Pony Phaeton, a four-wheeled carriage belonging to Queen Victoria. Her Majesty drove it herself, but a servant walked alongside, ever ready to apply the handbrake (think Billy Connolly's Mr Brown to Judi Dench's Queen Victoria). Arlington Court is 8 miles north of Barnstaple on the A39.

🛏️ Sleeping

★**Vintage Vardos**   CAMPSITE £
(📞0797 7535233; www.fishertonfarm.com; Higher Fisherton Farm, near Atherington; campsite per night £230-290; ⊙Easter-Oct; 🅿️) There's every chance you'll fall utterly in love with this enchanting encampment of restored Romany caravans. The three brightly painted wagons boast log burners, funky fabrics and snug sleeping platforms. Night lights in jam jars lead to a vast fire pit encircled by log benches, a hamper full of crockery and ranks of cast iron pans. There's even a bailer twine-sprung outdoor bed, so you can slumber under the stars. It's all done with love and humour, and is impossible to resist. You have to book the entire camp (which sleeps six to 12), which is 10 miles south of Barnstaple.

Broomhill Art Hotel   BOUTIQUE HOTEL £
(📞01271-850262; www.broomhillart.co.uk; Muddiford Rd, near Barnstaple; s/d £50/75; 🅿️) The owners of this chic retreat are passionate about contemporary art. The result? Cool, stylish bedrooms dotted with witty artwork, antiques and jolts of colour. Ask for a garden-view room and you can even do some sculpture spotting from your own easy chair.

Lower Yelland Farm   B&B £
(📞01271-860101; www.loweryellandfarm.co.uk; Fremington; s/d £40/80; 🅿️🛜) Breakfast on fresh eggs from rescue chickens and home-made jam at this charming 17th-century farmhouse. The cream rooms are light, calm and framed by flower boxes, while the Tarka Trail and a reserve teeming with birds are just 200 yards away. It's three miles west of Barnstaple off the B3233.

🍴 Eating

★**Mason's Arms**   FINE DINING ££
(📞01398-341231; www.masonsarmsdevon.co.uk; Knowstone; mains £18-25; ⊙noon-2 Tue-Sun, 7-9pm Tue-Sat) A surprise: a Michelin-starred eatery in a thatched 13th-century pub deep in rural north Devon. Expect modern takes on European classics. Try the smoked scallops with wasabi and vermouth sauce, or confit of

duck with red wine jus, but leave room for a chocolate and raspberry mousse made zingy by lime. The Mason's Arms is 20 miles south-east of Barnstaple – it's worth the drive.

Terra Madre BISTRO **££**
(📞 01271-850262; www.broomhillart.co.uk; Muddiford Rd, Muddiford; 3-course lunch/dinner £15/25; ⏰ 12.30-2pm Wed-Sun, 7-9pm Fri & Sat; ✈) The tables at Broomhill Sculpture Gardens' slow-food bistro overflow with local, organic produce, including Lundy Island crab, Exmoor Red Ruby beef and free-range chicken. Dishes are infused with Mediterranean flavours – they even make their own air-dried chorizo with free-range pork from a farm just 4 miles away. The evening jazz and tapas buffets are a snip at £13.50.

ℹ Information

Barnstaple Tourist Office (📞 01271-375000; www.staynorthdevon.co.uk; The Square; ⏰ 10am-5pm Mon-Sat)

ℹ Getting There & Away

BUS

National Express Includes services to London, Bristol and Birmingham.

Bus 21 (two per hour) Runs to Ilfracombe (40 minutes), via Braunton.

Bus 118 (two to six daily) Goes to Tavistock (1½ hours) via Bideford and Okehampton.

Bus 315 (seven daily, Monday to Saturday) Runs to Exeter (2¼ hours) via Bideford (25 minutes).

TRAIN

Tarka Line runs to Exeter (£10, 1 hr 15min, hourly Monday to Saturday, six on Sunday).

Bideford, Appledore & Around

POP 17,110

The graceful expanse of the Taw-Torridge estuary has shaped the communities along its banks for centuries and still does. Business-like Bideford stretches along a river quay, with shops, pubs and houses on the hills behind.

Three miles down river, pretty Appledore provides expansive views over miles of wide water towards distant clusters of white houses and shifting sand dunes. Lined with flower boxes and pastel-painted terraces, some of its streets are too narrow for cars; its an unusually tranquil place.

◉ Sights

RHS Rosemoor GARDENS
(📞 0845 265 8072; www.rhs.org.uk; adult/child £7.70/3.85; ⏰ 10am-6pm Apr-Sep, to 5pm Oct-Mar; 🅿) Run by the Royal Horticultural Society (RHS), this garden is a must-see source of green-fingered inspiration. One of only four RHS centres open to the public nationwide, its 26 enchanting hectares are a vivid, fragrant oasis, full of colour, serenity and a wealth of styles ranging from arboreta and croquet lawns to shade, terrace and town gardens. The fruit and veg section is an object lesson of rows, raised beds and containers. Other highlights include the tree ferns, bananas and ginger lillies in the exotic garden, the sweeps of colour in the cottage garden and Rosemoor's famous heavily-scented rose garden. Rosemoor is one mile south of Great Torrington, off the A3124.

Torrington 1646 INTERPRETATION CENTRE
(📞 01805-626146; www.torrington-1646.co.uk; South St, Great Torrington; adult/child £8/6; ⏰ tours 10am-2pm Tue-Thu Apr-Aug) Prepare for an earthy, funny, multisensory recreation of a key English Civil War battle. In the eponymous 1646 the Parliamentarians surged into Great Torrington, confronting and defeating those loyal to the King – a battle that ended Royalist resistance in the West Country. Tours are led by cheeky costumed guides who expound tales of leech-breeders, urine-takers and bum-rolls. They also tease visitors remorselessly; women who sit with crossed legs will be the butt of more than a few jokes. Book to be sure of a tour.

🛏 Sleeping & Eating

Raleigh House B&B **£**
(📞 01237-459202; www.appledorebandb.co.uk; 9 Myrtle S, Appledore; d £70; 🛜) You get the whole top floor to yourself in this tiny 18th-century cottage a few minutes' walk from Appledore's quay. The bedroom is sweetly furnished, the blue bathroom is gently sea-themed and there's a mini fridge in your lounge to chill milk and wine.

Bradbourne House B&B **££**
(📞 01237-474395; www.bradbournehouse.co.uk; 5 Marine Pde, Appledore; s/d £60/90; 🛜) With its cream and dark-green porticoed exterior, wooden spiral staircase and William Morris-style furnishings, there's more than a touch of class about this Georgian B&B. Pull up an elegant armchair to your own sash window, and get absorbed in the bustling estuary views.

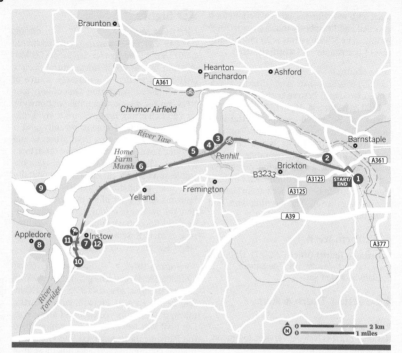

Cycling Tour
Tarka Trail

START BARNSTAPLE TRAIN STATION
END BARNSTAPLE TRAIN STATION
LENGTH 18 MILES; FOUR HOURS

Hire bikes at ❶ **Tarka Trail Cycle Hire** at Barnstaple train station. This tranquil, level, car-free route shadows the immense, sand-fringed River Taw, and combines cycling with paddling and birdwatching.

From Barnstaple train station, pick up Tarka Trail signs south towards Bideford and Meeth. Soon you're amid a lush landscape framed by the Taw and ❷ **salt marshes**; prime grazing land and a sea bass nursery. You're cycling on a disused, late-Victorian railway line, built because larger cargo ships couldn't navigate the Taw. Sweeping into ❸ **Fremington Quay** reveals views of that river. Make for the ❹ **Fremington Quay Café**, a tea stop set in the old station building; the terrace is an ideal place to watch the world go by. Here, photos reveal the quay's role in exporting the area's high-quality, fine-grained clay, which led to the local pottery industry.

Look out for ❺ **Wave Shelter** by Geoff Stainthorpe, an upturned boat-like structure that arches over the trail. It's one of a series of Sustrans-commissioned art installations that pepper the route.

Soon you're beside ❻ **Isley Marsh**, a RSPB reserve of salt marshes and tidal mudflats. Spot oystercatcher, curlew, little egret and grey heron and maybe kingfisher and osprey.

The broad, beautiful estuary views continue at ❼ **Instow**, an appealing array of stone shops and cottages lining up beside a sand-fringed shore. Far beyond on the other side of the estuary are ❽ **Appledore**'s white-washed houses; the massive dunes further north are the tip of ❾ **Braunton Burrows**. Dismount to discover more train-related history; Instow's disused railway station comes complete with milk churns on the former platform, and a restored 1873 ❿ **signal box**.

Instow's sandy ⓫ **beach** is perfect for a paddle; next eat at the funky ⓬ **Instow Arms** (food served noon to 9.30pm). Then saddle up for the view-filled return leg back to Barnstaple train station.

Appledore House B&B ££

(☑ 01237-421471; www.appledore-house.co.uk; Meeting St, Appledore; d £80-90, f £115, apt per week £750; P) The views from this former vicarage are simply superb with the sweeping Taw-Torridge estuary framed by Instow's sands. Stained glass and refined furnishings hint at the house's 1897 build date; bathrobes and bright fabrics bring things up-to-date. The top-floor, two-bedroom apartment is a swish, comfy bargain.

Bensons RESTAURANT ££

(☑ 01237-424093; www.bensonsonthequay.com; 20 The Quay, Appledore; mains £17; ☺7-9pm Tue-Sat) Much of the superb seafood dished up at this intimate eatery is landed on the quay directly opposite. Depending on that day's catch, you might get Torridge sea bass stuffed with wine-braised fennel, or pollock with garlic and lime. Booking is required.

🛈 Getting There & Away

Bus 21 (hourly) links Appledore with Bideford (15 minutes) and Barnstaple (1 hour).

Westward Ho!

POP 2120

Westward Ho! is the only place name in England with an exclamation mark, which seems a bit of a waste, really. But this low-key, family-friendly resort does boast a glorious stretch of beach.

The town owes its existence to the best-selling 1855 novel *Westward Ho!* by Charles Kingsley, which featured this stretch of coast. Developers targeted the spot, built a resort here and gave it the same name to cash in on the book's popularity.

◉ Sights & Activities

Beach &
Northam Burrows BEACH, WILDLIFE RESERVE

(P) Westward Ho!'s mind-expanding, 2-mile sandy beach is backed by Northam Burrows, a wildlife-rich expanse of grassy plains, sand dunes and salt marshes grazed by sheep and horses. Look out for wheatear, linnet, pied wagtail, stonechat, curlew and little egret. A pebble ridge sits between the burrows and the beach, forming a natural sea defense. It gets pushed back incrementally by high tides, and the stones used to be thrown back in gloriously eccentric English style by Potwallopers (only those locals who had two fires and a pot) at a wild, annual village bun-fight. These days the pebble management is done more prosaically by bulldozers, but the **Potwalloper's Festival**, with its music and marquees, still happens on the Spring Bank Holiday.

North Devon Surf School SURFING

(☑ 01237-474663; www.northdevonsurfschool.co.uk; Westward Ho!; half-/full day £28/50) Beside the beach at the Westward Ho! end of the Northam Burrows reserve.

🛏 Sleeping

Culloden House B&B £

(☑ 01237-479421; www.culloden-house.co.uk; Fosketh Hill; d £70-80; P ☂) It started life in 1865 as a gentleman's residence and there's still an air of Victorian charm about Culloden House, thanks to moulded ceilings and stained glass. The best bedrooms have expansive sea views – choose from brisk blues and white, or refined greens and creams.

🛈 Getting There & Away

Bus 21 runs to Bideford (15 minutes; half hourly) and Barnstaple (40 minutes).

Clovelly

POP 450

At this traffic-free fishing village white cottages cascade beside sheer cliffs and a crab-claw harbour curls out into a deep-blue sea. Cobbles are everywhere – smothering houses, garden walls and the incredibly steep lanes, giving the village the air of flowing down the hill. Inevitably it's a tourist honeypot and is sometimes branded artificial. But despite Clovelly's sometimes stage-set feel, around 98% of its houses have year-round tenants, which creates a tangible sense of community.

Clovelly is privately owned and you have to pay to get in via the vast **visitor centre** (☑ 01237-431781; www.clovelly.co.uk; Clovelly; adult/child £6.50/4; ☺9am-6.30pm Jun-Sep, 9.30am-5pm Apr-May & Oct, 10am-4pm Nov-Mar).

◉ Sights & Activities

Historic Village HISTORIC SITE

The cobbled lane down into Clovelly is so steep cars can't negotiate it. Instead supplies are brought in by sledge: look out for the big breadbaskets on runners leaning outside people's homes. Until the 1990s donkeys ferried goods up and down – today their descendants do photo ops from their stables near the visitor centre.

Charles Kingsley, author of the children's classic *The Water Babies*, spent much of his early life in Clovelly. You can visit his former house, the **Kingsley Museum** (High St; ☺9am-6.30pm Jun-Sep, 9.30am-5pm Apr-May & Oct, 10am-4pm Nov-Mar) FREE, which features an audio version of his poem *The Three Fishers*, about fishermen's wives waiting in vain for their husbands to return, a recurring theme locally.

The atmospheric **Fisherman's Cottage** (High St; ☺9am-6.30pm Jun-Sep, 9.30am-5pm Apr-May & Oct, 10am-4pm Nov-Mar) FREE recreates the interior of a 1930s village house, right down to the battered boots beside the door and the straw mattress in the attic. The village's two peaceful **chapels** (nearby) both add insight into Clovelly's unique atmosphere. At the beach, the first balconied house you see is the 15th-century **Crazy Kate's Cottage**; named after a fisherman's wife driven mad with grief when her husband was lost at sea.

Fishing & Boat Trips
FISHING, BOAT TRIPS

In its herring-fishing heyday 400 donkey-loads of fish were landed at Clovelly Quay in one day. Today you can buy wet fish, crab and lobster from the fish shop alongside, or charter a boat for fishing trips and journeys to Lundy Island. Try **Remo** (☎07966 172210), **Dave** (☎07817 974963) or **Clive** (☎07774 190359).

🍽 Sleeping & Eating

Donkey Shoe Cottage
B&B £

(☎01237-431601; www.donkeyshoecottage.co.uk; 21 High St; s/d £30/60) The location of this ancient terraced cottage halfway up Clovelly's crazily steep hill is superb. Bedrooms (which share bathrooms) boast surprisingly snazzy touches, with colour schemes ranging from raspberry to green. You can see the sea from all rooms, but the view is best from number 3, under the eaves.

★ Berridon Farm
CAMPSITE ££

(☎01409-241552; www.berridonfarm.co.uk; near Bradworthy;tentforthreenights£365-465;☺Easter–mid-Oct; P) At Berridon camping goes seriously comfy. Its five or six-person, insulated safari-style tents each sport a leather sofa and wood burner/oven, plus proper beds and a flushing loo. If it's wet out, head for the shabby-chic sitting-eating-playing space in a converted barn. Otherwise, sit on the veranda in the evening sun, sipping a West Country beer from the honesty shop, having

ordered locally-baked chocolate croissants for breakfast. You can even collect your own (free) eggs from the hen house in the field. It's all tucked away 11 miles south of Clovelly.

Red Lion
HOTEL, PUB £££

(☎01237-431237; www.clovelly.co.uk; The Quay; d £146-162) Not so much a room with a view, more a view with a room. Set right on Clovelly Quay, the hardest choice here is whether to look out over the sea or the harbour (both are captivating) from fresh bedrooms dotted with elegant, wicker Lloyd Loom-style furniture. Tuck into classy cooking in the restaurant (two/three courses £25/30, open 7pm to 8.30pm, booking required) or robust pub grub in the bar (mains £6 to £10, open noon to 2.30pm and 6pm to 8.30pm), watched over by the locally caught, stuffed shark's head on the wall.

❶ Getting There & Away

Bus 319 (four daily Monday to Saturday) runs between Clovelly, Hartland Village, Bideford (40 minutes) and Barnstaple (1 hour).

Hartland Peninsula

A rugged, right-angle of land, the Hartland Peninsula has the kind of coast that makes you gasp. It feels like the edge of Devon, and it is – the county goes no further west from here and only a few miles south before the cliffs surge off into Cornwall. Tucked away from traffic through-routes, its unspoilt coastline produces gorgeous sunsets and its remoteness ensures stunning star displays at night.

Hartland Quay is around four miles by road south of Hartland Point. The village of Hartland, with its shops and pubs, is a few miles inland.

◎ Sights & Activities

Hartland Abbey
HISTORIC BUILDING

(☎01237-441496; www.hartlandabbey.com; near Hartland; adult/child £10.50/4; ☺house 2-5pm, gardens 11.30am-5pm Sun-Thu Apr-Oct; P) History seems to seep from the walls of this enchanting, warm-grey manor house. Built in the 12th century, it was a monastery until Henry VIII grabbed it in the Dissolution; he then gave it to the sergeant of his wine cellar in 1539. Today its sumptuous interiors house a sequence of vivid murals, an ornate Alhambra Passage and a Regency library designed in the Strawberry Hill Gothic style.

The gardens were inspired by Gertrude Jekyll, a frequent guest, and are rich in camellias, hydrangeas, rhododendrons and azaleas. Hartland Abbey is a mile south of Hartland Point, and 5 miles west of Clovelly.

Hartland Quay   HARBOUR
(P) The towering cliffs at the 16th-century Hartland Quay are among the most spectacular in the region – the peninsula rises 350ft above sea level. Russet strata of sand and mudstone have been scrunched vertical by incredible natural force to stick out at crazy angles, not unlike a giant, deeply folded lasagne.

Shipwreck Museum   MUSEUM
(🖉 01237-441218; www.hartlandquayhotel.co.uk; Hartland Quay; admission £1; ⏱ 11am-4.30pm Easter-Oct; P) Artefacts and powerful photographs evoke some of the hundreds of vessels that have foundered on Hartland's shore.

Hartland Point   OUTDOORS
(P) The coast around Hartland Point offers superb hiking. Tucked just under the point is the short white column of a lighthouse, which was built in 1874. You can't go in but there's a viewing platform just to the west, where you can also see the rusting fragments of the coaster *Johanna*. She came to grief on New Year's Eve in 1982 (the crew were rescued by the Clovelly lifeboat); the ship's bell now sits in Hartland Quay's Shipwreck Museum.

🛏 Sleeping & Eating

Hartland Quay   HOTEL ££
(🖉 01237-441218; www.hartlandquayhotel.co.uk; Hartland Quay; s/d £50/100; ⏱ meals 11am-2.30pm & 6-9pm) The location is a grand one: just above spectacular Hartland Quay. The bedrooms of this long-established hotel are plain, but who cares. You're here for the view and most rooms look out onto a swirling sea. Locals pack the hotel's lively, friendly Wreckers Retreat Bar, which serves up no-nonsense pub grub (mains £9).

Longfurlong   COTTAGE £££
(🖉 01237-441337; www.longfurlongcottages.co.uk; near Hartland; four-person cottage per week £1300; P 🛜 🏊) Design styles at this cluster of beautifully converted former farm buildings range from country-cottage with beams, to more minimalistic lines. Each luxury pad gets unlimited use of the spa next door, so you can take a dip in the indoor or outdoor heated pools, sizzle in the sauna, then book a massage (from £30) in one of the candle-lit, fragranced treatment rooms. The village of Hartland and the North Devon shore are both around a mile away.

❶ Getting There & Away

Bus 319 (four daily Monday to Saturday) goes to Hartland village from Bideford (40 minutes) and Barnstaple, via Clovelly.

Bodmin & East Cornwall

Includes ➡

Bodmin 151
Around Bodmin 153
Lanhydrock 153
Bodmin Moor 153
Camelford &
the Northern Moor 153
Central &
Eastern Moor 156
Liskeard &
the Southern Moor 158

Best Places to Eat

➡ Woods Cafe (p153)

➡ Rising Sun (p158)

➡ Cowslip Cafe (p158)

➡ Hilltop Farm Shop (p156)

➡ Cornish Cheese Company (p159)

Best Places to Stay

➡ South Penquite Farm (p158)

➡ Yurt Works (p153)

➡ The Green (p159)

➡ Quirky Holidays (p158)

➡ Old Chapel House (p156)

Why Go?

Hugging the edge of the Devon border, the stark, barren expanse of Bodmin Moor is the county's wildest and weirdest landscape. Pockmarked by bogs and treeless heaths, Cornwall's 'roof' is often overlooked by visitors, but it's well worth taking the time to explore; lofty peaks loom on the horizon, stone circles are scattered across the hills, and ancient churches nestle at the foot of granite tors.

It's also home to Cornwall's highest peaks – Rough Tor (pronounced row-tor; 400m) and Brown Willy (420m) – as well as the infamous Beast of Bodmin Moor, a black catlike creature that's been seen for many years but has still not been conclusively captured on camera.

You're probably unlikely to spy the legendary cat, but on the upside you most likely won't spot many other tourists: Bodmin Moor is an under-explored corner of Cornwall that's skipped by most visitors making a beeline for the better-known attractions of the coast.

When to Go

➡ **Apr–Jun** These are often the best months to visit the moor, as they're usually when you'll encounter the most sunshine, along with colourful displays of spring wildflowers.

➡ **Jul & Aug** The summer months can swing either way: it could be hot and sunny one day, or carpeted in thick fog the next. Don't rely on the moor having good weather simply because it's sunny on the coast.

➡ **Sep & Oct** Can also be pleasant months to visit, with a good chance of late sunshine and rich autumnal colours.

➡ **All year** The changeable weather on the moor means it's vital to take precautions before venturing out: always check the forecast, pack an Ordnance Survey (OS) map, and definitely don't forget your waterproofs.

BODMIN

POP 14,500

On the western side of the moor is the stout market town of Bodmin, which grew up around a large 7th-century monastery founded by St Petroc, and later became one of the county's most important stannary towns. Although much of Bodmin's administrative power shifted to Truro in the late 19th century, Bodmin remained the seat of the county court until the mid-1990s. You can visit the old courtroom inside the town hall and the ruins of Bodmin Jail, Cornwall's most infamous lock-up, where lawbreakers were incarcerated or – in more serious cases – introduced to the hangman's noose.

The modern town has little to detain you, but it makes a useful launch-pad for venturing out onto nearby Bodmin Moor.

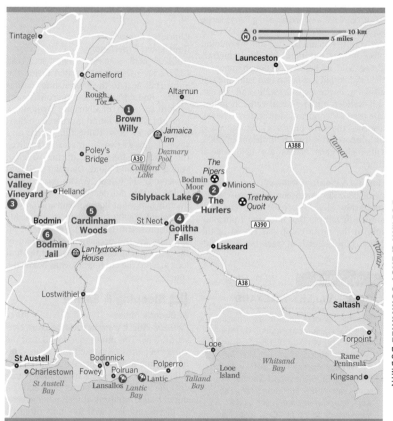

Bodmin & East Cornwall Highlights

1 Conquering the summit of Cornwall's highest hill, **Brown Willy** (p153)

2 Pondering the past around the eerie stone circle known as **The Hurlers** (p159)

3 Taking a tour around Cornwall's premier vineyard, **Camel Valley** (p152)

4 Picnicking by the cascading waters of **Golitha Falls** (p159)

5 Hiking or biking the trails of **Cardinham Woods** (p152)

6 Spotting spooks in the haunted setting of **Bodmin Jail** (p152)

7 Piloting a canoe across the choppy waters of **Siblyback Lake** (p159)

⊙ Sights & Activities

★ **Cardinham Woods** FOREST

(✆ 01208-72577; www.forestry.gov.uk/cardinham)
Just outside Bodmin, this large public forest is a great spot for a woody wander, and also has a network of mountain-bike trails if you're feeling more energetic. The Bodmin & Wenford Railway stops at nearby Coleslogget Halt, from where a 1.5-mile trail leads to Cardinham.

Bodmin Jail PRISON

(✆ 01208-76292; www.bodminjail.org; Berrycoombe Rd; adult/child £7.50/5.50; ⊙ 10am-dusk) Once the county's main prison, this forbidding place is now notorious for the numerous ghosts said to haunt it. Though much of the original jail has fallen into ruin, the ivy-grown walls are a spooky sight, and you can still wander round several cells, including one used for condemned prisoners. The jail also has the UK's only working 'execution pit', discovered during renovations in 2005. Late-night ghost walks are held several times a year.

Bodmin & Wenford Railway STEAM RAILWAY

(✆ 01208-73555; www.bodminrailway.co.uk; adult/child/family £12/6/33; ⊙ Mar-Oct) The old stretch of railway that once ran from Bodmin to the north coast was closed in the 1960s, but a stretch of track between Bod-

---

CAMEL VALLEY VINEYARD

Two miles west of Bodmin is Cornwall's most prestigious wine-maker, Camel Valley Vineyard (✆ 01208-77959; www.camelvalley.com; ⊙ 10am-5pm Mon-Sat), run by local entrepreneur Bob Lindo. It's been producing award-winning wines since 1989, including a range of world-class whites and rosés, and a sparkling bubbly that's Champagne in all but name. Aficionados say the wines have a fresh, light quality that comes from the mild climate, sunlight, and pure sea air. The top wine is Darnibole Bacchus, the only UK wine to be afforded its own 'geo-specific' status.

There's a range of tours around the vineyard available, all of which include the chance to try some of Bob's best vintages, and a wine shop where you can stock up on your favourites.

---

min and Boscarne Junction is still open to the vintage steam engines of the Bodmin & Wenford Railway. The carriages are still decked out in their 1950s livery, and the whole experience is bound to make you nostalgic for the days when train travel was more than a matter of simply getting from A to B. Allow two hours for the return trip.

The other end of the line at Boscarne Junction links up with the Camel Trail; bikes can be taken on the trains if there's space, but it's worth ringing ahead to make sure.

**Charlotte Dymond
Courtroom Experience** MUSEUM

(✆ 01208-76616; Shire Hall, Bodmin; adult/child £3.95/2.50; ⊙ 11am-4pm) Located inside the Shire Hall next to the tourist information centre, Bodmin's old county courtrooms explore the story of Charlotte Dymond, a local girl who was found murdered on Bodmin Moor in 1884. Using film, audio and some dodgy waxworks, the exhibit relives the infamous 1884 trial, during which a young farmhand (and Dymond's alleged boyfriend) Matthew Weeks was found guilty of the murder. Weeks was subsequently hanged at Bodmin Jail, and crowds of around 20,000 turned up to watch his execution (extra trains had to be laid on specially for the occasion). At the end of the tour you can cast your own verdict and look around the old holding cells below the court.

🛏 Sleeping & Eating

St Benet's Abbey B&B ££

(✆ 01208-216014; www.stbenetsabbey.co.uk; Lanivet; d £70-86) This atmospheric B&B near the village of Lanivet is packed with history. It's housed in a former abbey dating from 1411, although the rooms feel much more modern: the best have four-poster beds and coloured leaded windows. It feels a tad generic in places, but let's face it – how often do you get the chance to stay in a 15th-century abbey?

Bokiddick Farm B&B ££

(✆ 01208-831481; www.bokiddickfarm.co.uk; Lanivet; d £80) This farm B&B is a wee bit heavy on the florals, but as long as you don't mind flouncy bedspreads and brass bedsteads, you should be very happy here. Nice touches such as in-room fridges, fresh milk and a great farm-cooked breakfast add to the appeal.

South Tregleath Farm B&B ££
(☎ 01208-72692; www.south-tregleath.co.uk; d £65-
80; P 🖤) The farmstay goes fancy at this
fab nook on Bodmin Moor, where the three
rooms are all silky wood, wet rooms and
bamboo screens. Go for the Columbine
Room if you can – it's got the most space
and a patio – or book out the cottage, which
sleeps six. South Tregleath is still a working
farm: kids can help milk the cows and collect
eggs.

★ **Woods Cafe** CAFE ££
(☎ 01208-78111; www.woodscafecornwall.co.uk;
Cardinham Woods; mains £6-12; ⊙ 10.30am-
4.30pm) In an old woodsman's cottage lost
among the trees of Cardinham, this cracking
cafe has become a dining destination in its
own right – it's locally famous for its home-
baked cakes, cockle-warming soups and
sausage sarnies. There's even a yurt in the
garden if you feel like staying.

AROUND BODMIN

Lanhydrock
Located two-and-a-half miles from Bodmin,
the 16th-century manor of Lanhydrock (NT;
☎ 01208-265950; www.nationaltrust.org.uk/lanhyd
rock; adult/child £10.70/5.30, grounds only £6.30/
3.40; ⊙ house 11am-5pm Tue-Sat, grounds 10am-
6pm daily) offers a fascinating insight into *Upstairs, Downstairs* life in Victorian England.

The house was originally built for the
aristocratic Robartes clan, and still feels
very much like a family home. Highlights include the gentlemen's smoking room (lined
with old Etonian photos, moose heads and
tiger-skin rugs); the children's nursery, mov-
ingly strewn with abandoned toys belonging
to the Robartes children; and the original
kitchens with their huge ovens and pioneering water-cooled cold store. There's also a
fabulous plaster ceiling in the Long Gallery,
which somehow managed to escape a huge
fire in 1881 that gutted the rest of the house.

BODMIN MOOR

East of Bodmin, the scenery really starts
to get wild and windswept. The main A30
slices right through the centre of the moor,
while the A39 borders the moor to the north,
and the A38 frames it to the south. Each section of the moor has a slightly different feel:
the northern and central sections are largely
barren and treeless, with the scenery broken
only by shattered tors. The southern section
gets greener the further south you go, with
woodland and river valleys tumbling down
from the higher slopes.

The bus schedule is pretty much non-ex-
istent on Bodmin Moor, so you'll really need
your own car to explore.

Camelford & the Northern Moor
The nearest town to the northern reaches
of the moor is Camelford, which is said by
some to have King Arthur connections –
mainly due to the similarity of its name with
Camelot (Arthur's mythical castle) and Cam-
lann (the site of his epic final battle). In fact,
the name probably derives from 'cam-hayle',
meaning curving river.

The town's a quiet place these days, but it
makes a useful base for beginning the trek
to Rough Tor and Brown Willy, Cornwall's
highest hill. Despite its saucy name – a perennial source of amusement for Cornish
schoolkids – Brown Willy is actually a cor-
ruption of *bronn wennili*, Cornish for 'hill
of swallows'.

The best route starts from the car park at
Poldue Downs, 3 miles south of Camelford.

🏃 Activities

Hallagenna Riding HORSE RIDING
(☎ 01208-851500; www.hallagenna.co.uk; St Breward; per hr £20) One of the best ways to see the
moor is from the saddle. This well-established
riding stables offers hacks and treks from
£20 per hour, plus a 3-hour expedition including a pub stop and lunch at the Blisland
Inn (£60).

🛏 Sleeping

★ **Yurt Works** CAMPSITE £££
(☎ 01208-850670; www.yurtworks.co.uk; St Breward; yurts per week £260-520; P 🖤 🐾) 🌿 One of
Cornwall's very first yurt sites, and still hard
to beat. There are three to choose from –
Ash Field, Green Man and Oak Wood – all
in truly glorious wooded settings, and
equipped with proper beds, wood-burning
stoves, candle lanterns, barbecues and chill-
boxes. Each has its own 'ig-loo' and solar
shower.

West Country Moors

The southwest is famous for its white beaches and rolling fields, but its moors have a harsh beauty all of their own. Treeless, windswept and pockmarked by hills and rocky outcrops, these moors are as close as Britain gets to wilderness.

2

JULIAN ELLIOTT / GETTY IMAGES ©

ADAM BURTON / GETTY IMAGES ©

4

1. Bodmin Moor (p153)
Rock stacks dot the mystical landscape of the windswept moors.

2. Dartmoor National Park (p110)
Ponies in the wilds of Dartmoor, a haven for adventure-seekers.

3. Zennor (p228)
Gorse and heather cover the Zennor moorland, an area filled with archaeological Neolithic sites.

4. Exmoor National Park (p128)
Sheep graze at Exmoor, which offers extensive hiking and cycling paths.

3

ADAM WOOLFITT / CORBIS ©

★ **Old Chapel House** B&B ££

(☑ 01208-841834; www.theoldchapelhouse.co.uk; St Mabyn; s £55-65, d £75-110; P) Run by Des and Ginny Weston, who were formerly in charge of the lovely St Kew Inn, this spanking new little B&B near the village of St Mabyn has been beautifully refurbished. As its name suggests, it's in a converted chapel and has original stained glass in situ. There are only three rooms: top of the heap is Room 1, which still has its original cruck beams and romantic attic vibe.

Ekopod CAMPSITE ££

(☑ 01179-247877; www.canopyandstars.co.uk/our-places/ekopod; near Launceston; from £90 per night; P) ✿ Low-carbon camping in two geodesic domes surrounded by flower-filled fields and moorland views.

✕ Eating

★ **Hilltop Farm Shop** TEA ROOM £

(☑ 01840-211518; www.hilltopfarmshop.co.uk; Slaughterbridge; teas £3-6) Take your pick from the Cornish fudge, pasties and cheeses in the farm shop, or settle in for scones in the attached tea room. Staff will also pack you a hamper stuffed with goodies, all with Cornish credentials. It's in Slaughterbridge, 2 miles north of Camelford.

Old Inn PUB £

(☑ 01208-850711; www.theoldinnandrestaurant.co.uk; St Breward; mains £10-16) The main claim to fame of this village pub is that it's the highest in Cornwall (at around 720ft), and supposedly has a heritage that dates back to the 11th century, when it was a hostelry frequented by local monks. These days it's mostly a village hangout: the grub's decent, the welcome's warm, and there are fires to snuggle by.

Central & Eastern Moor

Standing in a desolate spot in the middle of the moor, beside the old coaching road through Bolventor, is **Jamaica Inn** (☑ 01566-86250; www.jamaicainn.co.uk), made famous by Daphne du Maurier's classic adventure story, published in 1936. The author apparently conceived the idea for the book when she got lost while riding on Bodmin Moor and took shelter at the inn, where she was entertained with spooky stories and smuggling yarns by the local parson from Altarnun Church – some of which provided the basis

for the book's plot. The inn now houses a small museum of smuggling, although sadly much of its period character has been swept away since du Maurier's day.

◉ Sights

Dozmary Pool LAKE

About a mile south from Jamaica Inn is the glassy expanse of Dozmary Pool, said by some to be the lake where Arthur was given his famous sword, Excalibur, by the Lady of the Lake.

It's also supposedly bottomless: another local legend concerns young Jan Tregeagle, who made a pact with the devil and in return was damned to spend his days emptying the neverending pool with a leaking limpet shell.

Just to the west is **Colliford Lake**, Cornwall's largest and highest reservoir.

Tamar Otter Wildlife Centre WILDLIFE CENTRE

(☑ 01566-785646; www.tamarotters.co.uk; North Petherwin, near Launceston; adult/child £7.50/4; ☉ 10.30am-6pm Apr-Oct) Generally, you'll need the skills of Ray Mears to spot otters in the wild, but this wildlife centre 5 miles outside Launceston guarantees a sighting. There's a population of British and Asian Short-Clawed otters, split between three families, which live in their own naturally constructed holts. Feeding time is at noon and 3pm daily. Elsewhere round the reserve you'll have the chance to see fallow deer, muntjac, pheasants and Scottish wildcats.

Launceston Castle CASTLE

(www.english-heritage.org.uk/daysout/properties/launceston-castle; adult/child £3.60/2.20; ☉ 10am-6pm) On the eastern edge of the moor is Launceston, another sturdy market town that's mainly worth visiting for this ruined 11th-century castle. A spiral staircase leads to the top of the tower battlements for wraparound views over the moor.

Launceston Steam Railway RAILWAY

(☑ 01566-775665; www.launcestonsr.co.uk; adult/child return £9.50/6.20) This dinky little enthusiasts' steam railway chugs for 2.5 miles between Launceston and the nearby hamlet of Newmills. You can choose to ride in open or closed carriages, but they're not quite as impressive as the ones on the Bodmin & Wenford Railway.

Stripple Stones RUINS

Near the hummock of Hawk's Tor are the Stripple Stones, a circular alignment that

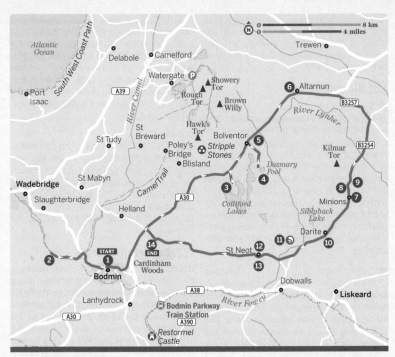

Driving Tour
Moorland Explorer

START BODMIN
FINISH BODMIN
DISTANCE 30 TO 40 MILES, 1 DAY

The moor can be easily covered in a day's drive. Begin in ❶ **Bodmin**, one of Cornwall's five original stannary towns, and the location of the notoriously haunted Bodmin Jail, now reduced to a supremely spooky ruin. From here, detour west to sample the vintages at the ❷ **Camel Valley Vineyard**, or take a tour around the vineyard with chief winemaker Bob Lindo. Pick up the A30 again for a drive past the silvery arcs of ❸ **Colliford Lake** and ❹ **Dozmary Pool**, both rich in fable and folklore.

As you pass through Bolventor, it's worth stopping in for a look around ❺ **Jamaica Inn**, made famous by the novel of the same name – although you'll find the du Maurier connections are pretty thin on the ground these days. A much better option for a pint and a ploughman's lunch is the Rising Sun, a cosy pub in nearby ❻ **Altarnun**.

From here, turn south along the B3257 and the B3254 to the village of ❼ **Minions**. Nearby you can hike to two of the moor's prehistoric monuments: the ❽ **Hurlers** and the ❾ **Cheesewring**, one made by man, the other by nature. Three miles south, near Darite, is ❿ **Trethevy Quoit**, a classic dolmen topped by an enormous flat capstone. More prehistoric ruins can be found nearby, but you'll need an OS map to find most of them.

Further west, a narrow back-road winds to the impressive cascade of ⓫ **Golitha Falls**, which makes a lovely place for a paddle and a picnic on a hot summer's day. Nearby, the parish church of ⓬ **St Neot** is blessed with some fabulous medieval stained glass that's worth a detour. Otherwise, continue on to the old slate mine at ⓭ **Carnglaze Caverns**, where you can venture underground to explore the caves and underwater pool.

Finish up with a walk around the forested trails of ⓮ **Cardinham Woods** and a proper Cornish cream tea at the Woods Cafe, nestled in a shady glade in the heart of the forest.

once enclosed 28 stones, although only four now remain standing. The site is west of the village of North Hill and a couple of miles north of Upton Cross; you'll definitely need an OS map to find it.

🛏 Sleeping

★ South Penquite Farm CAMPSITE £

(☑ 01208-850491; www.southpenquite.co.uk; Blisland; adult/child £8/4; P 🚲 📶) 🐾 As wonderfully out-of-the-way as you could possibly hope to be: a 200-acre organic farm surrounded by miles and miles of empty moor. Facilities include pine-clad loos, a solar-heated shower-block and a kids' play area. There are loads of activities on offer – from bushcraft sessions to art courses – and homemade lamb burgers and bangers are sold from Henry Jo's smoke-house. You're even allowed to make your own campfire.

★ Quirky Holidays CAMPSITE ££

(☑ 01579-370219; www.quirky-holidays-cornwall.co.uk; d £65-106; P) Quirky by name, quirky by nature. Three vintage carriages – a show-man's wagon, a wood-panelled steamroller wagon and an old ale-wagon, plus an old potting shed – have been lovingly reno-vated by enthusiast owners. Each has its own woodburner and is stuffed with period knick-knacks, and the country setting is to die for.

Lavethan B&B ££

(☑ 01208-850487; www.lavethan.com; Blisland; d £90; P) Set inside a Grade II–listed manor-house that's been around since the Domes-day Book, this heritage B&B offers posh rooms with floral drapes, old-fashioned bath tubs and antique rugs, plus a selection of self-catering cottages.

🍴 Eating

★ Rising Sun PUB ££

(☑ 01566-86636; www.therisingsuninn.co.uk; Al-tarnun; mains £9-16) Moorland travellers have been slaking their thirst for over 500 years at this delightfully rural pub, but it feels surprisingly up-to-date inside, with a mod-ern pub menu, a locally sourced ethos and a smart dining room. Ales come from Penpont Brewery just down the road. You're also wel-come to camp in the pub's field, but there's a three-night minimum.

Blisland Inn PUB £

(☑ 01208-850739; www.bodminmoor.co.uk/blisland inn; Blisland; drinks £3-5) Popular ale-drinker's pub, with toby jugs, vintage photos and beer-mats adorning the walls, and at least seven ales and a local scrumpy on tap. Look out for the blackboard tallying all the ales served since the owners arrived – nearly 3000 at the last count. Little wonder it was previously named Pub of the Year by the ale-quaffing aficionados at CAMRA (Campaign for Real Ale).

Cowslip Cafe CAFE £

(☑ 01566-772839; St Stephens, near Launceston; £4.50-6.95; ☉ 10am-5pm) On a farm just out-side Launceston, this excellent cafe makes most of its meals using veg from its own kitchen garden, and all the bread, fish and meat comes from within a radius of a few miles. Craft workshops are held throughout the week.

☆ Entertainment

Sterts OUTDOOR THEATRE

(☑ 01579-362382; www.sterts.co.uk; Upton Cross) Catch some culture surrounded by the wilds of the moor at this atmospheric alfresco theatre, near the village of Upton Cross. It's not quite as spectacular as the Minack, but at least there's a permanent awning to pro-tect you from the elements. The program changes seasonally; check the website to see what's on when.

Liskeard & the Southern Moor

The southern stretches of the moor are ar-guably its most beautiful, a wild swathe of tawny heaths, wooded copses and blustery lakes. It feels a little less desolate than the central moor, although it still has its wild spots – most notably the wild expanse of Twelve Men's Moor and the high point of Kilmar Tor (396m), a rocky pile of granite blocks that offers majestic views over the eastern moor. It's possible to walk to the summit, but you'll need a proper map, good boots and compass skills – if the mist sets in while you're walking, there's little else to guide your way.

The main town of Liskeard makes a useful access point, but like many of the moorland towns, it's looking a little ne-glected; shopping guru Mary Portas recently featured it in a high-profile television cam-paign to rescue Britain's high streets. The quiet village of St Neot is a prettier place to be based.

⊙ Sights & Activities

★ Golitha Falls
WATERFALL

FREE Around 1.25 miles west of St Cleer, these crashing waterfalls are one of the moor's renowned beauty spots on the moor. You can take a dip in the waterfall's pools, but the water is always icy-cold and the rocks are very slippy. Around the falls are the remains of the ancient oak woodland which once covered much of the moor. There is a car park half a mile's walk from the reserve near Draynes Bridge.

Prehistoric Sites
RUINS

The highest concentration of prehistoric sites is found in the southern moor. Near the small village of Minions, about 2 miles east of Siblyback Lake, the curious double stone circles known as **The Hurlers** are said to be the remains of men turned to stone for daring to play the Cornish sport of hurling on a Sunday. Nearby is the **Cheesewring**, a weird stack of granite stones that's said to be the work of local giants, but is actually the result of natural erosion. Three miles south near Darite is **Trethevy Quoit** – sometimes known as King Arthur's Quoit or the Giant's House – another example of Cornwall's distinctive Neolithic burial chambers, standing almost 15ft high.

In the middle of Twelve Men's Moor, the **Trewortha Bronze Age Farm** consists of a set of reconstructed roundhouses, faithfully built using thatch, timber, and traditional tools. It's on private land and is mainly used for educational purposes, but you can look over the site from the top of Kilmar Tor.

Carnglaze Caverns
CAVE

(🖉 01579-320251; www.carnglaze.com; adult/child £6/4; ⊙ 10am-5pm) Bodmin Moor's slate was once an important local export, and these deep caverns were cut out by hand by local miners, leaving behind a moody network of subterranean caves and a glittering underground pool. Concerts and plays are sometimes held inside the caves in summer. The caves are just outside St Neot and well signed.

Siblyback Water Park
WATER SPORTS

(🖉 01579-346522; www.swlakestrust.org.uk; ⊙ 9am-5pm) Siblyback is a huge lake offers a wealth of opportunity for getting out on the water, including windsurfing, rowing, waterskiing and wakeboarding. Mixed-use trails also run around the shoreline, and there's a small cafe.

Boat hire starts from around £10 per hour for a small rowing boat; canoeing and windsurfing taster sessions start from £34 for two hours.

Cornish Orchards
ORCHARD

(🖉 01503-269007; www.cornishorchards.co.uk; Duloe, Liskeard) This renowned orchard makes fruity apple juices and a range of exotic cider varieties, from traditional heritage scrumpy to raspberry and pear variants. You can pick them all up in the shop and have a free taste; they're in Duloe, 5 miles south from Liskeard.

🛏 Sleeping

Trussel Barn
B&B ££

(🖉 01579-340450; http://trusselbarn.wordpress.com; St Keyne; s £50-60, d £90; 🅿 🛜) An attractive barn-converted B&B about 2 miles from Liskeard, offering uncluttered modern rooms: go for the spacious Garden Room, with beams and terrace views, or the smaller Cyder Room, with its flashy bathroom and pond outlook. Two smaller rooms are also available for the kids or single travellers. There's also self-catering in The Buttery cottage.

★ The Green
COTTAGE £££

(🖉 01579-362253; www.thegreencornwall.co.uk; Upton Cross; from around £288 for 3 nights) Five impeccably appointed stone-fronted cottages looking across the moor to Caradon Hill. They're full of luxury touches: underfloor heating, open-plan kitchens, stripped wood floors and designer kitchens with dishwasher and fan ovens. The design is contemporary, and the grounds are dreamy: lawns, fields, woods, plus plans for a wild swimming pool.

✕ Eating

Crows Nest Inn
PUB ££

(🖉 01579-345930; near Darite; mains £10-14) Whitewashed walls, a roaring fire and a low-beamed interior make this 16th-century inn a welcome refuge when the moorland weather sets in, especially on Sunday for the generous roast.

Cornish Cheese Company
DELI

(🖉 01579-363660; www.cornishcheese.co.uk; Upton Cross, near Liskeard; ⊙ 10am-5pm Mon-Sat) Renowned local cheesemaker that has made its name with the powerful, pungent Cornish Blue, which you can buy in the traditional blue-and-white striped ceramic pots (£15.99 for 200g).

South Cornwall

Includes ➡

Falmouth, Truro &
the Roseland 161

Falmouth 161

Truro 170

The Roseland.............. 174

Southeast Cornwall... 180

Mevagissey &
Gorran Haven 181

Fowey.......................... 183

Looe 188

Tamar Valley 191

Best Places to Eat

➡ Oliver's (p165)

➡ The Wheelhouse (p164)

➡ Ferryboat Inn (p167)

➡ Hidden Hut (p176)

➡ Outlaw's Fish Kitchen (p190)

Best Places to Stay

➡ Highcliffe House (p164)

➡ Hotel Tresanton (p177)

➡ Roundhouse Barns (p177)

➡ Lugger Hotel (p174)

➡ Westcroft (p191)

Why Go?

It might lack the craggy granite cliffs and sea-blown grandeur of the north coast, but Cornwall's southern side has ample charms of its own: gentle creeks, green meadows, quaint harbours and world-renowned gardens such as Trebah, Trelissick, Heligan and Glendurgan, as well as the futuristic biomes of the Eden Project. It feels more pastoral than the craggy beauty of Penwith or the wild emptiness of Bodmin Moor: this is a place for quiet adventures, whether that's touring the back lanes and beaches of the Roseland, mooching around Mevagissey Harbour or kayaking on the Fal and Fowey Rivers.

The remote Rame Peninsula is particularly worth exploring. It's a fairly long drive from anywhere, so most visitors never make the effort, which means its lovely countryside and country houses are relatively quiet. It's also an easy trip from Plymouth thanks to the Torpoint ferry, which chugs across the beautiful Tamar Estuary.

When to Go

➡ **May** The Fowey Festival brings book readings, poetry events and live music to the streets of town.

➡ **Jul** Spectacular gigs light up the biomes during the Eden Sessions, which have become one of the county's top annual music events.

➡ **Sep** The Cornwall Food & Drink Festival, one of the county's largest food fairs, takes place on Lemon Quay. Top producers tout their wares, from pie-makers to microbreweries.

➡ **Oct** Falmouth celebrates its tradition of mollusc-rearing at the annual Oyster Festival. Mountains of oysters and mussels are devoured over the week-long event, and there are lots of chefs' demonstrations.

➡ **Dec** Wicker lanterns parade round Truro's streets during the City of Lights procession in the run-up to Christmas.

FALMOUTH, TRURO & THE ROSELAND

In contrast to the crags and breakers of the Atlantic coast, the area around Falmouth and the Roseland Peninsula presents a gentler side to the county. Sheltered from the brunt of the biting Atlantic winds, the coastline benefits from a balmy subtropical climate that allows exotic plants and trees to flourish along its valleys; it's no wonder that many of Cornwall's finest garden and country estates are found here. In previous centuries it was an important maritime area, and the old ports of Falmouth, St Mawes and Mevagissey are all worthy of investigation.

Falmouth

POP 20,775

If you're looking for Cornwall's coolest town, then the consensus seems to centre on Falmouth right now. Since the multi-million pound development of Falmouth University on the outskirts of nearby Penryn over the last decade, this ancient maritime harbour has become one of the county's most creative and quirky towns. From espresso bars to boutique beer taverns, vintage shops to cutting-edge design agencies, Falmouth seems to be where it's at these days.

It's all a far cry from the days when Falmouth earned its keep from the sea. Strategically situated at the end of the River Fal, overlooking the entrance to the Carrick Roads estuary, the port of Falmouth has been an important maritime hub for more than 500 years. The town sits at the edge of the world's third-deepest natural harbour, and flourished as a trading port after the river at Truro silted up. Falmouth's heyday was during the era of the Packet Service, which carried mail, bullion and supplies between Britain and its overseas colonies between 1689 and 1850.

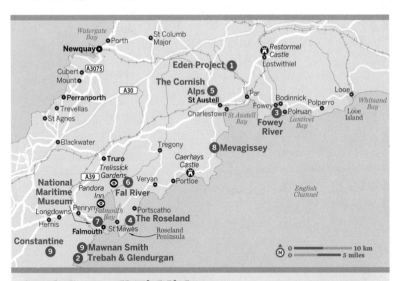

South Cornwall Highlights

❶ Marvelling at the biomes of the **Eden Project** (p182)

❷ Wandering round the valley gardens of **Trebah** (p167) and **Glendurgan** (p167)

❸ Piloting a kayak along the **Fowey River** (p185)

❹ Seeking out an empty beach on the **Roseland Peninsula** (p161)

❺ Exploring otherworldy pools and peaks around the **Cornish Alps** (p181)

❻ Catching a peaceful evening cruise along the **Fal River** (p170)

❼ Soaking up Falmouth's maritime history at the **National Maritime Museum** (p163)

❽ Going crabbing on **Mevagissey Harbour** (p181)

❾ Discovering some of south Cornwall's secret **gardens** (p168)

Falmouth

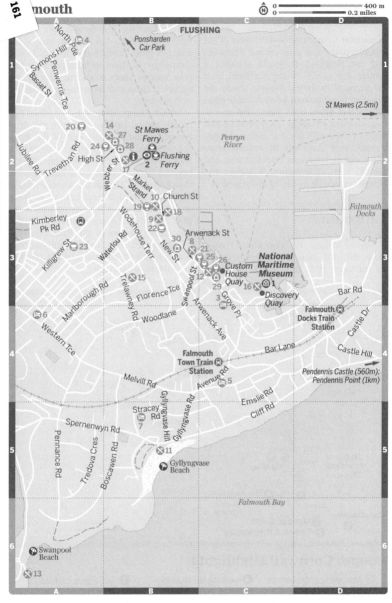

FLUSHING

Ponsharden
Car Park

St Mawes (2.5mi)

Penryn
River

St Mawes
Ferry

Flushing
Ferry

Market
Strand

Church St

Kimberley
Pk Rd

Arwenack St

**National
Maritime
Museum**

Falmouth
Docks

Custom
House
Quay

Discovery
Quay

Bar Rd

**Falmouth
Docks Train
Station**

Castle Dr

**Falmouth
Town Train
Station**

Bar Lane

Castle Hill

Melvill Rd

Avenue Rd

Pendennis Castle (560m);
Pendennis Point (1km)

Emslie Rd

Stracey
Rd

Cliff Rd

Gyllyngvase
Beach

Falmouth Bay

Swanpool
Beach

The days of the tall ships, tea clippers and naval galleons may be gone, but the town remains an important centre for shipping and repairs – you'll still see big ships moored up alongside the town docks, undergoing refurbishment and re-pairs. Since 2003 Falmouth has also been home to the Cornish outpost of the National Maritime Museum, an impressive multimedia affair that forms the centrepiece of the heavily redeveloped area around **Discovery Quay**.

Falmouth

◉ Top Sights
1 National Maritime Museum C3

◎ Sights
2 Prince of Wales Pier B2

⬢ Sleeping
3 Falmouth Townhouse C3
4 Greenbank A1
5 Highcliffe House C4
6 Sixteen Falmouth A4
7 St Michael's Hotel B5

⊗ Eating
8 Amanzi B3
9 Baker Tom's B3
10 Courtyard Deli B2
11 Gylly Beach Café B5
12 Harbour Lights C3
13 Indaba Fish on the Beach A6
14 Oliver's B2

15 Provedore B3
16 Stein's Fish & Chips C3
17 Stone's Bakery B2
18 The Wheelhouse ...SEAFOOD.........B3

◎ Drinking & Nightlife
19 Beerwolf Books B2
20 Boathouse A2
21 Chain Locker C3
22 Dolly's B3
23 Espressini A3
24 Hand Bar B2
25 Quayside C3
26 The Front C3

◎ Shopping
27 Jam B2
28 Mondo Trasho B2
29 Trago Mills C3
30 Willow & Stone B3

◉ Sights & Activities

★ **National Maritime Museum** MUSEUM
(www.nmmc.co.uk; Discovery Quay; adult/child £11/7.60; ☺10am-5pm) Sister to the Greenwich original, this is Falmouth's flagship attraction. It explores Britain's illustrious maritime history through a vast collection of yachts, gigs, schooners, trimarans and other groundbreaking sailing craft – many suspended from slender steel wires in the **Flotilla Gallery**, the heart of the complex.

Other highlights include the **Nav Station**, a hands-on exhibit exploring nautical navigation; the **Tidal Zone**, where underwater windows peer into the murky depths; and the **Lookout Tower**, offering a 360-degree panorama of Falmouth Bay. The museum also hosts various temporary exhibitions, so check the website for the latest news.

Outside the museum is the revamped Discovery Quay, home to an attractive collection of bars and bistros – including one of celebrity chef Rick Stein's fish and chips bars.

Pendennis Castle CASTLE
(EH; ☑01326-316594; adult/child £6.70/4; ☺10am-6pm Jul & Aug, 10am-5pm Apr-Jun & Sep, 10am-4pm Oct-Mar) Out on the promontory of **Pendennis Point**, west of the town centre, Pendennis Castle was constructed from 1540 to 1545 by Henry VIII as one of a chain of fortresses designed to defend the British mainland from Spanish and French invasion. Falmouth's deep harbour made it a key strategic asset, and Pendennis was built with its sister fortress of St Mawes in order to defend the entrance to the Carrick Roads.

The heart of the castle is its circular keep and Tudor gun-deck, where the battlements still bristle with vintage cannons. During the Civil War, the castle was engaged in a six-month siege under the command of Captain John Arundel of Trerice, during which the garrison resorted to eating the castle's dogs, rats and horses to survive; it was the last Royalist fortress in the southwest to fall. Elsewhere, you can visit the WWI-era guardhouse and the Half Moon Battery, designed to play a crucial role in the event of Nazi invasion during WWII. Underground are the guns' magazines and observation post.

Outdoor concerts are held in the grounds during summer. Less tuneful is the **Noonday Gun**, which rings out at noon sharp every day throughout July and August.

Town Beaches BEACH
Falmouth's bucket-and-spade beaches aren't quite up to north coast standards, but they're nice enough for paddling and sun-lounging. Nearest to town is **Gyllyngvase**, a flat sandy beach backed by the ever-popular Gylly Beach Café, about half a mile from the town centre. Fifteen minutes' walk along the coast path is the smaller beach of **Swanpool**, near a small inland lagoon populated

ots, ducks and mute swans, as ndaba Fish on the Beach cafe. miles further along the coast h, the quietest of the three, including a beach cafe, kayak nart restaurant, the Cove. The ... of the Scottish trawler, the *Ben Asdale*, can usually be seen just along the coast at low-tide.

All the beaches have car parks, but they fill up quickly in summer. Bus 500 stops at all three beaches en route to Trebah Gardens and the Helford Passage.

Festivals & Events

Falmouth Week REGATTA
(www.falmouthweek.co.uk) Held in mid-August, this busy festival is Cornwall's largest sailing regatta.

Falmouth Oyster Festival FOOD FESTIVAL
(www.falmouthoysterfestival.co.uk) You can feast on oysters, mussels and other crustaceans during this October festival, which also hosts cookery classes and culinary demos.

Sleeping

★ **Highcliffe House** B&B ££
(☑ 01326 314466; www.falmouth-hotel.co.uk; 22 Melvill Rd; r £92-135; ℗ 🛜) After a heavy revamp, this impressive affair is Falmouth's best B&B. Stylish and uncluttered, its rooms blend white walls, distressed furniture and retro pieces – a vintage-style radio here, an old angle-poise lamp there. We particularly liked Room 7 (the attic suite) and Room 4 for its town view.

Falmouth Townhouse HOTEL ££
(☑ 01326-312009; www.falmouthtownhouse.co.uk; Grove Pl; d £85-120) The choice for the design-conscious, in an elegant mansion overlooking the quay. Despite the heritage building, the feel is modernist: slate greys and funky scatter cushions throughout, plus walk-in showers and king-size TVs in rooms. Noise spillage from the downstairs bar may be an issue.

Sixteen Falmouth B&B ££
(☑ 01326-319920; www.sixteenfalmouth.co.uk; 16 Western Tce; d £75-90, f £90-130) There are four rooms to choose from at this elegant B&B: all are spacious and have mini-fridges, French antique furniture, plush fabrics and St Kitts bathstuffs. The house has Georgian style, and there's a woodburner to lounge by.

Budock Vean Hotel HOTEL £££
(☑ 01326-250288; www.budockvean.co.uk; Mawnan Smith; d £230-256; ℗ @ 🛜) Another stalwart on Cornwall's luxury-hotel scene, this riverside beauty sits on the Helford's north bank, with country-chic rooms (some with sitting rooms), four lounges, a health spa, tennis courts, 13 hectares of parkland and even a private jetty.

Greenbank HOTEL £££
(☑ 01326-312440; www.greenbank-hotel.co.uk; Harbourside; s £89-99, d £145-235; ℗) Ships in bottles and model boats cruise around the lobby of Falmouth's original upmarket hotel. Most rooms are classically styled, but only the more expensive have water views: ask for 'Deluxe' and 'Executive' for the most space.

St Michael's Hotel HOTEL £££
(☑ 01326-312707; www.stmichaelshotel.co.uk; Stracey Rd; r £108-236; ℗ 🛜 🛝) The pick of Falmouth's seafront hotels, with checks, stripes and slatted wood for that maritime feel. It's not worth skimping here: go for the biggest room you can afford.

Eating

Falmouth has some fine restaurants and cafes, plus a couple of artisan bakeries: **Stone's** (☑ 07791-003183; www.stonesbakery.co.uk; 28a High St) and **Baker Tom's** (www.bakertom.co.uk; 10b Church St), are both along the main street.

Harbour Lights FISH & CHIPS £
(www.harbourlights.co.uk; Arwenack St; fish & chips £6-8) Falmouth's classic chippie, serving the usual crispy cod and chips alongside special daily catches. Check the blackboard on the counter to see what's left – lemon sole and pollock often feature.

Provedore CAFE £
(☑ 01326-314888; www.provedore.co.uk; 43 Trelawney Rd; ⊙ cafe 8.30am-3.30pm Tue-Fri, 8.30am-12.45pm Sat; tapas bar 6.30-10pm Thu-Sat) Uphill from town, there's a dash of Riviera chic around this tapas bar. Students and arty types pack in for deli sandwiches and the inhouse espresso blend, as well as tapas on Thursday, Friday and Saturday.

★ **The Wheelhouse** SEAFOOD ££
(☑ 01326-318050; Upton Slip; mains £8-15; ⊙ 7-10pm Wed-Sat) Hidden down a narrow slip just off Arwenack St, this rough-and-ready seafood bar is another of Falmouth's hot-

ticket tables. Owners Tina and Matt keep the menu deliberately simple according to the day's catch: crab, lobster and mussels are chalked on the board, served with skinny chips and homemade mayonnaise. Nautical knick-knacks, old crockery and reclaimed furniture complete the fisherman's shack vibe. Bookings essential.

★ Oliver's   FRENCH ££
(☑ 01326-218138; www.oliversfalmouth.com; 33 High St; mains £12.95-19.95; ⊘ lunch noon-2pm, dinner 7-9pm Tue-Sun) This one-room bistro is fast becoming Falmouth's most sought-after address. The decor is bare-bones (plain white walls, plain pine tables) and the tables are sardine-can tight, but the diners don't seem to mind: they pack in for chef Ken Symons' Gallic-influenced grub. With 24-hours notice he'll even make you a 'party in a box' to eat at home. Book ahead.

Courtyard Deli   DELI, CAFE ££
(☑ 01326-319526; http:courtyarddeli.wordpress. com; 2 Bells Crt; mains £8-12; ⊘ 8.30am-5.30pm Mon-Wed, 8.30am-9.30pm Thu-Sat, 10.30am-4pm Sun) Small is beautiful, as this fabulous deli-diner ably demonstrates. Tempting charcuterie, homemade tarts, inventive salads and gourmet quiches fill the counter cabinets, and there are evening tapas sessions several times a week. It's up an easy-to-miss alley off Market St, next to Beerwolf Books.

Amanzi   AFRICAN ££
(☑ 01326-312678; www.amanzirestaurant.co.uk; 28 Arwenack St; mains £10.50-17; ⊘ 5-10pm Wed-Fri, noon-10pm Sat, 11am-9pm Sun) The produce at this zingy bistro is Cornish, but the flavours are much more exotic. African dishes feature heavily: start with falafels or *trinchado bunny-chow* (slow-cooked beef), then follow up with *espetado* (barbecued rump skewers) or *bobotie* (spiced lamb stew). Refreshingly different.

Gylly Beach Café   CAFE ££
(☑ 01326-312884; www.gyllybeach.com; Gyllyngvase Beach; mains £10.95-15.95; ⊘ 9am-11pm; ⊗) A great location and a decked patio over Gyllyngvase are the main draws at this lively beach restaurant. It covers all bases: fry-ups and pancakes for brekkie, platters of antipasti for lunch, quality steak, seafood and pasta after dark. It's open late for drinks but gets very busy.

Stein's Fish & Chips   FISH & CHIPS ££
(☑ 01841-532700; Discovery Quay; fish £7.85-9.25; ⊘ 12-2.30pm & 5-9pm) Rick Stein's only non-Padstow restaurant is on Falmouth's Discovery Quay. The menu is the same as his Padstow fish-and-chip shop: classic beer-battered cod and hake, alongside more unusual options such as monkfish and John Dory. Whether it's worth the premium price is a matter of opinion.

Cove   BRITISH ££
(☑ 01326-251136; www.thecovemaenporth.co.uk; Maenporth; lunch mains £10-15, dinner mains £17-25; ⊘ lunch noon-2pm, dinner 6.30-9.30pm; ☑) Overlooking Maenporth, this is the place for dining with a view. Chef Arty Williams is Cornish but infuses his menu with Mediterranean flavours: Falmouth Bay scallops with cauliflower purée, or plaice with sweet red onions and pancetta. Vegetarians are also well catered for. It's just behind Maenporth Beach, 2 miles from the town centre.

Indaba Fish on the Beach   SEAFOOD £££
(☑ 01326-311886; www.indabafish.co.uk; Swanpool; mains £13-22; ⊘ lunch daily, dinner Mon-Sat) Straightforward seafood served on a rocky bluff beside Swanpool: plump for fresh lobster and crab, goan seafood curry or classic surf-and-turf. Portions can be small and standards variable; the location's the draw.

🍷 Drinking & Nightlife

Falmouth's student crowd has ensured its nightlife has taken an upturn, but things can get rowdy on Friday and Saturday.

★ Beerwolf Books   PUB
(☑ 01326-618474; www.beerwolfbooks.co.uk; 3 Bells Crt; ⊘ noon-midnight daily) Quite possibly the greatest idea ever, anytime, anywhere: a pub and bookshop rolled into one, meaning you can browse for reading material before settling down for a pint of real ale. Boutique breweries such as Penryn's Rebel Brewery Co and Sussex-based Dark Star are represented at the bar. Dangerously attractive.

★ Espressini   CAFE
(39 Killigrew St; coffee from £2; ⊘ 8am-6pm Mon-Sat, 10am-4pm Sun; ⊗) Cornwall's best indie coffee house, bar none. Owner Rupert Ellis cut his teeth working for the big chains, but has branched out on his own with this bespoke venture. Indecisive drinkers beware: the choice of blends, roasts and coffee concoctions here are enough to fill a 6-foot long blackboard. Literally.

The Front
PUB

(☑01326-212168; Custom House Quay; ☺11am-11.30pm) The beer-buff's choice, named CAMRA's Kernow Pub of the Year in 2011. Old barrels, wonky stools and scuffed wood-floors make it feel like a proper old pub, but it's the local ale choice that draws in the punters – it changes daily. Mine's a pint of Heligan Honey.

Hand Bar
BAR

(☑01326-319888; 3 Old Brewery Yard; ☺noon-1am) Another of Falmouth's too-cool-for-school beer bars, fittingly situated in an old brewery yard off the old High St. The beer choice here showcases owner Pete Walker's knowledge, gained while running Leeds' North Bar: esoteric choices such as New York's Brooklyn Brewery and Bodmin's Harbour Brewing Co are both on tap.

Boathouse
PUB

(☑01326-315425; Trevethan Hill) Lively split-level pub offering great views across the river to Flushing, and decent food.

Chain Locker
PUB

(Quay St) A proper old sea-dog's pub, with the all-important low ceilings and hugger-mugger atmosphere.

Quayside
PUB

(Arwenack St) Along the quay from the Chain Locker, this is the pub for a sunset pint on a nice day, with plenty of picnic tables beside the harbour.

Dolly's
TEA ROOM

(☑01326-218400; www.dollysbar.co.uk; 21 Church St; ☺10am-10pm Tue-Thu, 10am-11pm Fri & Sat) Frilly and friendly, Dolly's has recaptured the delights of the old-fashioned English tea-room – complete with charity-shop lamps, bone china teapots and cake stands. It kicks into a different gear after-dark, with cocktails and jazz (plus a weekly knitting group).

🛍 Shopping

Jam
RECORDS

(☑info 219123; 32 High St) Music emporium-cum-cappuccino bar, with a just-so selection of vinyl and CDs, great coffee and leather sofas.

Willow & Stone
HOMEWARES

(☑01326-311388; www.willowandstone.co.uk; 18 Arwenack St) Falmouth's fix for design junkies, from antique ironmongery to enamel lamps.

Mondo Trasho
VINTAGE

(☑01326-212306; 31 High St; ☺10am-5pm) Vintage and retro togs, from classic Levis to re-claimed handbags.

Trago Mills
DEPARTMENT STORE

(☑01326-315738; www.trago.co.uk; Arwenack St; ☺9am-5.30pm) Owned by the Cornish mega-store near Liskeard, Trago's is an institution for cheap-and-cheerful goods.

ℹ Information

Fal River Information Centre (☑0905-3254 534; vic@falriver.co.uk; 11 Market Strand, Prince of Wales Pier; ☺9.30am-5.30pm Mon-Sat, 10am-4pm Sun) Small information centre run by the Fal River company.

ℹ Getting There & Away

BOAT

There are a number of ferries from Falmouth, most of which are listed on the useful Fal River website (www.falriverlinks.co.uk).

Ponsharden Park & Float Ferry (☑01326-319417; www.falriver.co.uk/getting-about/park-and-float; day pass per car with 2 passengers £12, up to 7 passengers £16; ☺10am-6pm May-Sep) Runs to Customs House Quay on the 500-space Ponsharden car park on the outskirts of Falmouth. The equivalent bus costs £5 return for up to seven people.

St Mawes Ferry (p177) runs from Prince of Wales Pier hourly from 8.30am to 6.15pm in winter, and three times per hour in summer.

Flushing Ferry (p169) Prince of Wales Pier to Flushing. Twice hourly year-round; children under four, dogs and bikes travel free.

Enterprise Boats (p170) Scenic river cruises between Truro and Falmouth.

BUS

Falmouth has good bus links. Most services leave from the Moor bus station in the centre of town.

Truro (First Bus 88, 45 minutes; two or three per hour) Also stops in Penryn and Devoran.

Penzance (First Bus 2, 1 hour 45 minutes, hourly) Runs via Penryn, Helston, Porthleven, Praa Sands and Marazion.

Helston and the Helford Passage (Western Greyhound Bus 35, 1 hour 15 minutes, four daily) Stops at Glendurgan, Trebah, Constantine and Gweek.

TRAIN

Falmouth is at the end of the branch line from Truro (£3.90, 20 minutes, hourly), stopping at Penryn, Falmouth Town and Falmouth Docks.

Trebah, Glendurgan & the Helford River

Several of Cornwall's great gardens lie to the south of Falmouth, on the north bank of the Helford River. The real showstoppers, Glendurgan and Trebah, can both be found on the banks of the Helford River, about 15 miles drive from Falmouth, and were founded by members of the Fox family, who made their fortune importing exotic plants from the New World.

Further west along the river near Port Navas is the Duchy of Cornwall Oyster Farm, the largest shellfish farm in the county. It's now run by the UK's premier oyster merchants, the Wright Brothers, who also own the nearby Ferryboat Inn (p167).

The villages and creeks around the Restronguet Estuary are also worth a detour.

Sights

Glendurgan   GARDENS
(NT; ☑ 01326-250906; www.nationaltrust.org.uk/glendurgan-garden; adult/child £6.80/3.50; ⊙ 10.30am-5.30pm Tue-Sun, open daily in Jul & Aug) Glendurgan was established by Alfred Fox in the 1820s to show off the many weird and wonderful plants being brought back from the far corners of the empire, from Himalayan rhododendrons to Canadian maples and New Zealand tree ferns. Tumbling down a stunning subtropical valley, the garden offers breathtaking views of the Helford, as well as a lovely ornamental maze and a secluded beach near Durgan village. The gardens are now owned by the National Trust.

Trebah   GARDENS
(☑ 01326-252200; www.trebahgarden.co.uk; adult/child £8.50/2.50; ⊙ 10am-4pm) Just west of Glendurgan is Trebah, planted in 1840 by Charles Fox, Alfred's younger brother. It's less formal, with gigantic rhododendrons, gunnera and jungle ferns lining the sides of a steep ravine leading down to the quay and shingle beach.

Charles Fox was a notorious polymath and stickler for detail; the story goes that he made his head gardener construct a scaffold to indicate the height of each tree, barking out his orders from an attic window via a megaphone and telescope. At the bottom of the gardens, near the Japanese-style bridge, look out for a plaque commemorating the 7500 troops from the 29th US Infantry Division who set sail for Omaha Beach from the nearby slipway on D-Day, many of them never to return.

There's a pleasant cafe and souvenir shop beside the ticket office. Half-price admission is offered if you arrive on the Western Greyhound Bus 500.

🍴 Eating

★ Ferryboat Inn   GASTROPUB ££
(☑ 01326-250625; Helford Passage; mains £8-18; ⊙ lunch & dinner) This riverside pub has had a complete revamp since being taken over by the Wright Brothers, Britain's premier oyster entrepreneurs. Gone are the dated furnishings; in comes wood, slate and an open-plan feel, plus a proper gastropub menu (oysters, shellfish and the Sunday roast are a particular strongpoint). Arrive early to bag an outside table. It's tricky to find; follow road directions to Trebah and Glendurgan and then look out for the signs. Buses 35 and 500 both stop at Helford Passage.

ℹ Getting There & Away

BUS
Bus 35 (four daily) from Falmouth travels through Mawnan Smith and stops at Glendurgan and Trebah.

BOAT
Helford Ferry (www.helford-river-boats.co.uk/theferry; adult/child single £5/2, return £6/3, bicycles £2 each way; ⊙ 9.30am-5pm Apr-Oct) There's been a ferry between the north and south banks of the Helford River since the Middle Ages. The current service leaves from in front of the Ferryboat Inn and runs to the jetty at Helford Village. The crossing takes around 15 minutes. Foot passengers, bikes, babies, pushchairs and dogs can all be carried.

Gweek & Constantine

At the western head of the Helford River near the village of Gweek, the 'ah' factor goes into overdrive at the National Seal Sanctuary (☑ 0871-423 2110; www.sealsanctuary.co.uk; adult/child £14.40/12; ⊙ 10am-5pm May-Sep, 9am-4pm Oct-Apr), which cares for sick and orphaned seals washed up along the Cornish coastline before returning them to the wild.

A couple of miles further north is the pretty village of Constantine, named after the 6th-century Cornish saint, and later a centre for mineral and granite mining. The village now has a lively arts scene thanks to the Tolmen Centre (☑ 01326-341353; http://constantinecornwall.com/tolmencentre), which stages regular theatre and music.

OFF THE BEATEN TRACK

FIVE SECRET GARDENS

Godolphin (☑ 01736-763194; www.nationaltrust.org.uk/godolphin; house & gardens adult/child £7.60/3.80, gardens only £5/2.50; ☺ house 10am-4pm Sun-Thu, gardens 10am-5pm daily) Wonderful 16th-century house and gardens near Helston, undergoing renovation by the National Trust.

Potager Garden (☑ 01326-341258; www.potagergarden.org; adult/child £2.50/free; ☺ 10am-5pm Fri-Sun) Gorgeous kitchen garden near Constantine, with a 100-foot greenhouse, craft workshops, outdoor games and a superb cafe.

Bonython (☑ 01326-240550; www.bonythonmanor.co.uk; Cury Cross Lanes; ☺ 10am-4.30pm Apr-Sep) This 20-acre estate near Helston includes allotments, herbaceous borders and a walled garden.

Penjerrick (☑ 01872-870105; www.penjerrickgarden.co.uk; adult/child £2.50/1; ☺ 1.30-4.30pm Sun, Wed & Fri Mar-Sep) Two gardens in one: exotic jungle plants in the Valley Garden; rhododendrons, magnolias and camellias in the Upper Garden. In Budock, near Falmouth.

Carwinion (☑ 01326-250258; www.carwinion.co.uk; Mawnan Smith; adult/child £4/free; ☺ 10am-5.30pm) Near Mawnan Smith, and worth a visit for rhododendrons and rare bamboo.

Penryn

These days you'll be hard-pushed to tell where Falmouth ends and Penryn begins. But in bygone days this was a proud market town in its own right, as well as the site of one of Cornwall's great seats of ecclesiastical learning, Glasney College (another casualty of Henry VIII's monastery-bashing antics during the Dissolution). The high street still has many attractive 18th and 19th century buildings (many of which are heritage listed), but the old riverside dock which once provided the town's livelihood is now mostly lined by shops and apartments. After decades in the doldrums, Penryn received a kick-start following the arrival of University College Falmouth, and its twisty alleyways are now home to a smattering of cafes, boutiques and food shops.

Of particular note is the **Higher Market Studio** (☑ 01326-374191; www.highermarketstudio.co.uk; 19 Higher Market St), which sells retro furniture and artworks.

✖ Eating & Drinking

★ **Miss Peapod's Kitchen Café**　CAFE **£**
(☑ 01326-374424; www.misspeapod.co.uk; Jubilee Wharf, Penryn; mains £5-10; ☺ 10am-4pm Sun-Thu, 10am-midnight Fri & Sat) What's not to adore about this riverfront cafe? Run with relaxed efficiency by Alice Marston and crew, and dotted with retro lamps and mix-and-match furniture, it's earned a passionate Penryn following thanks to its hearty wholefood, friendly vibe and packed program of film, music and live events – and the waterside deck is a stunner. Look out for late-night events and gigs on Friday and Saturday. It's part of the Jubilee Wharf development, which is also home to a seamstress, florist, bike shop and yoga school – check out the rooftop windmills as you drive towards Falmouth.

The Cornish Smokehouse　DELI **£**
(☑ 01326-376244; www.thecornishsmokehouse.com; Islington Wharf, Penryn; ☺ deli open 10am-4pm Wed-Fri) Duck, fish, cheese and game are just some of the things smoked in the kilns of this family-run smokehouse, which uses fruitwoods to give its goodies their distinctive smoky tang.

Earth & Water Deli　DELI **£**
(☑ 01326-259889; www.earthandwater.co.uk; 6 St Thomas St) Cute little deli on the high street in Penryn, selling great sandwiches, cheeses and other Cornish delights.

Rebel Brewing Company　BREWERY
(☑ 01326-378517; www.rebelbrewing.co.uk; Kernick Industrial Estate) This inventive young brewery is shaking things up on the ale scene: its 12 brews range from Hélène, a Belgian-style wheat beer to Penryn, a classic pale. Brewery tours (£12) last two hours, and there's a brew shop onsite.

Flushing & Mylor

Located directly across the Penryn River from Falmouth, the village of Flushing is one of Cornwall's prettiest, a colourful jumble of fishermen's cottages and sea-captain's cottages that are stacked along the waterfront and wooded hillsides. Originally known as Nankersey, the village became a busy fishing port during the 18th century, and many of the grand houses that are situated along the main approach to the village, St Peter's Hill, belonged to the merchants and captains who grew rich thanks to the Falmouth packet service.

There's not much fishing or sea-trading in Flushing these days (most of its pastel-coloured houses are holiday lets or second homes), although the village comes to life in late July for its annual regatta. At other times of year, it's a pleasant place for a wander, with a couple of good pubs and some peaceful walks along the riverbanks, including a trail to the nearby yachting harbour of Mylor.

Big Blue Watersports (☑01326-374044; www.bigbluewatersports.co.uk; single-seater kayaks £25/40 per half/full day) is based next to the harbour at Mylor, and rents out one- and two-seater kayaks, plus bikes and windsurfing equipment.

Eating & Drinking

Royal Standard PUB **££**
(☑01326-374250; St Peter's Hill; mains £8-14) Once the preferred haunt of Flushing's gig-rowers, but now a foodie's pub. The feel is modern, but there are still a few nautically-themed curios around: a rudder here, a vintage photo there – and there's a small garden out back.

Seven Stars PUB
(☑01326-374373; www.sevenstarsflushing.co.uk; Trefusis Rd) This is where the locals hang out in Flushing, a traditional village pub with benches on the street, an open log fire and plenty of beers on tap.

❶ Getting There & Away

Flushing is a 5-mile drive from Falmouth. A more entertaining way to arrive is aboard the **Flushing Ferry** (☑07974-799773; http://flushingferry.co.uk; adult/child £2.50/1), which runs regularly across the river from Falmouth.

Restronguet Creek & Devoran

Travelling north along the Fal River from Mylor, the next inlet is Restronguet Creek, perhaps the prettiest of the Fal's wooded tributaries. It runs west for about 2 miles all the way to the village of Devoran, once an important site for processing ore from the tin and copper mines, which was ferried here from the north coast mines aboard the old Redruth and Chacewater tramway.

Tucked at the bottom of a steep hill by the waters of Restronguet Creek, the thatched Pandora Inn (☑01326-372678; www.pandorainn.com; Restronguet Creek; mains £10-16) is one of Cornwall's landmark pubs, and has been here since the mid-1600s. It's the picture-perfect image of a smuggler's pub. Inside, blazing hearths, snug alcoves, low ceilings and ships-in-cabinets; outside, thatched roof, cob walls and a pontoon snaking out onto the creek. Hard to believe it almost burnt to the ground in 2011; thankfully, the ground floor remained largely intact, and it's since been rebuilt in seamless shipshape fashion.

Trelissick Gardens

Stretching for 200 hectares along the Carrick Roads, Trelissick (NT; ☑01872-862090; www.nationaltrust.org.uk/trelissick-garden; Feock; adult/child £7.20/3.60; ⊙10.30am-5.30pm Feb-Oct,

---

THE COAST-TO-COAST TRAIL

The disused tram track from Devoran to Portreath has been redeveloped as the Coast to Coast Cycle Trail, which runs for 11 miles past the old mine workings around Scorrier, Chacewater and the Poldice Valley. It's mostly flat and easy, although there are a few up-hill and off-road sections.

Bikes and maps can be hired at the Devoran end from Bissoe Bike Hire (☑01872-870341; www.cornwallcyclehire.com; ⊙9.30am-6.30pm summer, to 5pm winter), which also has a good cafe, and at the Portreath end from the Bike Barn (☑01209-891498; www.cornwallcycletrails.com; ⊙10.30am-5.30pm). There's car parking at both ends if you prefer to bring your own bike.

11am-4pm Nov-Jan) is another of Cornwall's showpiece estates. It's particularly popular for its walking trails, which meander through a patchwork of maintained woodland, working farmland and river estuary; deep-sea tankers can often be seen moored up along the Fal, near the King Harry Ferry. If you're only here to walk, you can just pay for the car park (free to NT members; otherwise £3.50).

The estate has been owned by several families, although for the bulk of its history it belonged to the Copeland family (of Copeland china fame) before being gifted to the National Trust in 1955. Although the estate's neo-Gothic mansion is closed to the public, you can still explore the ornamental gardens, renowned for their collections of rhododendrons, camellias and hydrangeas.

The gardens are on a minor road off the A39 between Falmouth and Truro; look out for the turn next to the Shell Garage at Playing Place. Beyond the gardens, the minor B3289 road runs all the way to the river, where the King Harry Ferry (☎ 01872-862312; www.falriver.co.uk/getting-about/ferries/king-harry-ferry) shuttles across the water to the Roseland.

Based near the gardens, Canoe Cornwall (☎ 07754-808639; www.canoecornwall.org.uk; £25 per person) is one of the only places in the county where you can take trips in traditional open-top wooden canoes (rather than plastic sit-on-top kayaks). Expeditions last around three hours and run along the Fal River.

Truro

POP 17,431

Dominated by the triumvirate spires of its mighty cathedral, built in the late 19th century, Truro is the county's capital and its main administrative and commercial centre. The city originally grew up around a medieval hilltop castle, and later became one of the county's four stannary towns and busiest ports. The town's maritime ambitions were scuppered, though, by the unexpected silting up of the river, and the town's quays (including Lemon Quay and Back Quay, both near the Hall for Cornwall) now exist only in name.

Traces of Truro's wealthy heritage remain in the smart Georgian townhouses and Victorian villas dotted around the city – especially along Strangways Terrace, Walsingham Place and Lemon St – although a rash of 60s and 70s architecture has done little to enhance the city's historic appeal.

These days it's the county's main centre for shopping and commerce. There are regular outdoor markets on the paved piazza at Lemon Quay (opposite the Hall for Cornwall) – check out the useful Enjoy Truro website (www.enjoytruro.co.uk) for all the latest goings-on.

◎ Sights & Activities

Truro Cathedral   CHURCH
(www.trurocathedral.org.uk; High Cross; suggested donation £4; ◷ 7.30am-6pm Mon-Sat, 9am-7pm Sun) Plonked like a neo-Gothic supertanker in the heart of town, Truro Cathedral dominates the city skyline from every angle. Built on the site of the 16th-century parish church of St Mary's (part of which now forms the cathedral's South Aisle), the cathedral was a massive technical undertaking for its architect John Loughborough Pearson. The foundation stones were laid in 1880 but the building wasn't completed until 1910 – the first new cathedral to be built in Britain since St Paul's. The cathedral's copper-topped central tower reaches 76m, while the shorter western spires are 61m.

Royal Cornwall Museum   MUSEUM
(☎ 01872-272205; www.royalcornwallmuseum.org.uk; River St; annual pass £5; ◷ 10am-4.45pm Mon-Sat) The Royal Cornwall Museum is Cornwall's oldest museum, and houses a varied range of exhibits covering the county's archaeological and historical past. In the main galleries the eclectic collection ranges from Celtic torcs to a ceremonial horse carriage, while the Rashleigh Gallery contains over 16,000 rare mineralogical specimens. Upstairs in the Treffry Gallery you'll find paintings by Stanhope Forbes and other Newlyn School artists alongside a small selection of old masters such as Rubens, Blake, Turner, Gainsborough and Van Dyck.

★ Enterprise Boats   BOAT TOUR
(☎ 01326-374241; www.enterprise-boats.co.uk; adult/child return £13/8) Two miles downriver from Truro's city centre, past the green expanse of Boscawen Park, is the riverside hamlet of Malpas, from where ferries chug out along the wooded banks of the River Fal all the way to Falmouth. Free double-deckers run from the Truro harbour-master's office to the pontoon at Malpas, although depending

Truro

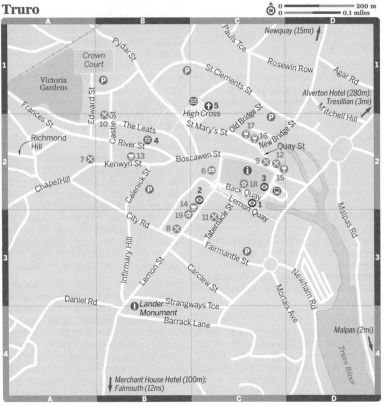

Truro

◎ Sights
1 Farmers Market	C2
2 Lemon St Market	C2
3 Pannier Market	C2
4 Royal Cornwall Museum	B2
5 Truro Cathedral	C1

🛏 Sleeping
| 6 Mannings Hotel | C2 |

⊗ Eating
7 Archie Brown's	A2
Baker Tom	(see 2)
8 Bustopher's	B3
9 Duke St Sandwich Deli	C2
10 Falmouth Bay Seafood Café	B2
11 Indaba Fish in the City	C3
12 Saffron	C2

🍷 Drinking & Nightlife
13 108 Coffee	B2
14 Blend 71	C2
15 Old Ale House	C2
16 Old Grammar School	C2
17 Vertigo	C2

✪ Entertainment
| 18 Hall for Cornwall | C2 |
| 19 Plaza Cinema | B3 |

on the tides you can often ride the boat all the way back to Truro. It's a wonderfully scenic trip that putters past wooded riverbanks and hidden inlets; some boats also stop at Trelissick en route.

🎆 Festivals & Events

City of Lights　　　　　　　FESTIVAL
(www.trurocityoflights.co.uk) Giant withy (wicker) lanterns are carried through the city centre during this December street parade.

🛏 Sleeping

Truro's hotels and B&Bs are on the dull side, but the city's central location makes it a useful overnight base.

Merchant House Hotel   HOTEL £
(☑ 01872-272450; www.merchant-house.co.uk; 49 Falmouth Rd; s £50-59, d £68-79; P) This Victorian house is handy for town, and refurbishment has brightened up the rooms with fresh colour schemes and contemporary furnishings. Some rooms have skylights, and there's parking – although the hotel's popular with coach tours so space can be hard to find.

Mannings Hotel   HOTEL ££
(☑ 01872-270345; www.manningshotels.co.uk; Lemon St; s £79, d £99-109; P 🛜) The city's best option is this efficient city-centre pad (formerly the Royal Hotel), geared towards the business crowd. Bold colours, wall-mounted TVs and sleek furniture keep things uncluttered, and there are 'aparthotels' for longer stays (£129). Cheaper rates at weekends.

Alverton Hotel   HOTEL £££
(☑ 01872-276633; www.thealverton.co.uk; Tregolls Rd; d £130-160; P 🛜) This converted convent is Truro's grandest hotel, but the style is more country than contemporary. Antique wardrobes, sleigh beds and drapes in the generous bedrooms; the best have views over the hotel's manicured grounds.

🍴 Eating

Archie Brown's   CAFE £
(☑ 01872-278622; www.archiebrowns.co.uk; 105-106 Kenwyn St; mains £4-12; ⊙ 9am-5pm Mon-Sat; 🛜 🖉) 🖉 The Truro outpost of Penzance's much-loved wholefood cafe, serving lovely salads and imaginative vegetarian mains, as well as a copious selection of herbal teas. The cafe's upstairs, and there's a wholefood and vitamin shop downstairs.

Baker Tom   BAKERY £
(☑ 01872-277496; www.bakertom.co.uk; breads £1-2) Young baker Tom Hazzledine has a growing reputation for his artisan breads and patisseries, and now has several shops across Cornwall. This bakery inside Lemon St market is the one that started it all.

Duke St Sandwich Deli   CAFE £
(10 Duke St; sandwiches £2.50-5; ⊙ 9am-5.30pm Mon-Sat) Build your own sandwich from Cornish ingredients here.

★ Falmouth Bay Seafood Café   SEAFOOD ££
(☑ 01872-278884; www.falmouthbayseafoodcafe. com; 10 Castle St; mains £13.95-22; ⊙ lunch noon-2.30pm, dinner 7.30-9pm Mon-Sat) Superior seafood is the *raison d'être* of this popular restaurant, from freshly-shucked Falmouth Bay oysters to huge seafood platters loaded with crab claws, mussels, langoustines and lobster (£28 for one person, £52 for two people). Often touted as Truro's top restaurant, and we'd hate to disagree.

Bustopher's   BISTRO ££
(☑ 01872-279029; www.bustophersbarbistro.com; 62 Lemon St; mains £10-18; ⊙ 10am-11pm daily) This longstanding Lemon St establishment has had a full contemporary refit and is now ideal for a swift, stylish bite. The interior's been lightened up with wood, chrome and an open kitchen, and the menu offers quality bistro food, including a different daily *plat du jour*. Businessy types cram in for lunchtime, and it gets busy at weekends.

Saffron   BRITISH ££
(☑ 01872-263771; www.saffronrestauranttruro.co.uk; 5 Quay St; mains £13.50-16.50; ⊙ lunch 11am-3pm Mon-Sat, dinner 5-11pm Tue-Sat) For ages this pint-sized restaurant was the only decent place to eat in town, and it's still a favourite – especially since the recent decor overhaul. The seasonal menu spices up Cornish with Spanish, Italian and French flavours: mutton with turnip dauphinoise, or seared pollock with saffron mash.

Indaba Fish in the City   SEAFOOD ££
(☑ 01872-274700; www.indabafish.co.uk/in-the-city; Tabernacle St; mains £12-18; ⊙ lunch noon-2.30pm, dinner 5-9.30pm Mon-Sat) This metro-modern diner is a good bet for fish, although the food is solid rather than spectacular: classic surf-and-turf, or Goan seafood curry. Industrial piping and leather seats give it a modern vibe, but the back-street location is slightly odd.

🍷 Drinking & Nightlife

Old Ale House   PUB
(Quay St; ⊙ noon-11pm) One of the last pubs in Truro to retain its traditional spit-and-sawdust skin, burnished wood, beer mats and all. Guest ales are chalked on blackboards, and there are live gigs at weekends.

Old Grammar School   PUB
(19 St Mary's St; ⊙ 10am-late; 🛜) Cool city bar, offering open-plan drinking with big tables and soft sofas to sink into. Lunch is served

from noon to 3pm; later it's cocktails, candles and imported Belgian and Japanese beers.

Vertigo
BAR

(15 St Mary's St; ☺10am-late; 🕿) Another of the buzzy bars around St Mary's St and Bridge St; the selling point at Vertigo is the quirky decor and delightful walled garden.

Heron
PUB

(Malpas; ☺11am-3pm & 7-11pm) Two miles from the city, this creekside pub serves good beer and grub, with outside benches where you can sip your pint overlooking the river.

★108 Coffee
CAFE

(☎07582-339636; www.108coffee.co.uk; 108c Kenwyn St; ☺7am-6pm Mon-Fri, 8am-6pm Sat) Set up in 2011 by unapologetic coffee-nuts Paul and Michelle, this is the place for a caffeine fix in Truro. The beans come courtesy of Cornwall's renowned coffee roasters Origin Coffee, and the flat whites and espressos are as good as any the county has to offer (you can even text your order ahead to save waiting). Light bites and cakes are also on offer.

Blend 71
CAFE

(☎01872-279686; www.blend71.co.uk; 71 Lemon St; ☺10am-5pm Mon-Sat) Another decent coffee stop, next door to the Plaza Cinema.

🛍 Shopping

Although the city centre is dominated by high-street chains, it's worth having a wander around the revamped Lemon St Market (www.lemonstreetmarket.co.uk; Lemon St; ☺10.30am-5.30pm Mon-Sat), home to several gift-shops, a barber, a cafe and Baker original shop, plus a smart gallery-c the upper level. Overhead, look out fc sculptures built for the City of Lights

Local butchers, bakers, cheese-makers and veg-growers set up shop at Truro's lively Farmers Market (www.trurofarmersmarket.co .uk; ☺9am-4pm) on nearby Lemon Quay on Wednesday and Saturday.

☆ Entertainment

Hall for Cornwall
HALL

(☎01872-262466; www.hallforcornwall.co.uk; Lemon Quay) The county's main venue for touring theatre and music.

Plaza Cinema
CINEMA

(☎01872-272894; www.wtwcinemas.co.uk; Lemon St) A four-screen cinema showing mainstream releases.

ℹ Information

Tourist Office (☎01872-274555; tic@truro. gov.uk; Boscawen St; ☺9am-5.30pm Mon-Fri, 9am-5pm Sat)

ℹ Getting There & Away

BUS

Truro is the county's main transport hub, with bus connections to most destinations in Cornwall.

Falmouth (First Bus 88, 45 minutes; two or three per hour) Stops in Penryn and Devoran.

St Ives (First Bus 14, 1½ hours; half-hourly Monday to Saturday, every 2 hours on Sunday) Via Chacewater, Redruth, Camborne and Hayle.

Penzance (First Bus 18, 1¾ hours; hourly Monday to Saturday)

WORTH A TRIP

TREGOTHNAN

Three miles from Truro near Tresillian is Tregothnan (☎01872-520000; www.tregothnan. co.uk) the feudal seat of the Boscawen family, whose heirs have inherited the title of Lord Falmouth for the last 600 years.

More recently, Tregothnan has found fame as the UK's first (and only) tea plantation. The temperate Cornish climate allows the cultivation of several rare-leaf teas, including assam, darjeeling and earl grey. Prices command a considerable premium (tea bags from £3.75 for 10 sachets, loose tea from £5 for 25g). Other goodies, including manuka honey produced by the estate's bees, are sold at the shop.

Tregothnan House is closed to the public, although the estate's botanic garden can be visited on a private tour with the head gardener Jonathan Jones (£65). It's open for group visits on various days throughout the year, when the admission drops to £30, so check the website for details.

The estate also has some gorgeous holiday cottages for rental, including several secluded cottages along the Fal's verdant creeks.

Newquay (Western Greyhound Bus 585/586, 50 minutes; half-hourly Monday to Saturday)

St Mawes (Western Greyhound Bus 550/551, 1 hour; hourly Monday to Saturday, every 2 hours Sunday) Stops in Tresillian, Probus and Tregony en route to Veryan, followed by Gerrans, Portscatho and St-Just-in-Roseland on the way to St Mawes.

Wadebridge (Western Greyhound Bus 594, 1 hour 10 minutes; hourly Monday to Saturday, one on Sunday) Runs to St Agnes in the opposite direction.

TRAIN

Truro is on the London Paddington–Penzance line (sample fares £3.90 to Redruth, £6.20 to Penzance & St Ives, £51.50 to £61.50 to London), and the smaller branch line to Penryn and Falmouth (£3.90).

The Roseland

East of Truro across the Fal River lies the rural Roseland, a lovely, quiet corner of the county, carpeted with arable fields, country lanes and little-visited inlets. This rural peninsula gets its name not from flowers, but from the Cornish word *ros,* meaning promontory. Dotted with tiny coastal villages and fringed with hidden beaches, the Roseland is a part of Cornwall that still seems to belong to a bygone age.

❶ Getting There & Away

By road, it's around 18 miles from Truro to the peninsula's largest town, St Mawes. The Western Greyhound 551 bus (half-hourly Monday to Saturday, five on Sunday) runs from Truro, stopping at Tregony and Veryan, where it becomes the 551 as it continues to St Mawes.

A quicker route is to catch a ferry. If you're on foot, the St Mawes Ferry (p177) shuttles pedestrians across from Falmouth several times an hour. If you're driving you'll need to catch the **King Harry Ferry** (☎ 01872-862312; www.falriver.co.uk/getting-about/ferries/king-harry-ferry; per car single/return £5/8, free for bicycles and pedestrians), which carries cars, cyclists and pedestrians across the river from the landing near Trelissick Garden.

Ferries shuttle back and forth throughout the day. The crossing only takes about twenty minutes, so if you've missed the boat, just join the queue and wait for the next one.

Tregony, Veryan & Portscatho

By road, the first town of note on the Roseland is Tregony, once an important market town and river port on the Fal's eastern tributary. Today it's a quiet village. As you drive past, look out for the almshouses on Tregony Hill, originally built in 1696 for the town's poor, and restored in 1895.

Four miles further south is Veryan, another sleepy country village that's home to a couple of art galleries and an excellent village pub. At the top of the hill above the village are its best-known landmarks: two circular roundhouses, whose lack of corners supposedly made them devil-proof (since there's nowhere to hide in the corners).

Another 7 miles south is the one-street village of Gerrans and the nearby port of Portscatho, formerly one of the busiest pilchard ports on Cornwall's south coast. The village boasts one of the county's largest granite breakwaters, alongside a smattering of galleries, knick-knack shops and second homes.

🛏 Sleeping

Treloan CAMPSITE **£**
(☎ 01872-580989; www.coastalfarmholidays.co.uk; Portscatho; pitches for 2 adults & car £15-24; ☺ year-round; ✴) This huge farm campsite is the best on the Roseland, occupying several spacious fields between Gerrans and Portscatho. There's ample space, even in summer, plus a wooden 'snug', and static caravans for hire if you prefer something more stable over your head than a sheet of canvas. During the summer, local artist Mac Dunlop holds weekly art and music sessions around the campsite fire: see www.caravanserai.info for details.

★ Lugger Hotel HOTEL **£££**
(☎ 01872-501322; www.luggerhotel.co.uk; Portloe; £99-175; 🛜) The consummate romantic hideaway, teetering on the harbour's edge in pretty Portloe. Sumptuous rooms dot the smugglers' inn and adjoining fishermen's cottages, with classy furnishings, decadent beds and the sound of waves breaking from your window; the restaurant's a spoil too.

Pollaughan Farm COTTAGES **£££**
(☎ 01872-580150; www.pollaughan.co.uk; £480-1480 per week; 🅿 🛜 ✴) Situated a quick drive from Porthcurnick Beach, this four-cottage complex is designed to suit the whole family: stressed-out parents, hyperactive kids, even homesick pets. Cottages range from country traditional to open-plan contemporary, and facilities include a wildlife lake and tennis court. Book well ahead.

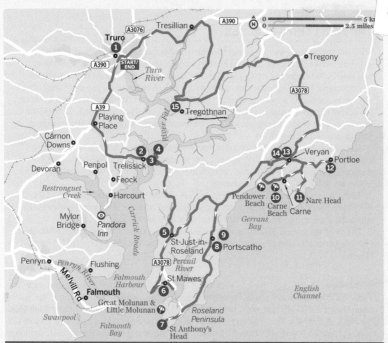

Driving Tour
The Roseland Peninsula

START TRURO
FINISH TRURO
LENGTH 48 MILES; 1 DAY

With its rolling fields, narrow lanes and out-of-the-way villages, the rural Roseland makes for an idyllic day's drive.

Start out in **1 Truro**, and head over to **2 Trelissick** for a wander around the riverside grounds and rhododendron gardens. Then join the queue for the historic **3 King Harry Ferry**, which has been transporting passengers over to Philleigh for nigh on a century. On the opposite side of the river, the old tearooms at **4 Smuggler's Cottage** near Tolverne are a picture of tranquillity now, but in 1944 the nearby quay was a major embarkation point for American troops setting sail for the D-Day landings.

Continue along the B3289 to the flower-filled churchyard of **5 St-Just-in-Roseland**, one of Cornwall's prettiest. Five miles further south brings you to the chichi harbour of **6 St Mawes**, with its curve of whitewashed cottages and medieval castle. Stop off for an excellent pub lunch at the Victory Inn or the Rising Sun.

From St Mawes, drive all the way around the River Percuil through the village of Gerrans to **7 St Anthony's Head**, crested by a lighthouse and the remains of a Victorian gun battery. Then it's back the way you came for a detour to the fishing village of **8 Portscatho** and the nearby beach of **9 Porthcurnick**, where you can indulge in a cream tea at the beachside Hidden Hut cafe.

Further along the coast takes you past the impressive sands of **10 Carne** to the National Trust–owned **11 Nare Head**, a fine place for a blustery walk. Afterwards you reach the squeeze-guts streets of **12 Portloe**, once the area's busiest pilchard harbour.

Inland is the village of **13 Veryan**, set around a central green and peaceful duck pond. Stop off at nearby **14 Melinsey Mill** to pick up some homemade crafts and cakes, then head back via the tea plantation at **15 Tregothnan** to journey's end in Truro.

THE ROSELAND'S BEACHES

They might not be as well-known as the north coast beaches, but the Roseland Peninsula has some beautiful beaches to explore. Largest of all are **Carne** and **Pendower**, two side-by-side beaches which join together at low tide to form one immense sweep of white sand. The beaches are signed from the A3078 between Veryan and Portscatho, but are accessed via a steep single-car lane. There's limited parking at the bottom. At the end of Pendower is a small cafe, **The Basking Shak** (Pendower Beach; £2-5; ⏲9am-5pm in season), which sells hot drinks and ice-cream, plus the house speciality – jumbo sausages wrapped in tortillas.

Further south towards Portscatho is **Porthcurnick**, a good family beach which has acres of sand at low tide, as well as the super Hidden Hut beach cafe. The nearest parking is at the Rosevine or the public car park in Portscatho. Either way, it's a walk of about 500m along the coast path to the beach.

To the south between Gerrans and St Anthony's Head is the secluded beach of **Porth Beor**, accessed via fields and a punishingly steep cliff trail and staircase. It's hard to find without a decent map, and not practical for families due to the difficult access.

The beaches around St Mawes are a better bet: **Great Molunan** and **Little Molunan** are perfect for paddling and can both be reached via the Place Ferry (p177) from St Mawes.

The Rosevine HOTEL **£££**
(☎01872-580206; www.rosevine.co.uk; Portscatho; 2-person studios £1000-1450 per week, family apt £1290-2480; P✿☰☺☻) This country house outside Portscatho is one of Cornwall's finest family-friendly hotels, with 2-person studios and family apartments, all self-contained and named after local beauty spots. It's very stylish, and the kids are superbly well-catered for, with playhouses, trampolines and climbing frames dotted round the grounds. Highly recommended if you're en famille.

✖ Eating & Drinking

⭐**Hidden Hut** CAFE **£**
(www.hiddenhut.co.uk; Porthcurnick Beach; meals £5-7.50; ⏲10am-5pm Mar-Oct) Hidden indeed: this coastal cabin cafe on Porthcurnick Beach is so tucked away, you might miss it even if you've been here before. The wooden cabin was built as a wartime lookout, but now serves delicious beach food: grilled cheese toasts, hot soups, proper cakes and super 'beach salads'. During summer, the hut also hosts pop-up 'feast nights' once or twice a week. The only seating is on benches, but with views like this, who wants to sit indoors? It's a 500m walk north to the hut from Portscatho.

Melinsey Mill CAFE **£**
(☎01872-501049; www.melinseymill.co.uk; near Veryan; mains £4-10; ⏲10am-5.30pm Apr-Oct Tue-Sun, open daily in Jul & Aug) Just outside Veryan, this 16th-century watermill has been converted into a delightful cafe and craft-shop, where you can pick up wacky withy sculptures made by owner Rick Hancocks. They also do a cracking cream tea, plus doorstep sandwiches and delicious homemade cakes.

New Inn PUB **££**
(☎01872-501362; www.newinnveryan.co.uk; Veryan; mains £8-14) Snug village pub near the green, frequented by a mainly local crowd. The pub has lots of atmosphere – fireplaces, woodburners, brass knick-knacks – and the food's decent enough.

Plume of Feathers PUB
(☎01872-580321; The Square, Portscatho) Cosy Portscatho pub dating from the 18th century. It's an old-style whitewashed pub, and all the better for it: expect worn wood, swirly carpets, plenty of locals and no-frills food (mains £9-14). It's owned by St Austell Brewery, so Tribute and Proper Job are on tap.

St Mawes & Around

Situated at the western tip of the Roseland, directly across the water from Falmouth, is the breezy seaside village of St Mawes. With its whitewashed cottages, well-kept gardens and sparkling waterfront location, it feels more ritzy Riviera than rural Roseland. It's been a favourite stop-off for sailors and yachties since the 1930s, and the addition of Olga Polizzi's renowned Hotel Tresanton has only added to the exclusive feel.

The village is named after the Celtic saint St Maudez, who is thought to have arrived in Cornwall from either Ireland or Brittany. St Mawes later became an important naval station thanks to its strategic position at the end of St Anthony's Head. Henry VIII built a 16th-century castle here in conjunction with the one across the water at Pendennis, and a naval gun battery remained on the nearby headland until after the end of WWII.

◎ Sights & Activities

★ St Mawes Castle
CASTLE

(EH; ☑ 01326-270526; adult/child £4.50/2.70; ☺ 10am-6pm Sun-Fri Jul-Aug, 10am-5pm Sun-Fri Mar-Jun & Sep-Nov, 10am-4pm Sat & Sun Nov-Mar) Strategically sited to command an uninterrupted field of fire over the entrance to the Carrick Roads, St Mawes is one of a string of coastal fortresses built by Henry VIII during the 16th century, and is also among the best preserved. The castle is laid out in the form of a clover, with circular towers around a central keep. It's approached via a classic drawbridge, and you can wander freely around the interior chambers and the outside gun-decks, which would have been mounted with heavy 'ship-sinking' cannons.

Ironically, the castle never really saw much action; the threat of Catholic invasion from Spain never materialised during Henry VIII's reign, and it was easily taken by parliamentarian forces during the Civil War.

St Anthony's Head
VIEWPOINT

The remains of a turn-of-the-century gun battery can still be seen along the point at St Anthony's Head. Just along the coast is the peninsula's 1835-built lighthouse, where you can now stay inside the lighthouse keeper's old cottage, Sally Port (☑ 01386-701177; www.ruralretreats.co.uk; from £910 for 5 nights).

St Mawes Kayaks
KAYAKING

(☑ 07971-846786; www.stmaweskayaks.co.uk; 2 hr £15, per day £30) Kayaks are ideal for exploring the waters off St Mawes, especially the quiet creeks along the Percuil River, and the nearby beaches of Great and Little Molunan. Single and two-seater sit-on kayaks are available.

⌕ Sleeping & Eating

★ Roundhouse Barns
COTTAGES £££

(☑ 01872-580038; www.roundhousebarnholidays.co.uk; cottages £695-945 per week; P ☀) Three sweet stone-fronted cottages, plus two B&B rooms, on a 3/4-acre private farm estate about 3 miles drive from St Mawes towards St Just.

Neutral colours, freestanding bathtubs, Neff appliances and goose-down duvets create a posh country vibe, and the grounds are lovely.

Hotel Tresanton
HOTEL £££

(☑ 01326-370055; www.tresanton.com; St Mawes; d £250-550; P ☎ ☀) Long the choice for sojourning celebs and film stars, Olga Polizzi's ritzy St Mawes establishment is still the queen of the castle in St Mawes. Chilled checks, sea stripes and deluxe fabrics in the bedrooms, plus little extras including a private cinema, motor launch and award-winning bistro. It's a wallet-buster, but one to remember.

Victory Inn
PUB ££

(☑ 01326-270324; www.victory-inn.co.uk; mains £10-18) Venerable village boozer tucked up an alley of the harbour, whitewashed on the outside, and decorated with hanging baskets in summer. It still has a bit of vintage character downstairs, but the upstairs restaurant is all twisted willow and muted tones. Good food, especially on Sunday for the roast.

Rising Sun
PUB ££

(☑ 01326-270233; www.risingsunstmawes.co.uk; St Mawes; mains £7-15) Gabled pub that does a roaring trade with visitors straight off the St Ives ferry. It has a little walled patio out front, and serves solid food as well as a decent carvery on Wednesday and Sunday. Upstairs rooms (rooms £98 to £142) are frilly and rather old-fashioned.

The Watch House
BISTRO ££

(☑ 01326-270038; www.watchhousestmawes.co.uk; 1 The Square; lunch mains £8-12, dinner mains £12-15; ☺ 11am-10pm Mon-Sat, 11am-9pm Sun) This relaxed restaurant on the St Mawes waterfront is where everyone wants to eat. The interior is suitably shipshape – clean lines, white tablecloths, sea-blue banquettes, wooden chairs – providing the setting for simple, unpretentious Mediterranean-style food, such as crab cakes with aioli and tomato compote, or Fal mussels with smoked bacon, Cornish cider and wild garlic. It's not quite fine-dining, but it'll definitely do.

❶ Getting There & Away

The **St Mawes Ferry** (☑ 01872-861910; www.falriver.co.uk/getting-about/ferries/st-mawes-ferry; adult/child return £9/4.50) potters across the water to Falmouth, while the little **Place Ferry** (adult/child return £6/4; ☺ half-hourly Apr-Oct) runs to nearby Place Creek, the starting point for several coastal walks and the beaches of Great and Little Molunan.

Gardens of the Southwest

Blessed with a balmy climate nurtured by the Gulf Stream, the southwest boasts an array of astonishing gardens. Many, such as Garden House, Heligan, Trelissick and Tresco's Abbey Gardens, date from the 18th and 19th centuries. Others, such as the Eden Project, feel like a vision from a sci-fi future.

VISITBRITAIN / BRITAIN ON VIEW / GETTY IMAGES ©

ELLEN ROONEY / GETTY IMAGES ©

1. Eden Project (p182)
The largest greenhouses on earth house palm trees, orchids, olive groves and a treetop walkway.

2. Trelissick Gardens (p169)
These 200-hectare gardens offer popular walking trails.

3. Lost Gardens of Heligan (p182)
A fairy grotto and 'Lost Valley' are features of these historic gardens.

4. Abbey Garden (p253)
This garden dates back to 1834 and boasts an impressive collection of more than 20,000 exotic plant species.

VISITBRITAIN / DANIEL BOSWORTH / GETTY IMAGES ©

OFF THE BEATEN TRACK

7TH RISE & THE LOST COTTAGE

If you really want to dodge the modern world for a while, this back-of-beyond cottage beside the banks of the Fal is the place to do it. Run by hunter, forager and diehard fisherman Thom Hunt, who trades under the name of 7th Rise (www.7thrise.co.uk; 1-day/ weekend course £95/249) and appeared on the *Three Hungry Boys* TV series, it's halfway between a bushcraft school and a spiritual retreat. Activities include catching and cleaning your own fish, foraging for marsh samphire and mussels, canoeing on the Fal, cooking in an underground oven and practising your skills on the makeshift shooting range.

The cottage is deliberately basic – outdoor shower, shack privy, communal bunks and no hot water – but that's all part of the backwoods experience. Thom's a man with a plan, and there are few places better to escape the stresses and strains of the 21st century.

St-Just-in-Roseland

The creekside church at St-Just-in-Roseland is quite possibly the prettiest in Cornwall – and in this ecclesiastically-minded county, there's no shortage of competition. Surrounded by a jumble of wildflowers and overhanging yews tumbling down to a boat-filled creek, the present church dates from the 13th century, but there was probably an oratory here as far back as the 6th century.

It's a gorgeous place to wander on a sunny day, with peaceful paths meandering among rhododendrons, magnolias and azaleas, and many lichen-covered gravestones, some of which are 300 years old or more. Look out for the signs as you reach St Just village.

The Roseland Inn (☑01872-580254; www. roselandinn.co.uk; Philleigh; mains £10-16) is a gorgeous little country pub just outside the hamlet of Philleigh, a couple of miles uphill from the King Harry Ferry. Outside it's covered with climbing roses and wisteria: inside it's all old pictures, brass whatnots and beams. The garden's a beauty, too.

The 500-year-old thatched Smuggler's Cottage (Tolverne), just uphill from the King Harry Ferry, has long been one of Cornwall's best-known riverside tea rooms, and was recently modernised by the Tregothnan estate. It was closed at the time of writing.

SOUTHEAST CORNWALL

East of the Roseland, Cornwall's south coast opens up through a string of beaches and ports that have long since swapped fishing gear for beach togs. Looe, Mevagissey and Polperro are among the most heavily touristed towns in Cornwall, although things are more upmarket in Fowey.

Further on is the Rame Peninsula, sometimes known as 'Cornwall's forgotten corner'. It's mainly worth visiting for its aristocratic estates, including Antony, Mount Edgcumbe and Port Eliot.

St Austell

Once a busy market town, St Austell's looking decidedly down in the dumps these days (and that's after the multi-million pound redevelopment of its town centre). Still, it's a handy spot for shopping and supplies before you venture out along the southeast coast.

Buses from St Austell are the 522 (hourly Monday to Saturday), 524 to Fowey (10 daily), 525 to Charlestown and Fowey (10 daily Monday to Saturday), 526 (hourly Monday to Saturday, four on Sunday) to Mevagissey, Heligan and Gorran Haven, and 527 (hourly Monday to Saturday, six on Sunday) from Newquay to St Austell and the Eden Project. St Austell is on the London Paddington-Penzance line, with connections along the branch line to Par.

Charlestown

In centuries past most of the china clay from the St Austell quarries was shipped out from Charlestown, but it's now a favourite location for film crews; several blockbusters and costume dramas have used its quayside as a backdrop. The town's seagoing heritage is explored at the Charlestown Shipwreck & Heritage Centre (☑01726-69897; www. shipwreckcharlestown.com; adult/child £5.95/2.95; ☺10am-5pm Mar-Oct). It houses a massive collection of objects and ephemera recovered from 150 global shipwrecks – ranging from telescopes, muskets, scrimshaw and coins to howitzer cannons and a few choice pieces from the *Titanic* and *Lusitania*.

Mevagissey & Gorran Haven

Eight miles from St Austell, Mevagissey is another of Cornwall's quintessential fishing ports, with the essential combination alleys, flower-fronted cottages and salty pubs. You'll still find second-hand bookshops and local galleries dotted round, and thankfully there's not a multi-national coffee shop in sight.

The town's impressive double-walled harbour still shelters a small fishing fleet, and it's one of the best places on the south coast for crab-lining: you'll be able to buy all the gear you need in the nearby shops. In summer, ferries (www.mevagissey-ferries.co.uk; adult/child single £7/4, return £12/6; ⊙May-Sep) run along the coast from Mevagissey Harbour to Fowey.

There's little sand to speak of in Mevagissey, but there's a large holiday beach in nearby Pentewan, and several more coves around the village of Gorran Haven and Dodman Point. First comes the grand shingle-sandy arc of Vault, which unfurls towards the headland west of Gorran, and has a small National Trust car park; the beach itself is a 15-minute walk downhill. Tiny Hemmick lies half a mile west around Dodman Point, between Penare and Boswinger; again, you have to park at the top of the hill and walk down.

🛏 Sleeping

Treveague Farm   CAMPSITE £
(☑01726-842295; www.treveaguefarm.co.uk; standard pitch £7-20, £2 extra with electric hookup; ⊙Apr-Oct) This large, popular, well-equipped campsite is just inland from Vault Beach,

about a mile south of Gorran Churchtown. There's lots of space for caravans and tents, but it gets packed in summer even so.

The Meadows   CAMPSITE £
(☑01726-844383; www.themeadowspentewanvalley.co.uk; sites £10-15; ⊙Easter-Oct) New owners have brought a fresh lease of life to this peaceful valley campsite, about halfway between St Austell and Mevagissey. A tinkling stream runs along one side, and the sites are well-spaced and shady. Breakfast baguettes, cakes, camping supplies and fresh eggs are sold in the shop, plus firepits to hire.

Boslinney Barn   B&B ££
(☑01726-843731; www.boslinney-barn.co.uk; Galowras, nr Mevagissey; d £80) A renovated barn between Meva and Gorran, with three stylish rooms tricked out with shiny wood, colourful rugs and reclaimed timber. Little artworks and rough-sawn doors add to the character.

Trevalsa Court   HOTEL £££
(☑01726-842468; www.trevalsa-hotel.co.uk; d £110-235; [P][🤚]) Mevagissey's hillside hotel is the top place to stay in town. Mahogany panels contrast with starchy tablecloths in the dining room, and the menu is good for fresh fish and local game. Rooms feel quaint, in creams, stripes and pastels; some are small, so aim for a Superior Sea View Double at least.

🍴 Eating

Fountain Inn   PUB ££
(☑01726-842320; St George's Sq, Mevagissey; pub meals £8-12) The oldest pub in Mevagissey has two bars in original oak and slate, plus a smugglers' tunnel to the harbour. For sustenance, there are St Austell ales and a menu of beer-battered cod and curries.

DON'T MISS

THE CORNISH ALPS

Alongside mining and fishing, Cornwall's other great industry in the 18th and 19th centuries was the extraction of 'white gold', otherwise known as china clay – a key component in everything from porcelain manufacture to medicines and paper coatings.

The heartland of the industry was the St Austell claypits, where a weird landscape of spoil heaps, mica dams and turquoise pools still looms on the horizon, earning them the local nickname of the 'Cornish Alps'.

The best way to explore is along the Clay Trails (www.claytrails.co.uk), a network of off-road routes suitable for pedestrians, horse riders and cyclists. One route starts at Wheal Martyn (☑01726-850362; www.wheal-martyn.com; adult/child £7.50/4.50; ⊙10am-5pm) country park and runs on to the Eden Project; another travels north from Eden to Bugle.

The park is about 2 miles from St Austell on the B3274; look out for signs for the China Clay Country Park.

OFF THE BEATEN TRACK

ROCHE ROCK

Clinging to a spur of contorted rock surrounded by barren heath, the curious tumble-down chapel on top of Roche Rock looks like a forgotten set from Monty Python's *Life of Brian*. The present chapel is thought to date from around the 15th century, although there was an oratory here long before. Local legends say that this was once the home of the hermit Ogrin, who was visited by the legendary lovers Tristan and Isolde while they were on the run from the wrath of King Mark.

You can still make out a few of the chapel's interior rooms, and the turret has majestic views all the way to Bodmin Moor.

The site is just outside Roche village; watch for the signs as you drive east on the A30 from Fraddon.

Barley Sheaf   PUB **££**
(☑ 01726-843330; www.barley-sheaf.co.uk; Gorran Churchtown; mains £8-14) Gorran Haven's village pub, the Llawnroc, has been turned into a rather soulless hotel, so this quaint country pub in nearby Gorran Churchtown is a much better bet. It's been here since 1837, and feels reassuringly lived-in: expect good grub and a mix of locals and visitors.

Caerhays Castle

West of Mevagissey, overlooking the gentle crescent of Porthluney Beach is Caerhays Castle (☑ 01872-501310; www.caerhays.co.uk; gardens adult/child £7.50/3.50, incl house tour £12.50/6; ⊙ gardens 10am-5pm mid-Feb–mid-Jun), a crenellated country mansion originally built for the Trevanions and later remodelled under the guidance of John Nash (who designed Buckingham Palace and Brighton Pavilion). The house is still a private residence, and is open for guided tours in spring, while the gardens are worth visiting for their wonderful displays of camellias, rhododendrons and magnolias.

A WWII pillbox can still be seen on the right-hand side of the beach. The house is on a narrow road between Portholland and Gorran Churchtown; it's reasonably well signposted, but you might find a map comes in handy.

Lost Gardens of Heligan

Before he embarked on his Eden adventure, Tim Smit's pet project was the Lost Gardens of Heligan (☑ 01726-845100; www.heligan.com; adult/child £11/6; ⊙ 10am-6pm Mar-Oct, 10am-5pm Nov-Feb). During the 19th century, Heligan was the family seat of the Tremayne family and one of Cornwall's great country gardens, but following the outbreak of WWI

(when most of its staff were killed) the garden and house slid into disrepair. Since the early 1990s, volunteers have restored the garden to its full splendour, complete with kitchen garden, fairy grotto and a 'Lost Valley' filled with palms and jungle plants.

Heligan is 1.5 miles from Mevagissey and 7 miles from St Austell. Western Greyhound's bus 526 runs regularly to Mevagissey, Gorran Haven and St Austell.

Eden Project

The space-age domes of the Eden Project (☑ 01726-811911; www.edenproject.com; adult/child £23.50/10.50; ⊙ 10am-6pm Apr-Oct, to 4.30pm Nov-Mar) scarcely need any introduction: since their opening in an abandoned clay pit in 2001, they've become one of Cornwall's most iconic – and most visited – sights.

The three giant greenhouses – the largest on earth – were dreamt up by former record producer Tim Smit, and recreate a stunning array of global habitats. Giant ferns, palms, banana trees, and delicate orchids fill the Humid Tropics Biome, while temperate plants such as cacti, lemon trees, vines, olive groves and aloes inhabit the Mediterranean Biome. Beyond the domes, 13 hectares of herbaceous borders, kitchen gardens and wild flower beds radiate out from the Core, Eden's inspiring education centre (constructed according to the Fibonacci sequence, one of nature's most fundamental building blocks).

The latest addition is a treetop walkway that allows you to stroll up amongst the canopy, right at the top of the biomes. It provides an exciting new perspective that allows you to see the trees literally from a bird's-eye perspective.

It's an amazing and hugely ambitious project that for once lives up to the hype. It's also a model of environmental sustainability – packaging is reused or recycled, power comes from sustainable sources or microgenerators, and rainwater is used to flush the loos. It's also worth visiting year-round: in summer, the biomes provide the backdrop for outdoor gigs at the Eden Sessions (www.edensessions.com); and in winter a full-size ice-rink springs up for the Time of Gifts.

Eden gets very busy; booking online allows you to dodge the queues and get a 10% discount, or 15% if you buy seven days in advance and stick to a specific day.

It's three miles by road from St Austell near Bodelva. You can catch buses from St Austell, Newquay, Helston, Falmouth and Truro, but arriving on foot or by bike snags you £4 off the admission price (and lets the kids in free).

Lostwithiel

High on a hilltop above Lostwithiel, 9 miles from St Austell on the A390, the ruined castle of Restormel (EH; adult/child £3.60/2.20; ☉10am-6pm Jul & Aug, 10am-5pm Apr-Jun & Sep, 10am-4pm Oct) was built by Edward the Black Prince (the first Duke of Cornwall), although he only stayed there twice during his life. It's one of the best-preserved circular keeps in the country, and affords brilliant views across the river and fields from its crenellated battlements.

Four miles southwest of Lostwithiel is another quaint and ancient village, Lerryn, which sits on the banks of the picturesque creek with which it shares its name. Lovely woodland trails wind along the banks of the river through the oak woodland of Ethy Park, and to the 14th century riverside church of St Winnow, about 1.5 miles west.

Back in Lerryn, the excellent Ship Inn (☎01208-872374; www.theshipinnlerryn.co.uk; Fore St, Lerryn; mains £8-10) makes an ideal place for a post-hike pint.

Fowey

In many ways, Fowey feels like Padstow's south-coast sister; a workaday port turned well-heeled holiday town, with a trim tumble of pastel-coloured houses, portside pubs and tiered terraces overlooking the china-blue harbour. The town's wealth was largely founded on the export of china clay from the St Austell pits, but it's been an important port since Elizabethan times; Fowey was a key link in the chain of defences protecting the British mainland against Catholic invasion.

These days Fowey is a prim place, with pricey yachts, fancy shops and brasseries sprinkled along its barnacled quays. It's quite a different place to the sleepy fishing port commemorated by the thriller writer Daphne du Maurier, who lived for many years at nearby Menabilly. The town is still at its busiest in mid-May, when it hosts the four-day Fowey Festival (www.foweyfestival.com), a literary and music festival.

☉ Sights

Readymoney Cove   BEACH
(admission free) From the town centre, the Esplanade leads down to little Readymoney Cove and the remains of the small Tudor fort of St Catherine's Castle.

TRISTAN & ISOLDE

The oft-told legend of *Tristan and Isolde* is one of the oldest of Cornish stories (reimagined by everyone from Béroul to Chaucer, Shakespeare, Wagner and Kneehigh Theatre), and has its legendary roots around Fowey. According to the story, the beautiful Irish maiden Iseult was betrothed to the Cornish King Mark, but fell in love with one of his knights, Tristan, with predictably tragic consequences.

Just outside town is the site of the Iron Age hillfort of Castle Dore, supposedly the site of King Mark's fortress, although little now remains save for a few raised banks. The Tristan Stone is another curiosity: standing by the main road into Fowey, this granite block is inscribed with the legend *Drustanus Hic Iacit/Filius Cunomorus* (here lies Drustanus, son of Cunomorus), and supposedly marks the site where Tristan's body was buried. Uproar ensued when the council recently announced plans to move the stone in order to make way for a housing estate.

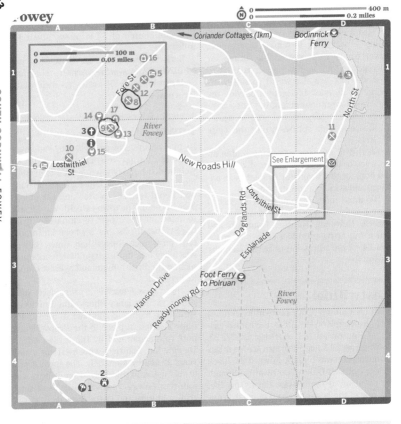

Fowey

⊙ Sights
1	Readymoney Cove	A4
2	St Catherine's Castle	A4
3	St Finbarrus Church	A2

⊕ Activities, Courses & Tours
4	Fowey River Expeditions	D1

⊟ Sleeping
5	Old Quay House	B1
6	Upton House	A2

⊗ Eating
7	Bistro	B1

TEA / CAKE
ICECR

8	Dwelling House	B1
9	Lazy Jack's Kitchen	B2
10	Lifebuoy Cafe	A2
11	Pinky Murphy's Café	D2
12	Sam's	B1

⊜ Drinking & Nightlife
13	King of Prussia	B2
14	Lugger	A1
15	Ship	A2

⊜ Shopping
16	Fowey Fish	B1
17	Webb St Company	B1

Polkerris Beach   BEACH
(www.polkerrisbeach.com) A couple of miles
west of Fowey, this is the area's largest and
busiest beach. It's especially popular for watersports: sailing lessons, windsurfing and
paddle-boarding are all on offer.

St Finbarrus Church   CHURCH
In the heart of town is the 15th-century
church of St Finbarrus, which marks the
southern end of the Saints' Way, a 26-mile
way-marked walking trail running all the
way to Padstow.

🏃 Activities

It's thought that Kenneth Grahame got the inspiration for *The Wind in the Willows* while wandering around Fowey's quiet creeks, so messing about on the river is a must. It's ideal for exploring by kayak, with lots of quiet inlets and plentiful birdlife. One of the loveliest sections is the area around Pont Pill Creek, where old oaks dangle their branches into the water, and if you're lucky you might spy herons, cormorants and the odd kingfisher.

Several operators run expeditions.

Encounter Cornwall   KAYAKING
(☑ 07976-466123; www.encountercornwall.com; Golant; adult/child £25/12.50) Three-hour trips from Golant, with a choice of creek or coast.

Fowey River Expeditions   KAYAKING
(☑ 01726-833627; www.foweyexpeditions.co.uk; 47 Fore St; £25 per person, under 8s free) Guided trips in single and double-seater kayaks.

🛏 Sleeping

Coriander Cottages   B&B £££
(☑ 01726-834998; www.foweyaccommodation.co.uk; Penventinue Lane; r £95-125; P) This cottage complex has something to suit all tastes: garden-view B&B rooms and deluxe open-plan barns powered by underground heat pumps and rainwater harvesting. The mix of old stone and contemporary fixtures is very convincing.

Old Quay House   HOTEL £££
(☑ 01726-833302; www.theoldquayhouse.com; 28 Fore St; d £180-325; P🛜) Fowey's upmarket trend continues at this exclusive quayside hotel. Natural fabrics, rattan chairs and tasteful tones characterise the interior, and the rooms are a mix of estuary-view suites and attic penthouses. Very Kensington; not at all Cornish.

Upton House   B&B £££
(☑ 01726-832732; www.upton-house.com; 2 Esplanade; d £160-240) A bonkers B&B that's gone for decorative overload: the four rooms are full of tongue-in-cheek touches, from neon pink flamingos to skull-print wallpaper. Owner Angelique Thompson holds regular soirées, and runs a retro clothing boutique downstairs.

🍴 Eating

Lifebuoy Cafe   CAFE £
(☑ 07715-075869; www.thelifebuoycafe.co.uk; 8 Lostwithiel St; mains £5-10; ⏱8am-5pm) Everyone's favourite brekkie stop in Fowey, this friendly cafe is a riot of character, from the bright furniture and polkadot bunting to the vintage action figures on the shelves. Wolf down a Fat Buoy brekkie or a classic fish-finger butty, washed down with a mug of good old English tea.

Dwelling House   CAFE £
(☑ 01726-833662; 6 Fore St; tea £3-6; ⏱10am-6.30pm summer, 10am-5.30pm Wed-Sun winter) Top spot for tea (20-plus varieties) and dainty cakes (decorated with sprinkles and icing swirls, and served on a proper cake stand).

Pinky Murphy's Café   CAFE £
(☑ 01726-832512; www.pinkymurphys.com; 19 North St; ⏱9am-5pm Mon-Sat, 9.30am-4pm Sun) You'll find everything from charcuterie platters to hot soups and homemade cupcakes at this colourful cafe. Pull up a beanbag and order the house special, Pinky's Cream Tease.

Lazy Jack's Kitchen   ICE CREAM £
(☑ 01726-832689; 4a Webb St; ice-creams £2-3; ⏱10am-5pm) The owners of the Lifebuoy Cafe have branched out with a coffee bar and ice cream shop, selling delicious Moomaid of Zennor ice cream.

Bistro   FRENCH ££
(☑ 01726-832322; www.thebistrofowey.co.uk; 24 Fore St; 2-/3-course menu £15.95/18.95; ⏱10am-11pm) Sparkling bistro dining on Fowey's main street, with a seasonal menu offering Cornish interpretations of Gallic classics: bouillabaisse, fish soup, roast cod loin, sole menunière. Mosaic floors and monochrome prints keep the dining area sleek and chic.

Sam's   BISTRO ££
(☑ 01726-832273; www.samsfowey.co.uk; 20 Fore St; mains £9.95-14.95) Much recommended local's caff, like a cross between *Cheers* and a backstreet French bistro. Squeeze into a booth, sink a beer and tuck into mussels, calamari rings or stacked-up Samburgers. New space has recently been added upstairs, but bookings aren't taken. They also run a sister venue, **Sam's on the Beach** (☑ 01726-812255), over at Polkerris.

🍷 Drinking & Nightlife

Fowey is swimming in pubs. The pink-fronted **King of Prussia** (www.kingofprussia. co.uk; Town Quay) is the best bet for a pint by the harbour, while on the main street you'll find the low-beamed **Lugger** (Fore St) and the **Ship** (☑ 01726-832230; Trafalgar Sq), one of

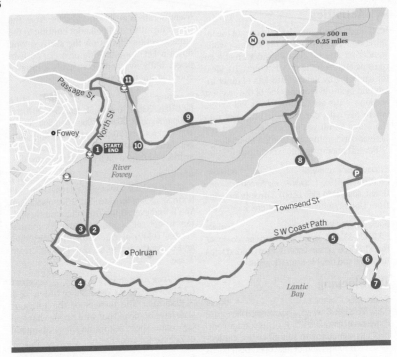

Walking Tour
Fowey, Polruan & Bodinnick

START FOWEY
FINISH FOWEY
DISTANCE 4 MILES; 2½ HOURS

Fowey offers a special mix of scenery, with coast, countryside and river on its doorstep. This fabulous walk factors in all three, and makes use of a couple of cross-river ferries.

Start in **1** **Fowey** at the town quay, next to the rosy-pink King of Prussia pub. From here, catch the foot ferry across the River Fowey, and disembark in the hugger-mugger village of **2** **Polruan**, a huddle of cottages and narrow streets stacked on a steep coastal cliffside. Take the coast path up to the village's **3** **blockhouse**, one of two such houses built around 1380, which would have enabled a chain to be raised across the harbour to prevent undesirable ships from entering it.

Climb up through town and pick up the path as it heads out past the black reefs known as the **4** **Washing Rocks**. From here, the trail begins to leave the village behind and heads out onto the coast path proper. After

a mile or so, you'll reach the hidden sands of **5** **Great** and **6** **Little Lantic Bay**, both offering secluded sun-lounging and swimming. Turn right to see the views from **7** **Pencarrow Head**, or turn left to reach the main road and the nearby National Trust car park. Follow the road round till you reach the little church of **8** **Lanteglos-by-Fowey**, and take the path downhill through the churchyard till you reach the creek.

At the bottom of the hill, the road leads across a footbridge to a path which bears left along the banks of **9** **Pont Pill Creek**, offering dreamy views of the river through the overhanging trees. At **10** **Penleath Point**, there's a lovely vantage point back across the river to Polruan and Fowey, as well as a small memorial to the novelist and scholar Sir Arthur Quiller-Couch, who lived in Fowey from 1891 until his death in 1944. From here, the trail winds on to **11** **Bodinnick**, where you can have a pint at the homely Bodinnick Inn while waiting for the ferry to carry you back to the northern end of Fowey.

Fowey's oldest buildings. It was once owned by John Rashleigh, who sailed against the Spanish Armada and was a contemporary of Francis Drake and Walter Raleigh.

The **Old Ferry** (☏ 01726-870237; www.oldferry inn.co.uk; Bodinnick) is a pleasant pub beside the Bodinnick slipway, and ideal for a crafty pint while you wait for the next crossing.

🛍 Shopping

Webb St Company   HOMEWARES
(☏ 01726-833838;   www.thewebbstreetcompany. co.uk; 2 Webb St) Sleek furniture, fancy light-fittings and other designer desirables fill the rooms of this elegant homeware shop near the harbour.

Fowey Fish   FISHMONGER
(☏ 01726-832422; www.foweyfish.com; 37 Fore St) Fowey's fresh fishmonger, with a fine wines shop next door.

ℹ Information

Fowey Tourist Information Centre (☏ 01726-833616; www.fowey.co.uk; 5 South St; ☺ 9.30am-5pm Mon-Sat, 10am-4pm Sun)

ℹ Getting There & Away

BOAT

From Fowey's quayside, a regular **foot ferry** (www.ctomsandson.co.uk/polruanferry.html; pedestrians & bikes £1) travels across to the neighbouring harbour at Polruan. A little further out of town the **Bodinnick Ferry** (www. ctomsandson.co.uk/bodinnickferry.html; car with 2 passengers/pedestrian/bicycle £4.50/1.30/1.60; ☺ last ferry around 8.45pm Apr-Oct, 7pm Nov-Mar) carries cars and bikes across the estuary, cutting miles off the onward journey to Looe.

BUS

The Western Greyhound 525/526 runs to St Austell (45 minutes, half-hourly Monday to Saturday, hourly on Sundays) via Par and Charlestown.

TRAIN

The nearest station to Fowey is 4 miles away in Par, on the main London-Penzance route. The station is the starting point of the branch line to Newquay (£4.40, 50 minutes).

Golant

This tiny village sits at the bottom of a steep hill about 2 miles from Fowey, on the west side of the Fowey River. It's a peaceful place,

ideal for a riverside pint and ploughman's lunch at the 19th-century **Fisherman's Arms** (☏ 01726-832453; mains £7-14; ☺ lunch noon-3pm, dinner 6-9pm). Afterwards you can wander along the banks of the river and spot birds on the creek, and see the remains of the village's little train station, disused since 1965.

Above the village is one of southeast Cornwall's best hostels, **Golant YHA** (☏ 0845-371 9019; golant@yha.org.uk; dm £16.50, r £36), which runs wildlife trips and badger-spotting expeditions along the river.

The 524/525 bus stops at the Golant turning, or you can follow the **Saint's Way** trail from Fowey.

Polperro

Even in a county where picturesque fishing harbours are ten-a-penny, it's hard not to fall for Polperro – a tight-packed warren of cob cottages, fishermens' stores and squeeze-guts alleyways, all set around a classic Cornish harbour. Unsurprisingly, this was once a smugglers' hideout, but Polperro's sea-going days are long done and dusted. The main industry is now tourism, and the village becomes a ghost town once the holiday season is over. Even so, it's an atmospheric place to wander. The main car park is 750m uphill from the village, from where it's a 15-minute stroll down to the quayside.

The quirky **Polperro Heritage Museum** (☏ 01503-273005; adult/child £2/50p; ☺ 10.30am-4.30pm) delves into the village's salty heritage with a chaotic collection of ships' wheels, model boats, vintage rum barrels and fishing memorabilia, as well as sepia-tinted 19th-century photographs by local man Lewis Harding. There's also a display relating to one of the town's most infamous smuggling escapades, when the crew of the local boat *Lottery* were involved in the murder of a customs officer.

Another Polperro peculiarity is the traditional guernsey sweater traditionally worn by the village's fishermen, known (somewhat confusingly) as the 'Polperro knitfrock'. If you'd like to learn how to knit your own, you'll find copies of *Cornish Guernseys & Knitfrocks* in the museum shop.

The coast path between Polperro and Looe is particularly scenic, especially around the sandy cove of **Talland Bay** – although recent landslips have made some sections inaccessible, so ask for updates before setting out.

✕ Eating & Drinking

Three Pilchards PUB **££**
(☑ 01503-272233; www.threepilchardspolperro.
co.uk; Quay Rd; mains £8-12) The pick of the
Polperro pubs, a classic with whitewashed
shutters and an atmospheric old bar. Sharp's
and St Austell ales, plus pub grub on the
blackboard.

Couch's Great House BISTRO **£££**
(☑ 01503-272554; www.couchspolperro.com; 3-/4-
course menu £28/32) Surprisingly swish bistro in a low-slung cottage near the harbour,
overseen by chef Richard McGeown, whose
previous gigs included working for Gordon
Ramsay, Marco Pierre White and Raymond
Blanc. This is old-school fine dining – amus-
es-gueles, meat in wine reductions, truffled
poached eggs – so it's not a place to turn up
to in shorts and a T-shirt.

❶ Getting There & Away

Bus 572 runs hourly Monday to Saturday to
Plymouth, with stops in Looe, St Germans and
Saltash. The 573 runs a couple of times an hour
to Liskeard via Looe.

Looe

Nestled in the crook of a steep-sided valley,
the twin towns of East and West Looe stand
on either side of a broad river estuary, connected by a multi-arched Victorian bridge
built in 1853. There's been a settlement
here since the days of the Domesday Book,
and the town thrived as a medieval port
before reinventing itself as a holiday resort for well-to-do Victorians: famously,
the town installed one of the county's
first 'bathing machines' beside Banjo Pier
(named for its circular shape) in around
1800, and it's been a popular beach retreat
ever since.

A couple of centuries on, the town beaches of East Looe, Second Beach and Mil-
lendreath are still bound to be crammed
on hot summer days; things are usually quieter across the river at Hannafore Beach,
backed by grassy banks for picnics, and
plenty of rock pools to delve in at low tide.

In contrast to Fowey, Looe still feels
behind-the-times when it comes to eating
out – chip shops and chintzy B&Bs still very
much rule the roost – but this might be set
to change thanks to *chef du jour* Nathan
Outlaw, who recently opened his first south
coast venture here, Outlaw's Fish Kitchen

(p190). Whether this will be enough to spark
Looe's culinary renaissance is debatable, but
it's certainly a welcome addition.

◉ Sights & Activities

Looe Island ISLAND
A mile offshore from Hannafore Point is
the densely wooded Looe Island (officially
known as St George's Island), a 22-acre nature reserve and a haven for marine wildlife.
The island has been inhabited since the early
12th century, when Benedictine monks established a chapel here. It was subsequently a favoured stash for local smugglers (the island's
main house was built by Customs officials to
keep a watch for smuggled contraband). In
1965 the island was occupied by Surrey sisters Babs and Evelyn Atkins, who established
the nature reserve and lived there for most
of their lives. Since 2000 the island has been
administered by the Cornwall Wildlife Trust,
which continues to protect the island's delicate habitat by monitoring visitor numbers.

Between May and September, trips are offered by the Islander (☑ 07814-139223; adult/
child return £6/4, plus £2.50/1 landing fee) from
the quayside near the lifeboat station, but
they're dependent on the weather and tides.
Check the blackboard on the quay for the
next sailing times, or call skipper Tim on
07814-139223.

Wild Futures
Monkey Sanctuary WILDLIFE RESERVE
(☑ 01503-262532; www.monkeysanctuary.org;
St Martins; adult/child/family £8/5/25; ⊗ 11am-
4.30pm Sat-Thu Mar-Nov) On the hills above
East Looe, the Wild Futures Monkey Sanctuary is home to a colony of ridiculously cute
woolly monkeys, smaller colonies of capuch-
in monkeys, patas monkeys and Barbary
macaques (mostly rescued from captivity),
as well as a roost of lesser horseshoe bats.

Boat Trips BOAT TOUR
Various boats set out from Buller Quay for
destinations along the coast – just head
along to the quay and check out the chalk-
boards, where the next sailings will be
chalked up. In summer, there are frequent
sailings to Fowey and Polperro.

Looe's also a great place to try your hand
at some sea-fishing: mackerel, conger and
shark are all regularly caught here. There
are lots of boats offering trips: for shark
trips, start with the Shark Fishing Club of
Great Britain (☑ 01503-262642; www.shark
anglingclubofgreatbritain.org.uk), or for more

OFF THE BEATEN TRACK

LANTIC & LANSALLOS

There are several little-known beaches strung along the coastline towards Looe, but they can be tricky to find without a decent map. Lansallos is a small patch of sand and shingle reached by a half-mile trail from Lansallos village; a second, even more remote beach called Palace Cove can be reached along the coast path. There's more space on the twin beaches of Great and Little Lantic, a pair of soft-sand coves reached via a steep cliff-path. Neither has facilities, but they're pretty much guaranteed crowd-free. There's also a National Trust (NT) campsite at Highertown Farm (✐01208-265211; www.campingninja.com/highertown; £5 per adult, £2.50 per child; ☺Apr-Nov), in a field above Lansallos.

The easiest way to reach the beaches is to take the foot ferry from Fowey to Polruan, then walk along the coast path; it's about 1.5 miles from Polruan to Lantic, 2.5 miles to Lansallos. Alternatively, you can drive from Lostwithiel, but parking is very limited.

general fishing, try Carrie Jane (✐07853-391090; www.fishing-cornwall.co.uk) or Mystique Fishing (✐01503-264530; www.mystique fishing.com).

🛏 Sleeping

Penvith Barns B&B £
(✐01503-240772; www.penvithbarns.co.uk; St-Martin-by-Looe; s £63-72, d £70-80; P 🖰 🐾) Escape the Looe crowds at this delightful rural barn conversion in the nearby hamlet of St-Martin-by-Looe, run by friendly owners Graham and Jules. Rooms range from small to spacious: The Piggery is tiny and tucked under the eaves, while The Dairy has enough space for a spare bed and sofa. Eggs come fresh from a flock of hens.

Botelet COTTAGES £
(✐01503-220225; www.botelet.com; Herodsfoot, Looe; d £100, cottages per week £310-1300, camping £7.50; P) The farmstay you've been dreaming of. Lost in lush farmland between Fowey and Looe, the Tamblyn family have created a haven of Cornish quiet: soothing B&B rooms (June to August only), a brace of cottages, a lovely secluded campsite and even a yurt. You won't want to leave.

Bay View Farm CAMPSITE £
(✐01503-265922; www.looebaycaravans.co.uk; sites £10-22, camping pods £25-40; ☺year-round) Clifftop campsite with an unbroken view across Looe Bay. It's quite exposed, and tents and caravans share facilities, but it's a great option when it's not too busy. Three camping pods are available, too.

Keveral Farm CAMPSITE £
(✐07772-155967; www.keveral.org; adult £4-5, child £2, cars £3) Join the genuine good life at this community farm near Seaton, five miles from Looe. It's home to ten adults and ten kids who grow their own veg, maintain the farm and live as greenly as possible. Camping areas split between an orchard and field, with a maximum of twenty tents per site – and if you fancy doing some work on the farm, you're welcome.

Barclay House B&B ££
(✐01503-262929; www.barclayhouse.co.uk; St Martins Rd, East Looe; d £125-165; P 🖰 🐾) Looe's most upmarket place to stay is beautifully positioned among terraced gardens above East Looe. The rooms are big and bold, finished in tones of aquamarine, gold and pistachio, and several also have bay windows, which offer memorable twilight views over the town. Cottages are available for longer stays.

Anchor Lights B&B ££
(✐01503-262334; www.anchorlights.co.uk; The Quay, West Looe; d £75-92) Despite the unprepossessing pebble-dash exterior, inside this B&B is light, bright and uncluttered. The four main rooms have brilliant views over the harbour, and are all named after local notables: aim for Colliver or Pengelly, or go for Piran if you're on a budget and don't mind bunkbeds.

Beach House B&B ££
(✐01503-262598; www.thebeachhouselooe.co.uk; Hannafore Point; d £90-140; P) Chintzy but cosy B&B in a modern double-gabled house overlooking Hannafore Point. The compact rooms are named after Cornish bays: top of the pile is Kynance, with a private balcony.

✗ Eating

There are plenty of cafes and teashops dotted along the main street in East Looe.

Sarah's Pasty Shop   BAKERY **£**
(☑ 01503-263973; www.sarahspastyshop.com; 6 Buller St; ⊙ 9am-4pm Mon-Sat, 10am-4pm Sun) Much-loved Looe pasty shop, with some controversial variations on the theme including lamb, mint and leek, chickpea and lentil and a 'breakfast fry-up' (with sausage, beans, egg, bacon and tomato). As usual, the traditional pasties are the best – but it's worth turning up on 'Fishy Friday' for the rather good mackerel, horseradish and pea pasty.

Treleavens   ICE CREAM **£**
(☑ 01840-770121; www.treleavens.co.uk; £2-4) Looe's renowned ice cream maker has an outlet near the harbour: creative flavours range from Cornish saffron, cardamom and blue cheese and pear. There are even a couple of diabetic-approved options.

Outlaw's Fish Kitchen   SEAFOOD
(www.outlaws.co.uk) Work on Nathan Outlaw's long-awaited Looe seafood restaurant was still underway at the time of writing – check the website for the latest news.

Squid Ink   BISTRO **£££**
(☑ 01503-262674; www.squid-ink.biz; Lower Chapel St; mains £16.50-19.75; ⊙ dinner 6-10pm Mon-Sat) Hunkered along a backstreet, framed by beams and cob walls, this creative bistro is a snug place to dine: start with seafood *amuses bouches*, then move on to buttery lemon sole or rich roast duck. A wee bit pricey, though.

ℹ Information

Looe Tourist Information Centre (☑ 01503-262072; www.visit-southeastcornwall.co.uk; The Guildhall, Fore St, East Looe; ⊙ 10am-5.30pm)

ℹ Getting There & Away

BUS

Bus 572 (hourly Monday to Saturday) Shuttles between Polperro and Plymouth, stopping at West and East Looe, St Germans (for Port Eliot) and Saltash.

Bus 573 (one or two per hour Monday to Saturday) Polperro to Liskeard via Looe.

TRAIN

The supremely scenic **Looe Valley Line** trucks for 9 miles along the valley to Liskeard (£3.90, 29 minutes, hourly), with grand views of woods and estuary. It's worth taking for the trip alone.

The Rame Peninsula

Flung out on Cornwall's eastern edge, the Rame Peninsula receives so few visitors it's often dubbed as 'Cornwall's forgotten corner'. Despite its proximity to Plymouth, which sits just across the River Tamar, and the regular ferry traffic from the Torpoint Ferry, the Rame Peninsula remains one of Cornwall's most unspoilt pockets, and it's a fine place to head when you want to give the crowds the slip. It's worth making a detour to the cute-as-a-button villages of Kingsand and Cawsand, both full of smuggling history.

Nearby, the impressive 3-mile expanse of Whitsand Bay provides one of the largest stretches of sand in southeast Cornwall.

◉ Sights

Mount Edgcumbe   HISTORIC BUILDING
(☑ 01752-822236; www.mountedgcumbe.gov.uk; adult/child £7.20/3.75; ⊙ 11am-4.30pm Sun-Thu Mar-Sep) Encompassing 865 acres, this Grade I-listed estate was built for the Earls of Edgcumbe, but is now owned by Cornwall and Plymouth City Councils. It's one of the earliest of Cornwall's estates, liberally sprinkled with follies, chapels, grottoes, pavilions and formal gardens. The house was built between 1547 and 1553, but was practically destroyed by German bombing in 1941. It's since been restored in lavish 18th-century style. The gardens are particularly lovely, and you can now get around by Segway if you don't fancy wearing out your shoe leather.

Antony House   HISTORIC BUILDING
(☑ 01752-812191; www.nationaltrust.org.uk/antony; adult/child £8.30/5.10, grounds only £4.40/2.20; ⊙ house 1-5pm Tue-Thu Mar-Nov, also open Sun in summer, gardens open from midday) Owned by the National Trust and still occupied by the Carew-Pole family, this house's main claim to fame are its decorative gardens, designed by the 18th-century landscape architect Humphry Repton and filled with outlandish topiary, some of which featured in Tim Burton's 2010 big-screen adaptation of *Alice in Wonderland*.

The house is 9 miles east of Looe or 6 miles west from Plymouth – the Torpoint Ferry stops a couple of miles away. Opening days vary through the year, so phone ahead or check the website.

PORT ELIOT

Stretching across the far eastern end of Cornwall, Port Eliot (☑ 01503-230211; www.porteliot.co.uk; house & grounds adult/child £8/4, grounds only £4/2; ⊙ 2-6pm Sat-Thu Mar-Jun & 1 week in July) is the family seat of the Earl of St Germans. The 6000-acre estate had been off-limits to the public for many years, but since 2008 has opened its doors for 100 days every year. The highlight of the house is the amazing Round Room, whose walls are almost entirely covered by a characteristically Bacchanalian mural by the late Plymouth artist Rovert Lenkiewicz. Outside, the Grade I–listed estate was part improved by Humphrey Repton, and offers dramatic views towards the Tamar estuary.

Port Eliot has also found notoriety thanks to its annual outdoor bash, the Port Eliot Festival (www.porteliotfestival.com), a quirky literary and musical shindig in late July.

Occasional trains from Plymouth stop at the tiny station of St Germans, on the edge of the estate; otherwise, you'll need your own transport. The vehicle entrance is along the B3249, about 9 miles east of Looe.

🛏 Sleeping & Eating

★ Westcroft
GUESTHOUSE ££

(☑ 01752-823216; www.westcroftguesthouse.co.uk; Kingsand; d £90-110; 🛜) Gorgeous guesthouse in charming Kingsand, offering three suites plastered in posh wallpaper and trendy fixtures: walk-in showers, clawfoot baths, iPod docks. Pick of the bunch is the Clocktower room, where the hot tub nestles under A-frame beams and you can hear the sea swash from your window. No parking.

The View
MODERN BRITISH ££

(☑ 01752-822345; www.theview-restaurant.co.uk; Treninnow Cliff Rd, Millbrook; dinner mains £15.50-19.75; ⊙ lunch noon-1.45pm Wed-Sun, dinner 7-8.45pm Wed-Sat) The name says it all. This restaurant sits in a stunning position on the cliffs above Whitsand Bay. It's a stylish treat, especially for classic seafood, meat and game.

❶ Getting There & Away

The Torpoint Ferry (www.tamarcrossings.org.uk; cars £1.50, motorbikes 30p, bikes & pedestrians free; ⊙ every 15min 9.30am-6.30pm, every 30min 6.30pm-6.30am) chugs across the River Tamar to Plymouth. The ferries run 24-hours a day, with a half-hourly service from 9.30pm to 6.30am.

Tamar Valley

Cutting a swathe through a gentle landscape of fields and woods, the mighty Tamar has marked the age-old dividing line between Devon and Cornwall for over a thousand years; it was officially declared as Cornwall's eastern edge in 936 by King Athelstan, the first unified English king.

Though it's spanned by around 20 bridges – including Brunel's Royal Albert rail bridge (built in 1859) and the more recent Tamar Bridge for cars (1961) – the Tamar is still an important psychological boundary for the Cornish, as demonstrated by the recent proposals to create a new cross-county 'Devonwall' constituency, which predictably met with howls of protest.

For most people, their only view of the Tamar is from the bridges as they travel in or out of the county, but the river is a deliciously peaceful area to explore if you have the time.

◉ Sights & Activities

Cotehele
HISTORIC BUILDING

(NT; ☑ 01579-351346; St Dominick; adult/child £9/4.50, grounds only £5.40/2.70; ⊙ house 11am-4pm Sat-Thu, gardens dawn-dusk daily) At the head of the Tamar Valley sits the Tudor manor of Cotehele, another of the Edgcumbe dynasty's modest country retreats. The cavernous great hall is the centrepiece, and the house has an unparalleled collection of Tudor tapestries, armour and furniture.

Outside, the gardens sweep down past the 18th-century Prospect Folly to Cotehele Quay, where there's a discovery centre exploring the history of the Tamar Valley and a vintage sailing barge, the Shamrock.

A short walk inland (or a shuttle bus) leads to the restored Cotehele Mill, where you can watch the original waterwheel grinding corn several days a week, and watch a furniture maker and potter at work.

Tamar Trails
CYCLING

(www.tamarvalley.org.uk/explore/access/walking/tamartrails) Much of the land is privately owned, but the new Tamar Trails have opened up 25km of hiking and biking trails which were previously off-limits to the public. The trails start at Bedford Sawmills car park, just off the A390 between Gunnislake and Tavistock, and wind their way along the banks of the river, passing through riverside copses and several disused mine-workings.

The Tamar was once a heavily industrialised landscape, with rich mineral lodes and several bustling river-ports, where copper and tin would be loaded before being shipped out across the country. Like many former mining areas, nature has now reclaimed the land, and wildflowers, butterflies and birds abound in summer. Unsurprisingly, the Tamar was declared an Area of Outstanding Natural Beauty (AONB) in 1995.

Canoe Tamar
CANOEING

(☑ 01822-833409; www.canoetamar.co.uk; adult/child £25/21) It'd be a shame to come to the Tamar and not see the river scenery close-up. Canoe Tamar leads daily expeditions up to the river's tidal limits in beautiful wooden Canadian canoes.

❶ Information

Tamar Valley Information Centre (☑ 01822-835030; www.tamarvalley.org.uk; ⊗ 10.30-3.30pm Mon-Fri) Offers general info on the Tamar area in Drakewalls, near Gunnislake.

❶ Getting There & Away

The scenic **Tamar Valley Line** (www.greatscenicrailways.com/tamar.html; day-pass adult/child £5.20/2.60) runs for 14 miles from Gunnislake to Plymouth, stopping at various small stations en route.

Newquay & the North Coast

Includes ➡

Bude 195

Boscastle................... 196

Port Isaac 198

Padstow..................... 201

Newquay & Around ...206

Perranporth to
Portreath 213

Perranporth................213

St Agnes &
Chapel Porth 213

Camborne, Redruth
& the Mining World
Heritage Site 216

Best Places to Eat

➡ Paul Ainsworth at No 6 (p204)

➡ Restaurant Nathan Outlaw (p201)

➡ Fifteen Cornwall (p212)

➡ No 4 Peterville (p215)

Best Places to Stay

➡ The Scarlet (p209)

➡ Elements Hotel (p195)

➡ Boscastle House (p197)

➡ Bedruthan Hotel (p209)

Why Go?

If it's the classic Cornish combination of lofty cliffs, sweeping bays and white-horse surf you're after, then Cornwall's north coast fits the bill. Battered by Atlantic breakers and whipped by sea winds, the shoreline between St Ives and Bude is arguably the county's most dramatic stretch of coast. Unsurprisingly, this was poet John Betjeman's favourite part of Cornwall, but it's far from a well-kept secret; you'll be sharing the scenery with everyone from weekend surfers to coasteerers and celebrity chefs.

The heart of the action is Newquay, north Cornwall's longstanding party town and the capital of the county's surf scene. The beaches are spectacular. If you prefer your sands quieter, head west towards the coastal villages of St Agnes and Perranporth, or east towards Padstow and its booming culinary culture. Even quieter are the out-of-the-way beaches east of the Camel Estuary towards Tintagel and Boscastle.

When to Go

➡ **May** Join the throngs for Padstow's raucous oss'-themed May Day celebrations, but remember to book your accommodation early – or better still, stay out of town.

➡ **Aug** Watch the pros in action at the Boardmasters surf and music festival, the largest event of its kind in the UK. The action centres around Fistral Beach.

➡ **Late Sep** This is a great time of year to enjoy the north coast's beaches in relative peace and quiet – with a bit of luck, you might even get some early autumn sun.

Newquay & the North Coast Highlights

1 Taking a bracing dip at **Bude's Sea Pool** (p195)

2 Strolling among the rockstacks at **Bedruthan Steps** (p206)

3 Seeking out the secret valley pool at **St Nectan's Glen** (p200)

4 Pondering the Arthurian legends of **Tintagel Castle** (p198)

5 Chowing down in Cornwall's culinary capital, **Padstow** (p201)

6 Catching a wave in **Newquay** (p206) or **Polzeath** (p200)

7 Exploring sea-caves and minestacks at **Chapel Porth** (p213)

8 Delving into Cornwall's mining past around **Camborne** and **Redruth** (p216)

BUDE & THE ATLANTIC HIGHWAY

Travelling west along the Atlantic Hwy from the Devon border (or the A39, as it's more prosaically known) carries you through some of the county's most inspiring coastal vistas. Every twist and turn in the road unfurls a fresh panorama of postcard views: wild headlands cloaked in gorse, villages nestled at the base of granite cliffs, and a seemingly neverending stretch of white-capped surf.

Much of the coastline around Bude is less frequented and feels slightly more remote than the well-known beaches around Newquay and Padstow, and with a bit of effort you'll discover several quiet coves even in the height of summer. Take your time: this is a road trip to be savoured.

Bude

First stop across the Cornish border is beachy Bude, which has been reeling in the day trippers and beachgoers since the Victorian tourist boom in the late 19th century. Tucked away at the end of the River Neet, Bude briefly flourished in the mid-19th century thanks to the construction of the Bude Canal, but the town's industrial ambitions were scuppered by the arrival of the railway, and the canal's now effectively a nature reserve. Heritage apart, it's Bude's beaches that warrant a visit.

◉ Sights

The closest beach to town is Summerleaze, a classic bucket-and-spade affair with lots of sand and plenty of space to paddle in. It's also home to the Bude Sea Pool (⊙10am-6pm May-Sep), an open-air lido dating from the 1930s. Be prepared for a chilly dip: the water's fed straight from the Atlantic, so it's bracing even at the best of times.

Directly to the north of town is Crooklets, a small sandy cove flanked by low bluffs that's home to Bude's Surf Life Saving Club. It gets busy in summer.

Bude's other beaches are a bit further afield. Northcott Mouth is great for rockpooling, with granite shelves exposed at low tide and a good sweep of pebbly sand. Further north is Sandymouth, a quiet beach with its own waterfall, followed by Duckpool, another secluded cove dominated by the craggy bulk of Steeple Point. These beaches are usually relatively quiet even in summer, although swimming can be dangerous due to strong rip tides.

Three miles south of town, Widemouth Bay (pronounced *widmuth*) is Bude's best family beach, offering good swimming and plenty of facilities, plus seasonal lifeguard cover. Though it looks like one long continuous stretch at low tide, it's officially two beaches (North and South) divided by the spiny spur of Black Rock.

⚡ Activities

Bude Surf Schools   SURFING
Bude has several low-key surf schools that make a great alternative to the hustle and bustle of the ones around Newquay. Most of Bude's beaches produce useable surf, but Crooklets and Widemouth Bay tend to be the most reliable. All the local surf schools provide equipment and minibus transport to the beach.

BSX Surf Centre   SURFING
(✐0870-7775511; www.budesurfingexperience.co.uk)

Big Blue Surf School   SURFING
(✐01288-331764; www.bigbluesurfschool.co.uk)

Raven Surf School   SURFING
(✐01288-353693; www.ravensurf.co.uk)

⨶ Sleeping

Dylan's Guesthouse   B&B £
(✐01288-354705; www.dylansguesthouseinbude. co.uk; Downs View; s £40-50, d £60-70; P) This snazzy B&B has rooms decked out in white linen, chocolate throws, pine furniture and quirky curios. Most look across the town's golf course and downlands.

Wooda Farm   CAMPSITE £
(✐01288-352069; www.wooda.co.uk; Poughill; sites £14-23) Huge, well-run campsite near Bude, which accommodates everything from caravans to campervans. It gets busy, though, so probably not ideal if you're after a wild camping vibe.

★ Elements Hotel   HOTEL ££
(✐01288-275066; www.elements-life.co.uk; Marine Dr; s £55, d £89-128; P) Eleven soothing rooms decorated in whites and creams, with big views from the outdoor deck, a gym and Finholme sauna, and surf lessons courtesy of nearby Raven Surf School. It is situated in a great detached position on the cliffs above Bude.

Bangor's Organic
B&B ££

(☑ 01288-361297; www.bangorsorganic.co.uk; Poundstock, Bude; d £95; P) An ecofriendly B&B near Poundstock, 7 miles from Bude. The house is elegantly Victorian and the rooms are fairly frilly, but the draw is the rural setting; it's set among 5 acres, and you'll find fresh-picked veg and just-laid eggs on the breakfast table.

The Beach at Bude
B&B £££

(☑ 01288-389800; www.thebeachatbude.co.uk; Summerleaze Cres; r £105-175; P 🖥) The main sell at this posh B&B are the fine views over Summerleaze beach, but the rooms are attractive too: spacious and smart, with super slate-lined bathrooms featuring his-and-hers sinks and fancy futuristic bathubs.

🍴 Eating

Scrummies
CAFE £

(Lansdown Rd; mains £6-8; ⊙ 8am-10pm) The best place for fish and chips in town (the skate and monkfish are caught by the owner). For something fancier, try their scallops and lobster (half/whole £12/24).

★ Life's A Beach
CAFE, BISTRO ££

(☑ 01288-355222; www.lifesabeach.info; Summerleaze; lunch mains £5-10, dinner mains £16-21.50; ⊙ 10.30am-3.30 pm & 7.30-11pm) Perched above Summerleaze, this beachside establishment has a split personality: by day it's a surfy cafe churning out ciabattas, coffees and ice cream, but by night it's a superior seafood venue serving bass fillet with braised fennel, and the house special, salt-baked bream with Moroccan dressing. The setting is fittingly beachy: blue walls, chalkboard menus, and a patio overlooking Summerleaze.

The Castle
MEDITERRANEAN ££

(☑ 01288-350543; www.thecastlerestaurant-bude.co.uk; The Wharf, Bude; lunch £8-12, mains £14-18; ⊙ 10am-9.30pm) Housed inside Sir Goldsworthy Gurney's faux folly in Bude, this restaurant is a relaxed place offering Mediterranean-influenced flavours. Chef Kit Davis honed his craft in the capital before setting up shop in Bude.

ℹ Information

Bude Tourist Office (☑ 01288-354240; www.visitbude.info; The Crescent; ⊙ 10am-5pm Mon-Sat, plus 10am-4pm Sun summer) Beside the main car park near the Castle.

ℹ Getting There & Away

Bus 595 (every two hours Monday to Saturday) from Bude stops at Widemouth Bay, Crackington Haven, Boscastle, Tintagel and Camelford.

Crackington Haven

More fantastic beaches lie to the south of Bude along the coast path. Two miles further south is rocky Millook, renowned for birdwatching and seal-spotting and a distinctive 'zigzag' cliff. Another 6 miles on is Crackington Haven, a popular and busy beach backed by imposing bluffs. Sandwiches, ice creams and beach supplies are sold at the nearby Cabin Cafe (☑ 01840-230238; www.cabincafe-crackington.co.uk; Crackington Haven; ⊙ 9am-5pm).

The most impressive scenery is at the Strangles, 12 miles south of Bude, where the perilously sheer cliffs plunge straight down into the booming surf. South along the coast path, the appropriately named High Cliff is the loftiest in Cornwall at 223m (731ft).

Boscastle

Cornwall's north shore has its share of pretty harbours, but few are quite as pretty as Boscastle. Nestled in the crook of a valley at the meeting point of three rivers (the Valency, Jordan and Paradise), it's the perfect Cornish port, filled with slate-roofed houses and an impressive Elizabethan-era harbour (built in 1584 by Sir Richard Grenville).

The village hit the headlines in August 2004 when freak rainfall caused a dramatic flash flood that swept away cars and devastated many buildings (although thankfully no-one lost their lives). There's precious little sign of the flood left now, though – and a series of river management schemes have hopefully ensured the flood was a freak occurrence rather than a regular event.

The wildflower-spotted cliffs provide the perfect backdrop for a blustery picnic, and the village's oddball Museum of Witchcraft (☑ 01840-250111; www.museumofwitchcraft.com; The Harbour; adult/child £4/3; ⊙ 10.30am-6pm Mon-Sat, 11.30am-6pm Sun Mar-Nov) is also well worth a peek. Founded by the occult expert and ex-MI6 spy Cecil Williamson in 1960, the museum's weird exhibits include witch's poppets (a kind of voodoo doll), divination pans, enchanted skulls, pickled beasts and a horrific 'witch's bridle', designed to extract confessions from suspected hags. Kids will love it.

🛏 Sleeping

Boscastle YHA   HOSTEL **£**
(🖉 01840-250928, 0845-371 9006; boscastle@yha.
org.uk; dm £18; ☺ Apr-Nov) Boscastle's shoebox-
sized hostel was all but washed away by
the floods in 2004, but it's been completely
renovated. It's in one of the village's oldest
buildings, beside the harbour, but be prepared for small dorms.

Orchard Lodge   B&B **££**
(🖉 01840-250418;   www.orchardlodgeboscastle.
co.uk; Gunpool Lane; d £89; P 🛜) A short walk
uphill, this is a thoroughly modern B&B,
crisply finished in slinky fabrics and cool
colours and run with efficiency by owners
Geoff and Shirley Barratt. Rates get cheaper
the longer you stay. No kids under 12.

⭐ Boscastle House   B&B **££**
(🖉 01840-250654; www.boscastlehouse.com; Tintagel Rd; s/d £55/120; P 🛜) The fanciest of
Boscastle B&Bs, this Victorian house overlooks the valley, with six rooms named after
Cornish legends. Charlotte has bay-window
views, Nine Windows has his-and-hers sinks
and a freestanding bath, while Trelawney
has space and its own sofa.

⭐ Belle Tents   CAMPSITE **££**
(🖉 01840-261556;   www.belletentscamping.co.uk;
Davidstow, near Camelford; £564-595 per week)
These stripey big-top style tents feel like
you're camping out with the circus. The 2.5-
acre site is divided into three family camping fields; all the tents have two bedrooms
with proper beds, rugs and solar lighting.
It's 6 miles from Boscastle.

Pencuke Farm   SELF-CATERING **££**
(🖉 01840-230360;   www.pencukefarm.co.uk;   St
Gennys; yurts from £259 per weekend, cottages
£339-799 per week) This organic farm, 1.5
miles from Crackington Haven, has a choice
of plush yurts or cosy self-catering cottages
(we particularly liked sleek Skyber Barn and
stone-fronted Appletree Cottage, which has
its original inglenook hearth). Fresh eggs
and just-baked bread are on sale in the
shop.

Old Rectory   B&B **££**
(🖉 01840-250225; www.stjuliot.com; St Juliot; d
£95-102; ☺ Mar-Nov; P) This house, a short
drive from Boscastle, was the home of St
Juliot's parson and the place where Thomas
Hardy wooed his wife-to-be. It's heavy on
the Victoriana – upholstered furniture, thick
drapes, sash windows – but the grounds are
gorgeous. There's more space in the stable,
with private entrance and woodburner.

🍴 Eating

Helsett Farm   ICE CREAM **£**
(☺ 10am-5pm) Local ice cream made just
outside Boscastle on an organic dairy farm.
It must be good, as it's sold at Harrod's and
Selfridges these days.

Boscastle Farm Shop   CAFE **£**
(🖉 01840-250827; www.boscastlefarmshop.co.uk;
cakes & teas £3-5; ☺ 10am-5pm; P) Half-a-mile
from the harbour on the B3263, this farm
shop sells its own produce, including ruby
red beef and possibly the best sausages on
the north coast. In the cafe, tall windows
look onto fields and coast – the perfect setting for a cream tea.

Wellington Hotel   HOTEL **£££**
(🖉 01840-250202; www.wellingtonhotelboscastle.
com; The Harbour; 2-/3-course menu £30/37.50)
This turreted coaching inn dates back to the
16th century (previous guests include King
Edward VII and Guy Gibson of Dambusters
fame). It's an old-fashioned place – flock
carpets, burnished furniture, upholstered
chairs – and the restaurant continues the
trad theme, with generous servings of Beef
Wellington and pork belly.

🍺 Drinking

Options for a pint include the Cobweb
(🖉 01840-250278; www.cobwebinn.co.uk; The Bridge;
mains £5-14), with a beer garden near the harbour; and the Napoleon (🖉 01840-250204;
High St; mains £6-12), a whitewashed inn in
the 'Top Town'.

ℹ Information

Boscastle Tourist Office (🖉 01840-250010;
www.visitboscastleandtintagel.com; The
Harbour; ☺ 10am-5pm Mar-Oct, 10.30am-4pm
Nov-Feb)

St Juliot

Inland from Boscastle along the River Valency, a 3-mile walking trail leads through old
oak woodland to a brace of historic churches:
pint-sized Minster (sometimes known as
St Merthiana's), partly dating from the 12th
century; and St Juliot, best known for its association with Thomas Hardy. Hardy arrived
here in 1870 as a young architect contracted to

oversee the church's restoration, and promptly fell head-over-heels for the rector's sister-in-law, Emma Lavinia Gifford (a tale recounted in his novel *A Pair of Blue Eyes*). Hardy buffs can even stay at the rectory where their love affair played out.

Trail leaflets for this walk and several others around Boscastle can be found at the tourist office.

Tintagel

The spectre of King Arthur looms large over Tintagel and its crumbling clifftop castle (EH; ☎01840-770328; www.english-heritage.org.uk/daysout/properties/tintagel-castle; Bossiney Rd; adult/child £5.90/3.50; ☉10am-6pm Apr-Sep, 10am-5pm Oct, 10am-4pm Nov-Mar). Though the ruins mostly date from the 13th century, archaeological digs have revealed the foundations of an earlier fortress, fuelling speculation that the legendary king was born at the castle as local legend claims. Fables aside, the site has been occupied since Roman times and served as a seasonal residence for Cornwall's Celtic kings, but the present castle is largely the work of Richard, Earl of Cornwall, who established the fortress to cash in on its Arthurian connections.

King Arthur notwithstanding, it's hard to think of a more soul-stirring spot for a stronghold. Part of the castle stands on a rock tower known as 'The Island', cut off from the mainland, and accessed via a wooden bridge and a dizzying set of cliff steps. Though much of the castle has long since crumbled, it's still possible to make out the footprint of the Great Hall and several other rooms. There's also a curious tunnel that's still puzzling archaeologists; it may have been used as a larder or cold store.

A short walk inland leads to the tiny Norman Church of St Materiana, in a windblown spot above Glebe Cliff. Below the castle is a small rocky beach with a hollow cavern that's inevitably been dubbed Merlin's Cave. It's only accessible at low tide.

After the natural splendour of the Tintagel headland, the village itself is a bit of a letdown, with a smattering of frilly tea rooms and souvenir shops. It's worth looking around the Old Post Office (NT; ☎01840-770024; www.nationaltrust.org.uk/tintagel-old-post-office; Fore St; adult/child £3.60/1.80; ☉10.30am-5.30pm), a 16th-century Cornish longhouse that was once the village post office.

The Mill House Inn (☎01840-770200; www.themillhouseinn.co.uk; Trebarwith; d £100-140; [P][⌂]) is a converted corn mill in Trebarwith, 2 miles from Tintagel. It has eight elegant rooms in calming creams and dark wood. They're a little quaint, with some old beams and poky corners, but the inn's smart pub and restaurant make up for any shortcomings.

Port Isaac

A few miles southwest of Tintagel is the teeny fishing harbour of Port Isaac, a cluster of cobbled alleyways, slender opes (alleys) and cob-walled cottages collected around a medieval harbour and slipway. Though still a working harbour, Port Isaac is best known as a filming location: the Brit film *Saving Grace* and the TV series *Doc Martin* have both used the village as a ready-made backdrop (a sign near the quayside directs tourists straight to Doc Martin's cottage).

More recently, the village has hit the charts thanks to the Fisherman's Friends (www.fishermansfriendsportisaac.co.uk), a group of local shanty singers whose albums have become global hits.

A short walk west leads to the neighbouring harbour of Port Gaverne, while a couple of miles west is Port Quin, now owned by the National Trust. Local folklore maintains that the entire fishing fleet of Port Quin was lost during a great storm in the late 17th century. The remaining families, including some 20 widows, were all subsequently relocated to Port Isaac.

🍴 Sleeping & Eating

Old School Hotel   HOTEL ££
(☎01208-880721; www.theoldschoolhotel.co.uk; Fore St, Port Isaac; d £103-160; [P][⌂]) A small hotel that was originally Port Isaac's schoolhouse. Appropriately, rooms are named after school subjects: top of the class are Latin, with its sleigh-bed and cupboard bathroom; Biology, with its sofa and church-style windows; and split-level Mathematics, with shared terrace and bunkbeds for the kids.

Fresh from the Sea   SEAFOOD £
(☎01208-880849; www.freshfromthesea.co.uk; 18 New Rd) Local man Calum Greehalgh takes out his boat daily in search of crab and lobster, then brings it back to sell at his quaint Port Isaac shop.

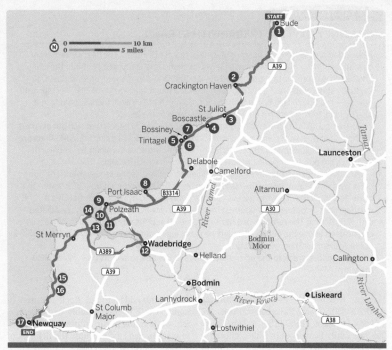

Driving Tour
North Coast Cruiser

START BUDE
FINISH NEWQUAY
DISTANCE 65 TO 70 MILES, 1 DAY

For a top-down, wind-in-your-hair road-trip, the north Cornish coast is hard to beat. This tour starts in ① **Bude**, and cruises south along the main A39 till you reach the village of Wainhouse Corner and the turn-off signed to ② **Crackington Haven**. The narrow road dips down towards the rocky beach, from where you can follow the coast path to High Cliff, the highest in Cornwall.

Follow the road as it loops back to the B3263, which runs past the church of ③ **St Juliot**, known for its Thomas Hardy connections, and drops into ④ **Boscastle**. Don't miss a walk along the harbour and an ice cream from Helsett Farm. From here, the coast road runs west to ⑤ **Tintagel** and its crumbling castle; en route, you'll pass through Trethevy, where trails lead to the pool of ⑥ **St Nectan's Glen** and the remote beach of ⑦ **Bossiney Haven**.

Continue onto the B3314, which runs through the old slate-mining village of Delabole and passes the turning to ⑧ **Port Isaac**, the seaside village that is the village of Portwenn in *Doc Martin*. You'll then reach the turn-off to the surfy village of ⑨ **Polzeath**, where you can stop for a cafe lunch, or head on to the lovely beach of ⑩ **Daymer Bay**.

South of Daymer, the road loops through ⑪ **Rock** and its ritzy restaurants, then heads to ⑫ **Wadebridge**. From here, continue till you reach a roundabout signed to ⑬ **Padstow**, and turn off onto the B3274. From this road you can reach Padstow's 'Seven Bays': Trevone and Harlyn are nearest to town, while Booby's Bay, Constantine, Treyarnon and Porthcothan all lie along the west side of ⑭ **Trevose Head**. It's worth taking the detour to the headland itself and its picturesque lighthouse.

South of Porthcothan, the B3276 unfurls past the rocks at ⑮ **Bedruthan Steps** and the beach at ⑯ **Mawgan Porth** before reaching journey's end in ⑰ **Newquay**.

OFF THE BEATEN TRACK

BOSSINEY HAVEN & TREBARWITH STRAND

A secluded and secret(ish) beach within easy reach of Tintagel, the tiny, tucked-away cove of Bossiney Haven is accessible via farmland and steep steps cut into the cliff. The beach is is practically submerged at high tide, and a tough walk up-and-down, so it usually stays pretty quiet. It's a great place for a picnic and an out-of-the-way dip, but beware – the tide rolls in fast. It's off the B3263 north of Tintagel; there's parking in a nearby field, from where it's a 10 minute walk down to the beach.

Further south is Trebarwith Strand, another fine sandy beach that's all but claimed by the tide at high water, and is accessed across rough rocks (flip-flops or surf shoes are a good idea). Follow the B3263 south from Tintagel, and spot the signs for Trebarwith. There's a big public car park, plus overspill parking in a nearby field.

In between the two beaches near the village of Trethevy is the secret swimming spot of St Nectan's Glen (www.st-nectansglen.co.uk; ⊙ 9.30am-5pm), where a 60ft waterfall tumbles across the slate into a kieve (plunge pool) fringed by ivy and shrubs. It's a mystical spot, supposedly frequented by fairies and pixies, and legendarily associated with King Arthur. The remains of a hermitage which supposedly belonged to St Nectan can be seen above the pool – although we're willing to bet there probably wasn't a cafe (£2-6; ⊙ 10am-5pm) here in his day.

The mile-long track to the pool starts opposite the bus stop in Trethevy; just follow the signs.

Harbour Kitchen BISTRO **££**
(⊋ 01208-880237; www.theharbourportisaac.com; 1 Middle St; mains £15.50-18.50; ⊙ 7am-9.30pm Tue-Sat) Emily Scott couldn't have chosen a better spot for her Cornish bistro – views of sea, harbour and boats fill its porthole windows. Her Mediterranean-influenced food is light and feminine, often using foraged ingredients and edible flowers, and has earned her many admirers. The dining room's tiny, so you'll need to book.

PADSTOW & AROUND

Rock & Polzeath

Across the estuary from Padstow is the exclusive enclave of Rock, now notorious as one of Cornwall's priciest postcodes thanks to an influx of cash-rich city-folk (hence the area's bevy of disparaging nicknames: Cornwall's St-Tropez, Kensington-on-Sea, etc). The village has received extra attention thanks to the arrival of celebrity seafood chef Nathan Outlaw, whose flagship restaurant has recently scooped its second Michelin star.

It's a far cry from the sleepy seaside backwater recalled so fondly by poet John Betjeman, who regularly holidayed in the area between the 1930s and 1960s. The coastline

and countryside around Rock featured in many of his poems, notably in *Trebetherick*, while in his poetic autobiography *Summoned by Bells*, he recounts the delights of arriving here on the coastal railway (now redeveloped as the Camel Trail).

While it's certainly changed, Betjeman's Rock hasn't quite disappeared. The dune-backed white sands of Daymer Bay are as glorious as ever, and outside the main holiday season between June and August, often largely deserted. Just along the coast is Polzeath, the area's main surfing beach and a lively location for some beach-lounging or adrenalin-fuelled outdoor activities. It's also worth walking inland to the quaint church of St Enodoc, where Betjeman was buried on a drizzly Cornish day in May 1984.

In season, the best way to visit Rock is aboard the Black Tor Ferry (p205) from Padstow.

 Activities

Era Adventures OUTDOOR ACTIVITIES
(⊋ 01208-862963; www.era-adventures.co.uk) One of the best multi-activity operators on the north coast, offering packages covering coasteering, surfing, sea-kayaking and guided mountain biking. The guides all have a background in lifeguarding or medical training, so you'll be in safe hands. It's based down a lane from Polzeath Village, signed to Valley Caravan Park & Era Adventures.

Surf's Up
SURFING

(📞 01208-862003; www.surfsupsurfschool.com; 2hr lessons from £26) Renowned local surf school that's been in business since 1995, with courses tailored for everyone from beginners to elite. The surf school is beside the main car park in Polzeath.

🛏 Sleeping

Dormy House
B&B ££

(📞 01208-863845; www.dmyhouserock.co.uk; Rock Rd; d £85; 🅿 🐕 🍽) Just up the road from the Outlaw restaurants, this B&B is suitably upmarket, with five rooms decorated with Anglo-Swedish style (courtesy of owners Anders and Trudie). The open-plan A-frame dining room is particularly fancy.

Cornish Tipi Holidays
CAMPSITE ££

(📞 01208-880781; www.cornishtipiholidays.co.uk; Pendoggett; per week £485-1100) Camp Sioux-style in a wooded valley near St Kew. Tepees are in communal 'village' fields, or pay a premium for a private site. All come with cool boxes, stoves, cooking gear and camp lanterns. BYO sense of adventure.

St Enodoc Hotel
HOTEL £££

(📞 01208-863394; www.enodoc-hotel.co.uk; Rock Rd; r £195-495; 🅿 🐕) As you'd expect, Nathan Outlaw's hotel screams style, but cheap it isn't. Rooms are elegantly furnished, with muted tones offset by colourful scatter cushions, cappuccino carpets, distressed dressers and artwork by Penzance painter Jessica Cooper.

🍴 Eating

Tube Station
CAFE £

(📞 01208-869200; www.tubestation.org; Polzeath; mains £6-12; ⏱ 10am-5pm) This surfy community centre-cum-cafe (part of the Methodist Church) has become a much-loved hangout in Polzeath, furnished with old sofas, slouchy beanbags and vintage surfboards.

St Kew Inn
GASTROPUB ££

(📞 01208-841259; www.stkewinn.co.uk; St Kew; mains £8-16; ⏱ 11am-3pm & 6-11pm) The best pub grub hereabouts can be found in the village of St Kew, about 6 miles drive east of Polzeath and Rock. It looks rustic, with a 16th-century stone exterior and an interior full of beams and flagstones – but the food's bistro standard, from sardines to minute steak. The beer garden's lovely, too.

⭐ Restaurant Nathan Outlaw
SEAFOOD £££

(📞 01208-862737; www.nathan-outlaw.com; Rock Rd, Rock; tasting menu £99; ⏱ dinner 7-9pm Tue-Sat) Since graduating from chef Rick Stein's shadow, seafood specialist Nathan Outlaw has earned himself a national reputation and two shiny Michelin stars – the only chef in Cornwall to do so. There's a choice of two Outlaw venues: foodies favour the exclusive (and expensive) Restaurant Nathan Outlaw, while the more relaxed Seafood & Grill (mains £16-25; ⏱ lunch noon-2.30pm, dinner 6-9.30pm) serves similar quality seafood at (slightly) more affordable prices. Nathan's style is surprisingly classic, and relies on the quality of the seafood rather than cheffy tricks to provide the fireworks. Both restaurants are at the St Enodoc Hotel.

Padstow
POP 3162

If there's one town that's synonymous with Cornwall's recent renaissance, it's Padstow, the undisputed capital of Cornwall's culinary scene, thanks to the efforts of one man – celebrity chef, TV star and local-food champion Rick Stein, who set up his first bistro here in 1975 and has gone on to create his own miniature gastronomic empire.

'OSS ANTICS

Padstow is famous for its annual street party, the 'Obby 'Oss ceremony, a May Day festival (or 2 May if it falls on a Sunday), believed to derive from an ancient pagan fertility rite. The ritual begins just before midnight on 30 April, when revellers announce to the innkeeper at the Golden Lion that summer is 'a-come'. At 10am the Blue Ribbon (or Peace) Oss – a man garbed in a hooped sailcloth dress and snapping horse headdress – dances around the town, accompanied by a baton-wielding 'teazer' and a retinue of musicians, dancers, singers and drummers, all singing the traditional May Song.

An hour later he's followed by the Old (or Red) Oss and, after a day of revelling and carousing, the 'osses are both 'stabled' for another year. It's all eerily reminiscent of The Wicker Man, but unlike Sgt Howie you'll need to book ahead if you plan to stay in town.

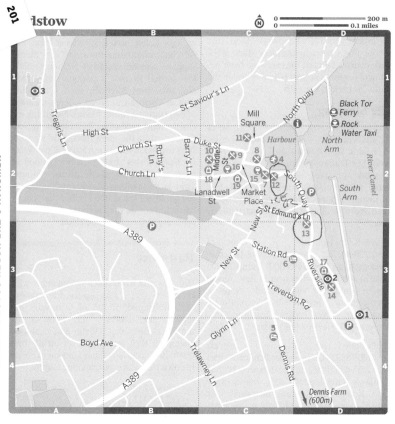

0 ——————— 200 m
0 ——————— 0.1 miles

Padstow

◉ Sights
1 National Lobster Hatchery D3
2 Padstow Seafood School D3
3 Prideaux Place A1

◔ Activities, Courses & Tours
4 Boat Trips C2

◔ Sleeping
5 Treann House C4
6 Treverbyn House C3

◉ Eating
7 Basement C2
8 Chough Bakery C2

9 Margot's Bistro C2
10 Paul Ainsworth at No 6 .... C2
11 Rojano's in the Square C2
12 Roskilly's C2
13 Seafood Restaurant D3
14 Stein's Fish & Chips D3

◔ Drinking & Nightlife
15 BinTwo C2
16 London Inn C2

◔ Shopping
17 Stein's Deli D3
18 Stein's Gift Shop C2
19 Stein's Patisserie C2

Since his arrival Padstow has become one of Cornwall's most cosmopolitan corners, with a profusion of posh boutiques and up-market eateries rubbing shoulders with the old pubs, pasty shops and lobster boats clus-tered around the town's old quay. The 'Stein Effect' has certainly transformed the place: Padstow feels more Kensington-chic than Cornish-quaint these days, and not every-one's enamoured of the change.

Whether the town's managed to hold on to its soul in the process is debatable, but it's still hard not to be charmed by the setting – especially outside summer, when the quayside throngs have thinned.

◎ Sights

National Lobster Hatchery NATURE DISPLAY
(☏01841-533877; www.nationallobsterhatchery.co.uk; South Quay; adult/child £3.50/1.50; ⊙10am-7.30pm Jul & Aug, 10am-5pm Apr-Jun & Sep-Oct, earlier closing Nov-Mar) Lobster-fishing has been a way of life on the north Cornish coast for centuries, but overfishing and pollution led to a dramatic decline in stocks during the 1970s and '80s, requiring dramatic action to ensure the industry's survival. Since 2004 the National Lobster Hatchery has been overseeing a sustainability project to help stocks recover. Baby lobsters are reared in holding tanks before being released into the wild.

Padstow Seafood School COOKING COURSE
(☏01841-532700; www.rickstein.com; Riverside, The Harbour; 1-day courses from £198) Masterclasses in everything from French fish to perfect sushi are on offer at Rick Stein's cookery school, which is above Stein's Fish & Chips. Courses are usually booked out months in advance; check the website for late availability.

Prideaux Place HISTORIC HOME
(☏01841-532411; www.prideauxplace.co.uk; house & grounds adult £7.50, grounds only £2; ⊙1.30-4pm Sun-Thu, grounds & tearoom 12.30-5.30pm Apr-Oct) Much favoured by directors of costume dramas, the stately manor was built by the Prideaux-Brune family, purportedly descendants of William the Conqueror. Guided tours last around an hour and take in state rooms, staircases and plaster ceilings, as well as a host of Prideaux-Brune heirlooms.

🏃 Activities

Camel Trail CYCLING
The old Padstow–Bodmin railway was closed in the 1950s as part of Dr Beeching's infamous rationalisation of Britain's railways. Thankfully, the route has now been re-invented as the Camel Trail, Cornwall's most popular bike path.

The flat, easygoing trail starts in Padstow and runs east through Wadebridge (5 miles from Padstow) along the Camel Estuary before continuing on through Bodmin (10.8 miles) to Poley's Bridge (18.3 miles) on Bodmin Moor. The Padstow–Wadebridge section makes a lovely half-day excursion, but it

gets crowded – an estimated 350,000 people tackle the Camel Trail every year. The Wadebridge–Bodmin section is usually quieter and, in its own rugged way, just as scenic.

Bikes can be hired from both ends. In Padstow, **Padstow Cycle Hire** (☏01841-533533; www.padstowcyclehire.com; South Quay; ⊙9am-5pm, to 9pm in summer) and **Trail Bike Hire** (☏01841-532594; www.trailbikehire.co.uk; Unit 6, South Quay; ⊙9am-6pm) hire out bikes for similar rates (£12 to £15 per day, more for tandems, trikes and tagalongs for kids). However, given Padstow's traffic problems, in summer you might find it easier to start the trail in Wadebridge and hire bikes from **Bridge Bike Hire** (☏01208-813050; www.bridgebikehire.co.uk) instead.

Boat Trips BOAT TOUR
(www.padstowboattrips.com) Between Easter and October, the **Jubilee Queen** (☏07836-798457; adult/child £10/5) runs scenic trips along the coastline, while **Padstow Sealife Safaris** (☏01841-521613; www.padstowsealifesafaris.co.uk; 1hr cruise adult/child £22.50/15, 2hr cruise £39/25) visits local seal and seabird colonies.

For something racier, 15-minute **speedboat trips** (£6) zip past the treacherous sandbank of Doom Bar and the beaches of Daymer Bay, Polzeath, Hawkers Cove and Tregirls.

The main Padstow Boat Trips website keeps listings of all the local operators.

🛏 Sleeping

Dennis Farm CAMPSITE £
(☏01841-533513; http://dennisfarm.wix.com/campsite; sites £20.50-23.50; ⊙Easter-Sep) Staying in Padstow doesn't have to break the bank thanks to this tents-only campsite situated in a lovely field beside the estuary. It's on the southern side of town, about a mile from the harbour; follow Dennis Rd onto Dennis Lane and look out for the signs near the lake. Unsurprisingly, it gets busy in summer, so book ahead.

Treyarnon Bay YHA HOSTEL £
(☏0845-371 9664; treyarnon@yha.org.uk; Tregonnan; dm from £15, r from £30; P @) A super 1930s-era beach hostel on the bluffs above Treyarnon Bay. Rooms are big and there's a good cafe, plus barbecues in summer. Bus 556 stops nearby at Constantine.

Treverbyn House B&B ££
(☏01841-532855; www.treverbynhouse.com; Station Rd; d £90-125; P) Harry Potter would feel at home at this turreted villa, complete

NEWQUAY & THE NORTH COAST PADSTOW

with four colour-coded rooms plus an ultra-romantic tower hideaway. Green and Yellow rooms have bay views; Lilac and Pink don't, so are cheaper. All are beautifully decorated with vintage rugs and antique fireplaces, and the breakfast jams are homemade with fruit from the garden.

Treann House
B&B ££

(☑ 01841-553855; www.treannhousepadstow.com; 24 Dennis Rd; d £100-130; P ⧬) Offering luxury that far outstrips its price point, this B&B shimmers with understated style. The three rooms (Cove, Bay and Estuary) are classic, with views over Padstow's rooftops, while the sitting room is blond wood and open plan. Breakfast's a treat: fresh berry pancakes, or poached eggs with asparagus and sweet potato hash – but then again, it should be, since the house is owned by Paul and Emma Ainsworth.

🍴 Eating

Stein's Fish & Chips
CAFE £

(South Quay; takeaway £6.65-10.95; ⊘ breakfast 9-11.30am, lunch noon-2.30pm, dinner 5-8pm) Get the Rick Stein experience on a budget at this posh fish-and-chips bar, where cod, haddock, monkfish, John Dory and bass are all on the deep-fried menu. The beef dripping batter ensures a super-crisp finish, especially accompanied by a beer like Chalky's Bite or Chalky's Bark (named after Stein's late, much-loved terrier).

Chough Bakery
BAKERY £

(☑ 01841-533361; www.thechoughbakery.co.uk; 1-3 The Strand; pasties £2-4) Award-winning family bakery whose traditional pasties have regularly scooped top prizes at the National Pasty Championships at the Eden Project.

Roskilly's
ICE CREAM £

(The Harbour; ice cream £2-3; ⊘ 9am-5pm) Harbourside outlet for the Lizard's renowned ice-cream maker.

Margot's Bistro
MODERN BRITISH ££

(☑ 01840-533441; www.margotsbistro.co.uk; 11 Duke St; lunch mains £8.50-11.50, dinner mains £13.50-17.50; ⊘ lunch noon-1.30pm Tue-Fri, dinner 7-9pm Tue-Sat) There's just one sitting and a handful of tables at this quaint bistro, but those in the know champion this as one of Padstow's secret gems. The menu takes its inspiration from the daily catch and the changing seasons, and owner-chef Adrian Oliver is a real character, so you're in for an offbeat – and occasionally chaotic – treat.

Rojano's in the Square
ITALIAN ££

(☑ 01841-532796; www.rojanos.co.uk; 9 Mill Sq; pizzas & pastas £7.95-12.95; ⊘ lunch noon-3pm, dinner 5-10pm) A smart pizza and pasta joint, now run by Paul Ainsworth, so standards are high and the cocktail list is great. Lots of options for the bambini, too.

Basement
CAFE ££

(☑ 01841-532846; 11 Broad St; lunch mains £5-10, dinner mains £10-14; ⊘ all day) Harbourside cafe that's good for a quick morning coffee, or a bowl of mussels for lunch.

Cornish Arms
GASTROPUB ££

(☑ 01841-520288; www.rickstein.com/the-cornish-arms.html; St Merryn; mains £5.95-16.50; ⊘ 11.30am-11pm) This country pub near the village of St Merryn is now owned by the Stein empire, and offers updated pub classics such as scampi-and-chips and pint-of-prawns, with a characteristically creative spin. The Sunday roast is phenomenally popular, so arrive early. It's a 3-mile drive from Padstow.

⭐ Paul Ainsworth at No 6
MODERN BRITISH £££

(☑ 01840-532093; www.number6inpadstow.co.uk; 6 Middle St; 2-/3-course set lunch £18/24, dinner mains £23-28; ⊘ lunch noon-2.45pm, dinner 6-10pm Tue-Sat) Paul Ainsworth is often touted as the heir to Stein's crown, a fact that was recently underlined by his first Michelin star. His flagship restaurant blends classic British and modern European in a smart townhouse setting. Ainsworth's trademark is taking humbler cuts such as lamb's liver and ox cheek, and treating them to a modern, playful and imaginative makeover. He's also a passionate champion of local produce, from Padstow monkfish and Porthilly oysters to Cornish saddleback pork. His signature dessert, 'A Trip to the Fairground', scooped top honours on BBC2's *Great British Menu* and is now a firm fixture at No 6. Is this Cornwall's best bistro? It might just be.

Seafood Restaurant
SEAFOOD £££

(☑ 01841-532700; www.rickstein.com; Riverside; mains £18-63.50; ⊘ lunch noon-2.30pm, dinner 6.30-10pm) The brick that built the Stein empire, and still the best of the bunch. It's less starchy than you might think, with a light-filled conservatory for pre-dinner tipples and a classy dining room draped with potted plants and local art. Unsurprisingly, seafood is the cornerstone: the seafood platter (£63.50) is a sight to behold. Stein rarely cooks here these days, but you'll still need military precision to get a table. Alternatively, you can just turn up and order sashimi, langoustines and oysters from the seafood bar.

Drinking

BinTwo WINE BAR

(📞 01841-532022; www.bintwo.com; The Drang; ⊙ 10am-8pm) A brilliant concept: a top-notch wine merchant where you can order top vintages by the glass, chased down by Padstow's best espressos. Young owner David McWilliam is a mine of oenological info.

London Inn PUB

(📞 01841-532554; 6-8 Lanadwell St) In business since 1803, this quaint old boozer is a reliable pint stop, with St Austell ales on tap. Old rudders, ships' wheels and even a croc's head adorn the main bar.

Shopping

Stein's Deli DELI

(South Quay; ⊙ 9am-7pm Mon-Sat, 10am-5pm Sun) A trove of gourmet goods: charcuterie, cheeses, biscuits, chutneys and mustards, all with a premium price-tag.

Stein's Patisserie BAKERY

(1 Lanadwell St; ⊙ 9am-5pm Mon-Sat, 10am-5pm Sun) Proper croissant and pains au chocolat, plus Stein's own take on the classic pasty.

Stein's Gift Shop GIFTS

(Middle St; ⊙ 9am-7pm Mon-Sat, 10am-5pm Sun) Stein-themed souvenirs (cookbooks, DVDs, chef's aprons) plus other fancy homewares.

ⓘ Information

Padstow Tourist Office (📞 01841-533449; www.padstowlive.com; North Quay; ⊙ 10am-5pm Mon-Sat)

ⓘ Getting There & Away

BUS

Bus 556 (hourly Monday to Saturday, four on Sunday) The most useful local bus runs between Padstow and Newquay with stops including Trevone, Harlyn, St Merryn, Constantine, Porthcothan, Bedruthan Steps, Newquay Airport, Watergate Bay and Porth.

Bus 555 (half-hourly Monday to Saturday, six on Sunday) Padstow to Bodmin via Little Petherick, St Issey and Wadebridge.

BOAT

Black Tor Ferry (www.padstow-harbour.co.uk/phc_ferry.html; adult/child return £3/2, bikes £3, dogs £1) Runs from Padstow to Rock year-round (pick-up/drop-off points depend on the tides). The first ferry is at 7.50am year-round. The last ferry is at 7.30pm in mid-July and August; 6.30pm June and September; 5.30pm April, May & October; and 4.30pm November to March.

Rock Water Taxi (📞 07778-105297; www.rock-watertaxi.com; adult/child single £5/3, return £7/4; ⊙ 7am-midnight Easter-Oct) The late-night option.

CAR

It's hard to find parking in Padstow in summer. There are two car parks along the harbourfront, plus a large car park at the top of town, from where it's a 10-minute walk downhill.

PADSTOW'S SEVEN BAYS

The headland west of Padstow is studded with a string of beaches known locally as 'the Seven Bays'.

Nearest to town are Trevone (1.5 miles from Padstow) and half-moon Harlyn (2 miles), which both offer good, safe swimming, with lifeguards in summer and surf/watersports schools. Nearby Mother Ivey's Bay (2.5 miles) is reached along the cliff path; it's usually quieter than its neighbours, despite the proximity of several local caravan parks.

Further west there are stunning, surf-battered views from Trevose Head, a notorious shipping hazard that was once used as a quarry, and has been topped by a lighthouse since the mid-19th century.

Near the headland are the cheek-by-jowl beaches of Booby's Bay (3.5 miles) and Constantine (4 miles), which lace together at low tides to form one great swash of rock and sand. Next comes Treyarnon (5 miles), with a natural rockpool that doubles as a swimming pool, followed by the slender cove of Porthcothan (6 miles).

Although it's not officially one of the Seven Bays, Hawker's Cove, 2 miles west of Padstow, is also worth seeking out. It's one of the best places to swim around Padstow when the tide's in. Between 1827 and 1967 it was home to Padstow's lifeboat before it moved near Trevose Head.

Wadebridge

Tucked at the eastern end of the Camel Estuary, the market town of Wadebridge grew up around its eponymous bridge, which was for centuries the only crossing over the River Camel. It receives less attention than its chi-chi coastal neighbours these days, but it's a lively and attractive town, with lots of local shops and eateries to explore. It also has admirable environmental credentials: it's aiming to become Cornwall's leading eco-town by generating all its energy from renewable sources over the next few years.

✕ Eating

Relish   DELI, CAFE **£**
(☏01208-814214; www.relishwadebridge.co.uk; Foundry Crt; mains £4.50-8.50; ⊘9am-5pm Tue-Sat) This fab cafe-deli is run by owner Hugo Hercod, who won the UK Barista Championship in 2008 – so the cappuccinos and espressos are top-notch, and supplied by several of the UK's top roasters (including London's Square Mile and Cornwall's own Origin). Follow up with a savoury scone laced with Godminster cheddar or a plate of goodies from the inhouse deli, and you've got one of the best little lunch stops in Cornwall.

The Picture & Coffee House   CAFE **£**
(☏01208-368191; www.picturesandcoffee.com; 33 Molesworth St; £3-10; ⊘10am-5pm, 10am-11pm Fri) This lively little local's hangout is lined with artworks and known for impromptu evening music sessions. Decent pizza and coffee, too.

Baker Tom's   BAKERY
(1, The Platt; ⊘9am-5pm Mon-Sat) North coast outpost of Cornwall's up-and-coming baker.

❶ Getting There & Away

Bus 584/595 (seven daily, four on Sunday) runs between Camelford and Wadebridge, stopping at Port Gaverne, Port Isaac, St Endellion and Port Quin. It's designated as the 595 in the opposite direction.

Bus 591/594 (hourly, three on Sunday) Via St Columb, then on to Truro and St Agnes.

Bus 591/593 (hourly, three on Sunday) Via St Columb to Newquay.

NEWQUAY & AROUND

Bright, breezy and brash: that's Newquay, Cornwall's premier party town and the spiritual home of British surfing. Perched above a cluster of golden beaches, Newquay's clifftop setting is fabulous, but the town's become better known for its after-dark antics – it's a favourite summer getaway for surfers, clubbers and stag parties, creating a drink-till-dawn atmosphere that's more Costa del Sol than Cornwall. The drab, concrete-heavy town centre doesn't do it any favours, either – but if it's white sand and wild nights you're after, Newquay definitely fits the bill.

WORTH A TRIP

BEDRUTHAN STEPS

South of Porthcothan, the B3276 coast road dips and rolls along a truly stirring stretch of coastline, surrounded by green fields and edged by wild, plunging cliffs. About 2 miles south of Porthcothan loom the stately rock stacks of **Bedruthan Steps** (Carnewas; www.nationaltrust.org.uk/carnewas-and-bedruthan-steps; East of Newquay), sometimes known as Carnewas. These mighty granite pillars have been carved out by the relentless action of thousands of years of wind and waves, and now make an ideal nesting spot for seabirds. The area is now owned by the National Trust, who also run the large car park and a cafe. You can also camp here in August (adult/child £7.50/4).

The beach itself is accessed via a steep staircase and is submerged at high tide. Towards the northern end is a rocky shelf known as **Diggory's Island**, which separates the main beach from another little-known cove. At low tide you can walk across from Bedruthan; otherwise you'll have to brave the crumbling Pentire Steps from the coast path.

Further towards Newquay is the deep sandy scoop of **Mawgan Porth**, a great swimming and paddling beach with lots of space. It's also home to Cornwall's top eco-chic hotel, The Scarlet (p209), perched on the bluffs above the beach.

Newquay

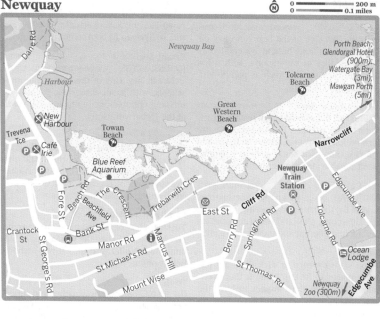

If you're looking for somewhere to base yourself within a stone's throw of the sand, then you're really spoilt for choice in Newquay, from Fistral's world-famous waves to Crantock's windblown dunes. Nearby Watergate Bay has become a centre for watersports, and is also home to Jamie Oliver's beachside Fifteen Restaurant.

It's hard to imagine these days, but a century ago Newquay was a quiet pilchard port. Until they were fished out in the early 20th century, the Newquay shoals were some of the largest in Cornwall (one catch in 1868 netted a record 16.5 million fish). The only remnant of this once-thriving industry is the 14th-century Huer's Hut, a lookout once used for spotting approaching shoals, perched on the headland between Towan and Fistral.

◉ Sights & Activities

Newquay is a haven for outdoor activities, from abseiling, kitesurfing and sea kayaking to the latest craze of coasteering, which combines clambering along the cliffs in a full-bodied wetsuit prior to taking a plunge into the briny blue. Obviously, it's also famous for its beaches, several of which are just a short walk from the town centre. Further afield, family travellers will find lots of activities to entertain younger minds.

Beaches

There's no doubt about it – Newquay's all about the beaches.

The three big draws are the ones closest to town: Great Western, Tolcarne and Towan, all of which get very busy in summer. Things are usually quieter out east at nearby Lusty Glaze and Porth, about a mile or so from the town centre. A little further on is the epic sweep of Watergate Bay, a huge crescent of flat sand, good for surfing, windsurfing, kiteboarding and other beach activities.

In the opposite direction, west beyond Pentire Head, lies Newquay's best-known beach – Fistral, a mecca for British surfers thanks to its constant swells.

If the town beaches are too hectic, you'll find more elbow room further afield. Three miles southwest is Crantock, sandwiched between the headlands of East and West Pentire, and backed by dunes and the fast-flowing River Gannel.

Further west is tiny Porth Joke (known locally as Polly Joke), but it's tricky to find and has no facilities. Families will be better off at Holywell Bay, with powder-soft sand plus rockpools and caves to explore at low tide.

Adventure Sports

Extreme Academy
ADVENTURE SPORTS
(☑ 01637-860840; www.extremeacademy.co.uk; Watergate Bay) One of the best Newquay operators, with a large base at Watergate Bay. They specialise in watersports, with a few more unusual options such as paddle-surfing and traction kiting.

Adventure Centre
ADVENTURE SPORTS
(☑ 01637-872444; www.adventure-centre.org; Lusty Glaze) On Lusty Glaze, the Adventure Centre runs multi-activity sessions on land, sea and cliff-face (note that some, such as ziplining, aren't suitable for younger children).

Ebo Centre
ADVENTURE SPORTS
(☑ 0800-781 6861; www.penhaleadventure.com; Holywell Bay) Surfing, coasteering, kayaking and kite sports, plus land-based activities including orienteering and mountain-biking.

Surfing

If you want to learn to surf, there are few better places in Britain to do it than Newquay – although don't expect to have the waves to yourself. Newquay's breaks are reliable, consistent and suitable for everyone from absolute beginners to elite surfers.

There are numerous schools to choose from. You'll get a more personal experience with a small local operator. Don't be afraid to ask questions before you book: maximum class size, instructors' accreditations, student-to-teacher ratio and so on. It's also a good idea to ask in advance about their policy on stag and hen parties: the better schools steer away from them, or at least keep them separate from other students. Some schools also specialise in female-only lessons, childrens' courses and so on. Expect to pay from around £30 for a two-hour lesson, including equipment. Hourly rates become cheaper the more hours you book.

O'Neill Surf Academy
SURFING
(☑ 01841-520052; www.oneillsurfacademy.co.uk) Perhaps the best-organised Newquay school, based at Watergate Bay and backed by the national O'Neill brand. Very well run, but often busy.

English Surf School
SURFING
(☑ 01637-879571; www.englishsurfschool.com) Another large school, linked with Rip Curl and staffed by instructors approved by the English Surfing Federation (including the British team coach).

Fistral Beach Surf School
SURFING
(☑ 01637-850737; www.fistralbeachsurfschool. co.uk) The only school actually based on Fistral, so likely to be booked out in summer.

Errant Surf School
SURFING
(☑ 07581-397038; www.errantsurfschool.co.uk; Trebarwith Cres) One of the best of the indie schools, with small class sizes, friendly tutors and optional one-to-one lessons. Based at the Trebarwith Hotel.

Kingsurf Surf School
SURFING
(☑ 01637-860091; www.kingsurf.co.uk) A good option if you prefer to avoid the Fistral hustle, this reliable school at Mawgan Porth has five young instructors and gets a tick for personal attention and small class sizes.

Family Attractions

There are lots of attractions in and around Newquay that'll keep the young 'uns entertained. Most offer discounts if you prebook tickets online.

Trerice
HISTORIC BUILDING
(NT; ☑ 01637-875404; www.nationaltrust.org.uk/ trerice; adult/child £7.20/3.60; ⊙ house 11am-5pm, gardens 10.30am-5pm mid-Feb–Oct) Built in 1751, the charming Elizabethan manor is most famous for the elaborate barrel-roofed ceiling of the Great Chamber, but has plenty of other intriguing features, including ornate fireplaces, original plasterwork and fine period furniture. Outside, the grounds contain a traditional Cornish orchard, a lawnmower museum and a bowling green where you can try traditional medieval sports: anyone for a game of slapcock?

Trerice is 3.3 miles southeast of Newquay. Bus 527 runs from Newquay to Kestle Mill, less than a mile from the house.

Blue Reef Aquarium
AQUARIUM
(☑ 01637-878134; www.bluereefaquarium.co.uk/ newquay; Towan Promenade; adult/child/family £9.75/7.50/32.50; ⊙ 10am-5pm) Touch-pools and deep-sea denizens on Towan Beach.

Newquay Zoo
ZOO
(☑ 01637-873342; www.newquayzoo.org.uk; Trenance Gardens; adult/child/family £11.50/9/33; ⊙ 9.30am-5pm Apr-Sep, 10am-5pm Oct-Mar) Red pandas, sloths, penguins, great-horned owls and a python called Monty (get it?).

Crealy Adventure Park
THEME PARK
(☑ 01841-540726; www.crealy.co.uk; adult/child/ under 92cm tall £16.95/9.95/free; ⊙ 10.30am-5.30pm) Rides including the Beast vertical

drop, a Viking ship, a Young Farmers' driving centre and the big-ticket Morgawr rollercoaster. Thorpe Park it isn't, but the kids will still have fun. It's 14 miles northeast from Newquay, off the A39 to Wadebridge.

St Eval Kart Circuit   KARTING
(☑01637-860160; www.cornwallkarting.com; St Eval, Wadebridge; per 10min adult £15, child £8-10; ⊙9.30am-6pm Mon-Sat) Cornwall's biggest go-kart centre, offering an all-weather track and four age-appropriate karts. It's 9 miles northeast of Newquay, near St Eval village.

Lappa Valley   STEAM RAILWAY
(☑01872-510317; www.lappavalley.co.uk; St Newlyn East; adult/child/family £11.70/9.25/36; ⊙closed winter) Ride the rails aboard Lilliputian-sized steam trains, 6 miles south of Newquay; look out for signs on the A392.

Dairyland Farm World   ANIMAL PARK
(☑01637-510246; www.dairylandfarmworld.com; adult £10.50, child £6-9.50; ⊙10am-5pm Mar-Oct) Sit on the ponies, pet the billy goats and milk the cows. Oo-ar. It's 6 miles southeast of Newquay, on the A3058 towards Summercourt.

Screech Owl Sanctuary   WILDLIFE PARK
(☑01726-860182; www.screechowlsanctuary.co.uk; Goss Moor, near St Columb; adult/child/family £9.50/7.50/29; ⊙10am-5pm Mar-Oct) Every type of owl you could wish to see – from giant eagle owls to snowy owls – plus a few emus, meerkats and ponies. It's 11 miles from Newquay; look out for signs on the A30 just after you pass Fraddon.

✦ Festivals & Events

Boardmasters   SURFING
(www.relentlessboardmasters.com) Surf and sports hit Fistral, while bands strut stages on Watergate Bay in early August.

🛏 Sleeping

Treago Farm   CAMPSITE £
(☑01637-830277; www.treagofarm.co.uk; Porth Joke; adult £7.25-9.50, child £3.50-4.50) Few campsites have such a swish setting as this, in the crook of the valley just behind Porth Joke. There are 81 grassy pitches, but it gets crowded in summer, so it might be better saved for the off-season. A sandy 500m trail leads straight to the beach. Porth (Polly) Joke is about 5 miles east from Newquay, sandwiched between Crantock and Holywell Bay. It's hard to find, so call ahead for directions.

Ocean Lodge   HOSTEL £
(☑01637-877701; www.oceanlodgenewquay.co.uk; Holywell Rd; ⊙dm £20-35; P🌐) The boxy building looks bland, but this is one of the better surf hostels, squeaky clean and with small ensuite dorms. There's a zingy downstairs bar and lounge, decorated with VW camper prints.

Glendorgal Hotel   HOTEL ££
(☑01637-874937; www.glendorgalhotel.co.uk; Lusty Glaze Rd, Porth Beach; d £102-192; P🌐) A decent hotel in a clifftop spot above Porth Beach. There are only 26 rooms, so it feels intimate. They're nicely finished, but a little on the small side and only a handful have proper sea views. The location's wonderful though, with headland and coves on your doorstep.

Newquay Townhouse   B&B ££
(☑01637-620009; www.newquaytownhouse.co.uk; 6 Tower Rd; £50-90) One of Newquay's best B&B choices. It's near the town centre, with stylish cream rooms livened up with stripy cushions, bright duvets and wicker furniture. Some have window seats, but only one has bay views.

★ **The Scarlet**   HOTEL £££
(☑01637-861600; www.scarlethotel.co.uk; Mawgan Porth; d £195-395; P🌐⊠) ✦ Cornwall's sexiest hotel by a country mile, and ecofriendly to boot (recycled rainwater, biomass boiler, renewable energy supplier). On the bluffs above Mawgan Porth, the hotel's rooms all boast eye-popping ocean views and defiantly modern design: minimalist bathrooms, statement furniture, industrial-chic materials and an outdoor 'wild pool'. The spa is a stunner, too. We particularly liked the 'Unique' rooms, which have their own little gardens and rooftop patios, reached via a spiral staircase.

★ **Bedruthan Hotel**   HOTEL £££
(☑01637-860555; www.bedruthan.com; Mawgan Porth; d from £158; P🌐⊠) Don't be put off by the boxy exterior: inside the Bedruthan offers contemporary rooms in bright primary colours and bold pattern prints, plus spacious villas and apartments for longer stays. Full-day kids' clubs and lots of organised activities have earned it a reputation as one of Cornwall's best hotels for families. There's lots of lively art and colourful furniture dotted around the lounge and library, making for a fun and quirky space to stay.

Food & Drink

Gone are the days when all the West Country had to offer was saffron buns and cream teas. These days it's one of Britain's best places to dine, with farmers markets, cutting-edge bistros and award-winning microbreweries – not to mention an unusually high quota of celebrity chefs.

1

2

4

1. Cream Teas (p270)
Enjoy a regional afternoon tea of scones with raspberry jam and cream.

2. Oysters
Fresh oysters served with seaweed on ice.

3. Cornish Pasties (p269)
These savoury snacks have received protected status from the European Commission and must always be crimped on the side.

4. Sharpham Vineyard (p77)
Take a tour or self-guided walk and tasting at this wine and cheese centre near Totnes.

3

The Hotel, Watergate Bay
HOTEL £££

(☏01637-860543; www.watergatebay.co.uk; Watergate Bay; d £125-360, ste £285-425; P☏) Fresh from a multi-million-pound refit, the Watergate is a beachside beauty. The rooms shine in slinky pinks, candy-stripes and sea-blues, partnered with wicker chairs, stripped wood and mini seaview balconies – but you're paying a lot for the premium location.

✖ Eating

Café Irie
CAFE £

(☏01637-859200; www.cafeirie.co.uk; 38 Fore St; lunch £3-8; ☉10am-5pm Mon-Sat) This oddball cafe's famous for its coffee and hot chocolate, plus veggie wraps, piping-hot jacket spuds and gooey cakes.

★ Jon's Bistro
FRENCH ££

(☏01637-860420; www.bre-penfarm.co.uk; Bre-Pen Farm; 3-course menu £20; ☉dinner 7-10pm Thu-Sat) This Frenchified bistro on a farm near Mawgan Porth is the north coast's best-kept secret. It's run by talented young chef Jon Harvey, who previously worked at Claridge's and Fifteen. His food is sophisticated and smart, but served without pomp or pretension. It's only open for dinner three nights a week (two in winter).

Beach Hut
BISTRO ££

(☏01637-860877; Watergate Bay; mains £8.95-15; ☉8.30am-9pm) If you can't get a table at Fifteen, head downstairs to this bistro by the sand. It's similarly beachy in feel, and the menu's simple surf 'n' turf: sticky pork ribs, 'extreme' burgers and a different fish every day. Wicker chairs and glass windows give it a shipshape feel.

New Harbour
BISTRO ££

(☏01637-874062; www.new-harbour.com; South Quay Hill; mains £12.95-17.50; ☉lunch noon-4.30pm, dinner 6-9.30pm) Most people never spot it, but Newquay actually still has a working quay – and this restaurant gets its seafood straight from the dayboats. It's away from the town hustle, and has atmospheric harbour views.

Lewinnick Lodge
GASTROPUB ££

(☏01637-878117; www.lewinnick-lodge.info; Pentire Head, Newquay; mains £10-18; ☉9am-11pm) Nestled on Pentire Head, the Lewinnick is good for a coffee with a coastal view, or a quick and easy lunch (think gourmet burgers and grilled steaks).

★ Fifteen Cornwall
ITALIAN £££

(☏01637-861000; www.fifteencornwall.com; Watergate Bay; 3-course lunch menu £28, 5-course dinner menu £60; ☉10am-9pm) Jamie Oliver's social enterprise restaurant on Watergate Bay is where everyone wants to eat. Underprivileged youngsters learn their trade in the kitchen preparing Oliver's trademark zesty, Italian-influenced food, while diners soak up the views and the buzzy, beachy vibe. It's a red-hot ticket: bookings essential.

❶ Information

Newquay Tourist Office (☏01637-854020; www.visitnewquay.com; Marcus Hill; ☉9.30am-5.30pm Mon-Sat, 9.30am-12.30pm Sun)

❶ Getting There & Away

TO & FROM THE AIRPORT

Newquay Cornwall Airport (p289) is 5 miles from town. Flight destinations vary; there are seasonal flights to Belfast, Edinburgh, Glasgow, Manchester and Newcastle, but at the time of writing the London connections were in flux. Check the website for the latest details.

Bus 556 travels to the airport from Newquay Bus Station (22 minutes, hourly in summer) plus Padstow and nearby villages. **Travel Cornwall** (☏01726-861108; www.travelcornwall.uk.com; adult £11.50) also runs prebooked taxibus services from Newquay.

There is no taxi rank at Newquay airport. Official transfers are provided by ecofriendly **BioTravel** (☏01637-880006; www.biotravel.co.uk). Local taxi firms offering airport transfers include **A2B Newquay Travel** (☏01637-875555; www.newquaytravel.co.uk), **Henver Cabs** (☏07928-825668; www.newquayairporttaxis.org) and **Carbis Cabs** (☏01637-260360; www.newquay-airport-taxis.co.uk). Guide prices: to/from Newquay £15 to £20; Padstow £25 to £30; Truro £40 to £50.

If you're driving, be very careful of parking outside the airport – there have been many reports of overzealous parking attendants slapping on tickets even if you leave your car for a second. There's now no free drop-off parking zone, either: the minimum charge is now £1 for 30 minutes. Long-stay parking costs £13/24.50/32 for one/two/three days, £7.50 per day for the next eight days, and no charge after that.

❶ Getting Around

BUS

Newquay's bus station is on Manor Rd.

Bus 88A (hourly Monday to Saturday) Truro and Falmouth.

Bus 585/586 (50 minutes, every half-hour Monday to Saturday, none on Sunday) The fastest buses to Truro. The 586 goes via St Columb, while the 585 goes via Crantock and Cubert.

Bus 591/594 (every half-hour Monday to Saturday, hourly on Sunday) Follows the coast via Crantock (14 minutes), Holywell Bay (25 minutes) and Perranporth (50 minutes), then on to Truro (1½ hours). The 594 also travels via St Agnes. Rather confusingly, the buses become the 592/593 in the opposite direction.

Newquay is at the end of the branch line to Par (£4.40, 50 minutes) on the main London–Penzance route. Other local destinations:
Truro (£5.70, 1 hour 20 minutes)
Penzance (£9.30, 2¼ hours)

PERRANPORTH TO PORTREATH

The craggy coastline between Perran and Portreath was once at the heart of Cornwall's mining boom. Two centuries ago, this blustery coast would have looked very different: spoil heaps and belching chimney stacks would have littered the landscape, but now their moody ruins provide nothing more than a ghostly reminder of Cornwall's past.

This is surfers' and walkers' country nowadays, with a wealth of rocky coves and white beaches to discover.

ⓘ Getting There & Away

The most useful local buses:
Bus 85 (hourly Monday to Saturday) Regular bus from Truro to St Agnes.
Bus 304 (hourly Monday to Friday, six on Saturday) Truro to Porthtowan.
Bus 591 (hourly) Newquay, Holywell Bay, Goonhavern and Perranporth.
Bus 594 (hourly) St Agnes to Truro.

Perranporth

East of Newquay, the coast road tracks through craggy scenery all the way to Perranporth, another breezy beach town blessed with a fabulous 3-mile stretch of sand. The town isn't much to look at – a sprawl of concrete chalets, holiday villas and clifftop bungalows – but the beach itself is an absolute stunner, sweeping in a great arc all the way to the grassy dunes of Penhale Sands.

The dune system here is the largest in Cornwall, and buried among them are the remains of a 6th-century oratory, the oldest such structure so far discovered in the county. It's dedicated to St Piran, Cornwall's Celtic saint; a campaign is underway to fund an archaeological survey and preserve the building for the future. At the southern edge of the beach, a staircase leads up the clifftop to Perran's sundial, built to commemorate the millennium and show Cornish time (rather than GMT).

Reliable swells make Perranporth popular with surfers and bodyboarders, and the level sands make it ideal for wind-powered sports such as kite-buggying, powerkiting and landboarding. Mobius Kite School (☎08456-430630; www.mobiusonline.co.uk; Cubert) has its home base in Perran, and offers taster sessions in all these sports, as well as guided mountain-bike trips.

The ivy-covered Bolingey Inn (☎01872-571626; Penwartha Rd, Bolingey; mains £10-16) is the best pub round Perranporth for food, and has a valley location about 2 miles drive inland.

Perran's venerable beachside bar, the Watering Hole (www.the-wateringhole.co.uk; Perranporth Beach), is great for a sundowner, with tables spilling onto the sand and local bands several nights a week.

St Agnes & Chapel Porth

Abandoned engine houses litter the hilltops around St Agnes, which once resounded to the thump and clang of mine pumps and steam engines, and now echoes only to the strains of crashing surf and calling gulls. Smart slate-roofed houses hint at the town's former prosperity as one of Cornwall's tin-mining boom towns: the local landmark of the Stippy Stappy consists of a terrace of miners' cottages built in a steeply stepped pattern down the hill to Trevaunance Cove.

◉ Sights & Activities

★Chapel Porth   COVE
(🅿) About 2 miles from St Agnes is one of Cornwall's most photogenic coves, Chapel Porth, a wild, rocky beach framed by steep, gorse-covered cliffs that's now owned by the National Trust. From the NT car park, you can clamber up the coast path to the famous engine stack of Wheal Coates, which still boasts its chimney and winding house. From

TOP CORNISH PASTIES

It's a fiercely contested title, but here are our picks of the county's top pasty shops.

Philps (p227) This longstanding Hayle baker is the traditionalist's choice, with pasties made to a time-honoured recipe.

Ann's Pasties (☑01326-290889; www.annspasties.co.uk; pasties £2.85; ☺9am-3pm Mon-Sat) Ann Muller's pasties are allegedly Rick Stein's favourites. You can only get them from her Lizard shop.

Chough Bakery (p204) A Padstow bakery that scooped top prize two years running at the county's annual pasty championships.

Pengenna Pasties (p224) Another traditional maker, with shops in St Ives, Bude and Tintagel. The pasties are huge and unusually crimped on top, not on the side.

Aunty May's (☑01736-364583; The Coombe, Newlyn) Pasties like your granny used to make, but with a flakier style of pastry. In Newlyn.

WC Rowe (www.wcrowe.com) Countywide baker that makes reliably good pasties.

here, the coast path winds along the surf-pounded cliffs around **Tubby's Head** and **St Agnes Head**.

The cove itself is great for exploring, especially at low tide, when the receding tide reveals many sea caves and rock pools. The **Chapel Porth Cafe** (☺10am-5pm) is a beloved local institution for hot chocolate, cheesy baguettes and the house speciality, hedgehog ice cream (vanilla ice cream topped with clotted cream and hazelnuts).

Trevaunance Cove   COVE
At the bottom of the steep coombe (valley) below St Agnes, this sandy beach is the town's main seaside playground, with beach huts to change in, rockpools to delve in, and the nearby Driftwood Spars pub to provide post-swim pints. **Koru Kayaking** (www.koru-kayaking.co.uk) runs trips from the cove.

At low tide, you can walk across the rocks to Trevellas Porth.

Trevellas Porth   COVE
This former mining valley is just across the rocks from Trevaunance Cove, and is locally known as Blue Hills, a reference to the blue heather that grows on the surrounding hills. The steep valley is littered with mine workings and chimneys, and there's a small sandy beach which offers super snorkelling around the offshore rock stacks. North of the beach, the coast path leads up to Perranporth Airfield, built during WWII but now used by local flying clubs.

At the rear of the valley is one of the last remaining tin workshops in Cornwall, the **Blue Hills Tin Stream** (☑01872-553341; www.bluehillstin.com; adult/child £5.50/3; ☺10am-4pm

Mon-Sat Jul-Aug, 10am-2pm Mon-Sat late-Mar–late-Oct). Guided tours take in the whole process, from mining and smelting through to casting and finishing.

If you're driving, the beach is about 2 miles east of St Agnes, on a turn-off from the B3285 (signed to Wheal Kitty). The road down is very steep and parking is limited; it might be easier to park at the small car park at the top of the hill and walk down.

The Beacon   VIEWPOINT
If you're feeling energetic, you can climb up to the area's highest viewpoint, The Beacon, which is about an hour's walk from St Agnes. From the top, the panorama stretches across most of Cornwall on a clear day; look out for the dark tors of Bodmin Moor to the east and the distinctive summit of Carn Brea in the west.

The beacon is just over a mile's walk from St Agnes town, and fairly well signposted from the village square; you can download a PDF at www.stagnes.com that details several circular routes.

Mount Hawke Skate Park   SKATEBOARDING
(☑01209-890705; www.mounthawke.com; ☺week-ends 1-8pm) Cornwall's only undercover skate park is just outside the village of Mount Hawke. Hours vary according to the school holidays, so phone ahead. It's tricky to find, so ask for directions.

🛏 Sleeping

Trevellas Manor Farm   CAMPSITE £
(☑01872-552238; www.trevellasmanorfarmcamp site.co.uk; sites £10-15) One of three campsites

scattered across the hills above Trevellas Porth. It's little more than a big grassy field with a couple of taps and a toilet block, but the coastal views are off the chart.

Beacon Cottage
CAMPSITE £
(☑ 01872-552347; www.beaconcottagefarmholidays.co.uk; sites for 2 adults £17-23) Mixed caravan-and-camping site, in a great clifftop spot between Chapel Porth and the Beacon.

Aramay
B&B ££
(☑ 01872-553546; www.aramay.com; Quay Rd; d £105-125; 🅿🛜) Not long on the scene, but with five fine rooms and a sweet St Agnes location, it won't stay secret for long. Try No 1, with contemporary crimson-and-cream decor and fireplace, or swanky No 3, with silky throws and views of the Stippy Stappy. Owner Amie is full of fun ideas: she'll even lend you a pair of wellies if you forget to bring your own.

Eating

Genki
CAFE £
(☑ 01872-555858; Quay Rd; mains £4-8; ⊗9am-5pm) This shack cafe on the road to Trevaunance Cove is perfect for quick paninis, homemade soups and cheese platters. The smoothies and coffee are pretty fancy too, but there are only a couple of picnic tables to sit down on.

Cornish Pizza Company
PIZZA £
(☑ 01872-553092; www.thecornishpizzacompany.co.uk; 68 Vicarage Rd; pizzas £8-9; ⊗5-9pm Tue-Sat) Gourmet pizzas in the centre of town, with the all-important crispy bases, and

all named after Cornish mines. Try Wheel Geevor with Cornish Blue cheese and roasted veg, or Wheal Alfred, with goat's cheese, sundried tomatoes and onion marmalade.

Lewsey Lou's
CAFE £
(☑ 01872-552126; www.lewseylous.co.uk; Trevaunance Cove; £4-6) Sustainable, line-caught, delicious fish and chips with celebrity cachet – the shop's owned by ex-England rugby player Josh Lewsey. It's steps from Trevaunance Cove, right opposite Driftwood Spars.

★No 4 Peterville
BISTRO ££
(☑ 01872-554245; Peterville Sq; mains £12-16.95; ⊗dinner 7-10.30pm Wed-Sat, brunch 10am-1pm Sat & Sun) For sit-down dining in St Agnes, look no further than this swish bistro beside the turning to Trevaunance Cove. It's a relaxed affair, with pine tables, candles in kilner jars and flowers in bottles on every table, and the food is classic British brasserie: lemon sole with wild garlic, or pork chop with pears and smoked crackling.

Driftwood Spars
PUB ££
(☑ 01872-552428; www.driftwoodspars.com; Trevaunance Cove, St Agnes; mains £10.95-16.95; ⊗10am-11pm) Hunkered in by Trevaunance Cove, the Driftwood is an old warhorse of a pub – it's been around for at least two centuries – but it's as popular as ever. The beamed bars are full of character, while the upstairs restaurant is light, bright and pine-filled. They brew their own ale, too: try light Lou's Brew or malty Bolster's Blood.

WORTH A TRIP

CARN BREA

Brooding on the horizon above the old mining towns of Redruth and Camborne is **Carn Brea**, a barren granite outcrop that's thought to have been occupied since at least 3500 BC. Various pieces of Neolithic pottery, flints and arrowheads have been discovered here, as well as the remains of ditches, enclosures and platforms for longhouses. It's not hard to see why ancient settlers chose this as a strongpoint: the 36˚ views stretch in all directions. On a clear day you can see all the way east to Bodmin Moor and west towards Land's End, as well as both north and south coasts.

The hilltop is now topped by a 90ft Celtic cross known as the **Basset Monument**, dedicated to the aristocratic mine-owning family, and a peculiar part-medieval **castle** that now houses (of all things) a Middle Eastern restaurant.

There are several trails to the top, including from the little hamlets of Carnkie and Carn Brea. The trails also form part of the **Mineral Tramways** (www.cornwall.gov.uk/default.aspx?page=13419), a network of cycling paths that wind amongst the old workings and disused mines surrounding Carn Brea.

Drinking

Apart from Driftwood Spars, the traditional drinking hole is the St Agnes Hotel (☎01872-552307; www.st-agnes-hotel.co.uk; Churchtown) on the village square, while the Tap House (☎01872-553095; www.the-taphouse.com; Peterville Sq) at the bottom of town attracts a younger crowd and hosts live gigs.

ℹ Information

St Agnes (www.st-agnes.com) Informative community website.

Porthtowan

Four miles southwest from St Agnes is the valley of Porthtowan, once a mining and milling site, but now a surfer's hangout. The sandy beach is pleasant enough, but the main reason most people drop by is for a beachside lunch at the Blue Bar (www.blue-bar.co.uk; Porthtowan; ⊙lunch & dinner), a surfy diner-bar with bold primary colours, an open-plan interior, and good grub (burgers, falafels, steaks and so on). Arrive early if you want to grab one of the patio tables or window seats – it's one of the north coast's most frequented sundowner spots.

There are surf shops by the beach, and a Moomaid of Zennor ice cream parlour.

Portreath

Another 4 miles southwest of Porthtowan is Portreath, from where vast quantities of Cornwall's mineral ore were once shipped out to Swansea for smelting. In its heyday in the mid-19th century, around 100,000 tonnes of ore were passing out of Portreath's harbour every year; in order to streamline the process a mineral tramway was built from Portreath to connect the harbour with the local mines, now reinvented as the 11-mile Coast to Coast Cycle Trail (p216).

Portreath's beach isn't the best, but it's good for bodyboarding.

Tehidy Woods

The 250-acre country park of Tehidy (www.cornwall.gov.uk/default.aspx?page=13240; ⊙8am-around 6pm) formerly belonged to the Bassets, one of Cornwall's four richest tin-mining families, who made their fortune from extensive mineral rights across west and central Cornwall.

The estate has been owned by the council since 1983 and run as public woodland, criss-crossed by trails, peaceful lakes, wildlife reserves and a golf course, as well as a good cafe (mains £4-8; ⊙9.30am-5pm).

There are several car parks dotted around the edge of the estate, including one at North Cliffs, on the B3301 coast road between Portreath and Gwithian.

Camborne, Redruth & the Mining World Heritage Site

Camborne and Redruth once sat slap bang at the deafening epicentre of Cornwall's mining industry. Many of the county's most prosperous and profitable mines could be found nearby, with names that hinted at their mineral wealth: Wheal Prosper, Wheal Fortune, Wheal Bounty and so on. Local mineowners grew fabulously rich on the proceeds, and built many smart townhouses in the area, but the towns entered a slow decline following the collapse of the tin industry in the mid-1850s. The long tradition of mining continued until 1998, when the county's last remaining mine at South Crofty, near Pool, closed down for good, sounding the death knell for an industry that had endured here for at least five centuries.

Since South Crofty's closure, there have been various attempts to restart the industry, fuelled by the steady rise in mineral prices over the last decade or so. But the prohibitive cost of draining the now-flooded shafts, coupled with increasing competition from the developing world, have so far meant that the plans haven't got much further than the drawing board.

Cornwall's mining heritage lives on, however. Since 2006, Cornwall's historic mining areas have formed part of the UK's newest Unesco World Heritage Site, the Cornwall and West Devon Mining Landscape (www.cornish-mining.org.uk). This site covers huge tracts of land around the county, with the largest concentration in St Just, St Agnes, Gwennap Camborne and Redruth.

⦿ Sights & Activities

Cornish Mines & Engines   MINE
(☎01209-315027; cornishmines@nationaltrust.org.uk) This mining centre near Redruth makes an ideal place to get acquainted with Cornwall's once-great industry. At the heart of the

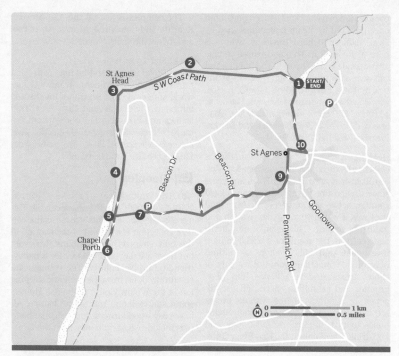

🏃 Coastal Walk
St Agnes Circular

START TREVAUNANCE COVE
FINISH TREVAUNANCE COVE
DISTANCE 5 MILES, 3 TO 4 HOURS

This walk takes in the beautiful windblown scenery around the old mining village of St Agnes, factoring in panoramic coastal views and a trip to the top of the area's highest point, The Beacon.

Start at ❶ **Trevaunance Cove**, where you can park in the car park opposite the Driftwood Spars pub. From here follow the coast path as it climbs steeply around the clifftops to ❷ **Newdowns Head**. Offshore there are two rocks known locally as the Bawden Rocks, or the Cow and Calf, which according to local legend were hurled there by the local giant Bolster. From here, the coast path tracks round to ❸ **St Agnes Head**, travelling through thick heather and gorse.

The trail then swings south, opening out onto the exposed cliffs around ❹ **Tubby's Head** before dropping down to the picturesque mine workings and chimney stacks at

❺ **Wheal Coates**, one of the most photographed in Cornwall. From here it's a steep walk downhill to the cove of ❻ **Chapel Porth**, where you can fuel up with a hot tea and hedgehog ice cream from the shack cafe.

From here, backtrack to the Wheal Coates mine ruins, and this time turn inland along the uphill path, which leads to a car park beside ❼ **Beacon Drive**. Turn left, then immediately right through Beacon Cottage Touring Park, where you'll see signs to the ❽ **Beacon**. The path climbs sharply up the heathery hilltop, with truly majestic views of St Agnes and the surrounding coastline, and inland towards Carn Brea.

From the top, there are several trails leading back towards Goonvrea Rd, from where it's an easy downhill stroll back into the centre of ❾ **St Agnes** village. Follow the road down through town past the St Agnes Hotel, and take the footpath down past the terraced houses known as the ❿ **Stippy Stappy**, which leads to Trevaunance Cove. Reward yourself with a well-earned pint of homebrewed ale and a ploughman's lunch at the Driftwood.

complex are two working beam engines, both once powered by steam boilers designed by local engineer Richard Trevithick (who was born in Redruth in 1771, and whose cottage at Penponds is now open to the public). You can see more mining gear in action at the nearby King Edward Mine (☑ 01209-61468; www.kingedwardmine.co.uk; Troon, near Camborne; adult/child £6/1.50; ☺ 10am-5pm daily Aug, 10am-5pm Wed-Mon Jul & Sep, 10am-5pm Wed-Sun Jun, 10am-5pm Wed-Thu & Sat & Sun May).

Heartlands   HERITAGE CENTRE
(www.heartlandscornwall.com; ☺ 10am-5pm Apr-Sep, 10am-4pm Oct-Mar) FREE For many years since the closure of the mines, the rugged country between Camborne, Redruth and Pool was a watchword for deprivation and industrial decline. This swanky new heritage centre is the result of a £22.3 million investment, and bills itself as a 'cultural playground': in other words, it's a mix of shops, artists' studios, galleries, kids' playgrounds and exhibition spaces, all tied together by a mining theme. Various events are held throughout the year, from engine house tours to prehistoric talks, and food and drink is available at the Red River Cafe.

The complex is just off the A30 between Redruth and Camborne; head towards Pool and follow the signs.

Great Flat Lode Trail   CYCLING
An off-road hiking-and-biking path that forms part of the Mineral Tramways network, and winds past several of the disused minestacks dotted around Carn Brea. Trail leaflets and bikes can be sourced from Explorer Cycle Hire (☑ 07709-835543; www.explorercyclehire.co.uk; adult hire half-/full-day £10/16, child £10/7) at Heartlands.

🛏 Sleeping

★ Little White Alice   COTTAGE
(☑ 01209-861000; www.littlewhitealice.co.uk; Carmenellis; P 🛜 🐕) ✎ This ecoconscious cottage collection is a bit out-of-the-way, up in the hilly country near Stithians Reservoir, but there are few better places for a family-friendly Cornish holiday. The cottages are beautifully done, from the romantic sleeping loft in the Willow House to the Ash House's spiral staircase and mezzanine lounge. All have cosy woodburners, and welcome hampers include eggs and honey from the farm.

West Cornwall & the Isles of Scilly

Includes ➡

West Cornwall 220
St Ives 220
The Penwith
Peninsula 227
Penzance 235
The Lizard 245
Helston 245
Lizard Point &
Around 247
Isles of Scilly 250
St Mary's 251

Best Places to Eat

➡ Tolcarne Inn (p240)

➡ Porthminster Beach Café (p225)

➡ Gurnard's Head (p229)

➡ Ben's Cornish Kitchen (p244)

Best Places to Stay

➡ Old Coastguard Hotel (p241)

➡ Artist Residence Penzance (p238)

➡ Venton Vean (p238)

➡ Boskerris (p224)

Why Go?

While most visitors head for the tourist honey pots of the north coast, the wild west of Cornwall receives fewer visitors outside the major draws of St Ives and Land's End. But the real beauty of this corner lies off the beaten track: it's a land where stone monuments rise up from the hilltops, ancient moorland butts up against gorse-topped cliffs, and forgotten mine stacks stand out in relief against the skyline.

With its sparkling seaside setting and artistic connections, the attractions of St Ives are very well-known, and the town can feel uncomfortably crowded between July and September, but time your visit for early spring or autumn and you'll find things quieter. Similarly, the main beaches around Gwithian, Sennen and the Lizard can be very busy, but many more remote coves can be reached via the coast path. And for a real escape, the lesser-visited islands of Scilly feel like a whole different world.

When to Go

➡ **May** St Mary's on the Isles of Scilly hosts the World Pilot Gig Championships over a weekend in early May. Accommodation is almost impossible to find, so you'll need to book at least six months' ahead.

➡ **Jun** Penzance stages its big summer street celebration during the Golowan Festival: try and visit on Mazey Day if you can, when the whole town turns out to party.

➡ **Dec** Christmas lights cover the harbour around Mousehole, and Penzance's pagan Montol Festival provides a slightly more alternative view of the festive season.

St Ives

POP 9870

Huddled at the end of a peninsula fringed by golden sands and glittering sea, St Ives is unquestionably one of Cornwall's prettiest coastal towns. Historically the town was an important pilchard harbour, but it reinvented itself as a haven for the arts after a stream of influential painters and sculptors set up studios here during the 1920s and '30s.

These days it's a blend of boutique chic and old-fashioned seaside. From the old harbour, a maze of cobbled alleys and

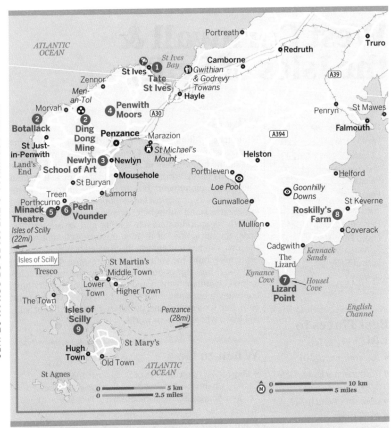

West Cornwall & the Isles of Scilly Highlights

1 Seeing the work of key St Ives artists at the **Tate St Ives** (p221)

2 Hiking to the picturesque ruins of **Botallack** and **Ding Dong Mine** (p229)

3 Bringing out your inner artist at the **Newlyn School of Art** (p240)

4 Seeking out the hillforts and stone circles scattered across the **Penwith Moors** (p227)

5 Watching a cliff-top play at the amazing **Minack Theatre** (p234)

6 Losing your inhibitions (and your swimsuit) on the nudist beach of **Pedn Vounder** (p234)

7 Sounding the fog-horn inside the historic **lighthouse** (p247) at Lizard Point

8 Trying some of Cornwall's best home-made ice-cream at **Roskilly's Farm** (p249)

9 Watching an evening gig race on the idyllic **Isles of Scilly** (p250)

switchback lanes lead up into a jumble of bistros, cafes and artists' galleries. The recent influx of big brands along the main street has done little to enhance St Ives' alternative character, but away from the centre you'll still find solitude along the quieter lanes of the old town, locally known as 'Downalong'.

Traffic (of all kinds) can be hellish during the peak season, and parking is both expensive and infuriating. There are large car parks around the edges of town, but a more peaceful way to arrive is aboard the single-carriage railway, which chugs its way along the coastline from St Erth and offers grandstand views over the Atlantic.

The town's name is a derivation of St Eia, who supposedly sailed here from Ireland on a leaf.

◉ Sights & Activities

St Ives boasts three fine town beaches. Furthest west is Porthmeor, just below the Tate, a broad sweep of yellow sand that's popular with the town's surfers, and has a small cafe beside the road.

Nearby, around the grassy headland known as the Island, is the little cove of Porthgwidden, which is the smallest and often the quietest of the town's beaches. At the rear of the beach are a line of vintage bathing huts and the cosy Porthgwidden Beach Café (☑ 01736-796791; www.porthgwidden cafe.co.uk; Porthgwidden Beach; mains £8.95-10.95; ☺ 9am-10pm in summer, closed all day Mon in winter): you can sit down inside for light meals of fresh mussels and haddock chowder, or just get a takeaway from the serving hatch.

The largest and loveliest of St Ives' beaches is Porthminster, with a horseshoe of soft golden sand that's sheltered by the cliffs. It's also where you'll find one of the town's swishest restaurants, the Porthminster Beach Café (p225).

Two miles east of town is the busy resort of Carbis Bay, worth a visit for its sheltered (if touristy) Blue Flag beach.

Tate St Ives   GALLERY
(☑ 01736-796226; www.tate.org.uk/stives; Porthmeor Beach; adult/child £7/4.50; ☺ 10am-5pm Mar-Oct, to 4pm Tue-Sun Nov-Feb) There's no shortage of galleries in St Ives, but the Tate St Ives is the centrepiece. Hovering like a white concrete curl above Porthmeor Beach, the gallery's architecture echoes its seaside setting. Themed exhibitions are matched

with a permanent collection rich in works by artists connected with the St Ives School. Terry Frost, Naum Gabo, Patrick Heron, Ben Nicholson, the potter Bernard Leach and the naive Cornish painter Alfred Wallis are all represented, alongside sculptures by Barbara Hepworth (you can buy a joint ticket with the Barbara Hepworth Museum for £10/7 for adult/child). The top-floor cafe has a glass-walled patio overlooking Porthmeor Beach.

Planning permission for a new £12.3m extension has recently been granted, which will allow more space for showing prize pieces from the museum's permanent collection. Work is scheduled for completion by late 2015.

You can receive a discount of £1 if you arrive by public transport and show your ticket.

Barbara Hepworth Museum   MUSEUM
(☑ 01736-796226; Barnoon Hill; adult/child £6/4; ☺ 10am-5pm Mar-Oct, 10am-4pm Tue-Sun Nov-Feb) Barbara Hepworth was one of the leading abstract sculptors of the 20th century, and a key figure in the St Ives art scene, so it's fitting that her former studio is now a museum (you can purchase a joint ticket with the Tate St Ives gallery for £10/7 per adult/child). The studio has remained untouched since her death in a fire in 1975, and the adjoining garden contains some of her most famous sculptures. Among the shrubs, look out for the harplike Garden Sculpture (Model for Meridian) and Four Square, the largest work Hepworth created.

Her art is also liberally sprinkled around town; there's a Hepworth outside the Guildhall, and her moving Madonna and Child inside St Ia Church commemorates her son Paul Skeaping, who was killed in an air crash in 1953.

0 — 200 m
0 — 0.1 miles
N

ATLANTIC
OCEAN

The Island

3

Porthgwidden Beach

Porthmeor Rd

Island Rd

Porthmeor Beach

Carncrows St
Teetotal St
St Eia St
Back Rd East

20

Porthgwidden Beach

Back Rd West

Fish St

28
5 24
23
26
17

1

Bunkers Hill

The Digey

Fore St

The Wharf

ICE CR

6
TATE

Porthmeor
TCE

Harbour

Smeaton's Pier

West Pl

Barnoon Hill

Bowling Green Tce

15
22

18
27
14
8

2

Ayr La

Richmond Pl

7

St Ives Bay

19

Parish Church

12

St Andrews St

St Ives Tourist Office

Bedford Rd

Tregenna Hill

Chapel St

Gabriel St

St Ia Church

Tregenna Pl

No 1 St Ives (240m);
Leach Pottery Studio
& Museum (1mi);
Zennor
(4.5mi)

Street-an-Pol

Skidden Hill

4
16

The Warren

OUR HOTEL

13

The Terrace

Tregenna Tce

Albert Rd

10

9
11

Porthminster Beach

21

St Ives Train Station

Primrose Valley

25

Blue Hayes (150m);
Boskerris (0.8mi);
Carbis Bay (1.5mi)

St Ives

⊙ **Sights**
1 Art Space C2
2 Barbara Hepworth Museum................B4
3 Chapel of St Nicholas..........................C1
4 New Millennium Gallery B5
   Salthouse Gallery.........................(see 5)
5 St Ives Society of Artists....................B2
6 Tate St Ives...A3
7 Wills Lane Gallery................................B4

⊕ **Activities, Courses & Tours**
8 St Ives Boats.......................................B4

⊜ **Sleeping**
9 11 Sea View Terrace............................B6
10 Little Leaf Guest House.......................A5
11 Organic Panda......................................B6
12 Treliska...B4
13 Trevose Harbour House......................C5

⊗ **Eating**
14 Alba...B4
15 Alfresco...B3
16 Blas Burgerworks B5
17 Moomaid of Zennor B3
18 Onshore...B4
19 Pengenna Pasties B4
20 Porthgwidden Beach Café...................D2
21 Porthminster Beach Café....................C6
22 Rum & Crab Shack B4
23 Seagrass...C3
24 The Loft...B2

⊙ **Drinking & Nightlife**
25 Porthminster Beach Cafe....................D7
26 Sloop Inn...C3
27 The Hub...B4

⊙ **Shopping**
28 Sloop Craft Market B2

Leach Pottery   GALLERY
(☏ 01736-796398; www.leachpottery.com; Higher Stennack; adult/child £5.50/4.50; ⊙ 10am-5pm Mon-Sat, 11am-4pm Sun) While Barbara Hepworth was breaking new sculptural ground, the potter Bernard Leach was hard at work reinventing British ceramics in his studio in Higher Stennack. Drawing inspiration from Japanese and Oriental sculpture, and using a unique hand-built 'climbing' kiln based on ones he had seen in Japan, Leach's pottery created a unique fusion of Western and Eastern ideas.

His former studio displays examples of his work, and has been enhanced by a brand-new museum and working pottery studio. The shop contains work by contemporary potters, as well as souvenirs from the Leach tableware range.

Chapel of St Nicholas   RELIGIOUS
On the grassy promontory known as the Island, between Porthmeor and Porthminster, is the tiny pre-14th-century Chapel of St Nicholas, patron saint of children and sailors. It's allegedly the oldest church in St Ives – and certainly the smallest.

Boat Trips   BOAT TOUR
From the harbourfront, several operators including St Ives Boats (☏ 0777-300 8000; www.stivesboats.co.uk; Wharf Rd; adult/child £10/8) offer fishing trips and scenic cruises, including to the grey seal colony on Seal Island. If you're really lucky, you might even spot a porpoise or a basking shark in summer.

⚑ Festivals & Events

St Ives September Festival   FESTIVAL
(www.stivesseptemberfestival.co.uk) Annual arts fest (in early September) featuring music, exhibitions and events.

⬛ Sleeping

Treliska   B&B £
(☏ 01736-797678; www.treliska.com; 3 Bedford Rd; d £65-85; ☏) The smooth decor at this B&B is attractive – chrome taps, wooden furniture, cool sinks – but it's the position that sells it, just steps from the town centre.

No 1 St Ives   B&B ££
(☏ 01736-799047; www.no1stives.co.uk; 1 Fern Glen; d £90-135; P☏) This renovated granite cottage bills itself as 'shabby chic', but it's nothing of the sort. It's a model of a modern B&B, and full of spoils – filtered water, goose-down duvets, iPod docks and White Company bathstuffs. Rooms vary in size, but all sport the same palette of white, cream and cappuccino.

11 Sea View Terrace   B&B ££
(☏ 01736-798440; www.11stives.co.uk; 11 Sea View Tce; d £100-135; P☏) Creams, checks and warm brown carpets distinguish this chic St Ives B&B. The two front 'suites' have lovely town and seaviews, while the rear one overlooks a garden patio; for more space there's a smart holiday flat (£500 to £950 per week).

Little Leaf Guest House   B&B ££
(☏ 01736-795427; www.littleleafguesthouse.co.uk; Park Ave; r £85-120; ☏) This six-room B&B is run with style and a smile by owners Danny and Lee. Rooms are sweet and simple, finished in creamy colours and pine furniture. Ask for Room two or five if you're a sucker for a sea view.

Organic Panda
B&B **££**

(☎ 01736-793890; www.organicpanda.co.uk; 1 Pednolver Tce; d £80-140; P 🗢) Removed from the St Ives hustle in nearby Carbis Bay, this sweet little B&B has an arty streak: spotty cushions and timber-salvage beds in the rooms, and the house is dotted with work by St Ives artists. Needless to say, brekkie is organic. Twenty-five percent discount for three-night stays.

Boskerris
HOTEL **£££**

(☎ 01736-795295; www.boskerrishotel.co.uk; Boskerris Rd; d £125-220; P 🗢) This 1930s guesthouse in Carbis Bay has had a makeover and, if you like your materials modern and your colours cool and contemporary, you won't go far wrong. Big bay views, a soothing seaside ambience and plenty of classy touches make it popular: book well ahead.

Trevose Harbour House
B&B **£££**

(☎ 01736-793267; www.trevosehouse.co.uk; 22 The Warren; d £135-185; 🗢) A swanky six-room townhouse on the winding Warren, restored with a sea-themed combo of fresh whites and stripy blues. It's been beautifully finished – Neal's Yard bathstuffs, iPod docks, and plenty of retro design pieces in the rooms – but it's pricey, even with the handy location near Porthminster.

Blue Hayes
HOTEL **£££**

(☎ 01736-797129; www.bluehayes.co.uk; Trelyon Ave, St Ives; r £110-240; P 🗢) A favourite of the Sunday supplements thanks to its manicured grounds, balustraded breakfast terrace and five supremely well-appointed rooms. The Trelyon Suite even has its own private roof terrace.

🍴 Eating

Rum & Crab Shack
SEAFOOD **£**

(☎ 01736-796353; Wharf Rd; mains £5.95-9.50; ⏱ 9am-9pm; 🗲) If the thought of cracking your own crab and eating it from the shell appeals, then this place is definitely for you (aprons and tools are provided). As you might expect, the rum choice ain't bad either, and scrowlers (aka sardines) on toast has to be the best-named dish in town.

Moomaid of Zennor
ICE CREAM **£**

(www.moomaidofzennor.com; The Wharf; from £2; ⏱ 9am-5pm) This ice cream maker is a local legend, and makes all its 30 flavours on the home farm just outside Zennor, using only their own milk and Rodda's clotted cream. Exotic concoctions include fig and mascarpone and pear cider sorbet.

Pengenna Pasties
BAKERY **£**

(www.pengennapasties.co.uk; 9 High St; pasties £3-4) Generously-stuffed pasties, with a controversial top crimp and flakier texture.

Blas Burgerworks
BURGERS **££**

(☎ 01736-797 272; www.blasburgerworks.co.uk; The Warren; burgers £5-10; ⏱ noon-10pm; 🗲) The burger becomes a work of art at Blas. Their 6oz burgers come in a smorgasbord of choices: served with Cornish blue or Davidstow cheddar, laced with beetroot and wild garlic mayo, or spiced with corn salsa and guacamole. There are veggie options, too: the halloumi stack with field mushroom and caper aioli was recently voted best veggie burger by the BBC's *Olive* magazine. There's not much room to sit, though – and beware of marauding seagulls if you opt for takeaway.

Alba
SEAFOOD **££**

(☎ 01736-797222; www.thealbarestaurant.com; Old Lifeboat House, Wharf Rd; mains £11-18; ⏱ lunch noon-2pm, dinner 5.30-10pm) This seafood restaurant blazed the gourmet trail in St Ives. Beige pine and crisp white tablecloths create a cool and contemporary space, while the menu offers a wealth of seafood. The best tables are near the window overlooking the harbour; ask when you book. Set menus (two-/three-courses £16.95/19.95) are available between 5.30pm and 7.30pm.

Alfresco CLOSED
BISTRO **££**

(☎ 01736-793737; info@alfrescocafebar.co.uk; The Wharf; 2-course dinner menu £16.95; ⏱ lunch noon-3pm Thu & Fri, dinner 7-9pm daily) Another seafood specialist with a Mediterranean twist. Look out for the mussels 'steamed in Cornish stingers' and the excellent Alfresco Chowder. When the sun's shining and the doors are open onto the wharf, it all feels deliciously continental.

Seagrass CLOSED
MODERN BRITISH **££**

(☎ 01736-793763; www.seagrass-stives.com; Fish St; dinner mains £13.25-19.95; ⏱ dinner 6-10pm year-round, lunch noon-2pm in summer) An attractive bistro just off the harbour, with a strong focus on seafood and game with a French-Italian flavour. Fish fans might like to go for the 'Oysters & Shells' menu: a fresh St Ives crab with chili jam, perhaps, or Helford oysters served with a red wine and shallot vinaigrette. The 2-/3-course early dining menu is fab value at £15.95/19.95, and served from 6pm to 7pm.

Onshore
PIZZA **££**

(☏ 01736-796000; The Wharf; pizzas £8-14; ⊙ 9am-10pm; ❖) Pizza, pizza and more pizza; wood-fired, and served with harbour views. It's a perfect family option.

The Loft
BISTRO **££**

(☏ 01736-794204; www.theloftrestaurantandterrace.co.uk; Norway Ln; dinner £14.95-22.95; ⊙ lunch noon-2pm, dinner 6-10pm; ❖) In a converted sail loft, this A-frame restaurant feels like dining inside a ship's galley. Expect simple, unfussy food: chicken supreme on herby potatoes, or seabass with lemon and caper butter.

★ Porthminster Beach Café
BISTRO **£££**

(☏ 01736-795352; www.porthminstercafe.co.uk; Porthminster Beach; lunch £10.50-16.50, dinner £10-22; ⊙ 9am-10pm) A finer sea-view location you simply will not find in St Ives – or anywhere in Cornwall, for that matter. Right beside Porthminster's sands, there's an echo of the French Riviera about this award-winning bistro, with its beach-cabin vibe and seasonal menu ranging from Provençal fish soup to pan-fried scallops. On sunny days, the premium tables are on the sun-trap patio – but they go lightning-quick, so think fast. Cornwall's best beach cafe? Quite possibly.

🍷 Drinking & Nightlife

The Hub
CAFE, BAR

(www.hub-stives.co.uk; The Wharf) Coffee, cake, ciabattas or cocktails, this open-plan cafe-bar is the heart of St Ives' social scene. Funky murals by local design collective A-Side Studio create a big-city vibe quite out of keeping with the quayside location. Tables spill onto the flagstones on hot days, while DJs provide late-night entertainment.

Sloop Inn
INN

(☏ 01736-796584; www.sloop-inn.co.uk; The Wharf; mains £5.95-15.95; ⊙ 11am-11pm Mon-Sat, 10am-10pm Sun) Old Speckled Hen, Doom Bar and Bass ales make this beam-ceilinged boozer a comfy favourite. Settle into a booth for the night, or bag one of the coveted wharfside tables – there's no better place for a pint and a crab butty when the sun's shining.

🛍 Shopping

The Sloop Craft Market (St Ives) is a treasure trove of artists' studios selling everything from handmade cards to silkscreen art. You can watch the artists at work through the studio windows: look out for handcrafted brooches, rings and pendants at Smith Jewellery (☏ 01736-799876; www.smithjewellery.com), stained-glass artwork by Debbie Martin (☏ 01736-796051); and one-off pieces of driftwood furniture by Beach Wood (☏ 01736-796051). It's at the back of the Sloop car park, just off the harbourfront.

The St Ives Society of Artists (☏ 01736-795582; www.stivessocietyofartists.com; Norway Sq) – one of Cornwall's oldest and most influential collectives, founded in 1929 – has its gallery in a converted church on Norway Sq, with a separate 'Mariners Gallery' in the crypt. Another well-respected name is the New Millennium Gallery (☏ 01736-793121; www.newmillenniumgallery.co.uk; Street-an-Pol), which houses one of the largest local collections in town.

Modern work is the focus at the Salthouse Gallery (☏ 01736-795003; http://salthousegallery.110mb.com; Norway Sq) and the Wills Lane Gallery (☏ 01736-795723; www.willslanegallery.co.uk; Wills Lane; ⊙ 10.30am-5.30pm Wed-Sat, 11am-4pm Sun), run by a former director of the Contemporary Art Society, while Art Space (☏ 01736-799744; www.artspace-cornwall.co.uk; The Wharf; ⊙ 10.30am-5.30pm summer, 11am-4.30pm winter) showcases talented local artists.

ℹ Information

St Ives Tourist Office (☏ 01736-796297; www.stivestic.co.uk; Street-an-Pol; ⊙ 9am-5.30pm Mon-Fri, 9am-5pm Sat, 10am-4pm Sun) Inside the Guildhall.

ℹ Getting There & Away

BUS

From April to October, the open-top Western Greyhound bus 300 runs three to five times daily between Penzance and St Ives via Land's End, taking in St Just and Zennor en route.

Other local buses:

Penzance (30 minutes, every half-hour Monday to Saturday, hourly on Sunday) Bus 17.

Truro (1½ hours, hourly) Bus 14, via Hayle, Camborne and Redruth.

Zennor (20 minutes, every 2 hours Monday to Saturday) Bus 508 stops at Towednack, Zennor, Gurnard's Head and New Mill (for Chysauster).

CAR

St Ives' narrow streets make it a living nightmare to drive around in summer. Unless you want to spend your time roasting slowly inside an automobile-shaped oven, avoid driving into the town centre at all costs.

The best idea is to park at one of the large car parks around the outskirts. The largest is Trenwith, which is a long walk uphill from town, but has 759 spaces in summer, 311 spaces in winter.

Other options are the car park next to the station (106 spaces) and the large car park next to the Island (155 spaces). There are also small car parks next to Porthmeor Beach, the Sloop, Smeaton's Pier, Park Avenue and next to the Barnoon apartments.

An even better plan is to park at the train stations at St Erth or Lelant Saltings and catch the train into St Ives – much less stressful.

TRAIN

The scenic branch line runs via Carbis Bay, Lelant, Lelant Saltings and St Erth (£3, 14 minutes, half-hourly), where it links up with the main London–Penzance line.

Gwithian & Godrevy Towans

Four miles drive east of St Ives over the Hayle Estuary, the dune-backed flats of Gwithian and Godrevy unfurl in a glimmering golden curve that joins together at low tide to form Hayle's much-lauded '3 miles of golden sand'. At the southwestern end is the Hayle Estuary, once a busy harbour, while at the opposite end, the Godrevy Lighthouse perches on a rocky island and is famous for inspiring Virginia Woolf's stream-of-consciousness classic *To the Lighthouse*.

The beaches are backed by acres of grassy dunes (known in Cornish as *towans*). While popular, there's usually ample space for everyone even in the height of summer. Both beaches have car parks, but unsurprisingly spaces can be hard to come by on busy days. Godrevy is National Trust-owned, so members can park for free assuming they can find a space; extra parking is usually available at a nearby field. A resident colony of grey seals can often be spotted at the bottom of a cliff near the point.

Gwithian's reliable breaks are a favourite for surfers, and make this a fine place to learn the ropes. The Gwithian Surf Academy (☑ 01736-757579; www.surfacademy.co.uk) is a well-known surf school, and one of only four BSA Schools of Excellence.

🛏 Sleeping

Gwithian Farm CAMPSITE £
(☑ 01736-753127; gwithianfarm.co.uk; sites £14-23; ☺ Apr-Sep) Brilliantly situated campsite in a field in Gwithian village, with full fa-cilities and a handy location for the beach. It's expensive for camping, though, and gets packed in summer.

✗ Eating & Drinking

Godrevy Café CAFE £
(☑ 01736-757999; www.godrevycafe.com; lunch £6-10; ☺ 10am-5pm) Split-level timber cafe beside the Godrevy car park, serving great coffee and lunches. Arrive early if you want to bag a table on the top-deck patio overlooking the beach.

Jam Pot Cafe CAFE £
(☑ 01736-759190; £2-5; ☺ 9am-5pm in summer) A sweet little beach-snack cafe, housed in a former fisherman's watch-hut that's now a listed building. It's near the main Gwithian car park.

Sunset Surf Cafe CAFE £
(☑ 01736-752575; www.sunset-surf.com; mains £4-8; ☺ breakfast & lunch) Part surf school, part beach cafe, and a perennial snack stop behind the Gwithian dunes. Surf lessons start from £30.

Sandsifter BAR
(☑ 01736-757809; www.sandsiftercornwall.com; ☺ 10am-11pm) For twilight drinks, the Sandsifter is the place; it often stays open late for gigs and club nights. Look out for the carpark just after the Godrevy turning. Mains cost £4 to £16.

Hayle

Set beside a wide river estuary, Hayle grew up as an industrial harbour during the great mining boom of the 18th and 19th centuries. Grand old Victorian buildings line the waterfront and the area around Foundry Square, but the town has never quite managed to recapture its former status, despite several mooted projects to redevelop the harbourfront.

Hayle's main attraction is Paradise Park (☑ 01736-751020; www.paradisepark.org.uk; adult/child £12.99/9.99; ☺ 10am-5pm in summer), a bird sanctuary with a population of parrots, parakeets, eagles, owls and other birds of prey. Feeding and display flights are held throughout the day: look out for one of the park's prize animals, Archie the Bald Eagle, who regularly takes centre stage. There's also an indoor Jungle Barn play centre which is handy if the summer weather takes an unfavourable turn.

TOP FARM SHOPS

Cornwall has lots of fantastic farm shops where you can pick up produce fresh from the fields.

Trevaskis Farm (☏01209-713931; www.trevaskisfarm.co.uk; 12 Gwinear Rd, Hayle; ⊙farm shop 9am-6pm summer, 9am-5pm winter) Near Gwithian, this farm shop sells meats, homemade chutneys and fresh fruit and veg. The restaurant also does vast Sunday roasts.

Trevathan Farm (☏01208-880164; www.trevathanfarm.com; ⊙10am-5pm) Pick your own fruit near Port Isaac.

Lobbs Farm Shop (☏01726-844411; St Ewe; ⊙9.30am-5pm Mon-Fri) Part of the Heligan Estate. Stock up on smoked fish, farm-reared meats and marmalades, or pick up a pre-packed hamper at this farm shop at the Lost Gardens of Heligan, 7 miles south of St Austell.

Kingsley Village (☏01726-861111; www.kingsleyvillage.com) Purpose-built shopping complex on the A30 near Fraddon, with a massive food hall, and excellent fresh fish and meat counters.

Gear Farm (☏01326-221150; www.gearfarmcornwall.co.uk; St Martin, Helston) The Lizard's organic operation, with meat and dairy supplied from a herd of Aberdeen Angus reared on the farm.

Eating & Drinking

★Philps   BAKERY £
(☏01736-755661; www.philpspasties.co.uk; 1 East Quay; pasties from £3) According to many local aficionados, Philps makes the best pasties in Cornwall, made to the same recipe laid down by the bakery's founder, Sam Philps, some sixty years ago.

Mr B's Ice-Cream   CAFE £
(☏01736-758580; www.mrbsicecream.co.uk; 24 Penpol Tce; ice creams £2-3; ⊙10am-5pm) Scores of flavours to choose from at this beloved Hayle ice cream parlour, including oddball choices such as jaffa cake, bakewell tart and damson plum.

Bucket of Blood   PUB
(☏01736-752378; ⊙11am-11pm Mon-Sat, noon-10pm Sun) A whitewashed, low-ceilinged inn just outside the town centre, sporting quite possibly the best name of any pub in Britain (apparently it harks back 200 years when a corpse was dumped down the pub well and made the water run red, an incident commemorated on the pub's sign).

❶ Getting There & Away

Bus X18 (hourly Monday to Saturday) Stops in Hayle en route from Penzance to Camborne and Truro.

The Penwith Peninsula

Taking its name from two Cornish words – *penn* (headland) and *wydh* (end) – Penwith juts like a crooked finger stretching from St Ives to the most westerly point on the British mainland at Land's End. Wild and remote, spotted with minestacks, ancient farmland and windswept moor, Penwith was originally one of the Cornish Hundreds (a network of administrative districts dating back to the Domesday Book) but the first settlers arrived long before – this corner of west Cornwall boasts one of Europe's highest concentrations of prehistoric sites, many of which predate Stonehenge and Avebury. Later Penwith became a hub of mining activity and the area now provides a fantastic insight into the unimaginably tough lives of Cornwall's tin miners.

A great way to tour the Penwith area is aboard the open-top double-decker bus 300 (Penwith Explorer), which runs from April to October.

❶ Getting There & Away

Various buses trundle around the villages between Penzance and St Ives.

Bus 1/1A (six daily Monday to Saturday) Runs from Penzance to Land's End (half the buses go via Sennen; the other half via Treen and Porthcurno).

Penwith Peninsula & Land's End

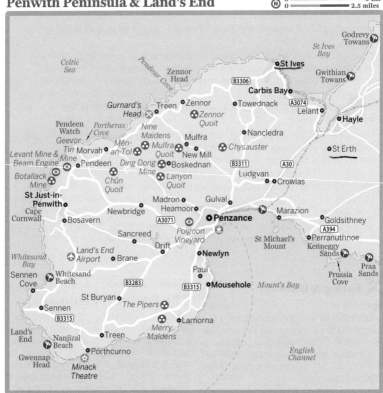

Bus 10A (at least one an hour Monday to Saturday) Runs from Penzance to St Just via Heamoor, Madron, Pendeen and Botallack.

Bus 300 (three to five daily April to October) An open-top double-decker that runs from Penzance to St Ives, then continues via Zennor, Pendeen, Geevor, Botallack and St Just to Land's End, and then circles back to Penzance via Sennen, Drift and Newlyn.

Bus 504 (two daily Monday to Saturday) Stops at Penzance to Lamorna, the Merry Maidens, Porthcurno, Land's End, Sennen and St Just.

Bus 508 (six daily Monday to Saturday) Stops at Towednack, Zennor, Gurnard's Head and New Mill (for Chysauster).

Zennor & Pendeen

The wild B3306 coast road between St Ives and St Just-in-Penwith is a jewel, winding through a panorama of granite-strewn moorland and patchwork fields, some of which date back to medieval times. This is a wild corner of Cornwall, and feels a long way from the prettified harbour towns and manicured beaches. Craggy tors and auburn heaths dominate the horizon, and broken cliffs tumble down into booming surf. It's scarcely populated now, but during Neolithic times this empty landscape was home to a string of ancient settlements, the remains of which can still be seen scattered amongst the granite rocks.

Five miles west of St Ives is the miniscule village of Zennor, set around the medieval Church of St Senara. DH Lawrence sojourned here between 1915 and 1917 before being drummed out of the village as a suspected communist spy (an episode recounted in his novel *Kangaroo*), but the village is best known for its associations with the local legend of the Mermaid of Zennor, who is said to have fallen in love with the singing voice of local lad Matthew Trewhella. A carved bench-end inside the church depicts the mermaid holding a mirror and comb. Her favourite haunt of **Pendour Cove** can be reached along the stunning coast path, as well as the ultra-hidden beach of **Veor Cove**, a great place for wild, secluded swimming.

Downhill from the church, the **Wayside Folk Museum** (admission £3; ⊙10.30am-5pm Sun-Fri May-Sep, 11am-5pm Sun-Fri Apr & Oct) houses curios gathered by Colonel 'Freddie' Hirst in the 1930s, from blacksmiths' hammers and reclaimed watermills to an 18th-century Cornish kitchen.

🛏 Sleeping & Eating

Zennor Backpackers HOSTEL **£**
(✆01736-798307; www.zennorbackpackers.net; dm/f £18.50/70) Inside Zennor's old chapel, this bright hostel has one family room, two four-bed dorms and four six-bed dorms, plus a very good cafe serving hot meals and homemade cakes.

Bodrifty Farm ROUNDHOUSE **££**
(✆07887-522788; www.bodriftyfarm.co.uk; from £130 per night) This isolated farm has something really special: an authentic reconstruction of a Celtic chieftain's roundhouse, built from timber and thatch, with its own firepit to keep the nights warm. But you won't be roughing it: the roundhouse has a handbuilt timber bed and its own luxurious (and very modern) bathroom block. The remains of a Celtic village can be seen nearby.

★ **Gurnard's Head** PUB **££**
(✆01736-796928; www.gurnardshead.co.uk; lunch £6.50-13.50, dinner £12.50-16.50; ⊙lunch noon-3pm, dinner 6.30-10pm) It's way out on the Zennor coast road, but you can't miss the Gurnard's – its name is written in big letters on the roof. Run by the Inkin brothers (who also run the Old Coastguard Hotel in Mousehole) this sublime country pub has defied its isolated location to become one of

---

WORTH A TRIP

MINING SITES

Tin mining was once the staple industry in West Cornwall, and deserted engine houses still punctuate the crag-backed coastline. **Geevor Tin Mine** (✆01736-788662; www. geevor.com; adult/child £10.50/6.50; ⊙9am-5pm Sun-Fri Mar-Oct, to 4pm Nov-Feb) was the last mine in West Cornwall to close (in 1990), and has since been resurrected as a fascinating museum. Above ground you can wander around the old machinery where the tin ore was extracted, while below ground you can take a guided tour into the mine itself – a maze of dank shafts and tunnels where miners worked for hours at a stretch, enduring ever-present dangers of rockfalls, air pollution and underground explosions. The mine is easy to spot on the B3306, just before you reach the village of Pendeen.

More mining heritage comes to life at the **Levant Mine & Beam Engine** (✆01736-786156; www.nationaltrust.org.uk/levant-mine; adult/child £6.50/3.20; ⊙11am-5pm Sun-Fri), one of the world's only working Cornish beam engines. These pioneering steam-powered engines were used to pump floodwater from the deep underground shafts and bring ore back to the surface, and transformed the Cornish mining industry into a world leader; the engine design was later exported across the world. It's in Trewellard, just past Pendeen; look out for the brown signs.

Clinging to the sea-battered cliffs nearby are the evocative remains of **Botallack Mine**. Sitting at the base of a rugged cliff and regularly battered by waves, it's perhaps the most picturesque of Penwith's crumbling minestacks. It's also renowned as one of Penwith's deepest mines; some of the shafts extend right out beneath the raging Atlantic waves, and it's said that the miners could sometimes hear the rumble of rocks overhead being moved around by the ocean currents. Various trails wind around the site; it's just along the coast from Levant Mine, so park there and walk.

Further west along the B3306 is the old minestack of **Carn Galver**, situated near the mining ruins of the Porthmeor Valley, while **Ding Dong Mine**, perched on the hilltops near the Mên-an-tol, is reputed to be Cornwall's oldest mine. Official records date back to the 17th century, although legend has it the mine has been working for over 2000 years, and was once visited by Jesus and Joseph of Arimathea. It's tricky to find; just before you reach Morvah, turn off the coast road towards Madron, drive past Lanyon Quoit and turn left when you see the sign to Bosiliack.

Cornwall's destination addresses (bookings are a must). Book-lined shelves, sepia prints, scruffy wood and rough stone walls create a reassuringly lived-in feel, and the menu offers cockle-warming fare: beef blade, pork shoulder, chicken breast and duck rillettes. Rooms are suitably cosy (double rooms £100 to £170), and all have a choice of moor or coastal views.

Tinner's Arms PUB **££**

(☎01736-792697; www.tinnersarms.com; mains £10.50-16.50) Built for masons working at St Senara's Church, this is a quintessential Cornish inn, complete with slate roof, roaring fireplaces and zero commercial clutter (no TV, no jukebox, no mobile signal). Next door, the 'White House' provides fresh, spotless rooms (singles/doubles £55/95).

Penwith's Ancient Sites

Penwith is littered with archaeological remains, built by Neolithic settlers sometime between 4000 BC and 2500 BC. They offer a fascinating insight into our ancestors' past, but some are very tricky to find; a detailed map such as the *Ordnance Survey Explorer 102* will come in very handy.

QUOITS & STONES

Most dramatic are the quoits (known elsewhere as dolmens): three or more upright stones topped by a capstone, built on top of a chamber tomb. Most were probably once covered by a barrow of earth or stones, but over the centuries the stones have been plundered or worn away to reveal the supporting structure.

Most impressive is Lanyon Quoit, topped by a 13.5-tonne capstone and situated right beside the road between Madron and Morvah. In the 18th century, the monument was tall enough to shelter a man on horseback, but an 1815 storm blew the quoit down and broke one of the four uprights; it was re-erected nine years later. Chûn Quoit (near the Chûn Castle hillfort) is also very well-preserved, although others such as Zennor Quoit and Mulfra Quoit haven't fared so well over the centuries.

Five miles southeast of Morvah is the curvy Mên-an-tol (Cornish for stone-of-the-hole), a weird formation consisting of two menhirs (monumental stones) flanking a hollow stone. Squeezing through the stone was said to be a cure for infertility and rickets.

HILLFORTS & SETTLEMENTS

The area is dotted with Iron Age hillforts, most of which date from around 1000 BC to 500 BC (although some were probably built on the site of earlier fortifications), including Chûn Castle, signposted from the road past Mên-an-tol and Lanyon Quoit. A pile of rubble and two upright stones are all that remains of the fortress, but in the 18th century the walls stood 4.5m high; much of the stone was subsequently plundered for local construction projects (including Penzance's north pier). Other ruined hillforts can be seen at Maen Castle near Sennen, Logan Rock near Treryn Dinas (p234) and Kenidjack, near St Just.

Marginally more intact is the Iron Age village of Chysauster (☎07831-757934; adult/child £3.60/2.20; ☺10am-6pm Jul & Aug, to 5pm Apr-Jun & Sep, to 4pm Oct), thought to have been built between 400 BC and AD 100. Consisting of eight stone-walled houses, each with its own central courtyard, it gives you a real sense of daily life during the Iron Age – you can still see the stone hearths and platforms used to grind corn, and wander the gardens where the residents kept livestock and grew arable crops.

Arguably even more atmospheric than Chysauster are the ruins of Carn Euny, another Bronze Age village that's half-hidden by trees, and is thought to date to around 500 BC. It's very hard to find without an Ordnance Survey (OS) map; head west from Penzance on the A30 to Land's End and look out for the brown 'Carn Euny' signs after you pass the turning to Drift. There's limited parking near the farmhouses at Brane, from where the hillfort's about a 500m walk.

STONE CIRCLES

Penwith's stone circles include the Merry Maidens, near Lamorna, which supposedly mark the petrified remains of a group of 19 girls turned to stone for dancing on the Sabbath. Nearby are the Pipers, who earned the same fate for tootling a tune on a Sunday. There's another circle east of the Mên-an-Tol, the Nine Maidens; the name derives from the Cornish word *maedn* (later *mên*) meaning stone.

Most picturesque of all is the Boscawen-un circle, about halfway between Penzance and Land's End on the A30. Follow directions as for Carn Euny, but ignore the turning and stay on the A30 for another half-mile till you reach Lands End Pine Ltd on your left; the track up to the circle starts directly opposite.

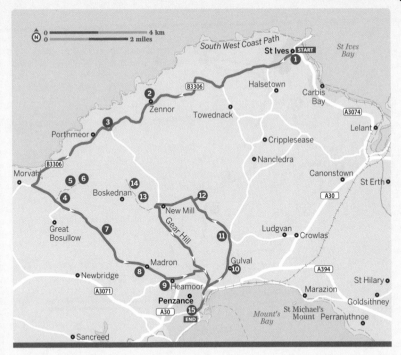

🏃 Driving Tour
Penwith's Prehistory

START ST IVES
FINISH PENZANCE
DISTANCE 26 MILES; 3 HOURS

This road-trip takes in Penwith's best-known ancient sites. Start the trip in **1 St Ives**, and head out on the B3306, signed to Zennor. The road climbs into majestic moorland scenery, dipping and winding along the clifftops all the way to **2 Zennor**, 6 miles west of St Ives. Continue along the B3306 to the renowned gastropub, the **3 Gurnard's Head**, which makes a great stop for lunch. Alternatively, stay on the road till you reach the next left-hand turn, signed to Penzance/Madron (you'll see a white cottage next to the turning). Stay on this road until you reach a small **4 layby** and farm gate on the left; it's easy to miss, so keep your eyes peeled. From here, an unsigned trail leads up to the ring-shaped stone known as the **5 Mên-an-tol**; if you wish, you can continue along the trail to the **6 Nine Maidens** stone circle. It's a mile there and back from the layby.

Back in the car, continue along the minor road for half-a-mile. You'll pass **7 Lanyon Quoit** on your left, one of the largest and best-preserved of Penwith's dolmens. You can walk up to the quoit by crossing over a drystone wall. From here, it's another couple of miles to the village of **8 Madron** and its holy well, one of Penwith's many sacred wells.

Continue downhill towards Penzance. When you reach the village of **9 Heamoor**, take the minor road signed left towards **10 Gulval**. Continue through the village and onto the B3311 towards Nancledra. Climb the hill to **11 Badger's Cross**, and take the next left signed to **12 Chysauster**, 0.75 miles after the turning. This is the southwest's most important Iron Age village, and you can wander freely around roundhouse remains.

Follow the road from Chysauster on to the nearby village of **13 Mulfra**, where you can see another impressive dolmen, **14 Mulfra Quoit**, before backtracking to **15 Penzance**.

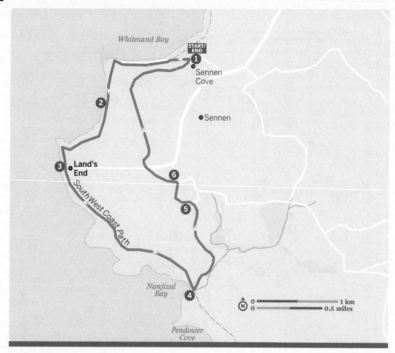

🏃 Walking Tour
Last Stop Cornwall

START SENNEN
FINISH SENNEN
DISTANCE AROUND 6 TO 7 MILES; 3 TO 4 HOURS

This hike is as far west as you can walk on mainland Britain; it starts at the lovely cove of Sennen and circles round via the end-of-everything headland of Land's End, taking in some of the wildest coastal scenery in all of Cornwall. A few of the tracks are easy to miss, so an Ordnance Survey (OS) map will come in handy.

Leave the car at the car park at ❶ **Sennen Cove**, and head west along the coast path, which climbs steeply past an old lookout station that's been refurbished by the National Trust. Head on along the coast path, and look out for the remains of ❷ **Maen Castle** on your right, a prehistoric hillfort dramatically sited on the cliffs. The surrounding area has been inhabited since Neolithic times; it's thought that many of the field boundaries were established by ancient settlers. This section is particularly spectacular in summer, when the wildflowers are a blaze of colour, and seabirds wheel and circle over the clifftops.

Continue on the coast path till you reach ❸ **Land's End**, where you can snap your picture next to the famous sign: 28 miles to Scilly, 874 miles to John O'Groats, 3147 to New York, and 1.5 miles out to sea to the famous Longships Lighthouse. From here it's another mile or so along the rather precarious coast path to the secluded beach of ❹ **Nanjizal**, reached by wooden steps. It's great for swimming, but the waves can be powerful so take care.

After your dip, take the path leading inland up the hillside; turn left when you reach a junction, and cross the fields till you arrive at ❺ **Trevilley Farm** and the nearby village of ❻ **Trevescan**, where you can reward yourself with a cream tea at the delightful Apple Tree Cafe. From here, head along the road till you come to the junction with the A30. You'll see a sign for a public bridleway directly opposite the turning, which leads all the way back down to Sennen.

❶ Information

You'll need a decent map to find many of the sites; some are well signposted and reached via well-trodden trails, while others are well off the beaten-track. The OS Explorer Map 102 covers the whole Penwith Peninsula (including Land's End) and details most of the area's ancient sites.

The useful pages at www.pznow.co.uk/historic1/circles.html provide some useful background info.

St Just-in-Penwith & Cape Cornwall

Not to be confused with its namesake on the Roseland, St-Just-in-Penwith (usually known simply as St Just) might not be the hive of activity it was during the heyday of Cornish tin mining, but it's still a hub for Penwith's artistic community. All roads lead to the Market Sq, ringed by grey granite buildings, the small parish church and the Plen-an-gwary, an open-air auditorium once used to stage outdoor theatre, mystery plays, Methodist sermons and Cornish wrestling.

Jutting out from the cliffs a couple of miles from St Just is Cape Cornwall, a rocky headland topped by an abandoned chimneystack (the remains of the Cape Cornwall Mine, which closed in 1875). Below the cape is the rocky beach of Priest's Cove, while nearby are the ruins of St Helen's Oratory, one of the first Christian chapels built in West Cornwall. There's a cafe near the point.

A century ago, the surrounding cliffs (especially Gurnard's Head) were among the most treacherous in Britain, accounting for hundreds of costly shipwrecks. To prevent further wrecks, construction of a new lighthouse at Pendeen Watch began in 1900. Standing barely 17m tall, the lighthouse was originally oil-powered, before being electrified in 1926 and automated in 1995.

Half a mile east of town is Portheras Cove, a lovely slash of sheltered sand reached via a 15-minute walk along the cliff path. The high cliffs around the beach take the brunt of the Atlantic winds, and the water is deep and crystal clear – although the remains of an exploded wreck in the 1960s still supposedly wash up from time to time, so take care.

Kegen Teg (🖉01736-788562; 12 Market Sq; meals £5-12; ⊙10am-5pm) is a cute little wholefood/vegetarian cafe on Market Square, usually full of St Just's arty types and boho mamas.

McFaddens (🖉01736-788136; www.mcfaddensbutchers.co.uk; Market Sq; pasties £2-4; ⊙9am-5.30pm Mon-Sat) is the traditional town butcher, and a local's tip for old-fashioned pasties.

Sennen

Tucked into the arc of Whitesand Bay, Sennen Cove (🅿) boasts Penwith's best surf and sand. With vivid blue waters and a mile of beach backed by dunes and marram grass, it's one of Cornwall's most impressive bays.

There's not much to the village itself save for the lifeboat station (in operation since 1853), a handful of shops, cafes and galleries and the venerable Old Success Inn.

When you've finished lazing about on the beach, Sennen makes a super spot for walks – the coast path allows access to several fabulous beaches nearby (see the Walking Tour, p232).

Now owned by St Austell Brewery, the Old Success Inn (🖉01736-871232; www.staustellbrewery.co.uk/old-success-inn.html; Sennen Cove; rooms £65-125, mains £5-15; ⊙11am-11pm) has been slaking the thirst of Sennen punters (and the local lifeboat crew) for centuries. It's looking smart after a refit: the restaurant grub is good, the rooms are comfy and the bar's as characterful as ever. There's a sea view deck, too, and they'll even pack you a hamper to take to the Minack Theatre (£6.95 to £16.95).

The Beach (🖉01736-871191; www.thebeachrestaurant.com; mains £8.75-14.95; ⊙breakfast, lunch & dinner) has been a feature in Sennen since the late '50s, but it feels Mediterranean-modern these days. Fish is landed by the cafe's own boat (named Rosebud). The cafe is light and airy inside, and the deck looks straight out over Whitesand Bay. There's a good kid's menu, too.

Land's End

A mile from Whitesand Bay, the Penwith Peninsula comes to a screeching halt at Land's End, the last port of call for charity walkers on the 874-mile slog from John O'Groats.

The scenery doesn't get much more dramatic – black granite cliffs and heather-covered headland teeter above the booming Atlantic surf, and in good weather you can glimpse the Isles of Scilly, 28 miles out to sea. Even the construction of a tacky theme park (🖉0871-720 0044; www.landsend-landmark.co.uk; adult/child £10/7; ⊙10am-5pm Easter-Oct,

10.30am-3.30pm Nov-Mar) on the headland in the 1980s hasn't quite spoiled the scenery, although it certainly hasn't helped – wiser heads will give it a wide berth and just pay for the car park (£3) and head off along the coast path instead. If you must take a peek, the rather lame attractions include an Arthur's Quest exhibit, a 4D film and a display on Air-Sea Rescue. Kids will probably most enjoy the Greeb Farm petting zoo and, of course, getting their picture snapped next to the Land's End sign.

The stretch of coast path which runs south from Land's End is as wild and beautiful as any in Cornwall, and windy pretty much year-round – umbrellas are never a good idea here. Looking west you might just be able to spy the silhouettes of the Isles of Scilly on a clear day but if not, you'll definitely be able to spy the famous Longships Lighthouse, perched on a rocky reef 1.25 miles out to sea. This is still an infamously dangerous patch of coastline, and the site of many wrecks, but the construction of the lighthouse was a formidable engineering challenge: the first one was built in 1795 but was frequently swamped by waves, and subsequently replaced in 1873 at the considerable cost of £43,870. Since then it's somehow withstood the worst of the Atlantic storms, and has been unmanned since 1988.

Just inland from the point in Trevescan is the arty Apple Tree Cafe (☑01736-872753; www.theappletreecafe.co.uk; mains £4-8; ☉10am-4pm), which makes its own bread and serves a superb sourdough burger.

Porchcurno

From Land's End, the coast path zigzags past a string of coves, including Nanjizal, Porthgwarra and teeny Porth Chapel, where you'll find the 'holy well' of St Levan (one of many holy wells sprinkled around Penwith) hidden amongst the cliffs.

Further east is Porthcurno, a golden wedge of sand, with a deep underwater shelf that makes for lively swimming (beware of strong waves and rip currents). Cut into the cliffs above the beach is the gravity-defying Minack Theatre (☑01736-810181; www.minack.com), dreamt up in the 1920s by local eccentric Rowena Cade and built largely by hand over the next 30-odd years. With its vertiginous seating and clifftop amphitheatre overlooking the Atlantic, it's an unforgettable place to watch a play – although aficionados always bring pillows, blankets

and umbrellas in case the weather takes centre stage. Above the theatre there's a cafe and visitor centre (adult/child £3.50/1.40; ☉9.30am-5.30pm Apr-Sep, 10am-4pm Oct-Mar) exploring the Rowena Cade story; you can wander around the auditorium on non-matinée days.

Long before the Minack, Porthcurno was a hub for Britain's burgeoning telecommunications network. During the 19th century, a network of subterranean cables owned by the Eastern Telegraph Company stretched from Porthcurno all the way to Spain, Gibraltar, northern France and India. The subterranean tunnels now house the Porthcurno Telegraph Museum (☑01736-810966; www.porthcurno.org.uk; adult/child £7.20/4.20; ☉10am-5pm daily Mar-Nov, 10am-5pm Sun & Mon Dec-Feb).

Treen & Logan Rock

A couple of miles from Porthcurno, just off the B3315, is the little village of Treen, best known for the geological oddity known as the Logan Rock. Perched on the headland near Treryn Dinas, the site of one of Cornwall's largest Iron Age hillforts, this massive boulder once famously rocked back and forth on its own natural pivot with only the slightest pressure; its name supposedly derives from the Cornish verb log, meaning 'to rock', often used to denote the motion of a drunken man.

The Logan Rock has been a tourist attraction since at least the 18th century, but became infamous after it was knocked off its perch by a young naval lieutenant, Hugh Goldsmith (the nephew of the Restoration playwright Oliver Goldsmith), in an attempt to show the physical prowess of the British Navy. Unfortunately, the locals were so incensed, Goldsmith was forced to restore the rock to its original position under threat of his naval commission – a task that required the efforts of 60 men, winches borrowed from Devonport Dockyard and a total cost of £130 8s 6d (a copy of the bill can be seen in the Logan Rock Inn). Sadly, Goldsmith's efforts were in vain: the Logan Rock hasn't rocked since.

The remote sandy beach of Pedn Vounder lies just west of Logan Rock. It's one of Cornwall's few naturist beaches, and well worth a walk if you don't mind the sight of a bit of bare flesh. It's also a wonderful beach in its own right, with a golden scoop of sand and a supremely secluded location.

🛏 Sleeping & Eating

Treen Farm CAMPSITE £
(☑07598-469322; www.treenfarmcampsite.co.uk;
adult £5, child £2-3, tent £2-4, car £1; ☺Apr-Oct)
This family-focused campsite is a beauty,
with views of Logan Rock and the coast near
Porthcurno. There's plenty of space in the
main field, plus a locally-stocked shop, and
loads of walks nearby. No bookings: pitches
are first-come, first-serve, so turn up early.

Logan Rock PUB ££
(☑01736-810495; www.theloganrock.co.uk; Treen;
mains £6-14; ☺10.30am-11pm, closed mid-after-
noon in winter) This village pub's been around
for four centuries, so it's crammed with old-
time atmosphere – head-scraping ceilings,
wooden seats, a crackling hearth and brassy
trinkets, plus a rather incongruous collection
of cricketing memorabilia in one corner.

Lamorna Cove

About halfway along the B3315 between Penzance and Porthcurno is the weeny cove of
Lamorna, a pocket of rocks, cliffs and pebbly
sand which was a popular subject for many
of the key artists of the Newlyn School. It
is particularly associated with the artist S. J.
'Lamorna' Birch who lived on the cove, and
his close associates Alfred Munnings and
Laura and Harold Knight (whose story was
recently dramatised in the film *Summer in
February*).

Just inland from the cove is **Trewoofe
House** (☑01736-810269; adult/child £3/free;
☺2-5pm Wed & Sun), with a 4-acre valley garden sprinkled with streams, ponds, cascades
and bluebell woodlands.

Lamorna's also home to a fantastically
luxurious complex of self-catering apartments, aptly dubbed **The Cove** (☑01736-
731411; www.thecovecornwall.co.uk; Lamorna Cove;
£115-375 per night, £1470-2625 per week; P ☀)
They're straight out of a glossy lifestyle
mag: stripped wood, plasma TVs, minimalist bathrooms and picture-window patios
opening onto a super swimming pool and
sweeping coastal views.

Penzance

POP 21,168
Gulls wheel overhead, fishing trawlers ply
the coast and there's a scent of brine on the
breeze around the old harbour town of Penzance. Stretching along the western edge of
Mount's Bay, Penzance has marked the end

WILD FOOD FORAGING

Longing for the good life? Then how
about a weekend delving through the
undergrowth in search of wild berries,
edible roots and the wild herb samphire
in the company of **Fat Hen** (☑01736-
810156; www.fathen.org; Boscawen-noon
Farm, St Buryan). Head forager-ecologist
Caroline Davey leads guided trips in
search of wild goodies, before retiring
to headquarters to see the raw materials transformed into something tasty
by the Fat Hen chefs. There are day
courses, or you can opt for a wild food
weekend (£165), which includes three
slap-up meals in the Goat Barn. Hedge-
row cocktails, anyone?

of the line for the Great Western Railway
since the 1860s, and the town still feels one
step removed from the rest of Cornwall. It's
faded in spots, but unlike many of its sister
towns along the coast, Penzance has resist-
ed the urge to over-gentrification and still
boasts the kind of rough-edged authenticity
Cornwall's daintier towns lost long ago.

Like Truro and Falmouth, Penzance's
wealth was founded largely on the booming
maritime trade of the 18th and 19th centuries,
and there are some fine Georgian and Regency townhouses dotted around town, especially
along Chapel St and Queen St; look out for the
extraordinary Egyptian House, which looks
like a cross between a Georgian townhouse
and an Egyptian sarcophagus, and was originally built for a wealthy local mineralogist,
John Lavin, as a geological museum.

☉ Sights

Penlee House Gallery & Museum GALLERY
(www.penleehouse.org.uk; Morrab Rd; adult/
child £4.50/3; ☺10am-5pm Mon-Sat Easter-Sep,
10.30am-4.30pm Mon-Sat Oct-Easter) Next to
the town library, the Penlee House Gallery
& Museum owns a fine collection of paintings by artists of the Newlyn and Lamorna
Schools, who were inspired by the colourful
characters and tough working conditions of
the fishermen and farmers who lived and
worked around Penwith in the late 19th
and early 20th centuries. Key figures of the
movement included Stanhope Forbes, Norman Garstin and Walter Langley (see p273
for more on the art of this region).

Penzance

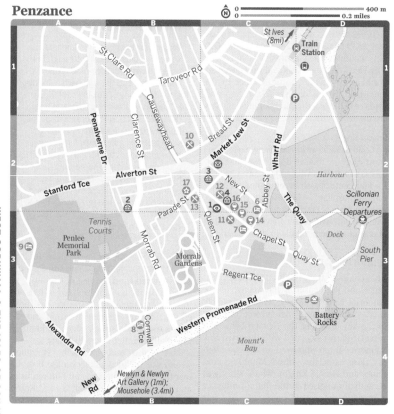

There's no permanent collection, so what you see is down to a bit of pot luck. Even if the art's not your thing, the lovely Morrab Gardens are well worth a stroll.

Across the gardens from the gallery, the Morrab Library (📞01736-364474; www.morrab library.org.uk; £3 for non-members; ⊙10am-4pm Tue-Fri, 10am-1pm Sat) is another little-known gem of old Penzance: a Georgian lending library with a wonderful collection of dusty old books, including many local interest titles and a super photographic archive. The library also holds regular readings and other literary events.

The Exchange   GALLERY
(www.theexchangegallery.co.uk; Princes St; ⊙10am-5pm Mon-Sat Easter-Sep, Wed-Sat Oct-Easter) FREE Housed in Penzance's former telecoms building, this cool gallery hosts regular exhibitions of contemporary art. The pulsating light installation outside is by the artist

Peter Freeman. It's the sister gallery to the Newlyn Art Gallery, a mile west along Penzance's prom.

Newlyn Art Gallery   GALLERY
(www.newlynartgallery.co.uk; ⊙10am-5pm Mon-Sat Easter-Sep, Wed-Sat Oct-Easter) On the edge of Newlyn, this historic gallery was founded in 1895 to display the work of the artists of the Newlyn School, but since 2007 the gallery's focus has been on contemporary art.

Chapel St   HISTORIC AREA
The cream of Penzance's heritage architecture can be seen along Chapel St, which is lined with a wealth of beautifully preserved Georgian buildings.

At the top end of the street is the bizarre Egyptian House, which looks like a cross between a Georgian townhouse and a sarcophagus, and was originally built for a wealthy mineralogist, John Lavin, as a geological museum.

Penzance

Sights
1 Egyptian House C2
2 Penlee House Gallery &
   Museum B2
3 The Exchange...C2
4 Union Hotel...C2

Activities, Courses & Tours
5 Jubilee Pool D3

Sleeping
6 Abbey Hotel..C2
7 Artist Residence Penzance C3
8 Summer House.......................................B4
9 Venton Vean A3

Eating
10 Archie Brown's.......................................B2
11 Assay House..C3
12 Bakehouse...C2
13 Honey Pot B2

Drinking & Nightlife
14 Admiral Benbow.....................................C3
15 Turk's Head C3
16 Zero Lounge C2

Entertainment
17 Acorn Arts Centre.................................B2

Further along the street is the **Union Hotel**, the first place to receive news of Nelson's death after the Battle of Trafalgar. It's also home to a Georgian Theatre dating from 1787, although this is not open to the public.

Also of interest is the little house which once belonged to the family of **Maria Branwell**, the mother of the Brontë sisters.

Tremenheere Sculpture Garden   GARDENS
(☎01736-448089; www.tremenheere.co.uk; garden admission adult £6.50, children 11-15yr £3; ☺10am-5pm Mon-Sat, 10am-4pm; ⊞) This inventive landscaped garden opened just outside Penzance in 2012. The gardens sit in a sheltered valley, landscaped with all kinds of exotic trees and shrubs that benefit from Penwith's balmy sub-tropical climate. They're also awash with artworks and installations: look out for a 'sky-view' chamber by James Turrell, a 'black mound' of tree stumps by David Nash and a 'Camera Obscura' by Billy Wynter, offering a unique panorama of the gardens and Mount's Bay. There's also a super cafe, the Lime Tree (lunches £8 to £14), next to the car park, and there are family events during the school holidays such as den-building workshops through to crafts sessions. See the website for details.

It's a bit difficult to find the first time. Look out for the left turning to Gulval as you head into Penzance, and follow the road through the village until you see signs for the gardens.

Trengwainton   GARDEN
(NT; ☎01736-363148; trengwainton@nationaltrust. org.uk; Madron; adult/child £6.30/3.15; ☺10am-5pm Sun-Thu mid-Feb–Nov) Two miles north of Penzance near Madron is the walled garden of Trengwainton, which is famous for its collection of ferns, shrubs, magnolias and rhododendrons, many of which were brought back by Cornish plant-hunters in the 19th century. Peculiarly, the kitchen garden was laid out to match the dimensions of Noah's Ark, but the main draw is the stunning vista over Mount's Bay. Admission is free for National Trust members.

Nearby is the **Madron Holy Well**, whose cure-all waters have been sought out by ailing pilgrims for at least six centuries. The ruins of the chapel date from the early Middle Ages, but the well was also a sacred site for pre-Roman Celts.

Activities

★ **Jubilee Pool**   SWIMMING
(www.jubileepool.co.uk; adult/child £4.30/3.20, family day-ticket £14; ☺10.30am-6pm May-Sep) Penzance's 19th-century promenade stretches along the sea wall between the South Pier and New Rd. At the eastern end is the Jubilee Pool, a stunning Art Deco lido built in 1935 to mark George V's silver jubilee. Since falling into disrepair in the 1980s, the triangular pool has been impeccably renovated and is now a listed monument – it even boasts its own poolside cafe. The views over Mount's Bay are utterly glorious, and on a sunny day you could almost convince yourself you're on the French Riviera – although the temperature of the water will shatter the illusion soon enough.

The rocky shoreline around the pool known as **Battery Rocks** has recently become the focus of a heated dispute over controversial proposals to transform it into a new terminal for ferries to Scilly. The issue was finally scuppered in 2011 when the Department for Transport decided that the environmental damage to the area would be too great, and shelved the plans indefinitely.

POLGOON VINEYARD

Braving the vicissitudes of the Cornish weather, former fish merchants John and Jim Coulson set up the Polgoon Vineyard (www.polgoon.com) on a derelict farm just outside Penzance in 2006. Since then they've developed a suite of vintages: the current crop includes a rosé and a red, as well as Peren (sparkling pear) and Aval (a champagne-style cider, also available in raspberry).

There are guided tours of the vineyard every Wednesday, Thursday and Friday at 2pm (£10 with 5 tastings), or you can guide yourself with a free map (£5 with 3 tastings). All Polgoon's vintages are on sale in the wine shop.

🎆 Festivals & Events

Golowan Festival   FESTIVAL
(www.golowan.com) Ten days of music, art and Cornish culture, plus a big street parade on Mazey Day. Held in Penzance in late June.

Newlyn Fish Festival   FESTIVAL
(www.newlynfishfestival.org.uk) Newlyn celebrates its piscatorial heritage at this festival, held over the August Bank Holiday.

🛏 Sleeping

Penzance YHA   HOSTEL £
(☏ 0845-371 9653; penzance@yha.org.uk; Castle Horneck, Alverton; dm from £14; P @) Penzance's excellent YHA is inside an 18th-century house on the edge of town. It's a rambling and friendly place, with a cafe, laundry and four- to 10-bed dorms, as well as a few private rooms. It's a 15-minute walk from the front; buses 5 and 6 stop nearby.

Noongallas Camping   CAMPSITE £
(☏ 01736-366698; www.kline.freeserve.co.uk; Noongallas, near Gulval; adult/child £6/3) Old-school, no-frills field camping north of Penzance, with two fields offering an uninterrupted outlook over Mount's Bay. It's quiet, relaxed and family-friendly: campers are allowed, caravans aren't. It's 1.5 miles outside Gulval; take the B3311 from Penzance and follow signs to Rosemorran/Polkinghorn.

★ **Artist Residence Penzance** B&B, HOTEL ££
(☏ 01736-365664; www.arthotelcornwall.co.uk; Chapel St; d £80-120; 🕲) This deliciously different new hotel on Chapel St is like sleeping inside an art gallery. All the rooms have their own bespoke design courtesy of a local artist: cartoony murals by Matt MacIvor, pop-art doves by Pinky Vision, butterfly wallpapers by Dolly Divine. They're furnished with hand-picked bits of retro furniture, and most peep across Penzance's rooftops. Bold, imaginative and brilliant fun.

★ **Venton Vean**   B&B ££
(☏ 01736-351294; www.ventonvean.co.uk; Trewithen Rd; £82-95) The picture of a modern B&B, finished in soothing greys, blues and pistachios, and furnished with stripped wooden floors, quirky design and a minimum of clutter. Rooms 1 and 2 are the most spacious; the former overlooks Penlee Park, while the latter has a window seat and its original fireplace. Breakfast choices include Mexican, Spanish, Full English and even smoked pollock with duck egg. Recommended.

Hotel Penzance   HOTEL ££
(☏ 01736-363117; www.hotelpenzance.com; Briton's Hill; d £109-125; 🕲) Perched on a hill with views across Mount's Bay, this townhouse hotel makes a pleasant Penzance base. Bedrooms are staid in style, with cream-and-magnolia colours, varnished desks and vintage lamps: the best have bay windows looking out to sea. The hotel's restaurant, the Bay, serves quality food. It is about 400m northeast of the train station.

Summer House   HOTEL ££
(☏ 01736-363744; www.summerhouse-cornwall. com; Cornwall Tce; s £105, d £120-150; P) Just off the Penzance prom, this former artist's house is now a stylish hotel, blending Knightsbridge chic with seaside accents.

Boutique Retreats   SELF-CATERING ££
(☏ 01872-270085; www.boutique-retreats.co.uk; Mousehole; per week £790-835; P 🕲) Boutique retreats indeed, these are halfway between holiday cottages and high-class hotels. Options range from Mousehole fishermen's cottages to a divine beach cabin at Porthkidney, near Hayle. All ooze style: slate tiles, modern kitchens, groovy furniture and modern art.

Abbey Hotel   HOTEL £££
(☏ 01736-366906; www.theabbeyonline.co.uk; Abbey St; d £90-200) A 17th-century sea-captain's house turned heritage hotel, off Chapel St. Its creaky rooms brim with antiques, vintage rugs and Victoriana, and there's a cool

secret garden hidden out back. Layouts are higgledy-piggledy: ask for Rooms One or Three, or the book-lined suite for maximum space. It's owned by former 60s fashion model Jean Shrimpton.

Hidden Hideaways   SELF-CATERING **£££**
(07887-522788; www.hiddenhideaways.co.uk; from around £550 per week) More posh places for rent: a cosy hut near Mousehole Harbour, a Penzance townhouse and a beautiful stilt-top printer's a mile north of Penzance.

Eating

Archie Brown's   CAFE **£**
(01736-362828; Bread St; mains £4-10; 9am-5pm Mon-Sat) Veggie salads, chunky sandwiches and hearty soups are what this much-loved wholefood cafe is all about, with filling eats in the cheerful 1st-floor cafe, and a smorgasbord of lentils, pulses and wholegrains in the ground-floor shop.

Honey Pot   CAFE **£**
(01736-368686; 5 Parade St; mains £4-10; 9am-5pm Mon-Sat) For afternoon tea and crumbly cakes, there's nowhere better in Penzance than the Honey Pot, opposite the Acorn Arts Centre. It attracts punters across the Penzance spectrum, from arty types supping cappuccinos to earth-mums tucking into fruit teas and homity pie. Naturally, nearly everything's homemade and local.

★**Coldstreamer Inn**   PUB **££**
(01736-362072; www.coldstreamer-penzance.co.uk; Gulval; mains £11-17.95; open daily from 10am) This inn in nearby Gulval is a real corker. Chef Tom Penhaul has a strong local pedigree, with stints at the now-defunct Abbey Restaurant and the Gurnard's Head, and his stylish, tasty food (steak with savoy cabbage, pork belly with celeriac purée) has earned many admirers, including a well-deserved mention in the Michelin pub guide.

Bakehouse   MEDITERRANEAN **££**
(01736-331331; www.bakehouserestaurant.co.uk; Chapel St; mains £9.95-19.50; 6.15-10pm Mon-Sat) Laid-back double-floored diner down an alley off Chapel St. Steaks take the honours: choose your cut and match it with your choice of sauce or spicy rub. Seafood and veggie options are more limited, but that doesn't seem to deter the punters – booking is advisable.

Assay House   BISTRO **££**
(01736-369729; 12-13 Chapel St; mains £14-17; breakfast & lunch daily, dinner Fri & Sat) Streetside bistro serving crispy fish goujons and tapas-style platters.

Drinking & Nightlife

Admiral Benbow   PUB
(01736-363448; 46 Chapel St, Penzance) On historic Chapel St, the salty old Benbow looks like it's dropped from the pages of *Treasure Island,* with nautical decor mostly reclaimed from shipwrecks: anchors, lanterns, figureheads and all.

Turk's Head   PUB
(Chapel St) Purportedly the town's oldest pub, there's been a tavern on the site of the Turk's Head since the 13th century. It was supposedly a favourite hangout for Penzance's 'free traders'; a subterranean smugglers tunnel once led straight to the harbour from the cellar (now the dining room). Skinner's and Sharp's ales on tap.

Zero Lounge   BAR
(Chapel St) In stark contrast to Chapel St's other pubs, this new boy is more urban chic than olde-worlde. There's a big open-plan bar serving quality coffees, beers and cocktails, and a sprawling patio out back that's popular with Penzance's trendy set.

Entertainment

Acorn Arts Centre   THEATRE
(www.acornartscentre.co.uk; Parade St) Lively arts centre hosting film, theatre, comedy and live bands. It's only open when there are events: see the website for the latest program.

Getting There & Away

For ferries to the Isles of Scilly, see p250.

BUS

Penzance is the main local bus hub. It's also served by National Express coaches. Useful connections include:

Newlyn/Mousehole (Bus 6/6A, 15 minutes, hourly) Bus 5 also runs every half-hour via Gwavas and Paul.

St Ives (Bus 17/17A/17B, 28 minutes, half-hourly, hourly on Sunday) The 17B runs a few times daily via Marazion.

Land's End (Bus 1/1A, 45 minutes, every 2 hours Monday to Saturday)

Truro (Bus X18, 1 hour, hourly Monday to Saturday)

ART COURSES IN PENWITH

Penwith's artistic heritage makes it an ideal place to mine your own creative side. The peninsula now has two art schools where you can learn everything from landscape painting to ceramics under the guidance of top Cornish artists.

In a prime spot overlooking Porthmeor Beach near the Tate, the **St Ives School of Painting** (☑ 01736-797180; www.stivesartschool.co.uk; 2-day courses from £150) was opened in 1938 by two young artists – Borlase Smart and Leonard Fuller – and was later attended by many of the leading lights of the St Ives School. It now runs courses focusing mainly on painting in watercolour, gouache, oils and other media. There are drop-in sessions on Monday, Wednesday, Friday and Saturday, as well as longer courses lasting from one to six days. The school forms part of the historic Porthmeor Studios, a collection of artists' rooms and fishermen's stores, parts of which date back to the 1800s. After decades of disrepair, the studios were recently restored thanks to a £4m grant.

On the other side of Penwith, the **Newlyn School of Art** (☑ 01736-365557; www.newlynartschool.co.uk; 2-day courses from £130) is an exciting new project run by local artist Henry Garfitt, who set up shop in 2012 in the old school at the top of Chywoone Hill. The range of courses on offer is comprehensive – ranging from experimental landscape painting to screen printing – and the roster of tutors reads like a Who's Who of the Cornish art scene. Classes are kept small (maximum of 10 people) and, unusually, are open to artists of mixed ability. If you just feel like dropping in, the Wednesday evening life class (£13) provides a good introduction.

TRAIN

Penzance is the last stop on the main line from London Paddington; trains run roughly hourly. For trains to St Ives, you need to change at St Erth.

Local destinations:

Truro (£6.20, 38 minutes)
Redruth (£5.10, 27 minutes)
St Ives (£3.10, 45 minutes)

Newlyn

Two miles along the Penzance prom, the salty old harbour of Newlyn has weathered the storms in the wider fishing industry and clung on as Britain's busiest working port. The old Cornish staple, the pilchard, has recently received a rebrand as the 'Cornish sardine' in an effort to boost consumer appeal (it's not entirely sleight of hand: pilchards are in fact simply juvenile sardines).

It's a briny old town where trawlers and dayboats bob in the harbour, and fishermen's stores and processing factories still occupy many of the harbour buildings. Although the town's last pilchard cannery closed in 2005, ending a tradition stretching back over three centuries, Newlyn still has many suppliers where you can pick up fish literally straight off the boats.

Eating

Jelbert's Ices   ICE CREAM £
(New Rd) This traditional ice-cream maker still does things the old-fashioned way. There's only one flavour (vanilla), made with Cornish clotted cream and served in old-school wafer cones.

Newlyn Cheese & Charcuterie   DELI £
(☑ 01736-368714; www.newlyncheese.co.uk; 1 New Rd; ⊙ 9am-5pm Mon-Sat Easter-Oct) Just along from Jelbert's Ices, this upmarket deli has a good selection of cold cuts and cheeses: try the Cornish Blue and Garlic Yarg.

★**Tolcarne Inn**   PUB ££
(☑ 01736-363074; www.tolcarneinn.co.uk; mains £12-18; ⊙ lunch noon-2.15pm, dinner 7-9pm, closed Sun eve & Mon) Now run by chef supremo Ben Tunnicliffe (who previously oversaw the renowned Abbey Restaurant in Penzance), this cosy Newlyn inn is fast gaining ground as one of the area's premium gastropubs. The ethos is refreshingly honest – top-quality fish, seafood and locally-sourced meat, served as simply as possible. It's deservedly becoming very popular, so bookings are advised, especially for Sunday lunch.

Shopping

The largest (and oldest) fishing family is W Stevenson & Sons, who owns the Newlyn market and runs two fish outlets on Harbour

Rd in Newlyn and Wharf Rd in Penzance (beneath the Wharfside Shopping Centre). You can buy direct from the fish shops, or place an order by phone or online; it's always worth phoning ahead if you're after something specific. Other Newlyn suppliers:

Trelawney Fish FOOD
(☑ 01736-361793; www.cornishfishonline.com; 78 The Strand; ☺ 8am-5pm Mon-Fri, 8am-1pm Sat) Fish shop and deli on the Newlyn harbour.

JH Turner FOOD
(☑ 01736-363726; www.jhturner.co.uk; The Coombe, Newlyn; ☺ 9am-3pm Mon-Fri) Stocks whatever's in season.

W Harvey & Sons FOOD
(☑ 01736-362983; www.crabmeat.co.uk; The Coombe, Newlyn; ☺ 8am-4.45pm Mon-Fri, 8am-11.45pm Sat) Specialists in crab and lobster.

Mousehole

In contrast to rough-and-ready Newlyn, the next-door harbour of Mousehole (pronounced *mowzel*) is a gentler affair. Once a bustling pilchard port, and now a hot spot for second homes, Mousehole's muddle of slate-roofed cottages, meandering lanes and granite quays is undeniably attractive, although the village is swamped by visitors throughout summer and the Christmas lights in December. Whatever you do, leave the car on the outskirts – or better still, follow the coast path on foot from Newlyn.

Mousehole's main claim to fame is being the home of stargazy pie, a baked pilchard pie in which the fish heads are left poking through the crust. It's eaten on 23rd December, Bawcock's Eve, in commemoration of Tom Bawcock, a local lad who ended a village famine by braving tempestuous seas to land a bounty of fish. The traditional recipe is still a closely-guarded secret at the village's hugger-mugger pub, the Ship Inn.

Halfway along the Newlyn road, look out for the old Penlee Lifeboat Station just below the cliff. On 19 December 1981 the *Solomon Browne* lifeboat went to the aid of the stricken coaster *Union Star,* which was being driven onto rocks near Lamorna by heavy seas. Both ships were lost with all hands; since then the boathouse has remained as a monument to the 16 men who lost their lives, and every year Mousehole's lights are dimmed on December 19 as an act of remembrance.

🛏 Sleeping

★ Old Coastguard Hotel HOTEL ££
(☑ 01736-731222; www.oldcoastguardhotel.co.uk; d £110-195; P 🛜 🐾) Now run by the owners of the Gurnard's Head, this coastal beauty has a much more relaxed atmosphere than it used to. Rooms are still classic – restrained colour schemes, stately beds – and the best ones obviously have a sea view. Seafood takes prominence in the smart sea-view restaurant, and there's a cliff garden for soaking up the rays. A seaside retreat par excellence.

🍴 Eating & Drinking

2 Fore St FRENCH ££
(☑ 01736-731164; www.2forestreet.co.uk; 2 Fore St; mains £9.75-15.50; ☺ lunch noon-2pm & dinner 6.30-9pm) Culinary sophistication on the Mousehole seafront. It's young but has already gained plenty of admirers, including *Harden's* and the *Good Food Guide.* Inside, stripped wood, cool colours and harbour views; outside, a sweet garden shaded by palms and canvas umbrellas. The menu wears its French influences on its sleeve, as you might expect from a head chef who trained under Raymond Blanc.

The Cornish Range SEAFOOD £££
(☑ 01736-731488; www.cornishrange.co.uk; 6 Chapel St; mains £11.50-20.95; ☺ dinner 5.30-9.30pm) Another well-respected Mousehole restaurant squeezed inside a former pilchard processing house. The food is elegant – roast sole with crab, or roast cod with tempura lobster – but it is expensive and feels claustrophobic when crowded. The restaurant's a short walk past the Ship Inn.

Ship Inn PUB
(☑ 01736-731234; www.shipmousehole.co.uk; South Cliff; mains £8.95-13.95) The old Ship dates (at least in parts) back to the 1700s and has lashings of period charm, with hefty fireplaces and leaded glass windows. Food is standard pub grub – steak pie, veggie chilli.

Marazion

Five miles east of Penzance, past the sandy curve of Long Rock, lies little Marazion, a pretty village lined with seafront houses and Victorian villas with an epic overlook across Mount's Bay.

Historic Southwest

The southwest packs nearly 5000 years of history into its rugged landscapes. From strange quoits and stone circles left behind by neolithic people to a catalogue of castles, churches and country houses, it's a place where the past is never too far away.

2

PAUL FELIX / GETTY IMAGES ©

1. Lanyon Quoit (p230)
This quoit bears a massive 13.5-tonne capstone.

2. Tintagel Castle (p198)
Tintagel is possibly the birthplace of the legendary King Arthur.

3. Merrivale Stone Rows (p117)
These monuments include a parallel stone row, a stone circle and burial chambers.

4. Buckland Abbey (p114)
This former Cistercian monastery became the home of Sir Francis Drake in 1851.

4

ANTHONY COLLINS / GETTY IMAGES ©

3

ADAM BURTON / GETTY IMAGES ©

ECO-ESCAPES

Lost in the remote countryside around Sancreed, the dreamy retreats offered by **Plan-It Earth** (☑ 01736-810660; www.plan-itearth.org.uk; Chyena, Sancreed; from £978 per week in summer; P ❀) are perfect for a green getaway. Owners Rachel and David have built two amazing roundhouses: a 'hobbit house' made from cord wood and cob, and a 'straw bale' house made from cob, straw and earth plaster. They're definitely not roughing it though, both come with composting loos and star-view roofs, and are furnished with sheepskin rugs, lanterns and wood-burners. Eco-adventure holidays and wild camping are also offered. Green and glorious.

Apart from a few attractive cafes and galleries, the village is mainly worth a visit as the jumping-off point for **St Michael's Mount** (NT; ☑ 01736-710507; www.stmichaelsmount.co.uk; castle & gardens adult/child £9.60/4.80; ⊙ house 10.30am-5.30pm Sun-Fri late Mar-Oct, gardens Mon-Fri Apr-Jun, Thu & Fri Jul-Sep) – the dramatic island abbey which sits at the centre of Mount's Bay and has become one of Cornwall's most iconic landmarks. Connected to the mainland by a cobbled causeway that's submerged by the rising tide, there's been a monastery here since at least the 5th century, but the island was used long before as a trading stop for Cornish tin and copper. After the Norman Conquest, the island was gifted to the Benedictine monks of Mont St Michel in Normandy, who raised a new chapel on the site in 1135. The mount later served as a fortified stronghold and is now the family seat of the St Aubyns, although since 1954 it has been under the stewardship of the National Trust.

At low tide, you can walk across the causeway from Marazion, or when the tide's up you can catch a ferry (£1) from the quay. The tiny chapel with its rose window and 15th-century alabaster panels is a highlight; there's also a rococo drawing room, ornate library, an island garrison and the grand Chevy Chase Room (named after a medieval hunting ditty, not the National Lampoon star). Around the edge, subtropical gardens cling precariously to the cliffs, with a cornucopia of blooms and shrubs nurtured by the temperate Gulf Stream.

🛏 Sleeping

St Michael's B&B   B&B **££**
(☑ 01736-711348; www.stmichaels-bedandbreakfast.co.uk; Fore St; d £88-98; P ☀) Good value B&B on the main street, with six individual rooms (3 & 5 have the best Mount's Bay views). The style is classic – expect brass beds, puffy duvets and antique dressers.

Mount Haven Hotel   HOTEL **£££**
(☑ 01736-710249; www.mounthaven.co.uk; Turnpike Rd; d £130-200; P ☀) Coastal hotel in private seafront grounds. Rooms are boxy, but most have balconies opening onto Mount's Bay. Ex-Masterchef contestant Lee Groves has recently taken over the restaurant, and it's fast becoming a destination dine.

🍴 Eating

⭐ **Ben's Cornish Kitchen**   BRITISH **££**
(☑ 01736-719200; www.benscornishkitchen.com; 1-/2-/3-course lunch menu £12/15/18, dinner mains £14-23; ⊙ lunch noon-2pm, dinner 6.30-8.30pm Tue-Sat; ☑) Young chef Ben Prior has really made waves since opening his Cornish kitchen on Marazion's main street. Diners now travel from far and wide to taste his exciting and imaginative cooking, which majors on Cornish flavours with a French influence: local pigeon, pork, turbot, and John Dory, laced with port reductions, confit shallots and rich bisque sauces. Often he just dreams up the menu on the day, and tailors the menu around customers' requested dishes – and you can't get more personal than that. It's so popular he's recently expanded upstairs. Definitely one to watch.

Perranuthnoe to Praa Sands

East of Marazion, the coast dips and dives past a series of sandy stretches, including the small beach of Perranuthnoe and the well-known family-friendly beach of Praa Sands.

In between is the rocky nook known as **Prussia Cove**, once a notorious smugglers' haunt thanks to the exploits of the infamous 'free trader' John Carter, the so-called King of Prussia (supposedly due to his resemblance to the Prussian monarch Frederick the Great). Born in 1770, Carter became one of Cornwall's best-known smugglers, running contraband cargoes of tea, rum and spices while simultaneously trying to avoid the attention of government preventive boats. He became something of a local hero, especially following the publication of a sensational account of his adventures by his brother Harry Carter.

The cove itself now forms part of the private Porth-en-Alls (☎01736-762014; www.prussiacove.co.uk) estate, which has several cottages available for rent. If you're not staying, there's a small public car park signposted off the A394, from where the coast path meanders steeply down to the rocky inlets of Bessy's Cove, King's Cove, Coule's Cove and Piskies Cove.

✖ Eating

Peppercorn Kitchen CAFE £
(☎01736-719584; www.peppercornkitchen.co.uk; Lynfield Yard; lunch £4.50-7.50; ☺10am-3pm) Exotic flavours of the Middle East come to sleepy Perranuthnoe courtesy of this spicy cafe, run by half-Afghan owner Lisa Durrani-Prior. Wolf down sausage hotpot or Bangladeshi dhal, then follow with one of the cafe's legendary giant meringues.

Victoria Inn PUB ££
(☎01736-710309; www.victoriainn-penzance.co.uk; Perranuthnoe; mains £11.50-18.95; ☺noon-3pm lunch daily, dinner 6-10pm Mon-Sat) The village's snug pub has also earned a loyal following for its food.

THE LIZARD

Cornwall's southern coastline takes a sudden wild turn around the Lizard Peninsula, where fields and heaths plunge into a melee of black cliffs, churning surf and saw-tooth rocks. Cut off from the rest of Cornwall by the River Helford, and ringed by treacherous seas, the Lizard was once an ill-famed graveyard for ships, and the peninsula still has a raw, untamed edge.

Although the Lizard is known for its wildlife, the peninsula's peculiar name actually comes from the old Celtic words 'lys ardh', meaning 'high court'.

❶ Getting There & Around

Buses on the Lizard are patchy. Bus 32 runs from Helston to Gunwalloe, Gweek, Coverack and St Keverne, while bus 33 stops at Poldhu, Mullion and the Lizard. Helston also has regular services to Penzance, Truro and Falmouth.

Perilously narrow streets lie in wait for unsuspecting drivers – take our advice and leave the car outside Cadgwith, Helford Village, Coverack and St Anthony.

Helston

The Lizard's main town is Helston, which started life as a bustling river port and one of the county's Stannary towns, where local tin was assayed and stamped. The town received another lease of life with the arrival of the naval airbase at Culdrose, which hosts a popular annual air-day in late July.

The best time to visit is on Flora Day (www.helstonfloraday.org.uk) on 8 May. Believed to be the last remnant of a pagan celebration marking the coming of spring, this ancient festival is a mix of street dance, musical parade and floral pageant. The two main events are the Hal-An-Tow, in which St Michael and the devil do battle; and the Furry Dance, which kicks off at noon and proceeds around the town's streets (participants take part by invitation only, and the dance is always led by a local couple).

Helston's short on places to eat, but it's well worth dropping into the lovely Blue Anchor Inn (☎01326-562821; www.spingoales.com; 50 Coinagehall St; ☺11am-11pm), which brews its own Spingo ale and has an old-fashioned skittles alley.

◉ Sights

Helston Folk Museum MUSEUM
(☎01326-564027; Market Pl; ☺10am-1pm Mon-Sat) FREE There's plenty of background on the Furry Dance at the town's quirky museum, where the displays include replica shopfronts, a 5-tonne cider press and a display on local hero Bob Fitzsimmons, the first man to simultaneously hold the world titles for middleweight, light heavyweight and heavyweight boxing.

OFF THE BEATEN TRACK

LOE BAR & LOE POOL

A mile south of Helston is the treacherous sandbank of Loe Bar – scene of many a shipwreck down the centuries – and Loe Pool, Cornwall's largest freshwater lake, said by some to be the resting place of King Arthur's magical blade, Excalibur. Walking trails wind their way around the lakeshore and the surrounding Penrose Estate, but swimming is dangerous due to unpredictable rip currents.

WEST CORNWALL & THE ISLES OF SCILLY HELSTON

Flambards THEME PARK
(☎ 01326-573404; www.flambards.co.uk; admission incl rides adult/child £17.95/12.50; ☺ opens 10.30am, last admission 2.30pm) Just outside town is Flambards, Cornwall's oldest theme park. Attractions include the wartime-themed Britain in the Blitz, an aviation gallery and a reconstructed Victorian village, plus various outdoor rides: there's a log flume, a rollercoaster and a spiralling Skyraker amongst other things. It's hardly Alton Towers, but it'll keep the kids entertained for an afternoon. Note that outside July and August, the rides only run on certain days, so it's worth phoning ahead to check.

Trelowarren

Trelowarren (☎ 01326-221224; www.trelowarren.com; Mawgan) FREE has been in the hands of the Vyvyan family for six centuries and sprawls over 1000 acres of land between Goonhilly and the Helford River. Several woodland walks and country trails wind across the estate, including one to the Halliggye Fougou, an underground chamber on the site of an old Iron Age hillfort.

The estate's stylish restaurant, New Yard (☎ 01326-221224; www.newyardrestaurant.co.uk; Trelowarren; mains £9.50-16; ☺ lunch 12.30-2pm & dinner 7-9pm Tue-Sat, lunch only on Sun), makes a luxurious place for lunch, but you'd be wise to book.

Porthleven & the Loe

Three miles southwest of Helston is Porthleven, a quiet port set around the massive walls of its stone quay, built to shelter the harbour from winter storms. The town has a burgeoning foodie scene, epitomised by the Wednesday-morning market and the Porthleven Food Festival (www.porthlevenfoodfestival.co.uk).

🛏 Sleeping & Eating

Copper Kettle B&B ££
(☎ 01326-562157; www.cornishcopperkettle.com; 33 Fore St; s £45, d £80-85) Delightful little four-room B&B, with all the guest rooms named after local coves, and freshly decorated with seaside stripes, colourful spots and chocolatey throws.

Beacon Crag B&B ££
(☎ 01326-573690; www.beaconcrag.com; d £80-95; P @) Built for an artist, this Victorian villa above Porthleven is one of the Lizard's loveliest B&Bs. Rooms are plainly furnished to make the most of the house's grandstand position.

★**Kota** RESTAURANT ££
(☎ 01326-562407; www.kotarestaurant.co.uk; Porthleven; mains £12-20; ☺ lunch 12-2pm, dinner 6-9pm) Malaysian meets Maori at this converted mill on Porthleven's harbour, overseen by head chef Jude Kereama, one of Cornwall's rising culinary stars. His pan-Asian food has won lots of plaudits, blending Pacific Rim flavours with Cornish ingredients. They've recently opened a cafe offshoot, Kota Kai, just along the harbour.

Kota Kai Bar & Kitchen CAFE ££
(☎ 01326-574411; www.kotakai.co.uk; mains £11.50-14.95; ☺ lunch noon-2pm & dinner 5.30-9.30pm; 🐾) On the first-floor of a waterfront building, this zingy cafe shows the same flair as its fine-dining original, Kota. Tuck into tuna ceviche or seafood laksa curry while watching the boats head from the harbour, then head off for a game of skittles in the back-room. Kids eat free with their parents from 5.30pm to 6.30pm. Look out for regular film nights.

Amélie's at the Smokehouse BRITISH ££
(☎ 01326-554000; www.ameliesporthleven.co.uk; mains £12-16; ☺ 10.30am-9pm) This popular harbourside bistro is a good bet for a light bite, with mains such as wood-fired pizzas, bouillabaisse, dressed crab and the rather excellent Bruneski burger, served in a brioche bap. Glass doors and local art make for an attractive interior. For a special treat, they also offer lots of Cornish treats in their lavish Gourmet Picnics (☎ 01326-554333; www.gourmetpicnics.co.uk; picnics £75-150).

Gunwalloe

Five miles from Porthleven, the out-of-the-way National Trust owned cove of Gunwalloe feels miles from anywhere. It's best-known for the tiny 15th-century Church of St Winwaloe, which is half-buried amongst the dunes behind the beach. There's also a golf course nearby.

Up on the headland, the hulking 200ft mass of Halzephron Cliff was an infamous shipwreck spot – in 1785, the Spanish ship *Vrijdag* was wrecked offshore along with its 2.5-tonne cargo of silver dollars, and local legend maintains that the pirate John Avery once buried a fabulous horde somewhere in the Gunwalloe dunes. Don't be surprised if you see a few metal-detectors hard at work on nearby **Dollar Cove**.

🛏 Sleeping & Eating

Barefoot Kitchen   B&B **££**
(✆01326-240517; www.barefootkitchen.com; B&B from £130 per night) This 'lifestyle' outfit covers many bases, with foraging courses, a surf school, a food and homewares shop, and two luxurious safari tents (£426 to £1110 per week) for clifftop glamping. There's also a range of accommodation, from a restored airstream and a countryside cabin to supremely posh B&B-cum-holiday apartment in the turreted Halzephron House.

Halzephron Inn   PUB **££**
(✆01326-240406; www.halzephron-inn.co.uk; mains £10.95-18.50) You couldn't ask for a better place for a pint than this 500-year-old pub, balanced on the cliffs above Gunwalloe. It's whitewashed, slate-roofed, and full of nooks and niches – and the food is always reliably good (especially the Sunday roast).

Mullion

Tucked away on the Lizard's west side is Mullion, handily placed for three of the peninsula's prettiest beaches: **Mullion Cove**, with a characteristically Cornish cluster of harbour, boats and cottages; **Polurrian**, the most remote and dramatic of the three, only accessible via the coast path; and **Poldhu**, favoured by families thanks to its facilities (and ice cream shop).

Poldhu's other claim to fame is as the site of the world's first radio transmission, sent from Poldhu Point across 2000 miles of the Atlantic to St John's in Newfoundland by the Italian engineer Guglielmo Marconi in 1901. The little **Marconi Centre** (✆01326-574441; http://marconi-centre-poldhu.org.uk; ⊙times vary, check website) was opened in 2001 to mark the centenary. Volunteer radio enthusiasts fill you in on the Marconi story, and there are short-wave radio sets to mess about with. A plaque in a nearby field marks the site of the original transmission station.

Lizard Point & Around

Five miles south from Mullion, Britain reaches its southernmost tip at Lizard Point, historically one of Britain's deadliest patches of coast. Hundreds of ships have come to grief around the point over the centuries, from Spanish treasure galleons to naval frigates. It's a mecca for scuba divers, as well as coastal walkers who flock to the clifftops to bask in the scenery.

With its conglomeration of fudge-sellers and souvenir shops, **Lizard village** makes a pretty disappointing gateway, so most people just park in the village and make the mile-long stroll down to the point itself. A steep track leads down to the long-disused lifeboat station and shingly cove. In May and June the Lizard is one of the best places in Cornwall to spot basking sharks, and if you're really lucky you might catch sight of a Cornish chough (for more on Cornwall's wildlife see Environment, p277).

Just inland from the point is the **Lizard Lighthouse Heritage Centre** (✆01326-290202; http://www.trinityhouse.co.uk/lighthouses/lighthouse_list/lizard.html?tab=visitor; admission with tour adult/child £7/4, without tour £2/1; ⊙11am-5pm Mar-Oct, check website for exact days). Commissioned in 1752, the lighthouse was automated in the '90s and since 2009 has housed a museum exploring the area's maritime history, encompassing everything from weather prediction to semaphore and shipwrecks. You can wander around the lighthouse grounds, but it's well worth taking the informative guided tour; ask nicely and the kids might even get to let off a blast from the station foghorn.

More craggy scenery can be found further east at **Housel Bay** and the wild promontories of Pen Olver and Bass Point. Further along the coast past Church Cove is **Cadgwith**, an idyllic huddle of thatched houses and fishermen's cottages at the foot of a lung-bustingly steep hill. Fishing boats still run out from the cove in pursuit of local crabs and lobsters, and you'll see their pots piled up beside the village beach – but it's an increasingly tough business these days, as documented by Monty Halls in his TV series *The Fisherman's Apprentice*.

It's worth walking up the cliffs to the 200ft collapsed blowhole called the **Devil's Frying Pan**, which gets its name from the way it spits out water during heavy seas.

Five miles from Lizard Point near Kuggar is **Kennack Sands**, a popular family paddling spot with plenty of sand, seaweed-stocked rockpools and beach shops.

🛏 Sleeping

★ Henry's Campsite CAMPSITE **£**
(📞 01326-290596; www.henryscampsite.co.uk;
Caerthillian Farm, the Lizard; adults £9.60, child 5-16
yr £5, under 4yr free; ⊙ year-round) Endearingly
eccentric campsite in a private subtropical
garden in Lizard village. Nearly all sites have
electric hook-ups and views of the sea, and
the Lizard's beaches, shops and pubs are all
within easy reach. There's a laundry block
and well-stocked shop, but the unisex loos
might not be to everyone's liking.

Lizard YHA HOSTEL **£**
(📞 0845-371 9550; www.yha.org.uk/hostel/lizard-
point; dm from £18, r £52) Even if you're not a
habitual hosteller, this YHA hostel boasts
the kind of location that might just convert
you. It's in a former Victorian hotel beside
the lighthouse above Lizard Point, so the
coastal vistas are out of this world; summer
BBQs and guided walks are a bonus.

Landewednack House B&B **££**
(📞 01326-290877;www.landewednack.uniquehome
stays.com; Church Cove; d £110-180; P ☎) A
slice of Lizard luxury: a restored rectory
surrounded by two green acres and a gorgeous pool. It's been carefully modernised
while retaining the house's heritage: the big
Cornish hearth is still in situ, while little
windows peep out over the grounds and the
house's private chef prepares yummy meals.

Housel Bay Hotel HOTEL **££**
(📞 01326-290417; www.houselbay.com; Housel
Bay; r from £90; P ☎) If you're after sleek lines
and stripped-back minimalism, then this
coastal hotel won't be for you – but if it's
wraparound views and vintage Victoriana
that lights your candle, then you'll be thoroughly happy here. Built by the renowned

Cornish architect Silvanus Trevail, this detached hotel is all faded charm: make sure
you ask for a sea view.

🍴 Eating

Lizard Pasty Shop BAKERY **£**
(📞 01326-290889; www.annspasties.co.uk; The
Lizard; pasties £2.95; ⊙ 9am-3pm Mon-Sat, plus
9am-2pm Sun Jul-Aug) Long before Rick Stein
bestowed his seal of approval on this Lizard
bakery, Ann Muller was already famous for
her pasty-making. Made by hand to a tried-
and-tested recipe, the steak's the star, but
wholemeal, veggie and cheese-and-onion
versions are also offered.

Cadgwith Cove Inn PUB **££**
(📞 01326-290513; www.cadgwithcoveinn.com;
mains £8-14) Cadgwith's fishermen have been
congregating in this thatched pub since
time immemorial, and if you're lucky you
might be treated to a traditional sea shanty
or two if the boys are in the mood. If not,
you'll just have to soak up the pub's low-
ceilinged atmosphere, or sup a pint of Otter
or Sharp's ale.

St Keverne & Around

Centred around a market square ringed
by stone cottages and two village pubs, St
Keverne is one of the Lizard's oldest market towns. The spire of the parish church
has been a vital day-mark for sailors and
fishermen for more than five centuries, and
the nearby coastline is dotted with attractive fishing ports, including **Porthoustock**,
Porthallow (locally pronounced *pralla*)
and the spectacular arc-shaped harbour
of **Coverack**, once an infamous haunt for
smuggled contraband, now a haven for the

DON'T MISS

KYNANCE COVE

The Lizard has some special coves, but top of the pile is **Kynance Cove**, an impossibly pretty pocket of coast tucked under towering cliffs and wildflower-strewn
headland. Once an important source of the red-green serpentine rock favoured by
the Victorians, the cove is now owned by the National Trust. A rough path leads down
from the cliff car park, allowing Kynance's panorama of rock stacks, arches, caves,
islands and vivid sapphire seas to unfurl in dramatic fashion. It's dreamy stuff, no matter whether the sun's blazing or the winter storms are raging – but take care when
swimming and be careful not to be cut off by the tide, especially if you're venturing to
Asparagus Island and Gull Rock.

There's also an excellent eco-friendly cafe just behind the beach, which does great
crab sandwiches and battered fish, and sells the usual beach supplies.

ROSKILLY'S FARM

Just outside St Keverne is Roskilly's Farm (☑ 01326-280479; www.roskillys.co.uk; meals £6-12; ☺ 10am-6pm), an ice cream maker and organic farm which has scooped several awards for its ice creams, yoghurts, fudges, sorbets and fruit jams. It's a lovely spot to spend an afternoon: there are several walking trails to explore around the farm, and light lunches are served at the Croust House cafe, housed in one of the old outbuildings. You can even watch the cows being milked in the viewing gallery at 4.30pm. Needless to say, it's also the best spot on the Lizard for an ice cream.

The farm is at Tregallast Barton, about a mile south of St Keverne. Look out for the signs as you head towards the village on the B3293.

Lizard's artistic community. Out to the east are the Manacles, a treacherous offshore reef that's a source of terror for sailors and delight for wreck divers.

Across the centre of the Lizard sprawl the barren Goonhilly Downs, home to one of the world's largest satellite stations. For some reason the Goonhilly dishes are all named after Arthurian characters; the oldest, Arthur, was built in 1961 and is now a listed monument.

🛏 Sleeping & Eating

Lovelane Caravans   CARAVAN, CAMPSITE £
(www.lovelanecaravans.com; Tregallast Barton; caravan per week £395-540) Kitsch connoisseurs will adore this place, with a collection of caravans tricked-out in retro designs – from a timber shepherd's hut to a five-berth hippie bus, all with gas hob, cool-box and woodburner. Camping is also available. Facilities are simple: lighting is provided by candles and paraffin lamps, and the toilet block only has one shower.

Coverack YHA   HOSTEL £
(☑ 0845-371 9014; www.yha.org.uk/hostel/coverack; School Hill; dm from £18, r from £36) Brilliantly located hostel inside a former gentleman's residence on the hillside above Coverack. Rooms are mostly modern, and a few have windows overlooking the bay.

Lifeboat House   CAFE ££
(☑ 01326-281212; www.lifeboathouse.com; mains £10-18; ☺ 10am-10pm) As its name hints, this Coverack cafe is located in the village's old lifeboat station, so as you'd expect, seafood figures heavily on the menu: megrim sole, monkfish tail, roast gurnard and so on. It's fairly cramped inside and doesn't take bookings, so arrive early if you want a window table – alternatively, you can just get fish-and-chips to take away.

The Helford

Flowing along the Lizard's northern edge, lined with overhanging oaks and hidden creeks, the River Helford feels far removed from the rest of the peninsula. There are few corners of Cornwall which have remained as naturally unspoilt, and it's a haven for marine wildlife, as well as one of Cornwall's last remaining oyster fisheries at Porth Navas. It's also infamous as one of the county's priciest places to buy a house – there's a liberal smattering of rock-star mansions and palatial houses sprinkled along the riverbanks.

The southern bank is much less accessible than the northern shore, and is ideal for exploring on foot. Helford River Boats (☑ 01326-250770; www.helford-river-boats.co.uk; adult/child £4/2; ☺ 9.30am-9.30pm Jun-Aug, 9.30am-5.30pm Apr, May, Sep & Oct) runs pedestrian ferries from Helford Passage (near Falmouth) to Helford village, and also hires out dinghies and motor boats if you prefer exploring solo.

If you're driving, park at the village car park, walk downhill and cross the bridge into the village. Drinks and snacks are sold at the Down by the Riverside Café (☑ 01326-231893; www.downbytheriverside.co.uk) beside the car park.

For a longer walk, the coast trail leads east to Frenchman's Creek (inspiration for Daphne du Maurier's classic tale of Cornish smuggling). To the west, the coast path leads to the village of St-Anthony-in-Meneage, picturesquely plonked beside Gillan Creek. Locals can sometimes be spotted trigging (cockle-picking) in the nearby mudflats – it's an annual tradition on Good Friday. Further still is the isolated headland of Nare Point, from where the views unfurl all the way to Pendennis Point.

Various local kayaking companies offer expeditions along the river, including **Koru Kayaking** (☑ 07794-321827; www.korukayaking.co.uk; 2hr trip £35) and **Aberfal Outdoor Pursuits** (☑ 07968-770756; www.aberfaloutdoorpursuits.co.uk; half/full day £35/50).

🍴 Eating

Shipwright Arms   PUB £
(☑ 01326-231235; Helford; mains £6-14) Thatched on top, beamed inside, blessed with to-die-for river views, the Helford's waterfront pub is an olde-worlde beauty. Betty Stogs, Doom Bar and Helford Creek cider behind the bar.

⭐ South Café   CAFE ££
(☑ 01326-231311; www.south-cafe.com; Manaccan; mains £12-24; ⊙ breakfast, lunch & dinner) Not what you'd expect in the uber-rural Lizard – a bistro that feels more Covent Garden than Cornwall. Take your pick from the burner-heated dining rooms or sheltered back garden, and sit back for a blend of English, French and Italian: lemon sole with caper butter, perhaps, or authentic bouillabaisse. Worth travelling for.

ISLES OF SCILLY

Sprinkled across the Atlantic Ocean 28 miles southwest of Land's End, the Isles of Scilly offer a taste of what life must have been like in England a century ago. Rush-hour traffic, trilling telephones and road-works seem like a distant memory as soon as you set foot on this miniature archipelago of around 140 tiny islands, only five of which are inhabited.

Peak season is from May to September, when you'll find most of the B&Bs and hotels are fully booked weeks ahead, while many businesses simply shut down in winter. Even the main island of St Mary's, which welcomes the vast majority of the islands' visitors, is hardly a bustling metropolis, and the smaller islands of Tresco, Bryher, St Martin's and St Agnes are home to just a few hardy castaways.

ℹ Information

Hospital (☑ 01720-422392; ⊙ 24hr)
Police Station (Garrison Lane, Hugh Town, St Mary's; ⊙ 9am-10pm)
Isles of Scilly Tourist Office (☑ 01720-422536; tic@scilly.gov.uk; Hugh Town, St Mary's; ⊙ 8.30am-6pm Mon-Fri, 9am-5pm Sat,

9am-2pm Sun May-Sep, shorter hrs in winter) The islands' only tourist office.
Radio Scilly (107.9FM; www.radioscilly.com) The islands' very own FM station.
Scilly Online (www.scillyonline.co.uk) A locally run website with lots of info on the islands.
Simply Scilly (www.simplyscilly.co.uk) The official tourist site.

ℹ Getting There & Away

AIR
The end of chopper flights to Scilly mean that the only way to get to the islands by air is now by plane. **Skybus** (☑ 0845-710 5555; www.islesofscilly-travel.co.uk) runs several daily flights from Land's End Airport (adult/child single £70/54) and Newquay (£85/66.50), plus at least one daily from Exeter and Bristol in summer.

Cheaper day-trip fares are available.

BOAT
The cheapest way to reach the islands is the **Scillonian Ferry** (☑ 0845-710 5555; www.ios-travel.co.uk; ⊙ Mar-Oct), which plies the choppy waters between Penzance and St Mary's (adult/child single £37.50/19). There's at least one daily crossing in summer (except on Sunday), dropping to four a week in the shoulder months. Day-trip returns cost adult/child £35/18, or there's a family ticket for 2 adults and up to 3 children which costs £75 per person. The ferry doesn't run from November to April.

ℹ Getting Around

BOAT
The **St Mary's Boatmen Association** (☑ 01720-423999; scillyboating.co.uk) runs regular day trips and ferry services from St Mary's to the outer islands, usually leaving in the early morning and returning in late afternoon. You don't need to book, but make sure you label your luggage clearly so it can be deposited at the right harbour. It also offers fishing, sightseeing and wildlife excursions.

The standard return fare for any island is adult/child £8.40/4.20, or £13/6.50 for a multi-island circular trip.

BUS
The only bus services are on St Mary's. The airport bus (£4) departs from Hugh Town 40 minutes before each flight, while the **Island Rover** (☑ 01720-422131; www.islandrover.co.uk; £8) offers a twice-daily sightseeing trip in a vintage bus in summer.

BIKE
Bikes are an ideal way of getting round the island of St Mary's; contact **St Mary's Bike Hire** (☑ 01720-

Isles of Scilly

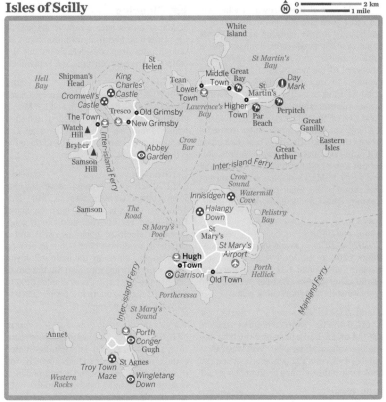

0 ————— 2 km
0 ————— 1 mile

422289; The Strand, High Town; bike hire per day around £10) or **Book A Bike** (📞01720-422786; www.bookabikeonscilly.co.uk; £12 per day).

TAXI

For taxis on St Mary's, try **Island Taxis** (📞01720-422126), **Scilly Cabs** (📞01720-422901) or **St Mary's Taxis** (📞01720-422555).

St Mary's

First stop on Scilly (unless you're arriving aboard your own private yacht) is St Mary's, the largest and busiest of the islands, and home to the vast majority of hotels, shops, restaurants and B&Bs. Just over 3 miles at its widest point, St Mary's is shaped like a crooked circle, with a claw-shaped peninsula at its southwestern edge – home to the island's capital, Hugh Town, and the docking point for the *Scillonian* ferry.

The main airport is a mile east near Old Town.

👁 Sights

Isles of Scilly Museum MUSEUM
(Church St; adult/child £2/50p; ⊙10am-4.30pm Mon-Fri, 10am-noon Sat Easter-Sep, 10am-noon Mon-Sat Oct-Easter, or by arrangement) The islands' main repository of knowledge, Hugh Town's museum contains an eclectic muddle of stuffed birds, Bronze Age artefacts and shipwreck booty (including muskets, a cannon and a ship's bell).

🏃 Activities

Towns & Beaches

Most of the action on St Mary's centres on Hugh Town, which sits on a low-lying sliver of land between the main island and the old Garrison. By Scilly standards, its positively hectic souvenir shops and cafes line the main thoroughfares of the Strand and Hugh St, while trippers dip their toes in at Town Beach and Porthcressa.

A mile east of Hugh Town, reached via the coast path around Peninnis Head, is the island's former harbour at Old Town, home to a few small cafes, a village pub, a working pottery and a pleasant beach. The graveyard of the nearby church contains a memorial to Augustus Smith, founder of the Abbey Garden, as well as the grave of former prime minister Harold Wilson, who often holidayed on the Scillys.

There are lots of small inlets scattered around the island's coastline, best reached on foot or by bike, including Porth Hellick, Watermill Cove and the relatively remote Pelistry Bay. St Mary's also has several ancient sites, notably the small Iron Age village at Halangy Down, a mile north of Hugh Town.

Tours

Island Sea Safaris BOAT TOUR
(☏01720-422732; www.islandseasafaris.co.uk) Offers trips to see local seabird and seal colonies (adult/child £32/25) and one-hour 'island taster' cruises (£23 per person). Also rents wetsuits and snorkelling gear.

Island Wildlife Tours WALKING TOUR
(☏01720-422212; www.islandwildlifetours.co.uk; half-/full day £6/12) Regular birdwatching and wildlife walks with local boy Will Wagstaff. A full-day walk costs £12 per person, or you can book for just the morning or afternoon for £6.

Scilly Walks WALKING TOUR
(☏01720-423326; www.scillywalks.co.uk; adult/child £5/2.50) Katharine Sawyer runs three-hour archaeological and historical tours, and visits to the off-islands (day trips adult/child £10/5).

CAMPING & SELF-CATERING ON SCILLY

There are loads of self-catering cottages available on Scilly – contact the tourist office for full listings, or call Island Properties (☏422082; St Mary's) or Sibley's Island Homes (☏01720-422431; www.sibleysonscilly.co.uk).

All the main islands, except Tresco, have a campsite, but you'll need to book well ahead in season.

➡ Garrison Campsite
➡ St Martin's Campsite (p255)
➡ Troytown Farm (p256)
➡ Bryher Campsite (p254)

🛏 Sleeping

St Mary's hotels have a captive market, so the prices tend to command a premium – although rates drop considerably outside the main months between June and September.

Belmont B&B £
(☏01720-423154; www.the-belmont.co.uk; Church Rd; s £37-75, d £64-82, f £102-125) Solid St Mary's guesthouse, in a double-fronted detached house 15 minutes' walk from the quay. The six rooms are clean and bright and the price is definitely right.

Garrison Campsite CAMPSITE £
(☏01720-422670; www.garrisonholidays.com; Tower Cottage, Garrison; sites £8.55-11) This 4-hectare site sits on the garrison above Hugh Town. Facilities are surprisingly good, including electrical hook-ups, wi-fi and a laundry-cum-shower block – but as ever on Scilly, the sea views are the main sell. If you don't want to bring your own kit, the campsite has pre-erected tents available (£105 to £125 for 3 nights and up to 2 people, £240 to £285 for up to 5 people).

Wingletang B&B ££
(☏01720-422381; www.wingletangguesthouse.co.uk; s £32-42, d £72-88) This granite-fronted cottage in the heart of Hugh Town is well over 200 years old, but the accommodation is surprisingly light inside. Magnolia walls and simple furnishings make it feel like a family home, and you're welcome to browse the little library of nature books.

St Mary's Hall Hotel HOTEL £££
(☏01720-422316; www.stmaryshallhotel.co.uk; Church St, Hugh Town; r £160-236; ☏) This Scilly mansion was originally built for a holidaying Italian nobleman. Grand staircases, objets d'art and wood-panelled walls give an upmarket feel, but the Godolphin and Count Leon rooms are standard considering the price; if you can, plump for one of the plush suites with their own sitting areas and a galley kitchen.

Star Castle Hotel HOTEL £££
(☏01720-422317; www.star-castle.co.uk; The Garrison; r incl dinner £176-344; ☏☀) Shaped like an eight-pointed star, this former fort on Garrison Point is one of Scilly's star hotels, with a choice of heritage-style castle rooms or more modern garden suites. It's a bit stuffy, but prices include dinner at a choice of restaurants.

GIG RACING

The six-oared wooden boats known as **pilot gigs** were once the traditional craft for navigating Cornwall's shorelines, used for transporting goods and passengers from tall ships which were too big to moor in the shallow coastal harbours.

These days the boats are used for gig racing, a highly competitive and physically demanding sport. You'll often spot local teams practising in the waters around St Mary's; organised races are held most weekends.

Every April or May St Mary's also hosts the **World Pilot Gig Championships**, the largest gig-racing regatta in the world. The event attracts teams from as far away as Holland, Canada and the USA.

 ### Eating

Both the island's big hotels have upmarket restaurants.

Dibble & Grub CAFE **££**
(☑ 01720-423719; www.dibbleandgrub.com; lunch £6-12, dinner £10-16; ☉ 10am-10pm in summer) Breezy new beach cafe beside Porthcressa, housed in the island's old fire station, and specialising in tapas.

**Juliet's
Garden Restaurant** RESTAURANT, CAFE **££**
(☑ 01720-422228; www.julietsgardenrestaurant. co.uk; mains £8-16; ☉ 10am-11pm summer) Fifteen minutes' walk from Hugh Town, just above Portloo Beach, this old barn on Seaways Farm began life as a tiny tearoom but has blossomed into the best place to eat on St Mary's. There's light lunches by day, candlelit fare by night, all treated with loving care and attention. The addition of the new Balcony Room has maximised the fine harbour views. There's also a small farm shop.

Tresco

A short boat hop across the channel from St Mary's brings you to Tresco, the second-largest island, once owned by the monks of Tavistock Abbey, now leased by locals from the Duchy of Cornwall.

It's a proper old-fashioned island getaway – for decades there was just one pub and one hotel on the island, although the recent arrival of the Flying Boat Club has brought a dash of razzle-dazzle to this tiny corner of Scilly.

Sights

Around the edge of the island are several well-hidden beaches, including the sand-and-shell beach of **Appletree Bay**, and the more grandiose curve of sand at **Pentle Bay**.

On the northwest side of the island are the ruins of two naval forts – **King Charles' Castle** was the first to be built in the 1550s, but was later superseded by the cannon tower of **Cromwell's Castle** nearby.

Abbey Garden GARDEN
(☑ 01720-424105; www.tresco.co.uk/see/abbey-garden; adult £12, under 16s free; ☉ 10am-4pm) One of Scilly's great attractions is this sub-tropical estate, first laid out in 1834 on the site of a 12th-century Benedictine priory by the horticultural visionary Augustus Smith. The gardens are now home to over 20,000 exotic species, from towering palms to desert cacti and crimson flame trees, all nurtured by the temperate gusts of the Gulf Stream. Admission also covers the **Valhalla collection**, made up of figureheads and nameplates salvaged from the many ships that have foundered off Tresco's shores.

Sleeping & Eating

All the accommodation is handled by **Tresco Island** (☑ 01720-422849; www.tresco.co.uk). The New Inn and Sea Garden Cottages offer rooms by the night, but most people either visit as a day-trip or rent out cottages by the week.

The New Inn INN **£££**
(☑ 01720-422844; d £140-230) Compared with Tresco's two wallet-shreddingly expensive hotels, the New Inn is a comparative bargain. The rooms are soothingly finished in buttery yellows and pale blues, although inevitably you'll have to fork out for a view.

Sea Garden Cottages COTTAGE **£££**
(☑ 01720-422849; contactus@tresco.co.uk; £160-210; ❀ ☏) This complex of self-contained cottages at the Island Hotel has nine properties available on a nightly basis. Checked tiles, wood and nautical pictures give them a suitably seaside feel, and rates include breakfast and dinner at the Ruin Beach Café.

Flying Boat Club APARTMENT **£££**
(☑ 01720-422849; contactus@tresco.co.uk; apt per
week £4500-5000; ✴ 🐾 🏊) Ludicrously lavish
sea-view houses with indoor pool and spa;
prices drop to a mere £1475 to £2000 in
winter.

New Inn INN **££**
(☑ 01720-422222; mains £8-18.50; ⊙ 10am-11pm)
The hub of the island's social scene, where
locals and trippers alike pack onto the shady
terrace of the Driftwood Bar for a refreshing
pint of Skinner's or Scilly ale accompanied
by a plate of beer-battered pollock or bangers and mash. Be warned though – the lack
of competition means prices are far from
cheap.

Other Inhabited Islands

Bryher

Just over 80 people live on the remote island of Bryher. Blanketed with heather and
bracken, and spotted with miniature hills,
it's a tough place to eke out an existence;
fishing and flower-growing are about the island's only industries, and even those aren't
what they once were.

Bryher's town is little more than a huddle of a couple of dozen houses dotted along
the shore overlooking the deep anchorage of
New Grimsby Channel, a favourite stop for
visiting yachts. From the modest summit of
Samson Hill, you can drink in one of the
finest views in all of Scilly, with a fantastic
panorama taking in most of the island chain.

Bryher's eastern side is exposed to the full
force of the Atlantic weather, and the appropriately named Hell Bay makes for a powerful sight during a winter gale. Things are
usually more tranquil to the south at Rushy
Bay and on the east side at Green Bay.

From the quay, Bryher Boats (☑ 01720-
422886) trundles across to deserted Samson Island, where a few ruined cottages are
all that's left of the last island settlers who
moved out in 1855. At low tide, the remains
of ancient fields swamped during the last ice
age become visible at Samson Flats.

🛏 Sleeping & Eating

Bryher Campsite CAMPSITE **£**
(☑ 01720-422886; www.bryhercampsite.co.uk;
sites £10) Bare-bones camping near the quay.
Hot showers and tractor transport from the
boat are included in the rates.

Hell Bay HOTEL **£££**
(☑ 01720-422947; www.hellbay.co.uk; d £135-320)
Pretty much the poshest place to stay in
Scilly – a true island getaway blending New
England-style furnishings with sunny golds,
sea blues and pale wood beams. Rooms
have sitting rooms, private balconies and,
of course, stunning sea views. There are a
range of categories, starting with the garden-view rooms ranging up to the supremely plush Emperor Suites.

Fraggle Rock CAFE, PUB **£**
(☑ 01720-422222; mains £6-14; ⊙ 10.30am-
4.30pm & 7-11pm; 🐾) This relaxed cafe also
doubles as Bryher's pub. The menu's mainly
pizzas, salads and burgers, and there are a
few local ales on tap and Fairtrade coffees
that help support the Cornwall Wildlife
Trust.

St Martin's

The third-largest and furthest north of the
islands, St Martin's is one of the main centres
for Scilly's flower-growing industry, and the
island's fields are a riot of colourful blooms
in season. It's also blessed with gin-clear waters and the kind of untouched sands you'd
more usually associate with St Lucia than
Cornwall.

The main settlement is Higher Town,
where you'll find the village shop and diving operation, but there are small clusters of
cottages in nearby Middle and Lower Town.

Seven miles offshore from the island is
the infamous Seven Stones reef, where the
oil tanker *Torrey Canyon* came aground in
1967, causing one of Britain's worst oil spills.
The vessel was bombed several times by the

WEST CORNWALL & THE ISLES OF SCILLY OTHER INHABITED ISLANDS

THE UNINHABITED ISLANDS

Still not left the outside world behind
enough? Don't fret – St Agnes Boating (☑ 422704; www.st-agnes-boating.
co.uk) offers day trips (around £15) to
the most remote corners of Scilly, including the little-visited beaches of the
Eastern Isles, the ruined church on
St Helen's, the many shipwreck spots
around the Western Rocks, and the
famous Bishops Rock Lighthouse,
a marvel of 19th-century engineering
raised on a narrow sliver of rock barely
46m long by 16m wide.

RAF in an attempt to sink the ship and burn off the spill; it eventually broke up several days later, but still polluted more than 120 miles of coastline around Cornwall and northern France.

◉ Sights

St Martin's Vineyard   VINEYARD
(☑ 01720-423418; www.stmartinsvineyard.co.uk) Rather improbably, the island is also home to Britain's most southwesterly (and certainly the smallest) winemaker. Tours of the vineyard, which began as a holiday hobby for owners Val and Graham Thomas, are offered from 11am to 4pm on weekdays throughout the summer.

North Farm Gallery   ART GALLERY
(☑ 01720-423028; ⊙ 10am-5pm Sun-Fri) A little art gallery and crafts shop next to St Martin's Bakery.

Beaches   BEACHES
The island's isolated beaches feel fantastically wild. **Par Beach** is right next to the main quay, while on the island's southern shore is **Lawrence's Bay**, which reveals a broad sweep of sandy flats at low tide. Along the island's northern side are **Great Bay** and **Little Bay**, arguably the finest beaches in Scilly; from the western end, you can cross to White Island at low tide.

Along the cliffs from Great Bay is the island's famous red-and-white striped **Day Mark**, a navigation aid dating back to 1683. Nearby is the ultra-secluded cove of **Perpitch**.

⚡ Activities

St Martin's Boat Services   BOAT TRIPS
(☑ 07831-585365; £8 per person) Scenic boat-trips around St Martin's and the other islands; there's a daily service to St Mary's and Tresco (except Sunday), and trips to Bryher and St Agnes every other day. There's no need to book, just turn up and pay cash on board.

There's usually a circular trip to the Eastern Isles once a week (£14).

Scilly Diving   DIVING
(☑ 01720-422848; www.scillydiving.com; Higher Town; s dives £43) Diving courses, and single dives for qualified divers.

🛌 Sleeping

St Martin's Campsite   CAMPSITE £
(☑ 01720-422888; www.stmartinscampsite.co.uk; sites £9-11; ⊙ Mar-Oct) Towards the western end of Lawrence's Bay, this site has 50 pitches spread across three fields, so it never feels crowded. Coin-operated laundry and showers are available, and water comes from the campsite's own bore-hole. Eggs and veg are even available for your morning fry-up. Book well ahead for July and August.

Polreath   B&B ££
(☑ 01720-422046; www.polreath.com; Higher Town; d £100-110, weekly stays only May-Sep) This friendly granite cottage is one of the only B&Bs on St Martin's – tiny and traditional, with a sunny conservatory serving cream teas, homemade lemonade and hearty evening meals.

🍴 Eating & Drinking

Adam's Fish & Chips   SEAFOOD £
(☑ 01720-422457; ⊙ 6-8.30pm Tue & Thu) The fish here is about as fresh as it gets – whatever's caught on the day is what ends up in your batter. It's run by Adam and Emma, who live and work on Little Arthur Farm nearby. Takeaway is available, but you'll need to book if you want one of the six tables.

St Martin's Bakery   BAKERY £
(☑ 01720-423444; www.stmartinsbakery.co.uk; ⊙ 9am-6pm Mon-Sat, 9am-2pm Sun) Now under new ownership, this tiny bakery turns out fresh bread, pastries, pizzas and quiches, as well as some of Scilly's best homemade pasties.

Seven Stones   PUB £
(☑ 01720-423560; www.sevenstonesinn.co.uk; mains £8-12; ⊙ 10am-11pm) Gorgeous pub and the island's only boozer, so it's the heart of the action every night of the week. There are super views of the other islands from the terrace.

Little Arthur Farm   CAFE, SHOP ££
(☑ 01720-422457; www.littlearthur.co.uk; St Martin's; ⊙ 10.30am-4pm daily, 6.30-8.30pm Mon-Fri) Live the good life at this wonderful wholefood cafe and sustainable farm just off Par Beach. All the produce is home-grown, from herbs and vegetables to ham, fruit and eggs – they even make their own shoes, for heaven's sake. Soups, sandwiches and scones are served up daily.

ℹ Information

St Martin's Post Office (www.stmartins-stores.co.uk; 9am-5.30pm Mon-Sat, 9-10am Sun) The island's post office and general store.

St Agnes

Even by Scilly standards, the rocky island of St Agnes is quiet. When the last day boats have departed for St Mary's, the island is all but deserted. The most southerly of the Scilly Isles, St Agnes is studded with peaceful coves, rugged reefs and a scattering of prehistoric sites, and it's a place many visitors never quite manage to reach.

The main quay is at Porth Conger, near the decommissioned Old Lighthouse, from where the road leads to two lovely inlets at Periglis Cove and St Warna's Cove, named after the patron saint of shipwrecks. The coast path between the coves passes the tiny Troytown Maze, a concentric maze of stones that's thought to be around two centuries old, but might be based on a prehistoric original.

The southern side of the island is mostly taken up by the bracken-strewn sweep of Wingletang Down, while on the east side the little beach of Covean is a handsome place to settle down for an afternoon sunbathe. At low tide a sandbar connects St Martin's with the small island of Gugh (pronounced *goo*), famous for its Bronze Age remains and the slanting menhir known as the Old Man of Gugh. Take care not to be cut off by the rising tide, which comes in fast and is too strong for swimming.

🛏 Sleeping

★ **Troytown Farm** CAMPSITE £
(☑ 01720-422360; www.troytown.co.uk; Troytown Farm; sites per adult £8.50, tents £2-8 depending on size; P) At the southwestern corner of the island. Originally a flower farm, it's now home to Scillys' only dairy herd, and offers field camping with wonderful sea views.

Covean Cottage B&B ££
(☑ 01720-422620; www.coveancottage.com; d £78-88) A little stone-walled cottage, with three pretty sea-view rooms. There's also a small cafe which serves brekkies and light meals cooked up by the owner.

🍴 Eating

★ **Turk's Head** PUB ££
(☑ 01720-422434; mains £8-14; ⊘ 10am-11pm) Britain's most southerly alehouse is a beauty. Model ships and seafaring photos line the walls, great pub food (swordfish, crab cakes, veggie chillis) is served up in the panelled bar, and you can carry your pint of homebrewed Turk's Head down to the slipway as the sun goes down. You might even be treated to a sea shanty if the lads are in the mood.

High Tide SEAFOOD ££
(☑ 01720-423869; mains £14-18; ⊘ dinner 6-10pm Mon-Sat) Quite possibly the remotest fish restaurant in Britain, run by a Kiwi chef and his artist wife. The menu's tiny as it's dictated by what turns up on the day, but it's a surprisingly sophisticated affair – think sea bass with samphire, or red mullet on bok choy.

Understand
Devon &
Cornwall

DEVON & CORNWALL TODAY.................258
Get up to speed on the hot local topics: food miles, second homes, mining matters and the future of tourism.

HISTORY 260
From ancient stones to modern architecture, the southwest packs an astonishing amount of history into a tiny space.

FOOD & DRINK.............................268
Renowned as a gourmet hot spot and celebrity-chef-packed zone, the southwest also leads the way in sustainable cuisine.

THE ARTS 273
West Cornwall has been a hotbed of artistic creativity since the early 19th century.

ENVIRONMENT.............................277
Coast and countryside, cities and surf: the varied landscape of Devon and Cornwall is a sight to behold.

Devon & Cornwall Today

From the thorny topics of tourism and holiday homes to the future of southwest food, here's a quick overview of some of the most important issues facing Devon and Cornwall over the next few years.

Best Books

Jamaica Inn (Daphne du Maurier; 1936) Classic thriller on Bodmin Moor.
The Levelling Sea (Philip Marsden; 2011) Covers Falmouth's maritime history.
And Then There Were None (Agatha Christie; 1939) Mystery on Burgh Island.
Vanishing Cornwall (Daphne du Maurier; 1967) Lyrical history of Cornwall.

Best Films

War Horse (2011) Spielberg filmed key scenes on Dartmoor.
Alice in Wonderland (2010) Cornwall's Antony House doubled as Wonderland in Tim Burton's version.
Summer in February (2013) Account of the Lamorna School of artists.
When The Whales Came (1989) Dreamy children's tale set on Scilly.

Resources

Cornwall Beaches (www.cornwall-beaches.co.uk) Online guide to the county's sands.
Love the Flavour (www.lovethe flavour.co.uk) Devon's best food and drink.
Cornwall and Devon Wildlife Trusts (www.cornwallwildlifetrust.org.uk & www.devonwildlifetrust.org) Great resource for wildlife enthusiasts.

The Second Home Issue

If there's one issue that still divides opinion in the southwest more than any other, it's the thorny question of second homes. According to the 2011 census, Cornwall now tops the league when it comes to holiday properties (more than 23,000 at the last count), with Devon only a short way behind.

While arguments rumble on about the economic benefit of these homes-away-from-home, there can be little doubt that the region's enduring popularity has contributed to rapidly rocketing house prices – especially in picturesque places such as Salcombe, St Mawes, Perranporth, Padstow and Fowey, which all now figure in the top 10 list of the most expensive places to buy property in the UK.

Across the region, the average house price is now more than £200,000, almost 10 times the average wage of around £22,000 – leaving many locals, and especially the region's young people, struggling to get onto the housing ladder.

It's a difficult problem to solve: the region's popularity with urban escapees and cash-rich retirees, coupled with limited space for house-building, inevitably means that house prices look set to continue rising in the coming years.

Grockles & Emmets

A century ago it was farming and fishing, but tourism is now by far and away the region's top-grossing industry. Recent figures indicate that tourism adds more than £9 billion to the region's coffers, and it's estimated that around one in five jobs now depend on the tourism industry in some form or other. The region's residents have a mixed relationship with the summer influx of grockles and emmets (as the locals either side of the Devon-Cornwall border refer to them): traffic jams, litter and overcrowded beaches are inevitable problems, but many towns and villages would now find it all but impossible to survive without the vital cash injection visitors bring.

The downside of this tourism boom is its unpredictability: Britain's recent economic troubles and spells of poor weather have badly impacted the region's tourist businesses, forcing many operators to the financial edge. Meanwhile, the increasing accessibility and affordability of foreign holidays has made it hard for Devon and Cornwall to attract new visitors, especially those from the younger demographic. Even high profile businesses such as the Eden Project aren't immune; the attraction was recently forced to lay off staff due to falling visitor numbers.

A Foodie Future?

It isn't all doom and gloom, however. One of the region's great success stories over the last decade has been its increasing focus on food. Several Michelin-starred restaurants are now dotted across the two counties, but it's the numerous homegrown businesses that have sprung up in recent years that are arguably more important for the future.

From coffee roasters and food-box companies to bakeries, vineyards and microbreweries, Devon and Cornwall are leading the way when it comes to Britain's culinary innovation. In a world where food miles and carbon footprints are on everyone's minds, these homegrown businesses all provide positive signs of Cornwall and Devon's growing reputation as a foodie destination – a fact that was underlined by the recent decision to grant 'geo-protected' status to the region's greatest gastronomic export, the Cornish pasty.

The local focus isn't just limited to food, either. Many towns across the southwest are exploring ways to take control of their own futures: take Wadebridge, for example, which is planning to be the southwest's greenest town by generating a third of its electricity from renewable sources by 2015, and has recently followed Totnes' lead by launching its own currency in an attempt to encourage people to shop more locally.

Tin Mining & Tidal Power

Another major success was the announcement in 2006 of World Heritage Status for the Cornwall & West Devon Mining Landscape, in recognition of the region's proud industrial heritage. The last working tin mine closed at South Crofty near Camborne in 1998, but there have been several attempts to revive the mine since, buoyed by the worldwide spike in mineral prices. Ironically, these projects have ruffled Unesco's feathers, who claim that the area's heritage status depends on the mines remaining closed for good. Instead, pioneering eco-projects such as the Wave Hub tidal power scheme and some of the UK's first 'solar farms' perhaps point the way towards an alternative – and greener – future.

POPULATION: **1.6 MILLION**

AREA: **10,270 SQ KM**

INFLATION: **2%**

UNEMPLOYMENT: **5%**

NUMBER OF PEOPLE WHO STATE CORNISH AS THEIR NATIONAL IDENTITY: **9.9%**

if Devon & Cornwall were 100 people

20 would work in tourism
8 would work in manufacturing
5 would work in agriculture or fishing
1 would work in mining or quarrying
66 would work in another job

belief systems
(% of population)

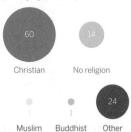

Christian	No religion
60	14

Muslim	Buddhist	Other
1	1	24

population per sq km

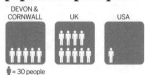

DEVON & CORNWALL   UK   USA

👤 ≈ 30 people

History

Whether it's gazing out from the battlements of a medieval castle or wandering among the menhirs of an ancient stone circle, you'll find Devon and Cornwall both have a wealth of history to explore. Mining, methodism and maritime exploration have all played a key role in shaping the region's past, and you'll encounter a litany of fascinating figures – from the swashbuckling explorer Francis Drake to the mythical figure of King Arthur, whose legendary name is linked to countless sites around the southwest.

Ancient Remains
....
Chysauster Iron Age Village, near Penzance
....
Grimspound Bronze Age Village, Dartmoor
....
Grey Wethers Stone Rows, Dartmoor
....
The Hurlers, Bodmin Moor
....
Mên-an-tol Stone, Penwith

Ancient Stones

It's thought that humans have inhabited southwest England for more than 100,000 years, but the first evidence of human settlement is a jawbone dating from around 35,000 BC, unearthed in Kents Cavern, near Torquay, during an excavation in 1927 (academic opinion is still divided as to whether the bone belongs to a Neanderthal or prehistoric ancestors of *Homo sapiens*). A similar argument continues to rage over the controversial issue of cannibalism: some evidence has emerged that seems to suggest early humans had no qualms about eating their deceased relatives, and may even have used their bones to make drinking vessels and dining implements.

The earliest settlers were tribes of hunter-gatherers, living seasonally from the land and travelling in pursuit of seasonal game, but the first signs of organised farming and animal domestication emerged around 4000 BC. Around this time prehistoric builders developed their taste for eye-catching architecture, and built many stone circles, menhirs, quoits and barrows across Devon, Dartmoor, Bodmin Moor, Penwith and the Isles of Scilly.

By 1800 BC there was already a thriving trade in gold, tin, bronze and copper between southwest mines and many parts of Europe and the Mediterranean. This trade continued following the arrival of the Celts, who established themselves in southwest Britain from around 1000 BC.

The Celts quickly conquered much of the area, establishing themselves in hilltop forts and coastal strongholds. The remains of several Bronze and Iron Age 'villages' can still be seen in many areas, including Dartmoor and Penwith: Chysauster, Carn Euny and Grimspound are perhaps the best preserved.

TIMELINE	To 4000 BC	4000–1500 BC	1000–500 BC
	The southwest is populated by tribes of nomadic hunter-gatherers.	First evidence of organised farming. Neolithic builders construct many dolmens, quoits, stone circles and menhirs.	Arrival of the first Celts on British shores. Celtic warriors establish hillforts and fortified settlements across the region, and gradually begin to integrate with native Britons.

Over the next few centuries, Celtic society flourished in southwest Britain and developed its own culture, architecture and language, but by the 1st century BC, a new wave of invaders had landed and brushed all but the hardiest Celtic defenders aside. *Veni, vidi, vici* – the Romans had arrived.

Roman Rule & the Coming Of The Kings

The first Roman landings in Britain were led by Julius Caesar in 55 BC. In AD 43 Aulus Plautius invaded Britain with around 20,000 troops, who were backed by reinforcements from the stuttering Emperor Claudius. Over the next five years, under the orders of their commander Vespasian, the legions rampaged through southern England.

Having wrested control of the area from the ruling Celtic tribes (the Durotriges in Dorset and Somerset, and the Dumnonii in Devon and Cornwall), the Romans set about building a network of roads, settlements, ports, temples and forts. A key garrison was stationed at Exeter (Isca Dumnoniorum to the Romans), which marked the western end of the Roman road to Lincoln known as the Fosse Way.

The Romans' grip on power lasted until the 4th century, when military pressures and dwindling resources forced their withdrawal from many of the empire's more far-flung outposts. By 410 the last legions had returned to Rome, and the so-called 'Dark Ages' had begun.

Over the next 500 years, southwest Britain was invaded by waves of Anglo-Saxon settlers, mainly tribes of Angles, Saxons, Jutes and Frisians from modern-day Germany, who first came as mercenaries in the Roman army. The native Celts were pushed back into their core strongholds in Wales, Dartmoor and Cornwall, creating pockets of Celtic culture, while the rest of the region was largely colonised by the Anglo-Saxons. Around this time a fearsome war leader – supposedly named Arthur or Arthurus – is said to have emerged to lead a counter-attack against the invading Saxons, checking their progress over 12 great battles, and launching the enduring legend of King Arthur.

The first Christian saints arrived in the southwest around this time, probably from Ireland, although their vessels were a little unconventional – St Ia is supposed to have sailed to the north Cornish coast on a giant leaf, while St Piran, patron saint of Cornwall, allegedly arrived aboard a granite millstone.

In the early 9th century, King Egbert and the armies of Wessex swept west and brought the whole of the southwest under Anglo-Saxon control. His grandson, King Alfred, led a series of campaigns against Viking incursions (and famously burnt some cakes while hiding on the island of Athelney). After a series of power struggles between various Anglo-Saxon kingdoms over the next century, King Edward (the Peacemaker) was crowned the first king of a unified England at Bath Abbey in 973.

55 BC	AD 410–600	838	939
Roman legions under Julius Caesar land in Britain and defeat native tribes, although some areas of west Cornwall and Devon remain effectively independent kingdoms.	Christianity is brought to the southwest by Irish missionaries (many of whom are subsequently made saints, including St Piran, the patron saint of Cornwall).	Armies of Wessex under King Egbert defeat the final alliance of Cornish and Viking warriors at Hingston Down.	Athelstan, king of Wessex and the first recognised king of a unified England, dies.

CASSITERIDES

The Middle Ages

Following the Norman conquest of 1066, the region came under the sway of feudal lords, who developed the area's potential for trade, agriculture and industry. Wool, tin and minerals became important exports, and a series of ports sprang up around the southwest coastline, notably at Fowey, Bristol, Looe, Saltash and Plymouth.

In 1305 Edward I recognised the importance of tin mining to the area by granting official charters to the Stannaries (tin-mining districts) and establishing five stannary towns in Cornwall (Truro, Lostwithiel, Launceston, Helston and Bodmin) and three more in Devon (Chagford, Ashburton and Tavistock). Among other functions, these towns had the right to assay tin to determine its quality before export. Cornwall also had its own Stannary Parliament, governed by its own system of taxes and laws; tin miners were effectively exempt from civil jurisdiction, and had the right to be tried according to Stannary law. Half a century later in 1337, Edward III established the Duchy of Cornwall for his son Edward, the 'Black Prince', a title that is still traditionally inherited by the heir to the throne.

The long-held rights of the Stannaries were a major factor in the 1497 'An Gof' rebellion, a popular uprising against taxes levied by Henry VII to fund a war against the Scots, which many believed eroded the Stannaries' right to govern their own affairs. Under leaders Thomas Flamank, a Bodmin lawyer, and Michael Joseph, a blacksmith (*an gof* in Cornish) from St Keverne, an army of 15,000 Cornishmen marched on London. Despite a series of battles, it was outclassed by the king's forces, and Flamank and Joseph were hanged, drawn and quartered before having their heads impaled on pikes outside London Bridge.

A similarly brutal end awaited the region's ecclesiastical institutions during Henry VIII's Dissolution. Nearly all of the region's abbeys, including Buckfast, Bodmin and Glasney College in Penryn, were abolished. Assets were stripped, buildings dismantled and most of the monks were forcibly retired or, in many cases, put to death. In the absence of the abbeys, the cathedral of Exeter flourished alongside smaller chapels and churches.

The Reformation also abolished the use of Latin in church services and introduced a new all-English Book of Common Prayer. This was the final straw for many devout worshippers in Cornwall and Devon, but the so-called Prayer Book Rebellion of 1549 was put down in similarly bloody fashion to the 'An Gof' rebellion 50 years before; the West Country armies were summarily crushed outside Exeter, and the leaders executed.

The Ancient Greeks referred to the British Isles as the 'Cassiterides', or Islands of Tin.

1050

Foundation of the first cathedral at Exeter, although the original building is substantially remodelled by successive bishops in the 12th and 13th centuries.

1201

King John grants the first charter to the Stannaries (tin-mining districts) of Cornwall. Further charters are granted in the early 13th century by Edward I.

KIM SAYER / GETTY IMAGES ©

➜ Exeter Cathedral (p44)

The New World

Religion was yet again the cause of troubles following the ascension of Elizabeth to the throne in 1558. Tensions between Protestant England and the mainly Catholic countries of southern Europe culminated in a series of skirmishes and battles, prompting Elizabeth to expand the navy's power to counter the increasing strength of Spanish fleets. The Queen also encouraged the practice of 'private enterprise' (otherwise known as piracy) on the open seas. Many of her favourite sea captains were born in the southwest, including the Cornish nobleman Sir Richard Grenville (born at Buckland Abbey in Devon); his cousin, Sir Walter Raleigh (born in Hayes Barton, East Devon); Sir John Hawkins (Plymouth); and his cousin, Sir Francis Drake (Tavistock).

In 1588 Philip II of Spain dispatched an armada of 130 warships to invade England and bring the island under Catholic rule. The Armada was sighted off the Lizard on 19 July, and the message was carried to London via a series of beacons along the south coast. Whether Drake was really bowling on Plymouth Hoe at the time of the invasion is unlikely, but he lost no time in organising his response: he set sail from Plymouth with a fleet of 55 ships. Over the next two weeks Drake fought a series of engagements against the Spanish fleet, culminating in the Battle of Gravelines on 29 July, in which 11 Spanish galleons were destroyed and the rest put to flight. Drake and Hawkins' subsequent exploits were rather less worthy of commendation: they were instrumental in establishing the first slave-trafficking routes with Africa, a trade that underpinned the growth of several southwest ports (especially Bristol and Plymouth) over the next two centuries.

The southwest also had a pivotal role to play in the move from Old to New World. Following Sir Francis Drake's circumnavigation of the globe from Plymouth in 1577 (a replica of his ship, the *Pelican,* renamed the *Golden Hind,* can be seen on Brixham Harbour), the city of Plymouth also witnessed the first voyage of the Pilgrim Fathers, who set sail from the Barbican on 16 September 1620 aboard the *Mayflower.* The pilgrims landed at Provincetown Harbour in present-day Massachusetts and founded the colony of New Plymouth, effectively marking the start of modern America.

Civil War

As in many other areas, the Civil War from 1642 to 1646 resulted in massive turmoil throughout the West Country. Broadly speaking, Cornwall declared itself for the king, Charles I, while loyalties varied widely across the rest of the region with neighbouring villages often declaring contradictory allegiances. Key battles were fought at Braddock Down,

Top 5 Castles

Dartmouth Castle
....
Pendennis Castle, Falmouth
....
Tintagel Castle
....
Restormel Castle, Lostwithiel
....
Berry Pomeroy Castle, near Totnes

1337	1348	1497	1588
The Duchy of Cornwall is established, and Edward the 'Black Prince' becomes the first Duke of Cornwall.	The Black Death, a form of flea-borne bubonic plague spread by rats and other rodents, reaches the southwest. The epidemic kills an estimated one-third of the population.	The 'An Gof' rebellion against Henry VII marches on London, but is quashed and its leaders executed. A second Cornish rebellion under Perkin Warbeck fails later the same year.	The Spanish Armada invasion fleet, first sighted off the Lizard Peninsula, is defeated by the Royal Navy fleet under the command of Sir Francis Drake, stationed at Plymouth.

Stratton, Lostwithiel, Lansdown (near Bristol) and Plymouth, but the tide of the war swept back and forth until a new commander, Oliver Cromwell, galvanised the Parliamentarian armies and led them towards a string of crushing victories, most notably at the Battle of Lostwithiel in 1644, which effectively ended Royalist control of the southwest. The Royalists eventually surrendered at Tresillian, 3 miles outside Truro, on 15 March 1646.

Forty years later, the Protestant Monmouth Rebellion broke out against the Catholic rule of James II, culminating in the last battle ever fought on English soil, at Sedgemoor in northern Somerset in 1646. The ringleaders of the rebellion were rounded up and tried in the 'Bloody Assizes' at Taunton Castle. Predictably, most of them ended up losing their heads.

Methodism

In 1743 the Methodist preacher John Wesley delivered his first sermon in St Ives. Preaching the virtues of temperance, piety and self-reliance, Wesley spent the next 20 years travelling the county and preaching to ever-larger crowds (in his journal in 1781, Wesley claims to have preached to around 20,000 people at Gwennap Pit, near St Day). Many Methodist chapels were built, including several by the famous Cornish Methodist Billy Bray (a former miner), and methodism was rapidly established as the region's predominant religion: by 1851 more than 60% of Cornwall's population classed themselves as Methodists.

Best History Museums

National Maritime Museum

Plymouth City Museum & Art Gallery

Porthcurno Telegraph Museum

Dartmouth Museum

Lizard Lighthouse Heritage Centre

The Age of Industry

Following the upheavals of the Civil War, the southwest developed as an industrial and maritime powerhouse over the next century. The huge demand for metals during the Industrial Revolution (particularly tin, iron and copper) heralded the beginning of the golden age of mining in Cornwall and west Devon, and the advent of new technologies such as steam power, beam engines and 'blast' extraction enabled the region's miners to reach previously inaccessible lodes of high-quality metals.

Mining in Cornwall boomed: in 1800 the county boasted 75 mines employing 16,000 people, but by 1837 this had mushroomed to 200 mines employing some 30,000 workers. Several local engineers played a key role in the industry's expansion. First came Dartmouth-born Thomas Newcomen (1664–1729), the pioneer of the earliest steam engines, which were subsequently used to power the pumps that extracted water from Devon and Cornwall's deep-shaft mines, greatly improving the mines' safety and efficiency. Then came Redruth-born Richard Trevithick (1771–1833), who devised the first steam-powered locomotive, which he named

1620	1720	1743
The Pilgrim Fathers set sail from Plymouth aboard the *Mayflower*, founding the colony of New Plymouth in Massachusetts in November the same year.	Thomas Newcomen builds an 'atmospheric engine' at Wheal Fortune Mine, in the Gwennap mining district, heralding the arrival of mechanised mining.	The preacher and theologian John Wesley delivers his first sermon in Cornwall, and begins the long process of Methodist conversion in the county.

OLEG ALBINSKY / GETTY IMAGES ©

➡ Replica of the *Mayflower*

THE MINER'S LIFE
••

While many mine-owners grew fabulously rich on the proceeds of their investments, the miners' lot was an altogether different story. Most tinners worked for between eight and 12 hours a day, descending hundreds of metres underground via metal ladders or rickety gigs into a network of pitch-black tunnels and cramped shafts, where the temperature routinely exceeded 40°C (little wonder that many miners preferred to work naked in an effort to stave off the heat). Explosions and rockfalls were routine hazards, and many of the mineral ores were contaminated with poisonous chemicals such as arsenic and 'mica dust', which penetrated the miners' lungs. As a result, few miners lived much longer than their early 30s.

For this, most miners received a weekly wage of around 4s, or £10 a year – barely enough to keep a family above starvation level. Consequently the miners' wives and children were often put to work at the mines as well; women known as 'bal maidens' did most of the sorting or 'dressing' of the ore above ground, while children were often employed below ground to squeeze into narrow shafts the burly miners couldn't reach. By 1839 it's thought that about 7000 children were hard at work down Cornwall's mines.

his 'Puffing Devil' and first demonstrated to an amazed Cornish crowd in 1801. Another gifted Cornishman had also done much to improve the miners' lot: the genius chemist Humphry Davy (1778–1829), who invented the safety lamp (sometimes known as the Davy lamp) in 1815, which prevented the lethal underground explosions caused by flammable gases being ignited by the miners' candles.

The industry continued to flourish until the mid-19th century, when mineral lodes in many mines were already beginning to fail, turning them into 'knackt bals' (exhausted mines). Much worse was to follow: a great financial panic in 1866 bankrupted many investors, while the discovery of huge mineral deposits in other areas of the globe – particularly Australia, Mexico and the western US – led to a crash in commodity prices and forced the closure of huge numbers of mines. Faced with joblessness and starvation, entire communities upped sticks and emigrated to Australia, Mexico and the western United States (a phenomenon referred to as the 'Cornish Diaspora'). It's thought that around a third of Cornwall's mining community had emigrated overseas by the end of the 19th century.

While mining was on the wane, the region's maritime trade continued to expand. Plymouth consolidated its status as a naval base, and Falmouth established itself as the home of the Falmouth Packet Service, which carried mail and goods around the Empire between 1689 and 1850.

1768	1801	1833	1859
James Cook sets out from Plymouth to record the transit of Venus across the Pacific Ocean, but inadvertently discovers Tahiti, New Zealand and Australia.	Redruth-born Richard Trevithick demonstrates his groundbreaking steam locomotive on Fore St in Camborne.	Isambard Kingdom Brunel begins construction of the groundbreaking Great Western railway line from London. The final section to Penzance is eventually completed in 1867.	The Brunel-designed Royal Albert Bridge over the River Tamar connects Cornwall to Devon.

SMUGGLING

In the late 18th century, rising customs duty on imported goods (especially luxury items such as brandy, gin and tea) led to a huge growth in smuggling along the southwest coastline. Cornwall's remote coves were perfect hideouts for the enterprising 'free traders', and the sight of government 'preventive' boats in pursuit of smuggling vessels off the southern Cornish coastline became commonplace.

But the government operatives were often fighting a losing battle. Widespread opposition to the taxes, coupled with the lucrative returns that could be made from handling contraband goods, meant that collusion between the smugglers and onshore communities was widespread.

Smuggling rapidly became a hugely profitable industry – according to some estimates, as much as four-fifths of the tea drunk in England in the late 19th century had escaped official duty – and some smugglers, such as Harry Carter and Jack Rattenbury, became local celebrities. Harry Carter even published his own autobiography.

Many of the West Country's newly rich industrial magnates lavished fortunes on grand country estates, or embarked on ambitious architectural projects designed to showcase the wealth and prestige of the English elite. The foundation of many of the southwest's finest landscaped gardens can trace their origins back to this period.

As the Industrial Revolution rolled on, pioneering engineers set about reinventing Britain's infrastructure, constructing tunnels, canals and railways to link Britain's industrial bases. Foremost among them was Isambard Kingdom Brunel, one of England's brightest engineering minds, who built everything from groundbreaking bridges to the first great transatlantic steamers. Perhaps Brunel's greatest achievement was the development of the Great Western Railway, which provided the first rapid link between London and Bristol in 1841, and was later extended into Devon and Cornwall.

In the mid-18th century a pound of tea cost at least 8s – roughly the same as a bottle of champagne and the average weekly wage of a manual labourer.

The Early 20th Century

The railway also brought a new phenomenon to the southwest: tourism. Rising living standards and better wages, coupled with the expanding rail network, brought swathes of trippers from the region's smog-choked cities to the southwest's shores. Many towns were quick to seize on the opportunity: Torquay, Paignton, Ilfracombe and Penzance grew rapidly to cater for the booming tourist trade, adding a plethora of promenades, piers and seaside villas. Over a century later, tourism remains one of the southwest's biggest industries, accounting for around 20% of the region's total income.

1940–42	1951	1973	1998
Plymouth endures heavy bombing raids by the Luftwaffe, and sustains heavy damage. Exeter is later damaged during the Baedeker Blitz.	Dartmoor becomes the southwest's first designated national park, followed three years later by Exmoor.	Britain joins the EEC (European Economic Community), opening up the region's fishing grounds to foreign trawlers for the first time.	The closure of South Crofty, the last working mine in Cornwall, results in thousands of job losses and an end to over 4000 years of metal mining in Cornwall.

As with many corners of England, the southwest suffered heavily during the Great War. Many rural regiments recruited their men en masse from local villages, which meant that entire populations could be wiped out in the space of just a few hours of fighting.

The region did little better in WWII, when its ports and manufacturing bases became key targets for the Luftwaffe. Plymouth fared the worst, and by the end of the Blitz huge swathes of the city centre had been reduced to rubble, while Exeter had been heavily damaged during the so-called Baedeker Raids (which deliberately targeted historic cities in an effort to dent the British morale).

Later in the war, the deep-water harbours around Falmouth and the Carrick Roads played a pivotal role in the preparations for D-Day, and marked the embarkation point for millions of American troops setting sail for the Normandy beaches.

Modern Industry

The last 50 years has been a period of fluctuating fortunes for the southwest. Traditional industries such as fishing and mining have almost completely disappeared (since the closure of South Crofty near Camborne in 1998, there are now no working mines in the region), and only Brixham and Newlyn retain sizeable fishing fleets. But the area's naval associations have continued, and Falmouth and Devonport Dockyard in Plymouth have both retained their shipyards – with 15 dry-docks and 4 miles of waterfront, Devonport is the largest naval base in Western Europe.

But the region's great growth industry over recent years has been tourism. Depending on which statistic you listen to, tourism adds between £4.5 and £8 billion to the region's coffers every year, and in some areas over half of all jobs are related to the wider tourist industry. Despite tourism's dominance, the southwest is slowly making the transition towards a more diversified economy: culture, food and the environment are particularly strong areas of growth. Exciting developments such as the Eden Project, as well as the conferral of Unesco World Heritage status for the Jurassic Coast and the Cornwall and West Devon Mining Landscape, have helped refocus attention on the region's history, heritage and creativity.

POTTED HISTORY

The main online resource for the Unesco Cornwall and West Devon Mining World Heritage Site is www.cornish-mining.org.uk, which has a list of all the key sites and a good potted history.

2001	2006	2011	2012
Foot and mouth strikes the southwest. The Eden Project opens in a disused Cornish clay pit. The Jurassic Coast becomes the UK's first natural World Heritage Site.	The Cornwall and West Devon Mining Landscape is recognised by Unesco for its cultural and historical importance.	After a long campaign, the Cornish pasty finally receives 'protected geographical indication' (PGI) status.	On 19 May 2012, the official Olympic Torch arrives at Land's End before making its journey around Britain, arriving in London 70 days later to mark the start of the Games.

Food & Drink

The southwest is Britain's happening foodie hot-spot. Whisk together a superb array of local, seasonal, organic produce, atmospheric eateries and a scattering of celebrity chefs. The result? The perfect culinary storm. But dishes here do more than fill bellies. They also bridge the disconnect between producer and consumer. Because food eaten on farms, vineyards and fish quays is different. You can see where it comes from, you can taste where it comes from – something no fancy flavourings can replicate.

Foodie Hubs

Padstow *Kick-started Cornwall's culinary renaissance.*

Torquay *Michelin-starred eatery; top-class fish.*

St Ives *Quaint harbour; imaginative food.*

Dartmouth *Pretty port; fine dining.*

Celebrity & Campaigning Chefs

When **Rick Stein** opened a restaurant in the quaint Cornish fishing village of Padstow in 1975, few realised he was about to transform a culinary landscape. By 1995, Stein's *Taste of the Sea* TV series had placed Cornwall firmly in the foodie spotlight; his show *Food Heroes* brought local produce to mainstream attention.

Others followed. **Hugh Fearnley-Whittingstall** set up River Cottage on the Devon–Dorset border in 1998; now you can dine at his farm River Cottage HQ (p61), his canteens in east Devon (p61) and Plymouth (p106), and learn how to grow vegetables, make bread and butcher meat.

Along with creating a small-screen lifestyle idyll, Fearnley-Whittingstall is also pushing for real change; 24,300 people signed up to Fish Fight, backing calls to cut the number of dead fish being thrown back into the seas.

So, crucially, the region's celebrity chefs are also campaigning chefs. **Jamie Oliver**, who battled for quality school dinners, brought Fifteen to a Newquay beach in 2006. This gourmet restaurant teaches underprivileged youngsters how to cook, and batches of apprentice chefs graduate each year. This is cooking as a community project.

High-profile eateries have a big impact on local towns. Stein has four eateries, three B&Bs and a hotel in Padstow, prompting critics to dub the port 'Padstein'. Others point to the jobs big-name chefs bring to areas badly in need of them.

And then there are chefs, famed in foodie circles, who dish up superb food: **Michael Caines** (Exeter and Gidleigh Park); **Nathan Outlaw** (Rock and Looe); **Paul Ainsworth** (Padstow) and **Mitch Tonks** (Dartmouth).

Local & Organic Produce

In Devon and Cornwall slow food is making fast progress. A whopping 27% of the UK's registered organic producers are southwest based, 11% more than the next biggest area, Wales. And all over the two counties producers and eateries are promoting the slow food ethos of placing importance on taste, quality and the production process itself.

The BBC 2012 Farmer of the Year, Guy Watson, has been pioneering organic food at **Riverford Farm** (www.riverford.co.uk), near Totnes, for more than 20 years. Now one of the UK's biggest organic delivery schemes, its innovative, on-farm field kitchen (p82) sees you eat produce harvested to order from just outside. Other top delivery schemes are the **Cornish Food Box Company** (www.thecornishfoodboxcompany.co.uk) and **Cornish Food Market** (www.cornishfoodmarket.co.uk).

Staples & Specialities

Devon and Cornwall's specialities speak eloquently of the counties' pasts, and shape present cultural identity. The Cornish pasty is a miner's lunch turned cultural icon, fish pies evoke desperately hard times and cider conjures up a subsistence economy.

Cornish Pasties

In the 13th century, these crinkly-edged half-moons of carbohydrate consisted of vegetables wrapped in pastry – many experts say originally no meat was actually involved. This creation delivered a portable, durable two-course lunch, and over the centuries, pasties became a staple of tin-mining communities. Those working underground in grim, arsenic-laced conditions didn't eat the crimped seam; instead it allowed them to hold their food without contaminating it.

When waves of impoverished Cornish miners emigrated in the mid-1800s, they took their pasty techniques with them, particularly to Australia and the US. Today, you can still pop out for a pasty in places as far from Cornwall as Adelaide and Arizona.

Annually, pasty production employs thousands of people, and brings millions of pounds into Cornwall's economy. In 2011 the savoury was finally awarded protected status by the European Commission, meaning only pasties with the following characteristics can be called 'Cornish pasties':

➡ Crimped on one side, never on top

➡ Must have at least 12.5% meat

➡ Must include swede, potato and onion, and a light peppery seasoning

➡ Has no flavourings or additives

➡ Must be made in Cornwall

For more, see the Cornish Pasty Association (www.cornishpastyassociation.co.uk).

Regional Oddities & Delicacies

Laverbread Patties of seaweed, oats and bacon, from north Devon and Exmoor.

Salcombe Smokies A south Devon speciality of richly flavoured, smoked mackerel.

Samphire Traditional regional delicacy; a coastal plant with a hint of asparagus.

Saffron Buns Yellow Cornish fruit cake; saffron is the legacy of the Phoenician tin trade.

Stargazy Pie Fish heads protrude from pastry in this communal Cornish pie.

Ice Cream Look out for Ottery Valley Dairy in east Devon, Roskilly's (p249) in St Keverne, Jelbert's (p240) in Newlyn, Salcombe Dairy in south Devon, Moomaid (p224) in Zennor and Helsett (p197) in Boscastle.

Top Eateries

Gidleigh Park (Chagford) Devon's best.

Restaurant Nathan Outlaw (Rock) Cornwall's finest.

Paul Ainsworth at No 6 (Padstow) Cornish cuisine.

Elephant (Torquay) Memorable Devon eatery.

FOOD & DRINK STAPLES & SPECIALITIES

DON'T MISS FOODIE EXPERIENCES

Wine Perfect your palate just yards from the vines at the region's beguiling wineries.

Picnics Watch from picturesque cliffs as the sun sets over the sea, surfers and your starter.

Rustic pubs Drink in centuries of history, culture and top cider and beer.

Seafood Watch fish being landed, then dine on gourmet delights or a super-tasty crab roll.

Cream teas Just-baked scones, homemade jam and so-thick-you-can-stand-your-spoon-up-in-it clotted cream.

Cream Teas

If the Cornish claim pasties as their own, Devonians do the same for cream teas. Some historians date the sweet snack back to the 10th century, when monks fed bread, cream and jam to workers repairing a Devon abbey after a Viking raid.

At its best a cream tea is a delightful combination of light scones, tasty homemade jam, a steaming brew and utterly gooey clotted cream. Locally there's heated debate about which to spread first: the jam or the cream. The Cornish plump for jam; Devonians cream.

Fish

The fruits of the southwest's seas provide a tasty, tangible link between food and place. Eating fish that's been landed a few yards away is special – still in buckets, it's sometimes even carried past diners by waterproofs-clad fishermen.

Rejoice in these negligible food miles in the ports of Newlyn, Falmouth, Padstow and Mevagissey in Cornwall; and Brixham, Torquay and Dartmouth in Devon. Some 40-plus species are still hauled in locally. Highlights include superb oysters, mussels, crab and lobster, line-caught sea bass and mackerel, and the freshest monkfish, John Dory and Dover sole.

Then there's the classic fish and chips. Wrapped in paper, dripping with vinegar and scattered with salt, it can be surprisingly good, especially in ports where the day's catch ends up in batter.

Cheese

Creamy, tangy, soft and hard, the southwest offers cheese lovers countless slices of gourmet heaven. Look out for these highlights:

Quickes Mouth-puckeringly strong cheddar, made near Exeter.

Cornish Yarg Gentle, nettle-wrapped and semi-hard.

Brie Try Cornish Country Larder, and Sharpham (Devon).

Blue Cheeses (aka the 'Blues') Exmoor (cow), Devon (cow), Harbourne (goat) and Beenleigh (sheep).

Cornish Blue A Gorgonzola-esque, gooey offering from the fringes of Bodmin Moor.

Davidstow Creamy, award-winning cheddar, with a 60-year heritage.

Cookery Courses

River Cottage (p61) Hugh Fearnley-Whittingstall's east Devon HQ. Learn butchery, baking or allotment gardening.

Fat Hen (p235) Wild food foraging in Cornwall's rugged far-western tip.

Padstow Seafood School (www.rickstein.com) Rick Stein's kitchen classroom.

Ashburton Cookery School (www.ashburtoncookeryschool.co.uk) An award-winning school offering 40 courses.

Etherington Meats (www.etherington-meats.co.uk) Teaches butchery.

Where to Eat & Drink

Bigger towns and cities have the widest variety of eateries and fly more diverse culinary flags. Booking is recommended at the more popular restaurants, especially at weekends in summer – at Rick Stein's Seafood Restaurant tables can be reserved a year in advance.

Pubs range from old-fashioned city boozers to time-warp village locals where the welcome is genuine, the fire is real and that horse brass has hung on that hook for centuries. Regional pub grub encompasses deeply satisfying cheese-rich ploughman's lunches and complex gastropub fare. Expect to pay around £8 for standard bar food, and from £13 for fancier dishes.

Low Food-Mile Eateries

Riverford Field Kitchen (Totnes) Exquisite meat and veg.

Fat Hen (West Cornwall) Wild-food foraging.

River Cottage (East Devon) Fearnley-Whittingstall's HQ.

Locals' Tips

Seahorse (Dartmouth) Charcoal-roasted seafood.

Ben's Cornish Kitchen (Penzance) Classy, unpretentious cooking.

Jon's Bistro (Newquay) Rustic cuisine.

Gorton's (Tavistock) Classical Dartmoor dishes.

Sloop Inn (p225), St Ives

Vegetarians & Vegans

In general vegetarians should encounter enough possibilities to make their stay enjoyable. As ever, the cities and bigger towns will cater to their needs better; in some rural and coastal areas, meat and fish dominate menus.

Predictably vegans fare worse except in larger towns and cities, but ethnic restaurants and counter-culture hubs such as Totnes and Falmouth boost prospects considerably.

Drinks

Devon & Cornwall Breweries

Beer Engine (p54) Devon microbrewery-cum-pub beside a railway; hence the brews, Rail Ale and Sleeper Heavy.

Blue Anchor Inn (www.spingoales.com; 50 Coinagehall St, Helston) They've been brewing Spingo ale in Helston for six centuries; ask at the bar to see the vats.

Dartmoor (www.dartmoorbrewery.co.uk) Set just yards from Dartmoor Prison, it's famous for its sweet-finishing Jail Ale.

Harbour (www.harbourbrewing.com) North Cornwall–based contemporary craft brewery; try their caramel-meets-toffee Amber Ale, or the citrusy India Pale.

Keltek (www.keltekbrewery.co.uk) Cornish offerings include mild Even Keel (3.4%) and superstrong Beheaded (7.6%).

Sharp's (www.sharpsbrewery.co.uk) This Rock-based brewery produces Doom Bar and ales inspired by Rick Stein's much-missed terrier: Chalky's Bark and Chalky's Bite.

Rebel (www.rebelbrewing.co.uk) Artisan real ales from Penryn (near Falmouth) include a dark, cloudy wheat beer, Nightshade, and the chocolate-vanilla Mexi-Cocoa.

Top Pubs

Turk's Head (Isles of Scilly) Britain's most southerly pub.

Warren House (Postbridge) Dartmoor institution.

Pandora (near Falmouth) Waterside smugglers' inn.

PLYMOUTH GIN

The Royal Navy ferried Plymouth Gin around the world in countless officers' messes, helping turn it into a leading global cocktail brand.

Skinners (www.skinnersbrewery.com) Truro operation with cheekily named tipples: Cornish Knocker, Ginger Tosser and Keel Over.

St Austell (www.staustellbrewery.co.uk) Runs 170 southwest pubs; brews Tribute, Proper Job and Tinners.

Cider

The southwest is rightly famous for ciders that conjure images of golden summers and hazy days. Centuries ago no farm would have been without its orchard; apples were pressed and then fermented to form the 'scrumpy', which was often drunk instead of water; then the H_2O was more toxic than the alcohol. Dazed but delighted labourers were paid partly in this golden currency – an average four-pint (2.25L) daily allowance increasing to a staggering eight pints during hay-making.

This deeply flavoured elixir was evocatively dubbed 'wine of wild orchards' by the writer Laurie Lee. The apple names alone are enough to give you a warm, fuzzy glow: Slack ma Girdle, Sops in Wine and Quench.

Excellent, small-scale producers include southeast Cornwall–based Cornish Orchards; south Devon–based Luscombe; and Helford Creek, near Helston.

Wine

The mild southwest weather ensures good conditions for vineyards, and sipping a chilled glass of white on a sun-drenched terrace, overlooking rows of vines feels more like Chablis than the southwest. These wineries are worth seeking out.

Sharpham (p77) Set in 200 stunning, south Devon hectares, wine ranges from £11 for a decent off-dry white to £23 for a rich red Pinot Noir-Precoce blend.

Camel Valley (p152) A north Cornwall award-winner; try its aromatic and appropriately named Bacchus (£13).

Polgoon (☑01736-333946; www.cornishwine.co.uk; Rosehill, Penzance) Near Penzance, produces award-winning still rosé and a champagne-style pear drink.

Yearlstone (p52) Take a tour, then eat and drink beside these east Devon vines.

Gin

Plymouth Gin (p101) is the oldest producing distillery in the world. For 200 years no British Royal Navy vessel left port without its own supply of the brand, helping it spread to drinking dens and the world's first cocktail bars. Today distillery tours allow you to sniff botanicals and carry out taste tests.

The Arts

Whether it's the unique quality of light, the landscapes or the sense of freedom, there's something about England's southwest that's proved irresistible for creative practitioners for decades. The region attracts waves of painters and sculptors; writers draw inspiration from West Country surroundings; theatre-makers revel in innovative spaces; filmmakers delight in cinematic surroundings; and ranks of enthused festival organisers ensure a packed arts calendar. Which means by exploring Devon and Cornwall's creative heritage, you get a richer visit today.

Painting & Sculpture

The Early Years

Cornwall's role as artistic magnet arguably began when JMW Turner toured the southwest in 1811 while painting watercolours for the engravings *Picturesque Views on the Southern Coast of England.* Turner travelled widely, but it was under Cornwall's wide-open skies that his passion for dreamy, ethereal landscapes found fullest expression. Many feel the artist's West Country sojourn played an important part in his enduring fascination with light, colour and form; the sketchbooks and canvases he produced there provide tantalising glimpses of his later, quasi-abstract experiments.

For Turner, though, it wasn't all about views. An observer of contemporary society, many of his paintings provide an insight into early-19th-century Cornish life. *St Mawes at the Pilchard Season* (1812) depicts a chaotic harbour filled with pilchard boats and bustling villagers, backed by a St Mawes Castle bathed in Turneresque sunlight. It's a moody contrast of social realism and romantic scenery and is intriguing both in terms of Turner's own work and the next major artistic movement to develop in Cornwall.

Impressionism

The Great Western Railway edging west of the Tamar in 1877 really put Cornwall on the artistic map. Now painters had relatively easy access to the county's landscapes, and they arrived in ever-increasing numbers as the century progressed.

The Impressionist movement had developed in Normandy and Brittany as Monet, Pissarro, Dégas and Eugène Boudin perfected painting *en plein air* (on location, rather than working from sketches in a studio), a technique designed to capture the immediacy of a scene. It encouraged others to travel to the southwest, among them the German-born artist Walter Sickert and the American James McNeill Whistler.

The Newlyn School

While some artists dabbled with the colours and forms of Impressionism, others took a markedly more figurative approach. In the early 1880s, a group of artists settled around the fishing port of Newlyn, spearheaded by Birmingham-born Walter Langley, Dubliner Stanhope Forbes and the Lincolnshire artist Frank Bramley. Following in the footsteps of the naturalistic French Barbizon School, the Newlyn artists set out to depict the day to day reality of people's lives in a representational way.

Top Galleries

Tate St Ives (St Ives)

Bernard Leach Pottery (St Ives)

The Barbara Hepworth Museum (St Ives)

Newlyn Art Gallery & Exchange (Penzance)

Penlee House (Penzance)

Courses

St Ives School of Painting

Dartington International Summer School (Totnes)

Newlyn School of Art

East Devon Art Academy (Sidmouth)

FESTIVALS

Port Eliot (p191) Uber-cool fiesta of literature, music and funky fun, centred around a Cornish stately home.

Ways With Words (p79) Top quality lit fest, at a gorgeous south Devon medieval estate.

Fowey (www.foweyfestival.com) Eclectic mix of literature and music, theatre and walks in this pretty harbour town.

Cornwall Film Festival (www.cornwallfilmfestival.com) Annual celebration of Cornish and international movie making.

Dartington International Summer School (p79) Month-long feast of musical styles ranging from early music and choral, via piano, to junk.

Animated Exeter (p48) Films include stop frame, puppetry and comics, plus talks and courses, too.

St Ives (p223) A September celebration of music and the arts.

They became particularly fascinated by Newlyn's fishermen, and documented their lives in close detail. Some canvases depicted such everyday tasks as net repair, sail rigging or fish sales on the quayside, while others exploited the natural drama and pathos of the fishermen's lot: poverty, hardship, storms and the ever-present danger of shipwrecks. Among the most characteristic paintings of the period are Stanhope Forbes' *The Health of the Bride*, depicting the marriage of a young sailor and his wife in a Newlyn inn; and Bramley's *A Hopeless Dawn*, which shows a distraught wife receiving the news that her husband has been lost at sea.

A lighter side of the Newlyn School is represented by artists such as Norman Garstin, whose *The Rain It Raineth Every Day* depicts a typically rainy scene on Penzance promenade and is now among the most prized possessions of the Penlee House Museum and Gallery in Penzance.

By 1884 there were at least 30 artists working either in Newlyn or the nearby towns of St Ives, Lelant and Falmouth. In 1889 Forbes and his wife Elizabeth formally established the first Newlyn School of Artists; a second colony of artists later developed in the nearby cove of Lamorna, forming the Lamorna Group (often referred to as the later Newlyn School).

The work of many of the key Newlyn and Lamorna artists – particularly Forbes, Bramley, Henry Scott-Tuke, Samuel John (Lamorna) Birch, Thomas Cooper Gotch and Walter Langley, as well as female artists Laura Johnson, Dod Procter and Elizabeth Forbes – became highly influential and prized, with many of the artists exhibiting their work in major London venues such as the Royal Academy and the National Gallery. Collectively they produced some of the West Country's best-known, and best-loved, works of art.

Eclectic Art

Verity (Ilfracombe) Damien Hirst's towering figure.

Lenkiewicz (Plymouth) Striking murals.

Tremenheere (Penzance) Contemporary sculpture; exotic gardens.

Beryl Cook (Plymouth) Pub-based cheery art.

The St Ives Schools

The next generation of artists reacted powerfully against the figurative concerns of their predecessors. The advent of modernism in the 1920s opened up the canvas far beyond the confines of representational painting – soon Cornwall became identified with a much more radical style of art.

Links between St Ives and the avant-garde go back to the mid-1920s, when the ground-breaking potter Bernard Leach established his first workshop in St Ives, in partnership with the Japanese ceramics artist Shoji Hamada. Leach was fascinated with the functions, shapes and forms of Oriental pottery and went on to develop a highly influential style, fusing Eastern philosophies with Western materials.

By the mid-1920s, the painters Cedric Morris, Christopher 'Kit' Wood and Ben Nicholson had followed in Leach's wake. During one visit to St Ives, Wood and Nicholson stumbled across the work of an entirely self-taught Cornish fisherman and painter, Alfred Wallis, whose naive style – which paid little heed to conventional rules of perspective, scale or composition – proved a powerful influence on the modernist artists, many of whom were seeking a return to the more primitive style of art that Wallis' work seemed to embody.

Within a few years Wallis found himself surrounded by a new artistic community that established itself in St Ives throughout the 1930s and early 1940s. At the forefront of this new movement were Nicholson and his wife, the young sculptor Barbara Hepworth; soon they were joined by their friend, the Russian sculptor Naum Gabo, a key figure of the Constructivist movement.

The three artists began developing experimental abstract work that echoed the post-war modernist movements and were inspired by West Cornwall's shapes, light and landscapes. Hepworth, in particular, became fascinated with her adopted home, and her distinctive combination of stone, metal and sinuous forms was clearly influenced by the rugged Cornish landscape and its industrial remains and ancient monuments.

Attracted by St Ives' burgeoning reputation as a centre for abstract art, a new wave of exciting young artists, including Wilhelmina Barns-Graham, Terry Frost, Patrick Heron, Roger Hilton and Peter Lanyon, helped consolidate the town's position as a hub of creativity and experimentation throughout the 1950s and '60s.

Recent Artists

Half a century on, west Cornwall remains an important centre for British art: Penwith claims a higher concentration of artists than anywhere else in the UK, outside London's East End. Among the best-known is St Just-based Kurt Jackson, who is famous for his expressive, often environmental-themed landscapes. He's also been artist-in-residence at the Eden Project.

The abstract experiments of the 1950s and '60s continues in the work of contemporary Cornish artists, including Trevor Bell, Noel Betowski and Jeremy Annear. Meanwhile, in Devon, Damien Hirst is linked to Ilfracombe. *Verity*, his 20m statue of a naked, pregnant, half-flayed woman, towers over the harbour mouth and his installations dot the walls of his restaurant, 11 The Quay (p140).

Literature

Devon and Cornwall have inspired countless writers. Often they reflect the counties' characters in their work, and sometimes specific locations in their books can still be tracked down today. Devon-born crime-writing legend Agatha Christie wove many local places into her novels. You can also visit her holiday home near Dartmouth, Greenway (p83).

Another West Country writer inextricably linked with the landscape she loved is Fowey-based Daphne du Maurier. Best known for romantic, dramatic novels such as *Rebecca*, she also wrote the short story that became the Alfred Hitchcock film *The Birds*. Cornwall's bleak moors and tree-fringed creeks feature strongly in her writings.

Other southwest literary connections include the popular poet and broadcaster Sir John Betjeman, who is buried near his Cornish home at Trebetherick on the River Camel; and the poet Charles Causley, who lived in and was inspired by west Cornwall. Richard Blackmore's 17th-century epic *Lorna Doone* is based on Exmoor; its atmosphere infuses the book. Similarly, Henry Williamson featured the landscape of his north Devon home in *Tarka the Otter*. And then there's Arthur Conan Doyle's *The Hound of the Baskervilles*, set on, and still deeply evocative of, Dartmoor.

Local Reads

....

Jamaica Inn (Bodmin Moor) Daphne du Maurier

....

The Hound of the Baskervilles (Dartmoor) Arthur Conan Doyle

....

Evil Under the Sun (Burgh Island) Agatha Christie

....

Lorna Doone (Exmoor) RD Blackmore.

FILM & TV LOCATIONS

War Horse (2011) Steven Spielberg shot his WWI epic amid Dartmoor's tors.

Alice in Wonderland (2010) Tim Burton filmed his Disney fantasy at Antony House, in East Cornwall.

Doc Martin (2004–) The north Cornish fishing village of Port Isaac doubles as Portwenn, home to grumpy medic Dr Ellingham (Martin Clunes).

Sense and Sensibility (1995) Ang Lee's version (starring Emma Thompson and Kate Winslet) was filmed at Plymouth's Saltram House.

Summer in February (2013) Dominic Cooper, Dan Stevens and the southwest Cornish coast star in this *plein-air* period drama about local painter Alfred Munnings.

Hound of the Baskervilles (1965) The BBC's classic version was filmed in the wilderness that inspired it: Dartmoor.

Theatre

Theatres

Minack
(Porthcurno) Cliff-side amphitheatre.

Drum *(Plymouth)*
Award-winning studio space.

Asylum
(St Agnes) Knee-high's magical, nomadic space.

Bike Shed *(Exeter)*
Profiles new writing.

Despite being 200 odd miles from London's West End, the turnover of the **Theatre Royal Plymouth** (p107) is only bettered by the National Theatre and the Royal Shakespeare Company (RSC). That's down in part to its innovative TR2 production centre, which features facilities for set, costume, prop-making, and stage-sized rehearsal spaces. It helps attract world premieres (such as Matthew Bourne's *Edward Scissorhands*) and secures work to produce key shows (*Legally Blonde* and *Shrek* for the West End, and *Mary Poppins,* the Australian tour). The theatre's award-winning Drum performance space pioneers new writing; highlights include *Love, Love, Love*; *The Empire* and *pool (no water)*.

In the **Minack Theatre** (p234), Cornwall has a stunning, unique performance space. Cut into the cliffs near Land's End, this amphitheater was started by indomitable Rowena Cade in the 1930s. The season runs from June to September and features touring and local productions.

Cornish-based theatre company **Kneehigh** (www.kneehigh.co.uk) is one of the most innovative and exciting in the UK. Joyful, anarchic and acclaimed productions include *Tristan & Yseult*, *Nights at the Circus*, *A Matter of Life and Death* (at the National), and *Cymbeline* (in association with the RSC). Also look out for their pop-up theatre, the Asylum, near St Agnes.

Environment

From sea-battered coast to rolling countryside, the southwest's landscapes are astonishingly varied, and it's a wonderful place to explore if you're an outdoors lover. To appreciate it at its best, it's worth getting off the beaten track – cycling along the backlanes or hiking along the coast path are both great ways of seeing parts of the counties that most visitors never reach.

Landscapes

Much of the West Country's landscape looks pristine, but in fact it's been worked and managed since the first human settlers arrived here some 10,000 years ago. Much of the peninsula was once covered by dense forest, but this was steadily cleared to make way for agriculture and industry. By the 19th century large swathes of Devon and Cornwall had effectively become an industrial landscape, pockmarked by slate and china clay quarries, tin and copper mines, and numerous slag mounds and spoil heaps. Though much of the old industry has disappeared, you can still see traces of it in the old mining country around St Agnes, Porthtowan, Portreath and Camborne, where shattered rock and industrial spoil lies just a few inches beneath the topsoil.

The coastline is undoubtedly the region's most distinctive landscape, with a unique combination of sandy beaches, rockpools, dunes, tidal marshes, estuaries and clifftops. Generally speaking, the Atlantic-facing north coast tends to be starker and wilder, characterised by high granite cliffs and large sandy beaches, while the southern coast is gentler, with fields, meadows and valleys replacing the lofty cliffs. The south coast is also notable for several large tidal estuaries that punctuate the shoreline, including the Helford, Fal, Fowey, Tamar and Dart. These sheltered creeks harbour unique subtropical microclimates that allow unusual plants, flowers and trees to flourish, and provide the perfect location for many of the region's great estates and landscaped gardens.

The southwest's other distinctive habitat is its moorland – notably the moors of Dartmoor, Exmoor, Bodmin and Penwith. These high upland moors are all located on the massive spine of granite that runs directly down the centre of Devon and Cornwall, formed by volcanic processes around 300 million years ago. This hard granite is much more erosion-resistant than other forms of rock, and has worn away more slowly than the surrounding landscape, leaving behind the barren peaks and strangely shaped rock formations known locally as tors. Incidentally, the same volcanic activity was also responsible for forming the rich mineral deposits that later underpinned Devon and Cornwall's mining industries.

National Parks & AONBs

The region has two designated national parks: Dartmoor, founded in 1951; and Exmoor, founded in 1954. Britain's National Parks operate in a slightly differently way to those in many other countries: rather than operating as strict nature reserves, they are run more as areas of environmental protection and natural conservation, where human activity is

GEOTHERMAL ENERGY

Cornwall's granite rocks are rich in natural radioactive isotopes, including thorium, potassium and uranium, leading to speculation that they could possibly be used as a source of geothermal energy.

allowed to coexist with areas of natural beauty in a managed way. Agriculture, forestry, residential housing and even some heavy industry (such as quarrying) are all theoretically allowed within the parks' boundaries, but strict rules on planning, land use and development ensure that the landscape remains largely unspoilt.

The parks are run by government-funded National Park Authorities who manage the landscape, ensure the welfare of the wildlife and natural environment, and oversee visitor activities within the parks' boundaries.

The area also has a number of AONBs (Areas of Outstanding Natural Beauty), which are protected in a similar way to the national parks, although the rules and regulations governing development, land usage and environmental protection are less rigorous. There are also many smaller nature reserves and SSSIs (Sites of Special Scientific Interest), established to protect specific habitats such as meadows, riverbanks, reed-beds, moors and mudflats.

Large sections of the southwest coastline are owned by the National Trust, an independent charity that manages many important sites on behalf of the general public.

Wildlife

Animals

The region's most famous residents are probably the miniature ponies that roam wild across many of its moors. Best-known is the Dartmoor pony, a stubby-legged, shaggy-maned steed that rarely grows much above 12 hands (roughly 4ft) high. Its cousins on Bodmin Moor and Exmoor are often slightly larger. Despite their diminutive dimensions, these hardy little ponies are astonishingly strong, and were originally bred as pack animals and beasts of burden.

Red deer are also fairly widespread on Exmoor and Dartmoor, although they're notoriously skittish creatures, so your best chance to see one is probably on a wildlife safari.

The region's wilder inhabitants include badgers, hares, many types of bat and, of course, several million rabbits. Foxes are also widespread, and since February 2005 have been protected (along with stags) by a ban on the traditional country pursuit of hunting with horses and hounds (much to the delight of animal activists and much to the chagrin of many country folk).

Along the riverbanks you might glimpse the odd stoat, vole or, if you're very lucky, a playful otter, which is slowly recovering after decades of decline. Sadly, the once-common native red squirrel hasn't been so fortunate – it has almost disappeared over the last 50 years thanks to the introduction of the more aggressive grey squirrel from the United States.

The hedgerows, coastlines and meadows of the southwest are also great for spotting butterflies and dragonflies – some of the more common varieties you might see include the tortoiseshell, hedge brown, red admiral and painted lady, as well as more elusive species such as the orange tip and silver-washed fritillary. Rarest of all is the Large Blue, which became extinct from the British Isles in 1979 but has since been re-introduced to five areas around the southwest.

Look out, too, for grass snakes, slow worms and adders (Britain's only poisonous snake), especially on areas of exposed moor and heathland during warm weather.

Bird Life

The southwest is a dream come true for twitchers. For a quick fix the coast is the best place to start: you're bound to catch sight of the most common birds, including the razorbill, guillemot, gannet, cormorant and, of course, one of several types of seagull. Most common of all is the herring gull,

JURASSIC COAST

The Jurassic Coast in Dorset and East Devon is one of the fastest-eroding stretches of coastline in Britain, making it a popular spot for fossil-hunters, who often find archaeological treasures revealed by the receding cliffs.

THE CORNISH CHOUGH

You won't have any trouble spotting a seagull around the coastline of Cornwall, but you'll be extremely lucky to catch sight of the elusive Cornish chough (pronounced *chuff*). A member of the crow family distinguished by its jet-black plumage and bright orange beak, this elegant bird is an enduring symbol of Cornish culture – legend has it that the chough embodies the spirit of King Arthur, and the bird even features on Cornwall's coat of arms.

The chough was once a common sight around the county's shores, but suffered a huge decline in the 20th century, probably due to intensive farming and a general decline in habitat. Happily, the first pair of choughs to nest in Cornwall for over 50 years arrived in 2002, and the success of recent breeding programs has led to hopes that the chough will again establish itself along the county's clifftops. The Lizard is one of the best places for chough-spotting.

distinguished by its grey plumage, light-coloured feet and black wingtips; if you're being harassed by a gull for a bite of your pasty or you've just been blessed from above, chances are it's thanks to a herring gull. Less common are the slightly darker black-backed gull and the smaller common gull (which, despite its name, actually isn't all that common). Gulls of all descriptions have become something of a nuisance in recent years thanks to the attentions of unsuspecting tourists and the growth in rubbish tips and street litter – whatever you do, don't feed them, as it only makes them bolder and certainly won't win you any friends among the locals.

There are also puffin colonies on the Isles of Scilly, Long Island near Boscastle and, in smaller numbers, on Lundy.

Inland, you might catch sight of birds of prey hovering above farmland and stretches of open countryside. Species to look out for include the sparrowhawk, kestrel and, most common of all, the buzzard. By night keep an ear cocked for the hoot of the barn owl or tawny owl in remote countryside.

River estuaries are also good for a spot of birdwatching, especially for wading birds, and various species of duck, grebe and goose. The estuaries around the Tamar and Exe Rivers in Devon, Dawlish Warren near Exmouth and Hayle in Cornwall promise especially rich pickings for twitchers.

West country beaches is a useful free app that covers the region's best sands. You can download it from www.thebeach-app.co.uk.

Sea Life

The most spectacular visitor to southwest waters is the basking shark, (the second-largest fish in the ocean after the whale shark), which can often be seen off the coast of Cornwall in the summer months. Despite its fearsome bulk – the average shark measures between 6m and 8m long – it's entirely harmless to humans, sustaining itself entirely on plankton and other forms of microscopic marine life. Some other species of shark, including the mako, porbeagle and blue shark, are rather less friendly, although you'll be unlikely to encounter them unless you happen to have hauled them up from the deep on a sea fishing trip.

Grey seals are another common sight along the southwest coastline. You might occasionally catch sight of a grey head or two bobbing in the waters off the Devon and Cornish coasts, but most of the region's seal colonies tend to cluster on small offshore islands, especially around the coasts of Cornwall and Scilly.

Sightings of dolphins and porpoises are rarer, but you might find them accompanying you if you take a boat trip. The best places for land-based sightings are generally the far westerly coastlines around Land's End, Cape Cornwall and West Penwith.

Jellyfish occasionally venture into southwest waters in the warmer months, and although poisonous or stinging species are unusual, it's best to steer clear if you see one.

Environmental Issues

Water pollution is obviously top of the environmental agenda. A few decades ago some of the region's beaches were in a sorry state, and it wasn't uncommon to find raw sewage and industrial effluents being pumped straight into the sea just a few miles from the most popular swimming spots. Happily, thanks to pressure put on local government by environmental NGOs and local campaign groups such as **Surfers Against Sewage** (www.sas.org.uk), the southwest has cleaned up its act and now boasts some of the most spotless coastline anywhere in Britain. Sixteen beaches in Devon and five in Cornwall currently hold the coveted Blue Flag award for water quality (for a full list, visit www.blueflag.org.uk). Dogs are banned on many beaches between April and October.

Other forms of pollution have proved more difficult to tackle. The region's agricultural industry has caused ongoing problems with pesticides and farming chemicals (especially nitrates and phosphates), which can seep into the water table, pollute river courses, poison fish and cause algal bloom. The problem is exacerbated by heavy rain, which washes topsoil into the rivers and seas.

Cornwall Wildlife Trust (www.cornwall-wildlifetrust.org.uk) manages many beauty spots and wildlife reserves across Cornwall. Devon has its own sister organisation.

Coastal erosion is another issue in many areas, especially along the southern coastline of Devon and Dorset, where landslips and rockfalls are a fact of life. Recent heavy rains and severe winter storms have accelerated erosion in many areas, and even caused several areas of the coast path to literally disappear into the sea.

Traffic and air pollution are also growing headaches, especially during peak holiday periods. The vast majority of visitors – around 80% – travel to the region by car, with all the attendant problems of parking, pollution and traffic jams. It's not always the easiest option, but you might find you have a much less stressful time if you leave the car at home and investigate some other ways of exploring the region: bikes, buses and branch railways are all useful for dodging the tailbacks on a hot summer's day.

Survival Guide

DIRECTORY A–Z....282

Accommodation........ 282

Climate................ 284

Dangers &
Annoyances............ 284

Discount Cards......... 285

Electricity 285

Food 285

Gay & Lesbian
Travellers 285

Health................. 286

Internet Access......... 286

Maps.................. 286

Money................. 286

Opening Hours 287

Telephone 287

Toilets................. 287

Tourist
Information 287

Travellers with
Disabilities............. 287

TRANSPORT.......288

GETTING
THERE & AWAY 288

Air 288

Bus 289

Car & Motorcycle....... 289

Train 289

Sea 289

GETTING AROUND...... 290

Air 290

Bicycle 290

Boat 290

Bus 290

Car & Motorcycle........291

Taxi 292

Train 292

Directory A–Z

Accommodation

B&Bs & Guesthouses

The great British B&B (bed and breakfast) is thriving across the West Country, ranging from larger, modern professional affairs to eccentric old-fashioned enclaves. Styles vary: there's crisp white linen in smart city streets, rustic rooms in remote villages, and clashing carpets in bucket n' spade resorts.

Some still have shared bathrooms but most are en suite (although bathrooms are often tiny). Most still serve the kind of belt-busting breakfast that means you don't have to eat till the evening.

Across the region, prices vary wildly. Expect to pay anything from £50 for a very basic double with shared bathroom, to £130 for a double, en suite room in a smarter guesthouse. Single travellers normally face a premium of anything between 25-50 percent.

Some further B&B tips:

➡ Booking by phone can be cheaper because some B&Bs have to pay an online transaction fee to third-party websites.

➡ Advance bookings are wise, and are essential in busy places during peak periods and in small villages.

➡ Some B&Bs don't take credit or debit cards and instead require cash or cheque.

➡ Rates rise at busy times, but some places cut prices for longer stays.

➡ When booking, check where the B&B actually is. In country areas postal addresses include the nearest town, which may be 20 miles away.

Bunkhouses & Camping Barns

Devon and Cornwall's bunkhouses and camping barns are basic, budget places to bed down for the night. They're usually in gorgeously rural locations and aimed primarily at hikers and cyclists.

Individual places vary but bunkhouses tend to have more facilities. Expect dorm style accommodation plus bathroom and cooking facilities, but you'll still need to bring a sleeping bag. Camping barns are more primitive – often just a sleeping platform, cold running water and a flush toilet – so bring all your camping kit except the tent.

Rates for both categories are around £8 to £15. Many are run by the Youth Hostels Association (YHA), which has five camping barns in Devon and Exmoor. The YHA also has two bunkhouses in Devon and Exmoor, and one bunkhouse in Cornwall. Other barns are independent – we provide details in the On The Road chapters.

Useful information sources:

Dartmoor National Park Authority (www.dartmoor.gov.uk)

Exmoor National Park Authority (www.exmoor-nationalpark.gov.uk)

Visit Cornwall (www.visitcornwall.com)

Youth Hostels Association (www.yha.org.uk)

Camping

CAMPSITES

Devon and Cornwall's campsites have progressed far beyond tap-and-toilet sites in farmers' fields, although thankfully remote, basic sites do still exist. In more popular tourist spots and around key resorts expect to find family-friendly sites full of facilities such as bouncy castles and pools.

BOOK YOUR STAY ONLINE

For more accommodation reviews by Lonely Planet authors, check out http://lonelyplanet.com/hotels/. You'll find independent reviews, as well as recommendations on the best places to stay. Best of all, you can book online.

The trend towards glamorous camping (or glamping) continues and both counties bristle with über-stylish Mongolian yurts, woodland ecopods and retro caravans – we've outlined the pick of the region's campsites throughout the guide.

The prices we quote are per pitch, per night for two people. Expect to pay more for campgrounds near popular resorts in peak season. Region-wide costs range from around £9 to £30.

Useful websites:

Camping & Caravanning Club (www.campingandcaravanning club.co.uk)

Visit Cornwall (www.visitcornwall .com)

Visit Devon (www.visitdevon .co.uk)

WILD CAMPING

On Dartmoor you can experience wild or backwoods camping at its best. Pitching a tent on certain parts of the open moor is allowed, provided you follow some simple, but strict, rules. They're available from the **Dartmoor National Park Authority** (DNPA; ☎01822-890414; www. dartmoor.gov.uk) and include:

➡ Only camp for one or two nights on the same spot.

➡ Don't pitch your tent on farmland, moorland enclosed by walls, flood plains or on archaeological sites.

➡ Pitch your tent at least 100m from any roads, and out of sight of them and any homes and farms.

➡ Use lightweight camping equipment, avoiding large family frame tents.

➡ Camp only in areas outlined in the *Where To Camp On Dartmoor* map, and follow the Camping Code of Conduct (available from the DNPA website).

Hostels

Be they official or unofficial, the southwest is peppered with hostels offering a cheap n' cheerful sleeping experi-

ence. The range is remarkable: recently-revamped YHA hostels in towns and villages, converted cliff-top cottages, funky backpackers in resorts, and surfer's crash pads in Cornwall. In the summer they're popular places so book ahead, while in the winter some close – check before turning up.

YHA HOSTELS

There are around 20 Youth Hostels Association (YHA) hostels scattered around Devon and Cornwall, making it perfectly possible to tour the region using them as bases. YHA hostels can have a more establishment feel than independent ones, but the 'youth' in the title is a misnomer; you can join however old you are. Facilities are modern and many offer en suite double and family rooms as well as dorms. Some specialise in activities. YHA membership is £16 for over 25s and £10 for those between 16 and 25. You don't have to join to stay, but get a £3 per-night discount if you are.

INDEPENDENT HOSTELS

With a distinctly backpacker vibe, the southwest's independent hostels are the place to revel in the region's chilled-out atmosphere. There's a good, region-wide network; expect to encounter cool city-centre pads, decks with beach views and no-one bothering about sandy feet.

Dorms are quite often mixed-sex, prices average around £15 for a bed, but some peak at £25 in high

season. Many have double rooms costing around £45. Some have internet and laundry facilities. The **Independent Hostels Guide** (www. independenthostelguide.co.uk) is a useful resource.

Hotels

Devon and Cornwall's hotels tend to be posher, bigger and have more facilities than the region's B&Bs. There are the usual UK chains, plus independent, business-oriented, smooth, corporate affairs. Others are boutique beauties – the kind of luxurious coastal and country house options that are travel experiences in themselves. We outline the best throughout the guide.

Prices & Booking

As befits one of the UK's top holiday destinations, prices in Devon and Cornwall take a hefty hike upwards in the high season, particularly from June to August. You may like to consider scheduling plans to take advantage of low-season deals. Prices also spike around Christmas, New Year, Easter and major bank holidays. If you're travelling within these peak times, booking ahead is pretty much essential.

Most B&Bs still include breakfast in their rates. Some quote prices per person and some quote prices per room. Hotels tend to outline room rates but occasionally tack breakfast on top. Special deals are often available at the last minute and out of the main holiday times. It can also be cheaper to book direct, by phone, with the hotel or B&B.

Pubs & Inns

The West Country's ancient inns offer fabulous meals, real ales and cosy places to sleep. They're also at the heart of community life – providing you with an authentic slice of local life. Accommodation is often stylish, but is occasionally seedy, with rooms a little too reminiscent of the atmosphere downstairs in the bar. You'll find the best inns in the west throughout this book.

Prices vary considerably, from £40/60 for a single/double to £90/150 and beyond.

Self-Catering

Self-catering can be a supremely flexible option, especially if you're travelling with kids. The range of properties to rent out is wide – all across the southwest there are snazzy flats, fishermen's cottages and country retreats waiting to be booked. These specialists can help you find your very own home-away-from-home:

Beach Retreats (☎01637-861005; www.beachretreats.co.uk)

Classic Cottages (☎01326-555555; www.classic.co.uk)

National Trust (☎0870-458 4422; www.nationaltrustcottages.co.uk)

Rural Retreats (☎01386-701177; www.ruralretreats.co.uk)

Stilwell's (☎0870-197 6964; www.stilwell.co.uk)

Unique Homestays (☎01637-881942; www.uniquehomestays.com)

West Country Cottages (☎01803-814000; www.westcountrycottages.co.uk)

Climate

Exeter

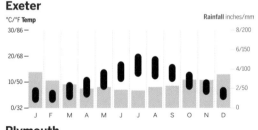

Plymouth

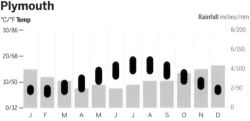

St Ives

Dangers & Annoyances

Compared to the world's trouble spots, England's southwest is a particularly safe place. But of course, crime can happen anywhere and you do still need to take care. Particular flashpoints can be at night amid concentrations of bars and clubs; avoid walking alone and beware of becoming embroiled in a fight.

Keep money and important documents out of sight in cars, and not just in city centres – remote moorland and coastal beauty spots are sometimes targeted by thieves. If you're in hostels take a padlock for the lockers and keep stuff packed away.

Beaches

The lifesaving charity, the **RNLI** (☎0845-045 6999; www.rnli.org.uk) has to rescue hundreds of people each year in the West Country. It advises:

➡ Use beaches with lifeguards.

➡ Read and obey safety signs.

➡ Never swim alone.

➡ Swim between red and yellow flags, and surf in water marked by black-and-white chequered flags. Coastguards also advise parents not let children use inflatables – if they do, an adult should attach a line and hold onto it.

Some of the biggest tidal ranges in the world occur in the southwest, and the sandy route out of that secluded cove can soon disappear under feet of water – people having to be rescued after getting cut off is a frequent event. Less dramatically, kit left on the sand when you go in to surf can be a soggy, scattered mess when you get back.

Times of high and low water are often outlined at popular beaches, as well as on local BBC TV and radio, and in newspapers. Small yellow booklets of tide times are available from newsagents and local shops (£1.40).

In recent decades, campaigners – particularly Cornwall-based **Surfers Against Sewage** (www.sas. org.uk) – have battled (and in part succeeded) to improve water quality. 'Blue Flags' are awarded to beaches with high water-quality standards, and good safety and environmental records. See the latest list at www.blueflag.org. But note, some of Devon and Cornwall's best beaches don't qualify for the award, not because water quality is bad, but because they don't have specific features (such as toilets, bins and drinking water).

Walking

While stunning to hike, the region's moors are also remote, so prepare for upland weather conditions. Warm, waterproof clothing, hats, water and sunscreen are essential. Parts of Dartmoor are used by the military for live-firing ranges; see p111.

Like the rest of Britain, the southwest's coastline is subject to erosion and occasionally rockfalls cause injury or even death. Unstable sections of the coastline are often fenced off and coastguards urge beach-users and walkers to obey warning signs.

Discount Cards

For regional rail and bus passes, see the start of our Transport chapter.

There are no region-wide, non-transport, discount cards for visitors, but sometimes two or more attractions team up with joint tickets that allow entry to both. We outline the key savings throughout our On The Road chapters.

Devon and Cornwall have a superb sprinkling of historic buildings and if you are visiting more than three or four properties, it is worth considering joining a heritage organisation for a year. The **National Trust**

(NT; ☎0870-458 4422; www. nationaltrustcottages.co.uk) has an excellent range of properties region-wide; members can park for free at their car parks too. Annual membership is from £42 for an adult, £70 for two and £73 for families.

English Heritage (EH; ☎0870-333 1181; www.english-heritage.org.uk) also has a good selection of properties available in the southwest. Annual adult membership costs £47 (£35 for over 60s) and allows up to six children free entry; joint adult membership costs £82 (joint senior £56).

Lonely Planet denotes National Trust and English Heritage sites by the abbreviations NT and EH.

Electricity

230V/50Hz

Food

See our Food & Drink guide on p268 for more on the southwest's fine cuisine.

Gay & Lesbian Travellers

The southwest generally mirrors the UK's relatively tolerant attitude to lesbians and gay men. Gay (and gay-friendly) clubs and bars can be found in the cities and bigger towns (such as Exeter, Torquay, Truro and Plymouth), although there is often not a huge range to choose from and sometimes gay venues do not exist at all.

The usual instincts about how open you want to be about your sexuality are the best guide; you can be the victim of homophobia, or not, in the most surprising places.

Even in the southwest's deepest rural areas, individual gay businesses, be they lesbian-owned B&Bs or exclusively gay hotels, are thriving – see the **Turing Network** (www.turingnetwork. org.uk), which has a wide-ranging, searchable database. Gay accommodation based in Devon and Cornwall also appears repeatedly in **Gay Times** (www.gaytimes. co.uk) and **Diva** (www.di-vamag.co.uk).

The **Intercom Trust** (☎0800-612 3010; www.inter-comtrust.org.uk) runs a lesbian and gay switchboard for Cornwall, Devon, Plymouth and Torbay.

Health

Adders

Britain's only venomous snake is not uncommon in the region's hills, moors and coast paths. Adders will only attack if harassed or threatened and although their venom poses little danger to a healthy adult human, the bite is very painful and does require medical attention. If you are bitten, don't panic. Immobilise the limb with a splint (eg a stick) and apply a bandage over the site firmly. Do not apply a tourniquet, or cut or suck the bite. Get the victim to medical help as soon as possible.

Sunburn

The coastline and outdoor lifestyle in Devon and Cornwall are often blamed for some of the highest malignant skin cancer rates in England and Wales. Experts remind UK nationals they still need sunscreen even if they're holidaying at home. Stay out of the sun between 11am and 3pm, cover up, use factor 15+ sunscreen and UV sunglasses and take extra care of children.

Ticks

Ticks are increasingly common in the region's countryside, some carry Lymes Disease – a relatively uncommon but potentially serious illness. To prevent bites use insect repellent and wear long trousers tucked into socks and long-sleeved shirts. At the end of the day, check that you're tick-free. If you are bitten, remove the tick as soon as possible by grasping it close to the skin with tweezers and twisting anti-clockwise. Lymes Disease may appear as an expanding, reddish round rash in the area of the bite, for up to 30 days later. Symptoms include influenza, mild headaches and aching muscles and joints. The condition is treatable with antibiotics but early diagnosis is best; if you think any of these symptoms may come from a tick bite, see a doctor.

Internet Access

Internet cafes feature in Devon and Cornwall's main cities and towns; prices range from around £1.50 to £3 per hour. You can get online at many hotels and hostels too. Public libraries often have free access but sometimes run booking systems and limit sessions to half an hour.

While not packed with wi-fi zones, most towns and cities have fair-to-good provision. Many hotels and a reasonable number of B&Bs also have wi-fi access, and (as elsewhere in the UK) cafes are another good option. Charges range from nothing to £5 per hour.

This book uses an internet icon (@) to show you can get online. The wi-fi icon (🛜) denotes wi-fi access.

Maps

If you're heading onto the region's smaller roads, a good regional atlas will save you frustration diversions. In remote areas you can't rely on signposts, or them mentioning places you're familiar with. In some more rural areas satnav systems are notorious for directing drivers down unnavigable roads.

The most useful maps have a scale of about 1:200,000 (three miles to one inch). The region's cities have their own A-Zs; look out too for good scale county-specific, or West-Country-specific map books. Most road atlases cost £8 to £12 and can be bought at petrol stations and bookshops.

For walkers and cyclists the **Ordnance Survey** (OS; www.shop.ordnancesurvey leisure.co.uk) Landranger series (£7) is good, with a scale of 1:50,000, but many prefer the detail of the Explorer range (£8), at 1:25,000.

Money

ATMs

ATMs (or cash machines) pepper cities and towns, but some of Devon and Cornwall's smaller communities simply don't have them, so a cheque book or small emergency stash of money is a good idea. Alternatives can be the stand-alone cash machines in convenience stores (as elsewhere, charges may apply).

Credit & Debit Cards

Visa and MasterCard credit cards, and debit cards such as Maestro, are widely accepted, but some of the region's smaller businesses, such as B&Bs or pubs, only take cash or cheque.

Most supermarkets and village shops have a cash-back system: if you spend more than £5 on your debit card, they also allow you to withdraw a small amount of cash, which is added to your bill.

Opening Hours

For details of opening hours of banks, museums, post offices, pubs, restaurants, cafes and shops, see p17.

Telephone

Mobile phone coverage in the region's towns and cities is good, as are signals in many, but not all, rural and coastal areas. Geography also means different networks have different zones where they provide poor or no reception – depending on the location and your provider, you could find your phone will not work. A few moorland or coastal areas have no signal at all. Payphones are common in towns and cities, with a reasonable number in rural areas.

Phones in the UK use GSM 900/1800, which is compatible with Europe and Australia but not with North America or Japan, although phones that work globally are increasingly common.

Useful Numbers & Codes

Lonely Planet lists the usual area codes (eg 01752 for Plymouth) separated from the local number by a hyphen; only the local number needs to be dialled from the same area. Useful numbers include:

International access code 00 to dial out of the UK

International direct dial code 44 to dial into the UK

International directory enquiries 118 505

Local directory enquiries 118 118, 118 500

Operator 100

To call somewhere outside the UK, dial 00, then the country code (1 for USA, 61 for Australia, etc), the area code (usually dropping the initial zero) and then the number.

To call England from abroad, dial your country's international access code, then 44 (the UK country code), then the area code (dropping the first 0), then the rest of the number.

Toilets

Public toilets tend to be relatively clean and plentiful, although sometimes unsavoury. Even rural petrol stations are likely to have a customer toilet. In some seasonal tourist areas the toilets are shut in the winter. Charges are rare, around 20p where they exist.

Tourist Information

Universally helpful and brimming with local knowledge, staff at tourist offices are an invaluable holiday resource. There are offices throughout the region; some information centres are also run by national parks. Tourist offices in the bigger cities are busier, larger and open for longer; we specify opening hours throughout the book.

Many have leaflets and free town maps. Some sell walking maps and local books and can help book accommodation (sometimes for a fee). Staff that are fluent in other languages aren't that common; French and to a lesser extent Spanish are the most likely specialities.

The regional tourist board, **Visit South West** (www.visit southwest.co.uk) has info on the region, and links through to county-specific websites.

Travellers with Disabilities

Disability access in the southwest, like elsewhere in the country, is patchy. In some places successful efforts have been made to make things accessible, in others they haven't and the situation is woeful. Sometimes best intentions are defeated by heritage and geography, in others more needs to be done.

Modern developments are required to have wheelchair access and in some places ramps, lifts and other facilities have been put into existing properties, but it's not universal. You might also find inconsistencies within buildings: a restaurant might have ramps and wheelchair-access toilets, but tables are 10in apart.

For long-distance travel, coaches can present problems, though staff will help where possible. On trains there's often more room and better facilities; in some modern carriages all the signs are repeated in Braille. If the train proves difficult to access there's normally a phone and a sign detailing how to request help. In cities and towns you may find buses with lower floors, but it's unlikely in rural areas. Some companies have taxis that take wheelchairs.

Exploring the region's wilder spaces can present challenges, but real efforts have been made. These include on the **South West Coast Path** (www.southwestcoastpath.com) where some more remote parts have been made more accessible. You can search for easier-access options on the trail's website.

The **Dartmoor National Park Authority** (www.dartmoor.gov.uk) produces the *Easy Going Dartmoor* booklet for less-mobile visitors (available online). This outlines facilities and has a good range of accessible routes to explore.

The **Good Access Guide** (www.goodaccessguide.co.uk) is a useful online resource.

Transport

GETTING THERE & AWAY

Devon and Cornwall sit, gloriously, at the far end of England, and getting there isn't always an easy exercise. Some visitors endure traffic jams, cramped coaches and delayed trains. At the same time, internal UK flights, reasonable rail links and travelling off-peak can help ease journeys; this chapter outlines how.

Flights, tours and rail tickets can be booked online at lonelyplanet.com/bookings.

Air

➡ The cost of flying to Devon and Cornwall from the rest of the UK varies dramatically depending on when you book and when you want to fly.

➡ A return flight to the region from within the British Isles is around £60 to £140 for an adult, including tax.

➡ Many prices rise at peak holiday times and at weekends.

➡ Save money by booking far in advance.

➡ If travelling from outside the UK, you'll often need to come via one of the country's key international airports, but there are links with a fair range of European cities.

➡ Flights to the Isles of Scilly leave from Exeter, Land's End and Newquay Airports. See p290.

Airlines

Recently, flights to Devon and Cornwall have been particularly subject to change. At the time of writing the following airlines were flying to the region. Airport websites have the latest details on which operators are running which route.

easyJet (☑0843-104 5000; www.easyjet.com) Summer season flights (Easter to October) between Newquay Cornwall Airport and London Southend and Liverpool.

FlyBe (☑0871-700 2000; www.flybe.com) UK services to Exeter include those from Belfast, the Channel Islands, Edinburgh, Glasgow, Manchester and Newcastle. European links include Amsterdam, Barcelona, Dublin, Dusseldorf, Geneva and Paris.

UK services to Newquay Cornwall Airport include year-round flights from Manchester, plus Easter to October flights from Belfast, Edinburgh and Newcastle.

LoganAir (☑0871-700 2000; www.flybe.com) Easter to October flights between Newquay Cornwall Airport and Glasgow. Operated by LoganAir; book through FlyBe.

Lufthansa (☑0871-945 974; www.lufthansa.com) Links Newquay Cornwall Airport and Dusseldorf between Easter and October.

CLIMATE CHANGE & TRAVEL

Every form of transport that relies on carbon-based fuel generates CO_2, the main cause of human-induced climate change. Modern travel is dependent on aeroplanes, which might use less fuel per mile per person than most cars but travel much greater distances. The altitude at which aircraft emit gases (including CO_2) and particles also contributes to their climate change impact. Many websites offer 'carbon calculators' that allow people to estimate the carbon emissions generated by their journey and, for those who wish to do so, to offset the impact of the greenhouse gases emitted with contributions to portfolios of climate-friendly initiatives throughout the world. Lonely Planet offsets the carbon footprint of all staff and author travel.

Airports

Exeter International
Airport (www.exeter-airport.co.uk) Routes from Belfast, the Channel Islands, Edinburgh, Glasgow, Manchester and Newcastle, plus links from European cities.

Land's End Airport
(☎01736-785231; www.landsendairport.co.uk; Kelynack, near St Just) This tiny airfield, 5 miles northwest of Penzance, offers flights to the Isles of Scilly.

Newquay Cornwall Airport (☎01637-860600; www.newquaycornwallairport.com) Direct, year-round flights from Manchester and the Isles of Scilly. Plus summer routes from London Southend, Belfast City, Dusseldorf, Edinburgh, Glasgow, Liverpool, Newcastle and Norwich. Beware the £5 per person departure tax.

St Mary's Airport (ISC; ☎01720-424330; www.scilly.gov.uk) Main gateway to the Isles of Scilly. Flights are Monday to Saturday only.

Bus

Travelling by bus to the southwest is cheap and reliable, but normally takes longer than the train. **National Express** (☎08717-818 178; www.nationalexpress.com) has a comprehensive network of services to Devon and Cornwall. Sample fares include London Victoria to Newquay (£35, 7½ hours, four daily) and Edinburgh to Exeter (£45, 18 hours, two daily). Special deals ('fun fares') can be a real bargain.

Car & Motorcycle

The vast majority of visitors to the southwest come by car, resulting in some serious traffic jams at peak times so try to avoid obvious Bank Holiday and school holiday travel periods.

London's circular M25 leads onto the M4, which links into the M5 around Bristol. The M5 winds south to Exeter, passing Exmoor National Park on the way. From the midlands and the north, the M6 links up with the M5 at Birmingham.

An alternative route west is the A303, which heads from the M3 towards Devon and Exmoor via Stonehenge. It has some quite prolonged single-lane stretches. Some 20 miles east of Exeter the A303 becomes the A30, it then skirts Dartmoor's northern fringe, heading on into Cornwall via Bodmin.

The 190-mile London-to-Exeter drive should take around 3½ hours; Birmingham to Newquay is 240 miles (five hours); Edinburgh to Penzance is 560 miles (10½ hours). Expect to add anything from half an hour to two hours (and beyond) for summer delays.

Train

Services between major cities and Devon and Cornwall tend to run at least hourly.

National Rail Enquiries
(☎08457-48 49 50; www.nationalrail.co.uk) has information on times and fares.

Travel times and costs vary (the latter wildly); advance booking and travelling off-peak cuts costs dramatically. Sample fares include London Paddington

to Penzance (£60, 5½ hours, nine daily) and Edinburgh to Plymouth (£125, 10 hours, every two hours).

First Great Western
(☎8457-000 125; www.firstgreatwestern.co.uk) Routes include those from London Paddington to Exeter, Penzance, Plymouth, Tiverton Parkway and Truro. It also runs services to Gatwick Airport and branch lines to Barnstaple, Exmouth, Falmouth, Looe, Newquay, St Ives and Torquay.

CrossCountry (☎0844-811 0124; www.crosscountrytrains.co.uk) Links the southwest with the midlands, and the north of England and Scotland. Stations served include Aberdeen, Birmingham, Bristol, Edinburgh, Glasgow, Leeds, Newcastle, Cardiff and the main southwest stations between Tiverton Parkway and Penzance.

South West Trains
(☎0845-600 0650; www.southwesttrains.co.uk) Runs services between London Waterloo and Axminster and Exeter.

Sea

Brittany Ferries (☎0871-244 1402; www.brittany-ferries.com) sails between Plymouth and Roscoff in France (6 to 8 hours; anywhere from two daily to three per week) and Santander in northern Spain (20 hours, one per week).

Prices vary dramatically; for cheap fares book early and take non-peak, non-weekend crossings. A 10-day, mid-week return in mid-August between Plymouth and Roscoff is £80 for foot passengers; £350 for a car and two adults. A similar Plymouth-Santander trip costs £230 for one on-foot passenger; £800 for a car and two passengers.

But off-season deals and special offers can bring the price down dramatically. Sample deals include £60 for a car and two passengers on the Plymouth-Roscoff route; and 20 percent off journeys between Plymouth and Santander.

GETTING AROUND

Devon and Cornwall are relatively compact destinations, with good concentrations of attractions and environments. The vast majority of people (locals and visitors) drive – and then complain about the traffic. If you're planning to leave the cities and tour rural areas, the car is the quickest way to get around, but for trips to relatively compact or urban areas, public transport might meet your needs.

The **Southwest Traveline** (☎0871-200 22 33; www.travelinesw.com) is a one-stop shop for all local bus, coach and train timetables. Calls cost 10p per minute, plus network charges.

Air

Skybus (☎0845-710 5555; www.islesofscilly-travel.co.uk) Run by Isles of Scilly Travel, the Skybus provides daily, year-round flights to St Mary's on the Isles of Scilly from Newquay (adult/child £170/130, 30 minutes) and Land's End (adult/child £140/110, 15 minutes) airports. Also offers daily Easter to October services from Exeter (adult/child £240/190, 1 hour).

Lundy Helicopter (☎01271-863636; www.lundyisland.co.uk; adult/child return £105/55) A seasonal helicopter service which only runs in the winter (late-October to late-March), linking North Devon's Lundy Island with nearby Hartland Point on the mainland.

Bicycle

The southwest has an appealing network of car-free or cyclist-friendly routes, with hundreds of miles of National Cycle Network routes. For info and maps try the sustainable transport charity, **Sustrans** (www.sustrans.org.uk). We also outline the pick of the West Country's cycle trails in Outdoor Activities.

The most enjoyable cycling weather tends to fall between spring and autumn. Because July and August are busy months, May, June and September make attractive alternatives.

Some basic rules cover where you can cycle. Bicycles are banned from motorways, but are allowed on other public roads. Pedaling Devon and Cornwall's 'A' roads, though, can be both dangerous and frightening; some of the busier 'B' roads are also unappealing. Cyclists can use public bridleways but must give way to other users. Be aware that you can't cycle on public footpaths, something that's a particular bone of contention in the southwest's moors and coast paths.

You can take a bike, for free, on all the national train companies in the southwest, but booking can be required and restrictions often apply at peak times.

Bike Hire

We specify bike-hire places throughout the guide. In general where there are well-used cycle paths, a good cycle-hire shop is often nearby. Expect to pay around £12 for a half-day rental.

Boat

Isles of Scilly Travel (☎0845-710 5555; www.islesofscilly-travel.co.uk) operates the archipelago's emblematic passenger ferry (the Scillonian III) between Penzance and the main island, St Mary's (adult/child return £76/40, 2 hours 40 minutes). The service is seasonal – it doesn't run in the winter. Between late April and early October there are between two and six sailings a week (Monday to Saturday only).

Once in the Isles of Scilly, a fleet of ferries shuttles between St Mary's and the smaller islands that surround it. Services are operated by the **St Mary's Boatmen's Association** (☎01720-423999; www.scillyboating.co.uk) and run at least daily between April and October, leaving St Mary's in the morning and returning in the afternoon. Adult/child returns cost £8.40/4.20.

The passenger vessel, **MS Oldenburg** (☎01271-863636; www.lundyisland.co.uk) sails to Lundy Island from either Bideford or Ilfracombe, once a day between April and late-October. The journey time is under two hours for both crossings. Fares are the same from either port: adult/child day return £35/18; period return (ie: anything longer than a day return) £62/31.

Bus

Regional Travel

National Express (☎08717-818 178; www.nationalexpress.com) runs frequent services between the region's cities, major towns and resorts. Sample direct services include Penzance to Torquay (£15, 4 hours, one daily) and Plymouth to Torquay (£7, 1 hour, one daily).

Key bus firms include the following:

First (www.firstgroup.com/ukbus) Major operator in South Devon, Dartmoor, Plymouth and West Cornwall.

Stagecoach (www.stagecoachbus.com) Runs local services in North Cornwall, Exeter and East Devon, North Devon and around Torquay.

Western Greyhound (www.westerngreyhound.com) Extensive services in Cornwall, including the north coast (covering Bude, Newquay, Padstow, St Ives and Tintagel), Bodmin Moor, St Austell and the far west (including Penzance, Porthcurno, Land's End and Sennen).

Within Cities

Devon and Cornwall's cities have good bus networks, although routes tend to be winding down by 10.30pm. City day passes (with names like Day Rover, Wayfarer or Explorer) can be good value. Expect to pay around £1.60 to £2 for a single fare.

Car & Motorcycle

Devon and Cornwall can't claim an extensive motorway network – there are none west of Exeter. While many stretches of the counties' key 'A' roads are dual carriageway, some aren't, and the lesser 'A' roads are rarely so.

Sometimes the sheer volume of traffic overwhelms the road network. Be aware: in the southwest in the summer, even on a clear road, when the sign before a bend says 'traffic queuing ahead' – it's probably going to be true.

The region's cities feature the usual ring roads, traffic jams and sometimes confusing one-way systems – Torquay and Exeter can be particularly bad. Many towns and cities have pedestrian-only central zones.

'A' roads and many 'B' roads have plenty of petrol and service stations. But it's worth filling up before heading off these main routes into rural areas, onto the moors or lesser-used coastal routes.

In the towns and cities fuel prices mirror those nationwide, but rise as you head into the countryside.

Bridge Tolls

There is a bridge toll for drivers leaving Cornwall on the A38 via the Tamar Bridge, near Plymouth. Rates are £1.50 for a car and £3.70 for touring vans over 3.5 tonnes. Charges apply eastbound only; you can pay by cash at the booths. The bridge is free for motorcyclists, pedestrians and cyclists.

Car Ferries

The Isles of Scilly and Lundy Island aside (see Boat section), you don't have to get on a boat to get around Devon and Cornwall, but it is an atmospheric way to explore the region. The deep rivers and wide estuaries

BUS PASSES

A range of bus passes cover cities and districts in Devon and Cornwall. We give a sample here, though cheaper passes, covering smaller areas, are also often available.

NAME	COMPANY	AREA	DURATION	PRICE: ADULT/CHILD/FAMILY
Day Explorer	Western Greyhound	Devon and Cornwall	1 day	£8.50/5.50/17
FirstDay Cornwall	First	Cornwall	1 day	£7/6/12
FirstDay Devon	First	Devon	1 day	£7.50/5.30/*
FirstDay Southwest	First	Devon and Cornwall	1 day	£7.60/6.20/18.70
FirstWeek Cornwall	First	Cornwall	7 days	£25/20/35
FirstWeek Devon	First	Devon	7 days	£37/22/58
MeggaRider Gold	Stagecoach	Devon and Cornwall	7 days	£25/*
MeggaRider	Stagecoach	Exeter	7 days	£13/*
MeggaRider	Stagecoach	North Devon	7 days	£10.50/*
MeggaRider	Stagecoach	Torbay	7 days	£17/*

* Note these items do not have child/family fares available.

PlusBus (www.plusbus.info) Adds bus travel around towns to your train ticket for £2 a day. Places covered in Devon and Cornwall are: Barnstaple, Bodmin, Brixham, Camborne & Redruth, Exeter, Falmouth & Penryn, Liskeard, Newquay, Newton Abbot, Paignton, Penzance, Plymouth, St Austell, Torquay, Totnes and Truro.

Ride Cornwall (adult/child/family £10/7.50/20) A day's off-peak travel in Cornwall on First and Western Greyhound buses, plus First Great Western and Cross Country trains.

that cut into the landscape sometimes make ferries the fastest, most scenic, route from A to B. At other times peak-period ferry queues make that 20-mile road detour seem like a better idea.

Some ferries take cars, people and bikes but some only carry foot passengers; we specify throughout the guide. The key car ferries run all year while some other routes are seasonal. If you miss the boat you can go by road (or sometimes path), although the detour can be significant, especially for cyclists and walkers.

The following are one-way, combined car and passenger fares. Unless specified, charges apply when travelling in both directions.

Bodinnick to Fowey Ferry Links mid and east Cornwall, cutting out the detour to Lostwithiel; £3.50.

Dartmouth Higher/Lower Ferry Crosses the River Dart at Dartmouth in Devon, providing a shortcut to Torquay; £4.70/4.

King Harry Ferry A short cut to the Roseland Peninsula; crossing the Fal River from near Trelissick Gardens to Philleigh, a few miles north of St Mawes; £5.

Torpoint Ferry Shuttles between Devon and Cornwall, a shortcut from the city of Plymouth to the Rame Peninsula; £1.50; charges apply eastbound only.

Car Hire

Rates echo those charged nationwide. The region's airports and cities, and many major towns, have car-hire outlets. Firms with a good presence in the region include Avis, Europcar and Hertz.

Avis (☑0844-581 0147; www.avis.co.uk)

Europcar (☑0871-384 1087; www.europcar.co.uk)

Hertz (☑0843-309 3099; www.hertz.co.uk)

National (☑0871-384 1140; www.nationalcar.co.uk) Has branches at Exeter and Newquay Cornwall airports.

Parking

Expect to pay from £1.40 to £1.60 for an hour and around £8 to £12 for the day. Sometimes a minimum two-hour rate is charged, while maximum durations are from 30 minutes onwards. Be aware, in some towns you won't have to buy a ticket to park overnight on one road, but will on a neighbouring one.

Charges at beaches, even remote ones, can also mount up; some cost per two/three hours £2.50/3.70, or £7 a day.

Parking can also be at a premium amid the winding, cobbled streets of the region's fishing villages and tourist hot spots. Many have park-and-ride systems, with costs ranging from around £2.50 to £5.

We identify hotels and B&Bs that have parking spaces by using a parking icon (**P**); when booking check if any spaces remain and if there's a charge.

Taxi

The southwest's towns and cities are well served by taxis, with ranks to be found near shopping centres, train stations and popular nightlife zones. In many rural areas there's also a reasonable network, partly because public transport is scarce and a taxi for four people often provides a fairly cost-effective means of getting around.

In the region's cities taxis cost around £3 to £4 per mile; in rural areas, it can be about half this. Taxi ranks are marked on Lonely Planet's maps; phone numbers for local firms are also given.

Train

Ticket Websites

Sites selling tickets from all train companies to all national destinations:

➡ www.thetrainline.com

➡ www.qjump.co.uk

➡ www.raileasy.co.uk

Train Passes

The following passes are accepted by all the national (but not private) train companies and can be bought either from them or at staffed stations:

Devon Day Ranger (adult/child £10/5) One day's unlimited travel on trains in the county.

Devon Evening Ranger (adult/child £5/2.50) Unlimited travel in Devon after 6pm.

Freedom of Devon and Cornwall Rover (adult/child £42/21) Three day's travel in any 7-day period across the two counties.

Freedom of Devon and Cornwall Rover (adult/child £64/32) Eight day's unlimited travel in any 15-day period.

RAIL VIEWS

Some of the region's train routes offer superb coastal and estuary views. It's definitely worth looking out the window between the following places:

➡ Exeter and Newton Abbot

➡ Plymouth and Gunnislake

➡ Plymouth and Liskeard

➡ St Erth and St Ives

➡ St Erth and Penzance

The website **Great Scenic Railways of Devon and Cornwall** (www.carfreedaysout.com) has a wealth of information, plus details of local walks.

Ride Cornwall Pass (adult/
child/family £10/7.50/20) Offers
one day's travel on the county's
buses and trains.

Main Lines

Services between Devon and
Cornwall's towns and cities
on the London Paddington
to Penzance mainline are
generally good. Trains normally run at least hourly,
sometimes more frequently.
The National Rail Enquiries
website (www.nationalrail.
co.uk) details train timetables and fares. Sample direct
services include Exeter to
Penzance (£25, 3 hours,
hourly), Plymouth to Truro
(£10, 1¼ hours, hourly) and
Truro to Exeter (£40, 2½
hours, hourly).

Branch Lines

Branch lines also fan out
from the main London–Pen-
zance intercity routes. Key
ones include Exeter to Barnstaple, Exeter to Exmouth,
Liskeard to Looe, Newton Abbot to Torquay and Paignton,
Par to Newquay, Plymouth to
Gunnislake, St Erth to St Ives
and Truro to Falmouth.

Steam Trains

The West Country's privately
operated steam trains ply
some stunning routes:
  **Bodmin and Wenford
Railway** (☑01208-73555;
www.bodminandwenfordrailway
.co.uk; adult/child/family
£12/6/33; ☺Mar-Oct) Scenic
journeys, skirting Bodmin
Moor.

  **Dartmouth Steam
Railway** (☑01803-555872;
www.dartmouthrailriver.
co.uk; Torbay Rd, Paignton;
adult/child/family return
£13.50/7.50/36; ☺4-9 trains
daily Mar-Nov) Links the
Torbay resort of Paignton
with Dartmouth.
  South Devon Railway
(☑01364-644370; www.south
devonrailway.org; adult/child
return £12/7; ☺4-9 trains daily
Apr-Oct) Shuttles between
Totnes and Buckfastleigh.
  **West Somerset Rail-
way** (☑01643-704996; www.
west-somerset-railway.co.uk;
24hr rover ticket adult/child
£17/8.50) Chugs between
Minehead on Exmoor and
Bishops Lydeard.

TRANSPORT TRAIN

Behind the Scenes

SEND US YOUR FEEDBACK

Things change – prices go up, schedules change, good places go bad and bad places go bankrupt. So if you find things better or worse, recently opened or long since closed, or you just want to tell us what you loved or loathed about this book, please get in touch and help make the next edition even more accurate and useful. We love to hear from travellers – your comments keep us on our toes and our well-travelled team reads every word. Although we can't reply individually to postal submissions, we always guarantee that your feedback goes straight to the appropriate authors, in time for the next edition. Each person who sends us information is thanked in the next edition – the most useful submissions are rewarded with a selection of digital PDF chapters.

Visit **lonelyplanet.com/contact** to submit your updates and suggestions or to ask for help. Our award-winning website also features inspirational travel stories, news and discussions.

Note: We may edit, reproduce and incorporate your comments in Lonely Planet products such as guidebooks, websites and digital products, so let us know if you don't want your comments reproduced or your name acknowledged. For a copy of our privacy policy visit lonelyplanet.com/privacy.

OUR READERS

Many thanks to the travellers who used the last edition and wrote to us with helpful hints, useful advice and interesting anecdotes:

Fabio Baldi, Franz Blaesi, Robyn Coates, Harry Hofman, Laura Sheil

AUTHOR THANKS
Oliver Berry

A big thank you to all the people who helped during research: Paul Ainsworth, Jayne Back, Hana Backland, Peter Bawden, Rupert Ellis, Justin Foulkes, Thom Hunt, Liz King, Lifebuoy Café, Anna Melton, Laura McKay, Emma Mustill, Origin Coffee and all the others I met along the way. Special thanks to Susie, Mo and Gracie; to Cliff Wilkinson for the gig; to Angela Tinson and Anthony Phelan for inhouse support; and to Belinda Dixon for digging out all those Devonian delights.

Belinda Dixon

Huge thanks go to: OTB for wise counsel; Cliff for the gig (again); LP's behind the scenes teams. Everyone encountered on Devon-wide travels for tips, facts and countless kindnesses. And JL for sharing the road trips (especially cycling, kayaking, and speed-hiking) and (still) making me smile.

ACKNOWLEDGMENTS

Climate map data adapted from Peel MC, Finlayson BL & McMahon TA (2007) 'Updated World Map of the Köppen-Geiger Climate Classification', Hydrology and Earth System Sciences, 11, 1633¬44.

Cover photograph: Walking path to the Wheal Coates Tin Mine, St Agnes, Cornwall, Pietro Canali/4corners.

THIS BOOK

This 3rd edition of Lonely Planet's *Devon & Cornwall* guidebook was researched and written by Oliver Berry and Belinda Dixon, who also wrote the previous two editions. The guidebook was commissioned in Lonely Planet's London office, and produced by the following:

Commissioning Editor Clifton Wilkinson

Coordinating Editors Susie Ashworth, Alison Ridgway

Senior Cartographers Jennifer Johnston, Anthony Phelan

Coordinating Layout Designer Frank Deim

Managing Editors Martine Power, Angela Tinson

Senior Editor Karyn Noble

Managing Layout Designer Chris Girdler

Assisting Editors Kate Daly, Kate Kiely, Jenna Myers

Assisting Cartographers Julie Dodkin, Mick Garrett, Rachel Imeson

Cover Research Naomi Parker

Internal Image Research Aude Vauconsant

Thanks to Ryan Evans, Larissa Frost, Jane Hart, Genesys India, Jouve India, Trent Paton, Kerri-anne Southway, Gerard Walker

Index

A

abbeys
  Buckland Abbey 114, **243**
  Cleeve Abbey 133
  Hartland Abbey 148-9
  St Benet's Abbey 152
  St Michael's Mount 13,
    244, **13**
accommodation 282-4, see
    also individual locations
activities 21-3, 30-5, see
    also individual activities
air travel 288-9, 290
animals 278, see also
    wildlife, individual
    species
Appledore 145-7
aquariums
  Blue Reef Aquarium 208
  Ilfracombe Aquarium 139
  National Marine Aquarium
    103
archaeological sites 260
  Bodmin Moor 159
  Dartmoor National
    Park 117
  Penwith 230, 231
area codes 17, 287
art galleries, see galleries
arts 20, 273-6, see also
    individual arts
Ashburton 120
ATMs 286

B

Bantham 97-8, **143**
Barnstaple 144-5
bathrooms 287
beaches 15, 18, 33, 284-5
  Bantham 97
  Bigbury-on-Sea 98
  Bossiney Haven 200

Map Pages **000**
Photo Pages **000**

Bude 195
Chapel Porth 213-14
Croyde 141
Dartmouth 86
Falmouth 163
Fistral 207
Godrevy 226
Gwithian 226
Kynance Cove 248
Lansallos 189
Lantic 189
Mullion 247
Newquay 207
Padstow's Seven Bays
    205
Perranporth 213
Perranuthnoe 244
Polkerris Beach 184
Porthcurno 234
Porthminster 221
Praa Sands 244-5
Readymoney Cove 183
Roseland Peninsula 176
Salcombe 93
Sennen Cove 233
St Ives 221
St Martin's 255
St Mary's 251
Torquay 66
Trebarwith Strand 200
Trevaunance Cove 214
Trevellas Porth 214
Westward Ho! 147
Bedruthan Steps 206, **5**
beer 271-2
Beer 61-3, **143**
bicycle travel, see cycling
Bideford 145-7
Bigbury-on-Sea 98
birdwatching 278-9
  Dawlish Warren 75
  Exminster Marshes
    Nature Reserve 46
  Fowey 185
  Hayle 226
  Millook 196

Northam Burrows 147
Slapton Ley 89
Topsham 55
boat travel 289-90
boat trips
  Dartmouth 85
  Looe 188
  Padstow 203
  Plymouth 104
  Salcombe 95
  St Ives 223
  St Martin's 255
  St Mary's 252
  Truro 170
Bodmin 39, 151-3, **151**
  accommodation 150
  climate 150
  food 150
  highlights 151
  travel seasons 150
Bodmin Moor 32, 153-9, **154**
books 20, 258, 275
Boscastle 196-7
Bossiney Haven 200
Bramley, Frank 273-4
Branscombe 61
Braunton 141-4
breweries 271-2
bridge tolls 291
British Fireworks
    Championships 23
Brixham 73-5
Bryher 254
Bude 195-6
budget 17
bus travel 289, 290-1
business hours 17
butterflies 278

C

Camborne 216-18
Camelford 153-6
camping 20, 282-3
Cape Cornwall 233
car travel 289, 291-2, see
    also driving tours

Carn Brea 215
castles
  Berry Pomeroy 83
  Castle Dore 183
  Castle Drogo 121
  Chûn Castle 230
  Dartmouth Castle 84
  Dunster Castle 133
  Launceston Castle 156
  Lydford Castle 123
  Maen Castle 230
  Okehampton Castle 125
  Pendennis Castle 163
  Powderham Castle 52
  Restormel 183
  St Catherine's Castle 183
  St Mawes Castle 177
  St Michael's Mount 244
  Tintagel Castle 198, **243**
  Totnes Castle 78
cathedrals, see churches &
    cathedrals
caves & tunnels
  Beer Quarry Caves 61
  Carnglaze Caverns 159
  Chapel Porth 214
  Kents Cavern 66
  Kynance Cove 248
  Merlin's Cave 198
cell phones 16, 287
Celtic rule 260-1
Chagford 121-3
Chapel Porth 213-14
Charlestown 180
cheese 270
children, travel with 36-7
Christie, Agatha 66, 67, 71,
    83, 275
churches & cathedrals
  Chapel of St Nicholas 223
  Church of St Winwaloe
    246
  Exeter Cathedral 10, 44-5,
    48, **10**, **262**
  Roche Rock 182
  St Finbarrus Church 184

St George's Church 133
St Pancras Church 119
Truro Cathedral 170
cider 272
Civil War 263-4
Clay Trails 181
climate 16, 21-3, *see also individual regions*
Clovelly 12, 147-8, **12, 142**
Coast to Coast Cycle Trail 169
Coleton Fishacre 88
Constantine 167
cooking courses 270
Cornish pasties 12, 214, 269, **12, 211**
Cornwall & West Devon Mining Landscape 216
Cornwall basics 16
Crackington Haven 196
cream teas 11, 270, **11, 210**
credit cards 287
Croyde 141-4
currency 16
cycling 35, 290, *see also* trails & paths
  Camel Trail 203
  Clay Trails 181
  Coast to Coast Cycle Trail 169
  Dartmoor National Park 110-11
  Exeter 46
  Exmoor National Park 128
  Great Flat Lode Trail 218
  Tamar Trails 192
cycling tours
  Granite Way 124, **124**
  Tarka Trail 146, **146**

D
dangers 284-5
Dartmoor National Park 10, 31-2, 39, 110-25, **100, 112, 10, 155**
  accommodation 99, 112
  activities 110-12
  climate 99
  food 99, 113
  highlights 100
  tourist information 110
  travel seasons 99
  travel to/from 113
  travel within 113
Dartmouth 83-8, **84**
  accommodation 86-7
  activities 85-6
  drinking 88

entertainment 88
festivals & events 86
food 87-8
history 83
sights 83-5
tourist information 88
travel to/from 88
deer 278
Devon basics 16
Devonshire teas 11, 270, **11, 210**
Devoran 169
disabilities, travellers with 287
Dittisham 86
diving 34, 255
Doc Martin 198
dolphins 279
Drake, Sir Francis 104, 263
drinks 271-2
driving, *see* car travel
driving tours
  Bodmin Moor 157, **157**
  Dartmoor National Park 115, **115**
  East Devon coast 56, **56**
  Exmoor National Park 136, **136**
  North Coast 199, **199**
  Penwith 231, **231**
  Roseland Peninsula 175, **175**
  South Devon 90, **90**
du Maurier, Daphne 275
Dulverton 130-2
Dunster 132-4

E
East Cornwall 39, 150-9, **151**
  accommodation 150
  climate 150
  food 150
  highlights 151
  travel seasons 150
East Devon 38, 42, 54-63, **43**
  accommodation 42
  climate 42
  food 42
  highlights 43
  travel seasons 42
economy 258-9
Eden Project 9, 182-3, **9**
Eden Sessions 22
electricity 285
emergency services 17
environment 277-80

environmental issues 280
erosion 280
events 21-3
exchange rates 17
Exeter 38, 43-54, **43, 44**
  accommodation 42, 48-9
  activities 46-8
  climate 42
  drinking 50-1
  entertainment 51
  festivals & events 48
  food 42, 50
  highlights 43
  history 43-4
  nightlife 50-1
  shopping 51
  sights 44-6
  tourist information 51
  tours 48
  travel seasons 42
  travel to/from 51
  travel within 52
Exeter Cathedral 10, 44-5, 48, **10, 262**
Exford 132
Exmoor National Park 15, 32, 39, 128-38, **127, 15, 155**
  accommodation 126, 129
  activities 128-9
  climate 126
  food 126
  highlights 127
  tourist information 129
  travel seasons 126
  travel within 129
Exmouth 57-9

F
Falmouth 161-6, **162**
  accommodation 164-6
  activities 163-4
  drinking 165-6
  festivals & events 164
  food 164-6
  nightlife 165-6
  shopping 166
  sights 163-4
  tourist information 166
  travel to/from 166
Fearnley-Whittingstall, Hugh 268
festivals 21-3, *see also individual locations*
  arts 274
  walking 32
films 258, 276
fish 270

fishing
  Beer 61
  Brixham 74
  Clovelly 148
  Dartmouth 85
  Looe 188
  Plymouth 103
  St Ives 223
Flora Day 21
Flushing 169
food 19, 259, 268-71, 285, *see also individual locations*
Forbes, Stanhope 273-4
Fowey 183-92, **184**
foxes 278

G
Gabo, Naum 275
galleries 273
  Barbara Hepworth Museum 221
  Exchange, The 236
  Leach Pottery 223
  Newlyn Art Gallery 236
  Penlee House Gallery & Museum 235
  Plymouth 101
  Spacex 46
  Tate St Ives 221
gardens
  Abbey Garden 253, **179**
  Bonython 168
  Broomhill Sculpture Gardens 144
  Carwinion 168
  Cockington Country Park 67
  Eden Project 9, 182-3, **9, 178**
  Elizabethan Garden 78
  Garden House 114
  Glendurgan 167
  Godolphin 168
  Greenway 83
  Lost Gardens of Heligan 13, 182, **13, 179**
  Penjerrick 168
  Potager Garden 168
  RHS Rosemoor 145
  St Michael's Mount 244
  Torre Abbey Gardens 69
  Trebah 167
  Tregothnan 173
  Trelissick Gardens 169-70, **179**
  Tremenheere Sculpture Garden 237
  Trengwainton 237

Garstin, Norman 274
gay travellers 285
gin 272
Glendurgan 167
Godrevy 226
Golant 187
Gorran Haven 181-2
Grand Western Canal 52, **109**
Gunwalloe 246-7
Gweek 167
Gwithian 226

H
Hartland Peninsula 148-9
Hartland Point 149, **11**
Hayle 226-7
health 286
Helford River 167
Helston 245-6
Hepworth, Barbara 221, 275
hiking, *see* walking
historic houses 20
history 260-7
Hope Cove 96-7
horse riding 35
    Bodmin Moor 153
    Clay Trails 181
    Dartmoor National Park 112
    Exmoor National Park 128, **108**

I
Ilfracombe 139-40
Impressionism 273
industrial age 264-5
internet access 286
internet resources 17, 258
Isles of Scilly 9, 40, 219, 250-6, **220**, **251**, **9**
    accommodation 219
    climate 219
    food 219
    highlights 220
    travel seasons 219
itineraries 24-9, **24**, **25**, **26**, **27**, **28-9**

J
Jackson, Kurt 275
jellyfish 280
Jurassic Coast 58

Map Pages **000**
Photo Pages **000**

K
kayaking 34
    Bigbury-on-Sea 98
    Exeter 48
    Fowey 185
    Plymouth 104
    Salcombe 94
    St Mawes 177
    Totnes 78
King Arthur 198, 261
Kingsbridge 91-2
Kynance Cove 248, **14**, **81**

L
Lamorna Cove 235
Ladram Bay 58, **19**
Land's End 227, 233-4, **228**
Langley, Walter 273-4
language 16
Leach, Bernard 274
lesbian travellers 285
lighthouses
    Bishops Rock Lighthouse 254
    Foreland Point 137
    Godrevy Lighthouse 226
    Hartland Point 149, **11**
    Lizard Lighthouse Heritage Centre 247
    Longships Lighthouse 234
    Lundy Island 140
    Pendeen Watch 233
    Smeaton's Tower 103
    St Anthony's Head 177
    Start Point Lighthouse 89
Liskeard 158-9
literature 20, 258, 275
Lizard Peninsula 14, 245-50, **14**
Lizard Point 247-8
Logan Rock 234, **80**
Looe 188-90
Lost Gardens of Heligan 13, 182, **13**, **179**
Lostwithiel 183
Lundy Island 140
Lydford 123
Lynmouth 137-8
Lynton 137-8

M
manors & stately homes
    Antony House 190
    Arlington Court 144
    Buckland Abbey 114
    Caerhays Castle 182

Coleton Fishacre 88
Cotehele 191
Greenway 83
Hartland Abbey 148
Lanhydrock 153
Mount Edgcumbe 190
Port Eliot 191
Prideaux Place 203
St Michael's Mount 244
Tregothnan 173
Trerice 208
maps 286
Mayflower 102, 103, 263, 264, **264**
Methodism 264
Mevagissey 181-2
Middle Ages 262
Millbrook Inn 93
mining 259, 262-3, 264, 265, 277
mining sites 259
    Camborne 216
    Cornish Mines & Engines 216
    Cornwall & West Devon Mining Landscape 216
    King Edward Mine 218
    Mining World Heritage Site 216
    Redruth 216
    Trevellas Porth 214
    West Cornwall 229
mobile phones 16, 287
money 16, 17, 285, 286-7
monkeys 188
Moretonhampstead 120-1
Morris, Cedric 275
motorcycle travel 289, 291-2
Mousehole 241, **143**
Mullion 247
museums 264
    Bakelite Museum 133
    Barbara Hepworth Museum 221
    Bill Douglas Centre 45
    City Museum & Art Gallery 103
    Cookworthy Museum of Rural Life 91
    Dartmoor Prison Heritage Centre 117
    Helston Folk Museum 245
    Isles of Scilly Museum 251
    Lyn & Exmoor Museum 137
    Maritime Museum 93

Museum of British Surfing 141
Museum of Witchcraft 196
National Maritime Museum 163
Penlee House Gallery & Museum 235
RAMM 46
Royal Cornwall Museum 170
Shipwreck Museum 149
Sidmouth museum 60
Tavistock Museum 114
Teignmouth & Shaldon Museum 75
Topsham Museum 55
Torquay Museum 66
Totnes Fashion & Textile Museum 78
Mylor 169

N
national parks & reserves 277-8
    Bodmin Moor 32, 153-9, **154**
    Braunton Burrows 141
    Dartmoor National Park 10, 31-2, 110-25, **100**, **112**, **10**, **155**
    Dawlish Warren 75
    Exminster Marshes Nature Reserve 46, 48
    Exmoor National Park 15, 32, 128-38, **127**, **15**, **108**, **155**
    Looe Island 188
    Northam Burrows 147
    Slapton Ley 89
Newlyn 240-1
Newlyn School 273-4
Newquay 12, 40, 206-13, **194**, **207**, **12**, **109**
    accommodation 193
    climate 193
    food 193
    highlights 194
    travel seasons 193
newspapers 286
Nicholson, Ben 275
North Coast 40, 195-206, **194**
    accommodation 193
    climate 193
    food 193
    highlights 194
    travel seasons 193

North Devon 39, 138-49, **127**
   accommodation 126
   climate 126
   food 126
   highlights 127
   travel seasons 126

O
'Obby 'Oss 21, 201
Okehampton 125
opening hours 17
otters 156
outdoor activities 18-19, 30-5
Outlaw, Nathan 188, 190, 200, 201, 268

P
Padstow 201-5, **202**
   accommodation 203-4
   activities 203
   drinking 205
   food 204-5
   shopping 205
   sights 203
   travel to/from 205
painting 273-5
pasties 12, 214, 269, **12, 211**
paths, see trails & paths
Penryn 168
Penwith Peninsula 227-35, **228**
Penzance 235-40, **236**
Perranporth 213, **81**
Perranuthnoe 244-5
planning 16-17
   calendar of events 21-3
   children, travel with 36-7
   Cornwall's regions 38-40
   Devon's regions 38-40
   internet resources 17
   itineraries 24-9, **24, 25, 26, 27, 28-9**
   travel seasons 21-3
Plymouth 39, 100-10, **100, 102**
   accommodation 99, 104-5
   activities 104
   climate 99
   drinking 106-7
   entertainment 107
   food 99, 105-6
   highlights 100
   history 101
   sights 101-4
   tourist information 107

travel seasons 99
travel to/from 107, 110
pollution 280
Polperro 187-8
Polzeath 200-1, **15**
ponies 278
population 259
Porlock 134-5
Port Eliot 191
Port Eliot Festival 22
Port Isaac 198-200
Porthcurno 234
Porthleven 246
Porthtowan 216
Portreath 216
Portscatho 174-6
Postbridge 118-19
Praa Sands 244-5
prehistoric sites, see archaeological sites
Princetown 117-18

Q
quoits
   Bodmin Moor 159
   Penwith 230, **242**

R
radio 286
Rame Peninsula 190-1
Redruth 216-18
religion 259
reserves, see national parks & reserves
Restronguet Creek 169
River Helford 249-50
road trips, see driving tours
Roche Rock 182
Rock 200-1
rock climbing 35
Roman rule 261
Roseland, the 174-80
Royal Cornwall Museum 170

S
safety 284-5
sailing 34
Salcombe 93-6, **94**
sculpture 273-5
seagulls 278-9
seals 167, 279
Sennen 233
sharks 279
Sidmouth 59-61
smuggling 266
snakes 286

South Cornwall 39, 160-92, **161**
   accommodation 160
   climate 160
   food 160
   highlights 161
   travel seasons 160
South Devon 38, 64, 77-98, **65**
   accommodation 64
   climate 64
   food 64
   highlights 65
   travel seasons 64
South Hams 14, **14**
South West Coast Path 11, 31, **11**
Southeast Cornwall 180-92
St Agnes (Cornwall) 213-16
St Agnes (Isles of Scilly) 256
St Austell 180
St Ives 11, 220-6, **222, 11, 271**
   accommodation 223-4
   drinking 225
   festivals & events 223
   food 224-5
   nightlife 225
   shopping 225
   sights 221-3
   tourist information 225
   travel to/from 225-6
St Ives School 274-5
St Juliot 197-8
St Keverne 248-9
St Martin's 254-5
St Mary's 251-3
St Mawes 176-7
St Michael's Mount 13, 244, **13**
Start Bay 89-91
stately homes, see manors & stately homes
Stein, Rick 268
St-Just-in-Penwith 233
St-Just-in-Roseland 180
stone circles 230
sunburn 286
surfing 33
   Bantham 97
   Bigbury-on-Sea 98
   Bude 195
   Croyde 141
   Gwithian 226
   Ilfracombe 139
   Newquay 12, 208, **12, 109**
   Polzeath 201
   Sennen Cove 233
   Westward Ho! 147

T
Tamar Valley 191-2
Tate St Ives 221
Tavistock 113-16
taxis 292
teas 11, 270, **11, 210**
Tehidy Woods 216
Teignmouth 75-6
telephone services 16, 17, 287
theatre 276
Thurlestone 97
ticks 286
time 16
Tintagel Castle 198, **243**
toilets 287
Topsham 55-7
Torquay 38, 65-76, **65, 68-9**
   accommodation 64, 70-2
   activities 70
   climate 64
   drinking 73
   festivals & events 70
   food 64, 72-3
   highlights 65
   history 66
   nightlife 73
   sights 66-9
   tourist information 73
   travel seasons 64
   travel to/from 73
   travel within 73
Totnes 77-82
tourist information 287, see also individual locations
tours, see cycling tours, driving tours, walking tours
trails & paths
   Camel Trail 203
   Clay Trails 181
   Coast to Coast Cycle Trail 169
   Granite Way 124, **124**
   Great Flat Lode Trail 218
   South West Coast Path 11, 31, **11**
   Tamar Trails 192
   Tarka Trail 146, **146**
train travel 289, 292-3
transport 288-93
travel seasons 16
travel to/from Cornwall 288-90
travel to/from Devon 288-90
travel within Cornwall 290-3

INDEX T-Z

travel within Devon 290-3
Trebah 167
Trebarwith Strand 200
Treen 234-5, **80**
Tregony 174-6
Tregothnan 173
Trelissick Gardens 169-70, **179**
Trelowarren 246
Tresco 253-4, **9**
Tristan and Isolde 183
Tristan Stone 183
Truro 170-4, **171**
tunnels, *see* caves & tunnels
Turner, JMW 273
TV 276, 286

V
vegetarian travellers 271
Veryan 174-6
visas 16

W
Wadebridge 206

walking 31-2, 285, *see also* trails & paths
Bodmin Moor 32
Dartmoor National Park 31-2, 111
Exeter 46
Exmoor National Park 32, 128-9
festivals 32
Lynmouth 137
Lynton 137
Princetown 117
safety 32
Teignmouth 76
walking tours
Beer to Branscombe 62, **62**
Dartmoor National Park 122, **122**
Exeter 47, **47**
Exmoor National Park 131, **131**
Fowey, Polruan & Bodinnick 186, **186**
Land's End 232, **232**
St Agnes 217, **217**

Torquay 71, **71**
West Cornwall 232, **232**
Wallis, Alfred 275
water sports 33-4
weather 16, 21-3, *see also individual regions*
websites 17
West Cornwall 40, 220-45, **220**
accommodation 219
climate 219
food 219
highlights 220
travel seasons 219
Westward Ho! 147
white-water rafting 33-4
Widecombe-in-the-Moor 119-20
wildlife 278-80
wildlife parks & reserves
Braunton Burrows 141
Dawlish Warren 75
Donkey Sanctuary 60
Exminster Marshes Nature Reserve 46, 48
Exmoor Owl & Hawk Centre 134

Looe Island 188
Northam Burrows 147
Wild Futures Monkey Sanctuary 188
wildlife watching 35
wine 272
wineries
Camel Valley Vineyard 152
Pebblebed Vineyard 55
Polgoon Vineyard 238
Sharpham Wine & Cheese 77, **211**
St Martin's Vineyard 255
Yearlstone Vineyard 52
Wood, Christopher 275
Woolf, Virginia 226
WWI 267
WWII 267

Z
Zennor 228-30, **155**
zoos
Living Coasts 66
Newquay Zoo 208
Paignton Zoo 66

Map Legend

Sights

- Beach
- Bird Sanctuary
- Buddhist
- Castle/Palace
- Christian
- Confucian
- Hindu
- Islamic
- Jain
- Jewish
- Monument
- Museum/Gallery/Historic Building
- Ruin
- Sento Hot Baths/Onsen
- Shinto
- Sikh
- Taoist
- Winery/Vineyard
- Zoo/Wildlife Sanctuary
- Other Sight

Activities, Courses & Tours

- Bodysurfing
- Diving/Snorkelling
- Canoeing/Kayaking
- Course/Tour
- Skiing
- Snorkelling
- Surfing
- Swimming/Pool
- Walking
- Windsurfing
- Other Activity

Sleeping

- Sleeping
- Camping

Eating

- Eating

Drinking & Nightlife

- Drinking & Nightlife
- Cafe

Entertainment

- Entertainment

Shopping

- Shopping

Information

- Bank
- Embassy/Consulate
- Hospital/Medical
- Internet
- Police
- Post Office
- Telephone
- Toilet
- Tourist Information
- Other Information

Geographic

- Beach
- Hut/Shelter
- Lighthouse
- Lookout
- Mountain/Volcano
- Oasis
- Park
- Pass
- Picnic Area
- Waterfall

Population

- Capital (National)
- Capital (State/Province)
- City/Large Town
- Town/Village

Transport

- Airport
- Border crossing
- Bus
- Cable car/Funicular
- Cycling
- Ferry
- Metro station
- Monorail
- Parking
- Petrol station
- S-Bahn/Subway station
- Taxi
- T-bane/Tunnelbana station
- Train station/Railway
- Tram
- Tube station
- U-Bahn/Underground station
- Other Transport

Note: Not all symbols displayed above appear on the maps in this book

Routes

- Tollway
- Freeway
- Primary
- Secondary
- Tertiary
- Lane
- Unsealed road
- Road under construction
- Plaza/Mall
- Steps
- Tunnel
- Pedestrian overpass
- Walking Tour
- Walking Tour detour
- Path/Walking Trail

Boundaries

- International
- State/Province
- Disputed
- Regional/Suburb
- Marine Park
- Cliff
- Wall

Hydrography

- River, Creek
- Intermittent River
- Canal
- Water
- Dry/Salt/Intermittent Lake
- Reef

Areas

- Airport/Runway
- Beach/Desert
- Cemetery (Christian)
- Cemetery (Other)
- Glacier
- Mudflat
- Park/Forest
- Sight (Building)
- Sportsground
- Swamp/Mangrove

OUR STORY

A beat-up old car, a few dollars in the pocket and a sense of adventure. In 1972 that's all Tony and Maureen Wheeler needed for the trip of a lifetime – across Europe and Asia overland to Australia. It took several months, and at the end – broke but inspired – they sat at their kitchen table writing and stapling together their first travel guide, *Across Asia on the Cheap*. Within a week they'd sold 1500 copies. Lonely Planet was born.

Today, Lonely Planet has offices in Melbourne, London, Oakland and Delhi, with more than 600 staff and writers. We share Tony's belief that 'a great guidebook should do three things: inform, educate and amuse'.

OUR WRITERS

Oliver Berry

Coordinating Author, Bodmin & East Cornwall, South Cornwall, Newquay & the North Coast, West Cornwall & the Isles of Scilly Oliver is a writer and photographer based in Cornwall. He has travelled the length and breadth of the British Isles for Lonely Planet, having worked on previous editions of the guides to Great Britain; Devon, Cornwall and Southwest England; and the Lake District. He also writes for national publications including *Lonely Planet Traveller*. For this book he tasted ale, hiked miles of trails and braved Cornwall's winter waters – and loved every minute.

Read more about Oliver at:
lonelyplanet.com/members/oliverberry

Belinda Dixon

Exeter & East Devon, Torquay & South Devon, Plymouth & Dartmoor, Exmoor & North Devon Belinda made a gleeful bolt for the sunny southwest for her postgrad, having been drawn there by the palm trees on campus. Like the best West Country limpets she's proved hard to shift since, and now writes and broadcasts in the region. Research highlights included the spectacular Teign Gorge hike; cycling the atmospheric Granite Way; and eating, driving and walking her way around Exmoor – magical. Belinda also wrote the Outdoor Activities, Travel with Children, Food & Drink, Arts, Directory A–Z and Transport chapters.

Read more about Belinda at:
lonelyplanet.com/members/belindadixon

Published by Lonely Planet Publications Pty Ltd
ABN 36 005 607 983
3rd edition – January 2014
ISBN 978 1 74220 203 7
© Lonely Planet 2014   Photographs © as indicated 2014
10 9 8 7 6 5 4 3 2 1
Printed in China